NAVE'S
TOPICAL BIBLE

CONDENSED EDITION

By

ORVILLE J. NAVE

Editor, *Nave's Study Bible*

D1462497

MOODY PRESS

CHICAGO

PREFACE TO CONDENSED EDITION

NAVE'S TOPICAL BIBLE has been a standard text for Bible scholars for over fifty years. It is the result of fourteen years of untiring study of the Word of God. The book is truly a digest of the Scriptures with more than 20,000 topics and sub-topics and 100,000 references to the Scriptures written out (not just references) under the topics.

In preparing this condensed edition, the publishers have selected nearly 1,000 of the most useful topics and sub-topics and have included the important verses under each topic. This book will prove an invaluable aid for study and preaching.

THE PUBLISHERS

Printed in the United States of America

ISBN 0-8024-0030-2

Moody Press, a ministry of the Moody Bible Institute, is designed for education, evangelization and edification. If we may assist you in knowing more about Christ and the Christian life, please write us without obligation to: Moody Press, c/o MLM, Chicago, Illinois 60610.

THE TOPICAL BIBLE

ABLUTION. Prov. 20:9. Who can say, I have made my heart clean, I am pure from my sin?

Acts 22:16. Arise, and be baptized, and wash away thy sins, calling on the name of the Lord.

1 Cor. 5:7. Purge out therefore the old leaven, that ye may be a new lump.

1 Cor. 6:11. But ye are washed, but ye are sanctified, but ye are justified in the name of the Lord Jesus, and by the Spirit of our God. 2 Cor. 7:1; Eph. 5:26.

Tit. 3:5. Not by works of righteousness which we have done, but according to his mercy he saved us, by the washing of regeneration, and renewing of the Holy Ghost; 6. Which he shed on us abundantly through Jesus Christ our Saviour;

Heb. 1:3. Who . . . when he had by himself purged our sins, sat down on the right hand of the Majesty on high.

Heb. 9:14. How much more shall the blood of Christ, who through the eternal Spirit offered himself without spot to God, purge your conscience from dead works to serve the living God? *chap.* 10:22.

Jas. 4:8. Cleanse *your* hands, ye sinners; and purify *your* hearts, ye doubleminded.

Rev. 1:5. Unto him that loved us, and washed us from our sins in his own blood.

ABOMINATION. Unclassified Scriptures Relating to: Deut. 22:5. The woman shall not wear that which pertaineth unto a man, neither shall a man put on a woman's garment: for all that do so *are* abomination unto the LORD thy God.

Prov. 6:16. These six *things* doth the LORD hate: yea, seven *are* an abomination unto him: 17. A proud look, a lying tongue, and hands that shed innocent blood, 18. A heart that deviseth wicked imaginations, feet that be swift in running to mischief, 19. A false witness *that* speaketh lies, and he that soweth discord among brethren.

Prov. 12:22. Lying lips *are* abomination to the LORD: but they that deal truly *are* his delight.

Prov. 16:5. Every one *that is* proud in heart *is* an abomination to the LORD: *though* hand *join* in hand, he shall not be unpunished.

Prov. 17:15. He that justifieth the wicked, and he that condemneth the just, even they both *are* abomination to the LORD.

Prov. 20:10. Divers weights, *and* divers measures, both of them *are* alike abomination to the LORD. *v.* 23

Prov. 21:27. The sacrifice of the wicked *is* abomination: how much more, *when* he bringeth it with a wicked mind?

Prov. 28:9. He that turneth away his ear from hearing the law, even his prayer *shall be* abomination.

ABORTION. Ex. 21:22. If men strive, and hurt a woman with child, so that her fruit depart *from her,* and yet no mischief follow: he shall be surely punished, according as the woman's husband will lay upon him; and he shall pay as the judges *determine.* 23. And if *any* mischief follow, then thou shalt give life for life.

As a judgment, Hos. 9:14. Of animals, caused by thunder, Psa. 29:9.

ABRAHAM, called also ABRAM. Son of Terah, Gen. 11:26,27. Marries Sarah, Gen. 11:29. Dwells in Ur, but removes to Haran, Gen. 11:31; Neh. 9:7; Acts 7:4, and Canaan, Gen. 12:4,5,6; Acts 7:4.

Divine call of, Gen. 12:1-3; Josh. 24:3; Neh. 9:7; Isa. 51:2; Acts 7:2,3; Heb. 11:8. Canaan given to, Gen. 12:1,7; 15:7-21; Ezek. 33:24. Dwells in Beth-el, Gen. 12:8. Sojourns in Egypt, Gen. 12:10-20;

26:1. Deferring to Lot, chooses Hebron, Gen. 13; 14:13; 35:27. Dwells in Gerar, Gen. 20; 21:22-34.

Defeats Chedorlaomer, Gen. 14:5-24; Heb. 7:1. Is blessed by Melchizedek, Gen. 14:18-20; Heb. 7:1-10.

God's covenant with, Gen. 15; 17:1-22; Mic. 7:20; Luke 1:73; Rom. 4:13; 15:8; Heb. 6:13,14; Gal. 3:6-18,29; 4:22-31. Called ABRAHAM, Gen. 17:5; Neh. 9:7. Circumcision of, Gen. 17:10-14,23-27. Angels appear to, Gen. 18:1-16; 22:11,15; 24:7. His questions about the destruction of the righteous and wicked in Sodom, Gen. 18:23-32. Witnesses the destruction of Sodom, Gen. 19:27,28. Ishmael born to, Gen. 16:3,15. Dwells in Gerar; deceives Abimelech concerning Sarah, his wife, Gen. 20. Isaac born to, Gen. 21:2,3; Gal. 4:22-30. Sends Hagar and Ishmael away, Gen. 21:10-14; Gal. 4:22-30.

Trial of his faith in the offering of Isaac, Gen. 22:1-19; Heb. 11:17; Jas. 2:21. Sarah, his wife, dies, Gen. 23:1,2. He purchases a place for her burial, and buries her in a cave, Gen. 23:3-20. Marries Keturah, Gen. 25:1. Provides a wife for Isaac, Gen. 24.

Children of, Gen. 16:15; 21:2,3; 25:1-4; 1 Chr. 1:32-34. Testament of, Gen. 25:5,6. Wealth of, Gen. 13:2; 24:35; Isa. 51:2. Age of, at different periods, Gen. 12:4; 16:16; 21:5; 25:7. Death, Gen. 15:15; 25:8-10. In Paradise, Matt. 8:11; Luke 13:28; 16:22-31.

Friend of God, Isa. 41:8; 2 Chr. 20:7; Jas. 2:23. Piety of, Gen. 12:7,8; 13:4,18; 18:19; 20:7; 21:33; 22:3-13; 26:5; Neh. 9:7,8; Rom. 4:16-18; 2 Chr. 20:7; Isa. 41:8; Jas. 2:23. A prophet, Gen. 20:7. Faith of, Gen. 15:6; Rom. 4:1-22; Gal. 3:6-9; Heb. 11:8-10, 17-19; Jas. 2:21-24. Unselfishness of, Gen. 13:9; 21:25-30. Independence of, in character, Gen. 14:23; 23:6-16.

Ancestors of, Idolatrous, Josh. 24:2. How regarded by his descendants, Matt. 3:9; Luke 13:16,28; 19:9; John 8:33-40,52-59.

ABSTEMIOUSNESS. Prov. 23:1-3.

Instances of: Daniel and his Hebrew companions, Dan. 1:8-16. John the Baptist, Matt. 11:18.

ABSTINENCE, TOTAL. From Intoxicating Beverages: Lev. 10:8. And the LORD spake unto Aaron, saying, 9. Do not drink wine nor strong drink, thou, nor thy sons with thee, when ye go into the tabernacle of the congregation, lest ye die: *it shall be* a statute for ever throughout your generations: 10. And that ye may put difference between holy and unholy, and between unclean and clean.

Num. 6:3. He shall separate *himself* from wine and strong drink, and shall drink no vinegar of wine, or vinegar of strong drink, neither shall he drink any liquor of grapes, nor eat moist grapes, or dried. 4. All the days of his separation shall he eat nothing that is made of the vine tree, from the kernels even to the husk.

Judg. 13:4. Now therefore beware, I pray thee, and drink not wine nor strong drink, and eat not any unclean *thing*: . . . 13. And the angel of the LORD said unto Manoah, Of all that I said unto the woman let her beware. 14. She may not eat of any *thing* that cometh of the vine, neither let her drink wine or strong drink.

Esth. 1:8. And the drinking *was* according to the law; none did compel; for so the king had appointed to all the officers of his house, that they should do according to every man's pleasure.

Prov. 23:20. Be not among winebibbers, 31. Look not thou upon the wine when it is red, when it giveth his colour in the cup, *when* it moveth itself aright. 32. At the last it biteth like a serpent, and stingeth like an adder.

Prov. 31:4. *It is* not for kings, O Lemuel, *it is* not for kings to drink wine; nor for princes strong drink:

Jer. 35:6. But they said, We will drink no wine: for Jonadab the son of Rechab our father commanded us, saying, Ye shall drink no wine, *neither* ye, nor your sons forever: 7. Neither shall ye build house, nor sow seed, nor plant vineyard, nor have *any:* but all your days ye shall dwell in tents; that ye may live many days in the land where ye *be* strangers. 8. Thus have we obeyed the voice of Jonadab the son of Rechab our father in all that he hath charged us, to drink no wine all our days, we, our wives, our sons, nor our daughters: 14. The words of Jonadab the son of Rechab, that he commanded his sons not to drink wine, are performed; for unto this day they drink none, but obey their father's commandment: notwithstanding I have spoken unto you, rising early and speaking; but ye hearkened not unto me.

Luke 1:15. For he shall be great in the sight of the Lord, and shall drink neither wine nor strong drink; and he shall be filled with the Holy Ghost, even from his mother's womb.

ACCUSATION. False: Ex. 23:1.
Thou shalt not raise a false report: put not thine hand with the wicked to be an unrighteous witness. 7. Keep thee far from a false matter; and the innocent and righteous slay thou not: for I will not justify the wicked.

Lev. 19:16. Thou shalt not go up and down *as* a talebearer among thy people; neither shalt thou stand against the blood of thy neighbour: I *am* the LORD.

Matt. 5:11. Blessed are ye, when *men* shall revile you, and persecute *you,* and shall say all manner of evil against you falsely, for my sake.

ADAM.
1. The first man. Creation of, Gen. 1:26-28; 2:7; 1 Cor. 15:45; 1 Tim. 2:13. History of, before he sinned, Gen. 1:26-30; 2:16-25. Temptation and sin of, Gen. 3; Job 31:33; Isa. 43:27; Hos. 6:7 [see *R. V.*]; Rom. 5:14-21; 1 Tim. 2:14. Subsequent history of, Gen. 3:20-24; 4:1,2,25; 5:1-5. His death, Gen. 5:5.

Progenitor of the human race, Deut. 32:8; Mal. 2:10. Brought sin into the world, 1 Cor. 15:22,45. Type of Christ, Rom. 5:14.

2. A name of Christ, 1 Cor. 15:45,47.

3. A city near the Jordan, Josh. 3:16.

ADJUDICATION AT LAW.
To Be Avoided: Prov. 17:14. The beginning of strife *is as* when one letteth out water: therefore leave off contention, before it be meddled with.

Prov. 20:3. *It is* an honour for a man to cease from strife: but every fool will be meddling.

Prov. 25:8. Go not forth hastily to strive, lest *thou know not* what to do in the end thereof, when thy neighbour hath put thee to shame. 9. Debate thy cause with thy neighbour *himself;* and discover not a secret to another: 10. Lest he that heareth *it* put thee to shame, and thine infamy turn not away.

Matt. 5:25. Agree with thine adversary quickly, whiles thou art in the way with him; lest at any time the adversary deliver thee to the judge, and the judge deliver thee to the officer, and thou be cast into prison.

ADOPTION. Gen. 15:3.
Spiritual: Deut. 14:1. Ye *are* the children of the LORD your God.

Deut. 27:9. Moses and the priests the Levites spake unto all Israel, saying, Take heed, and hearken, O Israel; this day thou art become the people of the LORD thy God.

2 Sam. 7:14. I will be his father, and he shall be my son.

Isa. 8:18. Behold, I and the children whom the LORD hath given me.

Isa. 63:16. Doubtless thou *art* our Father, though Abraham be ignorant of us, and Israel acknowledge us not: thou, O LORD, *art* our Father, our Redeemer; thy name *is* from everlasting. *v.* 8.

Matt. 5:9. Blessed *are* the peacemakers: for they shall be called the children of God. 45. That ye may be the children of your Father which is in heaven:

John 1:12. As many as received him, to them gave he [power] to become [the sons] of God, even to them that believe on his name: 13. Which were born, not of blood, nor of the will of the flesh, nor of the will of man, but of God. (R. V. [the right] [children])

John 11:52. And not for that nation only, but that also he should gather together in one the children of God that were scattered abroad.

Rom. 8:14. For as many as are led by the Spirit of God, they are the sons of God. 15. For ye have not received the spirit of bondage again to fear; but ye have received the Spirit of adoption, whereby we cry, Abba, Father. 16. The Spirit itself beareth witness with our spirit, that we are the children of God: 17. And if children, then heirs; heirs of God, and joint-heirs with Christ;

2 Cor. 6:17. Wherefore come out from among them, and be ye separate, saith the Lord, and touch not the unclean *thing;* and I will receive you, 18. And will be a Father unto you, and ye shall be my sons and daughters, saith the Lord Almighty.

Gal. 3:26. For ye are all the children of God by faith in Christ Jesus. 29. And if ye *be* Christ's, then are ye Abraham's seed, and heirs according to the promise.

Eph. 1:5. Having predestinated us unto the adoption of children by Jesus Christ to himself.

Phil. 2:15. That ye may be blameless and harmless, the sons of God, without rebuke, in the midst of a crooked and perverse nation, among whom ye shine as lights in the world.

Heb. 12:6. Whom the Lord loveth he chasteneth, and scourgeth every son whom he receiveth.

1 John 3:1. Behold what manner of love the Father hath bestowed upon us, that we should be called the sons of God: 2. Beloved, now are we the sons of God, and it doth not yet appear what we shall be: but we know that, when he shall appear, we shall be like him;

ADULTERY. Gen. 20:3. But God came to Abimelech in a dream by night, and said to him, Behold, thou *art but* a dead man, for the woman which thou hast taken; for she *is* a man's wife.

2 Sam. 12:14. Howbeit, because by this deed thou hast given great occasion to the enemies of the Lord to blaspheme, the child also *that is* born unto thee shall surely die.

Job 31:1. I made a covenant with mine eyes; why then should I think upon a maid?

Job 31:12. For it *is* a fire *that* consumeth to destruction, and would root out all mine increase.

Prov. 2:16. To deliver thee from the strange woman, *even* from the stranger *which* flattereth with her words; 18. Her house inclineth unto death, and her paths unto the dead. 19. None that go unto her return again, neither take they hold of the paths of life. *v.* 17.

Prov. 5:3. The lips of a strange woman drop *as* an honeycomb, and her mouth *is* smoother than oil: 4. But her end is bitter as wormwood, sharp as a two-edged sword. *vs.* 5-22.

Prov. 6:25. Lust not after her beauty in thine heart; neither let her take thee with her eyelids. 26. For by means of a whorish woman *a man is brought* to a piece of bread: and the adulteress will hunt for the precious life. 27. Can a man take fire in his bosom, and his clothes not be burned? 28. Can one go upon hot coals, and his feet not be burned? 29. So he that goeth in to his neighbour's wife; whosoever toucheth her shall not be innocent. 32. *But* whoso committeth adultery with a woman lacketh understanding: he *that* doeth it destroyeth his own soul. 33. A wound and dishonour shall he get; and his reproach shall not be wiped away.

Prov. 7:18. Come, let us take our fill of love until the morning: let us solace ourselves with loves. 19. For the goodman *is* not at home, he is gone a long journey: 20. He hath taken a bag of money with him, *and* will come home at the day appointed. 21. With her much fair speech she caused him to yield, with the flattering of her lips she forced him. 22. He goeth after her straightway, as an ox goeth to the slaughter, or as a fool to the correction of the stocks; 23. Till a dart strike through his liver; as a bird hasteth to the snare, and knoweth not that it *is* for his life.

Prov. 9:16. Whoso *is* simple, let him turn in hither: and *as for* him that wanteth understanding, she saith to him, 17. Stolen waters are sweet, and bread *eaten* in secret is pleasant. 18. But he knoweth not that the dead *are* there: *and that* her guests *are* in the depths of hell.

Prov. 30:18. There be three *things which* are too wonderful for me, yea, four which I know not: 19. The way of an eagle in the air; the way of a serpent upon a rock; the way of a ship in the midst of the sea; and the way of a man with a maid. 20. Such *is* the way of an adulterous woman; she eateth, and wipeth her mouth, and saith, I have done no wickedness.

Matt. 5:28. Whosoever looketh on a woman to lust after her hath committed adultery with her already in his heart. 32. Whosoever shall put away his wife, saving for the cause of fornication, causeth her to commit adultery: and whosoever shall marry her that is divorced committeth adultery. Mark 10:11,12; Luke 16:18.

Matt. 19:9. And I say unto you, Whosoever shall put away his wife, except *it be* for fornication, and shall marry another, committeth adultery: and whoso marrieth her which is put away doth commit adultery. Mark 10:11.

Acts 15:20. We write unto them, that they abstain from pollutions of idols, and *from* fornication, *v.* 29.

1 Cor. 5:9. I wrote unto you in an epistle not to company with fornicators: 10. Yet not altogether with the fornicators of this world, or with the covetous, or extortioners, or with idolaters: for then must ye needs go out of the world.

1 Cor. 6:15. Know ye not that your bodies are the members of Christ? shall I then take the members of Christ, and make *them* the members of an harlot? God forbid. 16. What? know ye not that he which is joined to an harlot *is* one body? for two, saith he, shall be one flesh. 18. Flee fornication. Every sin that a man doeth is without the body; but he that committeth fornication sinneth against his own body.

2 Pet. 2:9. The Lord knoweth how to deliver the godly out of temptations, and to reserve the unjust unto the day of judgment to be punished: 10. But chiefly them that walk after the flesh in the lust of uncleanness. 14. Having eyes full of adultery, and that cannot cease from sin; beguiling unstable souls:

Rom. 13:13. Let us walk honestly, as in the day; not in rioting and drunkenness, not in chambering and wantonness.

1 Cor. 5:11. I have written unto you not to keep company, if any man that is called a brother be a fornicator, . . . with such an one no not to eat. *vs.* 9,10.

John 8:10. Woman, where are those thine accusers? hath no man condemned thee? 11. She said, No man, Lord. And Jesus said unto her, Neither do I condemn thee: go, and sin no more.

Num. 5:29. This *is* the law of jealousies, when a wife goeth aside *to another* instead of her husband, and is defiled;

1 Cor. 6:9. Be not deceived: neither fornicators nor idolaters, nor adulterers, nor effeminate, nor abusers of themselves with mankind, 10. . . . Shall inherit the kingdom of God.

AFFLICTED. Duty to the:
Isa. 58:6. *Is* not this the fast that I have chosen? to loose the bands of wickedness, to undo the heavy burdens, and to let the oppressed go free, and that ye break every yoke? 7. *Is it* not to deal thy bread to the hungry, and that thou bring the poor that are cast out to thy house? when thou seest the naked, that thou cover him; and that thou hide not thyself from thine own flesh? 10. And *if* thou draw out thy soul to the hungry, and satisfy the afflicted soul; then shall thy light rise in obscurity, and thy darkness *be* as the noonday.

Matt. 25:34. Then shall the King say unto them on his right hand, Come, ye blessed of my Father, inherit the kingdom prepared for you from the foundation of the world: 35. For I was an hungred, and ye gave me meat: I was thirsty, and ye gave me drink: I was a stranger, and ye took me in: 36. Naked, and ye clothed me: I was sick, and ye visited me: I was in prison, and ye came unto me. 37. Then shall the righteous answer him, saying, Lord, when saw we thee an hungred, and fed *thee?* or thirsty, and gave *thee* drink? 38. When saw we thee a stranger, and took *thee* in? or naked, and clothed *thee?* 39. Or when saw we thee sick, or in prison, and came unto thee? 40. And the King shall answer and say unto them, Verily I say unto you, Inasmuch as ye have done *it* unto one of the least of these my brethren, ye have done *it* unto me. 41. Then shall he say also unto them on the left hand, Depart from me, ye cursed, into everlasting fire, prepared for the devil and his angels: 42. For I was an hungred, and ye gave me no meat: I was thirsty, and ye gave me no drink: 43. I was a stranger, and ye took me not in: naked, and ye clothed me not: sick, and in prison, and ye visited me not. 44. Then shall they also answer him, saying, Lord, when saw we thee an hungred, or athirst, or a stranger, or naked, or sick, or in prison, and did not minister unto thee? 45. Then shall he answer them, saying, Verily I say unto you, Inasmuch as ye did *it* not to one of the least of these, ye did *it* not to me.

Luke 10:30. And Jesus answering said, A certain *man* went down from Jerusalem to Jericho, and fell among thieves, which stripped him of his raiment, and wounded *him,* and departed, leaving *him* half dead. 31. And by chance there came down a certain priest that way: and when he saw him, he passed by on the other side. 32. And likewise a Levite, when he was at the place, came and looked *on him,* and passed by on the other side. 33. But a certain Samaritan, as he journeyed, came where he was; and when he saw him, he had compassion *on him,* 34. And went to *him,* and bound up his wounds, pouring in oil and wine, and set him on his own beast, and brought him to an inn, and took care of him. 35. And on the morrow when he departed,

he took out two pence, and gave *them* to the host, and said unto him, Take care of him: and whatsoever thou spendest more, when I come again, I will repay thee. 36. Which now of these three, thinkest thou, was neighbour unto him that fell among the thieves? 37. And he said, He that shewed mercy on him. Then said Jesus unto him, Go, and do thou likewise.

Phil. 2:1. If *there be* therefore any consolation in Christ, if any comfort of love, if any fellowship of the Spirit, if any bowels and mercies, 2. Fulfil ye my joy, that ye be likeminded, having the same love, *being* of one accord, of one mind.

1 Tim. 5:10. If she have relieved the afflicted, if she have diligently followed every good work.

Jas. 5:13. Is any among you afflicted? let him pray. Is any merry? let him sing psalms. 14. Is any sick among you? let him call for the elders of the church; and let them pray over him, anointing him with oil in the name of the Lord: 15. And the prayer of faith shall save the sick, and the Lord shall raise him up; and if he have committed sins, they shall be forgiven him.

AFFLICTIONS AND ADVERSITIES. Unclassified Scriptures Relating to:

2 Sam. 7:14. I will be his father, and he shall be my son. If he commit iniquity, I will chasten him with the rod of men, and with the stripes of the children of men:

Job 5:17. Behold, happy *is* the man whom God correcteth: therefore despise not thou the chastening of the Almighty: 18. For he maketh sore, and bindeth up: he woundeth, and his hands make whole.

Job 23:10. But he knoweth the way that I take: *when* he hath tried me, I shall come forth as gold.

Psa. 39:1. I said, I will take heed to my ways, that I sin not with my tongue: I will keep my mouth with a bridle, while the wicked is before me. 2. I was dumb with silence, I held my peace, *even* from good; and my sorrow was stirred. 3. My heart was hot within me; while I was musing the fire burned: *then* spake I with my tongue, 4. LORD, make me to know mine end, and the measure of my days, what it *is; that* I may know how frail I *am*.

Psa. 89:32. Then will I visit their transgression with the rod, and their iniquity with stripes.

Prov. 3:11. My son, despise not the chastening of the LORD; neither be weary of his correction: 12. For whom the LORD loveth he correcteth; even as a father the son *in whom* he delighteth.

Prov. 17:3. The fining pot *is* for silver, and the furnace for gold; but the LORD trieth the hearts. 22. A merry heart doeth good *like* a medicine: but a broken spirit drieth the bones.

John 15:2. Every branch in me that beareth not fruit he taketh away: and every *branch* that beareth fruit, he purgeth it, that it may bring forth more fruit.

John 16:33. In the world ye shall have tribulation;

2 Cor. 4:7. But we have this treasure in earthen vessels, that the excellency of the power may be of God, and not of us. 8. *We are* troubled on every side, yet not distressed; *we are* perplexed, but not in despair; 9. Persecuted, but not forsaken; cast down, but not destroyed; 10. Always bearing about in the body the dying of the Lord Jesus, that the life also of Jesus might be made manifest in our body. 11. For we which live are alway delivered unto death for Jesus' sake, that the life also of Jesus might be made manifest in our mortal flesh. 12. So then death worketh in us, but life in you. 16. For which cause we faint not; but though our outward man perish, yet the inward *man* is renewed day by day. 17. For our light affliction, which is but for a moment, worketh for us a far more exceeding *and* eternal weight of glory.

2 Cor. 11:23. In labours more abundant, in stripes above measure, in prisons more frequent, in deaths oft. 24. Of the Jews five times received I forty *stripes* save one. 25. Thrice was I beaten with rods, once

was I stoned, thrice I suffered shipwreck, a night and a day I have been in the deep; 26. *In* journeyings often, *in* perils of waters, *in* perils of robbers, *in* perils by *mine own* countrymen, *in* perils by the heathen, *in* perils in the city, *in* perils in the wilderness, *in* perils in the sea, *in* perils among false brethren; 27. In weariness and painfulness, in watchings often, in hunger and thirst, in fastings often, in cold and nakedness. 28. Beside those things that are without, that which cometh upon me daily, the care of all the churches. 29. Who is weak, and I am not weak? who is offended, and I burn not? 30. If I must needs glory, I will glory of the things which concern my infirmities.

Heb. 12:6. For whom the Lord loveth he chasteneth, and scourgeth every son whom he receiveth. 7. If ye endure chastening, God dealeth with you as with sons; for what son is he whom the father chasteneth not? 9. Furthermore, we have had fathers of our flesh which corrected *us* and we gave *them* reverence: shall we not much rather be in subjection unto the Father of spirits, and live?

Benefits of: Job 5:17. Behold happy *is* the man whom God correcteth: therefore despise not thou the chastening of the Almighty.

Lam. 3:27. *It is* good for a man that he bear the yoke in his youth. 28. He sitteth alone and keepeth silence, because he hath borne *it* upon him.

Rom. 5:3. And not only *so,* but we glory in tribulations also; knowing that tribulation worketh patience: 4. And patience, experience; and experience, hope:

Rom. 8:17. And if children, then heirs; heirs of God, and joint heirs with Christ; if so be that we suffer with *him,* that we may be also glorified together. 28. And we know that all things work together for good to them that love God, to them who are the called according to *his* purpose.

2 Cor. 4:17. For our light affliction, which is but for a moment, worketh for us a far more exceeding *and* eternal weight of glory;

Phil. 1:12. But I would ye should understand, brethren, that the things *which happened* unto me have fallen out rather unto the furtherance of the gospel; 13. So that my bonds in Christ are manifest in all the palace, and in all other *places;* 14. And many of the brethren in the Lord, waxing confident by my bonds, are much more bold to speak the word without fear. 19. For I know that this shall turn to my salvation through your prayer, and the supply of the Spirit of Jesus Christ,

Jas. 1:2. My brethren, count it all joy when ye fall into divers temptations; 3. Knowing *this,* that the trying of your faith worketh patience. 4. But let patience have *her* perfect work, that ye may be perfect and entire, wanting nothing.

12. Blessed *is* the man that endureth temptation: for when he is tried, he shall receive the crown of life, which the Lord hath promised to them that love him.

1 Pet. 1:7. That the trial of your faith, being much more precious than gold that perisheth, though it be tried with fire, might be found unto praise and honour and glory at the appearing of Jesus Christ.

1 Pet. 4:14. If ye be reproached for the name of Christ, happy *are ye;* for the Spirit of glory and of God resteth upon you: [on their part he is evil spoken of, but on your part he is glorified] [Omitted in R. V.].

Consolation In: Psa. 69:33. For the LORD heareth the poor, and despiseth not his prisoners.

Nah. 1:7. The LORD *is* good, a strong hold in the day of trouble; and he knoweth them that trust in him.

Matt. 5:4. Blessed *are* they that mourn: for they shall be comforted. 10. Blessed *are* they which are persecuted for righteousness' sake: for theirs is the kingdom of heaven. 11. Blessed are ye, when *men* shall revile you, and persecute *you,* and shall say all manner of evil against you falsely, for my sake. 12. Rejoice, and be exceeding glad: for great *is* your reward in heaven: for

so persecuted they the prophets which were before you.

Matt. 10:29. Are not two sparrows sold for a farthing? and one of them shall not fall on the ground without your father. 30. But the very hairs of your head are all numbered. [Luke 21:18.] 31. Fear ye not therefore, ye are of more value than many sparrows. Luke 12:6,7.

Matt. 11:28. Come unto me, all *ye* that labour and are heavy laden, and I will give you rest.

Matt. 14:27. But straightway Jesus spake unto them, saying, Be of good cheer; it is I; be not afraid. Mark 6:50.

Luke 7:13. And when the Lord saw her, he had compassion on her, and said unto her, Weep not.

John 14:1. Let not your heart be troubled: ye believe in God, believe also in me. 16. And I will pray the Father, and he shall give you another Comforter, that he may abide with you for ever; 18. I will not leave you comfortless: I will come to you. 27. Peace I leave with you, my peace I give unto you: not as the world giveth, give I unto you. Let not your heart be troubled, neither let it be afraid.

Rom. 8:36. As it is written, For thy sake we are killed all the day long; we are accounted as sheep for the slaughter. 37. Nay, in all these things we are more than conquerors through him that loved us. 38. For I am persuaded, that neither death, nor life, nor angels, nor principalities, nor powers, nor things present, nor things to come, 39. Nor height, nor depth, nor any other creature, shall be able to separate us from the love of God, which is in Christ Jesus our Lord.

2 Cor. 12:9. And he said unto me, My grace is sufficient for thee: for my strength is made perfect in weakness. Most gladly therefore will I rather glory in my infirmities, that the power of Christ may rest upon me.

Gal. 6:2. Bear ye one another's burdens, and so fulfil the law of Christ.

2 Thess. 2:16. Now, our Lord Jesus Christ himself, and God, even our Father, which hath loved us,

and hath given *us* everlasting consolation and good hope through grace, 17. Comfort your hearts, and stablish you in every good word and work.

2 Tim. 2:12. If we suffer, we shall also reign with *him:*

Heb. 4:15. For we have not an high priest which cannot be touched with the feeling of our infirmities: but was in all points tempted like as *we are, yet* without sin. 16. Let us therefore come boldly unto the throne of grace, that we may obtain mercy, and find grace to help in time of need.

Heb. 12:1. Wherefore, seeing we also are compassed about with so great a cloud of witnesses, let us lay aside every weight, and the sin which doth so easily beset *us*, and let us run with patience the race that is set before us, 2. Looking unto Jesus the author and finisher of *our* faith; who for the joy that was set before him endured the cross, despising the shame, and is set down at the right hand of the throne of God. 3. For consider him that endured such contradiction of sinners against himself, lest ye be wearied and faint in your minds. 4. Ye have not yet resisted unto blood, striving against sin.

Jas. 1:12. Blessed *is* the man that endureth temptation; for when he is tried, he shall receive the crown of life, which the Lord hath promised to them that love him.

1 Pet. 4:12. Beloved, think it not strange concerning the fiery trial which is to try you, as though some strange thing happened unto you: 13. But rejoice, inasmuch as ye are partakers of Christ's sufferings, that when his glory shall be revealed, ye may be glad also with exceeding joy. 14. If ye be reproached for the name of Christ, happy *are ye;* for the Spirit of glory and of God resteth upon you.

1 Pet. 5:7. Casting all your care upon him; for he careth for you. 9. Knowing that the same afflictions are accomplished in your brethren that are in the world.

Design of: Job 33:11. He putteth my feet in the stocks, he marketh all my paths. 16. Then he

openeth the ears of men, and sealeth their instruction, 17. That he may withdraw man *from his* purpose, and hide pride from man. 18. He keepeth back his soul from the pit, and his life from perishing by the sword. 19. He is chastened also with pain upon his bed, and the multitude of his bones with strong *pain:* 20. So that his life abhorreth bread, and his soul dainty meat. 21. His flesh is consumed away, that it cannot be seen; and his bones *that* were not seen stick out. 22. Yea, his soul draweth near unto the grave, and his life to the destroyers. 23. If there be a messenger with him, an interpreter, one among a thousand, to shew unto man his uprightness; 24. Then he is gracious unto him, and saith, Deliver him from going down to the pit; I have found a ransom. 25. His flesh shall be fresher than a child's: he shall return to the days of his youth: 26. He shall pray unto God, and he will be favourable unto him: and he shall see his face with joy: for he will render unto man his righteousness. 27. He looketh upon men, and *if any* say, I have sinned, and perverted *that which was* right, and it profited me not; 28. He will deliver his soul from going into the pit, and his life shall see the light. 29. Lo, all these *things* worketh God oftentimes with man, 30. To bring back his soul from the pit, to be enlightened with the light of the living.

Job 36:8. And if *they be* bound in fetters, *and* be holden in cords of affliction; 9. Then he sheweth them their work, and their transgressions that they have exceeded. 10. He openeth also their ear to discipline, and commandeth that they return from iniquity.

Psa. 66:10. For thou, O God, hast proved us: thou hast tried us, as silver is tried.

Psa. 107:10. Such as sit in darkness and in the shadow of death, *being* bound in affliction and iron; 11. Because they rebelled against the words of God, and contemned the counsel of the Most High: 12. Therefore he brought down their heart with labour; they fell down, and *there was* none to help. 13. Then they cried unto the Lord in their trouble, *and* he saved them out of their distresses. 14. He brought them out of darkness and the shadow of death, and brake their bands in sunder. 17. Fools, because of their transgression, and because of their iniquities, are afflicted.

Psa. 119:71. *It is* good for me that I have been afflicted; that I might learn thy statutes.

John 9:2. And his disciples asked him, saying, Master, who did sin, this man, or his parents, that he was born blind? 3. Jesus answered, Neither hath this man sinned, nor his parents: but that the works of God should be made manifest in him.

John 11:4. When Jesus heard *that,* he said, This sickness is not unto death, but for the glory of God, that the Son of God might be glorified thereby.

1 Cor. 11:32. But when we are judged, we are chastened of the Lord, that we should not be condemned with the world.

2 Cor. 1:4. Who comforteth us in all our tribulation, that we may be able to comfort them which are in any trouble, by the comfort wherewith we ourselves are comforted of God. 5. For as the sufferings of Christ abound in us, so our consolation also aboundeth by Christ. 6. And whether we be afflicted, *it is* for your consolation and salvation, which is effectual in the enduring of the same sufferings which we also suffer: or whether we be comforted, *it is* for your consolation and salvation.

2 Cor. 12:7. And lest I should be exalted above measure through the abundance of the revelations, there was given to me a thorn in the flesh, the messenger of Satan to buffet me, lest I should be exalted above measure.

Heb. 5:8. Though he were a Son, yet learned he obedience by the things which he suffered; 9. And being made perfect, he became the author of eternal salvation unto all them that obey him.

Heb. 12:5. And ye have forgotten the exhortation which speaketh unto you as unto children, My son, despise not thou the chastening of the Lord, nor faint when thou art rebuked of him: 6. For whom the Lord loveth he chasteneth, and scourgeth every son whom he receiveth. 7. If ye endure chastening, God dealeth with you as with sons; for what son is he whom the father chasteneth not? 8. But if ye be without chastisement, whereof all are partakers, then are ye bastards, and not sons. 9. Furthermore, we have had fathers of our flesh which corrected *us,* and we gave *them* reverence: shall we not much rather be in subjection unto the Father of spirits, and live? 10. For they verily for a few days chastened *us* after their own pleasure; but he for *our* profit, that *we* might be partakers of his holiness. 11. Now no chastening for the present seemeth to be joyous, but grievous: nevertheless, afterward it yieldeth the peaceable fruit of righteousness unto them which are exercised thereby.

1 Pet. 1:6. Wherein ye greatly rejoice, though now for a season, if need be, ye are in heaviness through manifold temptations: 7. That the trial of your faith, being much more precious than of gold that perisheth, though it be tried with fire, might be found unto praise and honour and glory at the appearing of Jesus Christ:

Rev. 2:10. Fear none of those things which thou shalt suffer: behold, the devil shall cast *some* of you into prison, that ye may be tried; and ye shall have tribulation ten days: be thou faithful unto death, and I will give thee a crown of life.

Despondency in: Psa. 22:1. My God, my God, why hast thou forsaken me? *why art thou so* far from helping me, *and from* the words of my roaring? 2. O my God, I cry in the daytime, but thou hearest not; and in the night season, and am not silent.

Prov. 24:10. *If* thou faint in the day of adversity, thy strength *is* small.

Luke 18:1. And he spake a parable unto them *to this end,* that men ought always to pray, and not to faint;

Job 21:17. How oft is the candle of the wicked put out! and *how oft* cometh their destruction upon them! *God* distributeth sorrows in his anger.

Psa. 90:7. For we are consumed by thine anger, and by thy wrath are we troubled. 15. Make us glad according to the days *wherein* thou hast afflicted us.

Obduracy in: Lev. 26:23. If ye will not be reformed by me by these things, but will walk contrary unto me; 24. Then will I also walk contrary unto you, and will punish you yet seven times for your sins. *vs.* 27,28.

Jer. 5:3. O LORD, *are* not thine eyes upon the truth? thou hast stricken them, but they have not grieved; thou hast consumed them, *but* they have refused to receive correction: they have made their faces harder than a rock; they have refused to return.

Hag. 2:17. I smote you with blasting and with mildew and with hail in all the labours of your hands; yet ye *turned* not to me, saith the LORD.

Rev. 16:9. And men were scorched with great heat, and blasphemed the name of God, which hath power over these plagues: and they repented not to give him glory. 10. And the fifth angel poured out his vial upon the seat of the beast; and his kingdom was full of darkness; and they gnawed their tongues for pain, 11. And blasphemed the God of heaven because of their pains and their sores, and repented not of their deeds. *v.* 21.

Prayer in: 1 Kin. 8:35. When heaven is shut up, and there is no rain, because they have sinned against thee; if they pray toward this place, and confess thy name, and turn from their sin when thou afflictest them: with *vs.* 36-50; 2 Chr. 6:24-39.

1 Chr. 5:20. They cried to God in the battle, and he was entreated of them; because they put their trust in him.

2 Chr. 14:11. And Asa cried unto the LORD his God, and said, LORD,

it is nothing with thee to help, whether with many, or with them that have no power: help us, O LORD our God; for we rest on thee, and in thy name we go against this multitude. O LORD, thou *art* our God; let not man prevail against thee.

2 Chr. 20:12. O our God, wilt thou not judge them? for we have no might against this great company that cometh against us; neither know we what to do; but our eyes *are* upon thee. *vs.* 4-13.

2 Chr. 33:12. And when he was in affliction, he besought the LORD his God, and humbled himself greatly before the God of his fathers. 13. And prayed unto him: and he was entreated of him, and heard his supplication, and brought him again to Jerusalem into his kingdom. Then Manasseh knew that the LORD he *was* God.

Neh. 9:32. Now therefore, our God, the great, the mighty, and the terrible God, who keepest covenant and mercy, let not all the trouble seem little before thee, that hath come upon us, on our kings, on our princes, and on our priests, and on our prophets, and on our fathers, and on all thy people, since the time of the kings of Assyria unto this day.

Job 16:20. My friends scorn me: *but* mine eye poureth out *tears* unto God.

Psa. 6:1. O LORD, rebuke me not in thine anger, neither chasten me in thy hot displeasure. 2. Have mercy upon me, O LORD; for I *am* weak: O LORD, heal me; for my bones are vexed. 3. My soul is also sore vexed; but thou, O LORD, how long? 4. Return, O LORD, deliver my soul: oh save me for thy mercies' sake. *vs.* 5-7.

Psa. 10:1. Why standest thou afar off, O LORD? *why* hidest thou *thyself* in times of trouble? 12. Arise, O LORD; O God, lift up thine hand: forget not the humble. *vs.* 13-15.

Psa. 16:1. Preserve me, O God: for in thee do I put my trust.

Psa. 20:1. The LORD hear thee in the day of trouble; the name of the God of Jacob defend thee; 2. Send thee help from the sanctuary, and strengthen thee out of Zion;

Psa. 27:11. Teach me thy way, O Lord, and lead me in a plain path, because of mine enemies. 12. Deliver me not over unto the will of mine enemies: for false witnesses are risen up against me, and such as breathe out cruelty.

Psa. 31:1. In thee, O Lord, do I put my trust; let me never be ashamed: deliver me in thy righteousness. 2. Bow down thine ear to me; deliver me speedily: be thou my strong rock, for an house of defence to save me. 3. For thou *art* my rock and my fortress, therefore for thy name's sake lead me, and guide me. 4. Pull me out of the net that they have laid privily for me: for thou *art* my strength. [*vs.* 15-18.] 9. Have mercy upon me, O Lord, for I am in trouble: mine eye is consumed with grief, *yea,* my soul and my belly. 14. But I trusted in thee, O Lord: I said, Thou *art* my God. 15. My times *are* in thy hand: deliver me from the hand of mine enemies, and from them that persecute me. 16. Make thy face to shine upon thy servant: save me for thy mercies' sake. 17. Let me not be ashamed, O Lord: for I have called upon thee.

Psa. 35:17. Lord, how long wilt thou look on? rescue my soul from their destructions, my darling from the lions. 19. Let not them that are mine enemies wrongfully rejoice over me: *neither* let them wink with the eye that hate me without a cause.

22. *This* thou hast seen, O Lord: keep not silence: O Lord, be not far from me. 23. Stir up thyself, and awake to my judgment, *even* unto my cause, my God and my Lord. 25. Let them not say in their hearts, Ah, so would we have it: let them not say, We have swallowed him up.

Psa. 38:21. Forsake me not, O Lord: O my God, be not far from me. 22. Make haste to help me, O Lord my salvation. *vs.* 1-22.

Psa. 39:13. O spare me, that I may recover strength, before I go hence, and be no more.

Psa. 40:13. Be pleased, O Lord,

to deliver me: O Lord, make haste to help me. 17. I *am* poor and needy; *yet* the Lord thinketh upon me: thou *art* my help and my deliverer; make no tarrying, O my God. Psa. 70:5.

Psa. 50:15. And call upon me in the day of trouble: I will deliver thee, and thou shalt glorify me.

Psa. 57:1. Be merciful unto me, O God, be merciful unto me: for my soul trusteth in thee: yea, in the shadow of thy wings will I make my refuge, until *these* calamities be overpast. 2. I will cry unto God most high; unto God that performeth *all things* for me.

Psa. 61:1. Hear my cry, O God; attend unto my prayer. 2. From the end of the earth will I cry unto thee, when my heart is overwhelmed: lead me to the rock *that* is higher than I.

Psa. 69:1. Save me, O God; for the waters are come in unto *my* soul.

Psa. 71:9. Cast me not off in the time of old age; forsake me not when my strength faileth.

Psa. 74:10. O God, how long shall the adversary reproach? shall the enemy blaspheme thy name for ever?

Psa. 79:11. Let the sighing of the prisoner come before thee; according to the greatness of thy power preserve thou those that are appointed to die; *vs.* 1-11.

Psa. 80:1. Give ear, O Shepherd of Israel, thou that leadest Joseph like a flock; thou that dwellest *between* the cherubims, shine forth.

Psa. 85:5. Wilt thou be angry with us for ever? wilt thou draw out thine anger to all generations? 6. Wilt thou not revive us again: that thy people may rejoice in thee? 7. Shew us thy mercy, O Lord, and grant us thy salvation.

Psa. 102:2. Hide not thy face from me in the day *when* I am in trouble; incline thine ear unto me: in the day *when* I call answer me speedily. 24. O my God, take me not away in the midst of my days:

Psa. 130:1. Out of the depths have I cried unto thee, O Lord. 2. Lord, hear my voice: let thine ears

AFFLICTIONS

be attentive to the voice of my supplications. *vs.* 1-8.

Isa. 51:9. Awake, awake, put on strength, O arm of the LORD; awake, as in the ancient days, in the generations of old.

Dan. 6:10. He kneeled upon his knees three times a day, and prayed, and gave thanks before his God, as he did aforetime.

Hab. 1:12. *Art* thou not from everlasting, O LORD my God, mine Holy One? we shall not die. O LORD, thou hast ordained them for judgment; and, O mighty God, thou hast established them for correction. 13. *Thou art* of purer eyes than to behold evil, and canst not look on iniquity: wherefore lookest thou upon them that deal treacherously, *and* holdest thy tongue when the wicked devoureth *the man that is* more righteous than he?

Matt. 15:28. Then Jesus answered and said unto her, O woman, great *is* thy faith: be it unto thee even as thou wilt.

Matt. 26:39. And he went a little farther, and fell on his face, and prayed, saying, O my Father, if it be possible, let this cup pass from me: nevertheless, not as I will, but as thou *wilt*. 42. He went away again the second time, and prayed, saying, O my Father, if this cup may not pass away from me, except I drink it, thy will be done. *v.* 44; Mark 14:36; Luke 22:42.

Luke 18:1. And he spake a parable unto them *to this end*, that men ought always to pray, and not to faint;

Acts 4:29. Now, Lord, behold their threatenings; and grant unto thy servants, that with all boldness they may speak thy word, 30. By stretching forth thy hand to heal; and that signs and wonders may be done by the name of thy holy child Jesus.

Acts 7:59. And they stoned Stephen, calling upon *God*, and saying, Lord Jesus, receive my spirit. 60. And he kneeled down, and cried with a loud voice, Lord, lay not this sin to their charge.

2 Cor. 12:8. For this thing I besought the Lord thrice, that it might depart from me.

Jas. 5:13. Is any among you afflicted? let him pray. Is any merry? let him sing psalms. 14. Is any sick among you? let him call for the elders of the church; and let them pray over him, anointing him with oil in the name of the Lord: 15. And the prayer of faith shall save the sick, and the Lord shall raise him up; and if he have committed sins, they shall be forgiven him. 16. Confess *your* faults one to another, and pray one for another, that ye may be healed. The effectual fervent prayer of a righteous man availeth much.

Resignation in: Job 13:15. Though he slay me, yet will I trust in him:

Lam. 3:22. *It is of* the LORD'S mercies that we are not consumed, because his compassions fail not. 23. *They are* new every morning: great *is* thy faithfulness.

Phil. 2:14. Do all things without murmurings:

1 Thess. 3:3. That no man should be moved by these afflictions: for yourselves know that we are appointed thereunto. *v.* 4.

2 Tim. 2:3. Endure hardness, as a good soldier of Jesus Christ.

Jas. 4:7. Submit yourselves therefore to God.

1 Pet. 2:20. For what glory *is it*, if, when ye be buffeted for your faults, ye shall take it patiently? but if, when ye do well, and suffer *for it*, ye take it patiently, this *is* acceptable with God.

1 Pet. 4:12. Beloved, think it not strange concerning the fiery trial which is to try you, as though some strange thing happened unto you: 13. But rejoice, inasmuch as ye are partakers of Christ's sufferings; that, when his glory shall be revealed, ye may be glad also with exceeding joy. 19. Wherefore, let them that suffer according to the will of God commit the keeping of their souls *to him* in well doing, as unto a faithful Creator.

1 Pet. 5:6. Humble yourselves therefore under the mighty hand of God, that he may exalt you in due time: 7. Casting all your care upon him; for he careth for you.

15

AGENCY, In Salvation of Men: Psa. 8:2 Out of the mouth of babes and sucklings hast thou ordained strength because of thine enemies, that thou mightest still the enemy and the avenger.

Matt. 4:19. And he saith unto them, Follow me, and I will make you fishers of men. Luke 5:10.

Luke 1:17. And he shall go before him in the spirit and power of Elias, to turn the hearts of the fathers to the children, and the disobedient to the wisdom of the just; to make ready a people prepared for the Lord.

John 15:16. Ye have not chosen me, but I have chosen you, and ordained you, that ye should go and bring forth fruit, and *that* your fruit should remain.

Jas. 5:20. Let him know, that he which converteth the sinner from the error of his way shall save a soul from death, and shall hide a multitude of sins.

See PREACHING.

In Executing Judgments: 1 Sam. 15:18. And the LORD sent thee on a journey, and said, Go and utterly destroy the sinners the Amalekites, and fight against them until they be consumed. with *vs.* 1-19.

2 Sam. 7:14. If he commit iniquity, I will chasten him with the rod of men, and with the stripes of the children of men:

Isa. 10:5. O Assyrian, the rod of mine anger, and the staff in their hand is mine indignation. 6. I will send him against a hypocritical nation, and against the people of my wrath will I give him a charge, to take the spoil, and to take the prey, and to tread them down like the mire of the streets.

Isa. 13:5. They come from a far country, from the end of heaven, *even* the LORD, and the weapons of his indignation, to destroy the whole land.

Jer. 51:20. Thou *art* my battle ax *and* weapons of war: for with thee will I break in pieces the nations, and with thee will I destroy kingdoms;

AGENCY, FREE MORAL. See CONTINGENCIES.

AGRICULTURE, Laws Concerning: Ex. 22:5. If a man shall cause a field or vineyard to be eaten, and shall put in his beast, and shall feed in another man's field; of the best of his own field, and of the best of his own vineyard, shall he make restitution.

6. If fire break out, and catch in thorns, so that the stacks of corn, or the standing corn, or the field, be consumed *therewith;* he that kindled the fire shall surely make restitution.

Ex. 34:21. Six days shalt thou work, but on the seventh day thou shalt rest: in earing time and in harvest thou shalt rest. Ex. 20:9; 23:12; Deut. 5:13,14.

Lev. 19:9. And when ye reap the harvest of your land, thou shalt not wholly reap the corners of thy field, neither shalt thou gather the gleanings of thy harvest. 10. And thou shalt not glean thy vineyard, neither shalt thou gather *every* grape of thy vineyard; thou shalt leave them for the poor and stranger: I *am* the LORD your God.

Deut. 22:10. Thou shalt not plow with an ox and an ass together.

Deut. 23:24. When thou comest into thy neighbour's vineyard, then thou mayest eat grapes thy fill at thine own pleasure; but thou shalt not put *any* in thy vessel. 25. When thou comest into the standing corn of thy neighbour, then thou mayest pluck the ears with thine hand: but thou shalt not move a sickle unto thy neighbour's standing corn. Matt. 12:1.

Deut. 24:19. When thou cuttest down thine harvest in thy field, and hast forgot a sheaf in the field, thou shalt not go again to fetch it: it shall be for the stranger, for the fatherless, and for the widow: that the LORD thy God may bless thee in all the work of thine hands. 20. When thou beatest thine olive tree, thou shalt not go over the boughs again: it shall be for the stranger, for the fatherless, and for the widow. 21. When thou gatherest the grapes of thy vineyard, thou shalt not glean *it* afterward: it shall be for the stranger, for the fatherless, and for the widow.

16

Prov. 3:9. Honor the LORD with thy substance, and with the first fruits of all thine increase: 10. So shall thy barns be filled with plenty, and thy presses shall burst out with new wine.

2 Cor. 9:6. But this *I say*, He which soweth sparingly shall reap also sparingly; and he which soweth bountifully shall reap also bountifully.

Gal. 6:7. Be not deceived; God is not mocked: for whatsoever a man soweth, that shall he also reap.

ALABASTER. A white stone. Vessels made of, Matt. 26:7; Mark 14:3; Luke 7:37.

ALIENS, strangers, heathen. To be treated with justice, Ex. 22:21; 23:9; Lev. 19:33,34; Deut. 1:16; 10:19; 24:14,17; 27:19.

ALLIANCES, Political: With idolaters forbidden, Ex. 23:32,33; 34:12-15; Deut. 7:2; Judg. 2:2; 2 Chr. 19:2; 20:37; Isa. 30:2; 31:1; Hos. 4:17; 5:13; 12:1; Ezek. 17:15. Ratification of: By oaths, Gen. 21:23; 26:28-31; Josh. 9:15-20; I Sam. 20:16,17; by giving the hand, Lam. 5:6.

ALMOND, a tree. Fruit of, Gen. 43:11. Aaron's rod of the, Num. 17:8. Bowls of candlestick in the tabernacle fashioned after the nuts of the, Ex. 25:33,34; 37:19,20.

ALMS. Enjoined, Deut. 15:7-11; Matt. 5:42; 19:21; Luke 12:33; 2 Cor. 9:5-7; Gal. 2:10; 1 Tim. 6:18; Heb. 13:16. To be given without ostentation, Matt. 6:1-4; Rom. 12:8; freely, 2 Cor. 9:6,7. Withholding, not of love, 1 John 3:17. Solicited by the unfortunate, John 9:8; Acts 3:2.

Instances of Giving: Zaccheus, Luke 19:8. Dorcas, Acts 9:36. Cornelius, Acts 10:2. The early Christians, Acts 2:44,45; 4:34-37; 6:1-3; 11:29,30; 24:17; Rom. 15:25-28; 1 Cor. 16:1-4; 2 Cor. 8:1-4; 9:1; Heb. 6:10.

ALOES. Used as perfume, Psa. 45:8; Prov. 7:17; Song 4:14; In embalming the dead, John 19:39. Lign-aloes, Num. 24:6.

ALPHA, a title of Christ, Rev. 1:8,11; 21:6; 22:13. Compare Isa. 41:4; 44:6; 48:12.

ALTRUISM, Disinterested Benevolence. Matt. 20:26. Whosoever will be great among you, let him be your minister; 27. And whosoever will be chief among you, let him be your servant: [Matt. 23:11.] 28. Even as the Son of man came not to be ministered unto, but to minister, and to give his life a ransom for many. Mark 10:43-45; Luke 22:26,27.

Rom. 15:1. We then that are strong ought to bear the infirmities of the weak, and not to please ourselves. 2. Let every one of us please *his* neighbour for *his* good to edification. 3. For even Christ pleased not himself; but, as it is written, The reproaches of them that reproached thee fell on me.

1 Cor. 10:24. Let no man seek his own, but every man another's [wealth]. 31. Whether therefore ye eat, or drink, or whatsoever ye do, do all to the glory of God. (R.V. [good])

2 Cor. 4:5. For we preach not ourselves, but Christ Jesus the Lord; and ourselves your servants for Jesus' sake.

2 Cor. 8:9. For ye know the grace of our Lord Jesus Christ, that, though he was rich, yet for your sakes he became poor, that ye through his poverty might be rich.

Phil. 2:3. *Let* nothing *be done* through strife or vainglory; but in lowliness of · mind let each esteem other better than themselves. 4. Look not every man on his own things, but every man also on the things of others. 5. Let this mind be in you, which was also in Christ Jesus: 6. Who, being in the form of God, thought it not robbery to be equal with God: 7. But [made] himself [of no reputation, and took upon him] the form of a servant, [and was] made in the likeness of men: 8. And being found in fashion as a man, he humbled himself, and became obedient unto death, even the death of the cross. (R.V. [emptied] [taking] [being])

AMBASSADORS. Figurative: Job 33:23; Obad. 1; 2 Cor. 5:20; Eph. 6:20.

17

AMBITION. Isa. 5:8. Woe unto them that join house to house, *that* lay field to field, till *there be* no place, that they may be placed alone in the midst of the earth!

Matt. 16:26. For what is a man profited, if he shall gain the whole world, and lose his own soul? or what shall a man give in exchange for his soul? Luke 9:25.

Mark 9:33. And he came to Capernaum: and being in the house he asked them, What was it that ye disputed among yourselves by the way? [Luke 22:24.] 34. But they held their peace: for by the way they had disputed among themselves, who *should be* the greatest.

Mark 10:35. And James and John, the sons of Zebedee, come unto him, saying, Master, we would that thou shouldest do for us whatsoever we shall desire. [Matt. 20:20.] 36. And he said unto them, What would ye that I should do for you? 37. They said unto him, Grant unto us that we may sit, one on thy right hand, and the other on thy left hand, in thy glory.

John 5:44. How can ye believe, which receive honour one of another, and seek not the honour that *cometh* from God only?

1 Tim. 3:1. This *is* a true saying, If a man desire the office of a bishop, he desireth a good work.

Jas. 4:1. From whence *come* wars and fightings among you? *come they* not hence, *even* of your lusts that war in your members? 2. Ye lust, and have not: ye kill, and desire to have, and cannot obtain: ye fight and war, yet ye have not, because ye ask not.

1 John 2:16. For all that *is* in the world, the lust of the flesh, and the lust of the eyes, and the pride of life, is not of the Father, but is of the world.

Instances of: Lucifer, Isa. 14:12-15. Eve, Gen. 3:5,6. The builders of Babel, Gen. 11:4. Aaron and Miriam, Num. 12:2-10. Korah and his co-conspirators, Num. 16:3-35. Abimelech, Judg. 9:1-6. Absalom, 2 Sam. 15:1-13; 18:18. Ahithophel, 2 Sam. 17:23. Adonijah, 1 Kin. 1:5. Sennacherib, 2 Kin. 19:23. Haman, Esth. 5:9-13; 6:6-9. Diotrephes, 3 John 9, 10.

AMBUSH. Instances of: At Ai, Josh. 8:2-22; Shechem, Judg. 9:25,34; Gibeah, Judg. 20:29-41. Near Zemaraim, 2 Chr. 13:13.

By Jehoshaphat, 2 Chr. 20:22. See ARMIES.

Figurative: Jer. 51:12.

AMETHYST, a precious stone, Ex. 28:19; 39:12; Rev. 21:20.

AMNESTY. For political offenses: To Shimei, 2 Sam. 19:16-23; to Amasa, 2 Sam. 19:13, with 17:25.

AMUSEMENTS AND WORLDLY PLEASURES. Belong to the works of the flesh, Gal. 5:19,21; are transitory, Job 21:12, 13; Heb. 11:25; vain, Eccl. 2:11; choke the word of God in the heart, Luke 8:14; formed a part of idolatrous worship, Ex. 32:4,6,19, with 1 Cor. 10:7; Judg. 16:23-25.

Lead to rejection of God, Job. 21:12-15; poverty, Prov. 21:17; disregard of the judgments and works of God, Isa. 5:12; Amos 6:1-6; terminate in sorrow, Prov. 14:13; lead to greater evil, Job 1:5; Matt. 14:6-8; the wicked seek for happiness in, Eccl. 2:1,8.

Indulgence in, a proof of folly, Eccl. 7:4; a characteristic of the wicked, Isa. 47:8; Eph. 4:17,19; 2 Tim. 3:4; Tit. 3:3; 1 Pet. 4:3; a proof of spiritual death, 1 Tim. 5:6; an abuse of riches, Jas. 5:1,5; wisdom of abstaining from, Eccl. 7:2,3; shunned by the primitive saints, 1 Pet. 4:3.

Abstinence from, seems strange to the wicked, 1 Pet. 4:4; denounced by God, Isa. 5:11,12; exclude from the kingdom of God, Gal. 5:21; punishment of, Eccl. 11:9; 2 Pet. 2:13; renunciation of, exemplified by Moses, Heb. 11:25.—*Bible Text Book.*

ANARCHY. Isa. 3:5. And the people shall be oppressed, every one by another, and every one by his neighbour: the child shall behave himself proudly against the ancient, and the base against the honourable. 6. When a man shall take hold of his brother of the house of his father, *saying,* Thou hast clothing, be thou our ruler, and *let* this ruin *be* under thy hand;

Gal. 5:13. For, brethren, ye have been called unto liberty; only *use* not liberty for an occasion to the flesh, but by love serve one another. 14. For all the law is fulfilled in one word, *even* in this; Thou shalt love thy neighbour as thyself.

ANATOMY, human, Job 10:11.

ANCHOR, Acts 27:29,30. FIGURATIVE: Heb. 6:19.

ANCIENT OF DAYS, an appellation of Jehovah, Dan. 7:9,13, 22.

ANDREW. An apostle. A fisherman, Matt. 4:18. Of Bethsaida, John 1:44. A disciple of John, John 1:40. Finds Peter, his brother, and brings him to Jesus, John 1:40-42. Call of, Matt. 4:18; Mark 1:16. His name appears in the list of the apostles in Matt. 10:2; Mark 3:18; Luke 6:14. Asks the Master privately about the destruction of the temple, Mark 13:3,4. Tells Jesus of the Greeks who sought to see him, John 12:20-22. Reports the number of loaves at the feeding of the five thousand, John 6:8. Meets with the disciples after the Lord's ascension, Acts 1:13.

ANGEL. One of the Holy Trinity: Trinitarian authorities interpret the Scriptures cited under this topic as referring to Christ, who according to this view was the divine presence in the wilderness. Called ANGEL, Acts 7:30,35; MINE ANGEL, Ex. 32:34; ANGEL OF GOD, Ex. 14:19; Judg. 13:6; 2 Sam. 14: 17,20; ANGEL OF THE LORD, Ex. 3:2; Judg. 2:1; ANGEL OF HIS PRESENCE, Isa. 63:9.

ANGEL. A Celestial Spirit: Called ANGEL OF THE LORD, Matt. 1:20,24; 2:13,19; 28:2; Luke 1:11; Acts 5:19; 8:26; 12:7,23; MORNING STARS, Job 38:7; HOSTS, Gen. 2:1; 32:2; Josh. 5:14; 1 Chr. 12:22; Psa. 33:6; 103:21; Luke 2:13; PRINCIPALITIES, POWERS, Eph. 3:10; Col. 1:16. Created, Gen. 2:1; Neh. 9:6; Col. 1:16. Of different orders Isa. 6:2; 1 Thess. 4:16; 1 Pet. 3:22; Jude 9; Rev. 12:7. Immortal, Luke 20:36. Worship God, Neh. 9:6; Phil. 2:9-11; Heb. 1:6. Not to be worshipped, Col. 2:18; Rev. 19:10;

22:8,9. Do not marry, Matt. 22:30; Mark 12:25; Luke 20:35. Are obedient, Psa. 103:20; Matt. 6:10; Luke 11:2; 1 Pet. 3:22; 2 Pet. 2:11; Jude 6. Have knowledge of, and interest in, earthly affairs, Matt. 24:36; Luke 15:7,10; 1 Tim. 5:21; 1 Pet. 1:12. To be judged by men, 1 Cor. 6:3. See FUNCTIONS OF, below.

Men called angels, 2 Sam. 19:27. Are examples of meekness, 2 Pet. 2:11; Jude 9. Are wise, 2 Sam. 14:17,20; mighty, Psa. 103:20; 2 Pet. 2:11; holy, Matt. 25:31; Mark 8:38; elect, 1 Tim. 5:21; innumerable, Deut. 33:2; 2 Kin. 6:17; Job 25:3; Psa. 68:17 [R. V. omits angels in v. 17]; Heb. 12:22; Jude 14.

Aspects of, Judg. 13:6; Isa. 6:2; Dan. 10:6; Matt. 28:3. See UNCLASSIFIED SCRIPTURES RELATING TO, below.

Functions of: Guard the way to the tree of life, Gen. 3:24. Law given by, Acts 7:53; Gal. 3:19; Heb. 2:2. Medium of revelation to prophets, 2 Kin. 1:15; Dan. 4:13-17; 8:19; 9:21-27; 10:10-20; Zech. 1:9-11; Acts 8:26; Gal. 3:19; Heb. 2:2; Rev. 1:1; 5:2-14; 7:1-3, 11-17; 8:2-13; chapters 9 to 20; 22:6,16.

Remonstrates with Balaam, Num. 22:22-27. Announces the birth of Samson, Judg. 13; of John the Baptist, Luke 1:11-20; of Jesus, Matt. 1:20,21; Luke 1:28-38; 2:7-15. Warns Joseph to escape to Egypt, Matt. 2:13. Minister to Jesus after the temptation, Matt. 4:11; Mark 1:13; John 1:51; during his passion, Luke 22:43. Present at the tomb of Jesus, Matt. 28:2-6; the ascension, Acts 1:11. Will be with Christ at his second coming, Matt. 25:31; Mark 8:38; 2 Thess. 1:7; Jude 14,15; at the judgment, Matt. 13:39, 41,49; 16:27; 24:31; 25:31; Mark 13:27.

MINISTRANT TO THE RIGHTEOUS: Gen. 16:7. And the angel of the LORD found her by a fountain of water in the wilderness, by the fountain in the way to Shur.

Gen. 24:7. He shall send his angel before thee. [Ex. 32:34; 33:2.] 40. The LORD, before whom I walk, will send his angel with thee, and prosper thy way;

1 Kin. 19:5. And as he lay and

slept under a juniper tree, behold, then an angel touched him, and said unto him, Arise *and* eat.

Psa. 34:7. The angel of the LORD encampeth round about them that fear him, and delivereth them.

Psa. 91:11. For he shall give his angels charge over thee, to keep thee in all thy ways. 12. They shall bear thee up in *their* hands, lest thou dash thy foot against a stone. Matt. 4:6; Luke 4:10,11.

Isa. 63:9. In all their affliction he was afflicted, and the angel of his presence saved them:

Dan. 6:22. My God hath sent his angel, and hath shut the lions' mouths, that they have not hurt me: forasmuch as before him innocency was found in me; and also before thee, O king, have I done no hurt.

Luke 16:22. The beggar died, and was carried by the angels into Abraham's bosom.

Acts 5:19. But the angel of the Lord by night opened the prison doors, and brought them forth, and said, 20. Go, stand and speak in the temple to the people all the words of this life.

Acts 12:7. And, behold, the angel of the Lord came upon *him*, and a light shined in the prison: and he smote Peter on the side, and raised him up, saying, Arise up quickly. And his chains fell off from *his* hands.

Heb. 1:7. And of the angels he saith, Who maketh his angels spirits, and his ministers a flame of fire. 14. Are they not all ministering spirits, sent forth to minister for them who shall be heirs of salvation?

Heb. 13:2. Be not forgetful to entertain strangers: for thereby some have entertained angels unawares.

2 Chr. 32:21. And the LORD sent an angel, which cut off all the mighty men of valour, and the leaders and captains in the camp of the king of Assyria. Isa. 37:36.

Psa. 35:5. Let them be as chaff before the wind: and let the angel of the LORD chase *them*. 6. Let their way be dark and slippery: and let the angel of the LORD persecute them.

Matt. 13:41. The Son of man shall send forth his angels, and they shall gather out of his kingdom all things that offend, and them which do iniquity; 42. And shall cast them into a furnace of fire: there shall be wailing and gnashing of teeth. *vs.* 49,50.

Rev. 9:15. And the four angels were loosed, which were prepared for an hour, and a day, and a month, and a year, for to slay the third part of men.

Unclassified Scriptures Relating to: Job 38:7. When the morning stars sang together, and all the sons of God shouted for joy?

Psa. 103:20. Bless the LORD, ye his angels, that excel in strength, that do his commandments, hearkening unto the voice of his word. 21. Bless ye the LORD, all *ye* his hosts; *ye* ministers of his, that do his pleasure.

Isa. 6:2. Above it stood the seraphims: each one had six wings; with twain he covered his face, and with twain he covered his feet, and with twain he did fly.

Ezek. 1:13. As for the likeness of the living creatures, their appearance *was* like burning coals of fire, *and* like the appearance of lamps: it went up and down among the living creatures; and the fire was bright, and out of the fire went forth lightning.

Dan. 4:17. This matter *is* by the decree of the watchers, and the demand by the word of the holy ones:

Matt. 18:10. Take heed that ye despise not one of these little ones; for I say unto you, That in heaven their angels do always behold the face of my Father which is in heaven.

Matt. 24:31. He shall send his angels with a great sound of a trumpet, and they shall gather together his elect from the four winds, from one end of heaven to the other. 36. Of that day and hour knoweth no *man*, no, not the angels of heaven,

Matt. 25:31. The Son of man shall come in his glory, and all the holy angels with him.

Luke 12:8. Whosoever shall confess me before men, him shall the

Son of man also confess before the angels of God: 9. But he that denieth me before men shall be denied before the angels of God. Mark 8:38.

Luke 15:10. There is joy in the presence of the angels of God over one sinner that repenteth. *v.* 7.

Acts 7:53. Who have received the law by the disposition of angels,

Heb. 2:7. Thou madest him a little lower than the angels; thou crownest him with glory and honour, and didst set him over the works of thy hands: with *v.* 5. Psa. 8:5.

16. For verily he took not on *him the nature of* angels; but he took on *him* the seed of Abraham.

1 Pet. 3:22. Who is gone into heaven, and is on the right hand of God; angels and authorities and powers being made subject unto him.

2 Pet. 2:11. Angels, which are greater in power and might, bring not railing accusation against them before the Lord.

Rev. 14:10. He shall be tormented with fire and brimstone in the presence of the holy angels,

Rev. 18:1. And after these things I saw another angel come down from heaven, having great power; and the earth was lightened with his glory. 2. And he cried mightily with a strong voice, saying, Babylon the great is fallen, is fallen, and is become the habitation of devils, and the hold of every foul spirit, and a cage of every unclean and hateful bird.

Fallen: Job 4:18; Matt. 25:41; 2 Pet. 2:4; Jude 6; Rev. 12:9.

ANGER. Gen. 4:6. And the LORD said unto Cain, Why art thou wroth? and why is thy countenance fallen?

Gen. 49:7. Cursed *be* their anger, for *it was* fierce; and their wrath, for it was cruel:

Prov. 12:16. A fool's wrath is presently known: but a prudent *man* covereth shame.

Prov. 14:17. *He that is* soon angry dealeth foolishly: 29. *He that is* slow to wrath *is* of great understanding: but *he that is* hasty of spirit exalteth folly.

Prov. 15:1. A soft answer turneth away wrath: but grievous words stir up anger. 18. A wrathful man stirreth up strife: but *he that is* slow to anger appeaseth strife.

Prov. 19:11. The discretion of a man deferreth his anger; and *it is* his glory to pass over a transgression. 12. The king's wrath *is* as the roaring of a lion: but his favour *is* as dew upon the grass. 19. A man of great wrath shall suffer punishment: for if thou deliver *him*, yet thou must do it again.

Prov. 22:24. Make no friendship with an angry man, and with a furious man thou shalt not go: 25. Lest thou learn his ways, and get a snare to thy soul.

Prov. 25:28. He that *hath* no rule over his own spirit *is like* a city *that is* broken down, *and* without walls.

Eph. 4:26. Be ye angry, and sin not: let not the sun go down upon your wrath: 31. Let all bitterness, and wrath, and anger, and clamour, and evil speaking, be put away from you, with all malice:

Col. 3:8. But now ye also put of all these; anger, wrath, malice,

1 Tim. 2:8. I will therefore that men pray every where, lifting up holy hands, without wrath and doubting.

Jas. 1:19. Wherefore, my beloved brethren, let every man be swift to hear, slow to speak, slow to wrath: 20. For the wrath of man worketh not the righteousness of God.

Of God: Psa. 103:8. The LORD *is* merciful and gracious, slow to anger, and plenteous in mercy. 9. He will not always chide: neither will he keep *his anger* for ever.

Psa. 106:23. Therefore he said that he would destroy them, had not Moses his chosen stood before him in the breach, to turn away his wrath, lest he should destroy *them*.

Jer. 10:10. But the LORD *is* the true God, he *is* the living God, and an everlasting king: at his wrath the earth shall tremble, and the nations shall not be able to abide his indignation.

Hos. 13:11. I gave thee a king in mine anger, and took *him* away in my wrath.

Rom. 1:18. For the wrath of God is revealed from heaven against all ungodliness and unrighteousness of men, who hold the truth in unrighteousness;

Heb. 3:11. So I sware in my wrath, They shall not enter into my rest. Heb. 4:3.

Rev. 14:10. The same shall drink of the wine of the wrath of God, which is poured out without mixture into the cup of his indignation; and he shall be tormented with fire and brimstone in the presence of the holy angels, and in the presence of the Lamb: 11. And the smoke of their torment ascendeth up for ever and ever: and they have no rest day nor night, who worship the beast and his image, and whosoever receiveth the mark of his name.

ANIMALS. Creation of, Gen. 1:24,25; 2:19; Jer. 27:5. Food of, Gen. 1:30. Named, Gen. 2:20. Ordained as food for man, Gen. 9:2,3; Lev. 11:3,9,21,22; Deut. 14:4-6,9,11,20. God's care of, Gen. 9:9, 10; Deut. 25:4; Job 38:41; Psa. 36: 6; 104:11,21; 147:9; Jonah 4:11; Matt. 6:26; 10:29; Luke 12:6,24; 1 Cor. 9:9. Under the curse, Gen. 3: 14; 6:7,17. Suffer under divine judgments, sent upon man, Jer. 7:20; 12:4; 21:6; Ezek. 14:13,17,19-21; Joel 1:18-20. Two of every sort preserved in the ark, Gen. 6:19,20; 7:2,3,5,9,14; 8:19. Suffered the plagues of Egypt, Ex. 8:17; 9:9,10, 19; 11:5. Perish at death, Eccl. 3:21; 12:7. Possessed of devils, Matt. 8:31,32; 5:13; Luke 8:33. Clean and unclean, Gen. 8:20; Lev. 7:21; 11; 20:25; Deut. 14:3-20; Acts 10:11-15; 1 Tim. 4:3-5. Offered in sacrifice, Gen. 4:4; 7:2-8; 8:20.

God's control of, Psa. 91:13; Isa. 11:6,8; 35:9; Luke 10:19. Instruments of God's will, Ex. chapters 8, 9 and 10:1-20; Num. 21:6; 22:28; Josh. 24:12; Jer. 8:17; Joel 1:4. Belong to God, Psa. 50:10-12. Sent in judgment, Lev. 26:22; Num. 21: 6,7; Deut. 8:15; 28:26; Ezek. 5:17; 14:15; 32:4; Rev. 6:8. Paul contends with, 1 Cor. 15:32. Nature of, Job 39; Psa. 32:9; 49:12; Eccl.

3:18-21. Habits of, Job 12:7,8; 37: 8; 39; 40:20; Psa. 29:9; 104:20-25; Isa. 13:21,22; 34:14; Jas. 3:7. Menstruation of, Jer. 2:24. Facts about breeding, Gen. 30:35-43; 31:8,9. Instincts of, Deut. 32:11; Job 35:11; 39; 40; 41; Psa. 59:6; 104; Prov. 6:6-8; 30:25-28; Jer. 8:7; Matt. 24:28. Abodes of, Job 24:5; 37:8; 39; Psa. 104:20-25; Isa. 34:14; Jer. 2:24; 50:39; Mark 1:13.

BEASTS. Symbolical: Isa. 30:6; Dan. 7,11,17,19; 8:4; Acts 10-12; Rev. 4:6-9; 5:6-14; 6:1-7; 7:11; 11:7; 13; 14:3,9,11; 15:2; 16:2,10-13; 17; 19:4,19,20; 20:4,10.

Cruelty to: INSTANCES OF: Balaam, Num. 22:22-33. Houghing horses, 2 Sam. 8:4; 1 Chr. 18:4.

Kindness to: INSTANCES OF: Jacob, in erecting booths for his cattle, Gen. 33:17. People of Gerar, in providing tents for cattle, 2 Chr. 14:15.

Laws Concerning: Ex. 20:10. But the seventh day *is* the sabbath of the LORD thy God: *in it* thou shalt not do any work, thou, nor thy son, nor thy daughter, thy manservant, nor thy maidservant, nor thy cattle, nor thy stranger that *is* within thy gates: Deut. 5:14.

Ex. 21:28. If an ox gore a man or a woman, that they die: then the ox shall be surely stoned, and his flesh shall not be eaten; but the owner of the ox *shall be* quit. 29. But if the ox were wont to push with his horn in time past, and it hath been testified to his owner, and he hath not kept him in, but that he hath killed a man or a woman; the ox shall be stoned, and his owner also shall be put to death. 30. If there be laid on him a sum of money, then he shall give for the ransom of his life whatsoever is laid upon him.

Ex. 22:1. If a man shall steal an ox, or a sheep, and kill it, or sell it; he shall restore five oxen for an ox, and four sheep for a sheep. 2. If a thief be found breaking up, and be smitten that he die, *there shall* no blood *be shed* for him. 3. If the sun be risen upon him, *there shall be* blood *shed* for him; *for* he should make full restitution; if he have nothing, then he shall be sold for his theft. 4. If the theft be certainly found in his hand alive, whether it be ox, or ass, or sheep; he shall restore double.

Ex. 23:5. If thou see the ass of him that hateth thee lying under his burden, and wouldest forbear to help him, thou shalt surely help with him. Deut. 22:4.

Deut. 22:6. If a bird's nest chance to be before thee in the way in any tree, or on the ground, *whether they be* young ones, or eggs, and the dam sitting upon the young, or upon the eggs, thou shalt not take the dam with the young: 7. *But* thou shalt in any wise let the dam go, and take the young to thee; that it may be well with thee, and *that* thou mayest prolong *thy* days.

10. Thou shalt not plow with an ox and an ass together.

Deut. 25:4. Thou shalt not muzzle the ox when he treadeth out *the corn.* 1 Tim. 5:18.

Prov. 12:10. A righteous *man* regardeth the life of his beast; but the tender mercies of the wicked *are* cruel.

ANOINTING. Figurative: Of Christ's kingly and priestly office, Psa. 45:7; 89:20; Isa. 61:1; Dan. 9:24; Luke 4:18; Acts 4:27; 10:38; Heb. 1:9. Of spiritual gifts, 2 Cor. 1:21; 1 John 2:20,27.

TYPIFIED: Ex. 40:13-15; Lev. 8:12; 1 Sam. 16:13: 1 Kin. 19:16. SYMBOLICAL: of Jesus, Matt. 26: 7-12; John 12:3-7.

ANT, Prov. 6:6-8; 30:25.

ANTEDILUVIANS. Worship God, Gen. 4:3,4,26. Occupations of, Gen. 4:2,3,20-22. Arts of, Gen. 4:2,3,20-22; 6:14-22. Enoch prophesies to, Jude 14,15. Noah preaches to, 2 Pet. 2:5. Wickedness of, Gen. 6:5-7. Destruction of, Gen. 7:1,21-23; Job 22:15-17; Matt. 24: 37-39; Luke 17:26,27; 2 Pet. 2:5.

ANTHROPOMORPHISMS, figures of speech, which attribute human forms, acts, and affections to God.

Gen. 11:5. And the LORD came down to see the city and the tower, which the children of men builded. 7. Go to, let us go down, and there confound their language, that they

may not understand one another's speech. Num. 11:25.

Gen. 18:21. I will go down now, and see whether they have done altogether according to the cry of it, which is come unto me; and if not, I will know. 33. And the LORD went his way, as soon as he had left communing with Abraham:

Ex. 14:24. And it came to pass, that in the morning watch the LORD looked unto the host of the Egyptians through the pillar of fire and of the cloud,

Hab. 1:13. *Thou art* of purer eyes than to behold evil, and canst not look on iniquity:

1 Pet. 3:12. For the eyes of the Lord *are* over the righteous, and his ears *are open* unto their prayers: but the face of the Lord *is* against them that do evil.

INTELLECTUAL FACULTIES ATTRIBUTED TO DEITY: Memory, Isa. 43:26; 63:11; assisted by tokens, Gen. 9:16. Reason, Isa. 1:18. Understanding, Psa. 147:5. Will, Rom. 9:19.

MISCELLANEOUS ACTS AND STATES OF MIND ATTRIBUTED TO: Walking, Gen. 3:8; Lev. 26:12; Deut. 23:14; Job 22:14; Hab. 3:15; resting, Gen. 2:2,3; Ex. 20:11; 31:17; Deut. 5:14; Heb. 4:4,10; fainteth not, Isa. 40: 28; amazement, Isa. 59:16; 63:5; Mark 6:6; laughing, Psa. 2:4; 37:13; 59:8; Prov. 1:26; sleeping, Psa. 44: 23; 78:65; grieved, Gen. 6:6; Judg. 10:16; Psa. 95:10; Heb. 3:10,17.

Oaths, Isa. 62:8; Heb. 6:16,17; 7:21,28.

See OATH.* See also ANGER OF GOD.

ANTICHRIST. Matt. 24:5, 23,24,26; Mark 13:6,21,22; Luke

* For various additional anthropomorphic expressions and terms, see FIGURATIVE, under the following topics: ARM, EAR, EYE, HAND: see also ANGER OF GOD, ARROW, FOOTSTOOL, HATRED OF GOD, JEALOUSY, SCEPTER, SWORD, THRONE, and such other terms as are used for anthropomorphic purposes.
For a more extended exemplification of anthropomorphic expressions, consult concordances under the terms above cited, and under various grammatical forms of the verbs HATE, HEAR, REPENT, SEE, SMELL, TALK, WALK, etc.

21:8; 2 Thess. 2:3-12; 1 John 2:18, 22; 4:3; 2 John 7. To be destroyed, Rev. 19:20; 20:10,15.

APOLLYON, angel of the bottomless pit, Rev. 9:11.

APOSTASY. Unclassified Scriptures Relating to: Deut. 32:15. He forsook God *which* made him, and lightly esteemed the Rock of his salvation.

1 Chr. 28:9. If thou forsake him, he will cast thee off for ever.

Jer. 17:5. Cursed *be* the man whose heart departeth from the LORD. 6. For he shall be like the heath in the desert, and shall not see when good cometh; but shall inhabit the parched places in the wilderness, *in* a salt land and not inhabited.

Ezek. 3:20. When a righteous *man* doth turn from his righteousness, and commit iniquity, and I lay a stumblingblock before him, he shall die: because thou hast not given him warning, he shall die in his sin, and his righteousness which he hath done shall not be remembered; but his blood will I require at thine hand.

John 15:6. If a man abide not in me, he is cast forth as a branch, and is withered; and men gather them, and cast *them* into the fire, and they are burned.

1 Cor. 9:27. But I keep under my body, and bring *it* into subjection: lest that by any means, when I have preached to others, I myself should be a castaway.

1 Tim. 4:1. Now the Spirit speaketh expressly, that in the latter times some shall depart from the faith, giving heed to seducing spirits, and doctrines of devils; 2. Speaking lies in hypocrisy; having their conscience seared with a hot iron;

Heb. 6:4. For *it is* impossible for those who were once enlightened, and have tasted of the heavenly gift, and were made partakers of the Holy Ghost, 5. And have tasted the good word of God, and the powers of the world to come, 6. If they shall fall away, to renew them again unto repentance; seeing they crucify to themselves the Son of God afresh, and put *him* to an open shame.

Heb. 10:26. For if we sin wilfully after that we have received the knowledge of the truth, there remaineth no more sacrifice for sins, 27. But a certain fearful looking for of judgment and fiery indignation, which shall devour the adversaries.

See BACKSLIDERS; REPROBACY.

APOSTLES. A title distinguishing the twelve disciples, whom Jesus selected to be intimately associated with himself, Luke 6:13.

Names of, Matt. 10:2. Now the names of the twelve apostles are these; The first, Simon, who is called Peter, and Andrew his brother; James *the son* of Zebedee, and John his brother; 3. Philip, and Bartholomew: Thomas and Matthew the publican; James *the son* of Alphæus, and Lebbæus, whose surname was Thaddæus; 4. Simon the Canaanite, and Judas Iscariot, who also betrayed him. Mark 3:16-19; Luke 6:13-16; Acts 1:13,26.

Selection of, Matt. 4:18-22; 9:9,10; 10:2-4; Mark 3:13-19; Luke 6:13-16; John 1:43.

Commission of, Matt. 10; 28:19,20; Mark 3:14,15; 6:7-11; 16:15; Luke 9:1-5; 22:28-30; John 20:23; 21:15-19; Acts 1; 2; 10:42. Unlearned, Matt. 11:25; Acts 4:13. Miraculous power given to, Matt. 10:1; Mark 3:15; 6:7; 16:17; Luke 9:1,2; 10:9,17; Acts 2:4,43; 5:12-16; 1 Cor. 14:18; 2 Cor. 12:12. Authority of, see COMMISSION OF, above, and Matt. 16:19; 18:18; 19:28.

Inspiration of, Matt. 10:27; 16:17-19; Luke 24:45; Acts 1:2; 13:9. Duties of, see COMMISSION OF, above, and Luke 24:48; John 15:27; Acts 1:8,21,22; 2:32; 3:15; 4:33; 5:32; 10:39-41; 13:31; 2 Pet. 1:16,18; 1 John 1:1-3. See MINISTER.

Moral state of, before Pentecost, Matt. 17:17; 18:3; 20:20-22; Luke 9:54,55. Slow to receive Jesus, as Messiah, Matt. 14:33. Forsake Jesus, Mark 14:50.

Fail to comprehend the nature and mission of Jesus, and the nature of the kingdom he came to establish, Matt. 8:25-27; 15:23; 16:8-12,21,22; 19:25; Mark 4:13; 6:51,

52; 8:17,18; 9:9,10,31,32; 10:13,14; Luke 9:44,45; 18:34; 24:19,21; John 4:32,33; 10:6; 11:12,13; 12:16; 13:6-8; 14:5-9,22; 16:6,17,18,32; 20:9; 21:12; Acts 1:6.

False: 2 Cor. 11:13; Rev. 2:2.

APOTHECARY, a compounder of drugs, Ex. 30:25,35; 37:29; 2 Chr. 16:14; Neh. 3:8. Ointment of, Eccl. 10:1.

APPETITE. Kept in subjection, Dan. 1:8-16; 1 Cor. 9:27.

APPLE, a fruit, Prov. 25:11; Song 2:3,5; 7:8; 8:5; Joel 1:12.

AQUILA AND PRISCILLA. Christians at Corinth, Acts 18:1-3, 18,19,26. Friendship of, for Paul, Rom. 16:3,4. Paul sends salutations to, 2 Tim. 4:19.

ARBITRATION. Instances of: The two harlots before Solomon, 1 Kin. 3:16-28. Urged by Paul, as a mode of action for Christians, 1 Cor. 6:1-8.

ARCHANGEL. 1 Thess. 4:16; Jude 9.

See ANGEL.

ARCHERY. Practised by Ishmael, Gen. 21:20; Esau, Gen. 27:3; Jonathan, 1 Sam. 20:20,36,37; sons of Ulam, 1 Chr. 8:40; Philistines, 1 Sam. 31:1-3; 1 Chr. 10:3; Persians, Isa. 13:17,18; people of Kedar, Isa. 21:17; Syrians, 1 Kin. 22:31-34; Israelites, 2 Sam. 1:18; 1 Chr. 5:18; 12:2; 2 Chr. 14:8; 26:14; Neh. 4:13; Zech. 9:13; Lydians, Jer. 46:9.

In war, Gen. 49:23; Judg. 5:11; 1 Sam. 31:3; Isa. 22:3; Jer. 4:29; 51:3; Zech. 10:4.

ARCHITECTURE, Heb. 3:3,4. **Figurative:** Eph. 2:21,22.

ARK. 1. NOAH'S. Directions for building of, Gen. 6:14-16. Noah and family preserved in, Gen. 6:18; 7:8; Matt. 24:38; Heb. 11:7; 1 Pet. 3:20. Animals saved in, Gen. 6:19, 20; 7:1-16.

2. OF BULRUSHES, Ex. 2:3.

3. IN THE TABERNACLE. Called ARK OF THE COVENANT, Num. 10:33; Deut. 31:26; Josh. 4:7; 1 Sam. 4:3; 2 Sam. 15:24; 1 Chr. 15:25; 17:1; Jer. 3:16; Heb. 9:4; OF THE TESTIMONY, Ex. 30:6; OF THE LORD, Josh. 4:11; 1 Sam. 4:6; 6:1; 2 Sam. 6:9; 1 Kin. 8:4; OF GOD, 1 Sam. 3:3; 4:11,17,22; 6:3;

14:18; 2 Sam. 6:7; 7:2; 15:25; 1 Chr. 13:12; 15:1,2,15,24; 16:1; OF GOD'S STRENGTH, 2 Chr. 6:41.

Sanctification of, Ex. 30:26. Ceremonies connected with, on the day of atonement, Lev. 16:13-15. Holy, 2 Chr. 8:11; 35:3.

An oracle of God, Num. 10:33; 14:44; Josh. 7:6-15; Judg. 20:27,28; 1 Sam. 4:3,4,7; 1 Chr. 13:3; 1 Chr. 16:4,37; 2 Chr. 6:41; Psa. 132:8.

Directions for making, Ex. 25:10-15; 35:12. Construction of, Ex. 37:1-5; Deut. 10:3.

Contents of: The law, Ex. 25:16, 21; 40:20; Deut. 10:5; 31:26; 1 Kin. 8:9; 2 Chr. 5:10. Aaron's rod, Num. 17:10; Heb. 9:4. Pot of manna, Ex. 16:33,34; Heb. 9:4.

Place of, Ex. 26:33; 40:21; 1 Sam. 3:3; 2 Sam. 7:2; Heb. 9:2-4.

How prepared for conveyance, Num. 4:5,6. Carried by Kohathites, Num. 3:30,31; 4:4,15; Deut. 10:8; 1 Chr. 15:2,15. On special occasions carried by priests: Crossing Jordan, Josh. 3:6,14; siege of Jericho, Josh. 6:6.

Taken to battle, Josh. 6:6-20; 1 Sam. 4:3-22. Captured by the Philistines, 1 Sam. 4:10,11; Psa. 78:61. Returned by the Philistines, 1 Sam. 6. Remains at the house of Abinadab, 1 Sam. 7:1,2; 2 Sam. 6:4; in the house of Obed-edom, 2 Sam. 6:9-11.

Set up in Shiloh, Josh. 18:1; Judg. 20:27,28; 1 ·Sam. 4:3,4; in Jerusalem, 2 Sam. 6:12-17; 1 Chr. 6:31; 15; 16:1. Removed from Jerusalem by Zadok at the time of Absalom's revolt, but returned by command of David, 2 Sam. 15:24-29. Transferred to Solomon's temple, 1 Kin. 8:6-9; 2 Chr. 5:2-9; 35:3.

Prophecy concerning, Jer. 3:16. In John's vision, Rev. 11:19.

ARM. Figurative Use of: Ex. 6:6. I will redeem you with a stretched out arm, and with great judgments:

Deut. 5:15. The LORD thy God brought thee out thence through a mighty hand and by a stretched out arm: Psa. 136:12.

Isa. 53:1. Who hath believed our report? and to whom is the arm of the LORD revealed?

See ANTHROPOMORPHISMS.

ARMAGEDDON, a symbolical name, Rev. 16:16.

ARMIES. Who of the Israelites were subject to service in, Num. 1:2,3; 26:2; 2 Chr. 25:5; who were exempt from service in, Num. 1:47-50; 2:33; Deut. 20:5-9; Judg. 7:3. Compulsory service in, 1 Sam. 14:52.

How officered: Commander-in-chief, 1 Sam. 14:50; 2 Sam. 2:8; 8:16; 17:25; 19:13; 20:23; generals of corps and divisions, Num. 2:3-31; 1 Chr. 27:1-22; 2 Chr. 17:12-19; captains of thousands, Num. 31:14, 48; 1 Sam. 17:18; 1 Chr. 28:1; 2 Chr. 25:5; of hundreds, Num. 31:14,48; 2 Kin. 11:15; 1 Chr. 28:1; 2 Chr. 25:5; of fifties, 2 Kin. 1:9; Isa. 3:3.

Children instructed in military arts, 2 Sam. 1:18.

Insubordination in, punished, Achan, Josh. 7. Check roll-call, 1 Sam. 14:17; Num. 31:48,49.

Panics: Isa. 30:17; among the Midianites, Judg. 7:21.

Figurative: Deut. 33:2; 2 Kin. 6:17; Psa. 34:7; 68:17; Rev. 9:16.

ARMOR, the equipment of a soldier, Jer. 46:3,4; Eph. 6:14-17.

Figurative: Rom. 13:12; 2 Cor. 6:7; 10:4; Eph. 6:11-17; 1 Thess. 5:8.

ARREST. Of Jesus, Matt. 26:57; Mark 14:46; Luke 22:54; John 18:12; apostles, Acts 5:17,18; 6:12; Paul and Silas, Acts 16:19; Paul, Acts 21:30. Paul authorized to arrest Christians, Acts 9:2.

ARROGANCE. 1 Sam. 2:3. Talk no more so exceeding proudly; let *not* arrogancy come out of your mouth: for the LORD *is* a God of knowledge, and by him actions are weighed.

Prov. 8:13. Pride, and arrogancy, and the evil way, and the froward mouth, do I hate.

Isa. 13:11. I will cause the arrogancy of the proud to cease, and will lay low the haughtiness of the terrible.

ARSON. Psa. 74:7,8. Law concerning, Ex. 22:6.

Instances of: By Samson, Judg. 15:4, 5; Absalom, 2 Sam. 14:30; Zimri, 1 Kin. 16:18.

ART. Primitive: Invention of musical instruments and instruments of iron and copper [*A. V.*, brass], Gen. 4:21,22. Carpentry, Gen. 6:14-16; Ex. 31:2-9. Of the apothecary or perfumer, Ex. 30:25, 35; armorer, 1 Sam. 8:12; baker, Gen. 40:1; 1 Sam. 8:13; barber, Isa. 7:20; Ezek. 5:1; brickmaker, Gen. 11:3; Ex. 5:7,8,18; calker, Ezek. 27:9,27; compounding confections, 1 Sam. 8:13; gardener, Jer. 29:5; John 20:15; goldsmith, Isa. 40:19; mariner, Ezek. 27:8,9; mason, 2 Sam. 5:11; 2 Chr. 24:12; musician, 1 Sam. 18:6; 1 Chr. 15:16; potter, Isa. 64:8; Jer. 18:3; Lam. 4:2; Zech. 11:13; refiner of metals, 1 Chr. 28:18; Mal. 3:2,3; ropemaker, Judg. 16:11; stonecutter, Ex. 20:25; 1 Chr. 22:15; shipbuilder, 1 Kin. 9:26; smelter of metals, Job 28:2; spinner, Ex. 35:25; Prov. 31:19; tailor, Ex. 28:3; tanner, Acts 9:43; 10:6; tentmaker, Gen. 4:20; Acts 18:3; weaver, Ex. 35:35; John 19:23; wine maker, Neh. 13:15; Isa. 63:3.

ARTISANS, SKILLFUL: Jubal, Gen. 4:21; Tubal-cain, Gen. 4:22; Bezaleel and Aholiab, Ex. 31:2-14; 35; 30-35; Hiram, 1 Kin. 7:13-51; 2 Chr. 2:13,14.

ASCETICISM, a philosophy that leads to severe austerities in subordinating the body to the control of the moral attributes of the mind. Extrème application of, rebuked by Jesus, Matt. 11:19; Luke 7:34; by Paul, Col. 2:20-23; 1 Tim. 4:1-4,8.

Instances of the Practice of: John the Baptist, Matt. 11:18; Luke 7:33. Those who practised celibacy "for the kingdom of heaven's sake," Matt. 19:12.

ASHES. Uses of, in purification, Num. 19:9,10,17; Heb. 9:13. A symbol of mourning, 2 Sam. 13:19; Esth. 4:1,3. Sitting in, Job 2:8; Isa. 58:5; Jer. 6:26; Ezek. 27:30; Jonah 3:6; Luke 10:13. Repenting in, Job 42:6; Dan. 9:3; Jonah 3:6; Matt. 11:21; Luke 10:13. Disguises in, 1 Kin. 20:38,41.

ASIA. Inhabitants of, in Jerusalem, at Pentecost, Acts 2:9; 21:27; 24:18. Paul and Silas forbidden by the Holy Ghost to preach in, Acts

16:6. Gospel preached in, by Paul, Acts 19; 20:4. Paul leaves, Acts 20:16. Churches of, 1 Cor. 16:19; Rev. 1:4,11.

ASP. A venomous serpent, Deut. 32:33; Job 20:14,16; Isa. 11:8; Rom. 3:13. Venom of, illustrates the speech of the wicked, Psa. 140:3; Rom. 3:13; injurious effects of wine, Deut. 32:33; Prov. 23:32. Deprived of venom, illustrates conversion, Isa. 11:8,9.

ASS. Domesticated: Herds of, Gen. 12:16; 24:35; 32:5; 34:28; Num. 31:34,45; 1 Chr. 5:21; Ezra 2:67; Neh. 7:69.

Jawbone of, used by Samson with which to slay Philistines, Judg. 15:15-17.

FIRSTLINGS OF, redeemed, Ex. 13:13; 34:20.

ASSASSINATION. David's abhorrence of, 2 Sam. 4:9-12. Laws prohibiting, Deut. 27:24.

Instances of: Of Eglon, by Ehud, Judg. 3:15-22; Abner, by Joab, 2 Sam. 3:27; Ish-bosheth, by the sons of Rimmon, 2 Sam. 4:5-7; Amnon, by Absalom, 2 Sam. 13:28,29; Amasa, by Joab, 2 Sam. 20:9,10; Joash, by his servants, 2 Kin. 12:20; Sennacherib, by his sons, 2 Kin. 19:37; Isa. 37:38.

ASSAULT AND BATTERY. Laws Concerning: Ex. 21:15. And he that smiteth his father, or his mother, shall be surely put to death.

26. And if a man smite the eye of his servant, or the eye of his maid, that it perish; he shall let him go free for his eye's sake. 27. And if he smite out his manservant's tooth, or his maidservant's tooth; he shall let him go free for his tooth's sake.

Matt. 5:38. Ye have heard that it hath been said, An eye for an eye, and a tooth for a tooth: 39. But I say unto you, That ye resist not evil: but whosoever shall smite thee on thy right cheek, turn to him the other also.

ASSURANCE. Produced by faith, Eph. 3:12; 2 Tim. 1:12; Heb. 10:22. Made full by hope, Heb. 6:11,19. Confirmed by love, 1 John 3:14,19; 4:18. Is the effect of righteousness, Isa. 32:17. Is abundant in the understanding of the gospel, Col. 2:2; 1 Thess. 1:5.

SAINTS- PRIVILEGED TO HAVE, of their election, Psa. 4:3; 1 Thess. 1:4; their redemption, Job 19:25; their adoption, Rom. 8:16; 1 John 3:2; their salvation, Isa. 12:2; eternal life, 1 John 5:13; the unalienable love of God, Rom. 8:38, 39; union with God and Christ, 1 Cor. 6:15; 2 Cor. 13:5; Eph. 5:30; 1 John 2:5; 4:13; peace with God by Christ, Rom. 5:1; preservation, Psa. 3:6; 8; 27:3-5; 46:1-3; answers to prayer, 1 John 3:22; 5:14,15; comfort in affliction, Psa. 73:26; Luke 4:18; 2 Cor. 4:8-10,16-18; continuance in grace, Phil. 1:6; a support in death, Psa. 23:4; a glorious resurrection, Job 19:26; Psa. 17:15; Phil. 3:21; 1 John 3:2; a kingdom, Heb. 12:28; Rev. 5:10; a crown, 2 Tim. 4:7,8; Jas. 1:12. Saints give diligence to attain, 2 Pet. 1:10,11; strive to maintain, Heb. 3:14,18. Confident hope in God restores, Psa. 42:11.

Exemplified: David, Psa. 23:4, 73:24-26; Paul, 2 Tim. 1:12; 4:18. —*Bible Text Book.*

See FAITH.

ASTROLOGY, Isa. 47:13; Jer. 10:1,2; Dan. 1:20; 2:27; 4:7; 5:7.

ASTRONOMY. Job 26:7. He stretcheth out the north over the empty place, *and* hangeth the earth upon nothing. 13. By his spirit he hath garnished the heavens; his hand hath formed the crooked serpent.

Job 38:31. Canst thou bind the sweet influences of Pleiades, or loose the bands of Orion? 32. Canst thou bring forth Mazzaroth in his season? or canst thou guide Arcturus with his sons? 33. Knowest thou the ordinances of heaven? canst thou set the dominion thereof in the earth?

Psa. 19:1. The heavens declare the glory of God; and the firmament sheweth his handywork. 2. Day unto day uttereth speech, and night unto night sheweth knowledge.

Isa. 13:10. For the stars of heaven and the constellations thereof shall not give their light: the sun shall be darkened in his

27

going forth, and the moon shall not cause her light to shine.

Isa. 47:13. Let now the astrologers, the stargazers, the monthly prognosticators, stand up, and save thee from *these things* that shall come upon thee.

Amos 5:8. *Seek him* that maketh the [seven stars] and Orion, and turneth the shadow of death into the morning, and maketh the day dark with night: that calleth for the waters of the sea, and poureth them out upon the face of the earth: The Lord *is* his name: [R. V. [Pleiades].

Sidereal Phenomena: Josh. 10:12. Then spake Joshua to the Lord in the day when the Lord delivered up the Amorites before the children of Israel, and he said in the sight of Israel, Sun, stand thou still upon Gibeon; and thou, Moon, in the valley of Ajalon. 13. And the sun stood still, and the moon stayed, until the people had avenged themselves upon their enemies.

Isa. 13:13. Therefore I will shake the heavens, and the earth shall remove out of her place, in the wrath of the Lord of hosts, and in the day of his fierce anger.

Isa. 34:4. And all the host of heaven shall be dissolved, and the heavens shall be rolled together as a scroll: and all their host shall fall down, as the leaf falleth off from the vine, and as a falling *fig* from the fig tree.

Matt. 24:29. Immediately after the tribulation of those days shall the sun be darkened, and the moon shall not give her light, and the stars shall fall from heaven, and the powers of the heavens shall be shaken: [Mark 13:24,25.] 35. Heaven and earth shall pass away, but my words shall not pass away.

Matt. 27:45. Now from the sixth hour there was darkness over all the land unto the ninth hour.

Luke 21:25. And there shall be signs in the sun, and in the moon, and in the stars;

2 Pet. 3:10. But the day of the Lord will come as a thief in the night; in the which the heavens shall pass away with a great noise, and the elements shall melt with fervent heat, the earth also and the works that are therein shall be burned up.

Rev. 12:3. And there appeared another wonder in heaven; and behold a great red dragon, having seven heads and ten horns, and seven crowns upon his heads. 4. And his tail drew the third part of the stars of heaven, and did cast them to the earth:

Rev. 13:13. And he doeth great wonders, so that he maketh fire come down from heaven on the earth in the sight of men,

ATHEISM. Psa. 10:4. The wicked in the pride of his countenance, *saith*, He will not require *it*. All his thoughts are, There is no God. Psa. 14:1. The fool hath said in his heart, *There is* no God. Psa. 53:1.

Arguments Against: Job 12:7. But ask now the beasts, and they shall teach thee; and the fowls of the air, and they shall tell thee: 8. Or speak to the earth, and it shall teach thee: and the fishes of the sea shall declare unto thee. 9. Who knoweth not in all these that the hand of the Lord hath wrought this? 10. In whose hand *is* the soul of every living thing, and the breath of all mankind. 11. Doth not the ear try words? and the mouth taste his meat? 12. With the ancient *is* wisdom; and in length of days understanding.

Rom. 1:19. Because that which may be known of God is manifest in them; for God hath shewed *it* unto them. 20. For the invisible things of him from the creation of the world are clearly seen, being understood by the things that are made, *even* his eternal power and Godhead; so that they are without excuse:

ATOMS OF MATTER, Prov. 8:26.

ATONEMENT. Made by Animal Sacrifices: Ex. 29:36. And thou shalt offer every day a bulock *for* a sin offering for atonement: and thou shalt cleanse the altar, when thou hast made an atonement for it, and thou shalt anoint it, to sanctify it.

Lev. 1:4. And he shall put his hand upon the head of the burnt offering; and it shall be accepted for him to make atonement for him.

Heb. 9:22. And almost all things are by the law purged with blood; and without shedding of blood is no remission.

Made by Jesus: Divinely ordained: Luke 2:30,31; Gal. 4:4,5; Eph. 1:3-12,17-22; 2:4-10; Col. 1:19,20; 1 Pet. 1:20; Rev. 13:8. A mystery, 1 Cor. 2:7, with context; 1 Pet. 1:8-12. Made but once, Heb. 7:27; 9:24-28; 10:10,12,14; 1 Pet. 3:18. Redemption by, Matt. 20:28; Acts 20:28; Gal. 3:13; 1 Tim. 2:6; Heb. 9:12; Rev. 5:9. Typified, Gen. 4:4, with Heb. 11:4; Gen. 22:2, with Heb. 11:17,19; Ex. 12:5, 11,14, with 1 Cor. 5:7; Ex. 24:8, with Heb. 9:20; Lev. 16:30,34, with Heb. 9:7,12,28; Lev. 17:11, with Heb. 9:22.

Unclassified Scriptures Relating to: Psa. 40:6. Sacrifice and offering thou didst not desire; mine ears hast thou opened: burnt offering and sin offering hast thou not required. 7. Then said I, Lo, I come: in the volume of the book *it is* written of me, 8. I delight to do thy will, O my God: yea, thy law *is* within my heart. Heb. 10:5-9.

Isa. 53:4. Surely he hath borne our griefs, and carried our sorrows: yet we did esteem him stricken, smitten of God, and afflicted. 5. But he *was* wounded for our transgressions, *he was* bruised for our iniquities: the chastisement of our peace *was* upon him; and with his stripes we are healed. 6. All we like sheep have gone astray; we have turned every one to his own way; and the LORD hath laid on him the iniquity of us all. 7. He was oppressed, and he was afflicted, yet he opened not his mouth: he is brought as a lamb to the slaughter, and as a sheep before her shearers is dumb, so he openeth not his mouth. 8. He was taken from prison and from judgment: and who shall declare his generation? for he was cut off out of the land of the living: for the transgression of my people was he stricken. 10. Yet it pleased the LORD to bruise him; he hath put *him* to grief: when thou shalt make his soul an offering for sin, he shall see *his* seed, he shall prolong *his* days, and the pleasure of the LORD shall prosper in his hand. 11. He shall see of the travail of his soul, *and* shall be satisfied: by his knowledge shall my righteous servant justify many; for he shall bear their iniquities. 12. Therefore will I divide him *a portion* with the great, and he shall divide the spoil with the strong; because he hath poured out his soul unto death: and he was numbered with the transgressors; and he bare the sin of many, and made intercession for the transgressors.

Zech. 13:1. In that day there shall be a fountain opened to the house of David and to the inhabitants of Jerusalem for sin and for uncleanness.

Matt. 26:28. For this is my blood of the new testament, which is shed for many for the remission of sins. Luke 22:20.

Luke 24:46. And said unto them, Thus it is written, and thus it behoved Christ to suffer, and to rise from the dead the third day: 47. And that repentance and remission of sins should be preached in his name among all nations, beginning at Jerusalem.

John 1:29. The next day John seeth Jesus coming unto him, and saith, Behold the Lamb of God, which taketh away the sin of the world. *v.* 36.

John 11:49. And one of them, *named* Caiaphas, being the high priest that same year, said unto them, Ye know nothing at all, 50. Nor consider that it is expedient for us, that one man should die for the people, and that the whole nation perish not. 51. And this spake he not of himself: but being high priest that year, he prophesied that Jesus should die for that nation;

Rom. 3:24. Being justified freely by his grace through the redemption that is in Christ Jesus. 25. Whom God hath set forth *to be* a propitiation through faith in his blood, to declare his righteousness for the remission of sins that are past, through the forbearance of God; 26. To declare, *I say*, at this time his righteousness: that he might be just, and the justifier of him which believeth in Jesus.

Rom. 4:25. Who was delivered for our offences, and was raised again for our justification.

2 Cor. 5:18. And all things *are* of God, who hath reconciled us to himself by Jesus Christ, and hath given to us the ministry of reconciliation; 19. To wit, that God was in Christ, reconciling the world unto himself, not imputing their trespasses unto them; and hath committed unto us the word of reconciliation.

Eph. 1:7. In whom we have redemption through his blood, the forgiveness of sins, according to the riches of his grace;

1 Tim. 2:5. For *there is* one God, and one mediator between God and men, the man Christ Jesus; 6. Who gave himself a ransom for all, to be testified in due time.

Tit. 2:14. Who gave himself for us, that he might redeem us from all iniquity, and purify unto himself a peculiar people, zealous of good works.

Heb. 1:3. Who being the brightness of *his* glory, and the express image of his person, and upholding all things by the word of his power, when he had by himself purged our sins, sat down on the right hand of the Majesty on high;

Heb. 2:9. That he by the grace of God should taste death for every man. 17. Wherefore in all things it behoved him to be made like unto *his* brethren, that he might be a merciful and faithful high priest in things *pertaining* to God, to make reconciliation for the sins of the people.

1 Pet. 2:24. Who his own self bare our sins in his own body on the tree, that we, being dead to sins, should live unto righteousness: by whose stripes ye were healed.

1 John 1:7. The blood of Jesus Christ his Son cleanseth us from all sin.

AVARICE. Eccl. 5:10. He that loveth silver shall not be satisfied with silver; nor he that loveth abundance with increase: this *is* also vanity. 11. When goods increase, they are increased that eat them: and what good *is there* to the owners thereof, saving the beholding *of them* with their eyes?

1 Tim. 3:2. A bishop then must be blameless, the husband of one wife, vigilant, sober, of good behaviour, given to hospitality, apt to teach; 3. Not given to wine, no striker, not greedy of filthy lucre; but patient, not a brawler, not covetous. Tit. 1:7.

1 Tim. 6:5. Perverse disputings of men of corrupt minds, and destitute of the truth, supposing that [gain is godliness: from such withdraw thyself.] 10. For the love of money is the root of all evil: which while some coveted after, they have erred from the faith, and pierced themselves through with many sorrows. (R. V. [godliness is a way of gain]).

Instances of: The descendants of Joseph, Josh. 17:14-18.

AXE. An implement, Deut. 19:5; 1 Sam. 13:20,21; 2 Sam. 12:31; Psa. 74:5,6. Elisha causes to swim, 2 Kin. 6:5,6. Battle-axe, Ezek. 26:9.

Figurative: Jer. 46:22; 51:20; Matt. 3:10.

BAAL. 1. An idol of the Phenicians, god of the sun. Wickedly worshiped by the Israelites in the time of the judges, Judg. 2:10-23; 1 Sam. 7:3,4; by the kingdom of Israel, 2 Kin. 17:16; Jer. 23:13; Hos. 1; 2; 13:1; under Ahab, 1 Kin. 16:31-33; 18:18; 19:18; Jehoram, 2 Kin. 3:2; by the Jews, 2 Kin. 21:3; 2 Chr. 22:2-4; 24:7; 28:2; 33:3. Jeremiah expostulates against the worship of, Jer. 2:8,23; 7:9.

Altars of, destroyed by Gideon, Judg. 6:25-32; by Jehoiada, 2 Kin. 11:18; by Josiah, 2 Kin. 23:4,5.

Prophets of, slain by Elijah, 1 Kin. 18:40. All worshipers of, destroyed by Jehu, 2 Kin. 10:18-25.

2. A Benjamite, 1 Chr. 8:30; 9:36.

3. A Reubenite, 1 Chr. 5:5.

4. A city in the tribe of Simeon, 1 Chr. 4:33. Called BAALATH-BEER, Josh. 19:8.

BABEL, a city in the plain of Shinar. Tower built, and tongues confused at, Gen. 11:1-9.

BABES. In the mouths of, is praise perfected, Matt. 21:16. A symbol of the guileless, Psa. 8:2; Matt. 11:25; Luke 10:21; of the children of the kingdom of heaven, Matt. 18:2-6; Mark 10:15; Luke 18:17.

Figurative: Of weak Christians, Rom. 2:20; 1 Cor. 3:1; Heb. 5:13; 1 Pet. 2:2.

BABYLON. 1. **City of:** Built by Nimrod, Gen. 10:10. In the land of Shinar, Gen. 10:10; 11:2. Tower of, Gen. 11:1-9. Capital of the kingdom of Babylon, Dan. 4:30; 2 Kin. 25:13; 2 Chr. 36:6,7,10,18, 20. Gates of, Isa. 45:1,2; Jer. 51:58. Walled, Jer. 51:44,58. Splendor of, Isa. 14:4.

Peter writes from, 1 Pet. 5:13.

Prophecies concerning, Psa. 87:4; 137:8,9; Isa. 13; 14:4-26; 21:1-10; 46:1,2; 47; 48:14,20; Jer. 21:4-10; 25:12-14; 27:1-11; 28:14; 32:28; 34:2,3; 42:11,12; 43; 46:13-26; 49:28-30; 50; 51; Ezek. 21:19; 26; 29:17-20; 30:10; 32:11; Dan. 2:21-38; 4:10-26; 5:25-29; 7; Hab. 1:5-11; Zech. 2:7-9.

Figurative: Rev. 14:8; 16:19; 17; 18.

2. **Empire of:** Founded by Nimrod, Gen. 10:10. Called Land of Shinar, Gen. 10:10; 11:2; 14:1, 9; Isa. 11:11; Dan. 1:2; Zech. 5:11; Sheshach, Jer. 25:26; 51; 41; Merathaim, Jer. 50:21. Called also Chaldea.

Divisions of, 2 Kin. 17:24; 24:7; Isa. 23:12,13; Dan. 3:1; Acts 7:4. Extent of, at the time of Nebuchadnezzar, Dan. 2:37,38; 4:1; 6:1; of Ahasuerus, Esth. 1:1; 8:9; 9:30.

Armies of, invade ancient Canaan, Gen. 14; Samaria, 2 Kin. 17:5-24; Judah, 2 Kin. 24:1-16. Jews carried to, 2 Kin. 25; 1 Chr. 9:1; 2 Chr. 33:11; 36:17-21; Jer. 32:2; 39; 52. Colonists from, sent to Samaria, Ezra 4:9,10, with 2 Kin. 17:29-32. Conquest of Egypt by, 2 Kin. 24:7.

Prophecies of conquests by, 2 Kin. 20:16-19; Jer. 20:4-7; 21; 22; 25:1-11; 27; 28; 29; 32:28, 29; 34;

36:29; 38:17, 18; 43:8-13; 46:13-26; Ezek. 12; 17; 19; 21; 24; 26; 29:18-20; 30; 32.

Prophetic denunciations against, Psa. 137:8,9; Isa. 13; 14:21; 43:14-17; 47; Jer. 50:51.

Government of: A limited monarchy, Esth. 1:13-19; 8:8; Dan. 6:8,14,17. Tyrannical, Esth. 3:7-15; Dan. 3.

BACA, valley of, Psa. 84:6.

BACKBITING. Psa. 15:1. Lord, who shall abide in thy tabernacle? who shall dwell in thy holy hill? 2. He that walketh uprightly, and worketh righteousness, and speaketh the truth in his heart. 3. *He that* backbiteth not with his tongue, nor doeth evil to his neighbour, nor taketh up a reproach against his neighbour.

Rom. 1:28. And even as they did not like to retain God in *their* knowledge, God gave them over to a reprobate mind, to do those things which are not convenient; 30. Backbiters, haters of God, despiteful,

2 Cor. 12:20. For I fear, lest, when I come, I shall not find you such as I would, and *that* I shall be found unto you such as ye would not: lest *there* be debates, envyings, wraths, strifes, backbitings, whisperings, swellings, tumults:

BACKSLIDERS. Deut. 4:9. Only take heed to thyself, and keep thy soul diligently, lest thou forget the things which thine eyes have seen, and lest they depart from thy heart all the days of thy life:

Deut. 8:11. Beware that thou forget not the Lord thy God, in not keeping his commandments, and his judgments, and his statutes, which I command thee this day: 12. Lest *when* thou hast eaten and art full, and hast built goodly houses, and dwelt *therein;* 13. And *when* thy herds and thy flocks multiply, and thy silver and thy gold is multiplied, 14. Then thine heart be lifted up, and thou forget the Lord thy God, which brought thee forth out of the land of Egypt, from the house of bondage;

Deut. 29:18. Lest there should be among you man, or woman, or family, or tribe, whose heart turneth away this day from the LORD our God, ... lest there should be among you a root that beareth gall and wormwood; vs. 18-28.

Psa. 44:20. If we have forgotten the name of our God, or stretched out our hands to a strange god; 21. Shall not God search this out? for he knoweth the secrets of the heart.

Jer. 17:13. O LORD, the hope of Israel, all that forsake thee shall be ashamed, and they that depart from me shall be written in the earth, because they have forsaken the LORD,

Hos. 11:7. And my people are bent to backsliding from me: though they called them to the most High, none at all would exalt him. 8. How shall I give thee up, Ephraim? how shall I deliver thee, Israel? how shall I make thee as Admah? how shall I set thee as Zeboim? mine heart is turned within me, my repentings are kindled together.

Jonah 2:4. Then I said, I am cast out of thy sight; yet I will look again toward thy holy temple.

Matt. 24:12. Because iniquity shall abound, the love of many shall wax cold.

Matt. 26:31. All ye shall be offended because of me this night: for it is written, I will smite the shepherd, and the sheep of the flock shall be scattered abroad.

Mark 8:38. Whosoever therefore shall be ashamed of me and of my words in this adulterous and sinful generation; of him also shall the Son of man be ashamed, when he cometh in the glory of his Father with the holy angels.

Luke 9:62. No man, having put his hand to the plough, and looking back, is fit for the kingdom of God.

Luke 17:32. Remember Lot's wife.

John 6:67. Then said Jesus unto the twelve, Will ye also go away?

John 15:6. If a man abide not in me, he is cast forth as a branch, and is withered; and men gather them, and cast them into the fire, and they are burned.

Gal. 1:6. I marvel that ye are so soon removed from him that called you into the grace of Christ unto another gospel: v. 7.

1 Tim. 6:10. The love of money is the root of all evil: which while some coveted after, they have erred from the faith, and pierced themselves through with many sorrows.

2 Tim. 2:12. If we deny him, he also will deny us:

2 Tim. 4:10. For Demas hath forsaken me, having loved this present world.

Heb. 6:4. It is impossible for those who were once enlightened, and have tasted of the heavenly gift, and were made partakers of the Holy Ghost, 5. And have tasted the good word of God, and the powers of the world to come, 6. If they shall fall away, to renew them again unto repentance; seeing they crucify to themselves the Son of God afresh, and put him to an open shame.

Heb. 10:26. If we sin wilfully after that we have received the knowledge of the truth, there remaineth no more sacrifice for sins, 27. But a certain fearful looking for of judgment and fiery indignation, which shall devour the adversaries.

38. If any man draw back, my soul shall have no pleasure in him.

Heb. 12:15. Looking diligently lest any man fail of the grace of God; lest any root of bitterness springing up trouble you, and thereby many be defiled;

2 Pet. 2:20. For if after they have escaped the pollutions of the world through the knowledge of the Lord and Saviour Jesus Christ, they are again entangled therein, and overcome, the latter end is worse with them than the beginning. 21. For it had been better for them not to have known the way of righteousness, than, after they have known it, to turn from the holy commandment delivered unto them.

2 John 9. Whosoever transgresseth, and abideth not in the doctrine of Christ, hath not God.

Promises to: 1 Kin. 8:33. When thy people Israel be smitten down before the enemy, because they have sinned against thee, and shall turn again to thee, and confess thy name, and pray, and make supplication unto thee in this house: 34. Then hear thou in heaven, and forgive the sin of thy people Israel, and bring them again unto the land which thou gavest unto their fathers. vs. 35-53.

2 Chr. 30:9. For if ye turn again unto the LORD, your brethren and your children shall find compassion before them that lead them captive, so that they shall come again into this land: for the LORD your God is gracious and merciful, and will not turn away his face from you, if ye return unto him.

Psa. 17:5. Hold up my goings in thy paths, that my footsteps slip not.

Psa. 56:13. For thou hast delivered my soul from death: wilt not thou deliver my feet from falling, that I may walk before God in the light of the living?

Jer. 3:4. Wilt thou not from this time cry unto me, My father, thou art the guide of my youth? 5. Will he reserve his anger for ever? will he keep it to the end?

Jer. 6:16. Thus saith the LORD, Stand ye in the ways, and see, and ask for the old paths, where is the good way, and walk therein, and ye shall find rest for your souls.

Hos. 14:4. I will heal their backsliding, I will love them freely: for mine anger has turned away from him.

Mal. 3:7. Even from the days of your fathers ye are gone away from mine ordinances, and have not kept them. Return unto me, and I will return unto you, saith the LORD of hosts. But ye said, Wherein shall we return?

Return of: Isa. 29:24. They also that erred in spirit shall come to understanding, and they that murmured shall learn doctrine.

Hos. 6:1. Come, and let us return unto the LORD: for he hath torn, and he will heal us; he hath smitten, and he will bind us up.

Backsliding of Israel: Psa. 106:13. They soon forgat his works; they waited not for his counsel: 14. But lusted exceedingly in the wilderness, and tempted God in the desert.

Isa. 63:17. O LORD, why hast thou made us to err from thy ways, and hardened our heart from thy fear?

Jer. 15:1. Thus saith the LORD unto me, Though Moses and Samuel stood before me, yet my mind could not be toward this people: cast them out of my sight, and let them go forth. vs. 2-14.

BADGER. [R. V., SEAL or POR-POISE.] Skins of, used for covering of tabernacle, Ex. 25:5; 26:14; 35:7,23; 36:19; 39:34; Num. 4:6,8,10, 11,12,14,25. For shoes, Ezek. 16:10. [R. V., SEALSKIN.]

BAGPIPE, [R. V.,] a musical instrument, Dan. 3:5.

BAKER, 1 Sam. 8:13; Jer. 37:21; Hos. 7:4,6. Pharaoh's chief baker, Gen. 40.

BALANCES. Used for weighing, Job 31:6; Isa. 40:12,15; Ezek. 5:1. Money weighed with, Isa. 46:6; Jer. 32:10. Must be just, Lev. 19:36; Prov. 16:11; Ezek. 45:10. False balances used, Hos. 12:7; Amos 8:5; Mic. 6:11; an abomination, Prov. 11:1; 20:23.

Figurative: Job 6:2; 31:6; Psa. 62:9; Isa. 40:12; Dan. 5:27; Rev. 6:5.

BALDNESS, Lev. 13:40,41. A judgment, Isa. 3:24; Jer. 47:5; 48:37; Ezek. 7:18. Artificial, a sign of mourning, Isa. 22:12; Jer. 16:6; Ezek. 27:31; 29:18; Amos 8:10; Mic. 1:16. Artificial, as an idolatrous practice, forbidden, Lev. 21:5; Deut. 14:1.

Instances of: Elisha, 2 Kin. 2:23.

BALL, playing at, Isa. 22:18.

BALM, a medicinal balsam, Gen. 37:25; 43:11; Jer. 8:22; 46:11; 51:8; Ezek. 27:17.

BANISHMENT, Ezra 7:26. Of Adam and Eve, from Eden, Gen. 3:22-24. Of Cain, to be "a fugitive and vagabond," Gen. 4:14. Of Jews, from Rome, Acts 18:2. Of John, to Patmos, Rev. 1:9.

BANNER. Figurative: Psa. 20:5; 60:4; Song 2:4; 6:4; Isa. 13:2.

BAPTISM. Mark 1:4. John did baptize in the wilderness, and preach the baptism of repentance for the remission of sins. 5. And there went out unto him all the land of Judæa, and they of Jerusalem, and were all baptized of him in the river of Jordan, confessing their sins.

Luke 7:29. All the people that heard *him*, and the publicans, justified God, being baptized with the baptism of John. 30. But the Pharisees and lawyers rejected the counsel of God against themselves, being not baptized of him.

John 3:23. And John also was baptizing in Ænon, near to Salim, because there was much water there: and they came, and were baptized.

Acts 1:5. John truly baptized with water; but ye shall be baptized with the Holy Ghost not many days hence. 22. Beginning from the baptism of John, unto that same day that he was taken up from us, must one be ordained to be a witness with us of his resurrection.

Acts 11:16. Then remembered I the word of the Lord, how that he said, John indeed baptized with water; but ye shall be baptized with the Holy Ghost. Acts 18:25.

Acts 19:3. And he said unto them, Unto what then were ye baptized? And they said, Unto John's baptism. 4. Then said Paul, John verily baptized with the baptism of repentance, saying unto the people, that they should believe on him which should come after him, that is, on Christ Jesus.

Christian: Matt. 28:19. Go ye therefore, and teach all nations, baptizing them in the name of the Father, and of the Son, and of the Holy Ghost:

Acts 2:38. Peter said unto them, Repent, and be baptized every one of you in the name of Jesus Christ for the remission of sins, and ye shall receive the gift of the Holy Ghost. 41. Then they that gladly received his word were baptized: and the same day there were added *unto them* about three thousand souls.

Acts 8:36. And as they went on *their* way, they came unto a certain water: and the eunuch said, See, *here is* water; what doth hinder me to be baptized? [37. Philip said, If thou believest with all thine heart, thou mayest. And he answered and said, I believe that Jesus Christ is the Son of God.] 38. And he com-

manded the chariot to stand still: and they went down both into the water, both Philip and the eunuch; and he baptized him. [Omitted in R. V.]

Acts 10:46. Then answered Peter, 47. Can any man forbid water, that these should not be baptized, which have received the Holy Ghost as well as we? 48. And he commanded them to be baptized in the name of the Lord.

Acts 19:4. Then said Paul, John verily baptized with the baptism of repentance, saying unto the people, that they should believe on him which should come after him, that is, on Christ Jesus. 5. When they heard *this,* they were baptized in the name of the Lord Jesus.

Rom. 6:3. Know ye not, that so many of us as were baptized into Jesus Christ were baptized into his death? 4. Therefore we are buried with him by baptism into death: that like as Christ was raised up from the dead by the glory of the Father, even so we also should walk in newness of life.

1 Cor. 1:13. Were ye baptized in the name of Paul? 14. I thank God that I baptized none of you, but Crispus and Gaius; 15. Lest any should say that I had baptized in mine own name. 16. And I baptized also the household of Stephanas: besides, I know not whether I baptized any other. 17. For Christ sent me not to baptize, but to preach the gospel:

1 Cor. 12:13. By one Spirit are we all baptized into one body, whether *we be* Jews or Gentiles, whether *we be* bond or free; and have been all made to drink into one Spirit.

Eph. 4:5. One Lord, one faith, one baptism,

Col. 2:12. Buried with him in baptism, wherein also ye are risen with *him* through the faith of the operation of God, who hath raised him from the dead.

Of the Holy Ghost: Joel 2:28. And it shall come to pass afterward, *that* I will pour out my spirit upon all flesh; and your sons and your daughters shall prophesy, your old men shall dream dreams, your young men shall see visions: 29. And also upon the servants and upon the handmaids in those days will I pour out my spirit.

Matt. 3:11. I indeed baptize you with water unto repentance: but he that cometh after me is mightier than I, whose shoes I am not worthy to bear: he shall baptize you with the Holy Ghost, and *with* fire:

Acts 2:4. And they were all filled with the Holy Ghost, and began to speak with other tongues, as the Spirit gave them utterance.

See HOLY SPIRIT.

BARLEY. A product of Egypt, Ex. 9:31; Palestine, Deut. 8:8; 1 Chr. 11:13; Jer. 41:8. Fed to horses, 1 Kin. 4:28. Used in offerings, Num. 5:15; Ezek. 45:15. Traffic in, 2 Chr. 2:10; Hos. 3:2. Tribute in, 2 Chr. 27:5. Priests estimated value of, Lev. 27:16; 2 Kin. 7:1; Rev. 6:6. Absalom burns Joab's field of, 2 Sam. 14:30.

Loaves of, John 6:9,13.

BARN, 2 Kin. 6:27; Job 39:12; Prov. 3:10; Joel 1:17; Hag. 2:19; Matt. 6:26; 13:30; Luke 12:18,24.

BARNABAS, called also JOSES. A prophet, Acts 13:1. An apostle, Acts 14:14. A Levite who gave his possessions to be owned in common with other disciples, Acts 4:36,37. Goes to Tarsus to find Paul, brings him to Antioch, Acts 9:25-27. Accompanies Paul to Jerusalem,. Acts 11:30. Returns with Paul to Antioch, Acts 12:25. Goes with Paul to Seleucia, Acts 13; to Iconium, Acts 14:1-7. Called Jupiter, Acts 14:12-18. Goes to Derbe, Acts 14:20. Is sent as a commissioner to Jerusalem, Acts 15; Gal. 2:1-9. Disaffected towards Paul, Acts 15:36-39. Is reconciled to Paul, 1 Cor. 9:6. Piety of, Acts 11:24. Devotion of, to Jesus, Acts 15:26.

BARREL, an earthen jar, 1 Kin. 17:12,14,16; 18:33.

BASIN. Made of gold, 1 Kin. 7:50; 1 Chr. 28:17; 2 Chr. 4:8,22; Ezra 1:10; 8:27; of brass, Ex. 27:3; 38:3; 1 Kin. 7:45.

BASKET, Gen. 40:16,17; Ex. 29:3,23,32; Lev. 8:2; Num. 6:15; Deut. 26:2; 28:5,17; 2 Kin. 10:7. Received the fragments after the miracles of the loaves, Matt. 14:20;

15:37; 16:9,10. Paul let down from the wall in, Acts 9:25; 2 Cor. 11:33.

BAT, Lev. 11:19; Deut. 14:18; Isa. 2:20.

BATH, a Hebrew measure for liquids, containing about eight gallons, three quarts, 1 Kin. 7:26,38; Ezra 7:22; Isa. 5:10; Ezek. 45:10, 11,14.

BEAN, 2 Sam. 17:28; Ezek. 4:9.

BEAR. Ferocity of, 2 Sam. 17:8; Prov. 17:12; 28:15; Isa. 11:7; 59:11; Lam. 3:10; Hos. 13:8; Amos 5:19. Killed by David, 1 Sam. 17:34-37. Two destroy the children of Beth-el, who mocked Elisha, 2 Kin. 2:24.

Figurative: Dan. 7:5; Rev. 13:2.

BEAUTY. Vanity of, Psa. 39:11. Prov. 6:25; 31:30; Isa. 3:24; Ezek. 16:14; 28:17. Consumeth away, Psa. 39:11; 49:14.

Instances of: Sarah, Gen. 12:11. Rebekah, Gen. 24:16. Rachel, Gen. 29:17. Joseph, Gen. 39:6. Moses, Ex. 2:2; Heb. 11:23. David, 1 Sam. 16:12,18. Bath-sheba, 2 Sam. 11:2. Tamar, 2 Sam. 13:1. Absalom, 2 Sam. 14:25. Abishag, 1 Kin. 1:4. Vashti, Esth. 1:11. Esther, Esth. 2:7.

Spiritual: 1 Chr. 16:29; Psa. 27:4; 29:2; 45:11; 90:17; 110:3; Isa. 52:7; Ezek. 16:14; Zech. 9:17.

BEE. In Palestine, Deut. 1:44; Judg. 14:8; Psa. 118:12; Isa. 7:18. Called by hissing, Isa. 7:18.

BELIEVER. See RIGHTEOUS.

BENEDICTIONS. Rom. 15:5. Now the God of patience and consolation grant you to be likeminded one toward another according to Christ Jesus: 6. That ye may with one mind *and* one mouth glorify God, even the Father of our Lord Jesus Christ.

13. Now the God of hope fill you with all joy and peace in believing, that ye may abound in hope, through the power of the Holy Ghost.

2 Cor. 13:14. The grace of the Lord Jesus Christ, and the love of God, and the communion of the Holy Ghost, *be* with you all. Amen.

2 Thess. 3:16. Now the Lord of peace himself give you peace always by all means. The Lord *be* with you all.

18. The grace of our Lord Jesus Christ *be* with you all. Amen.

BENEFICENCE. Psa. 41:1. Blessed *is* he that considereth the poor: the LORD will deliver him in time of trouble.

Psa. 112:9. He hath dispersed, he hath given to the poor; his righteousness endureth for ever; his horn shall be exalted with honour.

Prov. 3:27. Withhold not good from them to whom it is due, when it is in the power of thine hand to do *it*. 28. Say not unto thy neighbour, Go, and come again, and to morrow I will give; when thou hast it by thee.

Prov. 11:25. The liberal soul shall be made fat: and he that watereth shall be watered also himself.

Prov. 22:9. He that hath a bountiful eye shall be blessed; for he giveth of his bread to the poor.

Prov. 25:21. If thine enemy be hungry, give him bread to eat; and if he be thirsty, give him water to drink: 22. For thou shalt heap coals of fire upon his head, and the LORD shall reward thee.

Prov. 28:27. He that giveth unto the poor shall not lack: but he that hideth his eyes shall have many a curse.

Mark 9:41. For whosoever shall give you a cup of water to drink in my name, because ye belong to Christ, verily I say unto you, he shall not lose his reward.

Acts 11:29. Then the disciples, every man according to his ability, determined to send relief unto the brethren which dwelt in Judaea: 30. Which also they did, and sent it to the elders by the hands of Barnabas and Saul.

1 Cor. 13:3. And though I bestow all my goods to feed *the poor*, and though I give my body to be burned, and have not charity, it profiteth me nothing.

Gal. 2:10. Only *they would* that we should remember the poor; the same which I also was forward to do.

1 Tim. 5:8. But if any provide not for his own, and specially for those of his own house, he hath denied the faith, and is worse than an infidel. 16. If any man or woman that believeth have widows, let them relieve them, and let not the church be charged; that it may relieve them that are widows indeed.

1 Tim. 6:18. That they do good, that they be rich in good works, ready to distribute, willing to communicate;

Heb. 6:10. For God *is* not unrighteous to forget your work and labour of love, which ye have shewed toward his name, in that ye have ministered to the saints, and do minister.

Heb. 13:16. But to do good and to communicate forget not: for with such sacrifices God is well pleased.

Jas. 2:15. If a brother or sister be naked, and destitute of daily food, 16. And one of you say unto them, Depart in peace, be *ye* warmed and filled; notwithstanding ye give them not those things which are needful to the body; what *doth it* profit?

1 John 3:17. But whoso hath this world's good, and seeth his brother have need, and shutteth up his bowels *of compassion* from him, how dwelleth the love of God in him?

BEREAVEMENT. 1 Thess. 4:13. But I would not have you to be ignorant, brethren, concerning them which are asleep, that ye sorrow not, even as others which have no hope. 14. For if we believe that Jesus died and rose again, even so them also which sleep in Jesus will God bring with him. 15. For this we say unto you by the word of the Lord, that we which are alive *and* remain unto the coming of the Lord shall not prevent them which are asleep. 16. For the Lord himself shall descend from heaven with a shout, with the voice of the archangel, and with the trump of God: and the dead in Christ shall rise first: 17. Then we which are alive *and* remain shall be caught up together with them in the clouds, to meet the Lord in the air: and so shall we ever be with the Lord. 18. Wherefore comfort one another with these words.

BETHLEHEM. A city S. W. of Jerusalem, Judg. 17:7; 19:18. Called EPHRATAH and EPHRATH, Gen. 48:7; Psa. 132:6; Mic. 5:2; and BETH-LEHEM-JUDAH, Judg. 17:7-9; 19:1,18; Ruth 1:1; 1 Sam. 17:12. Rachel dies and is buried at, Gen. 35:16,19; 48:7. The city of Boaz, Ruth 1:1,19; 2:4; 4. Taken and held by the Philistines, 2 Sam. 23:14-16. Jeroboam converts it into a military stronghold, 2 Chr. 11:6. The city of Joseph, Matt. 2:5,6; Luke 2:4. Birthplace of Jesus, Mic. 5:2; Matt. 2; Luke 2:4,15. Herod slays the children of, Matt. 2:16-18.

2. A town of Zebulun, six miles W. of Nazareth, Josh. 19:15. Israel judged at, Judg. 12:10.

BETTING, by Samson, Judg. 14:12-19.

BIBLE. See LAW; WORD OF GOD.

BIGOTRY. Isa. 65:5. Which say, Stand by thyself, come not near to me; for I am holier than thou. These *are* a smoke in my nose, a fire that burneth all the day.

Mark 2:16. And when the scribes and Pharisees saw him eat with publicans and sinners, they said unto his disciples, How is it that he eateth and drinketh with publicans and sinners? Luke 15:2.

BIRDS. Creation of, on the fifth creative day, Gen. 1:20-30. Man's dominion over, Gen. 1:26,28; 9:2, 3; Psa. 8:5-8; Jer. 27:6; Dan. 2:38; Jas. 3:7. Appointed for food, Gen. 9:2,3; Deut. 14:11-20. What species were unclean, Lev. 11:13-20; Deut. 14:12-19.

Used for sacrifice, Divine care of, Job 38:41; Psa. 147:9; Matt. 10:29; Luke 12:6,24. Songs of, at the break of day, Psa. 104:12; Eccl. 12:4; Song 2:12. Domesticated, Job 41:5; Jas. 3:7; Solomon's proverbs of, 1 Kin. 4:33. Nests of, Psa. 104:17; Matt. 8:20; 13:32. Instincts of, Prov. 1:17. Habits of, Job 39:13-18,26-30. Migrate, Jer. 8:7.

Mosaic law protected the mother from being taken with the young, Deut. 22:6,7. Cages of, Jer. 5:27; Rev. 18:2.

Figurative: Isa. 16:2; 46:11; Jer. 12:9; Ezek. 39:4. Symbolical, Dan. 7:6.

BIRTHDAY. Celebrated by feasts, Gen. 40:20; Matt. 14:6. Cursed, Job 3; Jer. 20:14,18.

BIRTHRIGHT. Belonged to the firstborn, Deut. 21:15,16. Entitled the firstborn to a double portion of inheritance, Deut. 21:15-17; royal succession, 2 Chr. 21:3. An honorable title, Ex. 4:22; Psa. 89:27; Jer. 31:9; Rom. 8:29; Col. 1:15; Heb. 1:6; 12:23; Rev. 1:5.

Sold by Esau, Gen. 25:29-34; 27:36, with 25:33; Heb. 12:16; Rom. 9:12,13. Forfeited by Reuben, 1 Chr. 5:1,2. Set aside: That of Manasseh, Gen. 48:15-20; Adonijah, 1 Kin. 2:15; Hosah's son, 1 Chr. 26:10.

BISHOP. Acts 20:28. Take heed therefore unto yourselves, and to all the flock, over the which the Holy Ghost hath made you overseers [R. V., bishops], to feed the church of God, which he hath purchased with his own blood.

Tit. 1:7, For a bishop [marg. R. V., overseer] must be blameless, as the steward of God; not self-willed, not soon angry, [not given to wine], no striker, not given to filthy lucre; 8. But a lover of hospitality, a lover of good men, sober, just, holy, temperate; [R. V. no brawler]

BLASPHEMY. Ex. 20:7. Thou shalt not take the name of the LORD thy God in vain; for the LORD will not hold him guiltless that taketh his name in vain. Deut. 5:11.

2 Kin. 19:22. Whom hast thou reproached and blasphemed? and against whom hast thou exalted *thy* voice, and lifted up thine eyes on high? *even* against the Holy *One* of Israel. Isa. 37:23.

*Job 13:7. Will ye speak wickedly for God? and talk deceitfully for him? 8. Will ye accept his person? will ye contend for God? 9. Is it good that he should search you out? or as one man mocketh another, do ye *so* mock him? [*Interpreted by some authorities as blasphemy.]

Psa. 78:19. Yea, they spake against God; they said, Can God furnish a table in the wilderness? 20. Behold, he smote the rock, that the waters gushed out, and the streams overflowed; can he give bread also? can he provide flesh for his people?

Psa. 139:20. For they speak against thee wickedly, *and* thine enemies take *thy name* in vain.

Jer. 23:10. For the land is full of adulterers; for because of swearing the land mourneth;

Matt. 12:31. Wherefore I say unto you, All manner of sin and blasphemy shall be forgiven unto men: but the blasphemy *against* the *Holy* Ghost shall not be forgiven unto men: 32. And whosoever speaketh a word against the Son of man, it shall be forgiven him: but whosoever speaketh against the Holy Ghost, it shall not be forgiven him, neither in this world, neither in the *world* to come. Mark 3:29,30; Luke 12:10.

Col. 3:8. Put off all these; . . . blasphemy, filthy communication out of your mouth.

Jas. 5:12. Above all things, my brethren, swear not, neither by heaven, neither by the earth, neither by any other oath: but let your yea be yea; and *your* nay, nay; lest ye fall into condemnation.

BLESSING. Ex. 19:5. Now therefore, if ye will obey my voice indeed, and keep my covenant, then ye shall be a peculiar treasure unto me above all people: for all the earth *is* mine:

Ex. 20:6. And shewing mercy unto thousands of them that love me, and keep my commandments.

Deut. 11:26. Behold, I set before you this day a blessing and a curse; 27. A blessing, if ye obey the commandments of the LORD your God, which I command you this day: *v.* 28.

Josh. 1:8. This book of the law shall not depart out of thy mouth; . . . for then thou shalt make thy way prosperous, and then thou shalt have good success.

2 Chr. 27:6. So Jotham became mighty, because he prepared his ways before the LORD his God.

2 Chr. 31:10. Since *the people* began to bring the offerings into the house of the LORD, we have had enough to eat, and have left plenty;

for the LORD hath blessed his people and that which is left *is* this great store.

Job. 36:11. If they obey and serve *him,* they shall spend their days in prosperity, and their years in pleasures.

Prov. 3:1. My son, forget not my law; but let thine heart keep my commandments: 2. For length of days, and long life, and peace, shall they add to thee.

Prov. 16:7. When a man's ways please the LORD, he maketh even his enemies to be at peace with him.

Mal. 3:10. Bring ye all the tithes into the storehouse, that there may be meat in mine house, and prove me now herewith, saith the LORD of hosts, if I will not open you the windows of heaven, and pour you out a blessing, that *there shall* not *be room* enough *to receive it.*

Heb. 10:36. For ye have need of patience, that, after ye have done the will of God, ye might receive the promise.

Rev. 2:10. Be thou faithful unto death, and I will give thee a crown of life.

Spiritual, from God: Psa. 55: 22. Cast thy burden upon the LORD, and he shall sustain thee: he shall never suffer the righteous to be moved.

Psa. 81:10. Open thy mouth wide, and I will fill it.

Mal. 4:2. Unto you that fear my name shall the Sun of righteousness arise with healing in his wings;

John 1:16. Of his fulness have all we received, and grace for grace.

Acts 20:32. And now, brethren, I commend you to God, and to the word of his grace, which is able to build you up, and to give you an inheritance among all them which are sanctified.

2 Cor. 9:8. God *is* able to make all grace abound toward you; that ye, always having all sufficiency in all *things,* may abound to every good work:

Eph. 3:20. Now unto him that is able to do exceeding abundantly above all that we ask or think, according to the power that worketh in us,

Phil. 1:6. Being confident of this

very thing, that he which hath begun a good work in you will perform *it* until the day of Jesus Christ:

Phil. 2:13. It is God which worketh in you both to will and to do of *his* good pleasure.

Phil. 4:7. The peace of God, which passeth all understanding, shall keep your hearts and minds through Christ Jesus. 19. My God shall supply all your need according to his riches in glory by Christ Jesus.

Col. 1:11. Strengthened with all might, according to his glorious power, unto all patience and longsuffering with joyfulness; 12. Giving thanks unto the Father, which hath made us meet to be partakers of the inheritance of the saints in light:

Jas. 1:17. Every good gift and every perfect gift is from above, and cometh down from the Father of lights, with whom is no variableness, neither shadow of turning. *v.* 18.

1 John 1:9. If we confess our sins, he is faithful and just to forgive us *our* sins, and to cleanse us from all unrighteousness.

Psa. 23:1. The LORD *is* my shepherd; I shall not want. 5. Thou preparest a table before me in the presence of mine enemies: thou anointest my head with oil; my cup runneth over.

Psa. 34:10. The young lions do lack, and suffer hunger: but they that seek the LORD shall not want any good *thing*.

Psa. 68:19. Blessed *be* the Lord, *who* daily loadeth us *with benefits*, *even* the God of our salvation.

Psa. 103:2. Bless the LORD, O my soul, and forget not all his benefits: 3. Who forgiveth all thine iniquities; who healeth all thy diseases; 4. Who redeemeth thy life from destruction; who crowneth thee with loving kindness and tender mercies; 5. Who satisfieth thy mouth with good *things; so that* thy youth is renewed like the eagle's.

Psa. 145:15. The eyes of all wait upon thee; and thou givest them their meat in due season. 16. Thou openest thine hand, and satisfiest the desire of every living thing.

Matt. 10:29. Are not two sparrows sold for a farthing? and one of them shall not fall on the ground without your Father.

Luke 12:27. Consider the lilies how they grow: they toil not, they spin not; and yet I say unto you, that Solomon in all his glory was not arrayed like one of these.

1 Cor. 2:9. Eye hath not seen, nor ear heard, neither have entered into the heart of man, the things which God hath prepared for them that love him.

1 Cor. 16:2. Upon the first *day* of the week let every one of you lay by him in store, as [God hath prospered him]. [R. V. he may prosper]

Phil. 4:19. But my God shall supply all your need according to his riches in glory by Christ Jesus.

Deut. 26:15. Look down from thy holy habitation, from heaven, and bless thy people Israel, and the land which thou hast given us, as thou swarest unto our fathers, a land that floweth with milk and honey.

1 Chr. 4:10. Oh that thou wouldest bless me indeed, and enlarge my coast, and that thine hand might be with me, and that thou wouldest keep *me* from evil, that it may not grieve me!

Prov. 30:8. Give me neither poverty nor riches; feed me with food convenient for me:

BLINDNESS. Spiritual: Judg. 16:20. And he wist not that the LORD was departed from him.

Psa. 14:1. The fool hath said in his heart, *There is* no God. 4. Have all the workers of iniquity no knowledge?

Psa. 82:5. They know not, neither will they understand; they walk on in darkness:

Psa. 119:18. Open thou mine eyes, that I may behold wondrous things out of thy law.

Prov. 4:19. The way of the wicked *is* as darkness: they know not at what they stumble. Prov. 7:7-23.

Isa. 9:2. The people that walked in darkness have seen a great light: they that dwell in the land of the shadow of death, upon them hath the light shined.

Isa. 60:2. Darkness shall cover the earth, and gross darkness the people:

Jer. 17:9. The heart *is* deceitful above all *things*, and desperately [wicked]: who can know it? [R. V. sick]

Matt. 22:29. Jesus answered and said unto them, Ye do err, not knowing the scriptures, nor the power of God. Mark 12:24.

Acts 26:18. To open their eyes, *and* to turn *them* from darkness to light, and *from* the power of Satan unto God, that they may receive forgiveness of sins, and inheritance among them which are sanctified by faith that is in me.

Rom. 1:19. That which may be known of God is manifest in them; for God hath shewed *it* unto them.

1 Cor. 15:34. Some have not the knowledge of God: I speak *this* to your shame.

Col. 1:13. Who hath delivered us from the power of darkness, and hath translated *us* into the kingdom of his dear Son:

Tit. 1:16. They profess that they know God; but in works they deny *him,*

BLOOD. Heb. 9:22. And almost all things are by the law purged with blood; and without shedding of blood is no remission.

27. And as it is appointed unto men once to die, but after this the judgment: 28. So Christ was once offered to bear the sins of many; and unto them that look for him shall he appear the second time without sin unto salvation.

Of Christ: Matt. 26:28. For this is my blood of the new testament, which is shed for many for the remission of sins. Mark 14:24; Luke 22:20.

Rom. 3:24. Being justified freely by his grace through the redemption that is in Christ Jesus: 25. Whom God hath set forth *to be* a propitiation through faith in his blood, to declare his righteousness for the remission of sins that are past, through the forbearance of God;

Rev. 12:11. And they overcome

him by the blood of the Lamb, and by the word of their testimony;

BOASTING. Spiritual: Psa. 52:1. Why boastest thou thyself in mischief, O mighty man? the goodness of God *endureth* continually.

Rom. 3:27. Where *is* boasting then? It is excluded. By what law? of works? Nay: but by the law of faith. *vs.* 1-31.

1 Cor. 1:29. That no flesh should glory in his presence. *vs.* 17-31.

Eph. 2:8. For by grace are ye saved through faith; and that not of yourselves: *it is* the gift of God: 9. Not of works, lest any man should boast. 10. For we are his workmanship, created in Christ Jesus unto good works, which God hath before ordained that we should walk in them.

BOLDNESS. Of the Righteous: Prov. 14:26. In the fear of the LORD *is* strong confidence: and his children shall have a place of refuge.

Prov. 28:1. The wicked flee when no man pursueth: but the righteous are bold as a lion.

Eph. 3:12. In whom we have boldness and access with confidence by the faith of him.

Heb. 4:16. Let us therefore come boldly unto the throne of grace, that we may obtain mercy, and find grace to help in time of need.

Heb. 10:19. Having therefore, brethren, boldness to enter into the holiest by the blood of Jesus,

Heb. 13:6. So that we may boldly say, The Lord *is* my helper, and I will not fear what man shall do unto me.

1 John 2:28. And now, little children, abide in him; that, when he shall appear, we may have confidence, and not be ashamed before him at his coming.

1 John 4:17. Herein is our love made perfect, that we may have boldness in the day of judgment: because as he is, so are we in this world.

BOOK. Of Life: Ex. 32:32. Yet now, if thou wilt forgive their sin—; and if not, blot me, I pray thee, out of thy book which thou hast written. 33. And the LORD said unto Moses,

Whosoever hath sinned against me, him will I blot out of my book.

Psa. 69:28. Let them be blotted out of the book of the living, and not be written with the righteous.

Dan. 12:1. And at that time shall Michael stand up, the great prince which standeth for the children of thy people: and there shall be a time of trouble, such as never was since there was a nation even to that same time: and at that time thy people shall be delivered, every one that shall be found written in the book.

Luke 10:20. Notwithstanding in this rejoice not, that the spirits are subject unto you; but rather rejoice, because your names are written in heaven.

Phil. 4:3. I entreat thee also, true yokefellow, help those women which laboured with me in the gospel, with Clement also, and with other my fellowlabourers, whose names are in the book of life.

Rev. 3:5. He that overcometh, the same shall be clothed in white raiment; and I will not blot out his name out of the book of life, but I will confess his name before my Father, and before his angels.

Rev. 13:8. And all that dwell upon the earth shall worship him, whose names are not written in the book of life of the Lamb slain from the foundation of the world.

Rev. 17:8. And they that dwell on the earth shall wonder, whose names were not written in the book of life from the foundation of the world, when they behold the beast that was, and is not, and yet is.

Rev. 20:12. And I saw the dead, small and great, stand before God; and the books were opened: and another book was opened, which is the book of life: and the dead were judged out of those things which were written in the books, according to their works. 15. And whosoever was not found written in the book of life was cast into the lake of fire.

Rev. 21:27. And there shall in no wise enter into it any thing that defileth, neither whatsoever worketh abomination, or maketh a lie: but they which are written in the Lamb's book of life.

Rev. 22:19. And if any man shall take away from the words of the book of this prophecy, God shall take away his part out of the [book] of life, and out of the holy city, and from the things which are written in this book. [R. V. tree]

Of Remembrance: Psa. 56:8. Thou tellest my wanderings: put thou my tears into thy bottle: are they not in thy book?

Mal. 3:16. Then they that feared the LORD spake often one to another: and the LORD hearkened, and heard it, and a book of remembrance was written before him for them that feared the LORD, and that thought upon his name.

BORROWING. Ex. 22:14. And if a man borrow ought of his neighbour, and it be hurt, or die, the owner thereof being not with it, he shall surely make it good. 15. But if the owner thereof be with it, he shall not make it good: if it be an hired thing, it came for his hire.

Psa. 37:21. The wicked borroweth, and payeth not again:

Prov. 22:7. The rich ruleth over the poor, and the borrower is servant to the lender.

BOTTLE, Gen. 21:14. Made of skins, Josh. 9:4,13; Job 32:19; Psa. 119:83; Matt. 9:17; Mark 2:22; Luke 5:37,38; of clay, Isa. 30:14; Jer. 19:1,10; 48:12. Used as a lachrymatory, Psa. 56:8.

BOW. Figurative: Gen. 9:13. I do set my bow in the cloud, and it shall be for a token of a covenant between me and the earth. 14. And it shall come to pass, when I bring a cloud over the earth, that the bow shall be seen in the cloud: 15. And I will remember my covenant, which is between me and you and every living creature of all flesh; and the waters shall no more become a flood to destroy all flesh.

Rev. 4:3. And he that sat was to look upon like a jasper and a sardine stone: and there was a rainbow round about the throne, in sight like unto an emerald.

Rev. 10:1. And I saw another mighty angel come down from heaven, clothed with a cloud: and a rainbow was upon his head, and his face *was* as it were the sun, and his feet as pillars of fire:

BREAD. Figurative: Isa. 55:2; 1 Cor. 10:17; 2 Cor. 9:10. Christ, John 6:32-35.

Symbolical: Of the body of Christ, Matt. 26:26; Acts 20:7; 1 Cor. 11:23,24.

BREASTPLATE. Figurative: Isa. 59:17. For he put on righteousness as a breastplate, and an helmet of salvation upon his head;

Eph. 6:14. Stand therefore, having your loins girt about with truth, and having on the breastplate of righteousness;

1 Thess. 5:8. But let us, who are of the day, be sober, putting on the breastplate of faith and love; and for an helmet the hope of salvation.

BRIBERY. Ex. 23:8. And thou shalt take no gift: for the gift blindeth the wise, and perverteth the words of the righteous.

Deut. 16:19. Thou shalt not wrest judgment; thou shalt not respect persons, neither take a gift: for a gift doth blind the eyes of the wise, and pervert the words of the righteous.

Deut. 27:25. Cursed *be* he that taketh reward to slay an innocent person.

1 Sam. 8:1. And it came to pass, when Samuel was old, that he made his sons judges over Israel. 3. And his sons walked not in his ways, but turned aside after lucre, and took bribes, and perverted judgment.

Prov. 15:27. He that is greedy of gain troubleth his own house; but he that hateth gifts shall live.

Eccl. 7:7. A gift destroyeth the heart.

Amos 5:12. For I know your manifold transgressions and your mighty sins: they afflict the just, they take a bribe, and they turn aside the poor in the gate *from their right.*

Mic. 7:3. That they may do evil with both hands earnestly, the prince asketh, and the judge *asketh* for a reward;

BRIDE. Figurative: Psa. 45:10-17; Ezek. 16:8-14; Rev. 19:7,8; 21:2,9; 22:17.

BRIDEGROOM. Ornaments of, Isa. 61:10. Exempt from military duty, Deut. 24:5. Companions of, Judg. 14:11. Joy with, Matt. 9:15; Mark 2:19,20; Luke 5:34,35.
Figurative: Ezek. 16:8-14.

BUSYBODY. Lev. 19:16. Thou shalt not go up and down *as* a talebearer among thy people: neither shalt thou stand against the blood of thy neighbour: I *am* the LORD.

Prov. 20:3. *It is* an honour for a man to cease from strife: but every fool will be meddling.

2 Thess. 3:11. For we hear that there are some which walk among you disorderly, working not at all, but are busybodies. 12. Now them that are such we command and exhort by our Lord Jesus Christ that with quietness they work, and eat their own bread.

1 Tim. 5:13. And withal they learn *to be* idle, wandering about from house to house: and not only idle, but tattlers also and busybodies, speaking things which they ought not.

1 Pet. 4:15. But let none of you suffer as a murderer, or *as* a thief, or *as* an evil doer, or as a busybody in other men's matters.

CALEB. One of the two survivors of the Israelites permitted to enter the land of promise, Num. 14:30,38; 26:63-65; 32:11-13; Deut. 1:34-36; Josh. 14:6-15. Sent to Canaan as a spy, Num. 13:6. Brings favorable report, Num. 13:26-30; 14:6-9. Assists in dividing Canaan, Num. 34:19. Life of, miraculously saved, Num. 14:10-12. Leader of the Israelites after Joshua's death, Judg. 1:11,12. Age of, Josh. 14:7-10. Inheritance of, Josh. 14:6-15; 15:13-16. Descendants of, 1 Chr. 4:15.

CALF. Offered in sacrifice, Mic. 6:6. Golden, made by Aaron, Ex. 32; Deut. 9:16; Neh. 9:18; Psa. 106:19; Acts 7:41.

CALL. Of Abraham, Gen. 12:1. Now the LORD had said unto Abram, Get thee out of thy country, and from thy kindred, and from thy father's house, unto a land that I will shew thee:

Heb. 11:8. By faith Abraham,

when he was called to go out into a place which he should after receive for an inheritance, obeyed;

Moses: Ex. 3:4. And when the LORD saw that he turned aside to see, God called unto him out of the midst of the bush, and said, Moses, Moses. And he said, Here *am* I. 10. Come now therefore, and I will send thee unto Pharaoh, that thou mayest bring forth my people the children of Israel out of Egypt.

Aaron and His Sons: Ex. 28:1. And take thou unto thee Aaron thy brother, and his sons with him, from among the children of Israel, that he may minister unto me in the priest's office, *even* Aaron, Nadab and Abihu, Eleazar and Ithamar, Aaron's sons.

Heb. 5:4. And no man taketh this honour unto himself, but he that is called of God as *was* Aaron.

Joshua: Num. 27:18. And the LORD said unto Moses, Take thee Joshua the son of Nun, a man in whom *is* the spirit, and lay thine hand upon him;

Gideon: Judg. 6:11. And there came an angel of the LORD, and sat under an oak *was* in Ophrah, that *pertained* unto Joash the Abiezrite: and his son Gideon threshed wheat by the winepress, to hide *it* from the Midianites. 12. And the angel of the LORD appeared unto him, and said unto him, The LORD *is* with thee, thou mighty man of valour.

Samuel: 1 Sam. 3:8. And the LORD called Samuel again the third time. And he arose and went to Eli, and said, Here *am* I; for thou didst call me. And Eli perceived that the LORD had called the child.

Solomon: 1 Chr. 28:6. And he said unto me, Solomon thy son, he shall build my house and my courts: for I have chosen him *to be* my son, and I will be his father.

Amos: Amos 7:14. Then answered Amos, and said to Amaziah, I *was* no prophet, neither *was* I a prophet's son; but I *was* an herdman, and a gatherer of sycomore fruit: 15. And the LORD took me as I followed the flock, and the LORD

said unto me, Go, prophesy unto my people Israel.

Apostles: Matt. 4:18. And Jesus, walking by the sea of Galilee, saw two brethren, Simon called Peter, and Andrew his brother, casting a net into the sea: for they were fishers. 19. And he saith unto them, Follow me, and I will make you fishers of men. 20. And they straightway left *their* nets and followed him. [Mark 1:16,17.]

John 15:16. Ye have not chosen me, but I have chosen you, and ordained you, that ye should go and bring forth fruit, and *that* your fruit should remain:

The Rich Young Man: Mark 10:21. Then Jesus beholding him loved him, and said unto him, One thing thou lackest: go thy way, sell whatsoever thou hast, and give to the poor, and thou shalt have treasure in heaven: and come, take up the cross, and follow me. 22. And he was sad at that saying, and went away grieved: for he had great possessions.

Paul: Acts 9:15. But the Lord said unto him, Go thy way: for he [Paul] is a chosen vessel unto me, to bear my name before the Gentiles, and kings, and the children of Israel: 16. For I will shew him how great things he must suffer for my name's sake.

Rom. 1:1. Paul, a servant of Jesus Christ, called *to be* an apostle, separated unto the gospel of God.

All Who Are Called of God: Rom. 8:30. Moreover, whom he did predestinate, them he also called: and whom he called, them he also justified: and whom he justified, them he also glorified.

CAPITAL PUNISHMENT. See PUNISHMENT.

CAPITAL AND LABOR. Strife between, Matt. 21:33-41; Mark 12:1-9; Luke 20:9-16.

CAPTIVITY. Of the Israelites foretold, Lev. 26:33; Deut. 28:36; of the ten tribes, 2 Kin. 17:6,23,24; 18:9-12.

Of Judah in Babylon, prophecy of, Isa. 39:6; Jer. 13:19; 20:4; 25:2-11; 32:28, etc.; fulfilled, 2 Kin. 24:11-16; 25; 2 Chr. 36; Jer. 52:28-

30. Jews return from, Ezra, chapters 2; 3; 8.

Israelites in, promises to, Neh. 1:9.

As a judgment, Ezra 5:12; 9:7; Isa. 5:13; Jer. 29:17-19; Lam. 1:3-5; Ezek. 39:23,24.

CARE, Worldly: Psa. 39:6. Surely every man walketh in a vain shew: surely they are disquieted in vain: he heapeth up *riches*, and knoweth not who shall gather them.

Psa. 127:2. *It is* vain for you to rise up early, to sit up late, to eat the bread of sorrows: *for* so he giveth his beloved sleep.

Matt. 6:25. Therefore I say unto you, Take no thought [be not anxious, *R. V.*] for your life, what ye shall eat, or what ye shall drink; nor yet for your body, what ye shall put on.

Luke 21:34. Take heed to yourselves, lest at any time your hearts be overcharged with surfeiting, and drunkenness, and cares of this life, and *so* that day come upon you unawares.

1 Cor. 7:32. But I would have you without carefulness. He that is unmarried careth for the things that belong to the Lord, how he may please the Lord: 33. But he that is married careth for the things that are of the world, how he may please *his* wife.

Phil. 4:6. Be careful for nothing; but in every thing by prayer and supplication with thanksgiving let your requests be made known unto God.

2 Tim. 2:4. No man that warreth entangleth himself with the affairs of *this* life; that he may please him who hath chosen him to be a soldier.

Remedy for: Psa. 37:5. Commit thy way unto the LORD; trust also in him; and he shall bring *it* to pass.

Psa. 55:22. Cast thy burden upon the LORD, and he shall sustain thee: he shall never suffer the righteous to be moved.

Phil. 4:6. Be careful for nothing; but in every thing by prayer and supplication with thanksgiving let your requests be made known unto God. 7. And the peace of God, which passeth all understanding, shall keep your hearts and minds through Christ Jesus.

CELIBACY. Matt. 19:10. His disciples say unto him, If the case of the man be so with *his* wife, it is not good to marry. 11. But he said unto them, All *men* cannot receive this saying, save *they* to whom it is given. 12. For there are some eunuchs, which were so born from *their* mother's womb: and there are some eunuchs which were made eunuchs of men: and there be eunuchs, which have made themselves eunuchs for the kingdom of heaven's sake. He that is able to receive *it,* let him receive *it.*

1 Cor. 7:1. Now concerning the things whereof ye wrote unto me: *It is* good for a man not to touch a woman. 2. Nevertheless, *to avoid* fornication, let every man have his own wife, and let every woman have her own husband. 7. For I would that all men were even as I myself. But every man hath his proper gift of God, one after this manner, and another after that. 8. I say therefore to the unmarried and widows, It is good for them if they abide even as I. 9. But if they cannot contain, let them marry: for it is better to marry than to burn.

25. Now concerning virgins I have no commandment of the Lord: yet I give my judgment, as one that hath obtained mercy of the Lord to be faithful. 26. I suppose therefore that this is good for the present distress, *I say*, that *it is* good for a man so to be.

32. But I would have you without carefulness. He that is unmarried careth for the things that belong to the Lord, how he may please the Lord: 33. But he that is married careth for the things that are of the world, how he may please *his* wife. 34. There is a difference *also* between a wife and a virgin. The unmarried woman careth for the things of the Lord, that she may be holy both in body and in spirit: but she that is married careth for the things of the world, how she may please *her* husband.

1 Tim. 4:1. Now the Spirit speaketh expressly, that in the lat-

ter times some shall depart from the faith, giving heed to seducing spirits, and doctrines of devils; 2. Speaking lies in hypocrisy; having their conscience seared with a hot iron; 3. Forbidding to marry, *and commanding* to abstain from meats, which God hath created to be received with thanksgiving of them which believe and know the truth.

CHARACTER. Prov. 22:1. A *good* name *is* rather to be chosen than great riches, *and* loving favour rather than silver and gold. Eccl. 7:1.

Revealed in Countenance: Isa. 3:9. The shew of their countenance doth witness against them; and they declare their sin as Sodom, they hide *it* not. Woe unto their soul! for they have rewarded evil unto themselves.

Firmness of: Psa. 57:7. My heart is fixed, O God, my heart is fixed: I will sing and give praise. Psa. 108:1; 112:7.

Matt. 10:22. And ye shall be hated of all *men* for my name's sake: but he that endureth to the end shall be saved.

Heb. 13:9. Be not carried about with divers and strange doctrines.

Instability of: Prov. 24:21. My son, fear thou the Lord and the king: *and* meddle not with them that are given to change: 22. For their calamity shall rise suddenly; and who knoweth the ruin of them both?

Jer. 2:36. Why gaddest thou about so much to change thy way?

Hos. 6:4. O Ephraim, what shall I do unto thee? O Judah, what shall I do unto thee? for your goodness *is* as a morning cloud, and as the early dew it goeth away.

Eph. 4:14. That we *henceforth* be no more children, tossed to and fro, and carried about with every wind of doctrine, by the sleight of men, *and* cunning craftiness, whereby they lie in wait to deceive;

Jas. 1:6. But let him ask in faith, nothing [wavering]. For he that [wavereth] is like a wave of the sea driven with the wind and tossed. 7. For let not that man think that he shall receive any thing of the Lord. 8. A double minded man *is* unstable in all his ways. (R. V. [doubting] [doubteth])

Jas. 4:8. Draw nigh to God, and he will draw nigh to you. Cleanse *your* hands, ye sinners: and purify *your* hearts, ye double minded.

2 Pet. 2:14. Having eyes full of adultery, and that cannot cease from sin; beguiling unstable souls:

CHARITABLENESS. Prov. 10:12. Hatred stirreth up strifes: but love covereth all sins.

Prov. 17:9. He that covereth a transgression seeketh love; but he that repeateth a matter separateth *very* friends.

Matt. 18:21. Then came Peter to him, and said, Lord, how oft shall my brother sin against me, and I forgive him? till seven times? 22. Jesus saith unto him, I say not unto thee, Until seven times: but, Until seventy times seven.

Luke 17:3. Take heed to yourselves: If thy brother trespass against thee, rebuke him; and if he repent, forgive him. 4. And if he trespass against thee seven times in a day, and seven times in a day turn again to thee, saying, I repent; thou shalt forgive him.

1 Cor. 13:1. Though I speak with the tongues of men and of angels, and have not charity [R. V., love], I am become *as* sounding brass, or a tinkling cymbal.

13. And now abideth faith, hope, charity, these three; but the greatest of these *is* charity.

Gal. 6:1. Brethren, if a man be overtaken in a fault, ye which are spiritual, restore such an one in the spirit of meekness; considering thyself, lest thou also be tempted.

Eph. 4:32. And be ye kind one to another, tenderhearted, forgiving one another, even as God for Christ's sake hath forgiven you.

1 Pet. 3:9. Not rendering evil for evil, or railing for railing: but contrariwise blessing; knowing that ye are thereunto called, that ye should inherit a blessing.

1 Pet. 4:8. And above all things have fervent charity among yourselves: for charity shall cover a multitude of sins.

CHASTISEMENT. 2 Sam. 7:14. I will be his father, and he shall be my son. If he commit iniquity, I will chasten him with the rod of men, and with the stripes of the children of men:

Job 5:17. Behold, happy *is* the man whom God correcteth: therefore despise not thou the chastening of the Almighty:

Psa. 6:1. O LORD, rebuke me not in thine anger, neither chasten me in thy hot displeasure. Psa. 38:1.

Prov. 3:11. My son, despise not the chastening of the LORD; neither be weary of his correction: 12. For whom the LORD loveth he correcteth; even as a father the son *in whom* he delighteth.

Rev. 3:19. As many as I love, I rebuke and chasten: be zealous therefore, and repent.

CHASTITY. Ex. 20:14. Thou shalt not commit adultery.

Job 31:1. I made a covenant with mine eyes; why then should I think upon a maid?

Prov. 2:18. For her house inclineth unto death, and her paths unto the dead.

Prov. 5:20. And why wilt thou, my son, be ravished with a strange woman, and embrace the bosom of a stranger? 21. For the ways of man *are* before the eyes of the LORD, and he pondereth all his goings.

Matt. 5:28. But I say unto you, That whosoever looketh on a woman to lust after her hath committed adultery with her already in his heart.

Acts 15:20. But that we write unto them, that they abstain from pollutions of *idols,* and *from* fornication,

Eph. 5:3. But fornication, and all uncleanness, or covetousness, let it not be once named among you, as becometh saints:

1 Thess. 4:3. For this is the will of God, *even* your sanctification, that ye should abstain from fornication: 7. For God hath not called us unto uncleanness, but unto holiness.

CHILDREN. The Gift of God: Gen. 4:1. And Adam knew Eve his wife; and she conceived, and bare Cain, and said, I have gotten a man from the LORD.

Gen. 28:3. And God Almighty bless thee, and make thee fruitful, and multiply thee, that thou mayest be a multitude of people;

Psa. 127:3. Lo, children *are* an heritage of the LORD: *and* the fruit of the womb *is his* reward.

God's Care of: Psa. 10:14. Thou art the helper of the fatherless.

Jer. 49:11. Leave thy fatherless children, I will preserve *them* alive; and let thy widows trust in me.

A Blessing: Psa. 127:3. Lo, children *are* an heritage of the LORD: *and* the fruit of the womb *is his* reward. 4. As arrows *are* in the hand of a mighty man; so *are* children of the youth. 5. Happy *is* the man that hath his quiver full of them: they shall not be ashamed, but they shall speak with the enemies in the gate.

Prov. 17:6. Children's children *are* the crown of old men; and the glory of children *are* their fathers.

Commandments to: Ex. 20:12. Honour thy father and thy mother: that thy days may be long upon the land which the LORD thy God giveth thee. Deut. 5:16; Matt. 15:4; 19:19; Mark 10:19; Luke 18:20; Eph. 6:2,3.

Psa. 119:9. Wherewithal shall a young man cleanse his way? by taking heed *thereto* according to thy word.

Prov. 1:8. My son, hear the instruction of thy father, and forsake not the law of thy mother: 9. For they *shall be* an ornament of grace unto thy head, and chains about thy neck.

Eccl. 12:1. Remember now thy Creator in the days of thy youth, while the evil days come not, nor the years draw nigh, when thou shalt say, I have no pleasure in them.

Lam. 3:27. *It is* good for a man that he bear the yoke in his youth.

Eph. 6:1. Children, obey your parents in the Lord: for this is right.

1 Tim. 4:12. Let no man despise thy youth; but be thou an example of the believers, in word, in conversation, in charity, in spirit, in faith, in purity.

2 Tim. 2:22. Flee also youthful

lusts: but follow righteousness, faith, charity, peace, with them that call on the Lord out of a pure heart.

Instruction of: Deut. 6:6. And these words, which I command thee this day, shall be in thine heart: 7. And thou shalt teach them diligently unto thy children, and shalt talk of them when thou sittest in thine house, and when thou walkest by the way, and when thou liest down, and when thou risest up.

Prov. 22:6. Train up a child in the way he should go: and when he is old, he will not depart from it.

Joel 1:3. Tell ye your children of it, and *let* your children *tell* their children, and their children another generation.

John 21:15. Feed my lambs.

Prayer in Behalf of: Gen. 17:18. Abraham said unto God, O that Ishmael might live before thee!

2 Sam. 12:16. David therefore besought God for the child; and David fasted, and went in, and lay all night upon the earth.

Promises and Assurances to: Prov. 3:1. My son, forget not my law; but let thine heart keep my commandments: 2. For length of days, and long life, and peace, shall they add to thee.

Prov. 29:3. Whoso loveth wisdom rejoiceth his father:

Isa. 40:11. He shall gather the lambs with his arm, and carry *them* in his bosom.

Isa. 54:13. All thy children *shall be* taught of the Lord; and great *shall be* the peace of thy children.

Matt. 18:4. Whosoever therefore shall humble himself as this little child, the same is greatest in the kingdom of heaven. 5. And whoso shall receive one such little child in my name receiveth me. 10. Despise not one of these little ones; for I say unto you, That in heaven their angels do always behold the face of my Father which is in heaven. Mark 9:37; Luke 9:48.

Matt. 19:14. Jesus said, Suffer little children, and forbid them not, to come unto me: for of such is the kingdom of heaven. 15. And he laid *his* hands on them. Luke 18:15,16.

Mark 10:16. He took them up in his arms, put *his* hands upon them, and blessed them. *vs.* 13-15.

Acts 2:39. The promise is unto you, and to your children,

I John 2:12. Little children, . . . your sins are forgiven you for his name's sake. 13. Young men, . . . ye have overcome the wicked one. Little children, . . . ye have known the Father.

Of the Righteous, Blessed of God: Gen. 7:1. Come thou and all thy house into the ark; for thee have I seen righteous before me in this generation.

Gen. 19:12. And the men said unto Lot, Hast thou here any besides? son in law, and thy sons, and thy daughters, and whatsoever thou hast in the city, bring *them* out of this place:

2 Kin. 8:19. The Lord would not destroy Judah for David his servant's sake, as he promised him to give him alway a light, *and* to his children.

Psa. 103:17. But the mercy of the Lord *is* from everlasting to everlasting upon them that fear him, and his righteousness unto children's children; 18. To such as keep his covenant, and to those that remember his commandments to do them.

1 Cor. 7:14. The unbelieving husband is sanctified by the wife, and the unbelieving wife is sanctified by the husband: else were your children unclean; but now are they holy.

Correction of: Prov. 13:24. He that spareth his rod hateth his son: but he that loveth him chasteneth him betimes.

Prov. 19:18. Chasten thy son while there is hope, and let not thy soul spare for his crying.

Prov. 22:15. Foolishness *is* bound in the heart of a child; *but* the rod of correction shall drive it far from him.

Prov. 23:13. Withhold not correction from the child: for *if* thou beatest him with the rod, he shall not die. 14. Thou shalt beat him with the rod, and shalt deliver his soul from hell.

Prov. 29:15. The rod and reproof give wisdom: but a child left *to himself* bringeth his mother to shame. 17. Correct thy son, and he shall give thee rest; yea, he shall give delight unto thy soul.

Eph. 6:4. And, ye fathers, provoke not your children to wrath: but bring them up in the nurture and admonition of the Lord.

Col. 3:21. Fathers, provoke not your children *to anger,* lest they be discouraged.

Prov. 10:1. The proverbs of Solomon. A wise son maketh a glad father: but a foolish son *is* the heaviness of his mother.

Prov. 20:20. Whoso curseth his father or his mother, his lamp shall be put out in obscure darkness.

Worship, Attend Divine: Josh. 8:35. There was not a word of all that Moses commanded, which Joshua read not before all the congregation of Israel, with the women, and the little ones, and the strangers that were conversant among them.

2 Chr. 20:13. And all Judah stood before the LORD, with their little ones, their wives, and their children.

2 Chr. 31:16. Beside their genealogy of males, from three years old and upward, *even* unto every one that entereth into the house of the LORD, his daily portion for their service in their charges according to their courses;

Symbolical of the Regenerated: Mark 9:36. And he took a child, and set him in the midst of them: and when he had taken him in his arms, he said unto them, 37. Whosoever shall receive one of such children in my name, receiveth me: and whosoever shall receive me, receiveth not me, but him that sent me.

CHINESE. SINIM in Isa. 49:12 is believed by many authorities to be a reference to the Chinese.

CHOSEN, or Elected: 1 Pet. 2:9. But ye *are* a chosen generation, a royal priesthood, an holy nation, a peculiar people; that ye should shew forth the praises of him who hath called you out of darkness into his marvellous light:

CHURCH, the collective body of believers.

Unclassified Scriptures Relating to: Psa. 111:1. I will praise the LORD with *my* whole heart, in the assembly of the upright, and *in* the congregation.

Matt. 16:18. That thou art Peter, and upon this rock I will build my church; and the gates of hell shall not prevail against it.

Acts 7:38. This is he, that was in the church in the wilderness with the angel which spake to him in the mount Sina.

Acts 20:28. Take heed therefore unto yourselves, and to all the flock, over the which the Holy Ghost hath made you overseers, to feed the church of God, which he hath purchased with his own blood.

1 Cor. 12:28. And God hath set some in the church, first apostles, secondarily prophets, thirdly teachers, after that miracles, then gifts of healings, helps, governments, diversities of tongues.

Christ, Head of: Psa. 118:22. The stone *which* the builders refused is become the head *stone* of the corner. 23. This is the LORD'S doing; it *is* marvellous in our eyes. Matt. 21:42,43; Mark 12:10; Luke 20:17,18; I Pet. 2:7.

John 13:13. Ye call me Master and Lord: and ye say well; for *so* I am.

1 Cor. 3:11. For other foundation can no man lay than that is laid, which is Jesus Christ.

Col. 2:10. And ye are complete in him, which is the head of all principality and power: 19. The Head, from which all the body by joints and bands having nourishment ministered, and knit together, increaseth with the increase of God.

Col. 3:11. Christ *is* all, and in all.

Rev. 1:13. And in the midst of the seven candlesticks *one* like unto the Son of man,

Christian, Divinely Established: Eph. 2:20. And are built upon the foundation of the apostles and prophets, Jesus Christ himself being the chief corner *stone;* 21. In whom all the building fitly framed together groweth unto an holy temple in the Lord: 22. In whom ye also are builded together for an habitation of God through the Spirit.

Corruption in: Hos. 4:9. And there shall be, like people, like priest: and I will punish them for their ways, and reward them their doings.

Decrees of: Acts 16:4. And as they went through the cities, they delivered them the decrees for to keep, that were ordained of the apostles and elders which were at Jerusalem.

Duty of, to Ministers: Phil. 2:29. Receive him therefore in the Lord with all gladness; and hold such in reputation:

1 Thess. 5:12. And we beseech you, brethren, to know them which labour among you, and are over you in the Lord, and admonish you; 13. And to esteem them very highly in love for their work's sake.

1 Tim. 5:17. Let the elders that rule well be counted worthy of double honour, especially they who labour in the word and doctrine.

Heb. 13:17. Obey them that have the rule over you, and submit yourselves: for they watch for your souls, as they that must give account, that they may do it with joy, and not with grief: for that *is* unprofitable for you.

Government of, Acts 6:2. The twelve called the multitude of the disciples *unto them,* and said, It is not reason that we should leave the word of God, and serve tables. 3. Brethren, look ye out among you seven men of honest report, full of the Holy Ghost and wisdom, whom we may appoint over this business. 5. The saying pleased the whole multitude: and they chose Stephen, a man full of faith and of the Holy Ghost, and Philip, . . . 6. Whom they set before the apostles: and when they had prayed, they laid *their* hands on them.

Acts 13:1. There were in the church that was at Antioch certain prophets and teachers; as Barnabas, and Simeon, . . . 3. When they had fasted and prayed, and laid *their*

hands on them, they sent *them* away.

Acts 14:23. When they had ordained them elders in every church, and had prayed with fasting, they commended them to the Lord,

Acts 15:2. When therefore Paul and Barnabas had no small dissension and disputation with them, they determined that Paul and Barnabas, and certain other of them, should go up to Jerusalem unto the apostles and elders about this question. 13. And after they had held their peace, James answered, saying, Men *and* brethren, hearken unto me:

19. Wherefore my sentence is, that we trouble not them, which from among the Gentiles are turned to God: 20. But that we write unto them, that they abstain from pollutions of idols, and *from* fornication, and *from* things strangled, and *from* blood.

1 Cor. 7:17. As God hath distributed to every man, as the Lord hath called every one, so let him walk. And so ordain I in all churches.

1 Cor. 12:5. There are differences of administrations, but the same Lord. 28. God hath set some in the church, first apostles, secondarily prophets, thirdly teachers, after that miracles, then gifts of healings, helps, governments, diversities of tongues.

2 Cor. 2:6. Sufficient to such a man *is* this punishment, which *was inflicted* of many. 7. So that contrariwise ye *ought* rather to forgive *him,* and comfort *him,* lest perhaps such a one should be swallowed up with overmuch sorrow. *vs.* 2-11.

Eph. 4:11. He gave some, apostles; and some, prophets; and some, evangelists; and some, pastors and teachers; 12. For the perfecting of the saints, for the work of the ministry, for the edifying of the body of Christ:

1 Tim. 3:1. If a man desire the office of a bishop, he desireth a good work. 2. A bishop then must be blameless, . . . 5. (For if a man know not how to rule his own house, how shall he take care of the

church of God?) 8. Likewise *must* the deacons *be* grave, not doubletongued, not given to much wine, not greedy of filthy lucre; 9. Holding the mystery of the faith in a pure conscience. 10. And let these also first be proved; then let them use the office of a deacon, being *found* blameless. 11. Even so *must their* wives *be* grave, not slanderers, sober, faithful in all things. 12. Let the deacons be the husbands of one wife, ruling their children and their own houses well. 13. For they that have used the office of a deacon will purchase to themselves a good degree, and great boldness in the faith which is in Christ Jesus. *vs.* 1-13.

Jas. 5:14. Is any sick among you? let him call for the elders of the church; and let them pray over him, anointing him with oil in the name of the Lord: 15. And the prayer of faith shall save the sick. See MINISTER, DUTIES OF.

Rules of Discipline in, Rom. 16:17. Mark them which cause divisions and offences contrary to the doctrine which ye have learned; and avoid them.

1 Cor. 16:22. If any man love not the Lord Jesus Christ, let him be Anathema Maranatha.

Gal. 6:1. Brethren, if a man be overtaken in a fault, ye which are spiritual, restore such an one in the spirit of meekness; considering thyself, lest thou also be tempted.

2 Thess. 3:6. We command you, brethren, in the name of our Lord Jesus Christ, that ye withdraw yourselves from every brother that walketh disorderly, and not after the tradition which he received of us. 14. If any man obey not our word by this epistle, note that man, and have no company with him, that he may be ashamed. 15. Yet count *him* not as an enemy, but admonish *him* as a brother.

1 Tim 5:19. Against an elder receive not an accusation, but before two or three witnesses.

Tit. 1:13. Rebuke them sharply, that they may be sound in the faith;

Membership in: John 15:5. I am the vine, ye *are* the branches:

He that abideth in me, and I in him, the same bringeth forth much fruit; for without me ye can do nothing. 6. If a man abide not in me, he is cast forth as a branch, and is withered; and men gather them, and cast *them* into the fire, and they are burned.

Acts 2:41. Then they that gladly received his word were baptized: and the same day there were added *unto them* about three thousand souls.

Eph. 4:25. We are members one of another.

Eph. 5:30. We are members of his body, of his flesh, and of his bones.

Unity of: Psa. 133:1. Behold, how good and how pleasant *it is* for brethren to dwell together in unity!

John 10:16. Other sheep I have, which are not of this fold: them also I must bring, and they shall hear my voice; and there shall be one fold, *and* one shepherd.

John 17:11. Holy Father, keep through thine own name those whom thou hast given me, that they may be one, as we *are*. 21. That they all may be one; as thou, Father, *art* in me, and I in thee, that they also may be one in us: that the world may believe that thou hast sent me. 22. And the glory which thou gavest me I have given them; that they may be one, even as we are one: 23. I in them, and thou in me, that they may be made perfect in one; and that the world may know that thou hast sent me, and hast loved them, as thou hast loved me.

.Eph. 2:14. For he is our peace, who hath made both one, and hath broken down the middle wall of partition *between us;* 18. For through him we both have access by one Spirit unto the Father. 19. Ye are no more strangers and foreigners, but fellowcitizens with the saints, and of the household of God; 21. In whom all the building fitly framed together groweth unto an holy temple in the Lord:

Col. 3:11. There is neither Greek nor Jew, circumcision nor uncircumcision, Barbarian, Scythian, bond *nor* free: but Christ *is* all, and in all. 15. Let the peace of God rule in your hearts, to the which also ye are called in one body;

CITIZENS. Duties of: Ex. 22:28. Thou shalt not revile the gods, nor curse the ruler of thy people. Acts 23:5.

Ezra 6:10. That they may offer sacrifices of sweet savours unto the God of heaven, and pray for the life of the king, and of his sons.

Jer. 29:7. Seek the peace of the city whither I have caused you to be carried away captives, and pray unto the LORD for it: for in the peace thereof shall ye have peace.

Matt. 17:24. They that received tribute *money* came to Peter, and said, Doth not your master pay tribute? 25. He saith, Yes. And when he was come into the house, Jesus prevented him, saying, What thinkest thou, Simon? of whom do the kings of the earth take custom or tribute? of their own children, or of strangers? 26. Peter saith unto him, Of strangers. Jesus saith unto him, Then are the children free. 27. Notwithstanding, lest we should offend them, go thou to the sea, and cast an hook, and take up the fish that first cometh up; and when thou hast opened his mouth, thou shalt find a piece of money: that take, and give unto them for me and thee.

Matt. 22:17. Tell us therefore, What thinkest thou? Is it lawful to give tribute unto Caesar, or not? 18. But Jesus perceived their wickedness, and said, Why tempt ye me, *ye* hypocrites? 19. Shew me the tribute money. And they brought unto him a penny. 20. And he saith unto them, Whose *is* this image and superscription? 21. They say unto him, Caesar's. Then saith he unto them, Render therefore unto Caesar the things that are Caesar's; and unto God the things that are God's. Mark 12:14-17; Luke 20:22-25.

Rom. 13:1. Let every soul be subject unto the higher powers. For there is no power but of God: the powers that be are ordained of God. 2. Whosoever therefore resisteth the power, resisteth the ordi-

nance of God: and they that resist shall receive to themselves damnation.

Tit. 3:1. Put them in mind to be subject to principalities and powers, to obey magistrates,

1 Pet. 2:13. Submit yourselves to every ordinance of man for the Lord's sake: . . .

Rights of: Acts 16:37. They have beaten us openly uncondemned, being Romans, and have cast *us* into prison; and now do they thrust us out privily? nay verily; but let them come themselves and fetch us out.

Acts 19:38. Wherefore if Demetrius, and the craftsmen which are with him, have a matter against any man, the law is open, and there are deputies: let them implead one another. 39. But if ye enquire any thing concerning other matters, it shall be determined in a lawful assembly.

Acts 25:16. It is not the manner of the Romans to deliver any man to die, before that he which is accused have the accusers face to face, and have license to answer for himself concerning the crime laid against him. *vs.* 5:10; Acts 24:18, 19.

Loyal, INSTANCES OF: Israelites, Josh. 1:16-18; 2 Sam. 3:36,37; 15:23,30; 18:3; 21:17; 1 Chr. 12:38. David, 1 Sam. 24:6-10; 26:6-16; 2 Sam. 1:14. Hushai, 2 Sam. 17:15, 16. David's soldiers, 2 Sam. 18:12, 13; 23:15,16. Joab, 2 Sam. 19:5,6. Barzillai, 2 Sam. 19:32. Jehoiada, 2 Kin. 11:4-12; Mordecai, Esth. 2:21-23.

CIVIL SERVICE. School for: Dan. 1:3. And the king spake unto Ashpenaz the master of his eunuchs, that he should bring *certain* of the children of Israel, and of the king's seed, and of the princes; 4. Children in whom *was* no blemish, but well favoured, and skilful in all wisdom, and cunning in knowledge, and understanding science, and such as *had* ability in them to stand in the king's palace, and whom they might teach the learning and the tongue of the Chaldeans.

1 Kin. 11:28. And the man Jeroboam *was* a mighty man of valour: and Solomon seeing the young man that he was industrious, he made him ruler over all the charge of the house of Joseph.

Corruption in: Neh. 5:15. But the former governors that *had been* before me were chargeable unto the people, and had taken of them bread and wine, beside forty shekels of silver; yea, even their servants bare rule over the people: but so did not I, because of the fear of God.

Mark 15:15. And *so* Pilate, willing to content the people, released Barabbas unto them, and delivered Jesus, when he had scourged *him*, to be crucified.

Acts 24:26. He hoped also that money should have been given him of Paul, that he might loose him: wherefore he sent for him the oftener, and communed with him.

CLOSET. Used as a place for prayer, Matt. 6:6.

COCK CROWING. Matt. 26: 34,74,75; Mark 13:35; 14:30,68,72.

COLLUSION. In Sin: Lev. 20:4. And if the people of the land do any ways hide their eyes from the man, when he giveth of his seed unto Molech, and kill him not: 5. Then I will set my face against that man, and against his family, and will cut him off, and all that go a whoring after him, to commit whoredom with Molech, from among their people.

COLONIZATION. Of conquered countries and people, 2 Kin. 17:6,24; Ezra 4:9,10.

COLORS. Symbolical uses of. **Black:** A SYMBOL OF AFFLICTION AND CALAMITY. Job 3:5. Let darkness and the shadow of death stain it; let a cloud dwell upon it; let the blackness of the day terrify it.

Jude 13. Wandering stars, to whom is reserved the blackness of darkness for ever.

Blue: SYMBOL OF DEITY. Ex. 24:10; Jer. 10:9; Ezek. 1:26; 10:1. One of the predominating symbolical colors in the drapery and furnishings of the tabernacle and temple, and vestments of priests.

Ex. 25:3. And this *is* the offering which ye shall take of them; gold, and silver, and brass, 4. And blue, and purple, and scarlet, and fine linen, and goats' *hair*,

Ex. 26:1. Moreover thou shalt make the tabernacle *with* ten curtains *of* fine twined linen, and blue, and purple, and scarlet: *with* cherubims of cunning work shalt thou make them.

Crimson, Red, Purple, and Scarlet, SYMBOLS OF VARIOUS IDEAS: Of *iniquity*, Isa. 1:18; Rev. 17:3,4; 18:12,16; of *royalty*, Judg. 8:26; Dan. 5:7,16,29; Matt. 27:28; *prosperity*, 2 Sam. 1:24; Prov. 31:21; Lam. 4:5; *conquest*, Nah. 2:3; Rev. 12:3.

These colors figured largely in the symbolisms of the tabernacle furnishings, and priestly vestments and functions, *as types and shadows of the atonement*.

Ex. 25:3. And this *is* the offering which ye shall take of them; gold, and silver, and brass, 4. And blue, and purple, and scarlet, and fine linen, and goats' *hair*, 5. And rams' skins dyed red, and badgers' skins, and shittim wood.

White: SYMBOL OF HOLINESS. The high-priest's holy garments were of white linen, Lev. 16:4,32. Choir singers arrayed in white, 2 Chr. 5:12.

Psa. 51:7. Purge me with hyssop, and I shall be clean: wash me, and I shall be whiter than snow.

Eccl. 9:8. Let thy garments be always white;

Isa. 1:18. Come now, and let us reason together, saith the LORD: though your sins be as scarlet, they shall be as white as snow; though they be red like crimson, they shall be as wool.

COMMUNION. With God: John 14:16. And I will pray the Father, and he shall give you another Comforter, that he may abide with you for ever; 17. *Even* the Spirit of truth; whom the world cannot receive, because it seeth him not, neither knoweth him: but ye know him; for he dwelleth with you, and shall be in you. 18. I will not leave you comfortless: I will come to you. 23. Jesus answered and said unto him, If a man love me, he will keep my words: and my Father will love him, and we will come unto him, and make our abode with him.

1 Cor. 10:16. The cup of blessing which we bless, is it not the communion of the blood of Christ? The bread which we break, is it not the communion of the body of Christ? 17. For we *being* many are one bread, *and* one body: for we are all partakers of that one bread.

1 John 1:3. Truly our fellowship *is* with the Father, and with his Son Jesus Christ.

Rev. 3:20. Behold, I stand at the door, and knock: if any man hear my voice, and open the door, I will come in to him, and will sup with him, and he with me.

See FELLOWSHIP.

Of Saints: Psa. 55:14. We took sweet counsel together, *and* walked unto the house of God in company.

Psa. 133:1. Behold, how good and how pleasant *it is* for brethren to dwell together in unity!

Mal. 3:16. They that feared the LORD spake often one to another: and the LORD hearkened, and heard *it,* and a book of remembrance was written before him for them that feared the LORD, and that thought upon his name.

John 17:20. Neither pray I for these alone, but for them also which shall believe on me through their word; 21. That they all may be one; as thou, Father, *art* in me, and I in thee, that they also may be one in us: that the world may believe that thou hast sent me.

Rom. 12:15. Rejoice with them that do rejoice, and weep with them that weep.

2 Cor. 6:14. Be ye not unequally yoked together with unbelievers: for what fellowship hath righteousness with unrighteousness? and what communion hath light with darkness? 15. And what concord hath Christ with Belial? or what part hath he that believeth with an infidel? 16. And what agreement hath the temple of God with idols? for

ye are the temple of the living God; as God hath said, I will dwell in them, and walk in *them;* and I will be their God, and they shall be my people. 17. Wherefore come out from among them, and be ye separate, saith the Lord, and touch not the unclean *thing;* and I will receive you, 18. And will be a Father unto you, and ye shall be my sons and daughters, saith the Lord Almighty.

Eph. 5:11. And have no fellowship with the unfruitful works of darkness, but rather reprove *them.*

Jas. 5:16. Confess *your* faults one to another, and pray one for another, that ye may be healed.

COMMUNISM. Acts 2:44. And all that believed were together, and had all things common; 45. And sold their possessions and goods, and parted them to all *men,* as every man had need.

Acts 4:32. And the multitude of them that believed were of one heart and of one soul: neither said any *of them* that ought of the things which he possessed was his own; but they had all things common. 34. Neither was there any among them that lacked: for as many as were possessors of lands or houses sold them, and brought the prices of the things that were sold, 35. And laid *them* down at the apostles' feet: and distribution was made unto every man according as he had need. 36. And Joses, who by the apostles was surnamed Barnabas, (which is, being interpreted, The son of consolation,) a Levite, *and* of the country of Cyprus, 37. Having land, sold *it,* and brought the money, and laid *it* at the apostles' feet.

Acts 5:1. But a certain man named Ananias, with Sapphira his wife, sold a possession, 2. And kept back *part* of the price, his wife also being privy *to it,* and brought a certain part, and laid *it* at the apostles' feet.

COMPANY, Evil: Ex. 23:2. Thou shalt not follow a multitude to *do* evil;

2 Chr. 19:2. And Jehu the son of Hanani the seer went out to meet him, and said to king Jehosha-

phat, Shouldest thou help the ungodly, and love them that hate the LORD? therefore *is* wrath upon thee from before the LORD.

Psa. 1:1. Blessed *is* the man that walketh not in the counsel of the ungodly, nor standeth in the way of sinners, nor sitteth in the seat of the scornful.

Psa. 6:8. Depart from me, all ye workers of iniquity;

Psa. 84:10. For a day in thy courts *is* better than a thousand. I had rather be a doorkeeper in the house of my God, than to dwell in the tents of wickedness.

Prov. 1:10. My son, if sinners entice thee, consent thou not. 11. If they say, Come with us, . . . 14. Cast in thy lot among us; let us all have one purse: 15. My son, walk not thou in the way with them; refrain thy foot from their path:

Prov. 4:14. Enter not into the path of the wicked, and go not in the way of evil *men*. 15. Avoid it, pass not by it, turn from it, and pass away.

Prov. 16:29. A violent man enticeth his neighbour, and leadeth him into the way *that is* not good.

Prov. 20:19. Meddle not with him that flattereth with his lips.

Prov. 24:1. Be not thou envious against evil men, neither desire to be with them.

1 Cor. 5:6. Know ye not that a little leaven leaveneth the whole lump? 9. I wrote unto you in an epistle not to company with fornicators: 10. Yet not altogether with the fornicators of this world, or with the covetous, or extortioners, or with idolaters; for then must ye needs go out of the world. 11. But now I have written unto you not to keep company, if any man that is called a brother be a fornicator, or covetous, or an idolater or a railer, or a drunkard, or an extortioner; with such an one no not to eat. Gal. 5:9.

1 Cor. 15:33. Be not deceived: evil communications corrupt good manners.

2 Cor. 6:14. Be ye not unequally yoked together with unbelievers: for what fellowship hath righteousness with unrighteousness? and what

communion hath light with darkness? 15. And what concord hath Christ with Belial? or what part hath he that believeth with an infidel? 17. Wherefore come out from among them, and be ye separate, saith the Lord, and touch not the unclean *thing;*

COMPLICITY. Prov. 29:24. Whoso is partner with a thief hateth his own soul: he heareth cursing, and bewrayeth *it* not.

Rom. 1:32. Who knowing the judgment of God, that they which commit such things are worthy of death, not only do the same, but have pleasure in them that do them.

2 John 10. If there come any unto you, and bring not this doctrine, receive him not into *your* house, neither bid him God speed: 11. For he that biddeth him God speed is partaker of his evil deeds.

COMPROMISE. Before Litigation, Enjoined: Prov. 25:8. Go not forth hastily to strive, lest *thou know not* what to do in the end thereof, when thy neighbour hath put thee to shame. 9. Debate thy cause with thy neighbour *himself;* and discover not a secret to another: 10. Lest he that heareth *it* put thee to shame, and thine infamy turn not away.

Luke 12:58. When thou goest with thine adversary to the magistrate, *as thou art* in the way, give diligence that thou mayest be delivered from him; lest he hale thee to the judge, and the judge deliver thee to the officer, and the officer cast thee into prison. 59. I tell thee, thou shalt not depart thence, till thou hast paid the very last mite. Matt. 5:25,26.

CONCEIT. Prov. 3:5. Trust in the LORD with all thine heart; and lean not unto thine own understanding. 7. Be not wise in thine own eyes:

Prov. 26:12. Seest thou a man wise in his own conceit? *there is* more hope of a fool than of him.

Jer. 9:23. Thus saith the LORD, Let not the wise *man* glory in his wisdom, neither let the mighty *man* glory in his might, let not the rich *man* glory in his riches:

Luke 18:11. The Pharisee stood and prayed thus with himself, God, I thank thee, that I am not as other men *are*, extortioners, unjust, adulterers, or even as this publican. 12. I fast twice in the week, I give tithes of all that I possess.

Rom. 1:22. Professing themselves to be wise, they became fools,

Rom. 12:16. Be not wise in your own conceits.

CONCEPTION. Miraculous: By Sarah, Gen. 21:1,2; Rebekah, Gen. 25:21; Rachel, Gen. 30:22; Manoah's wife, Judg. 13:3-24; Hannah, 1 Sam. 1:19,20; Elisabeth, Luke 1:24,25,36,37,58; Mary, Matt. 1:18,20; Luke 1:31-35.

CONCUBINAGE. Laws Concerning: Ex. 21:7-11; Lev. 19:20-22; Deut. 21:10-14. Concubines might be dismissed, Gen. 21:9-14. Called WIVES, Gen. 37:2; Judg. 19:3-5. Children of, not heirs, Gen. 15:4; 21:10.

Practiced by Abraham, Gen. 16:3; 25:6; 1 Chr. 1:32; Nahor, Gen. 22:23,24; Jacob, Gen. 30:4; Eliphaz, Gen. 36:12; Gideon, Judg. 8:31; a Levite, Judg. 19:1; Caleb, 1 Chr. 2:46-48; Manasseh, 1 Chr. 7:14; Saul, 2 Sam. 3:7; David, 2 Sam. 5:13; 15:16; Solomon; 1 Kin. 11:3; Rehoboam, 2 Chr. 11:21; Abijah, 2 Chr. 13:21; Belshazzar, Dan. 5:2.

CONDESCENSION OF GOD. In reasoning with his creatures: Sets forth his reasons for sending the flood, Gen. 6:11-13. Enters into covenant with Abraham, Gen. 15:1-21; 18:1-22. Indulges Abraham's intercession for Sodom, Gen. 18:23-33. Warns Abimelech in a dream, Gen. 20:3-7. Reasons with Moses, Ex. 4:2-17. Sends flesh to the Israelites in consequence of their murmuring, Ex. 16:12. Indulges Moses' prayer to behold his glory, Ex. 33:18-23. Indulges Gideon's tests, Judg. 6:36-40. Reasons with Job, Job 38; 39; 40; 41. Invites sinners, saying, "Come now, and let us reason together," Isa. 1:18-20. Expostulates with backsliding Israel, Isa. 41:21-24; 43:1-19; 65:1-16; Jer. 3:1-15; 4:1-31; 7:1-34; Ezek. 18:25-32; 33:10-20; Hos. 2; Mic. 6:1-9; Mal. 3:7-15.

CONFEDERACIES. Instances of: Of kings, Gen. 14:1,2; Josh. 10:1-5; 11:1-5; 1 Kin. 20:1.

CONFESSION. Matt. 7:22. Many will say to me in that day, Lord, Lord, have we not prophesied in thy name? and in thy name have cast out devils? and in thy name done many wonderful works? 23. And then will I profess unto them, I never knew you: depart from me, ye that work iniquity.

Matt. 10:32. Whosoever therefore shall confess me before men, him will I confess also before my Father which is in heaven. 33. But whosoever shall deny me before men, him will I also deny before my Father which is in heaven. Luke 12:8.

John 12:42. Nevertheless among the chief rulers also many believed on him; but because of the Pharisees they did not confess *him*, lest they should be put out of the synagogue: 43. For they loved the praise of men more than the praise of God.

1 John 2:4. He that saith, I know him, and keepeth not his commandments, is a liar, and the truth is not in him.

CONFIDENCE. False: 1 Kin. 20:11. Let not him that girdeth on *his harness* boast himself as he that putteth it off.

Psa. 20:7. Some *trust* in chariots, and some in horses: but we will remember the name of the LORD our God. 8. They are brought down and fallen: but we are risen, and stand upright.

Psa. 33:16. There is no king saved by the multitude of an host: a mighty man is not delivered by much strength. 17. An horse *is* a vain thing for safety: neither shall he deliver *any* by his great strength.

Psa. 60:11. Give us help from trouble: for vain *is* the help of man. Psa. 108:12.

Prov. 16:25. There is a way that seemeth right unto a man, but the end thereof *are* the ways of death.

Prov. 23:4. Cease from thine own wisdom.

Prov. 26:12. Seest thou a man wise in his own conceit? *there is* more hope of a fool than of him.

Isa. 2:22. Cease ye from man, whose breath *is* in his nostrils: for wherein is he to be accounted of?

Isa. 5:21. Woe unto *them that are* wise in their own eyes, and prudent in their own sight!

Isa. 47:7. And thou saidst, I shall be a lady for ever: *so* that thou didst not lay these *things* to thy heart, neither didst remember the latter end of it.

10. Thou hast trusted in thy wickedness: thou hast said, None seeth me. Thy wisdom and thy knowledge, it hath perverted thee;

Jer. 6:14. They have healed also the hurt *of the daughter* of my people slightly, saying, Peace, peace; when *there is* no peace. Jer. 8:11.

Jer. 7:8. Behold, ye trust in lying words, that cannot profit.

Jer. 17:5. Thus saith the LORD; Cursed *be* the man that trusteth in man, and maketh flesh his arm, and whose heart departeth from the LORD.

Rom. 12:16. Be not wise in your own conceits.

1 Cor. 3:21. Let no man glory in men.

2 Cor. 1:9. But we had the sentence of death in ourselves, that we should not trust in ourselves, but in God.

Gal. 6:7. Be not deceived; God is not mocked: for whatsoever a man soweth, that shall he also reap. 8. For he that soweth to his flesh shall of the flesh reap corruption;

1 Thess. 5:3. When they shall say, Peace and safety; then sudden destruction cometh upon them, as travail upon a woman with child; and they shall not escape.

1 Tim. 6:17. Charge them that are rich in this world, that they be not highminded, nor trust in uncertain riches, but in the living God, who giveth us richly all things to enjoy;

Jas. 4:13. Go to now, ye that say, To day or to morrow we will go into such a city, and continue there a year, and buy and sell, and get gain: 14. Whereas ye know not what *shall be* on the morrow. 15. For that ye *ought* to say, If the Lord will, we shall live, and do this, or that.

CONNIVANCE. Prov. 10:10. He that winketh with the eye causeth sorrow: but a prating fool shall fall.

1 Sam. 3:11. And the LORD said to Samuel, Behold, I will do a thing in Israel, at which both the ears of every one that heareth it shall tingle. 12. In that day I will perform against Eli all *things* which I have spoken concerning his house: when I begin, I will also make an end. 13. For I have told him that I will judge his house for ever for the iniquity which he knoweth; because his sons made themselves vile, and he restrained them not.

CONSCIENCE. Job 27:6. My righteousness I hold fast, and will not let it go: my heart shall not reproach *me* so long as I live.

Matt. 6:22. The light of the body is the eye: if therefore thine eye be single, thy whole body shall be full of light. 23. But if thine eye be evil, thy whole body shall be full of darkness. If therefore the light that is in thee be darkness, how great is that darkness!

Acts 23:1. And Paul, earnestly beholding the council, said, Men *and* brethren, I have lived in all good conscience before God until this day.

Acts 24:16. And herein do I exercise myself, to have always a conscience void of offence toward God, and *toward* men.

Rom. 2:14. When the Gentiles, which have not the law, do by nature the things contained in the law, these, having not the law, are a law unto themselves: 15. Which shew the work of the law written in their hearts, their conscience also bearing witness, and *their* thoughts the mean while accusing or else excusing one another;

Rom. 7:15. For that which I do I allow not: for what I would, that do I not; but what I hate, that do I.

Rom. 9:1. I say the truth in Christ, I lie not, my conscience also bearing me witness in the Holy Ghost,

Rom. 14:22. Hast thou faith? have *it* to thyself before God. Happy is he that condemneth not himself in that thing which he alloweth. 23.

And he that doubteth is damned if he eat, because *he eateth* not of faith: for whatsoever *is* not of faith is sin.

1 Cor. 8:7. Howbeit *there is* not in every man that knowledge: for some with conscience of the idol unto this hour eat *it* as a thing offered unto an idol; and their conscience being weak is defiled.

1 Cor. 10:27. If any of them that believe not bid you *to a feast*, and ye be disposed to go; whatsoever is set before you, eat, asking no question for conscience sake. 28. But if any man say unto you, This is offered in sacrifice unto idols, eat not for his sake that shewed it, and for conscience sake: for the earth *is* the Lord's, and the fulness thereof: 29. Conscience, I say, not thine own, but of the other: for why is my liberty judged of another *man's* conscience?

Heb. 10:22. Let us draw near with a true heart in full assurance of faith, having our hearts sprinkled from an evil conscience, and our bodies washed with pure water.

1 John 3:20. If our heart condemn us, God is greater than our heart, and knoweth all things. 21. Beloved, if our heart condemn us not, *then* have we confidence toward God.

Guilty: Psa. 51:3. For I acknowledge my transgressions: and my sin is ever before me. 10. Create in me a clean heart, O God: and renew a right spirit within me.

Prov. 28:1. The wicked flee when no man pursueth: but the righteous are bold as a lion.

John 8:9. And they which heard *it,* being convicted by *their own* conscience, went out one by one, beginning at the eldest, *even* unto the last: and Jesus was left alone, and the woman standing in the midst.

1 Tim. 4:2. Speaking lies in hypocrisy; having their conscience seared with a hot iron;

Tit. 1:15. Unto the pure all things *are* pure: but unto them that are defiled and unbelieving *is* nothing pure; but even their mind and conscience is defiled.

CONSECRATION. Personal: Psa. 51:17. The sacrifices of God *are* a broken spirit: a broken and a contrite heart, O God, thou wilt not despise.

Rom. 6:13. Neither yield ye your members *as* instruments of unrighteousness unto sin: but yield yourselves unto God, as those that are alive from the dead, and your members *as* instruments of righteousness unto God.

16. Know ye not, that to whom ye yield yourselves servants to obey, his servants ye are to whom ye obey; whether of sin unto death, or of obedience unto righteousness?

Rom. 12:1. I beseech you therefore, brethren, by the mercies of God, that ye present your bodies a living sacrifice, holy, acceptable unto God, *which is* your reasonable service.

CONSISTENCY. Matt. 6:24. No man can serve two masters: for either he will hate the one, and love the other; or else he will hold to the one, and despise the other. Ye cannot serve God and mammon. Luke 16:13.

1 Cor. 10:21. Ye cannot drink the cup of the Lord, and the cup of devils: ye cannot be partakers of the Lord's table, and of the table of devils.

CONSPIRACY. Law Against: Ex. 23:1. Thou shalt not raise a false report: put not thine hand with the wicked to be an unrighteous witness.

2. Thou shalt not follow a multitude to *do* evil; neither shalt thou speak in a cause to decline after many to wrest *judgment;*

CONSTITUTION. Agreement Between the Ruler and People: Deut. 17:18. And it shall be, when he sitteth upon the throne of his kingdom, that he shall write him a copy of this law in a book out of *that which is* before the priests the Levites: 19. And it shall be with him, and he shall read therein all the days of his life: that he may learn to fear the LORD his God, to keep all the words of this law and these statutes, to do them: 20. That his heart be not lifted up

57

above his brethren, and that he turn not aside from the commandment, *to* the right hand, or *to* the left: to the end that he may prolong *his* days in his kingdom, he, and his children, in the midst of Israel.

2 Sam. 5:3. So all the elders of Israel came to the king of Hebron; and king David made a league with them in Hebron before the LORD: and they anointed David king over Israel.

CONTENTMENT. Psa. 16:6. The lines are fallen unto me in pleasant *places;* yea, I have a goodly heritage.

Psa. 37:7. Rest in the LORD, and wait patiently for him: fret not thyself because of him who prospereth in his way, 16. A little that a righteous man hath *is* better than the riches of many wicked.

Prov. 16:8. Better *is* a little with righteousness than great revenues without right.

Prov. 17:1. Better is a dry morsel, and quietness therewith, than an house full of sacrifices *with* strife. 22. A merry heart doeth good *like* a medicine:

Eccl. 5:12. The sleep of a labouring man *is* sweet, whether he eat little or much:

Eccl. 6:9. Better *is* the sight of the eyes than the wandering of the desire: *vs.* 7,8.

1 Cor. 7:17. As God hath distributed to every man, as the Lord hath called every one, so let him walk.

Gal. 5:26. Let us not be desirous of vain glory, provoking one another, envying one another.

1 Tim. 6:6. Godliness with contentment is great gain.

Heb. 13:5. *Be* content with such things as ye have: for he hath said, I will never leave thee, nor forsake thee.

CONTINENCE. Job 31:1. I made a covenant with mine eyes; why then should I think upon a maid?

Matt. 5:27. Ye have heard that it was said by them of old time, Thou shalt not commit adultery: 28. But I say unto you, That whosoever looketh on a woman to lust after her hath committed adultery

with her already in his heart.

1 Cor. 7:1. Now concerning the things whereof ye wrote unto me: *It is* good for a man not to touch a woman. 2. Nevertheless, *to avoid* fornication, let every man have his own wife, and let every woman have her own husband.

1 Cor. 9:27. But I keep under my body, and bring *it* into subjection: lest that by any means, when I have preached to others, I myself should be a castaway.

CONTINGENCIES. In Blessing of Man: Ex. 19:5. Now therefore, if ye will obey my voice indeed, and keep my covenant, then ye shall be a peculiar treasure unto me above all people: for all the earth *is* mine:

Lev. 26:3. If ye walk in my statutes, and keep my commandments, and do them; 4. Then I will give you rain in due season, and the land shall yield her increase, and the trees of the field shall yield their fruit. *vs.* 3-13.

Deut. 11:26. Behold, I set before you this day a blessing and a curse; 27. A blessing, if ye obey the commandments of the LORD your God, which I command you this day: 28. And a curse, if ye will not obey the commandments of the LORD your God, but turn aside out of the way which I command you this day, to go after other gods, which ye have not known.

Matt. 19:17. If thou wilt enter into life, keep the commandments.

John 15:7. If ye abide in me, and my words abide in you, ye shall ask what ye will, and it shall be done unto you.

Heb. 3:14. For we are made partakers of Christ, if we hold the beginning of our confidence stedfast unto the end;

Rev. 22:17. And whosoever will, let him take the water of life freely.

CONTRACTS. Between Abraham and Abimelech, concerning wells of water, Gen. 21:25-32; lated, Gen. 26:15. First contract between Laban and Jacob for Laban's daughter, Gen. 29:15-20, 27-30; violated, Gen. 29:23-27; second contract, Gen. 30:28-34; violated, Gen. 30:37-43; 31:7; for cattle, Gen. 30:27-29,31-34.

Lev. 6:1. And the LORD spake unto Moses, saying, 2. If a soul sin, and commit a trespass against the LORD, and lie unto his neighbour in that which was delivered him to keep, 4. Then it shall be, because he hath sinned, and is guilty, that he shall restore that which he took violently away, or the thing which he hath deceitfully gotten, or that which was delivered him to keep, or the lost thing which he hath found. 5. Or all that about which he hath sworn falsely; he shall even restore it in the principal, and shall add the fifth part more thereto, and give it unto him to whom it appertaineth, in the day of his trespass offering.

Matt. 20:13. But he answered one of them, and said, Friend, I do thee no wrong: didst not thou agree with me for a penny? 14. Take that thine is, and go thy way: I will give unto this last, even as unto thee. 15. Is it not lawful for me to do what I will with mine own? Is thine eye evil, because I am good? 16. So the last shall be first, and the first last:

Gal. 3:15. Brethren, I speak after the manner of men; Though it be but a man's covenant, yet if it be confirmed, no man disannulleth, or addeth thereto.

CONVERSATION. Eph. 4:29. Let no corrupt communication proceed out of your mouth, but that which is good to the use of edifying, that it may minister grace unto the hearers.

Col. 3:8. But now ye also put off all these; anger, wrath, malice, blasphemy, filthy communication out of your mouth.

Col. 4:6. Let your speech be alway with grace, seasoned with salt, that ye may know how ye ought to answer every man.

CONVICTION. Of Sin: Job 40:4. Behold, I am vile; what shall I answer thee? I will lay mine hand upon my mouth. 5. Once have I spoken; but I will not answer: yea, twice; but I will proceed no further.

Psa. 31:10. My life is spent with grief, and my years with sighing: my strength faileth because of mine iniquity, and my bones are consumed.

Isa. 6:5. Woe is me! for I am undone; because I am a man of unclean lips, and I dwell in the midst of a people of unclean lips: for mine eyes have seen the King, the LORD of hosts.

Luke 5:8. When Simon Peter saw it, he fell down at Jesus' knees, saying, Depart from me; for I am a sinful man, O Lord.

Acts 2:37. Now when they heard this, they were pricked in their heart, and said unto Peter and to the rest of the apostles, Men and brethren, what shall we do?

Acts 16:29. He called for a light, and sprang in, and came trembling, and fell down before Paul and Silas, 30. And brought them out, and said, Sirs, what must I do to be saved?

Rom. 2:15. Which shew the work of the law written in their hearts, their conscience also bearing witness, and their thoughts the mean while accusing or else excusing one another.

COUNSEL. Prov. 11:14. Where no counsel is, the people fall: but in the multitude of counsellors there is safety.

Prov. 15:22. Without counsel purposes are disappointed: but in the multitude of counsellors they are established.

Prov. 20:18. Every purpose is established by counsel: and with good advice make war.

Prov. 27:9. Ointment and perfume rejoice the heart: so doth the sweetness of a man's friend by hearty counsel.

COUNTRY. Love of: Psa. 137:1. By the rivers of Babylon, there we sat down, yea, we wept, when we remembered Zion. 2. We hanged our harps upon the willows in the midst thereof. 3. For there they that carried us away captive required of us a song; and they that wasted us required of us mirth, saying, Sing us one of the songs of Zion. 4. How shall we sing the LORD's song in a strange land? 5. If I forget thee, O Jerusalem, let

my right hand forget *her cunning.*
6. If I do not remember thee, let my tongue cleave to the roof of my mouth; if I prefer not Jerusalem above my chief joy.

COURAGE. Scriptures Relating to: Prov. 28:1. The wicked flee when no man pursueth: but the righteous are bold as a lion.

Ezek. 3:9. As an adamant harder than flint have I made thy forehead: fear them not, neither be dismayed at their looks, though they *be* a rebellious house.

1 Cor. 16:13. Watch ye, stand fast in the faith, quit you like men, be strong.

2 Tim. 1:7. For God hath not given us the spirit of fear; but of power, and of love, and of a sound mind.

COURT. Ecclesiastical: Matt. 18:15. Moreover if thy brother shall trespass against thee, go and tell him his fault between thee and him alone: if he shall hear thee, thou hast gained thy brother. 16. But if he will not hear *thee, then* take with thee one or two more, that in the mouth of two or three witnesses every word may be established. 17. And if he shall neglect to hear them, tell *it* unto the church: but if he neglect to hear the church, let him be unto thee as an heathen man and a publican. 18. Verily I say unto you, Whatsoever ye shall bind on earth shall be bound in heaven: and whatsoever ye shall loose on earth shall be loosed in heaven.

Civil: COMPOSITION OF, AND MODE OF PROCEDURE: Ex. 18:25. And Moses chose able men out of all Israel, and made them heads over the people, rulers of thousands, rulers of hundreds, rulers of fifties, and rulers of tens. 26. And they judged the people at all seasons: the hard causes they brought unto Moses, but every small matter they judged themselves.

Deut. 1:17. Ye shall not respect persons in judgment; *but* ye shall hear the small as well as the great; ye shall not be afraid of the face of man; for the judgment *is* God's: and the cause that is too hard for you, bring *it* unto me, and I will hear it.

Ruth 4:2. And he took ten men of the elders of the city, and said, Sit ye down here. And they sat down. . .

Mark 14:53. And they led Jesus away to the high priest: and with him were assembled all the chief priests and the elders and the scribes.

Mark 15:1. And straightway in the morning the chief priests held a consultation with the elders and scribes and the whole council and bound Jesus, and carried *him* away, and delivered *him* to Pilate. Matt. 26:54-71; Luke 22:50-71; John 18:13-28.

Acts 5:17. Then the high priest rose up, and all they that were with him, (which is the sect of the Sadducees,) and were filled with indignation, 18. And laid their hands on the apostles, and put them in the common prison.

Circuit: 1 Sam. 7:15. And Samuel judged Israel all the days of his life. 16. And he went from year to year in circuit to Beth-el, and Gilgal, and Mizpeh, and judged Israel in all those places. 17. And his return *was* to Ramah; for there *was* his house; and there he judged Israel; and there he built an altar unto the LORD.

Superior, and Inferior: Ex. 18:22. And let them judge the people at all seasons: and it shall be, *that* every great matter they shall bring unto thee, but every small matter they shall judge: so shall it be easier for thyself, and they shall bear *the burden* with thee.

Justice Required of: Ex. 23:2. Thou shalt not follow a multitude to *do* evil; neither shalt thou speak in a cause to decline after many to wrest *judgment:* 7. Keep thee far from a false matter; and the innocent and righteous slay thou not: for I will not justify the wicked. 8. And thou shalt take no gift: for the gift blindeth the wise, and perverteth the words of the righteous.

Deut. 1:16. And I charged your judges at that time, saying, Hear *the causes* between your brethren, and judge righteously between *every* man and his brother, and the stranger *that is* with him. 17. Ye shall not respect persons in judgment; *but* ye shall hear the small as well as the great; ye shall not be afraid of the face of man; for the judgment *is* God's: and the cause that is too hard for you, bring *it* unto me, and I will hear it.

2 Chr. 19:6. And said to the judges, Take heed what ye do: for ye judge not for man, but for the LORD, who *is* with you in the judgment. 7. Wherefore now let the fear of the LORD be upon you; take heed and do *it:* for *there is* no iniquity with the LORD our God, nor respect of persons, nor taking of gifts.

Sentence of, Final and Obligatory: Deut. 17:11. According to the sentence of the law which they shall teach thee, and according to the judgment which they shall tell thee, thou shalt do: thou shalt not decline from the sentence which they shall shew thee, *to* the right hand, nor *to* the left.

Contempt of: Deut. 17:12. And the man that will do presumptuously, and will not hearken unto the priest that standeth to minister there before the LORD thy God, or unto the judge, even that man shall die: and thou shalt put away the evil from Israel. 13. And all the people shall hear, and fear, and do no more presumptuously.

Corrupt: Prov. 17:15. He that justifieth the wicked, and he that condemneth the just, even they both *are* abomination to the LORD.

Isa. 5:23. Which justify the wicked for reward, and take away the righteousness of the righteous from him!

Isa. 10:1. Woe unto them that decree unrighteous decrees, and that write grievousness *which* they have prescribed; 2. To turn aside the needy from judgment, and to take away the right from the poor of my people, that widows may be their prey, and *that* they may rob the fatherless!

Mic. 3:11. The heads thereof judge for reward, and the priests thereof teach for hire, and the

prophets thereof divine for money.

Mic. 7:3. That they may do evil with both hands earnestly, the prince asketh, and the judge *asketh* for a reward; and the great *man,* he uttereth his mischievous desire: so they wrap it up.

Acts 24:26. He hoped also that money should have been given him of Paul, that he might loose him; wherefore he sent for him the oftener, and communed with him. 27. But after two years Porcius Festus came into Felix' room: and Felix, willing to shew the Jews a pleasure, left Paul bound.

Accused Spoke in His Own Defense: Mark 15:3. And the chief priests accused him of many things: but he answered nothing. 4. And Pilate asked him again, saying, Answerest thou nothing? behold how many things they witness against thee. 5. But Jesus yet answered nothing; so that Pilate marvelled.

Acts 4:8. Then Peter, filled with the Holy Ghost, said unto them, Ye rulers of the people, and elders of Israel,

Acts 7:1. Then said the high priest, Are these things so? 2. And he [Stephen] said, Men, brethren, and fathers, hearken;

Acts 26:1. Then Agrippa said unto Paul, Thou art permitted to speak for thyself. Then Paul stretched forth the hand, and answered for himself:

COURTSHIP. Ancient customs of: Suitor visited the maid, Judg. 14:7; women proposed marriage, Ruth 3:9-13.

COVETOUSNESS. Ex. 20:17. Thou shalt not covet thy neighbour's house, thou shalt not covet thy neighbour's wife, nor his manservant, nor his maidservant, nor his ox, nor his ass, nor any thing that *is* thy neighbour's. Deut. 5:21.

Psa. 119:36. Incline my heart unto thy testimonies, and not to covetousness.

Prov. 11:24. *There is* that withholdeth more than is meet, but *it tendeth* to poverty. 26. He that withholdeth corn, the people shall curse him:

Prov. 22:16. He that oppresseth

the poor to increase his *riches, and* he that giveth to the rich, *shall* surely *come* to want.

Eccl. 5:10. He that loveth silver shall not be satisfied with silver; nor he that loveth abundance with increase; this *is* also vanity. 11. When goods increase, they are increased that eat them: and what good *is there* to the owners thereof, saving the beholding *of them* with their eyes?

Isa. 5:8. Woe unto them that join house to house, *that* lay field to field, till *there be* no place, that they may be placed alone in the midst of the earth!

Isa. 56:11. Yea, *they are* greedy dogs *which* can never have enough, and they *are* shepherds *that* cannot understand: they all look to their own way, every one for his gain, from his quarter.

Matt. 16:26. What is a man profited, if he shall gain the whole world, and lose his own soul?

COWARDICE. Lev. 26:36. And upon them that are left *alive* of you I will send a faintness into their hearts in the lands of their enemies; and the sound of a shaking leaf shall chase them; and they shall flee, as fleeing from a sword; and they shall fall when none pursueth. 37. And they shall fall one upon another, as it were before a sword, when none pursueth: and ye shall have no power to stand before your enemies.

Deut. 32:30. How should one chase a thousand, and two put ten thousand to flight, except their Rock had sold them, and the LORD had shut them up?

Josh. 7:5. The hearts of the people melted, and became as water.

Judg. 7:3. Now therefore go to, proclaim in the ears of the people, saying, Whosoever *is* fearful and afraid, let him return and depart early from mount Gilead. And there returned of the people twenty and two thousand; and there remained ten thousand.

Prov. 28:1. The wicked flee when no man pursueth: but the righteous are bold as a lion.

Prov. 29:25. The fear of man bringeth a snare:

2 Tim. 4:16. At my first answer no man stood with me, but all *men* forsook me:

CREATURE. New Creature: 2 Cor. 5:17. Therefore if any man *be* in Christ, *he is* a new creature: old things are passed away; behold, all things are become new.

Gal. 6:15. For in Christ Jesus neither circumcision availeth any thing, nor uncircumcision, but a new creature.

CREDITOR. Laws Concerning: Ex. 22:25. If thou lend money to *any of* my people *that is* poor by thee, thou shalt not be to him as a usurer, neither shalt thou lay upon him usury. 26. If thou at all take thy neighbour's raiment to pledge, thou shalt deliver it unto him by that the sun goeth down: 27. For that *is* his covering only, it *is* his raiment for his skin: wherein shall he sleep? and it shall come to pass, when he crieth unto me, that I will hear; for I *am* gracious.

Lev. 25:14. And if thou sell ought unto thy neighbour, or buyest *ought* of thy neighbour's hand, ye shall not oppress one another: 15. According to the number of years after the jubilee thou shalt buy of thy neighbour, *and* according unto the number of years of the fruits he shall sell unto thee: 16. According to the multitude of years thou shalt increase the price thereof, and according to the fewness of years thou shalt diminish the price of it: for *according* to the number *of the years* of the fruits doth he sell unto thee. 17. Ye shall not therefore oppress one another; but thou shalt fear thy God: for I *am* the LORD your God.

35. And if thy brother be waxen poor, and fallen in decay with thee; then thou shalt relieve him: *yea, though he be* a stranger, or a sojourner; that he may live with thee. 36. Take thou no usury of him, or increase: but fear thy God; that thy brother may live with thee. 37. Thou shalt not give him thy money upon usury, nor lend him thy victuals for increase.

Matt. 5:42. Give to him that asketh thee, and from him that would borrow of thee turn not thou away.

Luke 6:34. And if ye lend *to them* of whom ye hope to receive, what thank have ye? for sinners also lend to sinners, to receive as much again.

Oppressions of: 2 Kin. 4:1. Now there cried a certain woman of the wives of the sons of the prophets unto Elisha, saying, Thy servant my husband is dead; and thou knowest that thy servant did fear the LORD: and the creditor is come to take unto him my two sons to be bondmen.

Job 22:6. For thou hast taken a pledge from thy brother for nought, and stripped the naked of their clothing.

Job 24:3. They drive away the ass of the fatherless, they take the widow's ox for a pledge. 9. They pluck the fatherless from the breast, and take a pledge of the poor. 10. They cause *him* to go naked without clothing, and they take away the sheaf *from* the hungry:

Prov. 22:26. Be not thou *one* of them that strike hands, *or* of them that are sureties for debts. 27. If thou hast nothing to pay, why should he take away thy bed from under thee?

Matt. 18:28. But the same servant went out, and found one of his fellowservants, which owed him an hundred pence: and he laid hands on him, and took *him* by the throat, saying, Pay me that thou owest. 29. And his fellowservant fell down at his feet, and besought him, saying, Have patience with me, and I will pay thee all. 30. And he would not: but went and cast him into prison, till he should pay the debt. 31. So when his fellowservants saw what was done, they were very sorry, and came and told unto their lord all that was done. 32. Then his lord, after that he had called him, said unto him, O thou wicked servant, I forgave thee all that debt, because thou desiredst me: 33. Shouldest not thou also have had compassion on thy fellowservant, even as I had pity on thee? 34. And his lord was wroth, and delivered him to the tormentors, till he should pay all that was due unto him. 35. So likewise shall my heavenly Father do also unto you, if ye from your hearts forgive not every one his brother their trespasses.

Merciful: Psa. 112:5. A good man sheweth favour, and lendeth: he will guide his affairs with discretion.

CRIME. Partial Lists of: Matt. 15:19. For out of the heart proceed evil thoughts, murders, adulteries, fornications, thefts, false witness, blasphemies: Mark 7:21,22.

Rom. 3:14. Whose mouth *is* full of cursing and bitterness: 15. Their feet *are* swift to shed blood: 16. Destruction and misery *are* in their ways: 17. And the way of peace have they not known: 18. There is no fear of God before their eyes.

Rom. 13:9. For this, Thou shalt not commit adultery, Thou shalt not kill, Thou shalt not steal, Thou shalt not bear false witness, Thou shalt not covet;

CROSS. Figurative: Matt. 10:38. And he that taketh not his cross, and followeth after me, is not worthy of me. Luke 14:27.

Mark 10:21. Then Jesus beholding him loved him, and said unto him, One thing thou lackest: go thy way, sell whatsoever thou hast, and give to the poor, and thou shalt have treasure in heaven: and come, take up the cross, and follow me.

Gal. 6:14. But God forbid that I should glory, save in the cross of our Lord Jesus Christ, by whom the world is crucified unto me, and I unto the world.

CROWN. Figurative: Isa. 28:5. In that day shall the LORD of hosts be for a crown of glory, and for a diadem of beauty, unto the residue of his people.

1 Cor. 9:25. And every man that striveth for the mastery is temperate in all things. Now they *do it* to obtain a corruptible crown; but we an incorruptible.

2 Tim. 4:8. Henceforth there is laid up for me a crown of righteousness, which the Lord, the righteous judge, shall give me at that day: and not to me only, but unto

all them also that love his appearing.

Jas. 1:12. Blessed is the man that endureth temptation: for when he is tried, he shall receive the crown of life, which the Lord hath promised to them that love him.

1 Pet. 5:4. And when the chief Shepherd shall appear, ye shall receive a crown of glory that fadeth not away.

Rev. 3:11. Behold, I come quickly: hold that fast which thou hast, that no man take thy crown.

CRUCIFIXION. Figurative:
Gal. 2:20. I am crucified with Christ:

Gal. 5:24. And they that are Christ's have crucified the flesh with the affections and lusts.

Gal. 6:14. But God forbid that I should glory, save in the cross of our Lord Jesus Christ, by whom the world is crucified unto me, and I unto the world.

CURIOSITY. Prov. 27:20. Hell and destruction are never full; so the eyes of man are never satisfied.

CURSE. Deut. 27:15. Cursed be the man that maketh any graven or molten image, an abomination unto the LORD, the work of the hands of the craftsman, and putteth it in a secret place: and all the people shall answer and say, Amen. 16. Cursed be he that setteth light by his father or his mother. And all the people shall say, Amen. 17. Cursed be he that removeth his neighbour's landmark. And all the people shall say, Amen. 18. Cursed be he that maketh the blind to wander out of the way. And all the people shall say, Amen. 19. Cursed be he that perverteth the judgment of the stranger, fatherless, and widow. And all the people shall say, Amen.

24. Cursed be he that smiteth his neighbour secretly. And all the people shall say, Amen. 25. Cursed be he that taketh reward to slay an innocent person. 26. Cursed be he that confirmeth not all the words of this law to do them. And all the people shall say, Amen.

DAMAGES AND COMPENSATION. Ex. 21:18. And if men strive together, and one smite another with a stone, or with his fist, and he die not, but keepeth his bed; 19. If he rise again, and walk abroad upon his staff, then shall he that smote him be quit: only he shall pay for the loss of his time, and shall cause him to be thoroughly healed.

28. If an ox gore a man or a woman, that they die: then the ox shall be surely stoned, and his flesh shall not be eaten; but the owner of the ox shall be quit. 29. But if the ox were wont to push with his horn in time past, and it hath been testified to his owner, and he hath not kept him in, but that he hath killed a man or a woman; the ox shall be stoned, and his owner also shall be put to death. 30. If there be laid on him a sum of money, then he shall give for the ransom of his life whatsoever is laid upon him. 31. Whether he have gored a son, or have gored a daughter, according to this judgment shall it be done unto him. 32. If the ox shall push a manservant or a maidservant; he shall give unto their master thirty shekels of silver, and the ox shall be stoned.

33. And if a man shall open a pit, or if a man shall dig a pit, and not cover it, and an ox or an ass fall therein; 34. The owner of the pit shall make it good, and give money unto the owner of them; and the dead beast shall be his.

Lev. 6:1. And the LORD spake unto Moses, saying, 2. If a soul sin, and commit a trespass against the LORD, and lie unto his neighbour in that which was delivered him to keep, or in fellowship, or in a thing taken away by violence, or hath deceived his neighbour; 3. Or have found that which was lost, and lieth concerning it, and sweareth falsely; in any of all these that a man doeth, sinning therein: 4. Then it shall be, because he hath sinned, and is guilty, that he shall restore that which he took violently away, or the thing which he hath deceitfully gotten, or that which was delivered him to keep, or the lost thing which he found, 5. Or all that about which he hath sworn falsely; he shall even restore it in the principal, and shall add the fifth part more thereto, *and* give it unto him to whom it appertaineth, in the day of his trespass offering.

DANCING. Ex. 15:20. And Miriam the prophetess, the sister of Aaron, took a timbrel in her hand; and all the women went out after her with timbrels and with dances.

Ex. 32:19. And it came to pass, as soon as he came nigh unto the camp, that he saw the calf, and the dancing: and Moses' anger waxed hot, and he cast the tables out of his hands, and brake them beneath the mount.

2 Sam. 6:14. And David danced before the LORD with all *his* might; and David *was* girded with a linen ephod. 15. So David and all the house of Israel brought up the ark of the LORD with shouting, and with the sound of the trumpet.

Psa. 149:3. Let them praise his name in the dance: let them sing praises unto him with the timbrel and harp.

DANIEL. A Jewish captive, called also BELTESHAZZAR. Educated at king's court, Dan. 1. Interprets visions, Dan. 2; 4; 5. Promotion and executive authority of, Dan. 2: 48,49; 5:11,29; 6:2. Conspiracy against, cast into the lions' den, Dan. 6.

Prophecies of, Dan. 4:8,9; chapters 7-12; Matt. 24:15.

Abstinence of, Dan. 1:8-16. Wisdom of, Dan. 1:17; Ezek. 28:3. Devoutness of, Dan. 2:18; 6; 9; 10; 12; Ezek. 14:14. Courage and fidelity of, Dan. 4:27; 5:17-23; 6:10-23. Worshiped by Nebuchadnezzar, Dan. 2:6.

DARKNESS. Figurative: OF SPIRITUAL BLINDNESS: Isa. 9:2. The people that walked in darkness have seen a great light: they that dwell in the land of the shadow of death, upon them hath the light shined. Matt. 4:16; Luke 1:79.

Isa. 42:16. And I will bring the blind by a way *that* they knew not; I will lead them in paths *that* they have not known: I will make dark-

ness light before them, and crooked things straight. These things will I do unto them, and not forsake them.

Isa. 50:10. Who *is* among you that feareth the LORD, that obeyeth the voice of his servant, that walketh *in* darkness, and hath no light? let him trust in the name of the LORD, and stay upon his God.

Psa. 18:11. He made darkness his secret place; his pavilion round about him *were* dark waters *and* thick clouds of the skies.

2 Cor. 4:6. For God, who commanded the light to shine out of darkness, hath shined in our hearts, to *give* the light of the knowledge of the glory of God in the face of Jesus Christ.

Heb. 12:18. For ye are not come unto the mount that might be touched, and that burned with fire, nor unto blackness, and darkness, and tempest,

DAVID. 1. King of Israel. Genealogy of, Ruth 4:18-22; 1 Sam. 16:11; 17:12; 1 Chr. 2:3-15; Matt. 1:1-6; Luke 3:31-38. A shepherd, 1 Sam. 16:11. Kills a lion and a bear, 1 Sam. 17:34-36. Anointed king, while a youth, by the prophet Samuel, and inspired, 1 Sam. 16:1, 13; Psa. 89:19-37. Chosen of God, Psa. 78:70.

Described to Saul, 1 Sam. 16:18. Detailed as armor bearer and musician at Saul's court, 1 Sam. 16:21-23. Slays Goliath, 1 Sam. 17. Love of Jonathan for, 1 Sam. 18:1-4. Popularity and discreetness of, 1 Sam. 18. Saul's jealousy of, 1 Sam. 18:8-30. Is defrauded of Merab, and given Michal to wife, 1 Sam. 18:17-27. Jonathan intercedes for, 1 Sam. 19:1-7. Probably writes Psalm 11 at this period of his life.

Conducts a campaign against, and defeats, the Philistines, 1 Sam. 19:8. Saul attempts to slay him; he escapes to Ramah, and dwells at Naioth, whither Saul pursues him, 1 Sam. 19:9-24. About this time writes Psalm 59. Returns, and Jonathan makes covenant with him, 1 Sam. 20. Escapes by way of Nob, where he obtains shewbread and Goliath's sword from Abime-

DAVID

lech, 1 Sam. 21:1-6; Matt. 12:3,4; to Gath, 1 Sam. 21:10-15. At this time probably writes Psalms 34, 35, 52, 56, 120. Recruits an army of insurgents, goes to Moab, returns to Hareth, 1 Sam. 22. Probably writes Psalms 17, 35, 52, 58, 64, 109, 142. Saves Keilah, 1 Sam. 23:1-13. Makes second covenant with Jonathan, 1 Sam. 23:16-18. Goes to the wilderness of Ziph, is betrayed to Saul, 1 Sam. 23:13-26. Writes a psalm on the betrayal, Psalm 54, and probably Psalms 22, 31, 140. Saul is diverted from pursuit of, 1 Sam. 23:27,28. At this time probably writes Psalm 12. Goes to En-gedi, 1 Sam. 23:29. Refrains from slaying Saul, 1 Sam. 24. Writes Psalm 57. Covenants with Saul, 1 Sam. 26. Marries Nabal's widow, Abigail, and Ahinoam, 1 Sam. 25. Dwells in the wilderness of Ziph, has opportunity to slay Saul, but takes his spear only, Saul is contrite, 1 Sam. 26. Flees to Achish and dwells in Ziklag, 1 Sam. 27. List of men who join him, 1 Chr. 12:1-22. Conducts an expedition against Amalekites, misstates the facts to Achish, 1 Sam. 27:8-12. At this time probably writes Psalm 141. Is refused permission to accompany the Philistines to battle against the Israelites, 1 Sam. 28:1,2; 29. Rescues the people of Ziklag, who had been captured by the Amalekites, 1 Sam. 30. Probably writes Psalm 13. Death and burial of Saul and his sons, 1 Sam. 31; 2 Sam. 21:1-14. Slays the murderer of Saul, 2 Sam. 1:1-16. Lamentation over Saul, 2 Sam. 1:17-27.

After dwelling one year and four months at Ziklag, 1 Sam. 27:7, goes to Hebron, and is anointed king by Judah, 2 Sam. 2:1-4,11; 5:5; 1 Kin. 2:11; 1 Chr. 3:4; 11:1-3. List of those who join him at Hebron, 1 Chr. 12:23-40. Ish-bosheth, son of Saul, crowned, 2 Sam. chapters 2-4. David wages war against, and defeats, Ish-bosheth, 2 Sam. 2:13-32; 3:4. Demands the restoration of Michal, his wife, 2 Sam. 3:14-16. Abner revolts from Ish-bosheth, and joins David, but is slain by Joab, 2 Sam. 3. Punishes Ish-bosheth's murderers, 2 Sam. 4.

Anointed king over all Israel, after reigning over Judah at Hebron seven years and six months, and reigns thirty-three years, 2 Sam. 2:11; 5:5; 1 Chr. 3:4; 11:1-3; 12:23-40; 29:27. Makes conquest of Jerusalem, 2 Sam. 5:6; 1 Chr. 11:4-8; Isa. 29:1. Builds a palace, 2 Sam. 5:11; 2 Chr. 2:3. Friendship of, with Hiram, king of Tyre, 2 Sam. 5:11; 1 Kin. 5:1. Prospered of God, 2 Sam. 5:10,12; 1 Chr. 11:9. Fame of, 1 Chr. 14:17. Philistines make war against, and are defeated by him, 2 Sam. 5:17,25.

Assembles thirty thousand men to escort the ark to Jerusalem with music and thanksgiving, 2 Sam. 6:1-5. Uzzah is stricken when he attempts to steady the ark, 2 Sam. 6:6-11. David is terrified, and leaves the ark at the house of Obed-edom, 2 Sam. 6:9-11. After three months brings the ark to Jerusalem with dancing and great joy, 2 Sam. 6:12-16; 1 Chr. 13. Organized the tabernacle service, 1 Chr. 9:22; 15:16-24; 16:4-6,37-43. Offers sacrifice, distributes gifts, and blesses the people, 2 Sam. 6:17-19. Michal upbraids him for his religious enthusiasm, 2 Sam. 6:20-23. Desires to build a temple, is forbidden, but receives promise that his seed should reign forever, 2 Sam. 7:12-16; 23:5; 1 Chr. 17:11-14; 2 Chr. 6:16; Psa. 89:3,4; 132:11,12; Acts 15:16; Rom. 15:12. Interpretation and fulfillment of this prophecy, Acts 13:22,23. At this time, probably, writes Psalms 15, 16, 24, 101, 138. Conquers the Philistines, Moabites, and Syria, 2 Sam. 8.

Treats Mephibosheth, the lame son of Saul, with great kindness, 2 Sam. 9:6; 19:24-30. Sends commissioners with a message of sympathy to Hanun, son of the king of Ammon; the message misinterpreted, and commissioners treated with indignity; David retaliates by invading his kingdom, and defeating the combined armies of the Ammonites and Syrians, 2 Sam. 10; 1 Chr. 19. Probably writes Psalms 18, 20, 21.

Commits adultery with Bathsheba, 2 Sam. 11:2-5. Wickedly causes the death of Uriah, 2 Sam.

66

11:6-25. Takes Bath-sheba to be his wife, 2 Sam. 11:26,27. Is rebuked by the prophet Nathan, 2 Sam. 12:1-14. Repents of his crime and confesses his guilt, Psa. 6; 32; 38; 39; 40; 51. Is chastised with grievous affliction on account of his crime, Psa. 38; 41; 69. Death of his infant son by Bath-sheba, 2 Sam. 12:15-23. Solomon is born to, 2 Sam. 12:24,25.

Ammonites defeated and tortured, 2 Sam. 12:26-31. Amnon's crime, his murder by Absalom, and Absalom's flight, 2 Sam. 13. Absalom's return, 2 Sam. 14:1-24. Absalom's usurpation, 2 Sam. 14; 15. David's flight from Jerusalem, 2 Sam. 15:13-37. He probably writes, at this time, Psalms 5, 7, 26, 61, 63, 69, 70, 86, 143. Shimei curses him, 2 Sam. 16. Crosses the Jordan, 2 Sam. 17:21-29. Absalom's defeat and death, 2 Sam. 18. Laments the death of Absalom, 2 Sam. 18:33; 19:1-4. Upbraided by Joab, 2 Sam. 19:5-7. David upbraids the priests for not showing loyalty amid the murmurings of the people against him, 2 Sam. 19:9-15. Shimei sues for clemency, 2 Sam. 19:16-23. Mephibosheth sues for the king's favor, 2 Sam. 19:24-30. Barzillai rewarded, 2 Sam. 19:31-40. Judah accused by the ten tribes of stealing him away, 2 Sam. 19:41-43. Returns to Jerusalem, 2 Sam. 20:1-3. At this time, probably, composes Psalms 27, 66, 122, 144.

Sheba's conspiracy against David, and his death, 2 Sam. 20. Makes Amasa general, 2 Sam. 19:13. Amasa is slain, 2 Sam. 20:4-10. Consigns seven sons of Saul to the Gibeonites to be slain to atone for Saul's persecution of the Gibeonites, 2 Sam. 21:1-14. Buries Saul's bones, and his sons', 2 Sam. 21:12-14.

Defeats the Philistines, 2 Sam. 21:15-22; 1 Chr. 20:4-8. Takes the military strength of Israel without divine authority, and is reproved, 2 Sam. 24; 1 Chr. 21; 27:24. Probably composes Psalms 30, 131. Marries Abishag, 1 Kin. 1:1-4. Probably composes Psalms 19, 111.

Reorganizes the tabernacle service, 1 Chr. 22-26; 2 Chr. 7:6; 8:14; 23:18; 29:27-30; 35:15; Ezra 3:10; 8:20.

Adonijah usurps the sceptre, Solomon appointed to the throne, 1 Kin. 1; 1 Chr. 23:1. Delivers his charge to Solomon, 1 Kin. 2:1-11; 1 Chr. 22:6-19; 28; 29. Probably composes Psalms 23, 145.

Last words of, 2 Sam. 23:1-7. Death of, 1 Kin. 2:10; 1 Chr. 29:28; Acts 2:29,30. Sepulcher of, Acts 2:29. Age of, at death, 2 Sam. 5:4,5; 1 Chr. 29:28. Length of reign, forty years, 1 Kin. 2:11; 1 Chr. 29:27,28.

Wives of, 2 Sam. 3:2-5; 11:3,27; 1 Chr. 3:5. Children born at Hebron, 2 Sam. 3:2-5; 1 Chr. 3:4; at Jerusalem, 2 Sam. 5:14-16; 1 Chr. 3:5-8; 14:4-7. Descendants of, 1 Chr. 3.

Civil and military officers of, 2 Sam. 8:16-18.

Lists of his heroes, and of their exploits, 2 Sam. 23; 1 Chr. 11; 12: 23-40.

Devoutness of, 1 Sam. 13:14; 2 Sam. 6:5, 14-18; 7:18-29; 8:11; 24: 25; 1 Kin. 3:14; 1 Chr. 17:16-27; 29:10; 2 Chr. 7:17; Zech. 12:8; Psa. 6; 7; 11; 13; 17; 22; 26; 27:7-14; 28; 31; 35; 37; 38; 39; 40:11-17, 42; 43; 51; 54; 55; 56; 57; 59; 60; 61; 62; 64:1-6; 66; 69; 70; 71; 86; 101; 108; 120:1-2; 140; 141; 142; 143; 144; Acts 13:22.

Justice in the administration of, 2 Sam. 8:15; 1 Chr. 18:14. Discreetness of, 1 Sam. 18:14,30. Meekness of, 1 Sam. 24:7; 26:11; 2 Sam. 16:11; 19:22,23. Merciful, 2 Sam. 19:23.

David as musician, 1 Sam. 16:21-23; 1 Chr. 15:16; 23:5; 2 Chr. 7:6; 29:26; Neh. 12:36; Amos 6:5; poet, 2 Sam. 22; see PSALMS OF DAVID: prophet, 2 Sam. 23:2-7; 1 Chr. 28: 19; Matt. 22:41-46; Acts 2:25-38; 4:25.

Type of Christ, Psa. 2; 16; 18:43; 69:7-9,20,21,26,29; 89:19-37. Jesus called son of, Matt. 9:27; 12:23; 15:22; 20:30,31; 21:9; 22:42; Mark 10:47,48; Luke 18:37,39.

Prophecies concerning him and his kingdom, Num. 24:17,19; 2 Sam. 7:11-16; 1 Chr. 17:9-14; 22;

2 Chr. 6:5-17; 13:5; 21:7; Psa. 89: 19-37; Isa. 9:7; 16:5; 22:20-25; Jer. 23:5; 33:15-26; Luke 1:32,33.

Chronicles of, written by Samuel, Nathan, and Gad, 1 Chr. 29:29,30.

2. A prophetic name for Christ, Jer. 30:9; Ezek. 34:23,24; 37:24, 25; Hos. 3:5.

DEACON, an ecclesiastic charged with the temporal affairs of the church. Ordained by the apostles, Acts 6:1-6. Qualifications of, 1 Tim. 3:8-13. The Greek word translated DEACON signifies SERVANT, and is so translated in Matt. 23:11; John 12:26. Also translated MINISTER, Mark 10:43; 1 Cor. 3:5; 1 Thess. 3:2.

DEAD. Psa. 49:15. But God will redeem my soul from the power of the grave: for he shall receive me.

Dan. 12:2. And many of them that sleep in the dust of the earth shall awake, some to everlasting life, and some to shame *and* everlasting contempt.

Luke 16:19. There was a certain rich man, which was clothed in purple and fine linen, and fared sumptuously every day: 20. And there was a certain beggar named Lazarus, which was laid at his gate, full of sores, 21. And desiring to be fed with the crumbs which fell from the rich man's table: moreover the dogs came and licked his sores. 22. And it came to pass, that the beggar died, and was carried by the angels into Abraham's bosom: the rich man also died, and was buried; 23. And in hell he lifted up his eyes, being in torments, and seeth Abraham afar off, and Lazarus in his bosom. 24. And he cried and said, Father Abraham, have mercy on me, and send Lazarus, that he may dip the tip of his finger in water, and cool my tongue; for I am tormented in this flame. 25. But Abraham said, Son, remember that thou in thy lifetime receivedst thy good things, and likewise Lazarus evil things: but now he is comforted, and thou art tormented. 26. And beside all this, between us and you there is a great gulf fixed: so that they which would

pass from hence-to you cannot; neither can they pass to us, that *would come* from thence. 27. Then he said, I pray thee therefore, father, that thou wouldst send him to my father's house: 28. For I have five brethren: that he may testify unto them, lest they also come into this place of torment. 29. Abraham saith unto him, They have Moses and the prophets; let them hear them. 30. And he said, Nay, father Abraham: but if one went unto them from the dead, they will repent. 31. And he said unto him, If they hear not Moses and the prophets, neither will they be persuaded, though one rose from the dead.

Luke 23:43. And Jesus said unto him, Verily, I say unto thee, To day shalt thou be with me in paradise.

John 11:25. Jesus said unto her, I am the resurrection, and the life: he that believeth in me, though he [were dead], yet shall he live: [R. V. die]

DEATH. Called Sleep: Deut. 31:16. And the LORD said unto Moses, Behold, thou shalt sleep with thy fathers;

Dan. 12:2. And many of them that sleep in the dust of the earth shall awake, some to everlasting life, and some to shame *and* everlasting contempt.

John 11:11. These things said he: and after that he saith unto them, Our friend Lazarus sleepeth; but I go, that I may awake him out of sleep.

Acts 7:60. And he kneeled down, and cried with a loud voice, Lord, lay not this sin to their charge. And when he had said this, he fell asleep.

Unclassified Scriptures Relating to: Gen. 2:17. In the day that thou eatest thereof thou shalt surely die.

2 Sam. 14:14. We must needs die, and *are* as water spilt on the ground, which cannot be gathered up again;

Job 16:22. When a few years are come, then I shall go the way *whence* I shall not return.

Psa. 68:20. Unto GOD the Lord

belong the issues from death. Deut. 32:39.

Psa. 103:14. He remembereth that we *are* dust. 15. *As for* man, his days *are* as grass: as a flower of the field, so he flourisheth. 16. For the wind passeth over it, and it is gone; and the place thereof shall know it no more.

Rom. 5:12. Wherefore, as by one man sin entered into the world, and death by sin; and so death passed upon all men, for that all have sinned: 14. Nevertheless death reigned from Adam to Moses, even over them that had not sinned after the similitude of Adam's transgression, who is the figure of him that was to come.

1 Cor. 15:21. For since by man *came* death, by man *came* also the resurrection of the dead. 22. For as in Adam all die, even so in Christ shall all be made alive. 26. The last enemy *that* shall be destroyed *is* death. 55. O death, where *is* thy sting? O grave, where *is* thy victory? 56. The sting of death *is* sin; and the strength of sin *is* the law. 57. But thanks *be* to God, which giveth us the victory through our Lord Jesus Christ.

Heb. 9:27. And as it is appointed unto men once to die, but after this the judgment:

Rev. 21:4. And God shall wipe away all tears from their eyes; and there shall be no more death, neither sorrow, nor crying, neither shall there be any more pain: for the former things are passed away.

2 Kin. 20:1. In those days was Hezekiah sick unto death. And the prophet Isaiah the son of Amoz came to him, and said unto him, Thus saith the LORD, Set thine house in order; for thou shalt die, and not live.

Psa. 39:4. LORD, make me to know mine end, and the measure of my days, what it *is; that* I may know how frail I *am.* 13. O spare me, that I may recover strength, before I go hence, and be no more.

Psa. 90:12. So teach *us* to number our days, that we may apply *our* hearts unto wisdom.

Phil. 1:21. For to me to live *is* Christ, and to die *is* gain.

Of the Righteous: Num. 23:10. Let me die the death of the righteous, and let my last end be like his!

Psa. 23:4. Though I walk through the valley of the shadow of death, I will fear no evil: for thou *art* with me; thy rod and thy staff they comfort me.

Psa. 49:15. God will redeem my soul from the power of the grave: for he shall receive me.

Psa. 73:24. Thou shalt guide me with thy counsel, and afterward receive me *to* glory.

Psa. 116:15. Precious in the sight of the LORD *is* the death of his saints.

Eccl. 7:1. A good name *is* better than precious ointment; and the day of death than the day of one's birth.

Luke 2:29. Lord, now lettest thou thy servant depart in peace, according to thy word:

Rom. 14:7. For none of us liveth to himself, and no man dieth to himself. 8. For whether we live, we live unto the Lord; and whether we die, we die unto the Lord: whether we live therefore, or die, we are the Lord's.

1 Cor. 15:51. Behold, I shew you a mystery; We shall not all sleep, but we shall all be changed, 52. In a moment, in the twinkling of an eye, at the last trump: for the trumpet shall sound, and the dead shall be raised incorruptible, and we shall be changed. 53. For this corruptible must put on incorruption, and this mortal *must* put on immortality. 54. So when this corruptible shall have put on incorruption, and this mortal shall have put on immortality, then shall be brought to pass the saying that is written, Death is swallowed up in victory. 55. O death, where *is* thy sting? O grave, where *is* thy victory? 56. The sting of death *is* sin; and the strength of sin *is* the law. 57. But thanks *be* to God, which giveth us the victory through our Lord Jesus Christ.

Rev. 14:13. And I heard a voice

from heaven saying unto me, Write, Blessed *are* the dead which die in the Lord from henceforth: Yea, saith the Spirit, that they may rest from their labours; and their works do follow them.

Of the Wicked: Job 34:20. In a moment shall they die, and the people shall be troubled at midnight, and pass away: and the mighty shall be taken away without hand.

Psa. 49:17. When he dieth he shall carry nothing away: his glory shall not descend after him. 19. He shall go to the generation of his fathers; they shall never see light.

Prov. 2:22. The wicked shall be cut off from the earth, and the transgressors shall be rooted out of it.

Prov. 11:7. When a wicked man dieth, *his* expectation shall perish: and the hope of unjust *men* perisheth.

Prov. 14:32. The wicked is driven away in his wickedness: but the righteous hath hope in his death.

Prov. 29:1. He, that being often reproved hardeneth *his* neck, shall suddenly be destroyed, and that without remedy. 16. When the wicked are multiplied, transgression increaseth:

Luke 12:20. But God said unto him, *Thou* fool, this night thy soul shall be required of thee: then whose shall those things be, which thou hast provided?

Spiritual: John 11:26. And whosoever liveth and believeth in me shall never die. Believest thou this?

Rom. 5:12. Wherefore, as by one man sin entered into the world, and death by sin; and so death passed upon all men, for that all have sinned: 15. But not as the offence, so also *is* the free gift. For if through the offence of one many be dead, much more the grace of God, and the gift by grace, *which is* by one man, Jesus Christ, hath abounded unto many.

Eph. 2:1. You *hath he quickened,* who were dead in trespasses and sins; 5. Even when we were dead in sins, hath quickened us together with Christ, (by grace ye are saved;) 6. And hath raised *us* up together, and made *us* sit together in heavenly *places* in Christ Jesus:

1 Tim. 5:6. But she that liveth in pleasure is dead while she liveth.

1 John 5:12. He that hath the Son hath life; *and* he that hath not the Son of God hath not life.

Second: Prov. 14:12. There is a way which seemeth right unto a man, but the end thereof *are* the ways of death.

Ezek. 18:4. The soul that sinneth, it shall die.

Matt. 7:13. Enter ye in at the strait gate: for wide *is* the gate, and broad *is* the way, that leadeth to destruction, and many there be which go in thereat:

Rom. 8:13. For if ye live after the flesh, ye shall die:

2 Thess. 1:9. Who shall be punished with everlasting destruction from the presence of the Lord, and from the glory of his power;

Rev. 20:14. And death and hell were cast into the lake of fire. This is the second death.

Figurative of Regeneration: Rom. 6:2. How shall we, that are dead to sin, live any longer therein? 3. Know ye not, that so many of us as were baptized into Jesus Christ were baptized into his death? 4. Therefore we are buried with him by baptism into death: that like as Christ was raised up from the dead by the glory of the Father, even so we also should walk in newness of life. 5. For if we have been planted together in the likeness of his death, we shall be also *in the likeness* of *his* resurrection: 6. Knowing this, that our old man is crucified with *him,* that the body of sin might be destroyed, that henceforth we should not serve sin. 7. For he that is dead is freed from sin. 8. Now if we be dead with Christ, we believe that we shall also live with him: 9. Knowing that Christ being raised from the dead dieth no more; death hath no more dominion over him. 10. For in that he died, he died unto sin once: but in that he liveth, he liveth unto God. 11. Likewise reckon ye also yourselves to be dead indeed unto sin, but alive unto

God through Jesus Christ our Lord.
Rom. 8:10. And if Christ *be* in you, the body *is* dead because of sin: but the Spirit *is* life because of righteousness. 11. But if the Spirit of him that raised up Jesus from the dead dwell in you, he that raised up Christ from the dead shall also quicken your mortal bodies by his Spirit that dwelleth in you.

DEBT. Rom. 13:8. Owe no man any thing, but to love one another: Deut. 24:10. When thou dost lend thy brother any thing, thou shalt not go into his house to fetch his pledge. 11. Thou shalt stand abroad, and the man to whom thou dost lend shall bring out the pledge abroad unto thee. 12. And if the man *be* poor, thou shalt not sleep with his pledge: 13. In any case thou shalt deliver him the pledge again when the sun goeth down, that he may sleep in his own raiment, and bless thee: and it shall be righteousness unto thee before the LORD thy God.

Neh. 5:3. *Some* also there were that said, We have mortgaged our lands, vineyards, and houses, that we might buy corn, because of the dearth. 4. There were also that said, We have borrowed money for the king's tribute, *and that upon* our lands and vineyards.

Prov. 11:15. He that is surety for a stranger shall smart *for it:* and he that hateth suretiship is sure.

DECISION. Deut. 30:19. I call heaven and earth to record this day against you, *that* I have set before you life and death, blessing and cursing: therefore choose life, that both thou and thy seed may live:

Josh. 23:8. But cleave unto the LORD your God, as ye have done unto this day.

John 8:31. Then said Jesus to those Jews which believed on him, If ye continue in my word, *then* are ye my disciples indeed;

1 Cor. 15:58. Be ye stedfast, unmoveable, always abounding in the work of the Lord, forasmuch as ye know that your labour is not in vain in the Lord.

1 Cor. 16:13. Watch ye, stand fast in the faith, quit you like men, be strong.

Gal. 6:9. Let us not be weary in well doing: for in due season we shall reap, if we faint not.

Phil. 4:1. Therefore, my brethren dearly beloved and longed for, my joy and crown, so stand fast in the Lord, *my* dearly beloved.

2 Thess. 3:13. Brethren, be not weary in well doing.

MOSES: Heb. 11:24. By faith Moses, when he was come to years, refused to be called the son of Pharaoh's daughter; 25. Choosing rather to suffer affliction with the people of God, than to enjoy the pleasures of sin for a season; 26. Esteeming the reproach of Christ greater riches than the treasures in Egypt: for he had respect unto the recompence of the reward.

JOSHUA: Josh. 24:15. As for me and my house, we will serve the LORD.

RUTH: Ruth 1:16. Thy people *shall be* my people, and thy God my God:

PSALMIST: Psa. 26:6. I will wash mine hands in innocency; so will I compass thine altar, O LORD: 11. But as for me, I will walk in mine integrity:

Psa. 56:12. Thy vows *are* upon me, O God: I will render praises unto thee.

Psa. 108:1. O God, my heart is fixed; I will sing and give praise, even with my glory. Psa. 57:7,8.

DEDICATION. Law concerning dedicated things, Lev. 27; Num. 18:14; 1 Chr. 26:26,27. Must be without blemish, Lev. 22:18-23; Mal. 1:14. Not redeemable, Lev. 27:28,29. Offering must be voluntary, Lev. 1:3; 22:19. See OFFERINGS; Vows.

Of the tabernacle, Num. 7. Solomon's temple, 1 Kin. 8; 2 Chr. 7:5. Second temple, Ezra 6:16,17. Of the wall of Jerusalem, Neh. 12:27-43. Of houses, Deut. 20:5. Of Samuel by his mother, 1 Sam. 1:11, 22.

DEMONS. Worship of, Lev. 17:7; Deut. 32:17; 2 Chr. 11:15; Psa. 106:37; Matt. 4:9; Luke 4:7; 1 Cor. 10:20,21; 1 Tim. 4:1; Rev.

13:4. Worship of, forbidden, Lev. 17:7; Zech. 13:2; Rev. 9:20.

Possession by, instances of: Saul, 1 Sam. 16:14-23; 1 Sam. 18:10,11; 19:9, 10. Two men of the Gadarenes, Matt. 8:28-34; Mark 5:2-20. The dumb man, Matt. 9:32,33. The blind and dumb man, Matt. 12:22; Luke, 11:14. The daughter of the Syrophenician, Matt. 15:22-29; Mark 7:25-30. The lunatic child, Matt. 17:14-18; Mark 9:17-27; Luke 9:37-42. The man in the synagogue, Mark 1:23-26; Luke 4:33-35. Mary Magdalene, Mark 16:9; Luke 8:2,3. The herd of swine, Matt. 8:30-32.

Cast out by Jesus, Matt. 4:24; 8:16; Mark 3:22; Luke 4:41.

Power over, given the disciples, Matt. 10:1; Mark 6:7; 16:17. Cast out by the disciples, Mark 9:38; Luke 10:17; by Peter, Acts 5:16; by Paul, Acts 16:16-18; 19:12; by Philip, Acts 8:7. Disciples could not expel, Mark 9:18,28,29. Sceva's sons exorcise, Acts 19:13-16. Parable of the man repossessed, Matt. 12:43-45.

Jesus falsely accused of being possessed of, Mark 3:22-30; John 7:20; 8:48; 10:20.

Testify to the divinity of Jesus, Matt. 8:29; Mark 1:23,24; 3:11; 5:7; Luke 8:28; Acts 19:15.

Adversaries of men, Matt. 12:45. Sent to foment trouble between Abimelech and the Shechemites, Judg. 9:23. Messages given false prophets by, 1 Kin. 22:21-23.

Believe and tremble, Jas. 2:19. To be judged at the general judgment, Matt. 8:29, with 2 Pet. 2:4; Jude 6.

Punishment of, Matt. 8:29; 25:41; Luke 8:28; 2 Pet. 2:4; Jude 6; Rev. 12:7-9.

DEPRAVITY OF MAN.

Gen. 6:5. And GOD saw that the wickedness of man *was* great in the earth, and *that* every imagination of the thoughts of his heart *was* only evil continually. 6. And it repented the LORD that he had made man on the earth, and it grieved him at his heart. 7. And the LORD said, I will destroy man whom I have created from the face of the earth; both man, and beast, and the creeping thing, and the fowls of the air; for it repenteth me that I have made them.

Job 14:4. Who can bring a clean *thing* out of an unclean? not one.

Job 15:14. What *is* man, that he should be clean? and *he which is* born of a woman, that he should be righteous? 15. Behold, he putteth no trust in his saints; yea, the heavens are not clean in his sight. 16. How much more abominable and filthy *is* man, which drinketh iniquity like water?

Psa. 14:1. The fool hath said in his heart, *There is* no God. They are corrupt, they have done abominable works, *there is* none that doeth good. 2. The LORD looked down from heaven upon the children of men, to see if there were any that did understand, *and* seek God. 3. They are all gone aside, they are *all* together become filthy: *there is* none that doeth good, no, not one. Psa. 53:1-3.

Psa. 51:5. Behold, I was shapen in iniquity; and in sin did my mother conceive me.

Psa. 130:3. If thou, LORD, shouldest mark iniquities, O Lord, who shall stand?

Prov. 20:9. Who can say, I have made my heart clean, I am pure from my sin?

Isa. 1:5. The whole head is sick, and the whole heart faint. 6. From the sole of the foot even unto the head *there is* no soundness in it; *but* wounds, and bruises, and putrifying sores: they have not been closed, neither bound up, neither mollified with ointment.

Isa. 53:6. All we like sheep have gone astray; we have turned every one to his own way;

Isa. 64:6. We are all as an unclean *thing,* and all our righteousnesses *are* as filthy rags; and we all do fade as a leaf; and our iniquities, like the wind, have taken us away.

Jer. 17:9. The heart *is* deceitful above all *things,* and desperately [wicked]: who can know it? [R. V. sick]

Matt. 12:34. O generation of vipers, how can ye, being evil, speak good things? for out of the abundance of the heart the mouth speaketh. 35. A good man out of the good treasure of the heart bringeth forth good things: and an evil man out of the evil treasure bringeth forth evil things.

Matt. 15:19. Out of the heart proceed evil thoughts, murders, adulteries, fornications, thefts, false witness, blasphemies: Mark 7:21-23.

Rom. 2:1. Thou art inexcusable, O man, whosoever thou art that judgest: for wherein thou judgest another, thou condemnest thyself; for thou that judgest doest the same things.

Rom. 5:6. For when we were yet without strength, in due time Christ died for the ungodly.

Rom. 11:32. For God hath concluded them all in unbelief, that he might have mercy upon all.

1 John 1:8. If we say that we have no sin, we deceive ourselves, and the truth is not in us. 10. If we say that we have not sinned, we make him a liar, and his word is not in us.

DESIRE. Spiritual: Psa. 24:6. This *is* the generation of them that seek him, that seek thy face, O Jacob.

Psa. 33:20. Our soul waiteth for the LORD: he *is* our help and our shield.

Psa. 34:10. They that seek the LORD shall not want any good *thing*.

Psa. 37:4. Delight thyself also in the LORD; and he shall give thee the desires of thine heart.

Psa. 42:1. As the hart panteth after the water brooks, so panteth my soul after thee, O God. 2. My soul thirsteth for God, for the living God: when shall I come and appear before God? 5. Why art thou cast down, O my soul? and *why* art thou disquieted in me? hope thou in God: for I shall yet praise him *for* the help of his countenance.

Psa. 51:1. Have mercy upon me, O God, according to thy lovingkindness: according unto the multitude of thy tender mercies blot out my transgressions. 2. Wash me throughly from mine iniquity, and cleanse me from my sin. 3. For I

acknowledge my transgressions: and my sin *is* ever before me. 4. Against thee, thee only, have I sinned, and done *this* evil in thy sight: that thou mightest be justified when thou speakest, *and* be clear when thou judgest.

Psa. 62:1. Truly my soul waiteth upon God: from him *cometh* my salvation.

Isa. 40:31. They that wait upon the LORD shall renew *their* strength; they shall mount up with wings as eagles;

Jer. 29:13. Ye shall seek me, and find *me*, when ye shall search for me with all your heart. Deut. 4:29.

DESPAIR. See DESPONDENCY.

DESPONDENCY. Num. 17: 12. And the children of Israel spake unto Moses, saying, Behold, we die, we perish, we all perish. 13. Whosoever cometh any thing near unto the tabernacle of the LORD shall die: shall we be consumed with dying?

Job 3:1. After this opened Job his mouth, and cursed his day. 2. And Job spake, and said, 3. Let the day perish wherein I was born, and the night *in which* it was said, There is a man child conceived.

Psa. 31:22. For I said in my haste, I am cut off from before thine eyes: nevertheless thou heardest the voice of my supplications when I cried unto thee.

Psa. 77:7. Will the Lord cast off for ever? and will he be favourable no more? 8. Is his mercy clean gone for ever? doth *his* promise fail for evermore? 9. Hath God forgotten to be gracious? hath he in anger shut up his tender mercies?

Prov. 13:12. Hope deferred maketh the heart sick: but *when* the desire cometh, *it is* a tree of life.

Jer. 8:20. The harvest is past, the summer is ended, and we are not saved.

Lam. 3:1. I *am* the man *that* hath seen affliction by the rod of his wrath. 2. He hath led me, and brought *me into* darkness, but not *into* light. 3. Surely against me is he turned: he turneth his hand *against me* all the day. 4. My flesh and my skin hath he made old; he hath broken my bones. 5. He hath builded against me, and compassed *me* with gall and travail. 6. He hath set me in dark places, as *they that be* dead of old. 7. He hath hedged me about, that I cannot get out: he hath made my chain heavy. 8. Also when I cry and shout, he shutteth out my prayer. 9. He hath enclosed my ways with hewn stone, he hath made my paths crooked. 10. He *was* unto me *as* a bear lying in wait, *and as* a lion in secret places. 11. He hath turned aside my ways, and pulled me in pieces: he hath made me desolate.

DILIGENCE. Jesus an example of, Mark 1:35; Luke 2:49.

Required by God in seeking him, 1 Chr. 22:19; Heb. 11:6; obeying him, Deut. 6:17; 11:13; hearkening to him, Isa. 55:2; striving after perfection, Phil. 3:13,14; cultivating Christian graces, 2 Pet. 1:5; keeping the soul, Deut. 4:9; keeping the heart, Prov. 4:23; labors of love, Heb. 6:10-12; following every good work, 1 Tim. 3:10; guarding against defilement, Heb. 12:15; seeking to be found spotless, 2 Pet. 3:14; making our calling sure, 2 Pet. 1:10; self-examination, Psa. 77:6; lawful business, Prov. 27:23; Eccl. 9:10; teaching religion, 2 Tim. 4:2; Jude 3; instructing children, Deut. 6:7; 11:19; discharging official duties, Deut. 19:18; saints should abound in, 2 Cor. 8:7.

Required in the service of God, John 9:4; Gal. 6:9. Is not in vain, 1 Cor. 15:58. Preserves from evil, Ex. 15:26. Leads to assured hope, Heb. 6:11. God rewards, Deut. 11:14; Heb. 11:6.

In temporal matters leads to favor, Prov. 11:27; prosperity, Prov. 10:4; 13:4; honor, Prov. 12:24; 22:29.

Figurative: Prov. 6:6-8.

Exemplified: Ruth, Ruth 2:17. Hezekiah, 2 Chr. 31:21. Nehemiah and his helpers, Neh. 4:6. Psalmist, Psa. 119:60. Apostles, Acts 5:42. Apollos, Acts 18:25. Titus, 2 Cor. 8:22. Paul, 1 Thess. 2:9. Onesiphorus, 2 Tim. 1:17.—*Bible Text Book.*

DIPLOMACY. 1 Cor. 9:20. And unto the Jews I became as a Jew, that I might gain the Jews; to them that are under the law, as under the law, that I might gain them that are under the law; 21. To them that are without law, as without law, (being not without law to God, but under the law to Christ,) that I might gain them that are without law. 22. To the weak became I as weak, that I might gain the weak: I am made all things to all *men,* that I might by all means save some. 23. And this I do for the gospel's sake, that I might be partaker thereof with *you.*

Instances of: Of Abimelech. Gen. 21:22,23; 26:26-31. The Gibeonites, in securing a league with the Israelites through deception, Josh. 9:3-16. Of Jephthah, with the king of Moab, unsuccessful, Judg. 11:12-28. Of Abigail, 1 Sam. 25:23-31. Of Hiram, to secure the good will of David, 2 Sam. 5:11. Of Toi, to promote the friendship of David, 2 Sam. 8:10. David, in sending Hushai to Absalom's court, 2 Sam. 15:32-37; 16:15-19; 17:1-14. The wise woman of Abel, 2 Sam. 20:16-22. Absalom winning the people, 2 Sam. 15:2-6. Solomon, in his alliance with Hiram, 1 Kin. 5:1-12; 9:10-14,26,27; 10:11.

DISCIPLESHIP, tests of, Matt. 10:32-39; Luke 14:26,27,33; John 21:15-19.

DISEASE. Sent from God, Lev. 14:34. As judgments, Psa. 107:17; Isa. 3:17. INSTANCES OF: Upon the Egyptians, see PLAGUES; upon Nabal, 1 Sam. 25:38; David's child, 2 Sam. 12:15; Gehazi, 2 Kin. 5:27; Jeroboam, 2 Chr. 13:20; Jehoram, 2 Chr. 21:12-19; Uzziah, 2 Chr. 26:17-20.

Threatened as judgments, Lev. 26:16; Deut. 7:15; 28:22,27,28,35; 29:22.

Healing of, from God, Ex. 15:26; 23:25; Deut. 7:15; 2 Chr. 16:12; Psa. 103:3; 107:20. In answer to prayer: Of Hezekiah, 2 Kin. 20:1-11; Isa. 38:1-8; David, Psa. 21:4; 116:3-8.

Miraculous healing of, a sign to

accompany the preaching of the Word, Mark 16:18. See MIRACLES. Physicians employed for, 2 Chr. 16:12; Jer. 8:22; Matt. 9:12; Mark 5:26; Luke 4:23. Remedies used, Prov. 17:22; 20:30; Isa. 38:21; Jer. 30:13; 46:11; poultices, 2 Kin. 20: 7; ointments, Isa. 1:6; Jer. 8:22; emulsions, Luke 10:34.

DISHONESTY. Lev. 6:2. If a soul sin, and commit a trespass against the LORD, and lie unto his neighbour in that which was delivered him to keep, or in fellowship, or in a thing taken away by violence, or hath deceived his neighbour; 3. Or have found that which was lost, and lieth concerning it, and sweareth falsely; in any of all these that a man doeth, sinning therein: 4. Then it shall be, because he hath sinned, and is guilty, that he shall restore that which he took violently away, or the thing which he hath deceitfully gotten, or that which was delivered him to keep, or the lost thing which he found, 5. Or all that about which he hath sworn falsely; he shall even restore it in the principal, and shall add the fifth part more thereto, *and* give it unto him to whom it appertaineth, in the day of his trespass offering. 6. And he shall bring his trespass offering unto the LORD, a ram without blemish out of the flock, with thy estimation, for a trespass offering, unto the priest: 7. And the priest shall make an atonement for him before the LORD: and it shall be forgiven him for any thing of all that he hath done in trespassing therein.

Lev. 19:13. Thou shalt not defraud thy neighbour, neither rob *him:* the wages of him that is hired shall not abide with thee all night until the morning.

Job 24:2. *Some* remove the landmarks; they violently take away flocks, and feed *thereof.* 3. They drive away the ass of the fatherless, they take the widow's ox for a pledge. 4. They turn the needy out of the way: the poor of the earth hide themselves together. 5. Behold, *as* wild asses in the desert, go they forth to their work; rising betimes for a prey: the wilderness *yieldeth* food for them *and* for *their* children. 6. They reap *every one* his corn in the field: and they gather the vintage of the wicked. 7. They cause the naked to lodge without clothing, that *they have* no covering in the cold. 8. They are wet with the showers of the mountains, and embrace the rock for want of a shelter. 9. They pluck the fatherless from the breast, and take a pledge of the poor. 10. They cause *him* to go naked without clothing, and they take away the sheaf *from* the hungry; 11. *Which* make oil within their walls, *and* tread *their* wine-presses, and suffer thirst.

Psa. 37:21. The wicked borroweth, and payeth not again:

Psa. 50:18. When thou sawest a thief, then thou consentedst with him,

Prov. 3:27. Withhold not good from them to whom it is due, when it is in the power of thine hand to do *it.* 28. Say not unto thy neighbour, Go, and come again, and to morrow I will give: when thou hast it by thee.

Prov. 11:1. A false balance *is* abomination to the LORD:

Prov. 20:10. Divers weights, *and* divers measures, both of them *are* alike abomination to the LORD. 14. *It is* naught, *it is* naught, saith the buyer: but when he is gone his way, then he boasteth.

Jer. 22:13. Woe unto him that buildeth his house by unrighteousness, and his chambers by wrong; *that* useth his neighbour's service without wages, and giveth him not for his work;

Amos 8:5. When will the new moon be gone, that we may sell corn? and the sabbath, that we may set forth wheat, making the ephah small, and the shekel great, and falsifying the balances by deceit?

DISOBEDIENCE TO GOD. Denunciations Against: Num. 14:11. And the LORD said unto Moses, How long will this people provoke me? and how long will it be ere they believe me, for all the signs which I have shewed among

DISSENSION

them? 12. I will smite them with the pestilence, and disinherit them, and will make of thee a greater nation and mightier than they. 22. Because all those men which have seen my glory, and my miracles, which I did in Egypt and in the wilderness, and have tempted me now these ten times, and have not hearkened to my voice; 23. Surely they shall not see the land which I sware unto their fathers, neither shall any of them that provoked me see it: 24. But my servant Caleb, because he had another spirit with him, and hath followed me fully, him will I bring into the land whereinto he went; and his seed shall possess it.

Deut. 18:19. And it shall come to pass, *that* whosoever will not hearken unto my words which he shall speak in my name, I will require *it* of him.

Deut. 28:15. But it shall come to pass, if thou wilt not hearken unto the voice of the LORD thy God, to observe to do all his commandments and his statutes which I command thee this day; that all these curses shall come upon thee, and overtake thee: 16. Cursed *shalt* thou *be* in the city, and cursed *shalt* thou *be* in the field. 17. Cursed *shall be* thy basket and thy store. 18. Cursed *shall be* the fruit of thy body, and the fruit of thy land, the increase of thy kine, and the flocks of thy sheep. 19. Cursed *shalt* thou *be* when thou comest in, and cursed *shalt* thou *be* when thou goest out.

DISSENSION, in churches, 1 Cor. 1:10-13; 3:3,4; 11:18,19.

DIVORCE. Mic. 2:9. The women of my people have ye cast out from their pleasant houses; from their children have ye taken away my glory for ever.

Mal. 2:14. Yet ye say, Wherefore? Because the LORD hath been witness between thee and the wife of thy youth, against whom thou hast dealt treacherously: yet *is* she thy companion, and the wife of thy covenant. 15. And did not he make one? Yet had he the residue of the spirit. And wherefore one? That he might seek a godly seed. Therefore take heed to your spirit, and let none deal treacherously against the wife of his youth. 16. For the LORD, the God of Israel, saith that he hateth putting away: for *one* covereth violence with his garment, saith the LORD of hosts: therefore take heed to your spirit, that ye deal not treacherously.

Matt. 5:31. It has been said, Whosoever shall put away his wife, let him give her a writing of divorcement: 32. But I say unto you, That whosoever shall put away his wife, saving for the cause of fornication, causeth her to commit adultery: and whosoever shall marry her that is divorced committeth adultery.

1 Cor. 7:10. And unto the married I command, *yet* not I, but the Lord, Let not the wife depart from *her* husband: 11. But and if she depart, let her remain unmarried, or be reconciled to *her* husband: and let not the husband put away *his* wife. 12. But to the rest speak I, not the Lord: If any brother hath a wife that believeth not, and she be pleased to dwell with him, let him not put her away. 13. And the woman which hath an husband that believeth not, and if he be pleased to dwell with her, let her not leave him. 14. For the unbelieving husband is sanctified by the wife, and the unbelieving wife is sanctified by the husband: else were your children unclean; but now are they holy. 15. But if the unbelieving depart, let him depart. A brother or a sister is not under bondage in such *cases:* but God hath called us to peace. 16. For what knowest thou, O wife, whether thou shalt save *thy* husband? or how knowest thou, O man, whether thou shalt save *thy* wife? 17. But as God hath distributed to every man, as the Lord hath called every one, so let him walk. And so ordain I in all churches.

Disobedience of the wife to the husband, a sufficient cause for, in the Persian empire, Esth. 1:10-22.

DOCTOR, a teacher, or master, Matt. 8:19; Luke 2:46; 5:17; Acts 5:34; 1 Tim. 1:7.

DOCTRINES. John 7:16. Jesus answered them, and said, My doctrine is not mine, but his that sent me. 17. If any man will do his will, he shall know of the doctrine [*R. V.*, teaching], whether it be of God, or *whether* I speak of myself.

Set forth by church councils, Acts 15:6-29.

False: Matt. 5:19. Whosoever therefore shall break one of these least commandments, and shall teach men so, he shall be called the least in the kingdom of heaven:

Matt. 15:9. In vain they do worship me, teaching *for* doctrines the commandments of men. 13. Every plant, which my heavenly Father hath not planted, shall be rooted up.

Eph. 4:14. Be no more children, tossed to and fro, and carried about with every wind of doctrine, by the sleight of men, *and* cunning craftiness, whereby they lie in wait to deceive;

Col. 2:4. This I say, lest any man should beguile you with enticing words. 8. Beware lest any man spoil you through philosophy and vain deceit, after the tradition of men, after the rudiments of the world, and not after Christ.

2 Tim. 2:14. Of these things put *them* in remembrance, charging *them* before the Lord that they strive not about words to no profit, *but* to the subverting of the hearers. 16. Shun profane *and* vain babblings: for they will increase unto more ungodliness. 17. And their word will eat as doth a canker: of whom is Hymenæus and Philetus; 18. Who concerning the truth have erred, saying that the resurrection is past already; and overthrow the faith of some.

Tit. 1:10. For there are many unruly and vain talkers and deceivers, specially they of the circumcision: 11. Whose mouths must be stopped, who subvert whole houses, teaching things which they ought not, for filthy lucre's sake. 14. Not giving heed to Jewish fables, and commandments of men, that turn from the truth.

Tit. 3:10. A man that is an heretic after the first and second admonition reject; 11. Knowing that he that is such is subverted, and sinneth, being condemned of himself.

Heb. 13:9. Be not carried about with divers and strange doctrines. For *it is* a good thing that the heart be established with grace; not with meats, which have not profited them that have been occupied therein.

2 Pet. 2:1. There were false prophets also among the people, even as there shall be false teachers among you, who privily shall bring in *damnable* [omitted in R. V.] heresies, even denying the Lord that bought them, and bring upon themselves swift destruction.

Jude 4. There are certain men crept in unawares, who were before of old ordained to this condemnation, ungodly men, turning the grace of our God into lasciviousness, and denying the only Lord God, and our Lord Jesus Christ. 11. Woe unto them! for they have gone in the way of Cain, and ran greedily after the error of Balaam for reward, and perished in the gainsaying of Core.

DOER. Of the Word: Matt. 7:21. Not every one that saith unto me, Lord, Lord, shall enter into the kingdom of heaven; but he that doeth the will of my Father which is in heaven.

Matt. 12:50. For whosoever shall do the will of my Father which is in heaven, the same is my brother, and sister, and mother.

Luke 11:28. But he said, Yea rather, blessed *are* they that hear the word of God, and keep it.

Rom. 2:13. For not the hearers of the law *are* just before God, but the doers of the law shall be justified.

2 Cor. 8:11. Now therefore perform the doing *of it;* that as *there was* a readiness to will, so *there may be* a performance also out of that which ye have.

Jas. 1:22. But be ye doers of the word, and not hearers only, deceiving your own selves.

DOUBTING. Job 30:20. I cry unto thee, and thou dost not hear me: I stand up, and thou regardest me *not*. 21. Thou art become cruel to me: with thy strong hand thou opposest thyself against me. Job 3; 16; 17; 23:15-17.

Psa. 31:22. I said in my haste, I am cut off from before thine eyes:

Psa. 42:5. Why art thou cast down, O my soul? and *why* art thou disquieted in me? hope thou in God: for I shall yet praise him *for* the help of his countenance. 6. O my God, my soul is cast down within me:

Prov. 24:10. *If* thou faint in the day of adversity, thy strength *is* small.

Jer. 15:18. Why is my pain perpetual, and my wound incurable, *which* refuseth to be healed? wilt thou be altogether unto me as a liar, *and as* waters *that* fail?

Matt. 8:26. And he said unto them, Why are ye fearful, O ye of little faith? Mark 4:40; Luke 8:25.

1 Pet. 1:6. Wherein ye greatly rejoice, though now for a season, if need be, ye are in heaviness through manifold temptations:

Exemplified: Gen. 15:8. And he said, Lord GOD, whereby shall I know that I shall inherit it?

Gen. 18:12. Therefore Sarah laughed within herself, saying, After I am waxed old shall I have pleasure, my lord being old also?

Ex. 3:11. And Moses said unto God, Who *am* I, that I should go unto Pharaoh, and that I should bring forth the children of Israel out of Egypt?

Jer. 1:6. Then said I, Ah, Lord GOD! behold, I cannot speak: for I *am* a child.

Matt. 11:2. Now when John had heard in the prison the works of Christ, he sent two of his disciples, 3. And said unto him, Art thou he that should come, or do we look for another?

Matt. 28:17. And when they saw him, they worshipped him: but some doubted.

John 14:8. Philip saith unto him, Lord, shew us the Father, and it sufficeth us.

DRAGON. Any terrible creature, as a venomous serpent, Deut. 32:33; Psa. 91:13; a sea serpent, Psa. 74:13; 148:7; Isa. 27:1; a jackal, Isa. 13:22; 34:13; 35:7; 43:20; Jer. 9:11; 10:22; 14:6; 49:33; 51:37; Mic. 1:8; Mal. 1:3.

A term applied to Pharaoh, Isa. 51:9; to Satan, Rev. 20:2.

Symbolical, Ezek. 29:3; 32:2; Rev. 12; 13; 16:13.

DREAM. Evanescent, Job 20:8. Vanity of, Eccl. 5:3, 7.

Revelations by, Num. 12:6; Job 33:15-17; Jer. 23:28; Joel 2:28; Acts 2:17. The dreams of the butler and baker, Gen. 40:8-23; Pharaoh, Gen. 41:1-36.

Interpreted by Joseph, Gen. 40:12, 13, 18, 19; 41:25-32; Daniel, Dan. 2:16-23, 28-30; 4. Delusive, Isa. 29:7, 8.

False prophets pretended to receive revelations through, Deut. 13:1-5; Jer. 23:25-32; 27:9; 29:8; Zech. 10:2.

Instances of: Of Abimelech, concerning Sarah, Gen. 20:3. Of Jacob, concerning the ladder, Gen. 28:12; the ring-straked cattle, Gen. 31:10-13; concerning his going down into Egypt, Gen. 46:2. Of Laban, concerning Jacob, Gen. 31:24. Of Joseph, concerning the sheaves, Gen. 37:5-10. Of the Midianite, concerning the cake of barley, Judg. 7:13. Of Solomon, concerning his choice of wisdom, 1 Kin. 3:3-15. Of Eliphaz, of a spirit speaking to him, Job 4:12-21. Of Daniel, concerning the four beasts, Dan. 7. Of Joseph, concerning Mary's innocence, Matt. 1:20,21; concerning the flight into Egypt, Matt. 2:13; concerning the return into Palestine, Matt. 2:19-22. Of Pilate's wife, concerning Jesus, Matt. 27:19. Cornelius' vision, concerning Peter, Acts 10:3-6. Peter's vision of the unclean beasts, Acts 10:10-16. Paul's vision of the man in Macedonia, crying, "Come over into Macedonia," Acts 16:9; relating to his going to Rome, Acts 23:11; concerning the shipwreck, and the safety of all on board, Acts 27:23,24.

DRUNKARD. Deut. 21:20. And they shall say unto the elders of his city, This our son *is* stubborn and rebellious, he will not obey our voice; *he is* a glutton, and a drunkard. 21. And all the men of his city shall stone him with stones, that he die: so shalt thou put evil away from among you; and all Israel shall hear, and fear.

Psa. 69:12. They that sit in the gate speak against me; and I *was* the song of the drunkards.

Prov. 23:21. For the drunkard and the glutton shall come to poverty: and drowsiness shall clothe *a man* with rags.

Joel 1:5. Awake, ye drunkards, and weep; and howl, all ye drinkers of wine, because of the new wine; for it is cut off from your mouth.

1 Cor. 5:11. But now I have written unto you not to keep company, if any man that is called a brother be a fornicator, or covetous, or an idolater, or a railer, or a drunkard, or an extortioner; with such an one no not to eat.

DRUNKENNESS. 1 Sam. 1:14. How long wilt thou be drunken? put away thy wine from thee.

Prov. 20:1. Wine *is* a mocker, strong drink *is* raging: and whosoever is deceived thereby is not wise.

Prov. 21:17. He that loveth wine . . . shall not be rich.

Isa. 5:11. Woe unto them that rise up early in the morning, *that* they may follow strong drink; that continue until night, *till* wine inflame them!

Jer. 25:27. Thus saith the LORD of hosts, the God of Israel; Drink ye, and be drunken, and spue, and fall, and rise no more, because of the sword which I will send among you.

Hos. 4:11. Whoredom and wine and new wine take away the heart.

Joel 1:5. Awake, ye drunkards, and weep; and howl, all ye drinkers of wine, because of the new wine; for it is cut off from your mouth.

Hab. 2:15. Woe unto him that giveth his neighbour drink, that [puttest thy bottle to *him*,] and makest *him* drunken also, that thou mayest look on their nakedness! [R. V. addest thy venom thereto]

Rom. 13:13. Let us walk honestly, as in the day; not in rioting and drunkenness, not in chambering and wantonness, not in strife and envying.

Eph. 5:18. Be not drunk with wine, wherein is excess.

Instances of: Noah, Gen. 9:21. Lot, Gen. 19:33. Nabal, 1 Sam. 25:36. Uriah, 2 Sam. 11:13. Amnon, 2 Sam. 13:28. Elah, 1 Kin. 16:9. Ben-hadad and his thirty-two confederate kings, 1 Kin. 20:16. Ahasuerus, Esth. 1:10,11. Belshazzar, Dan. 5:1-6.

Falsely Accused of: Hannah, 1 Sam. 1:12-16. Jesus, Matt. 11:19. The Apostles, Acts 2:13-15.

DUTY. Of Man to God: Deut. 6:5. And thou shalt love the LORD thy God with all thine heart, and with all thy soul, and with all thy might.

Josh. 23:11. Take good heed therefore unto yourselves, that ye love the LORD your God.

Matt. 4:10. Then saith Jesus unto him, . . . It is written, Thou shalt worship the Lord thy God, and him only shalt thou serve.

Matt. 22:21. Then saith he unto them. Render therefore unto Cæsar the things which are Cæsar's; and unto God the things that are God's.

36. Master, which *is* the great commandment in the law? 37. Jesus said unto him, Thou shalt love the Lord thy God with all thy heart, and with all thy soul, and with all thy mind. 38. This is the first and great commandment. 39. And the second *is* like unto it, Thou shalt love thy neighbour as thyself. 40. On these two commandments hang all the law and the prophets.

Luke 17:10. When ye shall have done all those things which are commanded you, say, We are unprofitable servants: we have done that which was our duty to do.

John 4:34. Jesus saith unto them, My meat is to do the will of him that sent me, and to finish his work.

John 14:15. If ye love me, keep my commandments. 21. He that hath my commandments, and keepeth them, he it is that loveth me:

John 15:14. Ye are my friends, if ye do whatsoever I command you.

Of Man to Man: Lev. 19:18. Thou shalt love thy neighbour as thyself: I *am* the LORD.

Isa. 58:6. *Is* not this the fast that I have chosen? to loose the bands of wickedness, to undo the heavy burdens, and to let the oppressed go free, and that ye break every yoke? 7. *Is it* not to deal thy bread to the hungry, and that thou bring the poor that are cast out to thy house? when thou seest the naked, that thou cover him; and that thou hide not thyself from thine own flesh?

Matt. 7:12. Therefore all things whatsoever ye would that men should do to you, do ye even so to them: for this is the law and the prophets.

Luke 10:25-37. The Good Samaritan.

EARTH. Created by God: Gen. 1:1. In the beginning God created the heaven and the earth.

2 Kin. 19:15. Thou hast made heaven and earth.

Psa. 90:2. Before the mountains were brought forth, or ever thou hadst formed the earth and the world, even from everlasting to everlasting, thou *art* God.

Psa. 102:25. Of old hast thou laid the foundation of the earth:

BY CHRIST, John 1:3. All things were made by him; and without him was not any thing made that was made. 10. He was in the world, and the world was made by him, and the world knew him not.

Heb. 1:10. And, Thou, Lord, in the beginning hast laid the foundation of the earth; and the heavens are the works of thine hands:

Destruction of: Isa. 24:19. The earth is utterly broken down, the earth is clean dissolved, the earth is moved exceedingly. 20. The earth shall reel to and fro like a drunkard, and shall be removed like a

cottage; and the transgression thereof shall be heavy upon it; and it shall fall, and not rise again.

2 Pet. 3:10. But the day of the Lord will come as a thief in the night; in the which the heavens shall pass away with a great noise, and the elements shall melt with fervent heat, the earth also and the works that are therein shall be burned up.

Rev. 21:1. And I saw a new heaven and a new earth: for the first heaven and the first earth were passed away; and there was no more sea.

EARTHQUAKES. Instances of: At Sinai, Ex. 19:18; Psa. 68:8; 77:18; 114:4-7; Heb. 12:26. When Korah, Dathan, and Abiram were swallowed up, Num. 16:31,32. When Jonathan and his armorbearer attacked the garrison at Gibeah, 1 Sam. 14:15. When the Lord revealed himself to Elijah in the still small voice, 1 Kin. 19:11. In Canaan, in the days of Uzziah, king of Judah, Amos 1:1; Zech. 14:5. At the crucifixion of Jesus, Matt. 27:51. At the resurrection of Jesus, Matt. 28:2. When Paul and Silas were in prison at Philippi, Acts 16:26.

Figurative: Psa. 60:2.

SYMBOLICAL: Rev. 6:12-14; 11:13; 16:18,20.

ECLIPSE. Of the sun and moon, Isa. 13:10; Ezek. 32:7,8; Joel 2:10, 31; 3:15; Amos 8:9; Mic. 3:6; Matt. 24:29; Mark 13:24; Acts 2:20; Rev. 6:12,13; 8:12.

Figurative: Isa. 60:19.

EGYPT. The country of. Called RAHAB, Psa. 87:4; 89:10; LAND OF HAM, Psa. 105:23; 106:22. Limits of, Ezek. 29:10. Fertility of, Gen. 13:10. Productions of, Num. 11:5; Psa. 78:47; Prov. 7:16; Isa. 19:5-9. Irrigation employed in, Deut. 11:10. Imports of, Gen. 37:25,36. Exports of, Prov. 7:16; Ezek. 27:7; of horses, 1 Kin. 10:28,29.

Famine in, Gen. 41; Acts 7:11. Armies of, Ex. 14:7; Isa. 31:1. Army of, destroyed in the Red Sea, Ex. 14:5-31; Isa. 43:17. Magi of, Gen. 41:8; Ex. 7:11; 1 Kin. 4:30; Acts 7:22. Priests of, Gen. 41:45; 47:22. Idols of, Ezek. 20:7,8.

Overflowed by the Nile, Amos 8:8; 9:5. Joseph's captivity in, and subsequent rule over, see JOSEPH. Civil war in, Isa. 19:2. The king acquires title to land of, Gen. 47:18-26. Abraham dwells in, Gen. 12:10-20; 13:1. Joseph takes Jesus to, Matt. 2:13-20.

Prophecies against, Gen. 15:13,14; Isa. 19; 20:2-6; 45:14; Jer. 9:25,26; 43:8-13; 44:30; 46; Ezek. chapters 29-32; Hos. 8:13; Joel 3:11; Zech. 10:11.

ELDER. Acts 16:4. And as they went through the cities, they delivered them the decrees for to keep, that were ordained of the apostles and elders which were at Jerusalem. 5. And so were the churches established in the faith, and increased in number daily.

Acts 20:17. And from Miletus he sent to Ephesus, and called the elders of the church. 28. Take heed therefore unto yourselves, and to all the flock, over the which the Holy Ghost hath made you overseers, to feed the church of God, which he hath purchased with his own blood. 29. For I know this, that after my departing shall grievous wolves enter in among you, not sparing the flock. 30. Also of your own selves shall men arise, speaking perverse things, to draw away disciples after them. 31. Therefore watch, and remember, that by the space of three years I ceased not to warn every one night and day with tears. 32. And now, brethren, I commend you to God, and to the word of his grace, which is able to build you up, and to give you an inheritance among all them which are sanctified.

1 Tim. 5:17. Let the elders that rule well be counted worthy of double honour, especially they who labour in the word and doctrine. 18. For the scripture saith, Thou shalt not muzzle the ox that treadeth out the corn. And, The labourer *is* worthy of his reward. 19. Against an elder receive not an accusation, but before two or three witnesses.

Tit. 1:6. If any be blameless, the husband of one wife, having faithful children not accused of riot or unruly. 7. For a bishop must be blameless, as the steward of God; not selfwilled, not soon angry, not given to wine, no striker, not given to filthy lucre; 8. But a lover of hospitality, a lover of good men, sober, just, holy, temperate; 9. Holding fast the faithful word as he hath been taught, that he may be able by sound doctrine both to exhort and to convince the gainsayers.

ELECTION. John 15:16. Ye have not chosen me, but I have chosen you, and ordained you, that ye should go and bring forth fruit, and *that* your fruit should remain: that whatsoever ye shall ask of the Father in my name, he may give it you.

Eph. 1:4. According as he hath chosen us in him before the foundation of the world, that we should be holy and without blame before him in love:

Eph. 2:10. For we are his workmanship, created in Christ Jesus unto good works, which God hath before ordained that we should walk in them.

2 Thess. 2:13. But we are bound to give thanks always to God for you, brethren beloved of the Lord, because God hath from the beginning chosen you to salvation through sanctification of the Spirit and belief of the truth:

ELEGY. David's, on Saul and Jonathan: 2 Sam. 1:17. And David lamented with his lamentation over Saul and over Jonathan his son: 19. The beauty of Israel is slain upon thy high places: how are the mighty fallen! 20. Tell *it* not in Gath, publish *it* not in the streets of Askelon; lest the daughters of the Philistines rejoice, lest the daughters of the uncircumcised triumph. 27. How are the mighty fallen, and the weapons of war perished!

On Abner: 2 Sam. 3:33. And the king lamented over Abner, and said, Died Abner as a fool dieth? 34. Thy hands *were* not bound, nor thy feet put into fetters: as a man falleth before wicked men, *so* fellest thou. And all the people wept again over him.

ELIJAH. The Tishbite, a Gileadite and prophet, called ELIAS in the authorized version of the N. T. Persecuted by Ahab, 1 Kin. 17:2-7; 18:7-10. Escapes to the wilderness, where he is miraculously fed by ravens, 1 Kin. 17:1-7. By divine direction goes to Zarephath, where he is sustained in the household of a widow, whose meal and oil are miraculously increased, 1 Kin. 17:8-16. Returns, and sends a message to Ahab, 1 Kin. 18:1-16. Meets Ahab and directs him to assemble the prophets of Baal, 1 Kin. 18:17-20. Derisively challenges the priests of Baal to offer sacrifices, 1 Kin. 18:25-29. Slays the prophets of Baal, 1 Kin. 18:40. Escapes to the wilderness from the fierceness of Jezebel, 1 Kin. 19:1-18. Fasts forty days, 1 Kin. 19:8. Despondency and murmuring of, 1 Kin. 19:10,14. Consolation given to, 1 Kin. 19:11-18. Flees to the wilderness of Damascus; directed to anoint Hazael king over Syria, Jehu king over Israel, and Elisha to be a prophet in his own stead, 1 Kin. 19:9-21. Personal aspect of, 2 Kin. 1:8.

Piety of, 1 Kin. 19:10,14; Luke 1:17; Rom. 11:2; Jas. 5:17. His translation, 2 Kin. 2:11. Appears to Jesus at his transfiguration, Matt. 17:3,4; Mark 9:4; Luke 9:30. Antitype of John the Baptist, Matt. 11:14; 16:14; 17:10-12; Mark 9:12, 13; Luke 1:17; John 1:21-25.

Miracles of: Increases the oil of the widow of Zarephath, 1 Kin. 17: 14-16. Raises from the dead the son of the woman of Zarephath, 1 Kin. 17:17-24. Causes rain after a drought of three and a half years, 1 Kin. 18:41-45; Jas. 5:17,18. Causes fire to consume the sacrifice, 1 Kin. 18:24,36-38. Calls fire down upon the soldiers of Ahaziah, 2 Kin. 1:10-12; Luke 9:54.

Prophecies of: Foretells a drought, 1 Kin. 17:3; the destruction of Ahab and his house, 1 Kin. 21:17-29; 2 Kin. 9:25-37; the death of Ahaziah, 2 Kin. 1:2-17; the plague sent as a judgment upon the people in the time of Jehoram, king of Israel, 2 Chr. 21:12-15.

ELISHA, successor to the prophet Elijah. Elijah instructed to anoint, 1 Kin. 19:16. Called by Elijah, 1 Kin. 19:19. Ministers unto Elijah, 1 Kin. 19:21. Witnesses Elijah's translation, receives a double portion of his spirit, 2 Kin. 2:1-15; 3:11. Mocked by the children of Beth-el, 2 Kin. 2:23,24. Causes the king to restore the property of the hospitable Shunammite, 2 Kin. 8:1-6. Instructs that Jehu be anointed king of Israel, 2 Kin. 9: 1-3. Life of, sought by Jehoram, 2 Kin. 6:31-33. Death of, 2 Kin. 13: 14-20. Bones of, restore a dead man to life, 2 Kin. 13:21.

Miracles of: Divides the Jordan, 2 Kin. 2:14. Purifies the waters of Jericho by casting salt into the fountain, 2 Kin. 2:19-22. Increases the oil of the woman whose sons were to be sold for debt, 2 Kin. 4:1-7. Raises from the dead the son of the Shunammite, 2 Kin. 4:18-37. Neutralizes the poison of the pottage, 2 Kin. 4:38-41. Increases the bread to feed one hundred men, 2 Kin. 4:42-44. Heals Naaman the leper, 2 Kin. 5:1-19; Luke 4:27. Sends leprosy as a judgment upon Gehazi, 2 Kin. 5:26,27. Recovers the ax that had fallen into a stream by causing it to float, 2 Kin. 6:6. Reveals the counsel of the king of Syria, 2 Kin. 6:12. Opens the eyes of his servant to see the hosts of the Lord, 2 Kin. 6:17. Brings blindness upon the army of Syria, 2 Kin. 6:18.

Prophecies of: Foretells a son to the Shunammite woman, 2 Kin. 4:16; plenty to the starving in Samaria, 2 Kin. 7:1; death of the unbelieving prince, 2 Kin. 7:2; seven years' famine in the land of Canaan, 2 Kin. 8:1-3; death of Benhadad, king of Syria, 2 Kin. 8:7-10; elevation of Hazael to the throne, 2 Kin. 8:11-15; the victory of Jehoash over Syria, 2 Kin. 13:14-19.

EMPLOYEE. Deut. 24:14. Thou shalt not oppress an hired servant *that is* poor and needy, *whether he be* of thy brethren, or of thy strangers that *are* in thy land within thy gates: 15. At his day thou shalt give *him* his hire, neither shall the sun go down upon it; for he *is* poor, and setteth his heart upon it: lest he cry against thee unto the Lord, and it be sin unto thee.

Ruth 2:4. And, behold, Boaz came from Beth-lehem, and said unto the reapers, The Lord *be* with you. And they answered him, The Lord bless thee.

Matt. 10:10. The workman is worthy of his meat.

Luke 10:7. The labourer is worthy of his hire.

1 Tim. 5:18. For the scripture saith, Thou shalt not muzzle the ox that treadeth out the corn. And, The labourer *is* worthy of his reward.

Jas. 5:4. Behold, the hire of the labourers who have reaped down your fields, which is of you kept back by fraud, crieth: and the cries of them which have reaped are entered into the ears of the Lord of sabaoth.

EMPLOYER. Lev. 25:43. Thou shalt not rule over him with rigour; but shalt fear thy God.

Deut. 5:14. The sabbath of the Lord thy God: *in it* thou shalt not do any work, thou, nor thy son, nor thy daughter, nor thy manservant, nor thy maidservant, nor thine ox, nor thine ass, nor any of thy cattle, nor thy stranger that *is* within thy gates; that thy manservant and thy maidservant may rest as well as thou.

Jer. 22:13. Woe unto him . . . *that* useth his neighbour's service without wages, and giveth him not for his work;

Matt. 20:1. For the kingdom of heaven is like unto a man *that is* an householder, which went out early in the morning to hire labourers into his vineyard.

ENEMY. Ex. 23:5. If thou see the ass of him that hateth thee lying under his burden, and wouldest forbear to help him, thou shalt surely help with him.

Job 31:29. If I rejoiced at the destruction of him that hated me, or lifted up myself when evil found him: 30. Neither have I suffered

my mouth to sin by wishing a curse to his soul.

Prov. 24:17. Rejoice not when thine enemy falleth, and let not thine heart be glad when he stumbleth: 18. Lest the Lord see *it,* and it displease him, and he turn away his wrath from him.

Prov. 25:21. If thine enemy be hungry, give him bread to eat; and if he be thirsty, give him water to drink: 22. For thou shalt heap coals of fire upon his head, and the Lord shall reward thee.

Matt. 5:43. Ye have heard that it hath been said, Thou shalt love thy neighbour, and hate thine enemy. 44. But I say unto you, Love your enemies, bless them that curse you, do good to them that hate you, and pray for them which despitefully use you, and persecute you;

ENGRAVING. In making idols, Ex. 32:4. On the stones set in the priest's breastplate, Ex. 28:9-11,21, 36; 39:8-14; in the priest's girdle, Ex. 39:6; in the priest's crown Ex. 39:30.

ENVY. Psa. 37:1. Fret not thyself because of evildoers, neither be thou envious against the workers of iniquity. 7. Fret not thyself because of him who prospereth in his way, because of the man who bringeth wicked devices to pass. Prov. 24:19.

Psa. 49:16. Be thou not afraid when one is made rich, when the glory of his house is increased;

Psa. 73:3. I was envious at the foolish, *when* I saw the prosperity of the wicked. *vs.* 17-20.

Prov. 14:30. A sound heart *is* the life of the flesh: but envy the rottenness of the bones.

Prov. 23:17. Let not thine heart envy sinners:

Prov. 27:4. Who *is* able to stand before envy?

Song 8:6. Jealousy *is* cruel as the grave: the coals thereof *are* coals of fire, *which hath* a most vehement flame.

Rom. 13:13. Let us walk honestly, as in the day; not in rioting and drunkenness, not in chambering and wantonness, not in strife and [envying]. [R. V. jealousy]

1 Cor. 13:4. Charity envieth not; Jas. 3:14. If ye have bitter envying and strife in your hearts, glory not, and lie not against the truth. 16. Where envying and strife *is*, there *is* confusion and every evil work.

Jas. 4:5. Do ye think that the scripture saith in vain, The spirit that dwelleth in us lusteth to envy?

1 Pet. 2:1. Laying aside all malice, and all guile, and hypocrisies, and envies, and all evil speakings,

EPHOD. A sacred vestment worn by the high priest. Described, Ex. 28:6-14,31-35; 25:7. Making of, Ex. 39:2-26. Breastplate attached to, Ex. 28:22-29. Worn by Aaron, Ex. 39:5.

Used as an oracle, 1 Sam. 23:9, 12; 30:7,8.

ESAU. Eldest of twin sons born to Isaac and Rebekah. Birth of, Gen. 25:19-26; 1 Chr. 1:34. Called Edom, Gen. 36:1,8. A hunter, Gen. 25:27,28. Beloved by Isaac, Gen. 25:27,28. Sells his birthright for a mess of pottage, Gen. 25:29-34; Mal. 1:2; Rom. 9:13; Heb. 12:16. Marries a Hittite, Gen. 26:34. His marriage a grief to Isaac and Rebekah, Gen. 26:35. Polygamy of, Gen. 26:34; 28:9; 36:2,3. Is defrauded of his father's blessing by Jacob, Gen. 27; Heb. 11:20. Meets Jacob on the return of the latter from Haran, Gen. 33:1. With Jacob, buries his father, Gen. 35:29. Descendants of, Gen. 36; 1 Chr. 1:35-57. Enmity of descendants of, toward descendants of Jacob, Obad. 10-14. Ancestor of Edomites, Jer. 49:8. Mount of Edom, called MOUNT OF ESAU, Obad. 8,9,18,19, 21. His name used to denote his descendants and their country, Deut. 2:5; Jer. 49:8,10; Obad. 6. Prophecies concerning, Obad. 18.

ESCAPE. None, from the Judgments of God: Gen. 3:7. And the eyes of them both were opened, and they knew that they *were* naked; and they sewed fig leaves together, and made themselves aprons.

Gen. 4:9. And the LORD said unto Cain, Where *is* Abel thy

brother? And he said, I know not: *Am* I my brother's keeper? 10. And he said, What hast thou done? the voice of thy brother's blood crieth unto me from the ground. 11. And now *art* thou cursed from the earth, which hath opened her mouth to receive thy brother's blood from thy hand.

Job 34:21. For his eyes *are* upon the ways of man, and he seeth all his goings. 22. *There is* no darkness, nor shadow of death, where the workers of iniquity may hide themselves.

Isa. 10:3. And what will ye do in the day of visitation, and in the desolation *which* shall come from far?. to whom will ye flee for help, and where will ye leave your glory?

Matt. 23:33. *Ye* serpents, *ye* generation of vipers, how can ye escape the damnation of hell?

Heb. 2:3. How shall we escape, if we neglect so great salvation; which at the first began to be spoken by the Lord, and was confirmed unto us by them that heard *him;*

ETERNITY. Psa. 41:13. Blessed *be* the LORD God of Israel from everlasting, and to everlasting.

Psa. 90:2. Before the mountains were brought forth, or ever thou hadst formed the earth and the world, even from everlasting to everlasting, thou *art* God.

2 Cor. 9:9. His righteousness remaineth for ever.

Jude 6. And the angels which kept not their first estate, but left their own habitation, he hath reserved in everlasting chains under darkness unto the judgment of the great day.

ETHIOPIA, a region in Africa, inhabited by the descendants of Ham. The inhabitants of, black, Jer. 13:23. Within the Babylonian empire, Esth. 1:1. Rivers of, Gen. 10:6; Isa. 18:1. Bordered Egypt on the S., Ezek. 29:10. Was called the land of Cush, mentioned in Gen. 10:6; 1 Chr. 1:9; Isa. 11:11. Warriors of, Jer. 46:9; 2 Chr. 12:3; Ezek. 38:5. Defeated by Asa, 2 Chr. 14:9-15; 16:8. Invaded Syria, 2 Kin. 19:9. Merchandise of, Isa.

45:14. Moses marries a woman of, Num. 12:1. Ebel-melech, at the court of Babylon, native of; kindly treats Jeremiah, Jer. 38:7-13; 39:15-18. Candace, queen of, Acts 8:27. A eunuch from, becomes a disciple under the preaching of Philip, Acts 8:27-39. Prophecies concerning the conversion of, Psa. 68:31; 87:4; Isa. 45:14; Dan. 11:43. Desolation of, Isa. 18:1-6; 20:2-6; 43:3; Ezek. 30: 4-9; Hab. 3:7; Zeph. 2:12.

EUCHARIST. Matt. 26:17. Now the first *day* of the *feast* of unleavened bread the disciples came to Jesus, saying unto him, Where wilt thou that we prepare for thee to eat the passover? 26. And as they were eating, Jesus took bread, and blessed *it*, and brake *it*, and gave *it* to the disciples, and said, Take, eat; this is my body. 27. And he took the cup, and gave thanks, and gave *it* to them, saying, Drink ye all of it; 28. For this is my blood of the new testament, which is shed for many for the remission of sins. 29. But I say unto you, I will not drink henceforth of this fruit of the vine, until that day when I drink it new with you in my Father's kingdom. 30. And when they had sung an hymn, they went out into the mount of Olives. Mark 14:22-24; Luke 22:19, 20; John 13:1-4.

Acts 2:42. And they continued stedfastly in the apostles' doctrine and fellowship, and in breaking of bread, and in prayers. 46. And they, continuing daily with one accord in the temple, and breaking bread from house to house, did eat their meat with gladness and singleness of heart, 47. Praising God, and having favour with all the people.

Acts 20:7. And upon the first *day* of the week, when the disciples came together to break bread, Paul preached unto them, ready to depart on the morrow; and continued his speech until midnight.

1 Cor. 11:23. For I have received of the Lord that which also I delivered unto you, That the Lord Jesus the *same* night in which he was betrayed took bread: 24. And when he had given thanks, he brake *it*, and said, Take, eat: this is my body, which is broken for you: this do in remembrance of me. 25. After the same manner also *he took* the cup, when he had supped, saying, This cup is the new testament in my blood: this do ye, as oft as ye drink *it*, in remembrance of me. 26. For as often as ye eat this bread, and drink this cup, ye do shew the Lord's death till he come. 27. Wherefore whosoever shall eat this bread, and drink *this* cup of the Lord, unworthily, shall be guilty of the body and blood of the Lord. 28. But let a man examine himself, and so let him eat of *that* bread, and drink of *that* cup. 29. For he that eateth and drinketh unworthily, eateth and drinketh [damnation] to himself, not discerning the Lord's body. 30. For this cause many *are* weak and sickly among you, and many sleep. 31. For if we would judge ourselves, we should not be judged. 32. But when we are judged, we are chastened of the Lord, that we should not be condemned with the world. [R. V. judgment]

EVIDENCE. Laws Concerning: Ex. 20:16. Thou shalt not bear false witness against thy neighbour.

Ex. 23:1. Thou shalt not raise a false report; put not thine hand with the wicked to be an unrighteous witness. 7. Keep thee far from a false matter; and the innocent and righteous slay thou not: for I will not justify the wicked.

Lev. 5:1. And if a soul sin, and hear the voice of swearing, and *is* a witness, whether he hath seen or known *of it;* if he do not utter *it*, then he shall bear his iniquity.

Num. 35:30. Whoso killeth any person, the murderer shall be put to death by the mouth of witnesses: but one witness shall not testify against any person to *cause him* to die.

Matt. 18:16. But if he will not hear *thee, then* take with thee one or two more, that in the mouth of two or three witnesses every word may be established.

Self-Criminating: Josh. 7:19. And Joshua said unto Achan, My son, give, I pray thee, glory to the

LORD God of Israel, and make confession unto him; and tell me now what thou hast done; hide *it* not from me. 20. And Achan answered Joshua, and said, Indeed I have sinned against the LORD God of Israel, and thus and thus have I done: 21. When I saw among the spoils a goodly Babylonish garment, and two hundred shekels of silver, and a wedge of gold of fifty shekels weight, then I coveted them, and took them; and, behold, they *are* hid in the earth in the midst of my tent, and the silver under it.

EVIL, Appearance of, to Be Avoided: Rom. 14:15. But if thy brother be grieved with *thy* meat, now walkest thou not charitably. Destroy not him with thy meat, for whom Christ died. 16. Let not then your good be evil spoken of: 21. *It is* good neither to eat flesh, nor to drink wine, nor *any thing* whereby thy brother stumbleth, or is offended, or is made weak.

1 Thess. 5:22. Abstain from all appearance of evil.

EXAMPLE, Bad, Admonitions Against: Lev. 20:23. And ye shall not walk in the manners of the nation, which I cast out before you: for they committed all these things, and therefore I abhorred them.

2 Chr. 30:7. Be not ye like your fathers, and like your brethren, which trespassed against the LORD God of their fathers, *who* therefore gave them up to desolation, as ye see.

Prov. 22:24. Make no friendship with an angry man; and with a furious man thou shalt not go: 25. Lest thou learn his ways, and get a snare to thy soul.

Jer. 17:2. Whilst their children remember their altars and their groves by the green trees upon the high hills.

Hos. 4:9. And there shall be, like people, like priest: and I will punish them for their ways, and reward them their doings.

1 Cor. 8:9. But take heed lest by any means this liberty of your's become a stumblingblock to them that are weak. 10. For if any man

see thee which hath knowledge sit at meat in the idol's temple, shall not the conscience of him which is weak be emboldened to eat those things which are offered to idols; 11. And through thy knowledge shall the weak brother perish, for whom Christ died? 12. But when ye sin so against the brethren, and wound their weak conscience, ye sin against Christ. 13. Wherefore, if meat make my brother to offend, I will eat no flesh while the world standeth, lest I make my brother to offend.

3 John 11. Beloved, follow not that which is evil, but that which is good. He that doeth good is of God: but he that doeth evil hath not seen God.

Good: Psa. 101:2. I will walk within my house with a perfect heart.

1 Thess. 1:6. And ye became followers of us, and of the Lord, having received the word in much affliction, with joy of the Holy Ghost:

1 Tim. 4:12. Let no man despise thy youth; but be thou an example of the believers, in word, in conversation, in charity, in spirit, in faith, in purity.

Tit. 2:7. In all things shewing thyself a pattern of good works: in doctrine *shewing* uncorruptness, gravity, sincerity, 8. Sound speech, that cannot be condemned; that he that is of the contrary part may be ashamed, having no evil thing to say of you.

God, Our: Lev. 19:2. Speak unto all the congregation of the children of Israel, and say unto them, Ye shall be holy: for I the LORD your God *am* holy.

Matt. 5:48. Be ye therefore perfect, even as your Father which is in heaven is perfect.

Luke 6:36. Be ye therefore merciful, as your Father also is merciful.

Christ, Our: John 13:13. Ye call me Master and Lord: and ye say well; for *so* I am. 14. If I then, *your* Lord and Master, have washed your feet; ye also ought to wash one another's feet. 15. For I have given you an example, that ye

should do as I have done to you.
34. A new commandment I give
unto you, That ye love one another;
as I have loved you, that ye also
love one another.

Rom. 15:2. Let every one of us
please *his* neighbour for *his* good to
edification. 3. For even Christ
pleased not himself; but, as it is
written, The reproaches of them
that reproached thee fell on me.

Phil. 2:5. Let this mind be in
you, which was also in Christ
Jesus:

Col. 3:13. Forbearing one another, and forgiving one another, if
any man have a quarrel against any:
even as Christ forgave you, so also
do ye.

1 Pet. 2:21. For even hereunto
were ye called: because Christ also
suffered for us, leaving us an example, that ye should follow his
steps:

Paul, Our: 1 Cor. 4:16. Wherefore I beseech you, be ye followers
of me.

1 Cor. 11:1. Be ye followers of
me, even as I also *am* of Christ.

Phil. 4:9. Those things, which ye
have both learned, and received, and
heard, and seen in me, do: and the
God of peace shall be with you.

2 Tim. 1:13. Hold fast the form
of sound words, which thou hast
heard of me, in faith and love which
is in Christ Jesus.

EXCUSES. Gen. 3:12. And the
man said, The woman whom thou
gavest *to be* with me, she gave me
of the tree, and I did eat. 13. And
the LORD God said unto the woman,
What *is* this *that* thou hast done?
And the woman said, The serpent
beguiled me, and I did eat.

Ex. 32:22. And Aaron said, Let
not the anger of my lord wax hot:
thou knowest the people, that they
are set on mischief.

Acts 24:25. And as he reasoned
of righteousness, temperance, and
judgment to come, Felix trembled,
and answered, Go thy way for this
time; when I have a convenient
season, I will call for thee.

EXPEDIENCY. 1 Cor. 6:12.
All things are lawful unto me, but
all things are not expedient: all

things are lawful for me, but I will
not be brought under the power of
any.

1 Cor. 9:19. For though I be
free from all *men,* yet have I made
myself servant unto all, that I might
gain the more. 20. And unto the
Jews I became as a Jew, that I
might gain the Jews; to them that
are under the law, as under the
law, that I might gain them that are
under the law; 21. To them that
are without law, as without law,
(being not without law to God, but
under the law to Christ,) that I
might gain them that are without
law. 22. To the weak became I as
weak, that I might gain the weak: I
am made all things to all *men,* that
I might by all means save some. 23.
And this I do for the gospel's sake,
that I might be partaker thereof
with *you.*

EXTORTION. Ezek. 22:12.
In thee have they taken gifts to
shed blood; thou hast taken usury
and increase, and thou hast greedily gained of thy neighbours by extortion, and hast forgotten me, saith
the Lord GOD.

Matt. 23:25. Woe unto you,
scribes and Pharisees, hypocrites!
for ye make clean the outside of
the cup and of the platter, but
within they are full of extortion
and excess.

1 Cor. 6:10. Nor thieves, nor
covetous, nor drunkards, nor re-
vilers, nor extortioners, shall inherit the kingdom of God.

EXTRADITION. 1 Kin. 18:7.
And as Obadiah was in the way,
behold, Elijah met him: and he
knew him, and fell on his face, and
said, *Art* thou that my lord Elijah?
10. *As* the LORD thy God liveth,
there is no nation or kingdom,
whither my lord hath not sent to
seek thee: and when they said, *He*
is not *there;* he took an oath of the
kingdom and nation, that they
found thee not.

Acts 9:2. And desired of him letters to Damascus to the synagogues,
that if he found any of this way,
whether they were men or women,
he might bring them bound unto
Jerusalem. 14. And here he hath

authority from the chief priests to bind all that call on thy name.

EXTRAVAGANCE. Prov. 21: 17. He that loveth pleasure *shall be* a poor man: he that loveth wine and oil shall not be rich. 20. *There is* treasure to be desired and oil in the dwelling of the wise; but a foolish man spendeth it up.

EYE. Anthropomorphic Uses of: Psa. 33:18. Behold, the eye of the LORD *is* upon them that fear him, upon them that hope in his mercy; 19. To deliver their soul from death, and to keep them alive in famine.

Psa. 121:3. He that keepeth thee will not slumber. 4. Behold, he that keepeth Israel shall neither slumber nor sleep. 5. The LORD *is* thy keeper:

Hab. 1:13. *Thou art* of purer eyes than to behold evil, and canst not look on iniquity: wherefore lookest thou upon them that deal treacherously, *and* holdest thy tongue when the wicked devoureth *the man that is* more righteous than he?

FAITH. Psa. 5:11. Let all those that put their trust in thee rejoice: let them ever shout for joy, because thou defendest them:

Psa. 7:1. O LORD my God, in thee do I put my trust: save me from all them that persecute me, and deliver me:

Psa. 32:10. He that trusteth in the LORD, mercy shall compass him about.

Psa. 36:7. How excellent *is* thy loving-kindness, O God! therefore the children of men put their trust under the shadow of thy wings.

Psa. 118:8. *It is* better to trust in the LORD than to put confidence in man. 9. *It is* better to trust in the LORD than to put confidence in princes.

Prov. 3:5. Trust in the LORD with all thine heart; and lean not unto thine own understanding.

Isa. 26:3. Thou wilt keep *him* in perfect peace, *whose* mind *is* stayed *on thee:* because he trusteth in thee.

Nah. 1:7. The LORD *is* good, a strong hold in the day of trouble; and he knoweth them that trust in him.

Luke 17:5. And the apostles said unto the Lord, Increase our faith.

Rom. 4:20. He staggered not at the promise of God through unbelief; but was strong in faith, giving glory to God;

Rom. 5:1. Therefore being justified by faith, [we] have peace with God through our Lord Jesus Christ: [R. V. let us]

Eph. 2:8. By grace are ye saved through faith; and that not of yourselves: *it is* the gift of God:

Eph. 6:16. Above all, taking the shield of faith, wherewith ye shall be able to quench all the fiery darts of the wicked.

1 Thess. 5:8. Putting on the breastplate of faith and love;

1 Tim. 4:10. For therefore we both labour and suffer reproach, because we trust in the living God, who is the Saviour of all men, specially of those that believe.

2 Tim. 4:7. I have fought a good fight, I have finished *my* course, I have kept the faith: 8. Henceforth there is laid up for me a crown of righteousness, which the Lord, the righteous judge, shall give me at that day: and not to me only, but unto all them also that love his appearing.

Enjoined: Ex. 14:13. Moses said unto the people, Fear ye not, stand still, and see the salvation of the LORD, which he will shew to you to day:

2 Chr. 16:9. The eyes of the LORD run to and fro throughout the whole earth, to shew himself strong in the behalf of *them* whose heart *is* perfect toward him.

Psa. 27:14. Wait on the LORD: be of good courage, and he shall strengthen thine heart:

Psa. 37:3. Trust in the LORD, and do good; *so* shalt thou dwell in the land, and verily thou shalt be fed.

Psa. 55:22. Cast thy burden upon the LORD, and he shall sustain thee: he shall never suffer the righteous to be moved.

Psa. 62:8. Trust in him at all times; ye people, pour out your heart before him: God *is* a refuge for us.

Jer. 49:11. Leave thy fatherless children, I will preserve *them* alive; and let thy widows trust in me.

Mark 11:22. And Jesus answering saith unto them, Have faith in God.

Luke 12:32. Fear not, little flock; for it is your father's good pleasure to give you the kingdom.

Exemplified: Gen. 6:22. Thus did Noah; according to all that God commanded him, so did he.

Num. 10:29. And Moses said unto Hobab, the son of Raguel the Midianite, Moses' father in law, We are journeying unto the place of which the LORD said, I will give it you: come thou with us, and we will do thee good: for the LORD hath spoken good concerning Israel.

Josh. 14:12. If so be the LORD *will be* with me, then I shall be able to drive them out, as the LORD said.

1 Chr. 28:20. And David said to Solomon his son, Be strong and of good courage, and do *it:* fear not, nor be dismayed: for the LORD God, even my God, *will be* with thee; he will not fail thee, nor forsake thee, until thou hast finished all the work for the service of the house of the LORD.

2 Chr. 14:11. And Asa cried unto the LORD his God, and said, LORD, *it is* nothing with thee to help, whether with many, or with them that have no power: help us, O LORD our God; for we rest on thee, and in thy name we go against this multitude.

2 Chr. 32:7. *There be* more with us than with him: 8. With him is an arm of flesh; but with us *is* the LORD our God to help us, and to fight our battles. And the people rested themselves upon the words of Hezekiah king of Judah.

Ezra 8:22. The hand of our God *is* upon all them for good that seek him;

Neh. 2:20. The God of heaven, he will prosper us; therefore we his servants will arise and build:

Job 13:15. Though he slay me, yet will I trust in him. 16. He also *shall be* my salvation:

Job 19:25. I know *that* my redeemer liveth, and *that* he shall stand at the latter *day* upon the earth: 26. And *though* after my skin *worms* destroy this *body*, yet in my flesh shall I see God: 27. Whom I shall see for myself, and mine eyes shall behold, and not another; *though* my reins be consumed within me.

Job 23:6. Will he plead against me with *his* great power? No; but he would put *strength* in me.

Psa. 4:3. The LORD hath set apart him that is godly for himself: the LORD will hear when I call unto him. 8. I will both lay me down in peace, and sleep: for thou, LORD, only makest me dwell in safety.

Psa. 11:1. In the LORD put I my trust: how say ye to my soul, Flee *as* a bird to your mountain?

Psa. 28:7. The LORD *is* my strength and my shield; my heart trusted in 'him, and I am helped:

Psa. 56:3. What time I am afraid, I will trust in thee.

Psa. 57:1. My soul trusteth in thee: yea, in the shadow of thy wings will I make my refuge, until *these* calamities be overpast.

Psa. 63:6. I remember thee upon my bed, *and* meditate on thee in the *night* watches. 7. Because thou hast been my help, therefore in the shadow of thy wings will I rejoice.

Psa. 70:5. Make haste unto me, O God: thou *art* my help and my deliverer;

Psa. 90:1. LORD, thou hast been our dwelling place in all generations.

Psa. 118:17. I shall not die, but live, and declare the works of the LORD.

Psa. 121:2. My help *cometh* from the LORD, which made heaven and earth. Psa. 124:8.

Eccl. 11:1. Cast thy bread upon the waters: for thou shalt find it after many days.

Dan. 6:16. *Now* the king spake and said unto Daniel, Thy God whom thou servest continually, he will deliver thee.

Hab. 1:12. *Art* thou not from everlasting, O LORD my God, mine Holy One? we shall not die.

Hab. 3:17. Although the fig tree shall not blossom, neither *shall* fruit *be* in the vines; the labour of the olives shall fail, and the fields shall yield no meat; the flock shall be cut off from the fold, and *there shall be* no herd in the stalls: 18. Yet I will rejoice in the LORD, I will joy in the God of my salvation. 19. The LORD God *is* my strength, and he will make my feet like hinds' *feet,* and he will make me to walk upon mine high places.

Luke 7:50. And he said to the woman, Thy faith hath saved thee; go in peace.

Acts 27:25. I believe God, that it shall be even as it was told me.

Heb. 11:4. By faith Abel offered unto God a more excellent sacrifice than Cain, by which he obtained witness that he was righteous, God testifying of his gifts: and by it he being dead yet speaketh. 5. By faith Enoch was translated that he should not see death; and was not found, because God had translated him: for before his translation he had this testimony, that he pleased God.

In Christ: Matt. 15:28. Then Jesus answered and said unto her, O woman, great *is* thy faith: be it unto thee even as thou wilt.

Mark 9:23. Jesus said unto him, If thou canst believe, all things *are* possible to him that believeth.

Luke 8:50. When Jesus heard *it,* he answered him, saying, Fear not: believe only, and she shall be made whole. Mark 5:36.

Luke 17:6. If ye had faith as a grain of mustard seed, ye might say unto this sycamine tree, Be thou plucked up by the root, and be thou planted in the sea; and it should obey you.

Luke 18:42. Jesus said unto him, Receive thy sight: thy faith hath saved thee.

John 1:12. But as many as received him, to them gave he [power] to become [the sons] of God, *even* to them that believe on his name: [R. V. the right] [R. V. children]

John 3:16. For God so loved the world, that he gave his only begotten Son, that whosoever believeth in him should not perish, but have everlasting life.

John 7:38. He that believeth on me, as the scripture hath said, out of his belly shall flow rivers of living water.

John 14:1. Let not your heart be troubled: ye believe in God, believe also in me.

Acts 16:31. Believe on the Lord Jesus Christ, and thou shalt be saved, and thy house.

Gal. 2:16. Knowing that a man is not justified by the works of the law, but by the faith of Jesus Christ, even we have believed in Jesus Christ, that we might be justified by the faith of Christ,

Eph. 3:12. In whom we have boldness and access with confidence by the faith of him. 17. That Christ may dwell in your hearts by faith;

Heb. 4:16. Let us therefore come boldly unto the throne of grace, that we may obtain mercy, and find grace to help in time of need.

In Christ, Exemplified: Matt. 14:33. Then they that were in the ship came and worshipped him, saying, Of a truth thou art the Son of God.

Matt. 16:16. Simon Peter answered and said, Thou art the Christ, the Son of the living God.

Mark 9:24. And straightway the father of the child cried out, and said with tears, Lord, I believe; help thou mine unbelief. John 9:38.

Luke 5:5. Simon answering said unto him, Master, we have toiled all the night, and have taken nothing: nevertheless at thy word I will let down the net.

John 20:28. Thomas answered and said unto him, My Lord and my God.

Rom. 8:35. Who shall separate us from the love of Christ? *shall* tribulation, or distress, or persecution, or famine, or nakedness, or peril, or sword? 37. Nay, in all these things we are more than conquerors through him that loved us.

Gal. 2:20. I am crucified with Christ: nevertheless I live; yet not

I, but Christ liveth in me: and the life which I now live in the flesh I live by the faith of the Son of God, who loved me, and gave himself for me.

Phil. 4:13. I can do all things through Christ which strengtheneth me.

2 Tim. 1:12. I know whom I have believed, and am persuaded that he is able to keep that which I have committed unto him against that day.

2 Tim. 4:18. The Lord shall deliver me from every evil work, and will preserve *me* unto his heavenly kingdom:

Trial of: 1 Chr. 29:17. I know also, my God, that thou triest the heart, and hast pleasure in uprightness.

Jas. 1:3. Knowing *this,* that the trying of your faith worketh patience. 12. Blessed *is* the man that endureth temptation: for when he [is tried], he shall receive the crown of life, which the Lord hath promised to them that love him. [R. V. hath been approved]

1 Pet. 1:7. That the trial of your faith, being much more precious than of gold that perisheth, though it be tried with fire, might be found unto praise and honour and glory at the appearing of Jesus Christ:

FAITHFULNESS. Matt. 10: 22. And ye shall be hated of all *men* for my name's sake: but he that endureth to the end shall be saved.

Luke 16:10. He that is faithful in that which is least is faithful also in much: and he that is unjust in the least is unjust also in much. 11. If therefore ye have not been faithful in the unrighteous mammon, who will commit to your trust the true *riches?* 12. And if ye have not been faithful in that which is another man's, who shall give you that which is your own?

1 Cor. 4:2. Moreover it is required in stewards, that a man be found faithful.

Rev. 2:10. Be thou faithful unto death, and I will give thee a crown of life.

FALSEHOOD. Ex. 23:1. Thou shalt not raise a false report: put not thine hand with the wicked to be an unrighteous witness.

Job 27:4. My lips shall not speak wickedness, nor my tongue utter deceit.

Psa. 10:7. His mouth is full of cursing and deceit and fraud: under his tongue *is* mischief and vanity.

Psa. 34:13. Keep thy tongue from evil, and thy lips from speaking guile. 1 Pet. 3:10.

Psa. 63:11. The mouth of them that speak lies shall be stopped.

Psa. 101:5. Whoso privily slandereth his neighbour, him will I cut off: 7. He that worketh deceit shall not dwell within my house: he that telleth lies shall not tarry in my sight.

Psa. 120:2. Deliver my soul, O LORD, from lying lips, *and* from a deceitful tongue. 3. What shall be done unto thee, thou false tongue? 4. Sharp arrows of the mighty, with coals of juniper.

Prov. 3:3. Let not mercy and truth forsake thee: bind them about thy neck; write them upon the table of thine heart:

Prov. 11:9. An hypocrite with *his* mouth destroyeth his neighbour:

Obad. 7. The men that were at peace with thee have deceived thee.

Col. 3:9. Lie not one to another, seeing that ye have put off the old man with his deeds;

1 Tim. 4:2. Speaking lies in hypocrisy; having their conscience seared with a hot iron;

Rev. 21:8. All liars shall have their part in the lake which burneth with fire and brimstone:

False Witness: Lev. 19:16. Thou shalt not go up and down *as* a talebearer among thy people: neither shalt thou stand against the blood of thy neighbour: I *am* the LORD. Ex. 20:16.

FAMILY. Instituted: Gen. 2:23. And Adam said, This *is* now bone of my bones, and flesh of my flesh: she shall be called Woman, because she was taken out of Man. 24. Therefore shall a man leave his father and his mother, and shall cleave unto his wife: and they shall be one flesh.

Government of: Gen. 3:16. Unto the woman he said, . . . thy desire *shall be* to thy husband, and he shall rule over thee.

Gen. 18:19. For I know him, that he will command his children and his household after him, and they shall keep the way of the LORD to do justice and judgment; that the LORD may bring upon Abraham that which he hath spoken of him.

1 Cor. 11:3. The head of the woman *is* the man; 7. The woman is the glory of the man. 8. For the man is not of the woman; but the woman of the man. 9. Neither was the man created for the woman; but the woman for the man.

Eph. 5:22. Wives, submit yourselves unto your own husbands, as unto the Lord. 23. For the husband is the head of the wife, even as Christ is the head of the church: and he is the saviour of the body. 24. Therefore as the church is subject unto Christ, so *let* the wives *be* to their own husbands in every thing.

Infelicity in: Prov. 11:22. *As* a jewel of gold in a swine's snout, *so is* a fair woman which is without discretion.

Prov. 15:17. Better *is* a dinner of herbs where love is, than a stalled ox and hatred therewith.

Prov. 19:13. A foolish son *is* the calamity of his father: and the contentions of a wife *are* a continual dropping.

Prov. 21:9. *It is* better to dwell in a corner of the housetop, than with a brawling woman in a wide house. [Prov. 25:24.] 19. *It is* better to dwell in the wilderness, than with a contentious and an angry woman.

Religion of the: Gen. 18:19. For I know him, that he will command his children and his household after him, and they shall keep the way of the LORD, to do justice and judgment; that the LORD may bring upon Abraham that which he hath spoken of him.

Deut. 11:19. And ye shall teach them your children, speaking of them when thou sittest in thine house, and when thou walkest by the way, when thou liest down, and when thou risest up. 20. And thou shalt write them upon the door posts of thine house, and upon thy gates:

Josh. 24:15. But as for me and my house, we will serve the LORD.

FASTING. **Unclassified Scriptures Relating to:** Ezra 8:21. Then I proclaimed a fast there, at the river of Ahava, that we might afflict ourselves before our God, to seek of him a right way for us, and for our little ones, and for all our substance.

Isa. 58:3. Wherefore have we fasted, *say they,* and thou seest not? *wherefore* have we afflicted our soul, and thou takest no knowledge? Behold, in the day of your fast we find pleasure, and exact all your labours.

Dan. 10:2. In those days I Daniel was mourning three full weeks. 3. I ate no pleasant bread, neither came flesh nor wine in my mouth, neither did I anoint myself at all, till three whole weeks were fulfilled.

1 Cor. 7:5. That ye may give yourselves to [fasting and] prayer; [Omitted in R. V.]

FEAR OF GOD. Ex. 20:18. And all the people saw the thunderings, and the lightnings, and the noise of the trumpet, and the mountain smoking: and when the people saw *it,* they removed, and stood afar off. 19. And they said unto Moses, Speak thou with us, and we will hear: but let not God speak with us, lest we die. 20. And Moses said unto the people, Fear not: for God is come to prove you, and that his fear may be before your faces, that ye sin not.

Deut. 5:29. O that there were such an heart in them, that they would fear me, and keep all my commandments always, that it might be well with them, and with their children for ever!

Josh. 24:14. Fear the LORD, and serve him in sincerity and in truth:

1 Sam. 2:30. Them that honour me I will honour, and they that de-

spise me shall be lightly esteemed.

1 Chr. 16:30. Fear before him, all the earth:

2 Chr. 19:7. Let the fear of the LORD be upon you; take heed and do it: for *there is* no iniquity with the LORD our God, 9. Thus shall ye do in the fear of the LORD, faithfully, and with a perfect heart.

Job 28:28. And unto man he said, Behold, the fear of the Lord, that *is* wisdom; and to depart from evil *is* understanding.

Psa. 19:9. The fear of the LORD *is* clean, enduring for ever:

Psa. 31:19. *Oh* how great *is* thy goodness, which thou hast laid up for them that fear thee;

Psa. 34:7. The angel of the LORD encampeth round about them that fear him, and delivereth them. 9. O fear the LORD, ye his saints: for *there is* no want to them that fear him. 11. Come, ye children, hearken unto me: I will teach you the fear of the LORD.

Psa. 86:11. Teach me thy way, O LORD; . . . unite my heart to fear thy name.

Psa. 96:4. The LORD *is* great, and greatly to be praised: he *is* to be feared above all gods. 9. Fear before him, all the earth.

Psa. 103:11. As the heaven is high above the earth, *so* great is his mercy toward them that fear him. 13. Like as a father pitieth *his* children, *so* the LORD pitieth them that fear him. 17. The mercy of the LORD *is* from everlasting to everlasting upon them that fear him,

Psa. 112:1. Blessed *is* the man *that* feareth the LORD, *that* delighteth greatly in his commandments.

Psa. 147:11. The LORD taketh pleasure in them that fear him.

Prov. 16:6. By the fear of the LORD *men* depart from evil.

Prov. 23:17. *Be thou* in the fear of the LORD all the day long.

Prov. 31:30. A woman *that* feareth the LORD, she shall be praised.

Eccl. 8:12. Surely I know that it shall be well with them that fear God, which fear before him:

Eccl. 12:13. Fear God, and keep his commandments: for this *is* the whole *duty* of man. Eccl. 5:7; 1 Pet. 2:17.

Isa. 50:10. Who *is* among you that feareth the LORD, . . . let him trust in the name of the LORD, and stay upon his God.

Acts 10:35. In every nation he that feareth him, and worketh righteousness, is accepted with him.

Jas. 2:19. The devils also believe, and tremble.

Job 31:4. Doth not he see my ways, and count all my steps?

FELLOWSHIP. With God:
Gen. 5:24. And Enoch walked with God: and he *was* not; for God took him.

Gen. 6:9. These *are* the generations of Noah: Noah was a just man *and* perfect in his generations, *and* Noah walked with God.

Ex. 33:14. And he said, My presence shall go *with thee,* and I will give thee rest. 15. And he said unto him, If thy presence go not *with me,* carry us not up hence.

Lev. 26:12. And I will walk among you, and will be your God, and ye shall be my people.

Zech. 2:10. Sing and rejoice, O daughter of Zion: for, lo, I come, and I will dwell in the midst of thee, saith the LORD.

1 John 1:3. Truly our fellowship *is* with the Father, and with his Son Jesus Christ.

With Christ: Matt. 18:20. For where two or three are gathered together in my name, there am I in the midst of them.

Mark 9:37. Whosoever shall receive one of such children in my name, receiveth me: and whosoever shall receive me, receiveth not me, but him that sent me.

John 15:4. Abide in me, and I in you. As the branch cannot bear fruit of itself, except it abide in the vine; no more can ye, except ye abide in me. 5. I am the vine, ye *are* the branches: He that abideth in me, and I in him, the same bringeth forth much fruit: for without me ye can do nothing. 7. If ye abide in me, and my words abide in you, ye shall ask what ye will, and it shall be done unto you. *vss.* 1-8.

John 17:21. That they all may be

one; as thou, Father, *art* in me, and I in thee, that they also may be one in us: that the world may believe that thou hast sent me.

1 Cor. 1:9. God *is* faithful, by whom ye were called unto the fellowship of his Son Jesus Christ our Lord.

1 Cor. 12:27. Now ye are the body of Christ, and members in particular.

Of the Holy Spirit: Rom. 8:9. But ye are not in the flesh, but in the Spirit, if so be that the Spirit of God dwell in you. Now if any man have not the Spirit of Christ, he is none of his.

1 Cor. 3:16. Know ye not that ye are the temple of God, and *that* the Spirit of God dwelleth in you?

Of the Righteous: Psa. 55:14. We took sweet counsel together, *and* walked unto the house of God in company.

Psa. 119:63. I *am* a companion of all *them* that fear thee, and of them that keep thy precepts.

Amos 3:3. Can two walk together, except they be agreed?

Mal. 3:16. Then they that feared the LORD spake often one to another: and the LORD hearkened, and heard *it*, and a book of remembrance was written before him for them that feared the LORD, and that thought upon his name.

John 13:34. A new commandment I give unto you, That ye love one another; as I have loved you, that ye also love one another.

1 Cor. 1:10. Now I beseech you, brethren, by the name of our Lord Jesus Christ, that ye all speak the same thing, and *that* there be no divisions among you; but *that* ye be perfectly joined together in the same mind and in the same judgment.

Gal. 6:2. Bear ye one another's burdens, and so fulfil the law of Christ. 10. As we have therefore opportunity, let us do good unto all *men*, especially unto them who are of the household of faith.

1 Thess. 5:11. Comfort yourselves together, and edify one another, even as also ye do.

Heb. 10:24. Let us consider one another to provoke unto love and to good works:

Heb. 13:1. Let brotherly love continue.

Jas. 5:16. Confess *your* faults one to another, and pray for one another, that ye may be healed.

1 Pet. 2:17. Love the brotherhood.

With the Wicked: Gen. 49:6. O my soul, come not thou into their secret; unto their assembly, mine honour, be not thou united:

Psa. 6:8. Depart from me, all ye workers of iniquity; for the LORD hath heard the voice of my weeping.

Prov. 29:24. Whoso is partner with a thief hateth his own soul: he heareth cursing, and bewrayeth *it* not.

1 Cor. 5:11. But now I have written unto you not to keep company, if any man that is called a brother be a fornicator, or covetous, or an idolater, or a railer, or a drunkard, or an extortioner; with such an one no not to eat.

1 Cor. 15:33. Be not deceived: evil communications corrupt good manners.

With the Wicked Forbidden: Ex. 34:12. Take heed to thyself, lest thou make a covenant with the inhabitants of the land whither thou goest, lest it be for a snare in the midst of thee: Judg. 2:2.

Num. 16:26. And he spake unto the congregation, saying, Depart, I pray you, from the tents of these wicked men, and touch nothing of their's, lest ye be consumed in all their sins.

Psa. 1:1. Blessed *is* the man that walketh not in the counsel of the ungodly, nor standeth in the way of sinners, nor sitteth in the seat of the scornful.

Prov. 1:10. My son, if sinners entice thee, consent thou not.

Prov. 4:14. Enter not into the path of the wicked, and go not in the way of evil *men*. 15. Avoid it, pass not by it, turn from it, and pass away.

Matt. 18:17. And if he shall neglect to hear them, tell *it* unto the church: but if he neglect to hear the church, let him be unto thee as an heathen man and a publican. Rom. 16:17. Now I beseech you, brethren, mark them which cause divisions and offences contrary to the doctrine which ye have learned; and avoid them.

FINE, a penalty. Ex. 22:1. If a man shall steal an ox, or a sheep, and kill it, or sell it; he shall restore five oxen for an ox, and four sheep for a sheep. 4. If the theft be certainly found in his hand alive, whether it be ox, or ass, or sheep; he shall restore double. 7. If a man shall deliver unto his neighbour money or stuff to keep, and it be stolen out of the man's house; if the thief be found, let him pay double. 8. If the thief be not found, then the master of the house shall be brought unto the judges, *to see* whether he have put his hand unto his neighbour's goods. 9. For all manner of trespass, *whether it be* for ox, for ass, for sheep, for raiment, *or* for any manner of lost thing, which *another* challengeth to be his, the cause of both parties shall come before the judges; *and* whom the judges shall condemn, he shall pay double unto his neighbour.

FIRE. Used as a signal in war, Jer. 6:1. Furnaces of, Dan. 3:6. Children caused to pass through, 2 Kin. 16:3; 17:17.

Miracles connected with: Miraculously descends upon, and consumes, Abraham's sacrifice, Gen. 15:17; David's, 1 Chr. 21:26; Elijah's, 1 Kin. 18:38; Solomon's at dedication of the temple, 2 Chr. 7:1 Display of, in the plagues of Egypt, Ex. 9:24; at Elijah's translation, 2 Kin. 2:11. Consumes the conspirators with Korah, Dathan, and Abiram, Num. 16:35; the captains and their fifties, 2 Kin. 1:9-12.

Torture by, Lev. 21:9; Jer. 29:22; Ezek. 23:25, 47; Dan. 3.

Pillar of fire, Ex. 13:21,22; 14:19, 24; 40:38; Num. 9:15-23.

Figurative: Of cleansing, Isa. 6:6,7; spiritual power, Psa. 104: 4; Jer. 20:9; Matt. 3:11; Luke 3:16; judgments, Deut. 4:24; 32:22; Isa. 33:14; Jer. 23:29; Amos 1:4,7,

10,12,14; 2:2; Mal. 3:2; Luke 12: 49; Rev. 20:9; of the destruction of the wicked, Matt. 13:42,50; 25:41; Mark 9:48; Rev. 9:2; 21:8.

EVERLASTING FIRE, Isa. 33:14; Matt. 18:8; 25:41; Mark 9:48:

A SYMBOL: Of God's presence, Gen. 15:17; in the burning bush, Ex. 3:2; on Sinai, Ex. 19:18. Tongues of, on the apostles, Acts 2:3.

FIRSTBORN, of man and beast, reserved to himself by God, Ex. 13:2,12-16; 22:29,30; 34:19,20; Lev. 27:26; Num. 3:13; 8: 17,18; Deut. 15:19-23; Neh. 10:36.

Redemption of, Ex. 13:13; 34:20; Lev. 27:27; Num. 3:40-51; 18:15-17. Levites taken instead of firstborn of the families of Israel, Num. 3:12,40-45; 8:16-18.

Of Egyptians slain, Ex. 11:5; 12: 12,29; 13:15; Num. 33:4; Psa. 78: 51; 105:36; 136:10. Of idolaters, sacrificed, Ezek. 20:26.

Birthright of the: Had precedence over the sons of the family, Gen. 4:7; a double portion of inheritance, Deut. 21:15-17; royal succession, 2 Chr. 21:3. Honorable distinction of, Ex. 4:22; Psa. 89: 27; Jer. 31:9; Rom. 8:29; Col. 1:15; Heb. 1:6; 12:23; Rev. 1:5. Sold by Esau, Gen. 25:29-34; 27:36; Rom. 9:12,13; Heb. 12:16. Forfeited by Reuben, Gen. 49:3,4; 1 Chr. 5:1,2. Set aside: that of Manasseh, Gen. 48:15-20; 1 Chr. 5:1; Adonijah, 1 Kin. 2:15; Hosah's son, 1 Chr. 26: 10.

FIRST FRUITS. First ripe of fruits, grain, oil, wine, and first of fleece, required as an offering, Ex. 22:29; Lev. 2:12-16; Num. 18:12; Deut. 18:4; 2 Chr. 31:5; Neh. 10: 35,37,39; Prov. 3:9; Jer. 2:3; Rom. 11:16. Offerings of, must be free from blemish, Num. 18:12; presented at the tabernacle, Ex. 22:29; 23:19; 34:26; Deut. 26:3-10; belonged to the priests, Lev. 23:20; Num. 18:12,13; Deut. 18:3-5; Freewill offerings of, given to the prophets, 2 Kin. 4:42.

Wave offering of, Lev. 23:10-14, 17. As a heave offering, Num. 15: 20; Neh. 10:37; Ezek. 44:30. To be offered as a thank offering upon entrance into the Land of Promise, Deut. 26:3-10.

Figurative: Rom. 8:23; 11:16; 1 Cor. 15:20,23; James 1:18.

FISH. Creation of, Gen. 1:20-22. Appointed for food, Gen. 9:2, 3. Clean and unclean, Lev. 11:9-12; Deut. 14:9,10. Taken with nets, Eccl. 9:12; Hab. 1:14-17; Matt. 4:21; Luke 5:2-6; John 21:6-8; hooks, Isa. 19: 8; Amos 4:2; Matt. 17:27; spears, Job 41:7.

Ponds for: in Heshbon, Song 7:4; in Egypt, Isa. 19:10. Traffic in, Neh. 13:16; John 21:13. Broiled, John 21:9-13; Luke 24:42. Miracles connected with: Jonah swallowed by, Jonah 1:17; 2; Matt. 12: 40; of the loaves and fishes, Matt. 14:19; 15:36; Luke 5:6; 9:13-17; coin obtained from mouth of, Matt. 17:27; great draught of, Luke 5:4-7; John 21:6; furnished to the disciples by Jesus after his resurrection, Luke 24:42; John 21:9-13.

Figurative: Ezek. 47:9,10.

FLATTERY. Psa. 78:36. Nevertheless they did flatter him with their mouth, and they lied unto him with their tongues. Rom. 16:18.

Prov. 20:19. Meddle not with him that flattereth with his lips.

Prov. 28:23. He that rebuketh a man afterwards shall find more favour than he that flattereth with the tongue.

Prov. 29:5. A man that flattereth his neighbour spreadeth a net for his feet.

Luke 6:26. Woe unto you, when all men shall speak well of you! for so did their fathers to the false prophets.

FOOD. Gen. 9:3. Every moving thing that liveth shall be meat for you; even as the green herb have I given you all things.

Psa. 23:5. Thou preparest a table before me in the presence of mine enemies: thou anointest my head with oil; my cup runneth over.

Psa. 103:5. Who satisfieth thy mouth with good *things; so that* thy youth is renewed like the eagle's.

Psa. 111:5. He hath given meat unto them that fear him: he will ever be mindful of his covenant.

Psa. 136:25. Who giveth food to all flesh: for his mercy *endureth* for ever.

Matt. 6:11. Give us this day our daily bread.

FOOL. Psa. 14:1. The fool hath said in his heart, *There is* no God. Psa. 53:1.

Psa. 107:17. Fools because of their transgression, and because of their iniquities, are afflicted.

Prov. 1:7. The fear of the Lord *is* the beginning of knowledge: *but* fools despise wisdom and instruction. 22. How long, ye simple ones, will ye love simplicity? and the scorners delight in their scorning, and fools hate knowledge?

Prov. 3:35. Shame shall be the promotion of fools.

Prov. 10:1. A foolish son *is* the heaviness of his mother.

23. *It is* as sport to a fool to do mischief:

Prov. 14:15. The simple believeth every word:

Prov. 15:20. A wise son maketh a glad father: but a foolish man despiseth his mother.

Prov. 20:3. *It is* an honour for a man to cease from strife: but every fool will be meddling.

Prov. 29:11. A fool uttereth all his mind: but a wise *man* keepeth it in till afterwards.

Eccl. 7:9. Be not hasty in thy spirit to be angry: for anger resteth in the bosom of fools.

FORGIVENESS. Of Enemies: Ex. 23:4. If thou meet thine enemy's ox or his ass going astray, thou shalt surely bring it back to him again. 5. If thou see the ass of him that hateth thee lying under his burden, and wouldest forbear to help him, thou shalt surely help with him.

Prov. 19:11. The discretion of a man deferreth his anger; and *it is* his glory to pass over a transgression.

Prov. 24:17. Rejoice not when thine enemy falleth, and let not thine heart be glad when he stumbleth: 29. Say not, I will do so to him as he hath done to me: I will render to the man according to his work.

Prov. 25:21. If thine enemy be hungry, give him bread to eat; and if he be thirsty, give him water to drink: 22. For thou shalt heap coals of fire upon his head, and the LORD shall reward thee. Rom. 12:20.

Matt. 5:7. Blessed *are* the merciful: for they shall obtain mercy. 39. Resist not evil:

Matt. 18:21. Then came Peter to him, and said, Lord, how oft shall my brother sin against me, and I forgive him? till seven times? 22. Jesus saith unto him, I say not unto thee, Until seven times: but, Until seventy times seven.

Mark 11:25. When ye stand praying, forgive, if ye have ought against any: that your Father also which is in heaven may forgive you your trespasses.

Luke 6:35. Love ye your enemies, and do good, and lend, hoping for nothing again; and your reward shall be great, and ye shall be the children of the Highest: for he is kind unto the unthankful and *to* the evil.

Rom. 12:14. Bless them which persecute you: bless, and curse not. 17. Recompense to no man evil for evil. 19. Avenge not yourselves, but *rather* give place unto wrath: for it is written, Vengeance *is* mine; I will repay, saith the Lord. 21. Be not overcome of evil, but overcome evil with good.

1 Cor. 4:12. Being reviled, we bless; being persecuted, we suffer it: 13. Being defamed, we intreat.

Eph. 4:32. Be ye kind one to another, tenderhearted, forgiving one another, even as God for Christ's sake hath forgiven you.

1 Pet. 3:9. Not rendering evil for evil, or railing for railing: but contrariwise blessing; knowing that ye are thereunto called, that ye should inherit a blessing.

FORM. In Religious Service:
I Chr. 15:13. For because ye *did it* not at the first, the LORD our God made a breach upon us, for that we sought him not after the due order. 14. So the priests and the Levites sanctified themselves to bring up the ark of the LORD God of Israel.

Matt. 12:3. But he said unto them, Have ye not read what David did, when he was an hungred, and they that were with him; 4. How he entered into the house of God, and did eat the shewbread, which was not lawful for him to eat, neither for them which were with him but only for the priests?

FORMALISM. 1 Sam. 15:22. And Samuel said, Hath the LORD *as great* delight in burnt offerings and sacrifices, as in obeying the voice of the LORD? Behold, to obey *is* better than sacrifice, *and* to hearken than the fat of rams.

Psa. 51:16. For thou desirest not sacrifice; else would I give *it:* thou delightest not in burnt offering. 17. The sacrifices of God *are* a broken spirit: a broken and a contrite heart, O God, thou wilt not despise.

Eccl. 5:1. Keep thy foot when thou goest to the house of God, and be more ready to hear, than to give the sacrifice of fools: for they consider not that they do evil.

Jer. 6:20. To what purpose cometh there to me incense from Sheba, and the sweet cane from a far country? your burnt offerings *are* not acceptable, nor your sacrifices sweet unto me.

Hos. 6:6. For I desired mercy, and not sacrifice; and the knowledge of God more than burnt offerings.

Amos 5:21. I hate, I despise your feast days, and I will not smell in your solemn assemblies. 22. Though ye offer me burnt offerings and your meat offerings, I will not accept *them:* neither will I regard the peace offerings of your fat beasts. 23. Take thou away from me the noise of thy songs; for I will not hear the melody of thy viols.

Mal. 1:10. Who is *there* even among you that would shut the doors *for nought?* neither do ye kindle *fire* on mine altar for nought. I have no pleasure in you, saith the LORD of hosts, neither will I accept an offering at your hand. 13. Ye said also, Behold, what a weariness *is it!* and ye have snuffed at it saith the LORD of hosts; and ye brought *that* which *was* torn, and the lame and the sick; thus ye brought an offering: should I accept this of your hand? saith the LORD. 14. But cursed *be* the deceiver, which hath in his flock a male, and voweth, and sacrificeth unto the Lord a corrupt thing: for I *am* a great King, saith the Lord of hosts, and my name *is* dreadful among the heathen.

Matt. 9:13. But go ye and learn what *that* meaneth, I will have mercy, and not sacrifice: for I am not come to call the righteous, but sinners to repentance.

Matt. 15:8. This people draweth nigh unto me with their mouth, and honoureth me with *their* lips; but their heart is far from me. 9. But in vain they do worship me, teaching *for* doctrines the commandments of men.

FRATERNITY. Gen. 13:8. And Abram said unto Lot, Let there be no strife, I pray thee, between me and thee, and between my herdmen and thy herdmen; for we *be* brethren

Psa. 133:1. Behold, how good and how pleasant *it is* for brethren to dwell together in unity!

Matt. 5:22. Whosoever is angry with his brother without a cause shall be in danger of the judgment: and whosoever shall say to his brother, Raca, shall be in danger of the council: but whosoever shall say, Thou fool, shall be in danger of hell fire. 23. Therefore if thou bring thy gift to the altar, and there rememberest that thy brother hath ought against thee; 24. Leave there thy gift before the altar, and go thy way; first be reconciled to thy brother, and then come and offer thy gift.

Matt. 18:15. Moreover if thy brother shall trespass against thee, go and tell him his fault between thee and him alone: if he shall hear thee, thou hast gained thy brother. 16. But if he will not hear *thee then* take with thee one or two more, that in the mouth of two or three witnesses every word may be established. 17. And if he shall neglect to hear them, tell *it* unto the church: but if he neglect to hear the church, let him be unto thee as an heathen man and a publican.

Matt. 25:40. And the King shall answer and say unto them, Verily I say unto you, Inasmuch as ye have done *it* unto one of the least of these my brethren, ye have done *it* unto me.

John 13:34. A new commandment I give unto you, That ye love one another; as I have loved you, that ye also love one another. chapter 15:12.

Rom. 12:10. *Be* kindly affectioned one to another with brotherly love; in honour preferring one another;

1 John 3:17. But whoso hath this world's good, and seeth his brother have need, and shutteth up his bowels *of compassion* from him, how dwelleth the love of God in him?

FRIENDS. Jesus calls his disciples, John 15:14, 15.

FRIENDSHIP. Psa. 41:9. Yea, mine own familiar friend, in whom I trusted, which did eat of my bread, hath lifted up *his* heel against me.

Psa. 55:12. For *it was* not an enemy *that* reproached me; then I could have borne *it:* neither *was it* he that hated me *that* did magnify *himself* against me; then I would have hid myself from him: 13. But *it was* thou, a man mine equal, my guide, and mine acquaintance. 14. We took sweet counsel together, *and* walked unto the house of God in company.

Prov. 11:13. A talebearer revealeth secrets: but he that is of a faithful spirit concealeth the matter.

Prov. 17:9. He that covereth a transgression seeketh love; but he that repeateth a matter separateth *very* friends. 17. A friend loveth at all times, and a brother is born for adversity.

Prov. 18:24. A man *that hath* friends must shew himself friendly: and there is a friend *that* sticketh closer than a brother.

Prov. 27:6. Faithful *are* the

wounds of a friend; but the kisses of an enemy *are* deceitful.

Amos 3:3. Can two walk together, except they be agreed?

FRUGALITY. Prov. 11:16. A gracious woman retaineth honour: and strong *men* retain riches.

Prov. 13:22. A good *man* leaveth an inheritance to his children's children: and the wealth of the sinner *is* laid up for the just.

Prov. 21:17. He that loveth pleasure *shall be* a poor man: he that loveth wine and oil shall not be rich. 20. *There is* treasure to be desired and oil in the dwelling of the wise; but a foolish man spendeth it up.

Prov. 22:3. A prudent *man* foreseeth the evil, and hideth himself: but the simple pass on, and are punished.

Prov. 31:27. She looketh well to the ways of her household, and eateth not the bread of idleness.

Eph. 4:28. Let him that stole steal no more: but rather let him labour, working with *his* hands the thing which is good, that he may have to give to him that needeth.

FURNACE. Uses of: For refining silver, Ezek. 22:22; Mal. 3:3; gold, Prov. 17:3. For melting lead and tin, Ezek. 22:20. For capital punishment, Shadrach, Meshach, and Abed-nego cast into, by Nebuchadnezzar, Dan. 3:6-26.

Figurative: Of affliction, Deut. 4:20; 1 Kin. 8:51; Psa. 12:6; Isa. 48:10; Jer. 11:4. Of lust, Hos. 7:4. Of hell, Mal. 4:1, Matt. 13:42, 50; Rev. 9:2.

GABRIEL, a messenger of God. Appeared to Daniel, Dan. 8:16; 9:21; to Zacharias, Luke 1:11-19; to Mary, Luke 1:26-29.

GALILEE. 1. The northern district of Palestine. A city of refuge in, Josh. 20:7, 21:32; 1 Chr. 6:76. Cities in, given to Hiram, 1 Kin. 9:11,12. Taken by king of Assyria, 2 Kin. 15:29. Prophecy concerning, Isa. 9:1; Matt. 4:15. Called GALILEE OF THE NATIONS, Isa. 9:1. Herod, tetrarch of, Mark 6:21; Luke 3:1; 23:6, 7. Jesus resides in, Matt. 17:22; 19:1; John

7:1,9. Teaching and miracles of Jesus in, Matt. 4:23,25; 15:29-31; Mark 1:14,28,39; 3:7; Luke 4:14, 44; 5:17; 23:5; John 1:43; 4:3,43-45; Acts 10:37. People of, receive Jesus, John 4:45,53. Disciples were chiefly from, Acts 1:11; 2:7. Women from, ministered to Jesus, Matt. 27:55,56; Mark 15:41; Luke 23:49,55. Jesus appeared to his disciples in, after his resurrection, Matt. 26:32; 28:7, 10, 16, 17; Mark 14:28; 16:7; John 21.

Routes from, to Judæa, Judg. 21:19; John 4:3-5. Dialect of, Mark 14:70. Called GENNESARET, Matt. 14:34; Mark 6:53. Churches in, Acts 9:31.

2. Sea of. Called SEA OF TIBERIAS, John 21:1; LAKE OF GENNESARET, LUKE 5:1; SEA OF CHINNERETH, Num. 34:11; Deut. 3:17; Josh. 13:27; of CHINNEROTH, Josh. 12:3. Jesus calls disciples on the shore of, Matt. 4:18-22; Luke 5:1-11. Jesus teaches from a ship on, Matt. 13:1-3. Miracles of Jesus on, Matt. 8:24-32; 14:22-33; 17:27; Mark 4:37-39; Luke 5:1-9; 8:22-24; John 21:1-11.

GALL. Any bitter or poisonous substance, as the bile, Job 16:13; venom of serpents, Job 20:14.

A bitter herb, Deut. 29-18. Given Jesus, Psa. 69-21; Matt. 27:34.

Figurative: Gall of bitterness, Acts 8:23.

GAMALIEL. A celebrated teacher. Speech of, before the Sanhedrin, Acts 5:33-40. Paul's teacher, Acts 22:3.

GAMES. Foot races, 1 Cor. 9:24,26; Gal. 2:2; Phil. 2:16; Heb. 12:1. Gladiatorial, 1 Cor. 4:9; 9:26; 15:32; 2 Tim. 4:7.

Figurative: Of the Christian life, 1 Cor. 9:24,26; Gal. 5:7; Phil. 2:16; 3:14; Heb. 12:1. Of a successful ministry, Gal. 2:2, Phil. 2:16. Fighting wild beasts, of spiritual conflict, 1 Cor. 4:9; 9:26; 15:32; 2 Tim. 47.

GENTILES. Acts 14:16. Who in times past suffered all nations to walk in their own ways.

Acts 17:4. And some of them

believed, and consorted with Paul and Silas; and of the devout Greeks a great multitude, and of the chief women not a few.

Rom. 1:21. Because that, when they knew God, they glorified *him* not as God, neither were thankful; but became vain in their imaginations, and their foolish heart was darkened.

Rom. 2:14. For when the Gentiles, which have not the law, do by nature the things contained in the law, these, having not the law, are a law unto themselves: 15. Which shew the work of the law written in their hearts, their conscience also bearing witness, and *their* thoughts the mean while accusing or else excusing one another.

1 Pet. 4:3. For the time past of *our* life may suffice us to have wrought the will of the Gentiles, when we walked in lasciviousness, lusts, excess of wine, revellings, banquetings, and abominable idolatries: 4. Wherein they think it strange that ye run not with *them* to the same excess of riot, speaking evil of *you.*

Prophecies of the Conversion of: Gen. 12:3. In thee shall all families of the earth be blessed. *v. 5.*

Psa. 2:8. Ask of me, and I shall give *thee* the heathen *for* thine inheritance, and the uttermost parts of the earth *for* thy possession.

Psa. 22:27. All the ends of the world shall remember and turn unto the Lord: and all the kindreds of the nations shall worship before thee.

Isa. 9:2. The people that walked in darkness have seen a great light: they that dwell in the land of the shadow of death, upon them hath the light shined.

Isa. 24:16. From the uttermost part of the earth have we heard songs, *even* glory to the righteous.

Isa. 40:5. The glory of the LORD shall be revealed, and all flesh shall see *it* together: for the mouth of the LORD hath spoken *it.*

Isa. 60:1. Arise, shine; for thy light is come, and the glory of the LORD is risen upon thee. 3. The Gentiles shall come to thy light, and kings to the brightness of thy rising.

Hag. 2:7. And I will shake all nations, and the desire of all nations shall come: and I will fill this house with glory, saith the LORD of hosts.

Zech. 6:15. They *that are* far off shall come and build in the temple of the LORD.

Zech. 8:22. Yea, many people and strong nations shall come to seek the LORD of hosts in Jerusalem, and to pray before the LORD.

Matt. 8:11. And I say unto you, That many shall come from the east and west, and shall sit down with Abraham, and Isaac, and Jacob, in the kingdom of heaven.

Matt. 19:30. But many *that are* first shall be last; and the last *shall be first.* Mark 10:31.

John 10:16. And other sheep I have, which are not of this fold: them also I must bring, and they shall hear my voice; and there shall be one fold, *and* one shepherd.

Acts 28:28. Be it known therefore unto you, that the salvation of God is sent unto the Gentiles, and *that* they will hear it.

GENTLENESS. Gal. 5:22. But the fruit of the Spirit is love, joy, peace, longsuffering, gentleness.

2 Tim. 2:24. And the servant of the Lord must not strive; but be gentle unto all *men,* apt to teach, patient, 25. In meekness instructing those that oppose themselves; if God peradventure will give them repentance to the acknowledging of the truth; 26. And *that* they may recover themselves out of the snare of the devil, who are taken captive by him at his will.

Tit. 3:1. Put them in mind . . . 2. To speak evil of no man, to be no brawlers, *but* gentle, shewing all meekness unto all men.

Jas. 3:17. But the wisdom that is from above is first pure, then peaceable, gentle, *and* easy to be intreated, full of mercy and good fruits, without partiality, and without hypocrisy.

GEOLOGY. Gen. 1:9. And God said, Let the waters under the heaven be gathered together unto one place, and let the dry *land* appear: and it was so. 10. And God called the dry *land* Earth; and the gathering together of the waters called he Seas: and God saw that *it was* good.

2 Sam. 22:16. And the channels of the sea appeared, the foundations of the world were discovered, at the rebuking of the LORD, at the blast of the breath of his nostrils.

Job 28:9. He putteth forth his hand upon the rock; he overturneth the mountains by the roots. 10. He cutteth out rivers among the rocks; and his eye seeth every precious thing. 11. He bindeth the floods from overflowing; and *the thing that is* hid bringeth he forth to light.

Psa. 24:1. The earth *is* the LORD's, and the fulness thereof; the world, and they that dwell therein. 2. For he hath founded it upon the seas, and established it upon the floods.

Psa. 136:6. To him that stretched out the earth above the waters:

Jer. 31:37. Thus saith the LORD; If heaven above can be measured, and the foundations of the earth searched out beneath, I will also cast off all the seed of Israel for all that they have done, saith the LORD.

2 Pet. 3:5. For this they willingly are ignorant of, that by the word of God the heavens were of old, and the earth standing out of the water and in the water; 6. Whereby the world that then was being overflowed with water, perished: 7. But the heavens and the earth, which are now, by the same word are kept in store, reserved unto fire against the day of judgment and perdition of ungodly men.

GETHSEMANE, a garden near Jerusalem. Jesus betrayed in, Matt. 26:36-50; Mark 14:32-46; Luke 22:39-49; John 18:1-2.

GIANTS, Gen. 6:4.

GIDEON. Call of, by an angel, Judg. 6:11,14. His excuses, Judg.

6:15. Promises of the Lord to, Judg. 6:16. Angel attests the call to, by miracle, Judg. 6:21-24. He destroys the altar of Baal, and builds one to the Lord, Judg. 6:25-27. His prayer tests, Judg. 6:36-40. Leads an army against, and defeats the Midianites, Judg. 6:33-35; 7; 8:4-12. Ephraimites chide, for not inviting them to join in the campaign against the Midianites, Judg. 8:1-3. Avenges himself upon the people of Succoth, Judg. 8:14-17. Israel desires to make him king, he refuses, Judg. 8:22-23. Makes an ephod which becomes a snare to the Israelites, Judg. 8:24-27. Had seventy sons, Judg. 8:30. Death of, Judg. 8:32. Faith of, Heb. 11:32.

GIFTS. Psa. 21:2. Thou hast given him his heart's desire, and hast not witholden the request of his lips.

Psa. 34:10. The young lions do lack, and suffer hunger: but they that seek the LORD shall not want any good *thing.*

Psa. 84:11. For the LORD God *is* a sun and shield: the LORD will give grace and glory: no good *thing* will he withhold from them that walk uprightly.

Eccl. 2:26. For *God* giveth to a man that *is* good in his sight wisdom, and knowledge, and joy: but to the sinner he giveth travail, to gather and to heap up, that he may give to *him that is* good before God. This also *is* vanity and vexation of spirit.

Matt. 11:28. Come unto me, all *ye* that labour and are heavy laden, and I will give you rest.

Rom. 6:23. For the wages of sin *is* death; but the gift of God *is* eternal life through Jesus Christ our Lord.

Rom. 8:32. He that spared not his own Son, but delivered him up for us all, how shall he not with him also freely give us all things?

Rom. 11:29. For the gifts and calling of God *are* without repentance.

Rom. 12:6. Having then gifts differing according to the grace that is given to us, whether prophecy, *let us prophesy* according to the proportion of faith; 7. Or ministry, *let us wait* on *our* ministering: or he that teacheth, on teaching; 8. Or he that exhorteth, on exhortation: he that giveth, *let him do it* with simplicity; he that ruleth, with diligence; he that sheweth mercy, with cheerfulness.

1 Cor. 7:7. But every man hath his proper gift of God, one after this manner, and another after that.

Jas. 1:17. Every good gift and every perfect gift is from above, and cometh down from the Father of lights, with whom is no variableness, neither shadow of turning.

GIVING. Rules for: Matt. 6:1. Take heed that ye do not your alms before men, to be seen of them: otherwise ye have no reward of your Father which is in heaven. 2. Therefore when thou doest *thine* alms, do not sound a trumpet before thee, as the hypocrites do in the synagogues and in the streets, that they may have glory of men. Verily I say unto you. They have their reward. 3. But when thou doest alms, let not thy left hand know what thy right hand doeth: 4. That thine alms may be in secret: and thy Father which seeth in secret himself shall reward thee openly.

1 Cor. 16:2. Upon the first *day* of the week let every one of you lay by him in store, as God hath prospered him, [R. V. he may prosper]

2 Cor. 8:11. Now therefore perform the doing *of it;* that as *there was* a readiness to will, so *there may be* a performance also out of that which ye have. 12. For if there be first a willing mind, *it is* accepted according to that a man hath, *and* not according to that he hath not. 14. But by an equality, *that* now at this time your abundance *may be a supply* for their want, that their abundance also may be *a supply* for your want: that there may be equality:

2 Cor. 9:6. But this *I say,* He which soweth sparingly shall reap also sparingly; and he which soweth bountifully shall reap also bountifully. 7. Every man according as

he purposeth in his heart, *so let him give;* not grudgingly, or of necessity: for God loveth a cheerful giver.

GLORIFYING GOD. Commanded, 1 Chr. 16:28; Psa. 22:23; Isa. 42:12. Due to him, 1 Chr. 16:29; for his holiness, Psa. 99:9; Rev. 15:4; mercy and truth, Psa. 115:1; Rom. 15:9; faithfulness and truth, Isa. 25:1; wondrous works, Matt. 15:31; Acts 4:21; judgments, Isa. 25:3; Ezek. 28:22; Rev. 14:7; deliverances, Psa. 50:15; grace to others, Acts 11:18; 2 Cor. 9:13; Gal. 1:24.

All, by nature, fail in, Rom. 3:23. The wicked averse to, Dan. 5:23; Rom. 1:21. Punishment for not, Dan. 5:23,30; Mal. 2:2; Acts 12:23; Rom. 1:21. Heavenly hosts engaged in, Rev. 4:11.

GLORY. God is, to his people, Psa. 3:3; Zech. 2:5. Christ is, to his people, Isa. 60:1; Luke 2:32. The gospel ordained to be, to saints, 1 Cor. 2:7. Of the gospel exceeds that of the law, 2 Cor. 3:9,10. The joy of saints is full of, 1 Pet. 1:8.

Spiritual: Is given by God, Psa. 84:11; is given by Christ, John 17:22; is the work of the Holy Ghost, 2 Cor. 3:18.

Eternal: Procured by the death of Christ, Heb. 2:10; accompanies salvation by Christ, 2 Tim. 2:10; inherited by saints, 1 Sam. 2:8; Psa. 73:24; Prov. 3:35; Col. 3:4; 1 Pet. 5:10; saints called to, 2 Thess. 2:14; 1 Pet. 5:10; saints prepared unto, Rom. 9:23; enhanced by afflictions, 2 Cor. 4:17; present afflictions not worthy to be compared with, Rom. 8:18; of the church shall be rich and abundant, Isa. 60:11-13; bodies of saints shall be raised in, 1 Cor. 15:43; Phil. 3:21; saints shall be, of their ministers, 1 Thess. 2:19,20; afflictions of ministers are, to saints, Eph. 3:13.

Temporal: Is given by God, Dan. 2:37; passeth away, 1 Pet. 1:24. The devil tries to seduce by, Matt. 4:8. Of hypocrites turned to shame, Hos. 4:7. Seek not, from man, Matt. 6:2; 1 Thess. 2:6. Of the wicked is in their shame, Phil. 3:19. Ends in destruction, Is. 5:14.

Of God: Exhibited in Christ, John 1:14; 2 Cor. 4:6; Heb. 1:3. Ascribed to God, Gal. 1:5.

Exhibited in his name, Deut. 28:58; Neh. 9:5; his majesty, Job 37:22; Psa. 93:1; 104:1; 145:5,12; Isa. 2:10; his power, Ex. 15:1,6; Rom. 6:4; his works, Psa. 19:1; 111:3; his holiness, Ex. 15:11.

Described as great, Psa. 138:5; eternal, Psa. 104:31; rich, Eph. 3:16; highly exalted, Psa. 8:1; 113:4.

Exhibited to Moses, Ex. 34:5-7; with Ex. 33:18-23; Stephen, Acts 7:55; his church, Deut. 5:24; Psa. 102:16.

Enlightens the church, Isa. 60:1,2; Rev. 21:11,23. Saints desire to behold, Psa. 63:2; 90:16. God is jealous of, Isa. 42:8. The earth is full of, Isa. 6:3. The knowledge of, shall fill the earth, Hab. 2:14.

GLUTTONY. Ex. 16:20. Notwithstanding they hearkened not unto Moses; but some of them left of it until the morning, and it bred worms, and stank: and Moses was wroth with them.

Num. 11:32. And the people stood up all that day, and all *that* night, and all the next day, and they gathered the quails; he that gathered least gathered ten homers: and they spread *them* all abroad for themselves round about the camp. 33. And while the flesh *was* yet between their teeth, ere it was chewed, the wrath of the LORD was kindled against the people, and the LORD smote the people with a very great plague.

Prov. 23:21. For the drunkard and the glutton shall come to poverty: and drowsiness shall clothe *a man* with rags.

Luke 12:19. And I will say to my soul, Soul, thou hast much goods laid up for many years; take thine ease, eat, drink, *and* be merry. 20. But God said unto him, *Thou* fool, this night thy soul shall be required of thee: then whose shall those things be, which thou hast provided?

Luke 21:34. And take heed to yourselves, lest at any time your hearts be overcharged with sur-feiting, and drunkenness, and cares of this life, and *so* that day come upon you unawares.

Rom. 13:13. Let us walk honestly, as in the day; not in rioting and drunkenness, not in chambering and wantonness, not in strife and envying. 14. But put ye on the Lord Jesus Christ, and make not provision for the flesh, to *fulfill* the lusts *thereof.*

1 Pet. 4:3. For the time past of *our* life may suffice us to have wrought the will of the Gentiles, when we walked in lasciviousness, lusts, excess of wine, revellings, banquetings, and abominable idolatries:

GOD. Unclassified Scriptures Relating to: Job 5:8 I would seek unto God, and unto God would I commit my cause:

Psa. 119:90. Thy faithfulness *is* unto all generations: thou hast established the earth, and it abideth. 91. They continue this day according to thine ordinances: for all *are* thy servants.

Psa. 148:3. Praise ye him, sun and moon: praise him, all ye stars of light. 4. Praise him, ye heavens of heavens, and ye waters that *be* above the heavens. 5. Let him praise the name of the Lord: for he commanded, and they were created. 6. He hath also stablished them for ever and ever: he hath made a decree which shall not pass.

Isa. 2:19. And they shall go into the holes of the rocks, and into the caves of the earth, for fear of the LORD, and for the glory of his majesty, when he ariseth to shake terribly the earth.

Isa. 64:3. When thou didst terrible things *which* we looked not for, thou camest down, the mountains flowed down at thy presence.

Access to: Deut. 4:7. For what nation *is there so* great, who *hath* God *so* nigh unto them, as the LORD our God *is* in all *things that* we call upon him *for?*

Psa. 24:3. Who shall ascend into the hill of the LORD? or who shall stand in his holy place? 4. He that hath clean hands, and a pure heart; who hath not lifted up his soul unto vanity, nor sworn deceitfully.

GOD

Psa. 27:4. One *thing* have I desired of the LORD, that will I seek after; that I may dwell in the house of the LORD all the days of my life, to behold the beauty of the LORD, and to inquire in his temple.

Psa. 43:2. O send out thy light and thy truth: let them lead me; let them bring me unto thy holy hill, and to thy tabernacles.

Psa. 145:18. The LORD *is* nigh unto all them that call upon him, to all that call upon him in truth.

Matt. 6:6. But thou, when thou prayest, enter into thy closet, and when thou hast shut thy door, pray to thy Father which is in secret; and thy Father which seeth in secret shall reward thee openly.

John 14:6. Jesus saith unto him, I am the way, the truth, and the life: no man cometh unto the Father, but by me.

Heb. 4:16. Let us therefore come boldly unto the throne of grace, that we may obtain mercy, and find grace to help in time of need.

Heb. 11:6. But without faith *it is* impossible to please *him:* for he that cometh to God must believe that he is, and *that* he is a rewarder of them that diligently seek him.

Jas. 4:8. Draw nigh to God, and he will draw nigh to you. Cleanse *your* hands, *ye* sinners; and purify *your* hearts, *ye* double minded.

1 Pet. 3:18. For Christ also hath once suffered for sins, the just for the unjust, that he might bring us to God, being put to death in the flesh, but quickened by the Spirit.

Creator: Gen. 1:1. In the beginning God created the heaven and the earth.

1 Chr. 16:26. For all the gods of the people *are* idols: but the LORD made the heavens.

Neh. 9:6. Thou hast made heaven, the heaven of heavens, with all their host, the earth, and all *things* that *are* therein, the seas, and all that *is* therein, and thou preservest them all.

Job 9:8. Which alone spreadeth out the heavens, and treadeth upon the waves of the sea. 9. Which maketh Arcturus, Orion, and Pleiades, and the chambers of the south.

Job 26:7. He stretcheth out the north over the empty place, *and* hangeth the earth upon nothing. 13. By his spirit he hath garnished the heavens; his hand hath formed the crooked serpent. *vss.* 8-12.

Job. 37:16. Dost thou know the balancings of the clouds, the wonderous works of him which is perfect in knowledge? 18. Hast thou with him spread out the sky, *which is* strong, *and* as a molten looking glass?

Psa. 8:3. When I consider thy heavens, the work of thy fingers, the moon and the stars, which thou hast ordained;

Psa. 24:1. The earth *is* the LORD's, and the fulness thereof; the world, and they that dwell therein. 2. For he hath founded it upon the seas, and established it upon the floods.

Rom. 11:36. Of him, and through him, and to him, *are* all things: to whom *be* glory for ever.

Heb. 1:1. God, . . . 2. Hath in these last days spoken unto us by *his* Son, whom he hath appointed heir of all things, by whom also he made the worlds;

Creator of Man: Gen. 1:26. God said, Let us make man in our image, after our likeness: 27. So God created man in his *own* image, in the image of God created he him; male and female created he them. Gen. 2:7.

Job 12:10. In whose hand *is* the soul of every living thing, and the breath of all mankind.

Psa. 95:6. Let us kneel before the LORD our maker.

Eccl. 12:1. Remember now thy Creator in the days of thy youth.

Eternity of: Deut. 33:27. The eternal God *is thy* refuge, and underneath *are* the everlasting arms:

Job 36:26. Neither can the number of his years be searched out.

Psa. 9:7. But the LORD shall endure for ever:

Psa. 41:13. Blessed *be* the LORD God of Israel from everlasting, and to everlasting.

Psa. 93:2. Thy throne *is* established of old: thou *art* from everlasting. Mic. 5:2.

Isa. 44:6. I *am* the first, and I *am* the last; and beside me *there is* no God.

Eph. 3:21. Unto him *be* glory in the church by Christ Jesus throughout all ages, world without end.

1 Tim. 1:17. Unto the King eternal, [immortal], invisible, the only wise God, *be* honour and glory for ever and ever. [R. V. incorruptible]

2 Pet. 3:8. One day *is* with the Lord as a thousand years, and a thousand years as one day.

Faithfulness of: Ex. 34:6. And the Lord passed by before him, and proclaimed, The Lord, The Lord God, merciful and gracious, longsuffering, and abundant in goodness and truth,

Ezra 9:9. For we *were* bondmen; yet our God hath not forsaken us in our bondage, but hath extended mercy unto us.

Psa. 92:1. *It is* a good thing to give thanks unto the Lord, and to sing praises unto thy name, O most High: 2. To shew forth thy lovingkindness in the morning, and thy faithfulness every night. 15. To shew that the Lord *is* upright: *he is* my rock, and *there is* no unrighteousness in him. *v.* 14.

Psa. 100:5. His truth *endureth* to all generations.

Psa. 103:17. The mercy of the Lord *is* from everlasting to everlasting upon them that fear him, and his righteousness unto children's children;

Psa. 121:3. He will not suffer thy foot to be moved: he that keepeth thee will not slumber. 4. Behold, he that keepeth Israel shall neither slumber nor sleep.

Lam. 3:23. Great *is* thy faithfulness.

John 8:26. He that sent me is true:

1 Cor. 10:13. God *is* faithful, who will not suffer you to be tempted above that ye are able;

2 Cor. 1:20. All the promises of God in him *are* yea, and in him Amen,

1 Thess. 5:24. Faithful *is* he that calleth you, who also will do *it*.

Fatherhood of: 2 Sam. 7:14. I will be his father, and he shall be my son. If he commit iniquity, I will chasten him with the rod of men, and with the stripes of the children of men:

Psa. 68:5. A father of the fatherless, and a judge of the widows, *is* God in his holy habitation.

Isa. 9:6. For unto us a child is born, unto us a son is given: and the government shall be upon his shoulder: and his name shall be called Wonderful, Counsellor, The mighty God, The everlasting Father, The Prince of Peace.

Hos. 1:10. *Ye are* the sons of the living God.

Matt. 3:17. And lo a voice from heaven, saying, This is my beloved Son, in whom I am well pleased.

Matt. 5:45. That ye may be the children of your Father which is in heaven:

Luke 2:49. And he said unto them, How is it that ye sought me? wist ye not that I must be about my Father's business?

Rom. 8:15. For ye have not received the spirit of bondage again to fear; but ye have received the Spirit of adoption, whereby we cry, Abba, Father.

Eph. 3:14. For this cause I bow my knees unto the Father of our Lord Jesus Christ.

1 John 3:1. Behold, what manner of love the Father hath bestowed upon us that we should be called the sons of God:

Foreknowledge of: 1 Sam. 23:10. Then said David, O Lord God of Israel, thy servant hath certainly heard that Saul seeketh to come to Keilah, to destroy the city for my sake. 11. Will the men of Keilah deliver me up into his hand? will Saul come down, as thy servant hath heard? O Lord God of Israel, I beseech thee, tell thy servant. And the Lord said, He will come down. 12. Then said David, Will the men of Keilah deliver me and my men into the hand of Saul? And the Lord said, They will deliver *thee* up.

Jer. 1:5. Before I formed thee

in the belly I knew thee; and before thou camest forth out of the womb I sanctified thee, *and* I ordained thee a prophet unto the nations.

Matt. 6:8. Your Father knoweth what things ye have need of, before ye ask him.

Acts 15:18. Known unto God are all his works from the beginning of the world.

See GOD, KNOWLEDGE OF, WISDOM OF; PREDESTINATION.

Glory of: Ex. 24:10. They saw the God of Israel: and *there was* under his feet as it were a paved work of a sapphire stone, and as it were the body of heaven in *his* clearness. 17. And the sight of the glory of the LORD *was* like devouring fire on the top of the mount in the eyes of the children of Israel.

Ex. 33:20. Thou canst not see my face: for there shall no man see me, and live. 22. It shall come to pass, while my glory passeth by, that I will put thee in a clift of the rock, *v.* 23.

Deut. 28:58. That thou mayest fear this glorious and fearful name, THE LORD THY GOD;

Job 37:22. With God *is* terrible majesty. *v.* 4.

Psa. 19:1. The heavens declare the glory of God; and the firmament sheweth his handywork. *vss.* 2-4.

Psa. 46:10. Be still, and know that I *am* God: I will be exalted among the heathen, I will be exalted in the earth.

Psa. 97:2. Clouds and darkness *are* round about him: righteousness and judgment *are* the habitation of his throne.

Isa. 6:1. I saw also the Lord sitting upon a throne, high and lifted up, and his train filled the temple. 3. And one cried unto another, and said, Holy, holy holy, *is* the LORD of hosts: the whole earth *is* full of his glory. *vss.* 1-5.

Isa. 52:10. The LORD hath made bare his holy arm in the eyes of all the nations; and all the ends of the earth shall see the salvation of our God.

Matt. 6:9. Our Father which art in heaven, Hallowed be thy name.

13. Thine is the kingdom, and the power, and the glory, for ever.

Goodness of: Psa. 33:5. The earth is full of the goodness of the LORD.

Psa. 34:8. O taste and see that the LORD *is* good:

Psa. 68:19. Blessed *be* the Lord, *who* daily loadeth us *with benefits, even* the God of our salvation.

Psa. 73:1. Truly God *is* good to Israel, *even* to such as are of a clean heart.

Psa. 107:8. Oh that *men* would praise the LORD *for* his goodness, and *for* his wonderful works to the children of men! 9. For he satisfieth the longing soul, and filleth the hungry soul with goodness.

Nah. 1:7. The LORD *is* good, a strong hold in the day of trouble;

Grace of: Gen. 46:4. I will go down with thee into Egypt; and I will also surely bring thee up *again:*

Lev. 26:11. I will set my tabernacle among you; and my soul shall not abhor you. 12. And I will walk among you, and will be your God.

Psa. 84:11. The LORD will give grace and glory:

Psa. 149:4. The LORD taketh pleasure in his people: he will beautify the meek with salvation.

Prov. 8:35. Whoso findeth me findeth life, and shall obtain favour of the LORD.

Zech. 2:5. For I, saith the LORD, will be unto her a wall of fire round about, and will be the glory in the midst of her.

Zech. 9:16. And the LORD their God shall save them in that day as the flock of his people: for *they shall be as* the stones of a crown, lifted up as an ensign upon his land.

Luke 1:28. Hail, *thou that art* highly favoured, the Lord *is* with thee: [blessed *art* thou among women.] 30. Fear not, Mary: for thou hast found favour with God. 66. The hand of the Lord was with him [Jesus]. [Omitted in R. V.]

John 15:15. I call you not servants; for the servant knoweth not what his lord doeth: but I have called you friends; for all things that I have heard of my Father I have made known unto you.

Heb. 4:16. Let us therefore come boldly unto the throne of grace, that we may obtain mercy, and find grace to help in time of need.

Guide: Gen. 12:1. Now the LORD had said unto Abram, Get thee out of thy country, and from thy kindred, and from thy father's house, unto a land that I will shew thee:

Ex. 13:21. And the LORD went before them by day in a pillar of a cloud, to lead them the way; and by night in a pillar of fire, to give them light; to go by day and night:

Num. 10:33. The ark of the covenant of the LORD went before them in the three days' journey, to search out a resting place for them.

2 Sam. 22:29. For thou *art* my lamp, O LORD: and the LORD will lighten my darkness.

Psa. 5:8. Lead me, O LORD, in thy righteousness because of my enemies; make thy way straight before my face.

Psa. 23:2. He maketh me to lie down in green pastures: he leadeth me beside the still waters. 3. He restoreth my soul: he leadeth me in the paths of righteousness for his name's sake.

Psa. 27:11. Teach me thy way, O LORD, and lead me in a plain path, because of mine enemies.

Psa. 32:8. I will instruct thee and teach thee in the way which thou shalt go: I will guide thee with mine eye.

Psa. 73:24. Thou shalt guide me with thy counsel, and afterward receive me *to* glory.

Psa. 78:52. But made his own people to go forth like sheep, and guided them in the wilderness like a flock.

Psa. 80:1. Give ear, O Shepherd of Israel, thou that leadest Joseph like a flock;

Psa. 107:7. And he led them forth by the right way, that they might go to a city of habitation.

Isa. 42:16. And I will bring the blind by a way *that* they knew not: I will lead them in paths *that* they have not known: I will made darkness light before them, and crooked

things straight. These things will I do unto them, and not forsake them.

Holiness of: Ex. 3:5. Draw not nigh hither: put off thy shoes from off thy feet, for the place whereon thou standest *is* holy ground. Josh. 5:15.

Ex. 15:11. Who *is* like unto thee, O LORD, among the gods? who *is* like thee, glorious in holiness,

Lev. 19:2. Ye shall be holy: for I the LORD your God *am* holy. Lev. 11:44; 20:26; 21:8.

1 Sam. 2:2. *There is* none holy as the LORD:

1 Chr. 16:10. Glory ye in his holy name: Psa. 105:3.

Psa. 18:30. *As for* God, his way *is* perfect:

Isa. 57:15. The high and lofty One that inhabiteth eternity, whose name *is* Holy;

Hab. 1:13. *Thou art* of purer eyes than to behold evil, and canst not look on iniquity:

Rev. 4:8. Holy, holy, holy, Lord God Almighty, Which was, and is, and is to come.

Human Forms and Appearance of: See ANTHROPOMORPHISMS.

Immutable:* Num. 23:19. God *is* not a man, that he should lie; neither the son of man, that he should repent: hath he said, and shall he not do *it?* or hath he spoken, and shall he not make it good?

Psa. 33:11. The counsel of the LORD standeth for ever, the thoughts of his heart to all generations.

Psa. 119:89. For ever, O LORD, thy word is settled in heaven.

Eccl. 3:14. Whatsoever God doeth, it shall be for ever: nothing can be put to it, nor anything taken from it:

Rom. 11:29. For the gifts and calling of God *are* without repentance.

Impartial: Deut. 10:17. For the LORD your God *is* God of gods, and Lord of lords, a great God, a mighty, and a terrible, which re-

*As deduced from the attributes, ETERNITY OF, KNOWLEDGE OF, AND SELF-EXISTENT, see each in its place.

gardeth not persons, nor taketh reward:

Rom. 2:6. Who will render to every man according to his deeds: 11. For there is no respect of persons with God.

Col. 3:25. But he that doeth wrong shall receive for the wrong which he hath done: and there is no respect of persons.

Incomprehensible: Ex. 20:21. And the people stood afar off, and Moses drew near unto the thick darkness where God *was*.

Job 11:7. Canst thou by searching find out God? canst thou find out the Almighty unto perfection?

Isa. 55:8. For my thoughts *are* not your thoughts, neither *are* your ways my ways, saith the LORD. 9. For *as* the heavens are higher than the earth, so are my ways higher than your ways, and my thoughts than your thoughts.

1 Cor. 2:16. For who hath known the mind of the LORD, that he may instruct him?

Infinite: 1 Kin. 8:27. Will God indeed dwell on the earth? behold, the heaven and heaven of heavens cannot contain thee; how much less this house that I have builded? 2 Chr. 2:6; 6:1,18.

Psa. 147:5. Great *is* our Lord, and of great power: his understanding *is* infinite.

Jer. 23:24. Do not I fill heaven and earth? saith the LORD.

Invisible: Ex. 33:20. Thou canst not see my face: for there shall no man see me, and live.

Job. 9:11. Lo, he goeth by me, and I see *him* not: he passeth on also, but I perceive him not.

John 1:18. No man hath seen God at any time; the only begotten Son, which is in the bosom of the Father, he hath declared *him*.

John 5:37. Ye have neither heard his voice at any time, nor seen his shape.

1 Tim. 1:17. Now unto the King eternal, [immortal], invisible, the only wise God, *be* honour and glory for ever and ever. [R. V. incorruptible]

Jealous: Ex. 20:5. I the LORD thy God *am* a jealous God, 7. The LORD will not hold him guiltless that taketh his name in vain. Deut. 5:9,11.

Ex. 34:14. Thou shalt worship no other god: for the LORD, whose name *is* Jealous, *is* a jealous God: Deut. 6:15.

Deut. 4:24. The LORD thy God *is* a consuming fire, *even* a jealous God.

Deut. 32:16. They provoked him to jealousy with strange *gods,* 21. They have moved me to jealousy with *that which is* not God; they have provoked me to anger with their vanities:

II Chr. 16:9. For the eyes of the LORD run to and fro throughout the whole earth, to shew himself strong in the behalf of *them* whose heart *is* perfect toward him.

Judge, and His Justice: Josh. 24:19. Ye cannot serve the LORD: for he *is* an holy God; he *is* a jealous God; he will not forgive your transgressions nor your sins. Ex. 20:5; 34:7.

1 Sam. 24:12. The LORD judge between me and thee, and the LORD avenge me of thee: but mine hand shall not be upon thee. 15. The LORD therefore be judge, and judge between me and thee, and see, and plead my cause, and deliver me out of thine hand.

1 Chr. 16:33. Then shall the trees of the wood sing out at the presence of the LORD, because he cometh to judge the earth.

Job 8:3. Doth God pervert judgment? or doth the Almighty pervert justice?

Psa. 7:9. The righteous God trieth the heart and reins. 11. God judgeth the righteous, and God is angry *with the wicked* every day. *v.* 8; Heb. 10:30.

Psa. 11:4. His eyes behold, his eyelids try, the children of men. 5. The LORD trieth the righteous: but the wicked and him that loveth violence his soul hateth. 7. The righteous LORD loveth righteousness; his countenance doth behold the upright.

Psa. 51:4. Against thee, thee only, have I sinned, and done *this* evil in thy sight: that thou mightest be justified when thou speakest, *and* be clear when thou judgest.

Psa. 89:14. Justice and judgment *are* the habitation of thy throne: mercy and truth shall go before thy face.

Psa. 96:13. He cometh to judge the earth: he shall judge the world with righteousness, and the people with his truth. *v.* 10.

Nah. 1:3. The LORD *is* slow to anger, and great in power, and will not at all acquit *the wicked:* 6. Who can stand before his indignation? and who can abide in the fierceness of his anger? his fury is poured out like fire, and the rocks are thrown down by him.

Acts 17:31. He hath appointed a day, in the which he will judge the world in righteousness by *that* man whom he hath ordained;

Rom. 1:32. Knowing the judgment of God, that they which commit such things are worthy of death,

1 John 1:9. If we confess our sins, he is faithful and just to forgive us *our* sins, and to cleanse us from all unrighteousness.

Jude 6. The angels which kept not their first estate, but left their own habitation, he hath reserved in everlasting chains under darkness unto the judgment of the great day.

Rev. 6:16. Fall on us, and hide us from the face of him that sitteth on the throne, and from the wrath of the Lamb: 17. For the great day of his wrath is come; and who shall be able to stand?

Knowledge of: Gen. 16:13. Thou God seest me:

Ex. 3:7. I have surely seen the affliction of my people which *are* in Egypt, and have heard their cry by reason of their taskmasters; for I know their sorrows; *vs.* 3, 9, 19, 20; Ex. 6:1; 11:1; 14:3,4.

Num. 14:27. I have heard the murmurings of the children of Israel, which they murmur against me.

Deut. 2:7. He knoweth thy walking through this great wilderness: these forty years the LORD thy God *hath been* with thee;

Deut. 31:21. I know their imagi-

nation which they go about, even now, before I have brought them into the land which I sware.

1 Sam. 2:3. The LORD *is* a God of knowledge, and by him actions are weighed. Gen. 20:6.

2 Kin. 19:27. I know thy abode, and thy going out, and thy coming in, and thy rage against me.

1 Chr. 28:9. The LORD searcheth all hearts, and understandeth all the imaginations of the thoughts:

2 Chr. 16:9. The eyes of the LORD run to and fro throughout the whole earth, to shew himself strong in the behalf of *them* whose heart *is* perfect toward him. Zech. 4:10.

Psa. 139:1. O LORD, thou hast searched me, and known *me.* 2. Thou knowest my downsitting and mine uprising, thou understandest my thought afar off. 3. Thou compassest my path and my lying down, and art acquainted *with* all my ways. 4. For *there is* not a word in my tongue, *but,* lo, O LORD, thou knowest it altogether.

Prov. 5:21. The ways of man *are* before the eyes of the LORD, and he pondereth all his goings.

Prov. 15:3. The eyes of the LORD *are* in every place, beholding the evil and the good.

Prov. 24:12. If thou sayest, Behold, we know it not; doth not he that pondereth the heart consider *it?* and he that keepeth thy soul, doth *not* he know *it?* Prov. 21:2.

Isa. 29:15. Woe unto them that seek deep to hide their counsel from the LORD, and their works are in the dark, and they say, Who seeth us? and who knoweth us? 16. Shall the thing framed say of him that framed it, He had no understanding?

Jer. 23:24. Can any hide himself in secret places that I shall not see him? saith the LORD. Do not I fill heaven and earth? saith the LORD.

Jer. 32:19. Great in counsel, and mighty in work: for thine eyes *are* open upon all the ways of the sons of men:

Ezek. 11:5. I know the things that come into your mind, *every one of* them.

Matt. 6:4. Thy Father which

GOD

seeth in secret himself shall reward thee openly. 8. Your Father knoweth what things ye have need of, before ye ask him.

Matt. 10:29. One of them shall not fall on the ground without your Father. 30. But the very hairs of your head are all numbered.

Luke 16:15. God knoweth your hearts:

Longsuffering of: Gen. 6:3. My spirit shall not always strive with man, for that he also *is* flesh: yet his days shall be an hundred and twenty years.

Num. 14:18. The LORD *is* longsuffering, and of great mercy, forgiving iniquity and transgression.

Isa. 30:18. And therefore will the LORD wait, that he may be gracious unto you, and therefore will he be exalted, that he may have mercy upon you:

Isa. 48:9. For my name's sake will I defer mine anger, and for my praise will I refrain for thee, that I cut thee not off. 11. For mine own sake, *even* for mine own sake, will I do *it:* for how should *my name* be polluted? and I will not give my glory unto another.

Matt. 23:37. O Jerusalem, Jerusalem, *thou* that killest the prophets, and stonest them which are sent unto thee, how often would I have gathered thy children together, even as a hen gathereth her chickens under *her* wings, and ye would not! Luke 13:34.

Acts 17:30. And the times of this ignorance God winked at; but now commandeth all men everywhere to repent:

Rom. 2:4. Despisest thou the riches of his goodness and forbearance and longsuffering; not knowing that the goodness of God leadeth thee to repentance?

1 Pet. 3:20. The longsuffering of God waited in the days of Noah,

Longsuffering of, Abused: Neh. 9:28. But after they had rest, they did evil again before thee: therefore leftest thou them in the hand of their enemies, so that they had the dominion over them:

Prov. 29:1. He, that being often reproved hardeneth *his* neck, shall

suddenly be destroyed, and that without remedy.

Eccl. 8:11. Because sentence against an evil work is not executed speedily, therefore the heart of the sons of men is fully set in them to do evil.

Love of: Deut. 4:37. Because he loved thy fathers, therefore he chose their seed after them, Deut. 9:29; I Kin. 8:51-53.

Deut. 23:5. The LORD thy God turned the curse into a blessing unto thee, because the LORD thy God loved thee.

Psa. 42:8. The LORD will command his lovingkindness in the daytime, and in the night his song *shall be* with me,

Psa. 103:13. Like as a father pitieth *his* children, *so* the LORD pitieth them that fear him.

Jer. 31:3. Yea, I have loved thee with an everlasting love: therefore with lovingkindness have I drawn thee.

John 3:16. God so loved the world, that he gave his only begotten Son, that whosoever believeth in him should not perish, but have everlasting life.

Rom. 5:8. God commendeth his love toward us, in that, while we were yet sinners, Christ died for us.

Eph. 2:4. God, who is rich in mercy, for his great love wherewith he loved us, 5. Even when we were dead in sins, hath quickened us together with Christ,

Heb. 12:6. Whom the Lord loveth he chasteneth,

Love of, Exemplified: Ex. 19:4. Ye have seen what I did unto the Egyptians, and *how* I bare you on eagles' wings, and brought you unto myself. 5. Ye shall be a peculiar treasure unto me above all people: 6. Ye shall be unto me a kingdom of priests, and an holy nation.

Lev. 26:12. I will walk among you, and will be your God, and ye shall be my people.

Deut. 4:20. The LORD hath taken you, and brought you forth out of the iron furnace, *even* out of Egypt, to be unto him a people of in heritance, as *ye are* this day.

Deut. 7:7. The Lord did not set his love upon you, nor choose you, because ye were more in number than any people; for ye *were* the fewest of all people: 8. But because the Lord loved you, 13. And he will love thee, and bless thee, and multiply thee:

2 Sam. 7:23. What one nation in the earth *is* like thy people, *even* like Israel, whom God went to redeem for a people to himself,

Psa. 4:3. The Lord hath set apart him that is godly for himself:

Psa. 73:1. Truly God *is* good to Israel, *even* to such as are of a clean heart.

Isa. 54:10. The mountains shall depart, and the hills be removed; but my kindness shall not depart from thee, neither shall the covenant of my peace be removed, saith the Lord that hath mercy on thee.

Isa. 66:13. As one whom his mother comforteth, so will I comfort you;

Jer. 32:41. I will rejoice over them to do them good, and I will plant them in this land assuredly with my whole heart and with my whole soul.

Zech. 2:8. He that toucheth you toucheth the apple of his eye.

Rom. 8:31. If God *be* for us, who *can be* against us? 32. He that spared not his own Son, but delivered him up for us all, how shall he not with him also freely give us all things? 39. Nor height, nor depth, nor any other creature, shall be able to separate us from the love of God, which is in Christ Jesus our Lord.

1 Cor. 2:9. Eye hath not seen, nor ear heard, neither have entered into the heart of man, the things which God hath prepared for them that love him. Isa. 64:4.

Mercy of: Gen. 18:26. If I find in Sodom fifty righteous within the city, then I will spare all the place for their sakes. *vs.* 27-32.

2 Sam. 12:13. Nathan said unto David, The Lord also hath put away thy sin; thou shalt not die.

2 Sam. 24:14. Let us fall now into the hand of the Lord; for his mercies *are* great: 16. When the angel stretched out his hand upon Jerusalem to destroy it, the Lord repented him of the evil, and said to the angel that destroyed the people, It is enough; stay now thine hand.

1 Chr. 16:34. O give thanks unto the Lord; for *he is* good; for his mercy *endureth* for ever.

Psa. 25:6. Remember, O Lord, thy tender mercies and thy lovingkindnesses; for they *have been* ever of old. 8. Good and upright *is* the Lord: therefore will he teach sinners in the way.

Psa. 30:5. His anger *endureth but* a moment; in his favour *is* life: weeping may endure for a night, but joy *cometh* in the morning.

Psa. 32:1. Blessed *is he whose* transgression *is* forgiven, *whose* sin *is* covered. 2. Blessed *is* the man unto whom the Lord imputeth not iniquity, 5. I said, I will confess my transgressions unto the Lord; and thou forgavest the iniquity of my sin.

Psa. 62:12. Unto thee, O Lord, *belongeth* mercy:

Ezek. 33:11. *As* I live, saith the Lord God, I have no pleasure in the death of the wicked; but that the wicked turn from his way and live: turn ye, turn ye from your evil ways; for why will ye die, O house of Israel?

Luke 1:50. His mercy *is* on them that fear him from generation to generation.

2 Cor. 12:9. My grace is sufficient for thee: for my strength is made perfect in weakness.

Tit. 3:5. Not by works of righteousness which we have done, but according to his mercy he saved us, by the washing of regeneration, and renewing of the Holy Ghost;

Heb. 4:16. Let us therefore come boldly unto the throne of grace, that we may obtain mercy, and find grace to help in time of need.

Jas. 4:8. Draw nigh to God, and he will draw nigh to you.

Jas. 5:11. The Lord is very pitiful, and of tender mercy. 15. If he have committed sins, they shall be forgiven him.

1 John 1:9. If we confess our sins, he is faithful and just to forgive us *our* sins, and to cleanse us from all unrighteousness.

Omnipotent: Gen. 18:14. Is any thing too hard for the LORD?

Job 42:2. I know that thou canst do every *thing,*

Matt. 19:26. With God all things are possible.

Rev. 19:6. The Lord God omnipotent reigneth.

Omnipresent: Gen. 28:16. Surely the LORD is in this place; and I knew *it* not.

Psa. 139:3. Thou compassest my path, and my lying down, 5. Thou hast beset me behind and before, and laid thine hand upon me. 7. Whither shall I go from thy spirit? or whither shall I flee from thy presence? 8. If I ascend up into heaven, thou *art* there: if I make my bed in hell, behold thou *art* there. 9. *If* I take the wings of the morning, *and* dwell in the uttermost parts of the sea; 10. Even there shall thy hand lead me, and thy right hand shall hold me.

Perfection of: 2 Sam. 22:31. *As for* God, his way *is* perfect; the word of the LORD *is* tried: Psa. 18:30.

Matt. 5:48. Be ye therefore perfect, even as your Father which is in heaven is perfect.

Personality of: Ex. 15:11. Who *is* like unto thee, O LORD, among the gods? who *is* like thee, glorious in holiness, fearful *in* praises, doing wonders?

Deut. 10:17. The LORD your God *is* God of gods, and Lord of lords,

2 Sam. 22:32. Who *is* God, save the LORD? and who *is* a rock, save our God? Psa. 18:31.

Jer. 32:27. I *am* the LORD, the God of all flesh: is there any thing too hard for me?

Hos. 13:4. Thou shalt know no god but me: for *there is* no saviour beside me.

John 14:9. He that hath seen me hath seen the Father; and how sayest thou *then,* Shew us the Father?

1 Tim. 2:5. *There is* one God,

and one mediator between God and men, the man Christ Jesus;

Power of: Num. 11:23. Is the LORD's hand waxed short? thou shalt see now whether my word shall come to pass unto thee or not. Deut. 11:2.

Deut. 7:21. The LORD thy God *is* among you, a mighty God and terrible.

1 Sam. 14:6. *There is* no restraint to the LORD to save by many or by few.

2 Chr. 16:9. The eyes of the LORD run to and fro throughout the whole earth, to shew himself strong in the behalf of *them* whose heart *is* perfect toward him,

Job 42:2. I know that thou canst do every *thing,*

Psa. 33:9. He spake, and it was *done;* he commanded, and it stood fast.

Psa. 46:6. The heathen raged, the kingdoms were moved: he uttered his voice, the earth melted.

Psa. 76:6. At thy rebuke, O God of Jacob, both the chariot and horse are cast into a dead sleep. 7. Who may stand in thy sight when once thou art angry?

Psa. 77:14. Thou *art* the God that doest wonders: thou hast declared thy strength among the people.

Psa. 89:8. O LORD God of hosts, who *is* a strong LORD like unto thee?

Psa. 144:5. Bow thy heavens, O LORD, and come down: touch the mountains, and they shall smoke.

Psa. 145:16. Thou openest thine hand, and satisfiest the desire of every living thing.

Isa. 50:2. Is my hand shortened at all, that it cannot redeem? or have I no power to deliver? behold, at my rebuke I dry up the sea, I make the rivers a wilderness: 3. I clothe the heavens with blackness, and I make sackcloth their covering.

Isa. 59:1. The LORD's hand is not shortened, that it cannot save: neither his ear heavy, that it cannot hear:

Dan. 3:17. Our God whom we serve is able to deliver us from the burning fiery furnace, and he will deliver *us* out of thine hand, O king.

Presence of: Gen. 28:16. Surely the LORD is in this place; and I knew *it* not.

Jer. 23:23. *Am* I a God at hand, saith the LORD, and not a God afar off? 24. Can any hide himself in secret places that I shall not see him? saith the LORD. Do not I fill heaven and earth? saith the LORD.

Jer. 32:18. The Great, the Mighty God, the LORD of hosts *is* his name; 19. Great in counsel, and mighty in work: for thine eyes *are* open upon all the ways of the sons of men: to give every one according to his ways, and according to the fruit of his doings:

Preserver: Gen. 28:15. I *am* with thee, and will keep thee in all *places* whither thou goest, and will bring thee again into this land; for I will not leave thee, until I have done *that* which I have spoken to thee of. Gen. 31:3,13.

Ex. 9:26. Only in the land of Goshen, where the children of Israel *were*, was there no hail.

Ex. 14:29. But the children of Israel walked upon dry *land* in the midst of the sea; and the waters *were* a wall unto them on their right hand, and on their left. 30. Thus the LORD saved Israel that day out of the hand of the Egyptians; and Israel saw the Egyptians dead upon the sea shore.

Ex. 23:20. I send an Angel before thee, to keep thee in the way, and to bring thee into the place which I have prepared. *vs.* 21-31.

Deut. 32:10. He found him in a desert land, and in the waste howling wilderness; he led him about, he instructed him, he kept him as the apple of his eye.

Deut. 33:12. The beloved of the LORD shall dwell in safety by him; *and the Lord* shall cover him all the day long, and he shall dwell between his shoulders. 25. Thy shoes *shall be* iron and brass; and as thy days, *so shall* thy strength *be*. 27. The eternal God *is thy* refuge, and underneath *are* the everlasting arms: and he shall thrust out the

enemy from before thee; and shall say, Destroy *them*.

2 Chr. 16:9. The eyes of the LORD run to and fro throughout the whole earth, to shew himself strong in the behalf of *them* whose heart *is* perfect toward him.

Psa. 41:1. Blessed *is* he that considereth the poor: the LORD will deliver him in time of trouble. 2. The LORD will preserve him, and keep him alive; *and* he shall be blessed upon the earth: and thou wilt not deliver him unto the will of his enemies. 3. The LORD will strengthen him upon the bed of languishing: thou wilt make all his bed in his sickness.

Psa. 46:1. God *is* our refuge and strength, a very present help in trouble. 5. God *is* in the midst of her; she shall not be moved: God shall help her, *and that* right early. 7. The LORD of hosts *is* with us; the God of Jacob *is* our refuge.

Psa. 50:15. Call upon me in the day of trouble: I will deliver thee, and thou shalt glorify me.

Psa. 84:11. For the LORD God *is* a sun and shield: the LORD will give grace and glory. no good *thing* will he withhold from them that walk uprightly.

Psa. 91:1. He that dwelleth in the secret place of the most High shall abide under the shadow of the Almighty. 3. Surely he shall deliver thee from the snare of the fowler, *and* from the noisome pestilence. 4. He shall cover thee with his feathers, and under his wings shalt thou trust: his truth *shall be thy* shield and buckler. 7. A thousand shall fall at thy side, and ten thousand at thy right hand; *but* it shall not come nigh thee. 9. Because thou hast made the LORD, *which is* my refuge, *even* the most High, thy habitation; 10. There shall no evil befall thee, neither shall any plague come nigh thy dwelling. 14. Because he hath set his love upon me, therefore will I deliver him: I will set him on high, because he hath known my name. 15. He shall call upon me, and I will answer him: I *will be* with him in trouble;

I will deliver him, and honour him. *vss*. 1-16.

Psa. 103:2. Bless the LORD, O my soul, and forget not all his benefits: 3. Who forgiveth all thine iniquities; who healeth all thy disease; 4. Who redeemeth thy life from destruction; who crowneth thee with lovingkindness and tender mercies; 5. Who satisfieth thy mouth with good *things; so that* thy youth is renewed like the eagle's.

Psa. 107:9. He satisfieth the longing soul, and filleth the hungry soul with goodness. 10. Such as sit in darkness and in the shadow of death, *being* bound in affliction and iron;

Psa. 112:4. Unto the upright there ariseth light in the darkness: *he is* gracious, and full of compassion, and righteous.

Psa. 121:3. He will not suffer thy foot to be moved: he that keepeth thee will not slumber. 4. Behold, he that keepeth Israel shall neither slumber nor sleep. 7. The LORD shall preserve thee from all evil: he shall preserve thy soul. 8. The LORD shall preserve thy going out and thy coming in from this time forth, and even for evermore. *vss*. 5,6.

Psa. 127:1. Except the LORD build the house, they labour in vain that build it: except the LORD keep the city, the watchman waketh *but* in vain.

Prov. 3:6. In all thy ways acknowledge him, and he shall direct thy paths. 23. Then shalt thou walk in thy way safely, and thy foot shall not stumble. 24. When thou liest down, thou shalt not be afraid: yea, thou shalt lie down, and thy sleep shall be sweet.

Prov. 14:26. In the fear of the LORD *is* strong confidence: and his children shall have a place of refuge.

Prov. 15:19. The way of the righteous *is* made plain.

Prov. 16:9. A man's heart deviseth his way: but the LORD directeth his steps.

Isa. 30:21. Thine ears shall hear a word behind thee, saying, This *is* the way, walk ye in it, when ye turn to the right hand, and when ye turn to the left.

Isa. 40:31. They that wait upon the LORD shall renew *their* strength; they shall mount up with wings as eagles; they shall run, and not be weary; *and* they shall walk, and not faint.

Isa. 43:2. When thou passest through the waters, I *will be* with thee; and through the rivers, they shall not overflow thee: when thou walkest through the fire, thou shalt not be burned; neither shall the flame kindle upon thee.

Isa. 46:4. And *even* to *your* old age I *am* he; and *even* to hoar hairs will I carry *you*: I have made, and I will bear; even I will carry, and will deliver *you*. *v*. 3.

Isa. 48:17. I *am* the LORD thy God which teacheth thee to profit, which leadeth thee by the way *that* thou shouldest go.

Isa. 54:17. No weapon that is formed against thee shall prosper; and every tongue *that* shall rise against thee in judgment thou shalt condemn. This *is* the heritage of the servants of the LORD, and their righteousness *is* of me, saith the LORD.

Isa. 58:11. The LORD shall guide thee continually, and satisfy thy soul in drought, and make fat thy bones: and thou shalt be like a watered garden, and like a spring of water, whose waters fail not.

Isa. 59:19. When the enemy shall come in like a flood, the Spirit of the LORD shall lift up a standard against him.

Ezek. 11:16. Thus saith the Lord GOD; . . . although I have scattered them among the countries, yet will I be to them as a little sanctuary in the countries where they shall come.

Providence of: Gen. 1:29. And God; said, Behold, I have given you every herb bearing seed, which *is* upon the face of all the earth, and every tree, in the which *is* the fruit of a tree yielding seed; to you it shall be for meat. 30. To every beast of the earth, and to every fowl of the air, and to every thing that creepeth upon the earth, wherein *there is* life, I *have given* every green herb for meat:

Gen. 8:22. While the earth remaineth, seed time and harvest, and cold and heat, and summer and winter, and day and night shall not cease.

Deut. 1:10. The Lord your God hath multiplied you, and, behold, ye *are* this day as the stars of heaven for multitude.

Deut. 2:7. The Lord thy God hath blessed thee in all the works of thy hand: he knoweth thy walking through this great wilderness: these forty years the Lord thy God *hath been* with thee; thou hast lacked nothing.

Deut. 4:4. Ye that did cleave unto the Lord your God *are* alive every one of you this day. *v.* 40; Num. 10:29; Deut. 6:2-25; 5:33; 12:28.

Deut. 15:4. Save when there shall be no poor among you; for the Lord shall greatly bless thee in the land which the Lord thy God giveth thee *for* an inheritance to possess it: 5. Only if thou carefully hearken unto the voice of the Lord thy God, . . . 6. For the Lord thy God blesseth thee, as he promised thee: and thou shalt lend unto many nations, but thou shalt not borrow; and thou shalt reign over many nations, but they shall not reign over thee. Deut. 26:19; 28:2-13.

Deut. 29:5. I have led you forty years in the wilderness: your clothes are not waxen old upon you, and thy shoe is not waxen old upon thy foot. Deut. 8:4.

Josh. 1:8. This book of the law shall not depart out of thy mouth; . . . for then thou shalt make thy way prosperous, and then thou shalt have good success.

1 Sam. 2:7. The Lord maketh poor, and maketh rich: he bringeth low, and lifteth up.

2 Chr. 20:17. Ye shall not *need* to fight in this *battle:* set yourselves, stand ye *still,* and see the salvation of the Lord with you, O Judah and Jerusalem: fear not, nor be dismayed; tomorrow go out against them: for the Lord *will be* with you. *vs.* 3-30.

2 Chr. 31:10. Since *the people* began to bring the offerings into the house of the Lord, we have had enough to eat, and have left plenty: for the Lord hath blessed his people; and that which is left *is* this great store.

Psa. 23:1. The Lord *is* my shepherd; I shall not want. 2. He maketh me to lie down in green pastures: he leadeth me beside the still waters. 3. He restoreth my soul: he leadeth me in the paths of righteousness for his name's sake. 4. Yea, though I walk through the valley of the shadow of death, I will fear no evil: for thou *art* with me; thy rod and thy staff they comfort me. 5. Thou preparest a table before me in the presence of mine enemies: thou anointest my head with oil; my cup runneth over. 6. Surely goodness and mercy shall follow me all the days of my life: and I will dwell in the house of the Lord for ever.

Psa. 34:7. The angel of the Lord encampeth round about them that fear him, and delivereth them. 9. O fear the Lord, ye his saints: for *there is* no want to them that fear him. 10. The young lions do lack, and suffer hunger: but they that seek the Lord shall not want any good *thing.*

Psa. 37:3. Trust in the Lord, and do good; *so* shalt thou dwell in the land, and verily thou shalt be fed.

Psa. 104:10. He sendeth the springs into the valleys, *which* run among the hills. 11. They give drink to every beast of the field: the wild asses quench their thirst. 12. By them shall the fowls of the heaven have their habitation, *which* sing among the branches. 13. He watereth the hills from his chambers: the earth is satisfied with the fruit of thy works. 14. He causeth the grass to grow for the cattle, and herb for the service of man: that he may bring forth food out of the earth; 15. And wine *that* maketh glad the heart of man, *and* oil to make *his* face to shine, and bread *which* strengtheneth man's heart. 16. The trees of the Lord are full *of sap;* the cedars of Lebanon, which he hath planted; 17. Where the birds make their nests: *as for* the stork, the fir trees *are* her house. 18. The high hills *are* a refuge for the wild goats; *and* the rocks for the conies. 19. He appointed the moon for seasons: the sun knoweth his going down. 24. O LORD, how manifold are thy works! in wisdom hast thou made them all: the earth is full of thy riches. 25. *So is* this great and wide sea, wherein *are* things creeping innumerable, both small and great beasts. 26. There go the ships: *there is* that leviathan, *whom* thou hast made to play therein. 27. These wait all upon thee; that thou mayest give *them* their meat in due season. 28. *That* thou givest them they gather: thou openest thine hand, they are filled with good. 29. Thou hidest thy face, they are troubled: thou takest away their breath, they die, and return to their dust. 30. Thou sendest forth thy spirit, they are created: and thou renewest the face of the earth.

Psa. 107:1. O give thanks unto the LORD, for *he is* good: for his mercy *endureth* for ever. 2. Let the redeemed of the LORD say *so*, whom he hath redeemed from the hand of the enemy; 3. And gathered them out of the lands, from the east, and from the west, from the north, and from the south. 4. They wandered in the wilderness in a solitary way; they found no city to dwell in. 5. Hungry and thirsty, their soul fainted in them. 6. Then they cried unto the LORD in their trouble, *and* he delivered them out of their distresses. 7. And he led them forth by the right way, that they might go to a city of habitation. 8. Oh that *men* would praise the LORD *for* his goodness, and *for* his wonderful works to the children of men! 9. For he satisfieth the longing soul, and filleth the hungry soul with goodness.

Psa. 128:2. Thou shalt eat the labour of thine hands: happy *shalt* thou *be*, and *it shall be* well with thee. 3. Thy wife *shall be* as a fruitful vine by the sides of thine house: thy children like olive plants

round about thy table. 4. Behold, that thus shall the man be blessed that feareth the LORD.

Prov. 10:22. The blessing of the LORD, it maketh rich, and he addeth no sorrow with it. 27. The fear of the LORD prolongeth days:

Hos. 2:8. She did not know that I gave her corn, and wine, and oil, and multiplied her silver and gold.

Hos. 11:3. I taught Ephraim also to go, taking them [by their] arms; but they knew not that I healed them. [R. V. on my]

Amos 4:7. And also I have withholden the rain from you, when *there were* yet three months to the harvest: and I caused it to rain upon one city, and caused it not to rain upon another city: one piece was rained upon, and the piece whereupon it rained not withered. 8. So two *or* three cities wandered unto one city, to drink water; but they were not satisfied: yet have ye not returned unto me, saith the LORD. 9. I have smitten you with blasting and mildew: when your gardens and your vineyards and your fig trees and your olive trees increased, the palmerworm devoured *them:* yet have ye not returned unto me, saith the LORD.

Hag. 2:19. Is the seed yet in the barn? yea, as yet the vine, and the fig tree, and the pomegranate, and the olive tree, hath not brought forth: from this day will I bless *you*.

Zech. 10:1. Ask ye of the LORD rain in the time of the latter rain; *so* the LORD shall make bright clouds, and give them showers of rain, to every one grass in the field.

Mal. 3:10. Bring ye all the tithes into the storehouse, that there may be meat in mine house, and prove me now herewith, saith the LORD of hosts, if I will not open you the windows of heaven, and pour you out a blessing, that *there shall* not *be room* enough *to receive it*. 12. All nations shall call you blessed: for ye shall be a delightsome land, saith the LORD of hosts. *v*. 11.

Matt. 5:45. He maketh his sun to rise on the evil and on the good, and sendeth rain on the just and on the unjust.

2 Cor. 9:8. And God *is* able to make all grace abound toward you; that ye, always having all sufficiency in all *things*, may abound to every good work: 9. (As it is written, He hath dispersed abroad; he hath given to the poor: his righteousness re- remaineth for ever. 10. Now he that ministereth seed to the sower both minister bread for *your* food, and multiply your seed sown, and in- crease the fruits of your righteous- ness;)

Providence of, Overruling Interpositions of the: Gen. 50:20. As for you, ye thought evil against me; *but* God meant it unto good, to bring to pass, as *it is* this day, to save much people alive. Gen. 45:5-7; Psa. 105:17; Acts 7:9,10.

2 Sam. 17:14. For the LORD had appointed to defeat the good counsel of Ahithophel, to the intent that the LORD might bring evil upon Absalom.

Neh. 6:16. And it came to pass, that when all our enemies heard *thereof*, and all the heathen that *were* about us saw *these things*, they were much cast down in their own eyes: for they perceived that this work was wrought of our God.

Prov. 19:21. *There are* many de- vices in a man's heart; nevertheless the counsel of the LORD, that shall stand.

Isa. 43:14. Thus saith the LORD, your redeemer, the Holy One of Israel; For your sake I have sent to Babylon, and have brought down all their nobles, and the Chaldeans, whose cry *is* in the ships.

Isa. 44:28. That saith of Cyrus, *He is* my shepherd, and shall per- form all my pleasure: even saying to Jerusalem, Thou shalt be built; and to the temple, Thy foundation shall be laid.

Rom. 8:28. All things work to- gether for good to them that love God, to them who are the called according to *his* purpose.

Phil. 1:12. But I would ye should understand, brethren, that the things *which happened* unto me have fallen out rather unto the furtherance of the gospel;

Providence of, Mysterious and Misinterpreted: Job 12:6. The tabernacles of robbers prosper, and they that provoke God are secure; into whose hand God bringeth *abundantly*.

Job 21:7. Wherefore do the wicked live, become old, yea, are mighty in power?

Psa. 10:5. Thy judgments *are* far above out of his sight:

Psa. 73:2. But as for me, my feet were almost gone; my steps had well nigh slipped. 3. For I was envious at the foolish, *when* I saw the pros- perity of the wicked. 13. Verily I have cleansed my heart *in* vain, and washed my hands in innocency. 14. For all the day long have I been plagued, and chastened every morn- ing. 15. If I say, I will speak thus; behold, I should offend *against* the generation of thy children. 16. When I thought to know this, it *was* too painful for me; 17. Until I went into the sanctuary of God; *then* understood I their end. *vss.* 4,5,12.

INSTANCES OF: Elijah's trials, 1 Kin. 19. Job's, Job 3:19-23, with chapters 1; 2. Israelites, Ex. 5:20- 23.

Righteousness of: Psa. 71:15. My mouth shall shew forth thy righteousness *and* thy salvation all the day; for I know not the num- bers *thereof*. 19. Thy righteousness also, O God, *is* very high, who hast done great things: O God, who *is* like unto thee!

Psa. 97:2. Clouds and darkness *are* round about him: righteousness and judgment *are* the habitation of his throne.

Psa. 111:3. His work *is* honour- able and glorious: and his right- eousness endureth for ever.

Psa. 119:137. Righteous *art* thou, O LORD, and upright *are* thy judg- ments. 142. Thy righteousness *is* an everlasting righteousness, and thy law *is* the truth. 144. The righteous- ness of thy testimonies *is* everlast- ing: *v.* 172.

Matt. 6:33. But seek ye first the kingdom of God, and his righteousness; and all these things shall be added unto you.

Rom. 9:14. What shall we say then? Is there unrighteousness with God? God forbid.

2 Tim. 4:8. Henceforth there is laid up for me a crown of righteousness, which the Lord, the righteous judge, shall give me at that day: and not to me only, but unto all them also that love his appearing.

1 John 2:1. And if any man sin, we have an advocate with the Father, Jesus Christ the righteous:

Saviour: Ex. 15:2. The LORD is my strength and song, and he is become my salvation:

Psa. 19:14. Let the words of my mouth, and the meditation of my heart, be acceptable in thy sight, O LORD, my strength, and my redeemer.

Psa. 25:5. Thou art the God of my salvation; on thee do I wait all the day.

Psa. 27:1. The LORD is my light and my salvation; whom shall I fear? the LORD is the strength of my life; of whom shall I be afraid?

Isa. 12:2. Behold, God is my salvation; I will trust, and not be afraid: for the LORD JEHOVAH is my strength and my song; he also is become my salvation.

Isa. 44:22. I have blotted out, as a thick cloud, thy transgressions, and, as a cloud, thy sins: return unto me; for I have redeemed thee.

Isa. 45:21. There is no God else beside me; a just God and a Saviour; there is none beside me. 22. Look unto me, and be ye saved, all the ends of the earth: for I am God, and there is none else.

Isa. 60:16. Thou shalt know that I the LORD am thy Saviour and thy Redeemer, the mighty One of Jacob.

John 3:16. God so loved the world, that he gave his only begotten Son, that whosoever believeth in him should not perish, but have everlasting life. 17. For God sent not his Son into the world to condemn the world; but that the world through him might be saved.

Rom. 1:16. I am not ashamed of the gospel of Christ: for it is the power of God unto salvation to every one that believeth:

Rom. 6:23. The gift of God is eternal life through Jesus Christ our LORD.

1 Cor. 1:18. For the preaching of the cross is to them that perish foolishness; but unto us which are saved it is the power of God.

Self-existent: Ex. 3:14. And God said unto Moses, I AM THAT I AM: and he said, Thus shalt thou say unto the children of Israel, I AM hath sent me unto you.

Deut. 32:40. For I lift up my hand to heaven, and say, I live for ever.

John 5:26. For as the Father hath life in himself; so hath he given to the Son to have life in himself;

Sovereign: Gen. 24:3. And I will make thee swear by the LORD, the God of heaven, and the God of the earth,

Ex. 15:18. The LORD shall reign for ever and ever.

Ex. 18:11. Now I know that the LORD is greater than all gods: for in the thing wherein they dealt proudly he was above them.

Neh. 9:6. Thou, even thou, art LORD alone; thou hast made heaven, the heaven of heavens, with all their host, the earth, and all things that are therein, the seas, and all that is therein, and thou preservest them all; and the host of heaven worshippeth thee.

Job. 41:11. Whatsoever is under the whole heaven is mine.

Psa. 10:16. The LORD is King for ever and ever: the heathen are perished out of his land.

Psa. 29:10. The LORD sitteth upon the flood; yea, the LORD sitteth King for ever.

Psa. 93:1. The LORD reigneth, he is clothed with majesty; the LORD is clothed with strength, wherewith he hath girded himself: the world also is stablished, that it cannot be moved. 2. Thy throne is established of old: thou art from everlasting.

Psa. 95:3. The LORD is a great God, and a great King above all gods. 4. In his hand are the deep places of the earth: the strength of the hills *is* his also. 5. The sea *is* his, and he made it: and his hands formed the dry *land*.

Dan. 4:3. His kingdom *is* an everlasting kingdom, and his dominion *is* from generation to generation. 17. The most High ruleth in the kingdom of men, and giveth it to whomsoever he will, and setteth up over it the basest of men.

Matt. 6:10. Thy kingdom come. Thy will be done in earth, as *it is* in heaven. 13. [Thine is the kingdom, and the power, and the glory, for ever.] [Omitted in R. V.]

Matt. 11:25. At that time Jesus answered and said, I thank thee, O Father, Lord of heaven and earth, Luke 10:21.

Rom. 14:11. *As* I live, saith the Lord, every knee shall bow to me, and every tongue shall confess to God.

1 Tim. 6:15. Which in his times he shall shew, *who is* the blessed and only Potentate, the King of kings, and Lord of lords;

Rev. 19:6. And I heard as it were the voice of a great multitude, and as the voice of many waters, and as the voice of mighty thunderings, saying Alleluia: for the Lord God omnipotent reigneth.

A Spirit: John 4:24. God *is* a Spirit: and they that worship him must worship *him* in spirit and in truth.

Truth: 1 Sam. 15:29. And also the Strength of Israel will not lie nor repent: for he *is* not a man, that he should repent.

Psa. 33:4. For the word of the Lord *is* right; and all his works *are done* in truth.

Psa. 43:3. O send out thy light and thy truth: let them lead me; let them bring me unto thy holy hill, and to thy tabernacles.

Psa. 89:14. Mercy and truth shall go before thy face.

Psa. 100:5. For the Lord *is* good; his mercy *is* everlasting; and his truth *endureth* to all generations.

Psa. 138:2. I will worship toward thy holy temple, and praise thy name for thy lovingkindness and for thy truth: for thou hast magnified thy word above all thy name.

John 8:26. But he that sent me is true; and I speak to the world those things which I have heard of him.

John 17:17. Sanctify them through thy truth: thy word is truth.

Ubiquitous: 1 Kin. 8:27. Will God indeed dwell on the earth? behold, the heaven and heaven of heavens cannot contain thee; how much less this house that I have builded? 2 Chr. 2:6; Acts 7:48,49.

1 Kin. 20:28. Thus saith the Lord, Because the Syrians have said, The Lord *is* God of the hills, but he *is* not God of the valleys, therefore will I deliver all this great multitude into thine hand, and ye shall know that I *am* the Lord.

Jer. 23:23. *Am* I a God at hand, saith the Lord, and not a God afar off? 24. Can any hide himself in secret places that I shall not see him? saith the Lord. Do not I fill heaven and earth? saith the Lord.

Unity of: Deut. 6:4. Hear, O Israel: The Lord our God *is* one Lord: Mark 12:29.

Gal. 3:20. Now a mediator is not *a mediator* of one, but God is one.

1 Tim. 2:5. For *there is* one God, and one mediator between God and men, the man Christ Jesus.

Jas. 2:19. Thou believest that there is one God; thou doest well: the devils also believe, and tremble.

Unsearchable: Deut. 29:29. The secret *things belong* unto the Lord our God:

Judg. 13:18. And the angel of the Lord said unto him, Why askest thou thus after my name, seeing it *is* secret? Gen. 32:29.

Job 11:7. Canst thou by searching find out God? canst thou find out the Almighty unto perfection?

Job 36:26. Behold, God *is* great, and we know *him* not, neither can the number of his years be searched out.

Job 37:5. Great things doeth he, which we cannot comprehend. 23. *Touching* the Almighty, we cannot find him out:

Psa. 92:5. O Lord, how great

are thy works! *and* thy thoughts are very deep.

Prov. 25:2. *It is* the glory of God to conceal a thing:

Isa. 55:9. For *as* the heavens are higher than the earth, so are my ways higher than your ways, and my thoughts than your thoughts.

Rom. 11:33. O the depth of the riches both of the wisdom and knowledge of God! how unsearchable *are* his judgments, and his ways past finding out! 34. For who hath known the mind of the Lord? or who hath been his counsellor?

Wisdom of: Psa. 104:24. O Lord, how manifold are thy works! in wisdom hast thou made them all: the earth is full of thy riches.

Psa. 136:5. Him that by wisdom made the heavens:

Psa. 147:5. Great *is* our LORD, and of great power: his understanding *is* infinite.

Prov. 3:19. The LORD by wisdom hath founded the earth; by understanding hath he established the heavens. 20. By his knowledge the depths are broken up, and the clouds drop down the dew.

Works of: Psa. 75:1. Unto thee, O God, do we give thanks, *unto thee* do we give thanks: for *that* thy name is near thy wondrous works declare.

Psa. 111:2. The works of the LORD *are* great, sought out of all them that have pleasure therein. 4. He hath made his wonderful works to be remembered: 6. He hath shewed his people the power of his works,

Psa. 139:14. I will praise thee; for I am fearfully *and* wonderfully made: marvellous *are* thy works: and *that* my soul knoweth right well.

See Job 9; and chapters 37-41; Psalms 8; 19; 89; 104; 111; 145; 147; 148; Jer. 10:12.

GODLESSNESS. Deut. 32:15. He forsook God *which* made him, and lightly esteemed the Rock of his salvation.

Psa. 2:2. The kings of the earth set themselves, and the rulers take counsel together, against the LORD,

and against his anointed. 4. He that sitteth in the heavens shall laugh: the Lord shall have them in derision.

Psa. 9:17. The wicked shall be turned into hell, *and* all the nations that forget God.

Psa. 14:2. The LORD looked down from heaven upon the children of men, to see if there were any that did understand, *and* seek God. 3. They are all gone aside, Psa. 53:2,3; Rom. 3:11,18.

Mal. 3:8. Will a man rob God? Yet ye have robbed me. But ye say, Wherein have we robbed thee?

John 5:44. How can ye believe, which receive honour one of another, and seek not the honour that *cometh* from God only?

John 15:23. He that hateth me, 1 teth my Father also. 24. But now h e they both seen and hated both me and my Father. 25. They hated me without a cause.

Rom. 1:21. When they knew God, they glorified *him* not as God, neither were thankful; but became vain in their imaginations, and their foolish heart was darkened. 22. Professing themselves to be wise, they became fools, 28. As they did not like to retain God in *their* knowledge, God gave them over to a reprobate mind,

Heb. 10:26. For if we sin wilfully after that we have received the knowledge of the truth, there remaineth no more sacrifice for sins, 27. But a certain fearful looking for of judgment and fiery indignation, which shall devour the adversaries.

GOLD.

Figurative: Eccl. 12:6; Jer. 51: 7; Lam. 4:1; 1 Cor. 3:12.

SYMBOLICAL: Dan: 2:32-45; Rev. 21:18,21.

GOLDEN RULE. Lev. 19:18. Thou shalt love thy neighbor as thyself: I *am* the LORD. Rom. 13:9; Gal. 5:14.

Matt. 7:12. Therefore all things whatsoever ye would that men should do to you, do ye even so to them; for this is the law and the prophets.

GOOD FOR EVIL. Matt. 5:44. But I say unto you, Love your enemies, bless them that curse you, do good to them that hate you, and pray for them which despitefully use you, and persecute you; 45. That ye may be the children of your Father which is in heaven:

Luke 6:32. For if ye love them which love you, what thank have ye? for sinners also love those that love them.

GOSPEL. Called GOSPEL OF THE KINGDOM, Matt. 4:23; 24:14; GOSPEL OF GOD, Rom. 1:1; 15:16; 1 Thess. 2:8; 1 Tim. 1:11; 1 Pet. 4: 17; GOSPEL OF JESUS CHRIST, Mark 1:1; GOSPEL OF CHRIST, Rom. 1:16; 1 Cor. 9:12,18; Gal. 1:7; Phil 1:27; 1 Thess. 3:2; THE Dispensation OF THE GRACE OF GOD, Eph. 3:2; THE GRACE OF GOD, Acts 20:24; GOSPEL OF SALVATION, Eph. 1:13; GOSPEL OF PEACE, Eph 6:15; THE KINGDOM OF GOD, Luke 16:16; GLORIOUS GOSPEL OF CHRIST, 2 Cor. 4:4; PREACHING OF JESUS CHRIST, Rom. 16:25; MYSTERY OF CHRIST, Eph. 3:4; MYSTERY OF THE GOSPEL, Eph. 6:19; WORD OF GOD, 1 Thess. 2:13; WORD OF CHRIST, Col. 3:16; WORD OF SALVATION, Acts 13:26; WORD OF RECONCILIATION, 2 Cor. 5:19; WORD OF TRUTH, Eph. 1:13; 2 Cor. 6:7; WORD OF FAITH, Rom. 10:8; WORD OF LIFE, Phil 2:16; MINISTRATION OF THE SPIRIT, 2 Cor. 3:8; DOCTRINE ACCORDING TO GODLINESS, 1 Tim. 6:3; FORM OF SOUND WORDS, 2 Tim. 1:13.

Likened to a mustard seed, Matt. 13:31,32; Mark 4:30-33; Luke 13: 18,19; good seed, Matt. 13:24-30, 36-43; leaven, Matt. 13:33; a pearl of great price, Matt. 13:45,46; Luke 13:20,21; a treasure hidden in a field, Matt. 13:44; a householder, Matt. 20:1-16; a feast, Luke 14:16-24.

Unclassified Scriptures Relating to: Matt. 4:23. And Jesus went about all Galilee, teaching in their synagogues, and preaching the gospel of the kingdom, and healing all manner of sickness and all manner of disease among the people.

Luke 2:10. And the angel said unto them, Fear not: for, behold, I bring you good tidings of great joy, which shall be to all people. 11. For unto you is born this day in the city of David a Saviour, which is Christ the Lord.

Luke 4:18. The Spirit of the Lord *is* upon me, because he hath anointed me to preach the gospel to the poor; he hath sent me to heal the brokenhearted, to preach deliverance to the captives, and recovering of sight to the blind, to set at liberty them that are bruised, 19. To preach the acceptable year of the Lord.

Luke 16:16. The law and the prophets *were* until John: since that time the kingdom of God is preached, and every man presseth into it. Acts 12:24; 19:20.

Luke 17:20. The kingdom of God cometh not with observation: 21. Neither shall they say, Lo here! or, lo there! for, behold, the kingdom of God is within you.

Acts 10:36. The word which *God* sent unto the children of Israel, preaching peace by Jesus Christ.

Acts 13:32. We declare unto you glad tidings, how that the promise which was made unto the fathers, 33. God hath fulfilled the same unto us their children, in that he hath raised up Jesus again;

Rom. 1:16. For I am not ashamed of the gospel [of Christ:] for it is the power of God unto salvation to every one that believeth; to the Jew first, and also to the Greek. 17. For therein is the righteousness of God revealed from faith to faith: as it is written, The just shall live by faith. [Omitted in R. V.]

Rom. 10:15. And how shall they preach, except they be sent? as it is written, How beautiful are the feet of them that preach the gospel of peace, and bring glad tidings of good things!

1 Cor. 1:18. The preaching of the cross is to them that perish foolishness; but unto us which are saved it is the power of God.

1 Cor. 15:1. I declare unto you the gospel which I preached unto you, which also ye have received, and wherein ye stand; 2. By which also ye are saved, if ye keep in

memory what I preached unto you, unless ye have believed in vain.

Eph. 6:15. And your feet shod with the preparation of the gospel of peace; 17. And take the helmet of salvation, and the sword of the Spirit, which is the word of God: 19. And for me, that utterance may be given unto me, that I may open my mouth boldly, to make known the mystery of the gospel, 20. For which I am an ambassador in bonds: that therein I may speak boldly, as I ought to speak.

Col. 1:5. The hope which is laid up for you in heaven, whereof ye heard before in the word of the truth of the gospel; 27. To whom God would make known what *is* the riches of the glory of this mystery among the Gentiles; which is Christ in you, the hope of glory:

1 Tim. 2:4. Who will have all men to be saved, and to come unto the knowledge of the truth.

Heb. 4:2. For unto us was the gospel preached, as well as unto them: but the word preached did not profit them, not being mixed with faith in them that heard *it*.

Rev. 14:6. And I saw another angel fly in the midst of heaven, having the everlasting gospel to preach unto them that dwell on the earth, and to every nation, and kindred, and tongue, and people,

Called the New Covenant: Jer. 31:33. But this *shall be* the covenant that I will make with the house of Israel; After those days, saith the LORD, I will put my law in their inward parts, and write it in their hearts; and will be their God, and they shall be my people.

Heb. 7:22. By so much was Jesus made a surety of a better [testament.] [R. V. covenant]

Heb. 8:6. But now hath he obtained a more excellent ministry, by how much also he is the mediator of a better covenant, which was established upon better promises.

Heb. 9:13. For if the blood of bulls and of goats, and the ashes of an heifer sprinkling the unclean, sanctifieth to the purifying of the flesh: 14. How much more shall the blood of Christ, who through the eternal Spirit offered himself without spot to God, purge your conscience from dead works to serve the living God? 15. And for this cause he is the mediator of the new testament, that by means of death, for the redemption of the transgressions *that were* under the first testament, they which are called might receive the promise of eternal inheritance.

Heb. 10:9. He taketh away the first, that he may establish the second.

Heb. 12:24. And to Jesus the mediator of the new covenant, and to the blood of sprinkling, that speaketh better things than *that* of Abel.

Prophecies Relating to: Psa. 46:4. *There is* a river, the streams whereof shall make glad the city of God, the holy *place* of the tabernacles of the most High.

Isa. 9:2. The people that walked in darkness have seen a great light: they that dwell in the land of the shadow of death, upon them hath the light shined. 6. For unto us a child is born, unto us a son is given: and the government shall be upon his shoulder: and his name shall be called Wonderful, Counsellor, The mighty God, The everlasting Father, The Prince of Peace. 7. Of the increase of *his* government and peace *there shall be* no end, upon the throne of David, and upon his kingdom, to order it, and to establish it with judgment and with justice from henceforth even for ever. The zeal of the LORD of hosts will perform this.

Isa. 29:18. In that day shall the deaf hear the words of the book, and the eyes of the blind shall see out of obscurity, and out of darkness. 24. They also that erred in spirit shall come to understanding, and they that murmured shall learn doctrine.

Isa. 40:9. O Zion, that bringest good tidings, get thee up into the high mountain; O Jerusalem, that bringest good tidings, lift up thy voice with strength; lift *it* up, be not afraid; unto the cities of Judah, Behold your God!

Isa. 52:7. How beautiful upon the

mountains are the feet of him that bringeth good tidings, that publisheth peace; that bringeth good tidings of good, that publisheth salvation; that saith unto Zion, Thy God reigneth!

Isa. 55:1. Ho, every one that thirsteth, come ye to the waters, and he that hath no money; come ye, buy, and eat; yea, come, buy wine and milk without money and without price.

Isa. 60:1. Arise, shine; for thy light is come, and the glory of the LORD is risen upon thee.

Isa. 61:1. The Spirit of the Lord GOD is upon me; because the LORD hath anointed me to preach good tidings unto the meek; he hath sent me to bind up the brokenhearted, to proclaim liberty to the captives, and the opening of the prison to *them that are* bound; 2. To proclaim the acceptable year of the LORD, and the day of vengeance of our God; to comfort all that mourn;

Matt. 24:14. And this gospel of the kingdom shall be preached in all the world for a witness unto all nations; and then shall the end come.

GOSSIP. Forbidden: Lev. 19: 16. Thou shalt not go up and down *as* a talebearer among thy people:

Psa. 50:20. Thou sittest *and* speakest against thy brother; thou slanderest thine own mother's son.

Prov. 11:13. A talebearer revealeth secrets: but he that is of a faithful spirit concealeth the matter.

GOVERNMENT. Paternal functions of, Gen. 41:25-57. Civil service school provided by, Dan. 1:3-20. Maintains a system of public instruction, 2 Chr. 17:7-9.

Mosaic: Ex. 18:24. So Moses hearkened to the voice of his father-in-law, and did all that he had said. 25. And Moses chose able men out of all Israel, and made them heads over the people, rulers of thousands, rulers of hundreds, rulers of fifties, and rulers of tens. 26. And they judged the people at all seasons: the hard causes they brought unto Moses, but every small matter they judged themselves.

Num. 11:16. And the LORD said unto Moses, Gather unto me seventy men of the elders of Israel, whom thou knowest to be the elders of the people, and officers over them; and bring them unto the tabernacle of the congregation, that they may stand there with thee. 17. And I will come down and talk with thee there: and I will take of the spirit which *is* upon thee, and will put *it* upon them; and they shall bear the burden of the people with thee, that thou bear *it* not thyself alone.

POPULAR, BY A NATIONAL ASSEMBLY, OR ITS REPRESENTATIVES: Accepted, and agreed to, the law given by Moses, Ex. 19:7,8; 24:3, 7; Deut. 29:10-15. Refused to make conquest of Canaan, Num. 14:1-10. Chose, or ratified, the chief ruler, Num. 27:18-23; 1 Sam. 10:24, with 1 Sam. 8:4-22; 11:14,15; 2 Sam. 3: 17-21; 5:1-3; 1 Chr. 29:22; 2 Chr. 23:3. Possessed veto power over the king's purposes, 1 Sam. 14:44, 45. The court in certain capital cases, Num. 35:12,24,25.

THE DELEGATED, SENATORIAL COUNCIL:

Ex. 19:7. And Moses came and called for the elders of the people, and laid before their faces all these words which the LORD commanded him. 8. And all the people answered together, and said, All that the LORD hath spoken we will do. And Moses returned the words of the people unto the LORD.

Ex. 24:1. And he said unto Moses, Come up unto the LORD, thou, and Aaron, Nadab, and Abihu and seventy of the elders of Israel; and worship ye afar off. 14. And he said unto the elders, Tarry ye here for us, until we come again unto you: and, behold, Aaron and Hur *are* with you: if any man have any matters to do, let him come unto them.

Deut. 27:1. And Moses with the elders of Israel commanded the people, saying, Keep all the commandments which I command you this day.

Acts 5:17. Then the high priest rose up, and all they that were with him, (which is the sect of the Sadducees,) and were filled with indignation, 18. And laid their hands on the apostles, and put them in the common prison.

A similar senate existed among the Egyptians, Gen. 50:7, with Gen. 41:37,38; Ex. 10:1,7; 12:30; 14:5; and among the Midianites and Moabites, Num. 22:4,7, and Gibeonites, Josh. 9:11.

EXECUTIVE OFFICERS OF TRIBES AND CITIES, CALLED PRINCES OR NOBLES, MEMBERS OF THE NATIONAL ASSEMBLY, Num. 1:4-16,44; 7:2,3,10, 11,18,24,54,84; 10:4; 16:2; 17:2,6; 27:2; 31:13,14; 32:2; 34:18-29; 36: 1; Josh. 9:15-21; 17:4; 22:13-32; 1 Kin. 21:11-13; Neh. 3:9,12,16,18,19.

Theocratic: Ex. 19:3. And Moses went up unto God, and the LORD called unto him out of the mountain, saying, Thus shalt thou say to the house of Jacob, and tell the children of Israel;

Deut. 29:1. These *are* the words of the covenant, which the LORD commanded Moses to make with the children of Israel in the land of Moab, beside the covenant which he made with them in Horeb.

Corruption in: 1 Kin. 21:10. And set two men, sons of Belial, before him, to bear witness against him, saying, Thou didst blaspheme God and the king. And *then* carry him out, and stone him, that he may die.

Prov. 25:5. Take away the wicked *from* before the king, and his throne shall be established in righteousness.

Mic. 3:1. And I said, Hear, I pray you, O heads of Jacob, and ye princes of the house of Israel; *Is it* not for you to know judgment? 2. Who hate the good, and love the evil; who pluck off their skin from off them, and their flesh from off their bones;

Duty of Citizens to: Matt. 22: 21. They say unto him, Cæsar's. Then saith he unto them, Render therefore unto Cæsar the things which are Cæsar's; and unto God the things that are God's. Luke 20: 25.

Rom. 13:1. Let every soul be subject unto the higher powers. For there is no power but of God: the powers that be are ordained of God.

Tit. 3:1. Put them in mind to be subject to principalities and powers, to obey magistrates, to be ready to every good work.

1 Pet. 2:13. Submit yourselves to every ordinance of man for the Lord's sake: whether it be to the king, as supreme; 14. Or unto governors, as unto them that are sent by him for the punishment of evildoers, and for the praise of them that do well. 15. For so is the will of God, that with well doing ye may put to silence the ignorance of foolish men: 16. As free, and not using *your* liberty for a cloke of maliciousness, but as the servants of God. 17. Honour all *men*. Love the brotherhood. Fear God. Honour the king.

God in: Psa. 22:28. For the kingdom *is* the LORD's: and he *is* the governor among the nations.

Prov. 8:15. By me kings reign, and princes decree justice. 16. By me princes rule, and nobles, *even* all the judges of the earth.

Dan. 5:18. O thou king, the most high God gave Nebuchadnezzar thy father a kingdom, and majesty, and glory, and honour;

Hos. 8:4. They have set up kings, but not by me: they have made princes, and I knew *it* not:

John 19:10. Then saith Pilate unto him, Speakest thou not unto me? knowest thou not that I have power to crucify thee, and have power to release thee? 11. Jesus answered, Thou couldest have no power *at all* against me, except it were given thee from above: therefore he that delivered me unto thee hath the greater sin.

GRACE OF GOD. Gen. 15:6. And he believed in the LORD; and he counted it to him for righteousness.

Rom. 3:24. Being justified freely by his grace through the redemption that is in Christ Jesus:

Rom. 4:4. Now to him that worketh is the reward not reckoned of grace, but of debt. 5. But to him that worketh not, but believeth on him that justifieth the ungodly, his faith is counted for righteousness. 16. Therefore *it is* of faith, that *it might be* by grace; to the end the promise might be sure to all the seed;

Rom. 5:2. By whom also we have access by faith into this grace wherein we stand, and rejoice in hope of the glory of God.

Rom. 11:5. Even so then at this present time also there is a remnant according to the election of grace. 6. And if by grace, then *is it* no more of works: otherwise grace is no more grace.

1 Cor. 15:10. By the grace of God I am what I am: and his grace which *was bestowed* upon me was not in vain; but I laboured more abundantly than they all: yet not I, but the grace of God which was with me.

Eph. 2:8. By grace are ye saved through faith; and that not of yourselves: *it is* the gift of God: 9. Not of works, lest any man should boast.

Growth in: Psa. 84:7. They go from strength to strength, *every one of them* in Zion appeareth before God.

Prov. 4:18. But the path of the just *is* as the shining light, that shineth more and more unto the perfect day.

Phil. 1:6. Being confident of this very thing, that he which hath begun a good work in you will perform *it* until the day of Jesus Christ: 9. And this I pray, that your love may abound yet more and more in knowledge and *in* all judgment; 10. That ye may approve things that are excellent; that ye may be sincere and without offense till the day of Christ; 11. Being filled with the fruits of righteousness, which are by Jesus Christ, unto the glory and praise of God.

Phil. 3:13. Brethren, I count not myself to have apprehended: but *this* one thing I *do*, forgetting those things which are behind, and reaching forth unto those things which are before, 14. I press toward the mark for the prize of the high calling of God in Christ Jesus. 15. Let

us therefore, as many as be perfect, be thus minded:

Col. 1:10. That ye might walk worthy of the Lord unto all pleasing, being fruitful in every good work, and increasing in the knowledge of God; 11. Strengthened with all might, according to his glorious power, unto all patience and long-suffering with joyfulness;

1 Thess. 3:12. And the Lord make you to increase and abound in love one toward another, and toward all *men*, even as we *do* toward you:

2 Thess. 1:3. We are bound to thank God always for you, brethren, as it is meet, because that your faith groweth exceedingly, and the charity of every one of you all toward each other aboundeth;

2 Pet. 3:18. But grow in grace, and *in* the knowledge of our Lord and Saviour Jesus Christ.

GRACES. Christian. Matt. 5:3. Blessed *are* the poor in spirit: for their's is the kingdom of heaven. 4. Blessed *are* they that mourn: for they shall be comforted. 5. Blessed *are* the meek: for they shall inherit the earth. 6. Blessed *are* they which do hunger and thirst after righteousness: for they shall be filled. 7. Blessed *are* the merciful: for they shall obtain mercy. 8. Blessed *are* the pure in heart: for they shall see God. 9. Blessed *are* the peacemakers: for they shall be called the children of God. 10. Blessed *are* they which are persecuted for righteousness' sake: for their's is the kingdom of heaven. 11. Blessed are ye, when *men* shall revile you, and persecute *you*, and shall say all manner of evil against you falsely, for my sake.

Rom. 5:3. And not only *so*, but we glory in tribulations also: knowing that tribulation worketh patience; 4. And patience, experience; and experience, hope: 5. And hope maketh not ashamed; because the love of God is shed abroad in our hearts by the Holy Ghost which is given unto us.

1 Cor. 13:1. Though I speak with the tongues of men and of angels, and have not charity, I am become

as sounding brass, or a tinkling cymbal.

Gal. 5:22. But the fruit of the Spirit is love, joy, peace, longsuffering, gentleness, goodness, [faith,] 23. Meekness, temperance: against such there is no law. [R. V. faithfulness]

2 Pet. 1:5. And beside this, giving all diligence, add to your faith virtue; and to virtue knowledge; 6. And to knowledge temperance; and to temperance patience; and to patience godliness: 7. And to godliness brotherly kindness; and to brotherly kindness charity. 8. For if these things be in you, and abound, they make *you that ye shall* neither *be* barren nor unfruitful in the knowledge of our Lord Jesus Christ. 9. But he that lacketh these things is blind, and cannot see afar off, and hath forgotten that he was purged from his old sins.

HADES. 1. **The unseen world,** tranlated hell in *A. V.,* but in the *R. V.* the word Hades is retained, Matt. 11:23; 16:18; Luke 10:15; 16:23; Acts 2:27.31; Rev. 1:18; 6:8; 20:13,14.

2. **Realm, or State, of the Dead,** USUALLY EXPRESSED IN HEBREW BY SHEOL AND IN GREEK BY HADES: 2 Sam. 22:6. The sorrows of hell compassed me about; the snares of death prevented me;

Psa. 6:5. For in death *there is* no remembrance of thee: in the grave who shall give thee thanks?

Psa. 17:15. As for me, I will behold thy face in righteousness: I shall be satisfied, when I awake, with thy likeness.

Psa. 49:15. But God will redeem my soul from the power of the grave: for he shall receive me.

Psa. 86:13. For great *is* thy mercy toward me: and thou hast delivered my soul from the lowest hell.

Luke 23:42. And he said unto Jesus, Lord, remember me when thou comest into thy kingdom. 43. And Jesus said unto him, Verily I say unto thee, Today shalt thou be with me in paradise.

2 Cor. 12:4. How that he was caught up into paradise, and heard unspeakable words, which it is not lawful for a man to utter.

HANGING. Capital punishment by, Gen. 40:19-22; Josh. 8:29; 2 Sam. 4:12; Esth. 7:10. The curse of death by, Deut. 21:22,23; Gal. 3:13.

HAPPINESS. Of the Wicked: Limited to this life, Psa. 17:14; Luke 16:25; short, Job 20:5; uncertain, Luke 12:20; vain, Eccl. 2:1, 7:6.

Is derived from their wealth, Job 21:13;

Of the Righteous: Job 5:17. Behold, happy *is* the man whom God correcteth: therefore despise not thou the chastening of the Almighty:

Psa. 40:8. I delight to do thy will, O my God: yea, thy law *is* within my heart.

Psa. 63:5. My soul shall be satisfied as *with* marrow and fatness; and my mouth shall praise *thee* with joyful lips:

Psa. 144:15. Happy *is that* people, that is in such a case: *yea,* happy *is that* people, whose God *is* the LORD.

Psa. 146:5. Happy *is he* that *hath* the God of Jacob for his help, whose hope *is* in the LORD his God:

Prov. 14:21. He that hath mercy on the poor, happy *is* he.

Prov. 16:20. Whoso trusteth in the LORD, happy *is* he.

Prov. 28:14. Happy *is* the man that feareth alway:

Isa. 12:2. Behold, God *is* my salvation; I will trust, and not be afraid: for the LORD JEHOVAH *is* my strength and *my* song; he also is become my salvation. 3. Therefore with joy shall ye draw water out of the wells of salvation.

Rom. 5:2. By whom also we have access by faith into this grace wherein we stand, and rejoice in hope of the glory of God.

1 Pet. 3:14. But and if ye suffer for righteousness' sake happy *are ye:* and be not afraid of their terror, neither be troubled:

1 Pet. 4:12. Beloved, think it not strange concerning the fiery trial which is to try you, as though some strange thing happened unto you:

13. But rejoice, inasmuch as ye are partakers of Christ's sufferings; that, when his glory shall be revealed, ye may be glad also with exceeding joy.

HATRED. Scriptures Relating to: Lev. 19:17. Thou shalt not hate thy brother in thine heart: thou shalt in any wise rebuke thy neighbour, and not suffer sin upon him.

Prov. 10:12. Hatred stirreth up strifes: but love covereth all sins.

18. He that hideth hatred *with* lying lips, and he that uttereth a slander, *is* a fool.

Prov. 15:17. Better *is* a dinner of herbs where love is, than a stalled ox and hatred therewith.

Matt. 5:43. Ye have heard that it hath been said, Thou shalt love thy neighbour, and hate thine enemy. 44. But I say unto you, Love your enemies, bless them that curse you, do good to them that hate you, and pray for them which despitefully use you, and persecute you;

Matt. 10:22. And ye shall be hated of all *men* for my name's sake: but he that endureth to the end shall be saved.

John 15:18. If the world hate you, ye know that it hated me before *it hated* you.

John 17:14. I have given them thy word; and the world hath hated them, because they are not of the world, even as I am not of the world.

Gal. 5:19. The works of the flesh are manifest, . . . 20. . . . . Hatred, variance, emulations, wrath,

1 John 2:9. He that saith he is in the light, and hateth his brother, is in darkness even until now. 11. He that hateth his brother is in darkness, and walketh in darkness, and knoweth not whither he goeth, because that darkness hath blinded his eyes.

HEARERS. Ezek. 33:30. Also, thou son of man, the children of thy people still are talking against thee by the walls and in the doors of the houses, and speak one to another, every one to his brother, saying, Come, I pray you, and hear what is the word that cometh forth from the LORD. 31. And they come unto thee as the people cometh, and they sit before thee *as* my people, and they hear thy words, but they will not do them: for with their mouth they shew much love, *but* their heart goeth after their covetousness. 32. And, lo, thou *art* unto them as a very lovely song of one that hath a pleasant voice, and can play well on an instrument: for they hear thy words, but they do them not.

Matt. 7:24. Therefore whosoever heareth these sayings of mine, and doeth them, I will liken him unto a wise man, which built his house upon a rock:

Rom. 2:13. For not the hearers of the law *are* just before God, but the doers of the law shall be justified.

Jas. 1:22. But be ye doers of the word, and not hearers only, deceiving your own selves.

HEART, seat of the affections. **Renewed:** Deut. 30:6; Psa. 51:10; Ezek. 11:19; 18:31; 36:26; Rom. 2:29; Eph. 4:23; Col. 3:10. Regenerated, John 3:3,7. Graciously affected of God, 1 Sam. 10:26; 1 Chr. 29:18; Ezra 6:22; 7:27; Prov. 16:1; 21:1; Jer. 20:9; Acts 16:14. Strengthened, Psa. 27:14; 112:8; 1 Thess. 3:13. Enlightened, 2 Cor. 4:6. Tried, 1 Chr. 29:17; Psa. 7:9; 26:2; Prov. 17:3; Jer. 11:20; 12:3; 20:12; 1 Thess. 2:4; Heb. 11:17; Rev. 2:2,10.

It should render to God obedience, Deut. 10:12; 11:13; 26:16; 1 Kin. 2:4; Psa. 119:1,12; Eph. 6:6 faith, Psa. 27:3; 112:7; Rom. 6:17; 10:10; trust, Prov. 3:5; love, Matt. 22:37; fear, Psa. 119:161; Jer. 32:40; fidelity, Neh. 9:8; zeal, 2 Chr. 17:16; Jer. 20:9.

It should seek God, 2 Chr. 19:3; 30:19; Ezra 7:10; Psa. 10:17; 84:2; be joyful, 1 Sam. 2:1; Psa. 4:7; 97:11; Isa. 65:14; Zech. 10:7; perfect, 1 Kin. 8:61: Psa. 101:2; upright, Psa. 97:11; 125:4; clean, Psa. 51:10; 73:1; pure, Psa. 24:4; Prov. 22:11; Matt. 5:8; 1 Tim. 1:5; 2 Tim. 2:22; Jas. 4:8; 1 Pet. 1:22; sincere, Luke 8:15; Acts 2:46; Eph. 6:5; Col. 3:22; Heb. 10:22; repentant,

HEART

Deut. 30:2; Psa. 34:18; 51:17; devout, 1 Sam. 1:13; Psa. 4:4; 9:1; 27:8; 77:6; 119:10,69,145; wise, 1 Kin. 3:9,12; 4:29; Job 9:4; Prov. 8:10; 10:8; 11:29; 14:33; 23:15; tender, 1 Sam. 24:5; 2 Kin. 22:19; Job 23:16; Psa. 22:14; Eph. 4:32; holy, Psa. 66:18; 1 Pet. 3:15; compassionate, Jer. 4:19; Lam. 3:51; lowly, Matt. 11:29.

The Unregenerate: Is full of iniquity, Gen. 6:5; 8:21; 1 Sam. 17:28; Prov. 6:14,18; 11:20; Eccl. 8:11; 9:3; Jer. 4:14,18; 17:9; Rom. 1:21. Loves evil, Deut. 29:18; Psa. 95:10; Jer. 17:5. Is a fountain of evil, Matt. 12:34,35; Mark 7:21. See DEPRAVITY. Is wayward, 2 Chr. 12:14; Psa. 101:4; Prov. 6:14; 11:20; 12:8; 17:20; Jer. 5:23; Heb. 3:10; blind, Rom. 1:21; Eph. 4:18. See BLINDNESS, SPIRITUAL. Is double, 1 Chr. 12:33; Psa. 12:2; Hos. 10:2; Jas. 1:6,8; Prov. 28:14; Isa. 9:9; 10:12; 46:12. See INSTABILITY. Is hard, Psa. 76:5; Ezek. 2:4; 3:7; 11:19; 36:26; Mark 6:52; 10:5; 16:14; John 12:40; Rom. 1:21; 2:5. See IMPENITENCE; OBDURACY. Is deceitful, Jer. 17:9. Is proud, 2 Kin. 14:10; 2 Chr. 25:19; Psa. 101:5; Prov. 18:12; 28:25; Jer. 48:29; 49:16. See PRIDE. Is subtle, Prov. 7:10. See HYPOCRISY. Is sensual, Ezek. 6:9; Hos. 13:6; Rom. 8:7. See LASCIVIOUSNESS. Is worldly, 2 Chr. 26:16; Dan. 5:20; Acts 8:21,22. Is judicially hardened, Ex. 4:21; Josh. 11:20; Isa. 6:10; Acts 28:26,27. Is malicious, Psa. 28:3; 140:2; Prov. 24:2; Eccl. 7:26; Ezek. 25:15. See MALICE. Is impenitent, Rom. 2:5. See IMPENITENCE. Is diabolical, John 13:2; Acts 5:3. Is covetous, Jer. 22:17; 2 Pet. 2:14. See COVETOUSNESS. Is foolish, Prov. 12:23; 22:15; Eccl. 9:3.

Unclassified Scriptures Descriptive of the Seat of the Affections: Deut. 6:5. And thou shalt love the LORD thy God with all thine heart, and with all thy soul, and with all thy might. 6. And these words, which I command thee this day, shall be in thine heart:

1 Sam. 16:7. For the LORD seeth not as man seeth; for man looketh on the outward appearance, but the LORD looketh on the heart.

2 Chr. 12:14. And he did evil, because he prepared not his heart to seek the LORD.

Psa. 22:26. Your heart shall live for ever.

Psa. 34:18. The LORD is nigh unto them that are of a broken heart; and saveth such as be of a contrite spirit.

Psa. 51:10. Create in me a clean heart, O God; and renew a right spirit within me. 17. The sacrifices of God are a broken spirit: a broken and a contrite heart, O God, thou wilt not despise.

Prov. 4:23. Keep thy heart with all diligence; for out of it are the issues of life.

Prov. 14:30. A sound heart is the life of the flesh:

Prov. 15:13. A merry heart maketh a cheerful countenance: but by sorrow of the heart the spirit is broken.

Prov. 20:9. Who can say, I have made my heart clean, I am pure from my sin?

Matt. 5:8. Blessed are the pure in heart: for they shall see God.

Matt. 15:18. But those things which proceed out of the mouth come forth from the heart; and they defile the man. 19. For out of the heart proceed evil thoughts, murders, adulteries, fornications, thefts, false witness, blasphemies: 20. These are the things which defile a man: but to eat with unwashen hands defileth not a man. Mark 7:21.

Known to God: 1 Kin. 8:39. Then hear thou in heaven thy dwelling place, and forgive, and do, and give to every man according to his ways, whose heart thou knowest; (for thou, even thou only, knowest the hearts of all the children of men;)

Job 16:19. Also now, behold, my witness is in heaven, and my record is on high.

Psa. 44:21. Shall not God search this out? for he knoweth the secrets of the heart.

Psa. 51:10. Create in me a clean heart, O God; and renew a right spirit within me.

Prov. 5:21. For the ways of man *are* before the eyes of the LORD, and he pondereth all his goings.

Luke 16:15. Ye are they which justify yourselves before men; but God knoweth your hearts:

Acts 1:24. And they prayed, and said, Thou, Lord, which knowest the hearts of all *men*, shew whether of these two thou hast chosen.

Rom. 8:27. And he that searcheth the hearts knoweth what *is* the mind of the Spirit, because he maketh intercession for the saints according to *the will of* God.

HEAVEN. God's Dwelling Place: Deut. 26:15. Look down from thy holy habitation, from heaven, and bless thy people Israel, and the land which thou hast given us, as thou swarest unto our fathers, a land that floweth with milk and honey. Zech. 2:13; Isa. 63:15.

1 Kin. 8:30. Hear thou in heaven thy dwelling place: and when thou hearest, forgive. *vs.* 39,43,49; 2 Chr. 6:18,21,27,30,33,35,39; Jer. 23:24.

2 Chr. 2:6. But who is able to build him an house, seeing the heaven and heaven of heavens cannot contain him? who *am* I then, that I should build him an house, save only to burn sacrifice before him?

Psa. 2:4. He that sitteth in the heavens shall laugh: the Lord shall have them in derision.

Isa. 66:1. Thus saith the LORD, The heaven *is* my throne, and the earth *is* my footstool:

Matt. 6:9. Our Father which art in heaven, Matt. 18:10,14; Mark 11:25,26.

Mark 16:19. So then after the Lord had spoken unto them, he was received up into heaven, and sat on the right hand of God.

Acts 7:49. Heaven *is* my throne.

Rev. 8:1. And when he had opened the seventh seal, there was silence in heaven about the space of half an hour.

The Future Dwelling Place of the Righteous: Job 3:17. There the wicked cease *from* troubling; and there the weary be at rest.

Psa. 16:11. In thy presence *is* fulness of joy; at thy right hand *there are* pleasures for evermore.

Psa. 17:15. As for me, I will behold thy face in righteousness: I shall be satisfied, when I awake, with thy likeness.

Psa. 23:6. I will dwell in the house of the LORD for ever.

Psa. 73:24. Thou shalt guide me with thy counsel, and afterward receive me *to* glory.

Isa. 33:17. Thine eyes shall see the king in his beauty: they shall behold the land that is very far off.

Dan. 12:3. They that be wise shall shine as the brightness of the firmament; and they that turn many to righteousness as the stars for ever and ever.

Mal. 3:17. They shall be mine, saith the LORD of hosts, in that day when I make up my jewels; and I will spare them, as a man spareth his own son that serveth him.

Matt. 5:3. Blessed *are* the poor in spirit: for their's is the kingdom of heaven. 8. Blessed *are* the pure in heart: for they shall see God. 12. Rejoice, and be exceeding glad: for great *is* your reward in heaven:

Matt. 6:20. Lay up for yourselves treasures in heaven, where neither moth nor rust doth corrupt, and where thieves do not break through nor steal: Luke 12:33.

Matt. 18:10. Take heed that ye despise not one of these little ones; for I say unto you, That in heaven their angels do always behold the face of my Father which is in heaven.

Luke 12:32. Fear not, little flock; for it is your Father's good pleasure to give you the kingdom.

Luke 16:22. The beggar died, and was carried by the angels into Abraham's bosom:

Luke 23:43. Verily I say unto thee, To day shalt thou be with me in paradise.

John 10:28. I give unto them eternal life; and they shall never perish, neither shall any *man* pluck them out of my hand.

John 14:2. In my Father's house are many mansions: if *it were* not *so*, I would have told you. I go to prepare a place for you. 3. If I go and prepare a place for you, I will come again, and receive you unto myself; that where I am, *there* ye may be also.

2 Cor. 12:4. How that he was caught up into paradise, and heard unspeakable words, which it is not lawful for a man to utter.

1 Thess. 4:17. We which are alive *and* remain shall be caught up together with them in the clouds, to meet the Lord in the air: and so shall we ever be with the Lord.

Rev. 7:9. Lo, a great multitude, which no man could number, of all nations, and kindreds, and people, and tongues, stood before the throne, and before the Lamb, clothed with white robes, and palms in their hands;

Rev. 21:1. I saw a new heaven and a new earth: for the first heaven and the first earth were passed away; and there was no more sea.

25. And the gates of it shall not be shut at all by day: for there shall be no night there. 27. There shall in no wise enter into it any thing that defileth, neither *whatsoever* worketh abomination, or *maketh* a lie: but they which are written in the Lamb's book of life.

The Physical Heavens: PHYSICAL HEAVENS, CREATION OF: Gen. 1:1. In the beginning God created the heaven and the earth.

Gen. 2:1. Thus the heavens and the earth were finished, and all the host of them.

Job 9:8. Which alone spreadeth out the heavens, and treadeth upon the waves of the sea.

PHYSICAL HEAVENS, DESTRUCTION OF: Isa. 34:4. And all the host of heaven shall be dissolved, and the heavens shall be rolled together as a scroll: and all their host shall fall down, as the leaf falleth off from the vine, and as a falling *fig* from the fig tree.

Heb. 1:10. And, Thou, Lord, in the beginning hast laid the foundation of the earth; and the heavens are the works of thine hands: 11. They shall perish; but thou remainest; and they all shall wax old as doth a garment; 12. And as a

vesture shalt thou fold them up, and they shall be changed: but thou art the same, and thy years shall not fail.

2 Pet. 3:10. But the day of the Lord will come as a thief in the night; in the which the heavens shall pass away with a great noise, and the elements shall melt with fervent heat, the earth also and the works that are therein shall be burned up. 12. Looking for and hasting unto the coming of the day of God, wherein the heavens being on fire shall be dissolved, and the elements shall melt with fervent heat?

New Heavens: Isa. 65:17. For, behold, I create new heavens and a new earth: and the former shall not be remembered, nor come into mind.

2 Pet. 3:13. Nevertheless we, according to his promise, look for new heavens and a new earth, wherein dwelleth righteousness.

Rev. 21:1. And I saw a new heaven and a new earth: for the first heaven and the first earth were passed away; and there was no more sea.

HEIR. Gal. 4:1,2.

Eccl. 2:18. Yea, I hated all my labour which I had taken under the sun: because I should leave it unto the man that shall be after me. 19. And who knoweth whether he shall be a wise *man* or a fool? yet shall he have rule over all my labour wherein I have laboured, and wherein I have shewed myself wise under the sun. This *is* also vanity.

Figurative: Rom. 8:14. For as many as are led by the Spirit of God, they are the sons of God. 16. The Spirit itself beareth witness with our spirit, that we are the children of God: 17. And if children, then heirs; heirs of God, and joint-heirs with Christ; if so be that we suffer with *him*, that we may be also glorified together.

Gal. 3:29. And if ye *be* Christ's, then are ye Abraham's seed, and heirs according to the promise.

Gal. 4:6. And because ye are sons, God hath sent forth the Spirit of his Son into your hearts, crying, Abba, Father. 7. Wherefore thou art no more a servant, but a son; and if a son, then an heir [of God through Christ.] [R. V. through God]

Tit. 3:7. That being justified by his grace, we should be made heirs according to the hope of eternal life.

Jas. 2:5. Hearken, my beloved brethren, Hath not God chosen the poor of this world rich in faith, and heirs of the kingdom which he hath promised to them that love him?

HELL. The word used in the King James Version of the *O. T.* to translate the Hebrew word SHEOL, signifying the unseen state in Deut. 32:22; 2 Sam. 22:6; Job 11:8; 26:6; Psa. 9:17; 16:10; 18:5; 55:15; 86:13; 116:3; 139:8; Prov. 5:5; 7:27; 9:18; 15:11,24; 23:14; 27:20; Isa. 5:14; 14:9,15; 28:15,18; 57:9; Ezek. 31:16,17; 32:21,27; Amos 9:2; Jonah 2:2; Hab. 2:5.

Translation of the Greek word HADES in *N. T.* of King James Version, the unseen world, Matt. 11:23; 16:18; Luke 10:15; 16:23; Acts 2:27,31; Rev. 1:18; 6:8; 20:13,14; of the Greek word GEHENNA, signifying the place of torment, Matt. 5:22,29,30; 10:28; 18:9; 23:15,33; Mark 9:43,45,47; Luke 12:5; Jas. 3:6; of the Greek word TARTARUS, signifying the infernal region, 2 Pet. 2:4.

SHEOL is also translated GRAVE in King James Version in Gen. 37:35; 42:38; 44:29,31; 1 Sam. 2:6; 1 Kin. 2:6,9; Job 7:9; 14:13; 17:13; 21:13; 24:19; Psa. 6:5; 30:3; 31:17; 49:14,15; 88:3; 89:48; 141:7; Prov. 1:12; 30:16; Eccl. 9:10; Song 8:6; Isa. 14:11; 38:10,18; Ezek. 31:15; Hos. 13:14; PIT, Num. 16:30,33; Job 17:16.

The English revisers insert the Hebrew word SHEOL in places where HELL, GRAVE, and PIT were used in the *A. V.* as translations of the word SHEOL, except in Deut. 32:22; Psa. 55:15; 86:13; and in the prophetical books. The American revisers invariably use SHEOL in the American text, where it occurs in the original.

The Future Abode of the Wicked: Psa. 9:17. The wicked shall be turned into hell, *and* all the nations that forget God.

Prov. 9:17. Stolen waters are sweet, and bread *eaten* in secret is pleasant. 18. But he knoweth not that the dead *are* there; *and that* her guests *are* in the depths of hell.

Prov. 23:13. Withhold not correction from the child: for *if* thou beatest him with the rod, he shall not die. 14. Thou shalt beat him with the rod, and shalt deliver his soul from hell.

Isa. 33:14. The sinners in Zion are afraid; fearfulness hath surprised the hypocrites. Who among us shall dwell with devouring fire? who among us shall dwell with everlasting burnings?

Matt. 3:12. Whose fan *is* in his hand, and he will throughly purge his floor, and gather his wheat into the garner; but he will burn up the chaff with unquenchable fire.

Matt. 7:13. Wide *is* the gate, and broad *is* the way, that leadeth to destruction, and many there be which go in thereat: *v.* 14.

Matt. 8:12. But the children of the kingdom shall be cast out into outer darkness: there shall be weeping and gnashing of teeth.

Matt. 16:18. And I say also unto thee, That thou art Peter, and upon this rock I will build my church; and the gates of hell shall not prevail against it.

Mark 9:43. It is better for thee to enter into life maimed, than having two hands to go into hell, into the fire that never shall be quenched: [44. Where their worm dieth not, and the fire is not quenched.] *vss.* 45-48. Matt. 5:29. [Omitted in R. V.]

Luke 16:23. In hell he lift up his eyes, being in torments, and seeth Abraham afar off, and Lazarus in his bosom. 24. And he cried and said, Father Abraham, have mercy on me, and send Lazarus, that he may dip the tip of his finger in water, and cool my tongue; for I am tormented in this flame. 26. Between us and you there is a great gulf fixed: so that they which would pass from hence to you cannot; neither can they pass to us, that *would come* from thence. *vss.* 25,28; Acts 1:25.

2 Thess. 1:9. Who shall be punished with everlasting destruction from the presence of the Lord, and from the glory of his power;

Rev. 19:20. And the beast was taken, and with him the false prophet . . . These both were cast alive into a lake of fire burning with brimstone.

Rev. 21:8. But the fearful, and unbelieving, and the abominable, and murderers, and whoremongers, and sorcerers, and idolaters, and all liars, shall have their part in the lake which burneth with fire and brimstone: which is the second death. Rev. 2:11.

HEREDITY. Gen. 5:3. And Adam . . . begat *a son* in his own likeness, after his image;

Psa. 51:5. Behold, I was shapen in iniquity; and in sin did my mother conceive me.

Psa. 58:3. The wicked are estranged from the womb: they go astray as soon as they be born, speaking lies.

Isa. 48:8. A transgressor from the womb.

John 3:6. That which is born of the flesh is flesh; and that which is born of the Spirit is spirit. 7. Marvel not that I said unto thee, Ye must be born again.

Rom. 5:12. By one man sin entered into the world, and death by sin; and so death passed upon all men, for that all have sinned:

HERESY. Propagandism of, forbidden under severe penalties, Deut. 13; Tit. 3:10,11; 2 John 10,11. Teachers of, among early Christians, Acts 15:24; 2 Cor. 11:4; Gal. 1:7; 2:4; 2 Pet. 2; Jude 3-16; Rev. 2:2. Paul and Silas accused of, Acts 16:20,21,23. Paul accused of, Acts 18:13. Disavowed by Paul, Acts 24:13-16.

HIGHWAYS. Figurative: Prov. 16:17. The highway of the upright *is* to depart from evil: he that keepeth his way preserveth his soul.

Isa. 35:8. And an highway shall be there, and a way, and it shall be called The way of holiness; the unclean shall not pass over it; but it *shall be* for those: the wayfaring men, though fools, shall not err *therein.* 9. No lion shall be there, nor *any* ravenous beast shall go up thereon, it shall not be found there; but the redeemed shall walk *there:* 10. And the ransomed of the LORD shall return, and come to Zion with songs and everlasting joy upon their heads: they shall obtain joy and gladness, and sorrow and sighing shall flee away.

Isa. 40:3. The voice of him that crieth in the wilderness, Prepare ye the way of the LORD, make straight in the desert a highway for our God. 4. Every valley shall be exalted, and every mountain and hill shall be made low: and the crooked shall be made straight, and the rough places plain: Matt. 3:3.

Matt. 7:13. Enter ye in at the strait gate: for wide *is* the gate, and broad *is* the way, that leadeth to destruction, and many there be which go in thereat: 14. Because strait *is* the gate, and narrow *is* the way, which leadeth unto life, and few there be that find it.

HOLIDAY. For rest. See SABBATH. One year in seven, Lev. 25:2-7.

HOLINESS. Gen. 17:1. I *am* the Almighty God; walk before me, and be thou perfect.

Ex. 19:6. Ye shall be unto me a kingdom of priests, and an holy nation.

Ex. 39:30. And they made the plate of the holy crown *of* pure gold, and wrote upon it a writing, *like* to the engravings of a signet, HOLINESS TO THE LORD. Ex. 28:36.

Lev. 10:8. And the LORD spake unto Aaron, saying, 9. Do not drink wine nor strong drink, thou, nor thy sons with thee, when ye go into the tabernacle of the congregation, lest ye die: *it shall be* a statute for ever throughout your generations: 10. And that ye may put difference between holy and unholy, and between unclean and clean;

Lev. 11:44. For I *am* the LORD your God: ye shall therefore sanctify yourselves, and ye shall be holy; for I *am* holy: neither shall ye defile yourselves with any manner of creeping thing that creepeth upon the earth.

Lev. 20:26. And ye shall be holy unto me: for I the LORD *am* holy, and have severed you from *other* people, that ye should be mine.

Deut. 14:2. Thou *art* an holy people unto the LORD thy God, and the LORD hath chosen thee to be a peculiar people unto himself. Deut. 26:19.

Psa. 32:2. Blessed *is* the man unto whom the LORD imputeth not iniquity, and in whose spirit *there is* no guile.

Psa. 73:1. Truly God *is* good to Israel, *even* to such as are of a clean heart.

Psa. 97:10. Ye that love the LORD, hate evil: he preserveth the souls of his saints;

Psa. 119:1. Blessed *are* the undefiled in the way, who walk in the law of the LORD. 2. Blessed *are* they that keep his testimonies, *and that* seek him with the whole heart. 3. They also do no iniquity: they walk in his ways.

Prov. 22:1. A *good* name *is* rather to be chosen than great riches, *and* loving favour rather than silver and gold. Eccl. 7:1.

Isa. 35:8. And an highway shall be there, and a way, and it shall be called The way of holiness; the unclean shall not pass over it; but it *shall be* for those: the wayfaring men, though fools, shall not err *therein*.

Isa. 60:1. Arise, shine; for thy light is come, and the glory of the LORD is risen upon thee. 21. Thy people also *shall be* all righteous:

Zech. 14:20. In that day shall there be upon the bells of the horses, HOLINESS UNTO THE LORD; and the pots in the LORD'S house shall be like the bowls before the altar.

John 17:23. I in them, and thou in me, that they may be made perfect in one;

Acts 24:16. And herein do I exercise myself, to have always a conscience void of offence toward God, and *toward* men.

Rom. 6:13. Neither yield ye your members *as* instruments of unrighteousness unto sin: but yield yourselves unto God, as those that are alive from the dead, and your members *as* instruments of righteousness unto God. 14. For sin shall not have dominion over you: for ye are not under the law, but under grace.

Rom. 11:16. For if the firstfruit *be* holy, the lump *is* also *holy:* and if the root *be* holy, so *are* the branches.

Rom. 12:1. I beseech you therefore, brethren, by the mercies of God, that ye present your bodies a living sacrifice, holy, acceptable unto God, *which is* your reasonable service.

1 Cor. 3:16. Know ye not that ye are the temple of God, and *that* the Spirit of God dwelleth in you? 17. If any man defile the temple of God, him shall God destroy; for the temple of God is holy, which *temple* ye are.

1 Cor. 5:7. Purge out therefore the old leaven, that ye may be a new lump, as ye are unleavened.

Phil. 2:15. Be blameless and harmless, the sons of God, without rebuke, in the midst of a crooked and perverse nation, among whom ye shine as lights in the world;

Phil. 4:8. Whatsoever things are true, whatsoever things *are* honest, whatsoever things *are* just, whatsoever things *are* pure, whatsoever things *are* lovely, whatsoever things *are* of good report; if *there be* any virtue, and if *there be* any praise, think on these things.

2 Tim. 2:19. Let every one that nameth the name of Christ depart from iniquity. 21. If a man therefore purge himself from these, he shall be a vessel unto honour, sanctified, and meet for the master's use, *and* prepared unto every good work. 22. Flee also youthful lusts: but follow righteousness, faith, charity, peace, with them that call on the Lord out of a pure heart. *vss.* 16,17.

2 Tim. 3:17. That the man of

God may be perfect, throughly furnished unto all good works.

Tit. 1:15. Unto the pure all things *are* pure:

Heb. 12:1. Let us lay aside every weight, and the sin which doth so easily beset *us*, and let us run with patience the race that is set before us,

Heb. 13:9. *It is* a good thing that the heart be established with grace;

Jas. 3:17. The wisdom that is from above is first pure, then peaceable, gentle, *and* easy to be intreated, full of mercy and good fruits, without partiality, and without hypocrisy.

2 Pet. 1:5. Giving all diligence, add to your faith virtue; and to virtue knowledge; 6. And to knowledge temperance; and to temperance patience; and to patience godliness; 7. And to godliness brotherly kindness; and to brotherly kindness charity. 8. For if these things be in you, and abound, they make *you that ye shall* neither *be* barren nor unfruitful in the knowledge of our Lord Jesus Christ. *vss.* 2-4.

HOLY SPIRIT, Gen. 1:2. And the Spirit of God moved upon the face of the waters.

Gen. 6:3. And the LORD said, My spirit shall not always strive with man.

Gen. 41:38. And Pharoah said unto his servants, Can we find *such a one* as this *is*, a man in whom the Spirit of God *is*?

Isa. 11:2. And the spirit of the LORD shall rest upon him, the spirit of wisdom and understanding, the spirit of counsel and might, the spirit of knowledge and of the fear of the LORD;

Isa. 32:15. Until the spirit be poured upon us from on high.

Isa. 42:1. Behold my servant, whom I uphold; mine elect, *in whom* my soul delighteth; I have put my spirit upon him: he shall bring forth judgment to the Gentiles.

Isa. 59:19. When the enemy shall come in like a flood, the Spirit of the LORD shall lift up a standard against him.

Isa. 61:1. The Spirit of the Lord GOD *is* upon me; because the LORD hath anointed me to preach good tidings unto the meek; he hath sent me to bind up the brokenhearted, to proclaim liberty to the captives, and the opening of the prison to *them that are* bound; Luke 4:18.

Isa. 63:10. But they rebelled, and vexed his holy Spirit:

Ezek. 36:27. And I will put my spirit within you, and cause you to walk in my statutes, and ye shall keep my judgments, and do *them*.

Zech. 4:6. Not by might, nor by power, but by my spirit, saith the LORD of hosts. *vs.* 1-7.

Matt. 1:18. Now the birth of Jesus Christ was on this wise: When as his mother Mary was espoused to Joseph, before they came together, she was found with child of the Holy Ghost. *v.* 20.

Matt. 3:11. I indeed baptize you with water unto repentance: but . . . he shall baptize you with the Holy Ghost, and *with* fire: [John 1:33; Acts 11:16.] 16. And Jesus, when he was baptized, went up straightway out of the water: and lo, the heavens were opened unto him, and he saw the Spirit of God descending like a dove, and lighting upon him: 17. And lo a voice from heaven, saying, This is my beloved Son, in whom I am well pleased. Mark 1:10; Luke 3:22; John 1:32.

Matt. 4:1. Then was Jesus led up of the spirit into the wilderness to be tempted of the devil.

Matt. 10:20. For it is not ye that speak, but the Spirit of your Father which speaketh in you. Mark 13:11.

Matt. 28:19. Baptizing them in the name of the Father, and of the Son, and of the Holy Ghost:

John 7:38. He that believeth on me, as the scripture hath said, out of his belly shall flow rivers of living water. 39. (But this spake he of the Spirit, which they that believe on him should receive: for the Holy Ghost was not yet *given;* because that Jesus was not yet glorified.)

John 14:16. I will pray the Father, and he shall give you another Comforter, that he may abide with you for ever; 17. *Even* the Spirit of truth; whom the world cannot receive, because it seeth him not, neither knoweth him: but ye know him; for he dwelleth with you, and shall be in you. 26. But the Comforter, *which is* the Holy Ghost, whom the Father will send in my name, he shall teach you all things, and bring all things to your remembrance, whatsoever I have said unto you.

John 15:26. When the Comforter is come, whom I will send unto you from the Father, *even* the Spirit of truth, which proceedeth from the Father, he shall testify of me:

John 16:7. Nevertheless I tell you the truth; It is expedient for you that I go away: for if I go not away, the Comforter will not come unto you; but if I depart, I will send him unto you. 8. And when he is come, he will reprove the world of sin, and of righteousness, and of judgment:

John 20:22. He breathed on *them*, and saith unto them, Receive ye the Holy Ghost:

Acts 1:5. For John truly baptized with water; but ye shall be baptized with the Holy Ghost not many days hence. 8. But ye shall receive power, after that the Holy Ghost is come upon you:

Acts 2:2. And suddenly there came a sound from heaven as of a rushing mighty wind, and it filled all the house where they were sitting. 3. And there appeared unto them cloven tongues like as of fire, and it sat upon each of them. 4. And they were all filled with the Holy Ghost, and began to speak with other tongues, as the Spirit gave them utterance.

Acts 4:8. Then Peter filled with the Holy Ghost, said unto them, Ye rulers of the people, and elders of Israel, 31. And when they had prayed, the place was shaken where they were assembled together; and they were all filled with the Holy Ghost, and they spake the word of God with boldness.

Acts 6:5. They chose Stephen, a man full of faith and of the Holy Ghost,

Acts 8:15. Who, when they were come down, prayed for them, that they might receive the Holy Ghost: 16. (For as yet he was fallen upon none of them: only they were baptized in the name of the Lord Jesus.) 17. Then laid they *their* hands on them, and they received the Holy Ghost.

Acts 9:31. Then had the churches rest . . . and walking in the fear of the Lord, and in the comfort of the Holy Ghost, were multiplied.

Acts 11:15. As I began to speak, the Holy Ghost fell on them, as on us at the beginning. 16. Then remembered I the word of the Lord, how that he said, John indeed baptized with water; but ye shall be baptized with the Holy Ghost.

Acts 13:2. As they ministered to the Lord, and fasted, the Holy Ghost said, Separate me Barnabas and Saul for the work whereunto I have called them. 4. So they, being sent forth by the Holy Ghost, departed unto Seleucia:

Acts 19:5. When they heard *this*, they were baptized in the name of the Lord Jesus. 6. And when Paul had laid *his* hands upon them, the Holy Ghost came on them; and they spake with tongues, and prophesied.

Rom. 5:5. The love of God is shed abroad in our hearts by the Holy Ghost which is given unto us. *vss.* 3-5.

Rom. 8:26. The Spirit also helpeth our infirmities: for we know not what we should pray for as we ought: but the Spirit itself maketh intercession for us with groanings which cannot be uttered. 27. And he that searcheth the hearts knoweth what *is* the mind of the Spirit, because he maketh intercession for the saints according to *the will of* God. *vss.* 1-27.

1 Cor. 3:16. Know ye not that ye are the temple of God, and *that* the Spirit of God dwelleth in you? I Cor. 6:19.

Gal. 4:6. Because ye are sons, God hath sent forth the Spirit of his Son into your hearts, crying, Abba, Father.

Gal. 6:8. He that soweth to the

Spirit shall of the Spirit reap life everlasting.

Eph. 2:18. Through him [Jesus Christ] we both have access by one Spirit unto the Father. 22. In whom ye also are builded together for an habitation of God through the Spirit.

1 Thess. 5:19. Quench not the Spirit.

1 Pet. 3:18. Christ also hath once suffered for sins, . . . being put to death in the flesh, but quickened by the Spirit:

Isa. 63:10. They rebelled, and vexed his holy Spirit: therefore he was turned to be their enemy,

Acts 7:51. Ye stiffnecked and uncircumcised in heart and ears, ye do always resist the Holy Ghost: as your fathers did, so do ye.

Eph. 4:30. And grieve not the holy Spirit of God, whereby ye are sealed unto the day of redemption.

Heb. 10:29. Of how much sorer punishment, suppose ye, shall he be thought worthy, who . . . hath done despite unto the Spirit of grace?

HOMICIDE. Accidental: Ex. 21:13. And if a man lie not in wait, but God deliver him into his hand; then I will appoint thee a place whither he shall flee. 28. If an ox gore a man or a woman, that they die: then the ox shall be surely stoned, and his flesh shall not be eaten; but the owner of the ox shall be quit. 29. But if the ox were wont to push with his horn in time past, and it hath been testified to his owner, and he hath not kept him in, but that he hath killed a man or a woman; the ox shall be stoned, and his owner also shall be put to death. 30. If there be laid on him a sum of money, then he shall give for the ransom of his life whatsoever is laid upon him.

Num. 35:11. Then ye shall appoint you cities to be cities of refuge for you; that the slayer may flee thither, which killeth any person at unawares.

Felonious, OR MURDER: Gen 4:9. And the LORD said . . . 10. What hast thou done? the voice of thy brother's blood crieth unto me from the ground. 11. And now art thou cursed from the earth, which hath opened her mouth to receive thy brother's blood from thy hand; v. 12.

Ex. 20:13. Thou shalt [not kill.] Deut. 5:17; Rom. 13:9. [R. V. do no murder]

Num. 35:20. But if he thrust him of hatred, or hurl at him by laying of wait, that he die; 21. Or in enmity smite him with his hand, that he die: he that smote him shall surely be put to death; for he is a murderer: the revenger of blood shall slay the murderer, when he meeteth him. 22. But if he thrust him suddenly without enmity, or have cast upon him any thing without laying of wait, 30. Whoso killeth any person, the murderer shall be put to death by the mouth of witnesses: but one witness shall not testify against any person to cause him to die. 31. Moreover ye shall take no satisfaction for the life of a murderer, which is guilty of death: but he shall be surely put to death.

Deut. 22:8. When thou buildest a new house, then thou shalt make a battlement for thy roof, that thou bring not blood upon thine house, if any man fall from thence.

Deut. 27:24. Cursed be he that smiteth his neighbour secretly. 25. Cursed be he that taketh reward to slay an innocent person. And all the people shall say, Amen.

Prov. 1:11. If they say, Come with us, let us lay wait for blood, let us lurk privily for the innocent without cause: 12. Let us swallow them up alive as the grave; and whole, as those that go down into the pit: 15. My son, walk not thou in the way with them; refrain thy foot from their path: 16. For their feet run to evil, and make haste to shed blood. Isa. 59:7.

Prov. 6:16. These . . . things doth the LORD hate: . . . 17. A proud look, a lying tongue, and hands that shed innocent blood.

Matt. 15:19. Out of the heart proceed evil thoughts, murders, Mark 7:21.

1 John 3:15. Whosoever hateth his brother is a murderer: and ye

know that no murderer hath eternal life abiding in him. *v.* 12.

Rev. 21:8. Murderers . . . shall have their part in the lake which burneth with fire and brimstone: which is the second death.

HONESTY. Lev. 19:35. Ye shall do no unrighteousness in judgment, in meteyard, in weight, or in measure. 36. Just balances, just weights, a just ephah, and a just hin, shall ye have: I *am* the LORD your God, which brought you out of the land of Egypt.

Deut. 25:13. Thou shalt not have in thy bag divers weights, a great and a small. 14. Thou shalt not have in thine house divers measures, a great and a small. 15. *But* thou shalt have a perfect and just weight, a perfect and just measure shalt thou have: that thy days may be lengthened in the land which the LORD thy God giveth thee. 16. For all that do such things, *and* all that do unrighteously, *are* an abomination unto the LORD thy God.

Psa. 24:4. He that hath clean hands, and a pure heart; who hath not lifted up his soul unto vanity, nor sworn deceitfully.

Prov. 11:1. A false balance *is* abomination to the LORD: but a just weight *is* his delight.

Luke 6:31. As ye would that men should do to you, do ye also to them likewise. Matt. 7:12.

Acts 24:16. And herein do I exercise myself, to have always a conscience void of offence toward God, and *toward* men.

2 Cor. 8:21. Providing for honest things, not only in the sight of the LORD, but also in the sight of men.

I Thess. 4:11. Study to be quiet, and to do your own business, and to work with your own hands, as we commanded you; 12. That ye may walk honestly toward them that are without, and *that* ye may have lack of nothing.

Heb. 13:18. Pray for us: for we trust we have a good conscience, in all things willing to live honestly.

HOPE. Psa. 31:24. Be of good courage, and he shall strengthen your heart, all ye that hope in the LORD.

Psa. 33:18. The eye of the LORD *is* upon them that fear him, upon them that hope in his mercy; 22. Let thy mercy, O LORD, be upon us, according as we hope in thee.

Psa. 39:7. Now, LORD, what wait I for? my hope *is* in thee.

Psa. 43:5. Why art thou cast down, O my soul? and why art thou disquieted within me? hope in God: for I shall yet praise him, *who is* the health of my countenance, and my God.

Psa. 71:5. Thou *art* my hope, O Lord GOD: *thou art* my trust from my youth. 14. I will hope continually, and will yet praise thee more and more.

Rom. 12:12. Rejoicing in hope;

1 Cor. 15:19. If in this life only we have hope in Christ, we are of all men most miserable.

Col. 1:5. The hope which is laid up for you in heaven, whereof ye heard before in the word of the truth of the gospel;

Heb. 11:1. Faith is the substance of things hoped for, the evidence of things not seen.

1 Pet. 3:15. *Be* ready always to *give* an answer to every man that asketh you a reason of the hope that is in you with meekness and fear:

HOSPITALITY. Ex. 22:21. Thou shalt neither vex a stranger nor oppress him: for ye were strangers in the land of Egypt.

Lev. 19:10. And thou shalt not glean thy vineyard, neither shalt thou gather *every* grape of thy vineyard; thou shalt leave them for the poor and stranger: I *am* the LORD your God.

Lev. 24:22. Ye shall have one manner of law, as well for the stranger, as for one of your own country: for I *am* the LORD your God.

Deut. 10:18. He doth execute the judgment of the fatherless and widow, and loveth the stranger, in giving him food and raiment. 19. Love ye therefore the stranger: for ye were strangers in the land of Egypt.

Deut. 27:19. Cursed *be* he that perverteth the judgment of the stranger, fatherless, and widow. And all the people shall say, Amen.

Luke 14:12. Then said he also to him that bade him, When thou makest a dinner or a supper, call not thy friends, nor thy brethren, neither thy kinsmen, nor *thy* rich neighbours; lest they also bid thee again, and a recompence be made thee. 13. But when thou makest a feast, call the poor, the maimed, the lame, the blind: 14. And thou shalt be blessed; for they cannot recompense thee: for thou shalt be recompensed at the resurrection of the just.

Rom. 12:13. Distributing to the necessity of saints; given to hospitality.

1 Tim. 3:2. A bishop then must be blameless, the husband of one wife, vigilant, sober, of good behaviour, given to hospitality, apt to teach;

1 Tim. 5:10. Well reported of for good works; if she have brought up children, if she have lodged strangers, if she have washed the saints' feet, if she have relieved the afflicted, if she have diligently followed every good work.

Heb. 13:2. Be not forgetful to entertain strangers: for thereby some have entertained angels unawares.

1 Pet. 4:9. Use hospitality one to another without grudging

HOUSE OF GOD. A place of prayer, Matt. 21:13; Mark 11:17; Luke 19:46. Holy, Eccl. 5:1; Isa. 62:9; Ezek. 43:12; 1 Cor. 3:17.

HUMILIATION AND SELF-AFFLICTION. Enjoined: Lev. 23:26. And the LORD spake unto Moses, saying, 27. Also on the tenth *day* of this seventh month *there shall be* a day of atonement: it shall be an holy convocation unto you; and ye shall afflict your souls, and offer an offering made by fire unto the LORD.

Ezra 8:21. Then I proclaimed a fast there, at the river of Ahava, that we might afflict ourselves before our God, to seek of him a right way for us, and for our little ones, and for all our substance.

2 Chr. 7:14. If my people, which are called by my name, shall humble themselves, and pray, and seek my face, and turn from their wicked ways; then will I hear from heaven, and will forgive their sin, and will heal their land.

HUMILITY. Deut. 15:15. And thou shalt remember that thou wast a bondman in the land of Egypt, and the LORD thy God redeemed thee:

Psa. 9:12. He forgetteth not the cry of the humble.

Psa. 22:6. But I *am* a worm, and no man; a reproach of men, and despised of the people. 26. The meek shall eat and be satisfied:

Psa. 86:1. Bow down thine ear, O LORD, hear me: for I *am* poor and needy.

Psa. 147:6. The LORD lifteth up the meek:

Prov. 11:2. With the lowly *is* wisdom.

Prov. 12:15. He that hearkeneth unto counsel *is* wise.

Prov. 15:33. Before honour *is* humility. Prov. 18:12.

Prov. 22:4. By humility *and* the fear of the LORD *are* riches, and honour, and life.

Prov. 27:2. Let another man praise thee, and not thine own mouth; a stranger, and not thine own lips.

Isa. 51:1. Look unto the rock *whence* ye are hewn, and to the hole of the pit *whence* ye are digged. Deut 32:7.

Matt. 5:3. Blessed *are* the poor in spirit: for their's is the kingdom of heaven. Luke 6:20.

Rom. 12:3. For I say, through the grace given unto me, to every man that is among you, not to think *of himself* more highly than he ought to think; but to think soberly, according as God hath dealt to every man the measure of faith.

1 Cor. 10:12. Let him that thinketh he standeth take heed lest he fall.

Gal. 5:26. Let us not be desirous of vain glory.

Jas. 4:6. God resisteth the proud, but giveth grace unto the humble. 10. Humble yourselves in the sight of the Lord, and he shall lift you up.

Gen. 32:10. I am not worthy of

the least of all the mercies, and of all the truth, which thou hast shewed unto thy servant;

Psa. 8:3. When I consider thy heavens, . . . 4. What is man, that thou art mindful of him? and the son of man, that thou visitest him? Job 7:17,18; Psa. 144:3,4.

Psa. 73:22. So foolish *was* I, and ignorant: I was *as* a beast before thee.

Isa. 38:15. I shall go softly all my years in the bitterness of my soul.

Rom. 7:18. I know that in me (that is, in my flesh,) dwelleth no good thing:

1 Cor. 15:10. By the grace of God I am what I am: . . . I laboured more abundantly than they all: yet not I, but the grace of God which was with me.

HUNGER.

Spiritual: Matt. 5:6. Blessed *are* they which do hunger and thirst after righteousness: for they shall be filled.

1 Pet. 2:2. As newborn babes, desire the sincere milk of the word, that ye may grow thereby:

HUNTING.
Authorized in the Mosaic law, Lev. 17:13. By Nimrod, Gen. 10:9. By Esau, Gen. 27: 3,5,30,33. By Ishmael, Gen. 21:20. Of lion, Job 10:16. Fowling, 1 Sam. 26:20; Psa. 140:5; 141:9,10; Prov. 1:17; Eccl. 9:12; Lam. 3:52; Amos 3:5.

HUSBAND.
Gen. 2:23. And Adam said, This *is* now bone of my bones, and flesh of my flesh: she shall be called Woman, because she was taken out of man. 24. Therefore shall a man leave his father and his mother, and shall cleave unto his wife: and they shall be one flesh. Matt. 19:5; Mark 10:7.

Deut. 24:5. When a man hath taken a new wife, he shall not go out to war, neither shall he be charged with any business: *but* he shall be free at home one year, and shall cheer up his wife which he hath taken.

Prov. 5:15. Drink waters out of thine own cistern, and running waters out of thine own well. 16. Let thy fountains be dispersed abroad, *and* rivers of waters in the streets. 17. Let them be only thine own, and not strangers' with thee. 18. Let thy fountain be blessed: and rejoice with the wife of thy youth. 19. *Let her be as* the loving hind and pleasant roe; let her breasts satisfy thee at all times; and be thou ravished always with her love.

Eccl. 9:9. Live joyfully with the wife whom thou lovest all the days of the life of thy vanity, which he hath given thee under the sun, all the days of thy vanity: for that *is* thy portion in *this* life, and in thy labour which thou takest under the sun.

Mal. 2:14. Yet ye say, Wherefore? Because the LORD hath been witness between thee and the wife of thy youth, against whom thou hast dealt treacherously: yet *is* she thy companion, and the wife of thy covenant. 15. And did not he make one? Yet had he the residue of the spirit. And wherefore one? That he might seek a godly seed. Therefore take heed to your spirit, and let none deal treacherously against the wife of his youth. 16. For the LORD, the God of Israel, saith that he hateth putting away: for *one* covereth violence with his garment, saith the LORD of hosts: therefore take heed to your spirit, that ye deal not treacherously.

1 Cor. 7:3. Let the husband render unto the wife due benevolence: and likewise also the wife unto the husband. 5. Defraud ye not one the other, except *it be* with consent for a time, that ye may give yourselves to fasting and prayer; and come together again, that Satan tempt you not for your incontinency.

1 Cor. 11:3. But I would have you know, that the head of every man is Christ; and the head of the woman *is* the man; and the head of Christ *is* God.

Eph. 5:22. Wives, submit yourselves unto your own husbands, as unto the Lord. 23. For the husband is the head of the wife, even as Christ is the head of the church: and he is the saviour of the body.

24. Therefore as the church is subject unto Christ, so *let* the wives *be* to their own husbands in everything. 25. Husbands, love your wives, even as Christ also loved the church, and gave himself for it; 31. For this cause shall a man leave his father and mother, and shall be joined unto his wife, and they two shall be one flesh.

Col. 3:18. Wives, submit yourselves unto your own husbands, as it is fit in the Lord. 19. Husbands, love *your* wives, and be not bitter against them.

1 Tim. 5:8. But if any provide not for his own, and specially for those of his own house, he hath denied the faith, and is worse than an [infidel.] [R. V. unbeliever]

I Pet. 3:7. Likewise, ye husbands, dwell with *them* according to knowledge, giving honour unto the wife, as unto the weaker vessel, and as being heirs together of the grace of life; that your prayers be not hindered.

HYPOCRISY. Psa. 52:4. Thou lovest all devouring words, O *thou* deceitful tongue.

Psa. 55:12. *It was* not an enemy *that* reproached me; then I could have borne *it:* neither *was it* he that hated me *that* did magnify *himself* against me; then I would have hid myself from him: 13. But *it was* thou, a man mine equal, my guide, and mine acquaintance. 14. We took sweet counsel together, *and* walked unto the house of God in company. 20. He hath put forth his hands against such as be at peace with him: he hath broken his covenant. 21. *The words* of his mouth were smoother than butter, but war *was* in his heart: his words were softer than oil, yet *were* they drawn swords.

Psa. 78:36. Nevertheless they did flatter him with their mouth, and they lied unto him with their tongues.

Prov. 20:14. *It is* naught, *it is* naught, saith the buyer: but when he is gone his way, then he boasteth.

Prov. 25:19. Confidence in an unfaithful man in time of trouble *is like* a broken tooth, and a foot out of joint.

Isa. 29:13. This people draw near *me* with their mouth, and with their lips do honour me, but have removed their heart far from me, and their fear toward me is taught by the precept of men. [Matt. 15:8.]

Jer. 17:9. The heart *is* deceitful above all *things* and desperately [wicked:] who can know it? [R. V. sick]

Obad. 7. The men that were at peace with thee have deceived thee, *and* prevailed against thee; *they that eat* thy bread have laid a wound under thee:

Matt. 3:7. O generation of vipers, who hath warned you to flee from the wrath to come? 8. Bring forth therefore fruits meet for repentance:

Matt. 7:5. Thou hypocrite, first cast out the beam out of thine own eye; and then shalt thou see clearly to cast out the mote out of thy brother's eye.

Matt. 15:7. *Ye* hypocrites, well did Esaias prophesy of you, saying, 8. This people draweth nigh unto me with their mouth, and honoureth me with *their* lips; but their heart is far from me. [Mark 7:6.] 9. But in vain they do worship me, teaching *for* doctrines the commandments of men.

Matt: 23:23. Woe unto you, scribes and Pharisees, hypocrites! for ye pay tithe of mint and anise and cummin, and have omitted the weightier *matters* of the law, judgment, mercy, and faith: these ought ye to have done, and not to leave the other undone. 24. *Ye* blind guides, which strain [at a] gnat, and swallow [a] camel. 25. Woe unto you, scribes and Pharisees, hypocrites! for ye make clean the outside of the cup and of the platter, but within they are full of extortion and excess. 26. *Thou* blind Pharisee, cleanse first that *which is* within the cup and platter, that the outside of them may be clean also. 27. Woe unto you, scribes and Pharisees, hypocrites! for ye are like unto whited sepulchres, which indeed appear beautiful outward, but are within full of dead *men's* bones, and of all uncleanness. 28. Even so ye also outwardly appear righteous unto men, but within ye are full of hypocrisy and iniquity.

Luke 6:46. Why call ye me, Lord, Lord, and do not the things which I say?

Luke 18:11. The Pharisee stood and prayed thus with himself, God, I thank thee, that I am not as other men *are*, extortioners, unjust, adulterers, or even as this publican. 12. I fast twice in the week, I give tithes of all that I possess.

I AM THAT I AM, a name of deity, Ex. 3:14; Rev. 1:4,11,17.

IDLENESS. Prov. 6:6. Go to the ant, thou sluggard; consider her ways, and be wise: 9. How long wilt thou sleep, O sluggard? when wilt thou arise out of thy sleep? 10. *Yet* a little sleep, a little slumber, a little folding of the hands to sleep: 11: So shall thy poverty come as one that travelleth, and thy want as an armed man. Prov. 24:33.

Prov. 10:4. He becometh poor that dealeth *with* a slack hand: 5. He that sleepeth in harvest *is* a son that causeth shame.

Prov. 14:23. In all labour there is profit: but the talk of the lips *tendeth* only to penury.

Prov. 18:9. He also that is slothful in his work is brother to him that is a great waster.

Prov. 20:4. The sluggard will not plow by reason of the cold: *therefore* shall he beg in harvest, and *have* nothing. 13. Love not sleep, lest thou come to poverty:

Prov. 23:21. Drowsiness shall clothe *a man* with rags.

Prov. 24:33. *Yet* a little sleep, a little slumber, a little folding of the hands to sleep: 34. So shall thy poverty come *as* one that travelleth; and thy want as an armed man.

1 Tim. 5:13. Withal they learn *to be* idle, wandering about from house to house; and not only idle, but tattlers also and busybodies, speaking things which they ought not.

IDOLATRY. Ex. 20:3. Thou shalt have no other gods before me.

4. Thou shalt not make unto thee any graven image, or any likeness *of any thing* that *is* in heaven above, or that *is* in the earth beneath, or that *is* in the water under the earth: 5. Thou shalt not bow down thyself to them, nor serve them: for I the LORD thy God am a jealous God, visiting the iniquity of the fathers upon the children unto the third and fourth *generation* of them that hate me; 6. And shewing mercy unto thousands of them that love me, and keep my commandments. 23. Ye shall not make with me gods of silver, neither shall ye make unto you gods of gold. Deut. 5:7-9.

Acts 17:16. Now while Paul waited for them at Athens, his spirit was stirred in him, when he saw the city wholly given to idolatry.

Rom. 1:25. Who changed the truth of God into a lie, and worshipped and served the creature more than the Creator,

Rev. 21:8. Idolaters . . . shall have their part in the lake which burneth with fire and brimstone: which is the second death. Rev. 22:15.

1 Kin. 18:27. Elijah mocked them, and said, Cry aloud: for he *is* a god; either he is talking, or he is pursuing, or he is in a journey, *or* peradventure he sleepeth, and must be awaked. Judg. 6:31; 1 Sam. 5:3,4.

Psa. 115:4. Their idols *are* silver and gold, the work of men's hands. 5. They have mouths, but they speak not: eyes have they, but they see not: 8. They that make them are like unto them; *so is* every one that trusteth in them. Psa. 96:5; 135:15-18; Isa. 2:8.

Isa. 45:20. They have no knowledge that set up the wood of their graven image, and pray unto a god *that* cannot save.

IGNORANCE. Job 36:26. God *is* great, and we know *him* not, neither can the number of his years be searched out. 29. Can *any* understand the spreadings of the clouds, *or* the noise of his tabernacle?

Prov. 27:1. Boast not thyself of

tomorrow; for thou knowest not what a day may bring forth.

Jer. 10:23. O LORD, I know that the way of man *is* not in himself: *it is* not in man that walketh to direct his steps.

Acts 1:7. It is not for you to know the times or the seasons, which the Father hath put in his own power.

Acts 17:23. For as I passed by, and beheld your devotions, I found an altar with this inscription, TO THE UNKNOWN GOD. Whom therefore ye ignorantly worship, him declare I unto you. 30. And the times of this ignorance God winked at; but now commandeth all men everywhere to repent:

Jas. 1:5. If any of you lack wisdom, let him ask of God, that giveth to all *men* liberally, and upbraideth not; and it shall be given him. 6. But let him ask in faith, nothing [wavering.] For he that [wavereth] is like a wave of the sea driven with the wind and tossed. [R. V. doubting doubteth]

Num. 15:24. Then it shall be, if *ought* be committed by ignorance without the knowledge of the congregation, that all the congregation shall offer one young bullock for a burnt offering, for a sweet savour unto the LORD.

IMAGINATION. Gen. 6:5. And GOD saw that the wickedness of man *was* great in the earth, and *that* every imagination of the thoughts of his heart *was* only evil continually.

Matt. 5:28. Whosoever looketh on a woman to lust after her hath committed adultery with her already in his heart.

IMMORTALITY. Gen. 5:24. Enoch walked with God: and he *was* not; for God took him.

2 Sam. 12:23. But now he is dead, wherefore should I fast? can I bring him back again? I shall go to him, but he shall not return to me.

2 Kin. 2:11. And it came to pass, as they still went on, and talked, that, behold, *there appeared* a chariot of fire, and horses of fire, and parted them both asunder: and

Elijah went up by a whirlwind into heaven.

Psa. 21:4. He asked life of thee, *and* thou gavest *it* him, *even* length of days for ever and ever.

Psa. 121:8. The LORD shall preserve thy going out and thy coming in from this time forth, and even for evermore.

Dan. 12:2. And many of them that sleep in the dust of the earth shall awake, some to everlasting life, and some to shame *and* everlasting contempt. 3. And they that be wise shall shine as the brightness of the firmament; and they that turn many to righteousness as the stars for ever and ever.

Mark 12:26. And as touching the dead, that they rise: have ye not read in the book of Moses, how in the bush God spake unto him, saying, I *am* the God of Abraham, and the God of Isaac, and the God of Jacob? 27. He is not the God of the dead, but the God of the living: ye therefore do greatly err.

John 17:2. As thou hast given him power over all flesh, that he should give eternal life to as many as thou hast given him. 3. And this is life eternal, that they might know thee the only true God, and Jesus Christ, whom thou hast sent.

Rom. 2:7. To them who by patient continuance in well doing seek for glory and honour and immortality, eternal life:

Rom. 6:23. For the wages of sin *is* death; but the gift of God *is* eternal life through Jesus Christ our Lord.

1 Tim. 4:8. Godliness is profitable unto all things, having promise of the life that now is, and of that which is to come.

1 John 2:17. The world passeth away, and the lust thereof: but he that doeth the will of God abideth for ever. 25. And this is the promise that he hath promised us, *even* eternal life.

IMPENITENCE. Lev. 26:21. If ye walk contrary unto me, and will not hearken unto me; I will bring seven times more plagues upon you according to your sins. *vss.* 22-24.

Deut. 29:19. And it come to pass, when he heareth the words of this curse, that he bless himself in his heart, saying, I shall have peace, though I walk in the imagination of mine heart, to add drunkenness to thirst: 20. The LORD will not spare him, but then the anger of the LORD and his jealousy shall smoke against that man, and all the curses that are written in this book shall lie upon him, and the LORD shall blot out his name from under heaven. 21. And the LORD shall separate him unto evil out of all the tribes of Israel, according to all the curses of the covenant that are written in this book of the law:

1 Sam. 15:23. For rebellion is as the sin of witchcraft, and stubbornness is as iniquity and idolatry. Because thou hast rejected the word of the LORD, he hath also rejected thee from being king.

Psa. 82:5. They know not, neither will they understand; they walk on in darkness:

Prov. 1:25. But ye have set at nought all my counsel, and would none of my reproof:

Prov. 21:29. A wicked man hardeneth his face:

Prov. 26:11. As a dog returneth to his vomit, so a fool returneth to his folly.

Jer. 7:13. I spake unto you, rising up early and speaking, but ye heard not; and I called you, but ye answered not;

Jer. 8:5. Why then is this people of Jerusalem slidden back by a perpetual backsliding? they hold fast deceit, they refuse to return.

Jer. 12:11. The whole land is made desolate, because no man layeth it to heart.

Matt. 23:37. O Jerusalem, Jerusalem, thou that killest the prophets, and stonest them which are sent unto thee, how often would I have gathered thy children together, even as a hen gathereth her chickens under her wings, and ye would not! 38. Behold, your house is left unto you desolate. Luke 13:34.

Mark 3:5. He looked round about on them with anger, being grieved for the hardness of their hearts,

Luke 16:31. And he said unto him, If they hear not Moses and the prophets, neither will they be persuaded, though one rose from the dead.

Acts 7:51. Ye stiffnecked and uncircumcised in heart and ears, ye do always resist the Holy Ghost: as your fathers did, so do ye.

Rom. 2:4. Despisest thou the riches of his goodness and forbearance and longsuffering; not knowing that the goodness of God leadeth thee to repentance? 5. After thy hardness and impenitent heart treasurest up unto thyself wrath against the day of wrath and revelation of the righteous judgment of God;

Heb. 12:17. For ye know how that afterward, when he would have inherited the blessing, he was rejected: for he found no place of repentance, though he sought it carefully with tears.

INCEST. Defined and Forbidden: Lev. 18:6. None of you shall approach to any that is near of kin to him, to uncover their nakedness. I am the LORD.

1 Cor. 5:1. It is reported commonly that there is fornication among you, and such fornication as is not so much as named among the Gentiles, that one should have his father's wife.

INCONSISTENCY. Matt. 7: 3. And why beholdest thou the mote that is in thy brother's eye, but considerest not the beam that is in thine own eye?

Matt. 23:3. All therefore whatsoever they bid you observe, that observe and do; but do not ye after their works: for they say, and do not. 4. For they bind heavy burdens and grievous to be borne, and lay them on men's shoulders; but they themselves will not move them with one of their fingers.

Rom. 2:1. Therefore thou art inexcusable, O man, whosoever thou art that judgest: for wherein thou judgest another, thou condemnest thyself; for thou that judgest doest the same things.

143

INDECISION. 1 Kin. 18:21. How long halt ye between two opinions? if the LORD be God, follow him: but if Baal, then follow him.

Matt. 6:24. No man can serve two masters: for either he will hate the one, and love the other; or else he will hold to the one, and despise the other. Ye cannot serve God and mammon.

Jas. 1:8. A double minded man is unstable in all his ways.

Jas. 4:17. To him that knoweth to do good, and doeth it not, to him it is sin.

INDUSTRY. Gen. 2:15. The LORD God took the man, and put him into the garden of Eden to dress it and to keep it.

Ex. 23:12. Six days thou shalt do thy work, and on the seventh day thou shalt rest: Deut. 5:13.

Prov. 10:4. He becometh poor that dealeth with a slack hand: but the hand of the diligent maketh rich. 5. He that gathereth in summer is a wise son:

Prov. 14:4. Where no oxen are, the crib is clean: but much increase is by the strength of the ox. 23. In all labour there is profit:

Prov. 31:27. She looketh well to the ways of her household, and eateth not the bread of idleness. vss. 13-27.

Rom. 12:11. [Not slothful in business;] fervent in spirit; serving the Lord; [R. V. In diligence not slothful]

Eph. 4:28. Let him that stole steal no more: but rather let him labour, working with his hands the thing which is good, that he may have to give to him that needeth.

1 Tim. 5:8. If any provide not for his own, and specially for those of his own house, he hath denied the faith, and is worse than an infidel.

INFIDELITY. Deut. 32:15. Jeshurun waxed fat, and kicked: thou art waxen fat, thou art grown thick, thou art covered with fatness; then he forsook God which made him, and lightly esteemed the Rock of his salvation.

2 Chr. 36:16. They mocked the messengers of God, and despised his words, and misused his prophets, until the wrath of the LORD arose against his people, till there was no remedy.

Job 21:14. They say unto God, Depart from us; for we desire not the knowledge of thy ways. 15. What is the Almighty, that we should serve him? and what profit should we have, if we pray unto him?

Matt. 12:24. When the Pharisees heard it, they said, This fellow doth not cast out devils, but by Beelzebub the prince of the devils. Mark 3:22; Luke 11:15; 16:14.

Matt. 27:39. And they that passed by reviled him, wagging their heads, 40. And saying, Thou that destroyest the temple, and buildest it in three days, save thyself. If thou be the Son of God, come down from the cross. 41. Likewise also the chief priests mocking him, with the scribes and elders, said, 42. He saved others; himself he cannot save. If he be the King of Israel, let him now come down from the cross, and we will believe him. 43. He trusted in God; let him deliver him now, if he will have him: for he said, I am the Son of God. 44. The thieves also, which were crucified with him, cast the same in his teeth.

INFIRMITY. Physical: Moses exempt from, Deut. 34:7; Caleb, Josh. 14:11.

INFLUENCE. Evil: 1 Kin. 11:3. And he had seven hundred wives, princesses, and three hundred concubines: and his wives turned away his heart.

1 Kin. 21:25. But there was none like unto Ahab, which did sell himself to work wickedness in the sight of the LORD, whom Jezebel his wife stirred up.

2 Kin. 21:9. But they hearkened not: and Manasseh seduced them to do more evil than did the nations whom the LORD destroyed before the children of Israel.

Prov. 22:24. Make no friendship with an angry man; and with a furious man thou shalt not go; 25.

Lest thou learn his ways, and get a snare to thy soul.

Prov. 29:12. If a ruler hearken to lies, all his servants *are* wicked.

Hos. 4:9. And there shall be, like people, like priest: and I will punish them for their ways, and reward them their doings.

Gal. 5:7. Ye did run well; who did hinder you that ye should not obey the truth? 8. This persuasion *cometh* not of him that calleth you. 9. A little leaven leaveneth the whole lump.

Good: 2 Kin. 15:2. Sixteen years old was he when he began to reign, and he reigned two and fifty years in Jerusalem. And his mother's name *was* Jecholiah of Jerusalem. 3. And he did *that which was* right in the sight of the LORD, according to all that his father Amaziah had done;

1 Cor. 7:16. For what knowest thou, O wife, whether thou shalt save *thy* husband? or how knowest thou, O man, whether thou shalt save *thy* wife ?

1 Thess. 1:7. Ye were ensamples to all that believe in Macedonia and Achaia.

Political: 2 Kin. 4:12. And he said to Gehazi his servant, Call this Shunammite. And when he had called her, she stood before him. 13. And he said unto him, Say now unto her, Behold, thou hast been careful for us with all this care; what *is* to be done for thee? wouldest thou be spoken for to the king, or to the captain of the host? And she answered, I dwell among mine own people.

Prov. 19:6. Many will intreat the favour of the prince: and every man *is* a friend to him that giveth gifts.

Matt. 20:20. Then came to him the mother of Zebedee's children with her sons, worshipping *him*, and desiring a certain thing of him. 21. And he said unto her, What wilt thou? She saith unto him, Grant that these my two sons may sit, the one on thy right hand, and the other on the left, in thy kingdom.

INGRATITUDE. Of Man to God: Deut. 32:6. Do ye thus requite the LORD, O foolish people and unwise? *is* not he thy father *that* hath bought thee? hath he not made thee, and established thee?

Judg. 10:11. *Did* not *I deliver you* from the Egyptians, and from the Amorites, 13. Yet ye have forsaken me, and served other gods: wherefore I will deliver you no more. 14. Go and cry unto the gods which ye have chosen; let them deliver you in the time of your tribulation. Neh. 9:25,35; Psa. 106: 7,21; Jer. 2:6,7.

1 Sam. 8:7. And the LORD said unto Samuel, Hearken unto the voice of the people in all that they say unto thee: for they have not rejected thee, but they have rejected me, that I should not reign over them.

1 Sam. 10:19. Ye have this day rejected your God, who himself saved you out of all your adversities and your tribulations; and ye have said unto him, *Nay*, but set a king over us.

2 Chr. 32:25. Hezekiah rendered not again according to the benefit *done* unto him; for his heart was lifted up: therefore there was wrath upon him, and upon Judah and Jerusalem.

Isa. 1:2. I have nourished and brought up children, and they have rebelled against me.

Jer. 5:7. How shall I pardon thee for this? thy children have forsaken me, and sworn by *them that are* no gods: when I had fed them to the full, they then committed adultery, 9. Shall I not visit for these *things?* saith the LORD: and shall not my soul be avenged on such a nation as this?

John 1:11. He came unto his own, and his own received him not.

INHERITANCE. Gen. 24:36. And Sarah my master's wife bare a son to my master when she was old: and unto him hath he given all that he hath.

1 Kin. 21:3. And Naboth said to Ahab, The LORD forbid it me, that I should give the inheritance of my fathers unto thee.

2 Chr. 21:3. And their father gave them great gifts of silver, and of gold, and of precious things,

with fenced cities in Judah: but the kingdom gave he to Jehoram; because he *was* the firstborn.

Figurative: Psa. 37:29. The righteous shall inherit the land, and dwell therein for ever.

Rom. 8:16. The Spirit itself beareth witness with our spirit, that we are the children of God: 17. And if children, then heirs; heirs of God, and joint-heirs with Christ; if so be that we suffer with *him*, that we may be also glorified together.

Eph. 1:11. In whom also we have obtained an inheritance, being predestinated according to the purpose of him who worketh all things after the counsel of his own will:

INJUSTICE. Ex. 22:21. Thou shalt neither vex a stranger, nor oppress him: 22. Ye shall not afflict any widow, or fatherless child.

Ex. 23:1. Thou shall not raise a false report: put not thine hand with the wicked to be an unrighteous witness.

2. Thou shalt not follow a multitude to *do evil;* neither shalt thou speak in a cause to decline after many to wrest *judgment:* 3. Neither shalt thou countenance a poor man in his cause.

Job 31:13. If I did despise the cause of my manservant or of my maidservant, when they contended with me: 14. What then shall I do when God riseth up? and when he visiteth, what shall I answer him?

Prov. 17:15. He that justifieth the wicked, and he that condemneth the just, even they both *are* abomination to the LORD.

Zeph. 3:5. The unjust knoweth no shame.

Luke 16:10. He that is unjust in the least is unjust also in much.

INSANITY. Prov. 26:18. Feigned by David, 1 Sam. 21:13-15. Sent as a judgment from God, Deut. 28:28; Zech. 12:4. Nebuchadnezzar's, Dan. 4:32-34. Jesus accused of, Mark 3:21; John 10:20. Paul, Acts 26:24,25. Cured by Jesus, Matt. 4:24; 17:15. Demoniacal: Saul, 1 Sam. 16:14; 18:10.

INSOMNIA. Instances of:

Ahasuerus, Esth. 6:1. Nebuchadnezzar, Dan. 6:18.

INSPIRATION. Ex. 19:6. These *are* the words which thou shalt speak unto the children of Israel.

Luke 12:12. For the Holy Ghost shall teach you in the same hour what ye ought to say. Matt. 10:19; Mark 13:11; Luke 21:14,15.

2 Tim. 3:16. All scripture *is* given by inspiration of God, and *is* profitable for doctrine, for reproof, for correction, for instruction in righteousness:

INSTABILITY. 1 Kin. 18:21. And Elijah came unto all the people, and said, How long halt ye between two opinions? if the LORD *be* God, follow him: but if Baal, *then* follow him. And the people answered him not a word.

Matt. 6:24. No man can serve two masters: for either he will hate the one, and love the other: or else he will hold to the one, and despise the other. Ye cannot serve God and mammon.

Matt. 12:25. And Jesus knew their thoughts and said unto them, Every kingdom divided against itself is brought to desolation; and every city or house divided against itself shall not stand:

John 5:35. He was a burning and a shining light: and ye were willing for a season to rejoice in his light.

Gal. 1:6. I marvel that ye are so soon removed from him that called you into the grace of Christ unto another gospel:

Eph. 4:14. That we *henceforth* be no more children, tossed to and fro, and carried about with every wind of doctrine, by the sleight of men, *and* cunning craftiness, whereby they lie in wait to deceive;

Rev. 2:4. I have *somewhat* against thee, because thou hast left thy first love.

INSTINCT. Of animals, Prov. 1:17; Isa. 1:3. Of birds, Jer. 8:7.

INSTRUCTION. Ezra 7:10. For Ezra had prepared his heart to seek the law of the LORD, and to do *it*, and to teach in Israel statutes and judgments.

Psa. 119:12. Blessed *art* thou, O

LORD: teach me thy statutes. *vss.* 3-125.

Jer. 32:33. And they have turned unto me the back, and not the face: though I taught them, rising up early and teaching *them,* yet they have not hearkened to receive instruction.

Rom. 2:18. And knowest *his* will, and approvest the things that are more excellent, being instructed out of the law;

1 Cor. 12:28. And God hath set some in the church, first apostles, secondarily prophets, thirdly teachers, after that miracles, then gifts of healings, helps, governments, diversities of tongues. 29. *Are* all apostles? *are* all prophets? *are* all teachers? *are* all workers of miracles?

Of Children: Ex. 10:2. And that thou mayest tell in the ears of thy son, and of thy son's son, what things I have wrought in Egypt, and my signs which I have done among them; that ye may know how that I *am* the LORD.

Ex. 13:8. And thou shalt shew thy son in that day, saying, *This is done* because of that *which* the LORD did unto me when I came forth out of Egypt.

Deut. 6:6. And these words, which I command thee this day, shall be in thine heart: 7. And thou shalt teach them diligently unto thy children, and shalt talk of them when thou sittest in thine house, and when thou walkest by the way, and when thou liest down, and when thou risest up. 8. And thou shalt bind them for a sign upon thine hand, and they shall be as frontlets between thine eyes. 9. And thou shalt write them upon the posts of thy house, and on thy gates.

Psa. 34:11. Come, ye children, hearken unto me: I will teach you the fear of the LORD.

Psa. 78:5. For he established a testimony in Jacob, and appointed a law in Israel, which he commanded our fathers, that they should make them known to their children: 6. That the generation to come might know *them, even* the children *which* should be born; *who* should arise and declare *them* to their children:

2 Tim. 3:15. And that from a child thou hast known the holy scriptures, which are able to make thee wise unto salvation through faith which is in Christ Jesus.

INTEGRITY. Gen. 18:19. For I know him, that he will command his children and his household after him, and they shall keep the way of the LORD, to do justice and judgment; that the LORD may bring upon Abraham that which he hath spoken of him.

Ex. 18:21. Moreover thou shalt provide out of all the people able men, such as fear God, men of truth, hating covetousness;

Deut. 16:19. Thou shalt not wrest judgment; thou shalt not respect persons, neither take a gift: for a gift doth blind the eyes of the wise, and pervert the words of the righteous.

Psa. 26:1. Judge me, O LORD; for I have walked in mine integrity: I have trusted also in the LORD; *therefore* I shall not slide. 2. Examine me, O LORD, and prove me; try my reins and my heart. 3. I have walked in thy truth.

Prov. 3:3. Let not mercy and truth forsake thee: bind them about thy neck; write them upon the table of thine heart: 4. So shalt thou find favour and good understanding in the sight of God and man.

Prov. 4:25. Let thine eyes look right on, and let thine eyelids look straight before thee. 26. Ponder the path of thy feet, and let all thy ways be established. 27. Turn not to the right hand nor to the left: remove thy foot from evil.

Prov. 10:9. He that walketh uprightly walketh surely:

Prov. 11:3. The integrity of the upright shall guide them: 5. The righteousness of the perfect shall direct his way:

2 Cor. 4:2. But have renounced the hidden things of dishonesty, not walking in craftiness, nor handling the word of God deceitfully; but by manifestation of the truth commending ourselves to every man's

conscience in the sight of God. 2 Cor. 5:11.

2 Cor. 8:21. Providing for honest things, not only in the sight of the Lord, but also in the sight of men.

Tit. 1:7. For a bishop must be blameless, as a steward of God:

1 Pet. 3:16. Having a good conscience; that whereas they speak evil of you, as of evildoers, they may be ashamed that falsely accuse your good conversation in Christ.

INTERCESSION. Ex. 32:9. And the LORD said unto Moses, I have seen this people, and, behold, it *is* a stiffnecked people: 10. Now therefore let me alone, that my wrath may wax hot against them, and that I may consume them: and I will make of thee a great nation. 11. And Moses besought the LORD his God, and said, LORD, why doth thy wrath wax hot against thy people, which thou hast brought forth out of the land of Egypt with great power, and with a mighty hand? 12. Wherefore should the Egyptians speak, and say, For mischief did he bring them out, to slay them in the mountains, and to consume them from the face of the earth? Turn from thy fierce wrath, and repent of this evil against thy people. 13. Remember Abraham, Isaac, and Israel, thy servants, to whom thou swarest by thine own self, and saidst unto them, I will multiply your seed as the stars of heaven, and all this land that I have spoken of will I give unto your seed, and they shall inherit *it* for ever. 14. And the LORD repented of the evil which he thought to do unto his people.

Num. 16:46. And Moses said unto Aaron, Take a censer, and put fire therein from off the altar, and put on incense, and go quickly unto the congregation, and make an atonement for them: for there is wrath gone out from the LORD; the plague is begun.

Deut. 5:5. (I stood between the LORD and you at that time, to shew you the word of the LORD: for ye were afraid by reason of the fire, and went not up into the mount;)

Deut. 9:18. And I fell down before the LORD, as at the first, forty days and forty nights: I did neither eat bread, nor drink water, because of all your sins which ye sinned, in doing wickedly in the sight of the LORD, to provoke him to anger.

1 Sam. 7:5. And Samuel said, Gather all Israel to Mizpeh, and I will pray for you unto the LORD.

1 Sam. 12:23. Moreover as for me, God forbid that I should sin against the LORD in ceasing to pray for you: but I will teach you the good and the right way:

Job 16:21. O that one might plead for a man with God, as a man *pleadeth* for his neighbour!

Isa. 62:6. I have set watchmen upon thy walls, O Jerusalem, *which* shall never hold their peace day nor night: ye that make mention of the LORD, keep not silence, 7. And give him no rest, till he establish, and till he make Jerusalem a praise in the earth.

Jer. 7:16. Therefore pray not thou for this people, neither lift up cry nor prayer for them, neither make intercession to me: for I will not hear thee.

Ezek. 22:30. And I sought for a man among them, that should make up the hedge, and stand in the gap before me for the land, that I should not destroy it: but I found none.

Eph. 6:18. Praying always with all prayer and supplication in the Spirit, and watching thereunto with all perseverance and supplication for all saints;

1 Tim. 2:1. I exhort therefore, that, first of all, supplications, prayers, intercessions, *and* giving of thanks, be made for all men; 2. For kings, and *for* all that are in authority;

1 John 5:16. If any man see his brother sin a sin *which is* not unto death, he shall ask, and he shall give him life for them that sin not unto death. There is a sin unto death: I do not say that he shall pray for it.

Ex. 32:31. Moses returned unto the LORD, and said, Oh, this people have sinned a great sin, and have made them gods of gold. 32. Yet now, if thou wilt forgive their sin—; and if not, blot me, I pray thee, out of thy book which thou hast written.

Dan. 9:3. And I set my face unto the LORD God, to seek by prayer and supplications, with fasting, and sackcloth, and ashes: 4. And I prayed unto the LORD my God, and made my confession, and said, O LORD, the great and dreadful God, keeping the covenant and mercy to them that love him, and to them that keep his commandments; 5. We have sinned, and have committed iniquity, and have done wickedly, and have rebelled, even by departing from thy precepts and from thy judgments: 6. Neither have we hearkened unto thy servants the prophets, which spake in thy name to our kings, our princes, and our fathers, and to all the people of the land. 7. O Lord, righteousness *belongeth* unto thee, but unto us confusion of faces, as at this day; to the men of Judah, and to the inhabitants of Jerusalem, and unto all Israel, *that are* near, and *that are* far off, through all the countries whither thou hast driven them, because of their trespass that they have trespassed against thee. 8. O LORD, to us *belongeth* confusion of face, to our kings, to our princes, and to our fathers, because we have sinned against thee. 9. To the Lord our God *belong* mercies and forgiveness, though we have rebelled against him;

Matt. 5:44. Pray for them which despitefully use you, and persecute you;

Eph. 3:14. For this cause I bow my knees unto the Father of our Lord Jesus Christ, 15. Of whom the whole family in heaven and earth is named. 16. That he would grant you, according to the riches of his glory, to be strengthened with might by his Spirit in the inner man; 17. That Christ may dwell in your hearts by faith; that ye, being rooted and grounded in love, 18. May be able to comprehend with all saints what *is* the breadth, and length, and depth, and height; 19. And to know the love of Christ,

which passeth knowledge, that ye might be filled with all the fulness of God.

Gen. 19:22. Haste thee, escape thither; for I cannot do any thing till thou be come thither.

INTEREST. Income from loaning money, usually called usury in the scriptures, but not generally signifying unlawful or unjust rates.

Deut. 23:19. Thou shalt not lend upon usury to thy brother; usury of money, usury of victuals, usury of any thing that is lent upon usury: 20. Unto a stranger thou mayest lend upon usury; but unto thy brother thou shalt not lend upon usury: that the LORD thy God may bless thee in all that thou settest thine hand to in the land whither thou goest to possess it.

Ezek. 22:12. In thee have they taken gifts to shed blood; thou hast taken usury and increase, and thou hast greedily gained of thy neighbours by extortion, and hast forgotten me, saith the Lord GOD.

INTERPRETATION. Of dreams, see DREAM. Of foreign tongues, 1 Cor. 14:9-19.

JESTING. Foolish, forbidden, Eph. 5:4. See Matt. 12:36.

JESUS, THE CHRIST. History of: Genealogy of, Matt. 1:1-17; Luke 3:23-38.

Facts before the birth of: The Angel Gabriel appears to Mary [Nazareth], Luke 1:26-38. Mary visits Elisabeth [Hebron?], Luke 1:39-56. Mary's *magnificat* [Hebron?], Luke 1:46-55. An angel appears to Joseph concerning Mary, Matt. 1:18-25.

Birth of [Bethlehem], Luke 2:1-7.

Angels appear to the shepherds, Luke 2: 8-20.

Magi visit [Bethlehem], Matt. 2:1-12.

Circumcision of [Bethlehem], Luke 2:21. Is presented in the temple [Jerusalem], Luke 2:21-38.

Flight into, and return from, Egypt, Matt. 2:13-23.

Disputes with the doctors in the temple [Jerusalem], Luke 2:41-52.

Is baptized by John [Jordan], Matt. 3:13-17; Mark 1:9-11; Luke 3:21-23.

Temptation of [Desert of Judæa], Matt. 4: 1-11; Mark. 1:12,13; Luke 4:1-13.

John's testimony concerning him, John 1:1-18.

Testimony of John the Baptist concerning [Bethabara], John 1:19-34.

Disciples adhere to, John 1:35-51.

Miracle at Cana of Galilee, John 2:1-12.

Drives the money changers from the temple [Jerusalem], John 2:13-25. Nicodemus comes to [Jerusalem], John 3:1-21.

Baptizes [Ænon], John 3:22, with chapter 4:2.

Returns to Galilee, Matt. 4:12; Mark 1:14; Luke 4:14; John 4:1-3.

Visits Sychar, and teaches the Samaritan woman, John 4:4-42.

Teaches in Galilee, Matt. 4:17; Mark 1:14,15; Luke 4:14,15; John 4:43-45.

Heals a nobleman's son of Capernaum [Cana of Galilee], John 4:46-54.

Is rejected by the people of Nazareth, dwells at Capernaum, Matt. 4:13-16; Luke 4:16-31.

Chooses Peter, Andrew, James, and John as disciples, miracle of the draught of fishes [Capernaum], Matt. 4:18-22; Mark 1:16-20; Luke 5:1-11.

Preaches throughout Galilee, Matt. 4:23-25; Mark. 1:35-39; Luke 4:42-44.

Heals a demoniac [Capernaum], Mark 1:21-28; Luke 4:31-37.

Heals Peter's mother-in-law [Capernaum], Matt. 8:14-17; Mark 1:29-34; Luke 4:38-41.

Heals a leper in Galilee, Matt. 8:2-4; Mark 1:40-45; Luke 5:12-16.

Heals a paralytic [Capernaum], Matt. 9:2-8; Mark 2:1-12; Luke 5:17-26.

Calls Matthew [Capernaum], Matt. 9:9; Mark 2:13,14; Luke 5:27,28.

Heals an impotent man at the pool of Bethesda on the Sabbath day, is persecuted, and makes his defense, John 5.

Defines the law of the Sabbath on the occasion of his disciples plucking the ears of corn [Capernaum], Matt. 12:1-8; Mark 2:23-28; Luke 6:1-5.

Heals a man having a withered hand [Capernaum], Matt. 12:9-14; Mark 3:1-6; Luke 6:6-11.

Withdraws from Capernaum to the Sea of Galilee, where he heals many, Matt. 12:15-21; Mark 3:7-12.

Goes up into a mountain and calls and ordains twelve disciples [Galilee], Matt. 10:2-4; Mark 3:13-19; Luke 6:12-19.

Delivers the "Sermon on the Mount" [Galilee], Matt. 5; 6; 7; Luke 6:20-49.

Heals the servant of the centurion [near Capernaum], Matt. 8:5-13; Luke 7:1-10.

Raises from the dead the son of the widow of Nain, Luke 7:11-17.

Receives the message from John the Baptist [Galilee], Matt. 11:2-19; Luke 7-18-35.

Upbraids the unbelieving cities about Capernaum, Matt. 11:20-30.

Anointed by a sinful woman [Capernaum], Luke 7:36-50.

Preaches in the cities of Galilee, Luke 8:1-3.

Heals a demoniac, and denounces the scribes and Pharisees [Galilee], Matt. 12:22-37; Mark 3:19-30; Luke 11:14-26.

Replies to the scribes and Pharisees who seek a sign from him [Galilee], Matt. 12:38-45 Luke 11:16-36.

Denounces the Pharisees and other hypocrites [Galilee], Luke 11:37-54.

Discourses to his disciples [Galilee], Luke 12:1-59.

Parable of the barren fig tree [Galilee], Luke 13:6-9.

Parable of the sower [Sea of Galilee], Matt. 13:1-23; Mark 4:1-25; Luke 8:4-18.

Parable of the tares, and other teachings [Galilee], Matt. 13:24-53; Mark 4:26-34.

Crosses the Sea of Galilee, and stills the tempest, Matt. 8:18-27; Mark 4:35-41; Luke 8:22-25.

Miracle of the swine [Gadara], Matt. 8:28-33; Mark 5:1-21; Luke 8:26-40.

Returns to Capernaum, Matt. 9:

1; Mark 5:21; Luke 8:40.

Eats with publicans and sinners, and discourses on fasting [Capernaum], Matt. 9:10-17; Mark 2:15-22; Luke 5:29-39.

Raises to life the daughter of Jairus, and heals the woman who has the issue of blood [Capernaum], Matt. 9:18-26; Mark 5:22-43; Luke 8:41-56.

Heals two blind men, and casts out a dumb spirit [Capernaum], Matt. 9:27-34.

Returns to Nazareth, Matt. 13:53-58; Mark 6:1-6.

Teaches in various cities in Galilee, Matt. 9:35-38.

Instructs his disciples, and empowers them to heal diseases and cast out unclean spirits, Matt. 10; Mark 6:6-13; Luke 9:1-6.

Herod falsely supposes him to be John, whom he had beheaded, Matt. 14:1,2,6-12; Mark 6:14-16,21-29; Luke 9:7-9.

The twelve return; he goes to the desert; multitudes follow him; he feeds five thousand [Sea of Galilee], Matt. 14:13-21; Mark 6:30-44; Luke 9:10-17; John 6:1-14.

Walks on the sea [Galilee], Matt. 14:22-36; Mark 6:45-56; John 6:15-21.

Teaches in the synagogue in Capernaum, John 6:22-65.

Disciples forsake him [Capernaum], John 6:66-71.

He justifies his disciples in eating without washing their hands [Capernaum], Matt. 15:1-20; Mark 7:1-23.

Heals the daughter of the Syrophenician woman [Tyre and Sidon], Matt. 15:21-28; Mark 7:24-30.

Heals a dumb man [Decapolis], Matt. 15:29-31; Mark 7:31-37.

Feeds four thousand, Matt. 15:32-39; Mark 8:1-9.

Refuses to give a sign to the Pharisees [region of Magdala], Matt. 16:1-4; Mark 8:10-12.

Cautions his disciples against the leaven of hypocrisy [Sea of Galilee], Matt. 16:4-12; Mark 8:13-21.

Heals a blind man [Bethsaida], Mark 8:22-26.

Foretells his death and resurrection [near Cæsarea Philippi], Matt.

16:21-28; Mark 8:31-38; 9:1; Luke 9:21-27.

Is transfigured, Matt. 17:1-13; Mark 9:2-13; Luke 9:28-36.

Heals a demoniac [Cæsarea Philippi], Matt. 17:14-21; Mark 9:14-29; Luke 9:37-43.

Foretells his death and resurrection [Galilee], Matt. 17:22,23; Mark 9:30-32; Luke 9:43-45.

Miracle of tribute money in the fish's mouth, Matt. 17:24-27.

Reproves the ambition of his disciples [Capernaum], Matt. 18:1-35; Mark 9:33-50; Luke 9:46-50.

Reproves the intolerance of his disciples, Mark 9:38,39; Luke 9:49, 50.

Journeys to Jerusalem to attend the Feast of Tabernacles, passing through Samaria, Luke 9:51-62; John 7:2-11.

Commissions the seventy [Samaria], Luke 10:1-16.

Heals ten lepers, Luke 17:11-19.

Teaches in Jerusalem at the Feast of Tabernacles, John 7:14-53; 8.

Answers a lawyer, who tests his wisdom with the question, "What shall I do to inherit eternal life?" by the parable of the good Samaritan [Jerusalem], Luke 10:25-37.

Hears the report of the seventy [Jerusalem], Luke 10:17-24.

Teaches in the house of Mary, Martha, and Lazarus, in Bethany, Luke 10:38-42.

Teaches his disciples to pray, Luke 11:1-13.

Heals a blind man, who, because of his faith in Jesus, was excommunicated, John 9.

Teaches in Jerusalem, John 9:39-41; 10:1-21.

Teaches in the temple at Jerusalem, at the Feast of Dedication, John 10:22-39.

Goes to Bethabara to escape violence from the rulers [E. of the Jordan], John 10:40-42; 11:3-16.

Returns to Bethany, and raises Lazarus from the dead, John 11:1-46.

Escapes to the city of Ephraim from the conspiracy led by Caiaphas, the high priest [Judæa], John 11:47-54.

Journeys toward Jerusalem to attend the passover; heals many who are diseased, and teaches the people [Peræa], Matt. 19:1,2; Mark 10:1; Luke 13:10-35.

Dines with a Pharisee on the Sabbath [Peræa], Luke 14:1-24.

Teaches the multitude the conditions of discipleship [Peræa], Luke 14:25-35.

Enunciates the parables of the lost sheep, the lost piece of silver, prodigal son, unjust steward [Peræa], Luke 15:1-32; 16:1-13.

Reproves the hypocrisy of the Pharisees [Peræa], Luke 16.

Enunciates the parable of the rich man and Lazarus [Peræa], Luke 16:19-31.

Teaches his disciples concerning offenses, meekness, and humility [Peræa], Luke 17:1-10.

Teaches the Pharisees concerning the coming of his kingdom [Peræa], Luke 17:20-37.

Enunciates the parables of the unjust judge, and the Pharisee and publican praying in the temple [Peræa], Luke 18:1-14.

Interprets the law concerning marriage and divorce [Peræa], Matt 19:3-12; Mark 10:2-12.

Blesses little children [Peræa], Matt. 19:13-15; Mark 10:13-16; Luke 18:15-17.

Receives the rich young ruler, who asks what he shall do to inherit eternal life [Peræa], Matt. 19: 16-22; Mark 10:17-22; Luke 18:18-24.

Enunciates the parable of the vineyard [Peræa], Matt. 20:1-16.

Foretells his death and resurrection [Peræa], Matt. 20:17-19; Mark 10:32-34; Luke 18:31-34.

Listens to the mother of James and John in behalf of her sons [Peræa], Matt. 20:20-28; Mark 10:35-45.

Heals two blind men at Jericho, Matt. 20:29-34; Mark 10:46-50; Luke 18:35-43.

Visits Zacchæus, Luke 19:1-10.

Enunciates the parable of the pounds [Jericho], Luke 19:11-28.

Goes to Bethany six days before the passover, John 12:1-9.

Triumphal entry into Jerusalem, while the people throw palm branches in the way, Matt. 21:1-11; Mark 11:1-11; Luke 19:29-44; John 12:12-19.

Enters the temple, Matt. 21:12; Mark 11:11; Luke 19:45.

Drives the money changers out of the temple, Matt. 21:12,13; Luke 19:45,46.

Heals the infirm in the temple, Matt. 21:14.

Teaches daily in the temple, Luke 19:47,48.

Performs the miracle of causing the barren fig tree to wither, Matt. 21:17-22; Mark 11:12-14,20-22.

Enunciates the parable of the two sons, Matt. 21:28-31; the parable of the wicked husbandmen, Matt. 21:33-46; Mark 12:1-12; Luke 20:9-19; of the marriage, Matt. 22: 1-14; Luke 14:16-24.

Tested by the Pharisees and Herodians, and enunciates the duty of the citizen to his government, Matt. 22:15-22; Mark 12:13-17; Luke 20:20-26.

Tried by the Sadducees concerning the resurrection of the dead, Matt. 22:23-33; Mark 12:18-27; Luke 20:27-40; and by a lawyer, Matt. 22:34-40; Mark 12:28-34.

Exposes the hypocrisies of the scribes and Pharisees, Matt. 23; Mark 12:38-40; Luke 20: 45-47.

Extols the widow who casts two mites into the treasury, Mark 12: 41-44; Luke 21:1-4.

Verifies the prophecy of Isaiah concerning the unbelieving Jews, John 12:37-50.

Foretells the destruction of the temple, and of Jerusalem, Matt. 24; Mark 13; Luke 21:5-36.

Laments over Jerusalem, Matt. 23:37; Luke 19:41-44.

Enunciates the parables of the ten virgins and of the talents, Matt. 25:1-30.

Foretells the scenes of the day of judgment [Mount of Olives], Matt. 25:31-46.

Anointed with the box of precious ointment [Bethany], Matt. 26:6-13; Mark 14:3-9; John 12:1-8.

Last passover, and institution of the sacrament of the holy eucharist, Matt. 26:17-30; Mark 14:12-25; Luke 22:7-20.

Washes the disciples' feet, John 13:1-17.

Foretells his betrayal, Matt. 26:23; Mark 14:18-21; Luke 22:21; John 13:18.

Accuses Judas of his betrayal, Matt. 26:21-25; Mark 14:18-21; Luke 22:21-23; John 13:21-30.

Teaches his disciples, and comforts them with promises, and promises the gift of the Holy Spirit, John 14; 15; 16.

Last prayer [Jerusalem], John 17.

Repairs to Gethsemane [Mount of Olives], Matt. 26:30,36-46; Mark 14:26,32-42; Luke 22:39-46; John 18:1.

Is betrayed and apprehended [Gethsemane], Matt. 26:47-56; Mark 14:43-54,66-72; Luke 22:47-53; John 18:2-12.

Trial, before Caiaphas [Jerusalem], Matt. 26:57,58,69-75; Mark 14:53,54,66-72; Luke 22:54-62; John 18:13-18,25-27.

Tried by the council, Matt. 26:59-68; Mark 14:55-65; Luke 22:63-71; John 18:19-21.

Led by the council to Pilate, Matt. 27:1,2,11-14; Mark 15:1-5; Luke 23:1-5; John 18:28-38.

Arraigned before Herod, Luke 23:6-12.

Tried before Pilate, Matt. 27:15-26; Mark 15:6-15; Luke 23:13-25; John 18:39,40; 19:1-16.

Mocked by the soldiers, Matt. 27:27-31; Mark 15:16-20.

Is led away to be crucified, Matt. 27:31-34; Mark 15:20-23; Luke 23:26-32; John 19:16,17.

Crucified, Matt. 27:35-56; Mark 15:24-41; Luke 23:33-49; John 19:18-30.

Taken from the cross and buried, Matt. 27:57-66; Mark 15:42-47; Luke 23:50-56; John 19:31-42.

Arises from the dead, Matt. 28:2-15; Mark 16:1-11; Luke 24:1-12; John 20:1-18.

Is seen by Mary Magdalene, Matt. 28:1-10; Mark 16:9; John 20:11-17; by Peter, Luke 24:34; 1 Cor. 15:5.

Appears to two disciples who journey to Emmaus, Mark 16:12,13; Luke 24:13-35.

Appears in the midst of the disciples, when Thomas is absent [Jerusalem], Mark 16:14-18; Luke 24:36-49; John 20:19-23; when Thomas was present [Jerusalem], John 20:26-29; at the Sea of Galilee, Matt. 28:16; John 21:1-14; to the apostles and upwards of five hundred brethren on a mountain in Galilee, Matt. 28:16-20, with Acts 10:40-42. See also Acts 13:31; 1 Cor. 15:6,7.

Appears to James, and also to all the apostles [Jerusalem], Acts 1:3-8; 1 Cor. 15:7.

Ascends to heaven [Bethany], Mark 16:19,20; Luke 24:50-53; Acts 1:9-12.

Appears to Paul, Acts 9:3-17; 18:9; 22:14,18; 23:11; 26:16; 1 Cor. 9:1; 15:8.

Stephen's vision of, Acts 7:55,56.

Appears to John on Patmos, Rev. 1:10-18.

Miscellaneous Facts Concerning: Brethren of, Matt. 13:55; Mark 6:3; 1 Cor. 9:5; Gal. 1:19. Sisters of, Matt. 13:56; Mark 6:3.

Was with the Israelites in the wilderness, 1 Cor. 10:4,9; Heb. 11:26; Jude 5.

John 8:12. Then spake Jesus again unto them, saying, I am the light of the world: he that followeth me shall not walk in darkness, but shall have the light of life.

Ascension of: Psa. 47:5. God is gone up with a shout, the LORD with the sound of a trumpet.

Psa. 68:18. Thou hast ascended on high, thou hast led captivity captive: Eph. 4:8.

Mark 16:19. After the Lord had spoken unto them, he was received up into heaven, and sat on the right hand of God.

Acts 1:9. When he had spoken these things, while they beheld, he was taken up; and a cloud received him out of their sight.

Acts 3:21. Whom the heaven must receive until the time of restitution of all things.

Heb. 1:3. When he had by himself purged our sins, sat down on the right hand of the Majesty on high;

Heb. 4:14. We have a great high

priest, that is passed into the heavens, Jesus the Son of God,

Compassion of: Isa. 40:11. He shall feed his flock like a shepherd: he shall gather the lambs with his arm, and carry *them* in his bosom, *and* shall gently lead those that are with young.

Isa. 42:3. A bruised reed shall he not break, and the smoking flax shall he not quench:

Isa. 63:9. In all their affliction he was afflicted, and the angel of his presence saved them: in his love and in his pity he redeemed them; and he bare them, and carried them all the days of old. *vss.* 7,8.

Matt. 8:3. And Jesus put forth *his* hand, and touched him, saying, I will; be thou clean. And immediately his leprosy was cleansed.

Matt. 9:36. When he saw the multitudes, he was moved with compassion on them, because they fainted, and were scattered abroad, as sheep having no shepherd.

John 11:34. And said, Where have ye laid him? They said unto him, Lord, come and see. 35. Jesus wept.

Heb. 4:15. We have not an high priest which cannot be touched with the feeling of our infirmities; but was in all points tempted like as *we are, yet* without sin.

Creator: John 1:3. All things were made by him; and without him was not any thing made that was made. 10. He was in the world, and the world was made by him,

1 Cor. 8:6. *There is but* one God, the Father, of whom *are* all things, and we in him; and one Lord Jesus Christ, by whom *are* all things, and we by him.

Col. 1:16. By him were all things created, that are in heaven, and that are in earth, visible and invisible, whether *they be* thrones, or dominions, or principalities, or powers: all things were created by him, and for him: 17. And he is before all things, and by him all things consist.

Death of: Gen. 3:15. And I will put enmity between thee and the woman, and between thy seed and her seed; it shall bruise thy head, and thou shalt bruise his heel. Heb. 2:14.

Psa. 22:1. My God, my God, why hast thou forsaken me? *why art thou so* far from helping me, *and from* the words of my roaring? [Matt. 27:46.] 13. They gaped upon me *with* their mouths, *as* a ravening and a roaring lion. 16. They pierced my hands and my feet. 18. They part my garments among them, and cast lots upon my vesture. Luke 23:34; John 19:23,24.

Psa. 34:20. He keepeth all his bones: not one of them is broken. John 19:36.

Isa. 53:7. He was oppressed, and he was afflicted, yet he opened not his mouth: he is brought as a lamb to the slaughter, and as a sheep before her shearers is dumb, so he openeth not his mouth.

Matt. 16:21. From that time forth began Jesus to shew unto his disciples, how that he must go unto Jerusalem, and suffer many things of the elders and chief priests and scribes, and be killed, and be raised again the third day. Luke 9:22.

Luke 12:50. I have a baptism to be baptized with; and how am I straitened till it be accomplished!

John 10:11. I am the good shepherd: the good shepherd giveth his life for the sheep. 15. I lay down my life for the sheep.

John 18:11. The cup which my Father hath given me, shall I not drink it?

1 Cor. 2:2. For I determined not to know anything among you, save Jesus Christ, and him crucified.

Design of His Death: Gen: 3: 15. I will put enmity between thee and the woman, and between thy seed and her seed; it shall bruise thy head, and thou shalt bruise his heel.

Isa. 53:4. Surely he hath borne our griefs, and carried our sorrows: yet we did esteem him stricken, smitten of God, and afflicted. 5. But he *was* wounded for our transgressions, *he was* bruised for our iniquities: the chastisement of our peace *was* upon him; and with his stripes we are healed. 6. All we like sheep have gone astray; we have turned every one to his own way; and the LORD hath laid on him the iniquity of us all.

Zech. 9:11. By the blood of thy covenant I have sent forth thy prisoners out of the pit wherein *is* no water.

Matt. 20:28. The Son of man came not to be ministered unto, but to minister, and to give his life a ransom for many. Mark 10:45.

Luke 24:26. Ought not Christ to have suffered these things, and to enter into his glory?

John 1:29. Behold the Lamb of God, which taketh away the sin of the world.

John 3:16. For God so loved the world, that he gave his only begotten Son, that whosoever believeth in him should not perish, but have everlasting life.

John 12:24. Except a corn of wheat fall into the ground and die, it abideth alone; but if it die, it bringeth forth much fruit.

Rom. 3:24. Justified freely by his grace through the redemption that is in Christ Jesus.

Rom. 5:6. When we were yet without strength, in due time Christ died for the ungodly.

1 Cor. 15:3. Christ died for our sins according to the scriptures;

Col. 2:14. Blotting out the handwriting of ordinances that was against us, which was contrary to us, and took it out of the way, nailing it to his cross; 15. *And* having spoiled principalities and powers, he made a show of them openly, triumphing over them in it.

Heb. 2:9. We see Jesus, who was made a little lower than the angels for the suffering of death, crowned with glory and honour; that he by the grace of God should taste death for every man.

Heb. 10:14. By one offering he hath perfected for ever them that are sanctified. 17. Their sins and iniquities will I remember no more.

Rev. 5:9. Thou wast slain, and hast redeemed us to God by thy blood out of every kindred, and tongue, and people, and nation; 10. And hast made us unto our God

kings and priests: and we shall reign on the earth.

Death of, Voluntary: Isa. 50:6. I gave my back to the smiters, and my cheeks to them that plucked off the hair: I hid not my face from shame and spitting.

Isa. 53:12. He . . . poured out his soul unto death: and he was numbered with the transgressors; and he bare the sin of many, and made intercession for the transgressors.

Matt. 26:53. Thinkest thou that I cannot now pray to my Father, and he shall presently give me more than twelve legions of angels? 54. But how then shall the scriptures be fulfilled, that thus it must be?

Luke 22:42. Father, if thou be willing, remove this cup from me: nevertheless not my will, but thine, be done.

Divinity of: Mal. 3:1. The Lord, whom ye seek, shall suddenly come to his temple, even the messenger of the covenant, whom ye delight in: behold, he shall come, saith the LORD of hosts. Matt 11:10.

Matt. 1:23. Behold, a virgin shall be with child, and shall bring forth a son, and they shall call his name Emmanuel, which being interpreted is, God with us. Isa. 7:14.

Matt. 8:29. And, behold, they cried out, saying, What have we to do with thee, Jesus, thou Son of God? art thou come hither to torment us before the time? Luke 8:28.

Mark 5:6. But when he saw Jesus afar off, he ran and worshipped him, 7. And cried with a loud voice, and said, What have I to do with thee, Jesus, *thou* Son of the most high God? I adjure thee by God, that thou torment me not.

Luke 4:12. And Jesus answering said unto him, It is said, Thou shalt not tempt the Lord thy God.

John 1:1. In the beginning was the Word, and the Word was with God, and the Word was God, 2. The same was in the beginning with God. . . . And the Word became flesh and dwelt among us.

John 5:17. Jesus answered them, My Father worketh hitherto, and I work. 23. That all *men* should honour the Son, even as they honour the Father. He that honoureth not the Son honoureth not the Father which hath sent him.

John 10:30. I and *my* Father are one.

John 20:28. Thomas answered and said unto him, My Lord and my God.

Acts 20:28. Take heed . . . feed the church of God, which he hath purchased with his own blood.

Phil. 2:6. Who, being in the form of God, thought it not [robbery to be equal] with God: *vss.* 5-11. [R. V. a prize to be on an equality]

Heb. 1:8. But unto the Son *he saith*, Thy throne, O God, *is* for ever and ever; a sceptre of righteousness *is* the sceptre of thy kingdom.

Eternity of: Mic. 5:2. Out of thee shall he come forth unto me *that is* to be ruler in Israel; whose goings forth *have been* from of old, from everlasting.

John 1:1. In the beginning was the Word, and the Word was with God, and the Word was God.

Col. 1:17. He is before all things, and by him all things consist.

Heb. 13:8. Jesus Christ the same yesterday, and to day, and for ever.

Rev. 1:8. I am Alpha and Omega, the beginning and the ending, saith the Lord, which is, and which was, and which is to come, the Almighty.

Exaltation of: Mark 16:19. After the Lord had spoken unto them, he was received up into heaven, and sat on the right hand of God.

Luke 24:26. Ought not Christ to have suffered these things, and to enter into his glory?

John 7:39. The Holy Ghost was not yet *given:* because that Jesus was not yet glorified.

John 17:5. Now, O Father, glorify thou me with thine own self with the glory which I had with thee before the world was.

Heb. 12:2. Who for the joy that was set before him endured the cross, despising the shame, and is

set down at the right hand of the throne of God.

Example, an: Matt. 11:29. Take my yoke upon you, and learn of me; for I am meek and lowly in heart, and ye shall find rest unto your souls.

John 13:15. For I have given you an example, that ye should do as I have done to you.

Rom. 15:7. Wherefore receive ye one another, as Christ also received us to the glory of God.

Eph. 5:2. Walk in love, as Christ also hath loved us, and hath given himself for us an offering and a sacrifice to God for a sweetsmelling savour.

I Pet. 1:15. As he which hath called you is holy, so be ye holy in all manner of [conversation;] *v.* 16. [R. V. living]

1 Pet. 2:21. For even hereunto were ye called: because Christ also suffered for us, leaving us an example, that ye should follow his steps: 22. Who did no sin, neither was guile found in his mouth: 23. Who, when he was reviled, reviled not again; when he suffered, he threatened not; but committed *himself* to him that judgeth righteously:

1 John 2:6. He that saith he abideth in him ought himself also so to walk, even as he walked.

Holiness of: Psa. 45:7. Thou lovest righteousness, and hatest wickedness: Heb. 1:9.

Isa. 53:9. He had done no violence, neither *was any* deceit in his mouth.

Jer. 23:5. I will raise unto David a righteous Branch.

Luke 1:35. That holy thing which shall be born of thee shall be called the Son of God.

Luke 4:34. I know thee who thou art; the Holy One of God.

John 8:46. Which of you convinceth me of sin?

2 Cor. 5:21. For he hath made him *to be* sin for us, who knew no sin; that we might be made the righteousness of God in him.

Heb. 4:15. We have not an high priest which cannot be touched with the feeling of our infirmities; but was in all points tempted like as *we are, yet* without sin.

Heb. 7:26. Such an high priest became us, *who is* holy, harmless, undefiled, separate from sinners, and made higher than the heavens;

1 Pet. 1:19. A lamb without blemish and without spot:

1 Pet. 2:22. Who did no sin, neither was guile found in his mouth:

1 John 3:5. In him is no sin.

Humanity of: Deut. 18:15. The LORD thy God will raise up unto thee a Prophet from the midst of thee, of thy brethren, like unto me; unto him ye shall hearken;

John 1:14. And the Word was made flesh, and dwelt among us, (and we beheld his glory, the glory as of the only begotten of the Father,) full of grace and truth.

Gal. 4:4. But when the fulness of the time was come, God sent forth his Son, made of a woman, made under the law,

Phil. 2:7. But [made himself of no reputation, and took upon him] the form of a servant, and was made in the likeness of men: 8. And being found in fashion as a man, he humbled himself, and became obedient unto death, even the death of the cross. [R. V. emptied himself, taking]

1 Tim. 2:5. For *there is* one God, and one mediator between God and men, the man Christ Jesus;

Humility of: Zech. 9:9. Lowly, and riding upon an ass, and upon a colt the foal of an ass. Matt. 21:5.

2 Cor. 8:9. For ye know the grace of our Lord Jesus Christ, that, though he was rich, yet for your sakes he became poor, that ye through his poverty might be rich.

2 Cor. 10:1. I Paul myself beseech you by the meekness and gentleness of Christ,

Incarnation of: Psa. 2:7. The Lord hath said unto me, Thou *art* my Son; this day have I begotten thee. Acts 13:33.

Matt. 13:55. Is not this the carpenter's son? is not his mother called Mary? and his brethren, James, and Joses, and Simon, and Judas? 56. And his sisters, are they not all with us?

Matt. 22:45. If David then called him Lord, how is he his son?

Luke 1:30. And the angel said unto her, Fear not, Mary: for thou hast found favour with God. 31. And, behold, thou shalt conceive in thy womb, and bring forth a son, and shalt call his name JESUS. 32. He shall be great, and shall be called the Son of the Highest: and the Lord God shall give unto him the throne of his father David: 33. And he shall reign over the house of Jacob for ever; and of his kingdom there shall be no end.

John 1:14. The Word was made flesh, and dwelt among us, (and we beheld his glory, the glory as of the only begotten of the Father,) full of grace and truth.

John 7:42. Hath not the scripture said, That Christ cometh of the seed of David, and out of the town of Bethlehem, where David was?

Rom. 1:3. His Son Jesus Christ our Lord, which was made of the seed of David according to the flesh;

Gal. 4:4. When the fulness of the time was come, God sent forth his Son, made of a woman, made under the law,

1 John 1:1. That which was from the beginning, which we have heard, which we have seen with our eyes, which we have looked upon, and our hands have handled, of the Word of life;

Intercession of: See JESUS, MEDIATION OF.

Judge: Psa. 72:2. He shall judge thy people with righteousness, and thy poor with judgment.

Mic. 5:1. They shall smite the judge of Israel with a rod upon the cheek.

Luke 3:17. Whose fan *is* in his hand, and he will throughly purge his floor, and will gather the wheat into his garner; but the chaff he will burn with fire unquenchable. Matt. 3:12.

Acts 17:31. He hath appointed a day, in the which he will judge the world in righteousness by *that* man whom he hath ordained;

whereof he hath given assurance unto all *men,* in that he hath raised him from the dead.

Rom. 2:16. In the day when God shall judge the secrets of men by Jesus Christ according to my gospel.

Rom. 14:10. We shall all stand before the judgment seat of Christ.

Jas. 5:9. Behold, the judge standeth before the door.

Justice of: 2 Sam. 23:3. The God of Israel said, the Rock of Israel spake to me,[He] that ruleth over men [must be just, ruling] in the fear of God. [R. V. One] [R. V. righteously, that ruleth]

King: Gen. 49:10. The sceptre shall not depart from Judah, nor a lawgiver from between his feet, until Shiloh come; and unto him *shall* the gathering of the people *be.*

Num. 24:17. I shall see him, but not now: I shall behold him, but not nigh: there shall come a Star out of Jacob, and a Sceptre shall rise out of Israel.

Psa. 132:11. The LORD hath sworn *in* truth unto David; he will not turn from it; Of the fruit of thy body will I set upon thy throne. 17. There will I make the horn of David to bud: I have ordained a lamp for mine anointed. 18. His enemies will I clothe with shame: but upon himself shall his crown flourish.

Mic. 5:2. Out of thee shall he come forth unto me *that is* to be ruler in Israel; whose goings forth *have been* from of old, from everlasting.

Matt. 2:2. Where is he that is born King of the Jews? for we have seen his star in the east, and are come to worship him.

Matt. 21:5. Behold, thy King cometh unto thee, meek, and sitting upon an ass, and a colt the foal of an ass.

Matt. 27:11. And Jesus stood before the governor: and the governor asked him, saying, Art thou the King of the Jews? And Jesus said unto him, Thou sayest.

Luke 1:32. He shall be great, and shall be called the Son of the Highest: and the Lord God shall give unto him the throne of his father David:

Phil. 2:9. God also hath highly exalted him, and given him a name which is above every name: 10. That at the name of Jesus every knee should bow, of *things* in heaven, and *things* in earth, and *things* under the earth; 11. And *that* every tongue should confess that Jesus Christ *is* Lord, to the glory of God the Father.

1 Tim. 6:15. *Who is* the blessed and only Potentate, the King of kings, and Lord of lords; 16. Who only hath immortality, dwelling in the light which no man can approach unto; whom no man hath seen, nor can see; to whom *be* honour and power everlasting.

Kingdom of: ITS NATURE. Matt. 18:3. And said, Verily I say unto you, Except ye be converted, and become as little children, ye shall not enter into the kingdom of heaven. 4. Whosoever therefore shall humble himself as this little child, the same is greatest in the kingdom of heaven.

John 18:36. Jesus answered, My kingdom is not of this world: if my kingdom were of this world, then would my servants fight, that I should not be delivered to the Jews: but now is my kingdom not from hence.

PROPHECIES CONCERNING UNIVERSALITY OF THE KINGDOM OF: Gen. 12:3. In thee shall all families of the earth be blessed.

Psa. 2:8. Ask of me, and I shall give *thee* the heathen *for* thine inheritance, and the uttermost parts of the earth *for* thy possession.

Psa. 47:8. God reigneth over the heathen: God sitteth upon the throne of his holiness.

Psa. 65:2. O thou that hearest prayer, unto thee shall all flesh come.

Psa. 68:31. Princes shall come out of Egypt; Ethiopia shall soon stretch out her hands unto God. 32. Sing unto God, ye kingdoms of the earth; O sing praises unto the Lord;

Psa. 86:9. All nations whom thou hast made shall come and

worship before thee, O Lord; and shall glorify thy name.

Psa. 113:3. From the rising of the sun unto the going down of the same the LORD's name *is* to be praised.

Psa. 138:4. All the kings of the earth shall praise thee, O LORD, when they hear the words of thy mouth. 5. Yea, they shall sing in the ways of the LORD: for great *is* the glory of the LORD.

Isa. 11:6. The wolf also shall dwell with the lamb, and the leopard shall lie down with the kid; and the calf and the young lion and the fatling together; and a little child shall lead them.

Jer. 16:19. The Gentiles shall come unto thee from the ends of the earth, and shall say, Surely our fathers have inherited lies, vanity, and *things* wherein *there is* no profit. 20. Shall a man make gods unto himself, and they *are* no gods? 21. Therefore, behold, I will this once cause them to know, I will cause them to know mine hand and my might; and they shall know that my name *is* The LORD.

Jer. 31:34 They shall teach no more every man his neighbour, and every man his brother, saying, Know the LORD: for they shall all know me, from the least of them unto the greatest of them, saith the LORD: for I will forgive their iniquity, and I will remember their sin no more.

Matt. 8:11. Many shall come from the east and west, and shall sit down with Abraham, and Isaac, and Jacob, in the kingdom of heaven.

1 Cor. 15:24. Then *cometh* the end, when he shall have delivered up the kingdom to God, even the Father; when he shall have put down all rule and all authority and power. 25. For he must reign, till he hath put all enemies under his feet.

Phil. 2:10. That at the name of Jesus every knee should bow, of *things* in heaven, and *things* in earth, and *things* under the earth; 11. And *that* every tongue should confess that Jesus Christ *is* Lord, to the glory of God the Father.

Heb. 8:11. And they shall not teach every man his neighbour, and every man his brother, saying, Know the Lord: for all shall know me, from the least to the greatest.

Rev. 17:14. These shall make war with the Lamb, and the Lamb shall overcome them: for he is Lord of lords, and King of kings: and they that are with him *are* called, and chosen, and faithful.

Psa. 46:9. He maketh wars to cease unto the end of the earth; he breaketh the bow, and cutteth the spear in sunder; he burneth the chariot in the fire.

Isa. 42:4. He shall not fail nor be discouraged, till he have set judgment in the earth: and the isles shall wait for his law.

Dan. 7:9. I beheld till the thrones were cast down, and the Ancient of days did sit, whose garment *was* white as snow, and the hair of his head like the pure wool: his throne *was like* the fiery flame, *and* his wheels *as* burning fire. 10. A fiery stream issued and came forth from before him: thousand thousands ministered unto him, and ten thousand times ten thousand stood before him: the judgment was set, and the books were opened. 11. I beheld then because of the voice of the great words which the horn spake: I beheld *even* till the beast was slain, and his body destroyed, and given to the burning flame. 12. As concerning the rest of the beasts, they had their dominion taken away: yet their lives were prolonged for a season and time. 13. I saw in the night visions, and, behold, *one* like the Son of man came with the clouds of heaven, and came to the Ancient of days, and they brought him near before him. 14. And there was given him dominion, and glory, and a kingdom, that all people, nations, and languages, should serve him: his dominion *is* an everlasting dominion, which shall not pass away, and his kingdom *that* which shall not be destroyed. 27. And the kingdom and dominion, and the greatness of the kingdom under the whole heaven, shall be given to the people of the saints of the most High, whose kingdom *is* an everlasting kingdom, and all dominions shall serve and obey him.

Love of: Prov. 8:17. I love them that love me; and those that seek me early shall find me. 31. My delights *were* with the sons of men.

Isa. 40:11. He shall feed his flock like a shepherd: he shall gather the lambs with his arm, and carry *them* in his bosom, *and* shall gently lead those that are with young.

Isa. 42:3. A bruised reed shall he not break, and the smoking flax shall he not quench:

Isa. 63:9. In all their affliction he was afflicted, and the angel of his presence saved them: in his love and in his pity he redeemed them; and he bare them, and carried them all the days of old. *vss.* 7,8.

Matt. 8:17. Himself took our infirmities, and bare *our* sicknesses. Isa. 53:4.

Matt. 14:14. Jesus went forth, and saw a great multitude, and was moved with compassion toward them, and he healed their sick.

Mark 10:14. But when Jesus saw *it*, he was much displeased, and said unto them, Suffer the little children to come unto me, and forbid them not: for of such is the kingdom of God.

Luke 7:13. When the Lord saw her, he had compassion on her, and said unto her, Weep not.

John 13:1. Jesus . . . having loved his own which were in the world . . . loved them unto the end.

John 15:9. As the Father hath loved me, so have I loved you: continue ye in my love.

Eph. 5:2. Walk in love, as Christ also hath loved us, and hath given himself for us an offering and a sacrifice to God for a sweetsmelling savour.

Mediation of: Isa. 53:10. Yet it pleased the Lord to bruise him; he hath put *him* to grief: when thou shalt make his soul an offering for sin, he shall see *his* seed, he shall prolong *his* days, and the pleasure

of the Lord shall prosper in his hand. 11. He shall see of the travail of his soul, *and* shall be satisfied: by his knowledge shall my righteous servant justify many; for he shall bear their iniquities. 12. Therefore will I divide him *a portion* with the great, and he shall divide the spoil with the strong; because he hath poured out his soul unto death: and he was numbered with the transgressors; and he bare the sin of many, and made intercession for the transgressors.

Luke 22:31. And the Lord said, Simon, Simon, behold, Satan hath desired *to have* you, that he may sift *you* as wheat: 32. But I have prayed for thee, that thy faith fail not:

Luke 23:33. And when they were come to the place which is called Calvary, there they crucified him, 34. Then said Jesus, Father, forgive them; for they know not what they do.

John 17:9. I pray . . . for them which thou hast given me; for they are thine.

1 Tim. 2:5. For *there is* one God, and one mediator between God and men, the man Christ Jesus;

Heb. 13:15. By him therefore let us offer the sacrifice of praise to God continually, that is, the fruit of *our* lips giving thanks to his name.

Meekness of: Isa. 42:2. He shall not cry, nor lift up, nor cause his voice to be heard in the street.

Isa. 53:7. He was oppressed, and he was afflicted, yet he opened not his mouth: he is brought as a lamb to the slaughter, and as a sheep before her shearers is dumb, so he openeth not his mouth. Acts 8:32.

Matt. 11:29. Learn of me; for I am meek and lowly in heart:

Matt. 21:5. Tell ye the daughter of Sion, Behold, thy King cometh unto thee, meek, and sitting upon an ass, and a colt the foal of an ass.

Luke 22:27. I am among you as he that serveth.

John 13:5. He poureth water into

a basin, and began to wash the disciples' feet, and to wipe *them* with the towel wherewith he was girded. 14. If I then, *your* Lord and master, have washed your feet; ye also ought to wash one another's feet.

Phil. 2:7. Made himself of no reputation, and took upon him the form of a servant, and was made in the likeness of men: 8. And being found in fashion as a man, he humbled himself, and became obedient unto death, even the death of the cross.

1 Pet. 2:23. Who, when he was reviled, reviled not again; when he suffered, he threatened not; but committed *himself* to him that judgeth righteously:

Messiah: Acts 9:22. Saul . . . confounded the Jews which dwelt at Damascus, proving that this is very Christ.

Acts 28:23. He expounded and testified the kingdom of God, persuading them concerning Jesus, both out of the law of Moses, and *out* of the prophets,

Miracles of: Water made wine, John 2:1-11.

Heals the nobleman's son, John 4:46-54.

First miraculous draught of fishes, Luke 5:1-11.

Demoniac in the synagogue healed, Mark 1:23-26. Luke 4:33-36.

Heals Simon's wife's mother, Matt. 8:14,15; Mark 1:29-31; Luke 4:38,39.

Heals diseases in Galilee, Matt. 4:23,24; Mark 1:34.

Miracles at Jerusalem, John 2:23.

Cleanses the leper, Matt. 8:1-4; Mark 1:40-45; Luke 5:12-16.

Heals the paralytic, Matt. 9:1-8; Mark 2:1-12; Luke 5:17-26.

Heals the impotent man, John 5:1-16.

Restores the withered hand, Matt. 12:9-13; Mark 3:1-5; Luke 6:6-11.

Heals multitudes from Judah, Jerusalem, and coasts of Tyre and Sidon, Luke 6:17-19.

Heals the centurion's servant, Matt. 8:5-13; Luke 7:1-10.

Heals demoniacs, Matt. 8:16,17; Luke 4:40,41.

Raises the widow's son, Luke 7:11-16.

Heals in Galilee, Luke 7:21,22.

Heals a demoniac, Matt. 12:22-37; Mark 3:19-30; Luke 11:14,15, 17-23.

Stills the tempest, Matt. 8:23-27; Mark 4:35-41; Luke 8:22-25; Matt. 14:32.

Healing of the diseased in the land of Gennesaret, Matt. 14:34-36.

The demoniacs in Gadara healed, Matt. 8:28-34; Mark 5:1-20; Luke 8:26-39.

Raises Jairus's daughter, Matt. 9:18,19,23-26; Mark 5:22-24, 35-43; Luke 8:41,42, 49-56.

Heals the woman with the issue of blood, Matt. 9:20-22; Mark 5:25-34; Luke 8:43-48.

Opens the eyes of two blind men in the house, Matt. 9:27-31.

A devil cast out and a dumb man cured, Matt. 9:32,33.

Five thousand fed, Matt. 14:15-21; Mark 6:35-44; Luke 9:12-17: John 6:5-14.

Heals sick in Galilee, Matt. 14:14.

Walking on the sea, Matt. 14:22-33; Mark 6:45-52; John 6:14-21.

The daughter of the Syrophenician healed, Matt. 15:21-28; Mark 7:24-30.

Healing of lame, blind, dumb, and maimed, near the Sea of Galilee, Matt. 15:30.

Four thousand fed, Matt. 15:32-39; Mark 8:1-9.

One deaf and dumb cured, Mark 7:31-37.

One blind cured, Mark 8:22-36.

Lunatic child healed, Matt. 17:14-21; Mark 9:14-29; Luke 9:37-43.

Piece of money in the fish's mouth, Matt. 17:24-27.

The ten lepers cured, Luke 17:11-19.

Opening the eyes of one born blind, John 9.

Raising of Lazarus, John 11:1-54.

Woman with the spirit of infirmity cured, Luke 13:10-17.

The dropsy cured, Luke 14:1-6.

Two blind men cured near Jericho, Matt. 20:29-34; Mark 10:46-52; Luke 18:35-43.

The fig tree blighted, Matt. 21:17-22; Mark 11:12-14, 20-24.

Healing of Malchus's ear, Luke 22:49-51.

Second draught of fishes, John 21:6.

Not particularly described, Matt. 4:23,24. 14:14; 15:30; Mark 1:34; Luke 6:17-19; 7:21,22; John 2-23; 3:2. Resurrection, Matt. 28:6; Mark 16:6; Luke 24:6; John 20:1-18. Holds the vision of his disciples, that they should not recognize him, Luke 24:16,31,35. His appearances and disappearances, Luke 24:15,31,36-45; John 20:19,26. Opening the understanding of his disciples, Luke 24:45. His ascension, Luke 24:51; Acts 1:9.

Mission of: Zech. 13:1. In that day there shall be a fountain opened to the house of David and to the inhabitants of Jerusalem for sin and for uncleanness.

Matt. 1:21. For he shall save his people from their sins.

Matt. 20:28. Even as the Son of man came not to be ministered unto, but to minister, and to give his life a ransom for many. Mark 10:45.

Luke 4:18. The Spirit of the Lord *is* upon me, because he hath anointed me to preach the gospel to the poor: he hath sent me to heal the brokenhearted, to preach deliverance to the captives, and recovering of sight to the blind, to set at liberty them that are bruised, 19. To preach the acceptable year of the Lord. 43. And he said unto them, I must preach the kingdom of God to other cities also: for therefore am I sent.

John 4:34. My meat is to do the will of him that sent me, and to finish his work.

John 9:39. And Jesus said, For judgment I am come into this world, that they which see not might see; and that they which see might be made blind.

John 10:10. I am come that they might have life, and that they might have *it* more abundantly.

John 18:37. To this end was I born, and for this cause came I into the world, that I should bear witness unto the truth.

Names, Appellations, and Titles of: Adam, 1 Cor. 15:45. Advocate, 1 John, 2:1. Almighty, Rev. 1:8. Alpha and Omega, Rev. 1:8. Amen, Rev. 3:14. Angel, Gen. 48:16; Ex. 23:20,21. Angel of his presence, Isa. 63:9. Anointed, Psa. 2:2. Apostle, Heb. 3:1. Arm of the Lord, Isa. 51:9,10. Author and finisher of our faith, Heb. 12:2.

Beginning and end of the creation of God, Rev. 3:14; 22:13. Beloved, Eph. 1:6. Bishop, 1 Pet. 2:25. Blessed and only Potentate, 1 Tim. 6:15. Branch, Jer. 23:5; Zech. 3:8. Bread of life, John 6:48. Bridegroom, Matt. 9:15. Bright and morning star, Rev. 22:16. Brightness of the Father's glory, Heb. 1:3.

Captain of the Lord's host, Josh. 5:14. Captain of salvation, Heb. 2:10. Carpenter, Mark 6:3. Carpenter's son, Matt. 13:55. Chief Shepherd, 1 Pet. 5:4. Chief corner stone, 1 Pet. 2:6. Chiefest among ten thousand, Song 5:10. Child, Isa. 9:6; Luke 2:27,43. Chosen of God, 1 Pet. 2:4. Christ, Matt. 1:16; Luke 9:20. The Christ, Matt. 16:20; Mark 14:61. Christ, a King, Luke 23:2. Christ Jesus, Acts 19:4; Rom. 3:24; 8:1; 1 Cor. 1:2; 1 Cor. 1:30; Heb. 3:1; 1 Pet. 5:10,14. Christ Jesus our Lord, 1 Tim. 1:12; Rom. 8:39. Christ of God, Luke 9:20. Christ, the chosen of God, Luke 23:35. Christ the Lord, Luke 2:11. Christ the power of God, 1 Cor. 1:24. Christ the wisdom of God, 1 Cor. 1:24. Christ, the Son of God, Acts 9:20. Christ, Son of the Blessed, Mark 14:61. Commander, Isa. 55:4. Consolation of Israel, Luke 2:25. Corner stone, Eph. 2:20. Counsellor, Isa. 9:6. Covenant of the people, Isa. 42:6.

David, Jer. 30:9. Daysman, Job 9:33. Dayspring, Luke 1:78. Day star, 2 Pet. 1:19. Deliverer, Rom. 11:26. [Desire] of all nations, Hag. 2:7. Door, John 10:7. [R. V. desirable things]

Elect, Isa. 42:1. Emmanuel, Isa. 7:14. Ensign, Isa. 11:10. Eternal life, 1 John 5:20. Everlasting Father, Isa. 9:6.

Faithful and True, Rev. 19:11. Faithful witness, Rev. 1:5. Faithful and true witness, Rev. 3:14. Finisher of faith, Heb. 12:2. First and last, Rev. 1:17; 2:8; 22:13. First begotten, Heb. 1:6. First begotten of the dead, Rev. 1:5. Firstborn, Psa. 89:27. Foundation, Isa. 28:16. Fountain, Zech. 13:1. Forerunner, Heb. 6:20. Friend of sinners, Matt. 11:19.

Gift of God, John 4:10. Glory of Israel, Luke 2:32. God, John 1:1. God blessed for ever, Rom. 9:5. God manifest in the flesh, 1 Tim. 3:16. God of Israel, the Saviour, Isa. 45:15. God of the whole earth, Isa. 54:5. God our Saviour, 1 Tim. 2:3. God's dear Son, Col. 1:13. God with us, Matt. 1:23. Good Master, Matt. 19:16. Governor, Matt. 2:6. Great shepherd of the sheep, Heb. 13:20.

Head of the church, Eph. 5:23. Heir of all things, Heb. 1:2. High priest, Heb. 4:14. Head of every man, 1 Cor. 11:3. Head of the church, Col. 1:18. Head of the corner, Matt. 21:42. Holy child Jesus, Acts 4:30. Holy one, Psa. 16:10; Acts 3:14. Holy one of God, Mark 1:24. Holy one of Israel, Isa. 41:14; 54:5. Holy thing, Luke 1:35. Hope [our], 1 Tim. 1:1. Horn of salvation, Luke 1:69.

I Am, John 8:58. Image of God, Heb. 1:3. Israel, Isa. 49:3.

Jehovah, Isa. 40:3. Jehovah's fellow, Zech. 13:7. Jesus, Matt. 1:21. Jesus Christ, Matt. 1:1; John 1:17; 17:3; Acts 2:38; 4:10; 9:34; 10:36; 16:18; Rom. 1:1,3,6; 2:16; 5:15,17; 6:3; 1 Cor. 1:1,4; 1 Cor. 2:2; 2 Cor. 1:19; 4:6; 4:6; 13:5; Gal. 2:16; Phil. 1:8; 2:11; 1 Tim. 1:15; Heb. 13:8; 1 John 1:7; 2:1. Jesus Christ our Lord, Rom. 1:3; 6:11,23; 1 Cor. 1:9; 7:25. Jesus Christ our Saviour, Tit. 3:6. Jesus of Nazareth, Mark 1:24; Luke 24:19. Jesus of Nazareth, King of the Jews, John 19:19. Jesus, the King of the Jews, Matt. 27:37. Jesus, the Son of God, Heb. 4:14. Jesus, the Son of Joseph, John 6:42. Judge, Acts 10:42. Just man, Matt. 27:19. Just one, Acts 3:14; 7:52; 22:14. Just person, Matt. 27:24.

King, Matt. 21:5. King of Israel, John 1:49. King of the Jews, Matt. 2:2. King of saints, Rev. 15:3. King of kings, 1 Tim. 6:15; Rev. 17:14. King of glory, Psa. 24:7-10. King of Zion, Matt. 21:5. King over all the earth, Zech. 14:9.

Lamb, Rev. 5:6,8; 6:16; 7:9,10, 17; 12:11; 13:8,11; 14:1,4; 15:3; 17:14; 19:7,9; 21:9,14,22,23,27. Lamb of God, John 1:29. Lawgiver, Isa. 33:22. Leader, Isa. 55:4. Life, John 14:6. Light, John 8:12. Light, everlasting, Isa. 60:20. Light of the world, John 8:12. Light to the Gentiles, Isa. 42:6. Light, true, John 1:9. Living bread, John 6:51. Living stone, 1 Pet. 2:4. Lion of the tribe of Judah, Rev. 5:5. Lord, Rom. 1:3. Lord of lords, Rev. 17:14; 19:16. Lord of all, Acts 10:36. Lord our righteousness, Jer. 23:6. Lord God Almighty, Rev. 15:3. Lord from heaven, 1 Cor. 15:47. Lord and Saviour Jesus Christ, 2 Pet. 1:11; 3:18. Lord Christ, Col. 3:24. Lord Jesus, Acts 7:59; Col. 3:17; 1 Thess. 4:2. Lord Jesus Christ, Acts 11:17; 16:31; 20:21; Rom. 5:1,11; 13:14. Lord Jesus Christ our Saviour, Tit. 1:4. Lord of glory, Jas. 2:1. Lord of Hosts, Isa. 44:6. Lord, mighty in battle, Psa. 24:8. Lord of the dead and living, Rom. 14:9. Lord of the sabbath, Mark 2:28. Lord over all, Rom. 10:12. Lord's Christ, Luke 2:26. Lord, strong and mighty, Psa. 24:8. Lord, the our righteousness, Jer. 23:6. Lord, your holy one, Isa. 43:15. Lord, your redeemer, Isa. 43:14.

Man Christ Jesus, 1 Tim. 2:5. Man of sorrows, Isa. 53:3. Master, Matt. 23:8. Mediator, 1 Tim. 2:5. Messenger of the covenant, Mal. 3:1. Messiah, John 1:41. Messiah the Prince, Dan. 9:25. Mighty God, Isa. 9:6. Mighty one of Israel, Isa. 30:29. Mighty one of Jacob, Isa. 49:26. Mighty to save, Isa. 63:1. Minister of the sanctuary, Heb. 8:2. Morning star, Rev. 22:16. Most holy, Dan. 9:24. Most mighty, Psa. 45:3.

Nazarene, Matt. 2:23.

JESUS, THE CHRIST

Offspring of David, Rev. 22:16. Only begotten, John 1:14. Only begotten of the Father, John 1:14. Only begotten Son, John 1:18. Only wise God, our Saviour, Jude 25.

Passover, 1 Cor. 5:7. Plant of renown, Ezek. 34:29. Potentate, 1 Tim. 6:15. Power of God, 1 Cor. 1:24. Physician, Matt. 9:12. Precious corner stone, Isa. 28:16. Priest, Heb. 7:17. Prince, Acts 5:31. Prince of life, Acts 3:15. Prince of peace, Isa. 9:6. Prince of the kings of the earth, Rev. 1:5. Prophet, Deut. 18:15,18; Matt. 21:11; Luke 24:19. Propitiation, 1 John 2:2.

Rabbi, John 1:49. Rabboni, John 20:16. Ransom, 1 Tim. 2:6. Redeemer, Isa. 59:20. Resurrection and life, John 11:25. Redemption, 1 Cor. 1:30. Righteous branch, Jer. 23:5. Righteous judge, 2 Tim. 4:8. Righteous servant, Isa. 53:11. Righteousness, 1 Cor. 1:30. Rock, 1 Cor. 10:4. Rock of offense, 1 Pet. 2:8. Root of David, Rev. 5:5; 22:16. Root of Jesse, Isa. 11:10. Rose of Sharon, Song 2:1. Ruler in Israel, Mic. 5:2.

Salvation, Luke 2:30. Sanctification, 1 Cor. 1:30. Sanctuary, Isa. 8:14. Saviour, Luke 2:11. Saviour, Jesus Christ, 2 Tim. 1:10; Tit. 2:13; 2 Pet. 1:1. Saviour of the body, Eph. 5:23. Saviour of the world, 1 John 4:14. Sceptre, Num. 24:17. Second man, 1 Cor. 15:47. Seed of David, 2 Tim. 2:8. Seed of the woman, Gen. 3:15. Servant, Isa. 42:1. Servant of rulers, Isa. 49:7. Shepherd, Matt. 14:27. Shepherd and bishop of souls, 1 Pet. 2:25. Shepherd, chief, 1 Pet. 5:4. Shepherd, good, John 10:11. Shepherd, great, Heb. 13:20. Shepherd of Israel, Psa. 80:1. Shiloh, Gen. 49:10. Son of the Father, 2 John 3. Son of God, see JESUS, SON OF GOD. Son of Man, see JESUS, SON OF MAN. Son of the blessed, Mark 14:61. Son of the highest, Luke 1:32. Son of David, Matt. 9:27. Star, Num. 24:17. Sun of righteousness, Mal. 4:2. Surety, Heb. 7:22. Stone, Matt. 21:42. Stone of stumbling, 1 Pet. 2:8. Sure foundation, Isa. 28:16.

Teacher, John 3:2. True God, 1 John 5:20. True vine, John 15:1. Truth, John 14:6.

Unspeakable gift, 2 Cor. 9:15. Very Christ, Acts 9:22. Vine, John 15:1.

Way, John 14:6. Which is, which was, which is to come, Rev. 1:4. Wisdom, Prov. 8:12. Wisdom of God, 1 Cor. 1:24. Witness, Isa. 55:4; Rev. 1:5. Wonderful, Isa. 9:6. Word, John 1:1. Word of God, Rev. 19:13. Word of life, 1 John 1:1.

Those who use his name must depart from evil, 2 Tim. 2:19.

Obedience of: Psa. 40:8. I delight to do thy will, O my God; yea, thy law *is* within my heart.

Isa. 50:5. The Lord GOD hath opened mine ear, and I was not rebellious, neither turned away back. 6. I gave my back to the smiters, and my cheeks to them that plucked off the hair: I hid not my face from shame and spitting.

Matt. 26:39. O my Father, if it be possible, let this cup pass from me: nevertheless not as I will, but as thou *wilt*. 42. He went away again the second time, and prayed, saying, O my Father, if this cup may not pass away from me, except I drink it, thy will be done. Mark 14:36; Luke 22:42.

Heb. 5:8. Though he were a Son, yet learned he obedience by the things which he suffered;

Omnipotence of: Isa. 9:6. The government shall be upon his shoulder: and his name shall be called Wonderful, Counsellor, The mighty God, The everlasting Father, The Prince of Peace.

Isa. 40:10. Behold, the Lord GOD will come with strong *hand*, and his arm shall rule for him: behold, his reward *is* with him, and his work before him.

Matt. 10:1. When he had called unto *him* his twelve disciples, he gave them power *against* unclean spirits, to cast them out, and to heal all manner of sickness and all manner of disease. Mark 6:7; Luke 9:1.

Matt. 28:18. Jesus came and spake unto them, saying, All power is given unto me in heaven and in earth.

Heb. 7:25. He is able also to save them to the uttermost that come unto God by him,

Omnipresence of: Matt. 28:20. Lo, I am with you alway, *even* unto the end of the world.

Omniscience of: Matt. 9:4. And Jesus knowing their thoughts said, Wherefore think ye evil in your hearts?

Matt. 12:25. And Jesus knew their thoughts, and said unto them, Every kingdom divided against itself is brought to desolation; and every city or house divided against itself shall not stand:

Matt. 24:25. Behold, I have told you before.

Mark 5:30. Jesus, immediately knowing in himself that virtue had gone out of him, turned him about in the press, and said, Who touched my clothes?

Luke 6:8. He knew their thoughts,

John 6:64. Jesus knew from the beginning who they were that believed not, and who should betray him.

John 18:4. Jesus therefore, knowing all things that should come upon him, went forth, and said unto them, Whom seek ye?

Parables of: The wise and foolish builders, Matt. 7:24-27; Luke 6:47,49.

Two debtors, Luke 7:41-47.

The rich fool, Luke 12:16-21.

The servants waiting for their Lord, Luke 12:35-40.

Barren fig tree, Luke 13:6-9.

The sower, Matt. 13:3-9,18-23; Mark 4:1-9,14-20; Luke 8:5-8,11-15.

The tares, Matt. 13:24-30,36-43.

Seed growing secretly, Mark 4: 26-29.

Mustard seed, Matt. 13:31,32; Mark 4:30-32; Luke 13:18,19.

Leaven, Matt. 13:33; Luke 13: 20,21.

Hid treasure, Matt. 13:44.

Pearl of great price, Matt. 13: 45,46.

Dragnet, Matt. 13:47-50.

Unmerciful servant, Matt. 18: 23-35.

Good Samaritan, Luke 10:30-37.

Friend at midnight, Luke 11:5-8.

Good shepherd, John 10:1-16.

Great supper, Luke 14:15-24.

Lost sheep, Luke 15:3-7; Matt. 18:12-14.

Lost piece of money, Luke 15: 8-10.

The prodigal and his brother, Luke 15:11-32.

The unjust steward, Luke 16:1-9.

Rich man and Lazarus, Luke 16: 19-31.

Importunate widow, Luke 18:1-8.

Pharisee and publican, Luke 18: 9-14.

Laborers in the vineyard, Matt. 20:1-16.

The pounds, Luke 19:11-27.

The two sons, Matt. 21:28-32.

Wicked husbandmen, Matt. 21: 33-44; Mark 12:1-12; Luke 20:9-18.

Marriage of the king's son, Matt. 22:1-14.

Fig tree leafing, Matt. 24:32; Mark 13:28,29.

Man taking a far journey, Mark 13:34-37.

Ten virgins, Matt. 25:1-13.

Talents, Matt. 25:14-30.

The vine, John 15:1-5.

Perfections of: Not classified under foregoing topics: Psa. 45:2. Thou art fairer than the children of men: grace is poured into thy lips:

Mic. 5:4. He shall stand and feed in the strength of the LORD, in the majesty of the name of the LORD his God;

1 Cor. 1:24. Christ the power of God, and the wisdom of God.

2 Cor. 4:4. Christ, who is the image of God,

Col. 1:19. It pleased *the Father* that in him should all fulness dwell;

Heb. 1:3. Who being the brightness of *his* glory, and the express image of his person,

Power of, To Forgive Sins: Acts 5:31. Him hath God exalted with his right hand *to be* a Prince and a Saviour, for to give repentance to Israel, and forgiveness of sins:

Col. 3:13. As Christ forgave you, so also *do* ye.

Prayers of: Matt. 14:23. He went up into a mountain apart to pray: and when the evening was come, he was there alone. Mark 6:46.

Matt. 15:36. And he took the seven loaves and the fishes, and gave thanks, and brake *them*.

Matt. 19:13. Then were there brought unto him little children, that he should put *his* hands on them, and pray:

Luke 6:12. He went out into a mountain to pray, and continued all night in prayer to God.

Heb. 5:7. Who in the days of his flesh, when he had offered up prayers and supplications with strong crying and tears unto him that was able to save him from death, and was heard in that he feared;

Pre-Existence of: Psa. 102:25. Of old hast thou laid the foundation of the earth: and the heavens *are* the work of thy hands.

Prov. 8:22. The LORD possessed me in the beginning of his way, before his works of old. 23. I was set up from everlasting, from the beginning, or ever the earth was.

John 1:1. In the beginning was the Word, and the Word was with God, and the Word was God. 2. The same was in the beginning with God. 3. All things were made by him; and without him was not any thing made that was made.

Priesthood of: Appointed and called by God, Heb. 3:1,2; 5:4,5; after the order of Melchizedek, Psa. 110:4, with Heb. 5:6; 6:20; 7:15,17; superior to Aaron and the Levitical priests, Heb. 7:11,16,22; 8:1,2,6. Consecrated with an oath, Heb. 7: 20,21. Has an unchangeable priesthood, Heb. 7:23,28. Is of unblemished purity, Heb. 7:26,28; faithful, Heb. 3:2. Needed no sacrifice for himself, Heb. 7:27.

Offered himself a sacrifice, Heb. 9:14,26. His sacrifice superior to all others, Heb. 9:13,14,23. Offered sacrifice but once, Heb. 7:27. Made reconciliation, Heb. 2:17. Obtained redemption for us, Heb. 9:12. Entered into heaven, Heb. 4:14; 10:12. Sympathizes with saints, Heb. 2:18; 4:15. Intercedes, Heb. 7:25; 9:24. Blesses, Num. 6:23-26, with Acts

3:26. On his throne, Zech. 6:13. Appointment of, an encouragement to steadfastness, Heb. 4:14.

Typified: Melchizedek, Gen. 14: 18-20. Aaron and his sons, Ex. 40: 12-15.—*Bible Text-Book.*

Prophecies Concerning: COM-ING OF: Gen. 3:15. And I will put enmity between thee and the woman, and between thy seed and her seed; it shall bruise thy head, and thou shalt bruise his heel.

Gen. 12:3. In thee shall all families of the earth be blessed.

Job 19:25. For I know *that* my redeemer liveth, and *that* he shall stand at the latter *day* upon the earth:

Psa. 118:22. The stone *which* the builders refused is become the head *stone* of the corner.

Jer. 23:5. Behold, the days come, saith the LORD, that I will raise unto David a righteous Branch, and a King shall reign and prosper, and shall execute judgment and justice in the earth. 6. In his days Judah shall be saved, and Israel shall dwell safely: and this *is* his name whereby he shall be called, THE LORD OUR RIGHTEOUSNESS.

Zech. 9:9. Rejoice greatly, O daughter of Zion; shout, O daughter of Jerusalem: behold, thy King cometh unto thee: he *is* just, and having salvation; lowly, and riding upon an ass, and upon a colt the foal of an ass.

John 8:56. Your father Abraham rejoiced to see my day: and he saw *it*, and was glad.

Rom. 1:2. (Which he had promised afore by his prophets in the holy scriptures,) 3. Concerning his Son Jesus Christ our Lord,

PROPHECIES CONCERNING THE FU-TURE GLORY AND POWER OF: Mark 14:62. And Jesus said, I am: and ye shall see the Son of man sitting on the right hand of power and coming in the clouds of heaven.

1 Pet. 3:22. Who is gone into heaven, and is on the right hand of God; angels and authorities and powers being made subject unto him.

Rev. 5:5. The Lion of the tribe of Juda, the Root of David, hath prevailed to open the book, and to loose the seven seals thereof. 12. Worthy is the Lamb that was slain to receive power, and riches, and wisdom, and strength, and honour, and glory, and blessing.

Prophet: Deut. 18:15. The LORD thy God will raise up unto thee a Prophet from the midst of thee, of thy brethren, like unto me; unto him ye shall hearken; 18. I will raise them up a Prophet from among their brethren, like unto thee and will put my words in his mouth; and he shall speak unto them all that I shall command him. Acts 3:22,23; 7:37.

Luke 13:33. Nevertheless I must walk to day, and to morrow, and the *day* following: for it cannot be that a prophet perish out of Jerusalem.

Received: Matt 12:23. And all the people were amazed, and said, Is not this the son of David?

Matt. 21:8. A very great multitude spread their garments in the way; others cut down branches from the trees and strawed *them* in the way.

Mark 12:37. The common people heard him gladly.

Luke 5:1. As the people pressed upon him to hear the word of God, 26. They were all amazed, and they glorified God, and were filled with fear, saying, We have seen strange things to day.

Luke 7:16. There came a fear on all: and they glorified God, saying, That a great prophet is risen up among us; and, That God hath visited his people.

Luke 12:1. There were gathered together an innumerable multitude of people, insomuch that they trode one upon another.

Luke 21:38. And all the people came early in the morning to him in the temple, for to hear him. John 8:2.

John 12:42. Nevertheless among the chief rulers also many believed on him; but because of the Pharisees they did not confess *him*, lest they should be put out of the synagogue:

Rejected: Isa. 53:1. Who hath believed our report? and to whom is the arm of the LORD revealed? 2. For he shall grow up before him as a tender plant, and as a root out of a dry ground: he hath no form nor comeliness; and when we shall see him, *there is* no beauty that we should desire him. 3. He is despised and rejected of men; a man of sorrows, and acquainted with grief: and we hid as it were *our* faces from him: he was despised, and we esteemed him not. 4. We did esteem him stricken, smitten of God, and afflicted.

Matt. 8:34. And, behold, the whole city came out to meet Jesus: and when they saw him, they besought *him* that he would depart out of their coasts. Mark 5:17; Luke 8:37.

Matt. 17:17. Jesus answered and said, O faithless and perverse generation, how long shall I be with you? how long shall I suffer you?

Mark 6:3. Is not this the carpenter, the son of Mary, the brother of James, and Joses, and of Juda, and Simon? and are not his sisters here with us? And they were offended at him.

Luke 17:25. But first must he suffer many things, and be rejected of this generation.

Luke 22:67. Art thou the Christ? tell us. And he said unto them, If I tell you, ye will not believe:

John 1:11. He came unto his own, and his own received him not.

John 7:3. His brethren therefore said unto him, Depart hence, and go into Judæa, that thy disciples also may see the works that thou doest. 5. For neither did his brethren believe in him.

John 9:16. Therefore said some of the Pharisees, This man is not of God, because he keepeth not the sabbath day. Others said, How can a man that is a sinner do such miracles? And there was a division among them.

John 15:18. If the world hate you, ye know that it hated me before *it hated* you.

I Cor. 1:18. For the preaching of the cross is to them that perish, foolishness; but unto us which are saved it is the power of God. 23. But we preach Christ crucified, unto the Jews a stumblingblock, and unto the Greeks foolishness;

1 Pet. 2:4. A living stone, disallowed indeed of men, but chosen of God, *and* precious.

Relation of, to the Father: Psa. 110:1. The LORD said unto my Lord, Sit thou at my right hand, until I make thine enemies thy footstool.

Isa. 42:1. Behold my servant, whom I uphold; mine elect, *in whom* my soul delighteth; I have put my spirit upon him:

Isa. 61:1. The Spirit of the Lord GOD *is* upon me; because the LORD hath anointed me to preach good tidings unto the meek; he hath sent me to bind up the brokenhearted,

Mark 10:40. But to sit on my right hand and on my left hand is not mine to give; but *it shall be given to them* for whom it is prepared.

Mark 13:32. But of that day and *that* hour knoweth no man, no, not the angels which are in heaven, neither the Son, but the Father.

John 1:1. In the beginning was the Word, and the Word was with God, and the Word was God. 2. The same was in the beginning with God. 14. And the Word was made flesh, and dwelt among us, (and we beheld his glory, the glory as of the only begotten of the Father,) full of grace and truth.

John 4:34. Jesus saith unto them, My meat is to do the will of him that sent me, and to finish his work.

John 7:16. Jesus answered them, and said, My doctrine is not mine, but his that sent me.

John 10:15. As the Father knoweth me, even so know I the Father: and I lay down my life for the sheep.

John 12:44. Jesus cried and said, He that believeth on me, believeth not on me, but on him that sent me.

John 14:13. And whatsoever ye shall ask in my name, that will I do, that the Father may be glorified in the Son.

John 17:5. And now, O Father, glorify thou me with thine own self with the glory which I had with thee before the world was.

Rom. 8:32. He that spared not his own Son, but delivered him up for us all,

1 Cor. 11:3. The head of Christ *is* God.

1 Cor. 15:24. Then *cometh* the end, when he shall have delivered up the kingdom to God, even the Father; when he shall have put down all rule and all authority and power. 27. For he hath put all things under his feet. But when he saith all things are put under *him, it is* manifest that he is excepted, which did put all things under him. 28. And when all things shall be subdued unto him, then shall the Son also himself be subject unto him that put all things under him, that God may be all in all.

Phil 2:6. Who, being in the form of God, thought it not [robbery] to be equal with God: [R. V. a prize]

Resurrection of: Psa. 16:9. My flesh also shall rest in hope. 10. For thou wilt not leave my soul in hell; neither wilt thou suffer thine Holy One to see corruption.

Matt. 12:40. As Jonas was three days and three nights in the whale's belly; so shall the Son of man be three days and three nights in the heart of the earth.

Matt. 26:32. But after I am risen again, I will go before you into Galilee. Mark 14:28.

Matt. 28:6. He is not here: for he is risen, as he said. Come, see the place where the Lord lay. 7. And go quickly, and tell his disciples that he is risen from the dead; and, behold, he goeth before you into Galilee; there shall ye see him: lo, I have told you. Mark 16:6,7; Luke 24:5-7; John 20:1-18.

Luke 18:33. And they shall scourge *him*, and put him to death: and the third day he shall rise again.

Acts 1:3. To whom also he shewed himself alive after his passion by many infallible proofs, being seen of them forty days and speaking of the things pertaining to the kingdom of God:

Acts 3:15. And killed the Prince of life, whom God hath raised from the dead; whereof we are witnesses.

Rom. 1:4. Declared *to be* the Son of God with power, according to the spirit of holiness, by the resurrection from the dead:

Rom. 10:9. If thou shalt confess with thy mouth the Lord Jesus, and shalt believe in thine heart that God hath raised him from the dead, thou shalt be saved.

1 Thess. 4:14. For if we believe that Jesus died and rose again, even so them also which sleep in Jesus will God bring with him.

Saviour: Zech. 9:9. Shout, O daughter of Jerusalem: behold, thy king cometh unto thee: he *is* just, and having salvation;

Mal. 4:2. Unto you that fear my name shall the Sun of righteousness arise with healing in his wings; and ye shall go forth, and grow up as calves of the stall.

Matt. 1:21. Thou shalt call his name JESUS: for he shall save his people from their sins.

Luke 1:68. Blessed *be* the Lord God of Israel; for he hath visited and redeemed his people, 69. And hath raised up an horn of salvation for us in the house of his servant David;

Luke 2:11. Unto you is born this day in the city of David a Saviour, which is Christ the Lord. 30. Mine eyes have seen thy salvation, 31. Which thou hast prepared before the face of all people; 32. A light to lighten the Gentiles, and the glory of thy people Israel.

Luke 19:10. The Son of man is come to seek and to save that which was lost. Luke 15:4-10.

Acts 5:31. Him hath God exalted with his right hand *to be* a Prince and a Saviour, for to give repentance to Israel, and forgiveness of sins.

Acts 15:11. We believe that through the grace of the Lord Jesus Christ we shall be saved,

Acts 16:31. Believe on the Lord Jesus Christ, and thou shalt be saved, and thy house.

Rom. 4:25. Who was delivered for our offences, and was raised again for our justification.

Rom. 6:23. The gift of God *is* eternal life through Jesus Christ our Lord.

Second Coming of: Matt. 16:27. The Son of man shall come in the glory of his Father with his angels; and then he shall reward every man according to his works.

Matt. 24:42. Watch therefore: for ye know not what hour your LORD doth come.

Matt. 26:64. Hereafter shall ye see the Son of man sitting on the right hand of power, and coming in the clouds of heaven.

1 Cor. 15:23. Christ the firstfruits; afterward they that are Christ's at his coming.

Rev. 22:12. Behold, I come quickly; and my reward *is* with me, to give every man according as his work shall be. 20. He which testifieth these things saith, Surely I come quickly. Amen. Even so, come, Lord Jesus.

Shepherd: JESUS THE TRUE: Foretold, Gen. 49:24; Isa. 40:11; Ezek. 34:23; 37:24. The chief, 1 Pet. 5:4. The good, John 10:11,14. The great, Mic. 5:4; Heb. 13:20.

His sheep he knows, John 10:14, 27. He calls, John 10:3. He gathers, Isa. 40:11; John 10:16. He guides, Psa. 23:3; John 10:3,4. He feeds, Psa. 23:1,2; John 10:9. He cherishes tenderly, Isa. 40:11. He protects and preserves, Jer. 31:10; Ezek. 34:10; Zech. 9:16; John 10:28. He laid down his life for, Zech. 13:7; Matt. 26:31; John 10:11,15; Acts 20:28. He gives eternal life to, John 10:28.

Typified: David, 1 Sam. 16:11.

Son of God: Matt. 3:17. Lo a voice from heaven, saying, This is my beloved Son in whom I am well pleased. Mark 1:11; Luke 3:22.

Mark 1:1. The beginning of the gospel of Jesus Christ, the Son of God;

John 1:1. In the beginning was the Word, and the Word was with God, and the Word was God.

John 9:35. Jesus . . . said unto him, Dost thou believe on the Son of God? 36. He answered and said, Who is he, Lord, that I might believe him? 37. Jesus said unto him, Thou hast both seen him, and it is he that talketh with thee.

John 17:1. Father, the hour is come; glorify thy Son, that thy Son also may glorify thee: vss. 1-26.

Acts 3:13. The God of our fathers, hath glorified his Son Jesus;

Sufferings of: Matt. 26:38. Then saith he unto them, My soul is exceeding sorrowful, even unto death: tarry ye here, and watch with me.

Matt. 27:26. Then released he Barabbas unto them: and when he had scourged Jesus, he delivered him to be crucified. 27. Then the soldiers of the governor took Jesus into the common hall, and gathered unto him the whole band of soldiers. 28. And they stripped him, and put on him a scarlet robe. 29. And when they had platted a crown of thorns, they put it upon his head, and a reed in his right hand: and they bowed the knee before him, and mocked him, saying, Hail, King of the Jews! 30. And they spit upon him, and took the reed, and smote him on the head. 31. And after that they had mocked him, they took the robe off from him, and put his own raiment on him, and led him away to crucify him. 35. And they crucified him, and parted his garments, casting lots: that it might be fulfilled which was spoken by the prophet. They parted my garments among them, and upon my vesture did they cast lots. 36. And sitting down they watched him there;

Mark 15:34. At the ninth hour Jesus cried with a loud voice, saying, Eloi, Eloi, lama sabachthani? which is, being interpreted, My God, my God, why hast thou forsaken me?

Mic. 5:1. They shall smite the judge of Israel with a rod upon the cheek.

Luke 22:44. Being in an agony he prayed more earnestly: and his sweat was as it were great drops of blood falling down to the ground.

Rev. 19:13. He was clothed with a vesture dipped in blood: and his name is called The Word of God.

Teacher: Matt. 4:23. And Jesus went about all Galilee, teaching in their synagogues, and preaching the gospel of the kingdom.

Luke 4:15. And he taught in their synagogues, being glorified of all.

Temptation of: Matt. 4:1. Then was Jesus led up of the spirit into the wilderness to be tempted of the devil.

Heb. 4:15. For we have not an high priest which cannot be touched with the feeling of our infirmities; but was in all points tempted like as we are, yet without sin.

Unchangeable: Heb. 13:8. Jesus Christ the same yesterday, and to day, and for ever.

Worship of: Luke 5:8. When Simon Peter saw it, he fell down at Jesus' knees, saying, Depart from me; for I am a sinful man, O Lord.

Luke 24:52. They worshipped him, and returned to Jerusalem with great joy:

Phil. 2:10. At the name of Jesus every knee should bow, of things in heaven, and things in earth, and things under the earth; 11. And that every tongue should confess that Jesus Christ is Lord, to the glory of God the Father.

JONAH, called also JONAS. A prophet of Israel, 2 Kin. 14:25. Sent by God to warn Nineveh, Jonah 1:1,2. Disobedience and punishment of, Jonah 1:3-17. Repentance and deliverance of, Jonah 2; Matt. 12:40. Brought Ninevites to repentance, Jonah 3; Matt. 12:41. Displeased with God's mercy to Nineveh; reproved, Jonah 4. Is a sign, Matt. 16:4; Luke 11:29,30.

JONATHAN. Son of Saul, 1 Sam. 14:49. Victory of, over the Philistine garrison of Geba, 1 Sam. 13:3,4,16; over Philistines at Michmash, 1 Sam. 14:1-18. Under Saul's curse pronounced against any who might take food before he was avenged of his enemies, 1 Sam. 14: 24-30,43. Rescued by the people, 1 Sam. 14:43-45. Love of, for David, 1 Sam. 18:1-4; 19:1-7; 20; 23:16-18. Killed in battle with Philistines, 1 Sam. 31:2,6; 1 Chr. 10:2; 2 Sam. 21:12-14. Buried by inhabitants of Jabesh-gilead, 1 Sam. 31: 11-13. Mourned by David, 2 Sam.

JOSHUA

1:12,17-27. Son of, cared for by David, 2 Sam. 4:4; 9; 1 Chr. 8:34.

JOSEPH. Son of Jacob, Gen. 30:24. Personal appearance of, Gen. 39:6. His father's favorite child, Gen. 33:2; 37:3,4,35; 48:22; 1 Chr. 5:2, John 4:5. His father's partiality for, excites the jealousy of his brethren, Gen. 37:4,11,18-28; Psa. 105:17; Acts 7:9. His prophetic dreams of his fortunes in Egypt, Gen. 37:5-11. Sold into Egypt, Gen. 37:27,28. Is falsely reported to his father as killed by wild beasts, Gen. 37:29-35. Is bought by Potiphar, an officer of Pharaoh, Gen. 37:36. Is prospered of God, Gen. 39:2-5,21,23. Is falsely accused, and cast into prison; is delivered by the friendship of another prisoner, Gen. 39; 40; Psa. 105:18. Is an interpreter of dreams: of the two prisoners, Gen. 40:5-23; of Pharaoh, Gen. 41:1-37. His name is, changed to Zaphnath-paaneah, Gen. 41:45. Is promoted to authority next to Pharaoh at thirty years of age, Gen 41:37-46; Psa. 105:19-22. Takes to wife the daughter of the priest of On, Gen. 41:45. Provides against the years of famine, Gen. 41:46-57. Exports the produce of Egypt to other countries, Gen. 41: 57. Sells the stores of food to the people of Egypt, exacting of them all their money, flocks and herds, lands and lives, Gen. 47:13-26. Exempts the priests from the exactions, Gen. 47:22,26.

His father sends down into Egypt to buy corn, Gen. 42; 43; 44. Reveals himself to his brethren; sends for his father; provides the land of Goshen for his people; and sustains them during the famine, Gen. chapters 45; 46; 47:1-12. His two sons, Gen. 41:50,52. See EPHRAIM; MANASSEH. Mourns the death of his father, Gen. 50:1-14. Exacts a pledge from his brethren to convey his remains to Canaan, Gen. 50:24, 25; Heb. 11:22, with Ex. 13:19; Josh. 24:32; Acts 7-16. Death of, Gen. 50:22-26.

Kindness of heart, Gen. 40:7,8. His integrity, Gen. 39:7-12; humility, Gen. 41:16; 45:7-9; wisdom, Gen. 41:33-57; piety, Gen. 41:51,

52; faith, Gen. 45:5-8. Was a prophet, Gen. 41:38,39; 50:25; Ex. 13:19. God's providence with, Gen. 39:2-5; Psa. 105:17-22. His sons conjointly called JOSEPH, Deut. 33: 13-17. Descendants of, Gen. 46:20; Num. 26:28-37.

JOSHUA. Called also JEHOSHUA, and JEHOSHUAH, and OSHEA. Son of Nun, Num. 13:8; 1 Chr. 7: 27. Intimately associated with Moses, Ex. 24:13; 32:17; 33:11. A religious zealot, Num. 11:28. Sent with others to view the promised land, Num. 13:8. Makes favorable report, Num. 14:6-10. Rewarded for his courage and fidelity, Num. 14:30,38; 32:12. Commissioned, ordained, and charged with the responsibilities of Moses' office, Num. 27:18-23; Deut. 1:38; 3:28; 31:3,7, 23; 34:9. Divinely inspired, Num. 27:18; Deut. 34:9; Josh. 1:5,9; 3:7; 8.8. His life miraculously preserved when he made a favorable report of the land, Num. 14:10. Promises to, Josh. 1:5-9. Leads the people into the land of Canaan, Josh. chapters 1-4; Acts 7:45; Heb. 4:8. Renews circumcision of the children of Israel; reëstablishes the passover; has a vision of the angel of God, Josh. 5. Besieges and takes Jericho, Josh. 6. Takes Ai, Josh. 7; 8. Makes a league with the Gibeonites, Josh. 9:3-27. The kings of the six nations of the Canaanites confederate against him, Josh. 9:1,2; make war upon the Gibeonites; are defeated and slain, Josh. 10. Defeats seven other kings, Josh. 10:28-43. Makes conquest of Hazor, Josh. 11. Completes the conquest of the whole land, Josh. 11:23. List of the kings whom Joshua smote, Josh. 12. Allots the land, Josh. chapters 13-19. Sets the tabernacle up in Shiloh, Josh. 18:1. Sets apart cities of refuge, Josh. 20; forty-eight cities for the Levites, Josh. 21. Exhortation of, before his death, Josh. 23;24. Survives the Israelites who refused to enter Canaan, Num. 26:63-65. His portion of the land, Josh. 19:49,50. Death and burial of, Josh. 24:29,30. Esteem in which he was held, Josh. 1:16-18. Faith of, Josh. 6:16. Military genius of, as exhibited at the

defeat of the Amalekites, Ex. 17:13;
at Ai, Josh. 8; in Gibeon, Josh. 10;
at Hazor, Josh. 11. Age of, at
death, Judg. 2:8.

JOY. 1 Chr. 16:27. Glory and
honour *are* in his presence; strength
and gladness *are* in his place.

Job 8:21. Till he fill thy mouth
with laughing, and thy lips with rejoicing.

Psa. 4:7. Thou hast put gladness
in my heart, more than in the time
that their corn and their wine increased.

Psa. 30:5. Weeping may endure
for a night, but joy *cometh* in the
morning.

Psa. 33:21. Our heart shall rejoice in him, because we have trusted in his holy name.

Psa. 104:34. My meditation of
him shall be sweet: I will be glad
in the LORD.

Psa. 126:5. They that sow in
tears shall reap in joy.

Acts 13:52. The disciples were
filled with joy, and with the Holy
Ghost.

Rom. 15:13. Now the God of
hope fill you with all joy and peace
in believing, that ye may abound in
hope, through the power of the
Holy Ghost.

Gal. 5:22. The fruit of the Spirit
is love, joy, peace,

Phil. 4:4. Rejoice in the Lord
alway: *and* again I say, Rejoice.

1 Thess. 5:16. Rejoice evermore.

JUDAS. Surnamed Iscariot.
Chosen as an apostle, Matt. 10:4;
Mark 3:19; Luke 6:16; Acts 1:17.
Treasurer of the disciples, John 12:
6; 13:29. His covetousness exemplified by his protest against the breaking of the box of ointment, John
12:4-6; by his bargain to betray Jesus for a sum of money, Matt. 26:
14-16; Mark 14:10,11; Luke 22:3-6;
John 13:2. His apostasy, John 17:
12. Betrays the Lord, Matt. 26:47-
50; Mark 14:43-45; Luke 22:47-49;
John 18:2-5; Acts 1:16-25. Returns
the money to the rulers of the Jews,
Matt. 27:3-10. Hangs himself, Matt.
27:5; Acts 1:18. Prophecies concerning, Matt. 26:21-25; Mark 14:
18-21; Luke 22:21-23; John 13:18-

26; 17:12; Acts 1:16,20, with Psa.
41:9; 109:8; Zech. 11:12,13.

JUDGE. Psa. 82:2. How long
will ye judge unjustly, and accept the
persons of the wicked? 3. Defend the
poor and fatherless: do justice to
the afflicted and needy. 4. Deliver
the poor and needy: rid *them* out
of the hand of the wicked.

Prov. 24:23. These *things* also
belong to the wise. *It is* not good
to have respect of persons in judgment.

John 7:24. Judge not according
to the appearance, but judge righteous judgment.

JUDGMENT. 1 Chr. 16:33.
Then shall the trees of the wood
sing out at the presence of the
LORD, because he cometh to judge
the earth.

Psa. 9:7. But the LORD shall endure for ever: he hath prepared his
throne for judgment.

Eccl. 12:14. God shall bring
every work into judgment, with
every secret thing, whether *it be*
good, or whether *it be* evil.

Ezek. 18:20. The soul that sinneth, it shall die.

Dan. 7:9. I beheld till the thrones
were cast down, and the Ancient of
days did sit, whose garment *was*
white as snow, and the hair of his
head like the pure wool: his throne
was like the fiery flame, *and* his
wheels *as* burning fire. 10. A fiery
stream issued and came forth from
before him: thousand thousands
ministered unto him, and ten thousand times ten thousand stood before
him: the judgment was set, and the
books were opened.

Matt. 12:36. Every idle word
that men shall speak, they shall
give account thereof in the day of
judgment.

Matt. 16:27. The Son of man
shall come in the glory of his Father
with his angels; and then he shall
reward every man according to his
works. Mark 8:38.

Matt. 25:41. Then shall he say
also unto them on the left hand,
Depart from me, ye cursed, into
everlasting fire, prepared for the
devil and his angels.

Rev. 1:7. Behold, he cometh with

clouds; and every eye shall see him, and they *also* which pierced him: and all kindreds of the earth shall wail because of him.

Jer. 17:10. I the LORD search the heart, *I* try the reins, even to give every man according to his ways, *and* according to the fruit of his doings.

Matt. 12:37. By thy words thou shalt be justified, and by thy words thou shalt be condemned.

1 Cor. 3:8. Every man shall receive his own reward according to his own labour.

JUSTICE. Ex. 23:1. Thou shalt not raise a false report: put not thine hand with the wicked to be an unrighteous witness. 2. Thou shalt not follow a multitude to *do* evil; neither shalt thou speak in a cause to decline after many to wrest *judgment*.

Prov. 17:26. To punish the just *is* not good, *nor* to strike princes for equity.

Isa. 1:17. Learn to do well; seek judgment, relieve the oppressed, judge the fatherless, plead for the widow.

1 Cor. 13:6. Rejoiceth not in iniquity, but rejoiceth in the truth;

See COURT; JUDGE.

JUSTIFICATION. Psa. 32:2. Blessed *is* the man unto whom the LORD imputeth not iniquity, Rom. 4:6.

Isa. 50:8. *He is* near that justifieth me; who will contend with me? let us stand together: who *is* mine adversary? let him come near to me.

Isa. 53:11. He shall see of the travail of his soul, *and* shall be satisfied: by his knowledge shall my righteous servant justify many; for he shall bear their iniquities.

Zech. 3:4. Take away the filthy garments from him. And unto him he said, Behold, I have caused thine iniquity to pass from thee, and I will clothe thee with [change of raiment.] [R. V. rich apparel]

Acts 13:39. By him all that believe are justified from all things, from which ye could not be justified by the law of Moses.

Rom. 4:5. But to him that worketh not, but believeth on him that justifieth the ungodly, his faith is counted for righteousness. 20. He staggered not at the promise of God through unbelief; but was strong in faith, giving glory to God; 21. And being fully persuaded that, what he had promised, he was able also to perform. 22. And therefore it was imputed to him for righteousness.

Rom. 5:1. Being justified by faith [we] have peace with God through our Lord Jesus Christ: 9. Much more then, being now justified by his blood, we shall be saved from [wrath] through him. [R. V. let us] [R. V. wrath of God]

KEY. Judg. 3:25. A symbol of authority, Isa. 22:22; Matt. 16:19; Rev. 1:18; 3:7; 9:1; 20:1.

KIDNAPPING, forbidden, Ex. 21:16; Deut. 24:7.

Instance of: Judg. 21:20-23.

KINDNESS. Lev. 19:34. *But* the stranger that dwelleth with you shall be unto you as one born among you, and thou shalt love him as thyself; for ye were strangers in the land of Egypt.

Deut. 22:1. Thou shalt no see thy brother's ox or his sheep go astray, and hide thyself from them, thou shalt in any case bring them again unto thy brother. *vss.* 2-4.

Matt. 5:7. Blessed *are* the merciful: for they shall obtain mercy. 42. Give to him that asketh thee, and from him that would borrow of thee turn not thou away. Luke 6: 30.

Matt. 25:34. Then shall the King say unto them on his right hand, Come, ye blessed of my Father, inherit the kingdom prepared for you from the foundation of the world: 35. For I was an hungred, and ye gave me meat: I was thirsty, and ye gave me drink: I was a stranger and ye took me in: 36. Naked, and ye clothed me: I was sick, and ye visited me: I was in prison, and ye came unto me.

Acts 20:35. I have shewed you all things, how that so labouring ye ought to support the weak, and to remember the words of the Lord Jesus, how he said, It is more blessed to give than to receive.

Rom. 15:1. We then that are strong ought to bear the infirmities of the weak, and not to please ourselves. 2. Let every one of us please *his* neighbour for *his* good to edification. 5. The God of patience and consolation grant you to be likeminded one toward another according to Christ Jesus:

Eph. 4:32. And be ye kind one to another, tenderhearted, forgiving one another, even as God for Christ's sake hath forgiven you.

Heb. 5:2. Who can have compassion on the ignorant, and on them that are out of the way; for that he himself also is compassed with infirmity.

1 Pet. 4:8. Above all things have fervent charity among yourselves: for charity shall cover the multitude of sins.

LABOR. Gen. 3:19. In the sweat of thy face shalt thou eat bread, till thou return unto the ground; for out of it wast thou taken: for dust thou *art*, and unto dust shalt thou return.

Ex. 20:9. Six days shalt thou labour, and do all thy work: 10. But the seventh day *is* the sabbath of the LORD thy God: *in it* thou shalt not do any work, thou, nor thy son, nor thy daughter, nor thy manservant, nor thy maidservant, nor thy cattle, nor thy stranger that *is* within thy gates: 11. For *in* six days the LORD made heaven and earth, the sea, and all that in them *is*, and rested the seventh day: wherefore the LORD blessed the sabbath day, and hallowed it.

Deut. 24:14. Thou shalt not oppress an hired servant *that is* poor and needy, *whether he be* of thy brethren, or of thy strangers that *are* in thy land within thy gates: 15. At his day thou shalt give *him* his hire, neither shall the sun go down upon it; for he *is* poor, and setteth his heart upon it: lest he cry against thee unto the LORD, and it be sin unto thee.

Eccl. 5:12. The sleep of a labouring man *is* sweet, whether he eat little or much: but the abundance of the rich will not suffer him to sleep.

Acts 20:35. I have shewed you all things, how that so labouring ye ought to support the weak, and to remember the words of the Lord Jesus, how he said, It is more blessed to give than to receive.

I Thess. 4:11. Study to be quiet, and to do your own business, and to work with your own hands, as we commanded you;

LASCIVIOUSNESS. Prov. 2:16. To deliver thee from the strange woman, *even* from the stranger *which* flattereth with her words; 17. Which forsaketh the guide of her youth, and forgetteth the covenant of her God. 18. For her house inclineth unto death, and her paths unto the dead.

Prov. 5:3. For the lips of a strange woman drop *as* an honeycomb, and her mouth *is* smoother than oil: 4. But her end is bitter as wormwood, sharp as a twoedged sword. 5. Her feet go down to death; her steps take hold on hell. 8. Remove thy way far from her, and come not nigh the door of her house:

Mark 7:21. For from within, out of the heart of men, proceed evil thoughts, adulteries, fornications, murders,

Rom. 13:13. Let us walk honestly, as in the day; not in rioting and drunkenness, not in chambering and wantonness, not in strife and envying.

1 Cor. 9:27. But I keep under my body, and bring *it* into subjection: lest that by any means, when I have preached to others, I myself should be a castaway.

2 Cor. 12:21. I shall bewail many which have sinned already, and have not repented of the uncleanness and fornication and lasciviousness which they have committed.

Eph. 5:5. For this ye know, that no whoremonger, nor unclean person, nor covetous man, who is an idolater, hath any inheritance in the kingdom of Christ and of God.

LAW. Psa. 19:7. The law of the LORD *is* perfect, converting the soul: the testimony of the LORD *is* sure, making wise the simple. 8. The statutes of the LORD *are* right, rejoicing the heart: the commandment of the LORD is pure, enlightening the eyes. 9. The fear of the LORD is clean, enduring for ever: the judgments of the LORD are true and righteous altogether.

Psa. 119:1. Blessed are the undefiled in the way, who walk in the law of the LORD. 2. Blessed are they that keep his testimonies, and that seek him with the whole heart.

Prov. 28:4. They that forsake the law praise the wicked: but such as keep the law contend with them.

Matt. 22:21. Then saith he unto them, Render therefore unto Cæsar the things which are Cæsar's; and unto God the things that are God's. Luke 20:22-25.

1 John 5:3. This is the love of God, that we keep his commandments: and his commandments are not grievous.

Matt. 5:17. Think not that I am come to destroy the law, or the prophets: I am not come to destroy, but to fulfil. 18. For verily I say unto you, Till heaven and earth pass, one jot or one tittle shall in no wise pass from the law, till all be fulfilled. 19. Whosoever therefore shall break one of these least commandments, and shall teach men so, he shall be called the least in the kingdom of heaven: but whosoever shall do and teach them, the same shall be called great in the kingdom of heaven. 20. For I say unto you, That except your righteousness shall exceed the righteousness of the scribes and Pharisees, ye shall in no case enter into the kingdom of heaven. 27. Ye have heard that it was said by them of old time, Thou shalt not commit adultery: 28. But I say unto you, That whosoever looketh on a woman to lust after her hath committed adultery with her already in his heart.

John 1:17. For the law was given by Moses, but grace and truth came by Jesus Christ.

Acts 15:1. And certain men which came down from Judæa taught the brethren, and said, Except ye be circumcised after the manner of Moses, ye cannot be saved. 6. And the apostles and elders came together for to consider of this matter. 19. Wherefore my sentence is, that we trouble not them, which from among the Gentiles are turned to God: 20. But that we write unto them, that they abstain from pollutions of idols, and from fornication, and from things strangled, and from blood.

Rom. 8:3. For what the law could not do, in that it was weak through the flesh, God sending his own Son in the likeness of sinful flesh, and for sin, condemned sin in the flesh.

Gal. 2:3. But neither Titus, who was with me, being a Greek, was compelled to be circumcised: 4. And that because of false brethren unawares brought in, who came in privily to spy out our liberty which we have in Christ Jesus, that they might bring us into bondage: 5. To whom we gave place by subjection, no, not for an hour; that the truth of the gospel might continue with you.

Col. 2:14. Blotting out the handwriting of ordinances that was against us, which was contrary to us, and took it out of the way, nailing it to his cross;

Heb. 10:1. For the law having a shadow of good things to come, and not the very image of the things, can never with those sacrifices which they offered year by year continually make the comers thereunto perfect.

LEFT-HANDED, Judg. 3:15; 20:16.

LEGISLATION, class, forbidden, Ex. 12:49; Lev. 24:22; Num. 9:14; 15:15,29; Gal. 3:28.

Supplemental, concerning Sabbath-breaking, Num. 15:32-35; inheritance, Num. 27:1-11.

LENDING. Lev. 25:35. If thy brother be waxen poor, and fallen in decay with thee; then thou shalt relieve him: yea, though he be a stranger, or a sojourner; that he may live with thee. 36. Take thou no usury of him, or increase: but fear thy God; that thy brother may live with thee.

Deut. 15:20. Unto a stranger thou mayest lend upon usury; but unto thy brother thou shalt not lend upon usury: that the LORD thy God may bless thee in all that thou settest thine hand to in the land whither thou goest to possess it.

Psa. 37:25. I have been young, and *now* am old: yet have I not seen the righteous forsaken, nor his seed begging bread. 26. *He is* ever merciful, and lendeth; and his seed *is* blessed.

Psa. 112:5. A good man sheweth favour, and lendeth: he will guide his affairs with discretion.

Prov. 19:17. He that hath pity upon the poor lendeth unto the LORD; and that which he hath given will he pay him again.

Matt. 5:42. Give to him that asketh thee, and from him that would borrow of thee turn not thou away.

Luke 6:35. But love ye your enemies, and do good, and lend, hoping for nothing again; and your reward shall be great, and ye shall be the children of the Highest: for he is kind unto the unthankful and *to* the evil.

LIARS. All men liars, Psa. 116: 11. Satan a, John 8:44,55. Prohibited the Kingdom of Heaven, Rev. 21:8.

LIBERALITY. Ex. 22:29. Thou shalt not delay *to offer* the first of thy ripe fruits, and of thy liquors: the firstborn of thy sons shalt thou give unto me. 30. Likewise shalt thou do with thine oxen, *and* with thy sheep: Ex. 13:2,12.

Ex. 25:1. And the LORD spake unto Moses, saying, 2. Speak unto the children of Israel, that they bring me an offering: of every man that giveth it willingly with his heart ye shall take my offering.

Ex. 35:5. Take ye from among you an offering unto the LORD: whosoever *is* of a willing heart, let him bring it, an offering of the LORD; gold, and silver, and brass,

Deut. 15:7. If there be among you a poor man of one of thy brethren within any of thy gates in thy land which the LORD thy God giveth thee, thou shalt not harden thine heart, nor shut thine hand from thy poor brother: 8. But thou shalt open thine hand wide unto him, and shalt surely lend him sufficient for his need, *in that* which he wanteth. 11. For the poor shall never cease out of the land: therefore I command thee, saying, Thou shalt open thine hand wide unto thy brother, to thy poor, and to thy needy, in thy land.

1 Chr. 29:5. Who *then* is willing to consecrate his service this day unto the LORD?

Psa. 41:1. Blessed *is* he that considereth the poor: the LORD will deliver him in time of trouble. 2. The LORD will preserve him, and keep him alive; *and* he shall be blessed upon the earth: and thou wilt not deliver him unto the will of his enemies. 3. The LORD will strengthen him upon the bed of languishing: thou wilt make all his bed in his sickness.

Psa. 76:11. Vow, and pay unto the LORD your God: let all that be round about him bring presents unto him that ought to be feared.

Psa. 112:5. A good man sheweth favour, and lendeth: he will guide his affairs with discretion. 9. He hath dispersed, he hath given to the poor; his righteousness endureth for ever; his horn shall be exalted with honour.

Prov. 3:9. Honour the LORD with thy substance, and with the firstfruits of all thine increase: 10. So shall thy barns be filled with plenty, and thy presses shall burst out with new wine.

Prov. 11:24. There is that scattereth, and yet increaseth; 25. The liberal soul shall be made fat: and he that watereth shall be watered also himself.

Prov. 13:7. There is that maketh himself rich, yet *hath* nothing: *there is* that maketh himself poor, yet *hath* great riches.

Prov. 19:6. Many will intreat the favour of the prince: and every man *is* a friend to him that giveth gifts. 17. He that hath pity upon the poor lendeth unto the LORD; and that which he hath given will he pay him again.

Prov. 22:9. He that hath a

bountiful eye shall be blessed; for he giveth of his bread to the poor.

Prov. 28:27. He that giveth unto the poor shall not lack:

Eccl. 11:1. Cast thy bread upon the waters: for thou shalt find it after many days.

Isa. 60:17. For brass I will bring gold, and for iron I will bring silver, and for wood brass, and for stones iron: I will also make thy officers peace, and thine exactors righteousness.

Hag. 2:18. *Even* from the day that the foundation of the LORD's temple was laid, consider *it.* 19. Is the seed yet in the barn? yea, as yet the vine, and the fig tree, and the pomegranate, and the olive tree, hath not brought forth: from this day will I bless *you.*

Mal. 3:10. Bring ye all the tithes into the storehouse, that there may be meat in mine house, and prove me now herewith, saith the LORD of hosts, if I will not open you the windows of heaven, and pour you out a blessing, that *there shall* not *be room* enough *to receive it.* 11. And I will rebuke the devourer for your sakes, and he shall not destroy the fruits of your ground; neither shall your vine cast her fruit before the time in the field, saith the LORD of hosts. 12. And all nations shall call you blessed: for ye shall be a delightsome land, saith the LORD of hosts.

Matt. 19:21. Jesus said unto him, If thou wilt be perfect, go *and* sell that thou hast, and give to the poor, and thou shalt have treasure in heaven: and come *and* follow me. 22. But when the young man heard that saying, he went away sorrowful: for he had great possessions.

Luke 3:10. And the people asked him, saying, What shall we do then? 11. He answereth and saith unto them, He that hath two coats, let him impart to him that hath none; and he that hath meat, let him do likewise.

Luke 6:38. Give, and it shall be given unto you; good measure, pressed down, and shaken together, and running over, shall men give into your bosom. For with the same measure that ye mete withal it shall be measured to you again. Matt. 5:42.

Luke 11:41. But rather give alms of such things as ye have:

Acts 10:4. And when he looked on him, he was afraid, and said, What is it, Lord? And he said unto him, Thy prayers and thine alms are come up for a memorial before God.

Acts 20:35. I have shewed you all things, how that so labouring ye ought to support the weak, and to remember the words of the Lord Jesus, how he said, It is more blessed to give than to receive.

Rom. 12:8. He that giveth, *let him do it* with [simplicity;] 13. Distributing to the necessity of saints; given to hospitality. [R. V. liberality]

1 Cor. 13:3. And though I bestow all my goods to feed *the poor,* and though I give my body to be burned, and have not charity, it profiteth me nothing.

2 Cor. 8:12. If there be first a willing mind, *it is* accepted according to that a man hath, *and* not according to that he hath not.

2 Cor. 9:6. He which soweth sparingly shall reap also sparingly; and he which soweth bountifully shall reap also bountifully. 7. Every man according as he purposeth in his heart, *so let him give;* not grudgingly, or of necessity: for God loveth a cheerful giver. 8. God *is* able to make all grace abound toward you; that ye, always having all sufficiency in all *things* may abound to every good work: [*v.* 9.] 10. He that ministereth seed to the sower both minister bread for *your* food, and multiply your seed sown, and increase the fruits of your righteousness;

LIFE. Brevity and Uncertainty of: 1 Sam. 20:3. Truly *as* the LORD liveth, and *as* thy soul liveth, *there is* but a step between me and death.

2 Sam. 14:14. We must needs die, and *are* as water spilt on the

ground, which cannot be gathered up again;

1 Chr. 29:15. We *are* strangers before thee, and sojourners, as *were* all our fathers: our days on the earth *are* as a shadow, and *there is* none abiding.

Job 8:9. (We *are but of* yesterday, and know nothing, because our days upon earth *are a* shadow:)

Psa. 39:4. LORD, make me to know mine end, and the measure of my days, what it *is; that* I may know how frail I *am.*

Psa. 90:9. All our days are passed away in thy wrath: we spend our years as a tale *that is told.* 10. The days of our years *are* threescore years and ten; and if by reason of strength *they be* fourscore years, yet *is* their strength labour and sorrow; for it is soon cut off, and we fly away.

Psa. 103:14. He knoweth our frame; he remembereth that we *are* dust. 15. *As for* man, his days *are* as grass: as a flower of the field, so he flourisheth. 16. For the wind passeth over it, and it is gone; and the place thereof shall know it no more.

Luke 12:20. But God said unto him, *Thou* fool, this night thy soul shall be required of thee: then whose shall those things be, which thou hast provided?

Everlasting: Psa. 121:8. The LORD shall preserve thy going out and thy coming in from this time forth, and even for evermore.

Isa. 25:8. He will swallow up death in victory;

Dan. 12:2. And many of them that sleep in the dust of the earth shall awake, some to everlasting life, and some to shame *and* everlasting contempt.

1 John 2:25. And this is the promise that he hath promised us, *even* eternal life.

From God: Gen. 2:7. The LORD God formed man *of* the dust of the ground, and breathed into his nostrils the breath of life; and man became a living soul.

Job 27:3. All the while my breath *is* in me, and the spirit of God *is* in my nostrils;

Psa. 68:20. Unto GOD the LORD *belong* the issues from death.

Eccl. 12:7. Then shall the dust return to the earth as it was: and the spirit shall return unto God who gave it.

Spiritual: John 3:3. Jesus answered and said unto him, Verily, verily, I say unto thee, Except a man be born again, he cannot see the kingdom of God.

John 5:24. Verily, verily, I say unto you, He that heareth my word, and believeth on him that sent me, hath everlasting life, and shall not come into condemnation; but is passed from death unto life.

John 11:25. Jesus said unto her, I am the resurrection, and the life: he that believeth in me, though he [were dead,] yet shall he live: 26. And whosoever liveth and believeth in me shall never die. [R. V. die]

John 20:31. But these are written, that ye might believe that Jesus is the Christ, the Son of God; and that believing ye might have life through his name.

LIGHT. Psa. 27:1. The LORD *is* my light and my salvation; whom shall I fear? the LORD *is* the strength of my life; of whom shall I be afraid?

Psa. 119:105. Thy word *is* a lamp unto my feet, and a light unto my path. 130. The entrance of thy words giveth light; it giveth understanding unto the simple.

Matt. 5:14. Ye are the light of the world. A city that is set on a hill cannot be hid. 16. Let your light so shine before men, that they may see your good works, and glorify your Father which is in heaven.

John 1:4. In him was life; and the life was the light of men. 5. And the light shineth in darkness; and the darkness comprehended it not.

LONGEVITY. Ex. 20:12. Honour thy father and thy mother: that thy days may be long upon the land which the LORD thy God giveth thee.

Job 5:26. Thou shalt come to *thy* grave in a full age, like as a shock of corn cometh in in his season.

Psa. 91:16. With long life will I satisfy him, and shew him my salvation.

Prov. 3:1. My son, forget not my law; but let thine heart keep my commandments: 2. For length of days, and long life, and peace, shall they add to thee.

Prov. 10:27. The fear of the LORD prolongeth days: but the years of the wicked shall be shortened.

LONGSUFFERING. 1 Cor. 13:4. Charity suffereth long, *and* is kind; 7. Beareth all things, believeth all things, hopeth all things, endureth all things.

Gal. 5:22. But the fruit of the Spirit is love, joy, peace, longsuffering, gentleness, goodness, [faith,] [R. V. faithfulness]

LORD'S DAY. See SABBATH.

LOST, The. See WICKED, PUNISHMENT OF.

LOVE. Of Children for Parents: See CHILDREN.

Of God: See GOD, LOVE OF.

Of Man for God: Deut. 6:5. And thou shalt love the LORD thy God with all thine heart, and with all thy soul, and with all thy might.

Josh. 23:11. Take good heed therefore unto yourselves, that ye love the LORD your God.

Psa. 18:1. I will love thee, O LORD, my strength.

Psa. 31:23. O love the LORD, all ye his saints:

Psa. 37:4. Delight thyself also in the LORD; and he shall give thee the desires of thine heart.

Psa. 73:25. Whom have I in heaven *but thee?* and *there is* none upon earth *that* I desire beside thee. 26. My flesh and my heart faileth: *but* God *is* the strength of my heart, and my portion for ever.

Rom. 8:28. And we know that all things work together for good to them that love God,

Of Man for Jesus: Matt. 10: 37. He that loveth father or mother more than me is not worthy of me: and he that loveth son or daughter more than me is not worthy of me. *v.* 38.

John 21:17. Lord, thou knowest all things; thou knowest that I love thee.

I Cor. 16:22. If any man love not the Lord Jesus Christ, let him be Anathema Maran-atha.

1 Pet. 2:7. Unto you therefore which believe *he is* precious:

Of Man for Man: Lev. 19:18. Thou shalt love thy neighbour as thyself: I *am* the LORD. 34. *But* the stranger that dwelleth with you shall be unto you as one born among you, and thou shalt love him as thyself; for ye were strangers in the land of Egypt:

Prov. 15:17. Better *is* a dinner of herbs where love is, than a stalled ox and hatred therewith.

John 13:14. If I then, *your* Lord and Master, have washed your feet; ye also ought to wash one another's feet.

John 15:12. This is my commandment, That ye love one another, as I have loved you.

Eph. 5:2. Walk in love, as Christ also hath loved us, and hath given himself for us an offering and a sacrifice to God for a sweetsmelling savour.

1 Thess. 4:9. As touching brotherly love ye need not that I write unto you: for ye yourselves are taught of God to love one another.

1 Pet. 2:17. Honour all *men.* Love the brotherhood.

Prov. 24:17. Rejoice not when thine enemy falleth, and let not thine heart be glad when he stumbleth: 18. Lest the LORD see *it,* and it displease him, and he turn away his wrath from him.

Heb. 13:1. Let brotherly love continue. 2. Be not forgetful to entertain strangers: for thereby some have entertained angels unawares.

Of Money: The root of evil, 1 Tim. 6:10.

LUKEWARMNESS. Figurative: Jer. 9:3. They are not valiant for the truth upon the earth;

Hos. 6:4. O Ephraim, what shall I do unto thee? O Judah, what shall I do unto thee? for your goodness *is* as a morning cloud, and as the early dew it goeth away.

LUST. Ex. 20:17. Thou shalt

not covet thy neighbour's house, thou shalt not covet thy neighbour's wife, nor his manservant, nor his maidservant, nor his ox, nor his ass, nor any thing that *is* thy neighbour's.

1 Cor. 9:27. But I keep under my body, and bring *it* into subjection: lest that by any means, when I have preached to others, I myself should be a castaway.

2 Tim. 2:22. Flee also youthful lusts:

Tit. 2:12. Teaching us that, denying ungodliness and worldly lusts, we should live soberly, righteously, and godly, in this present world;

1 John 2:16. For all that *is* in the world, the lust of the flesh, and the lust of the eyes, and the pride of life, is not of the Father, but is of the world. 17. And the world passeth away, and the lust thereof: but he that doeth the will of God abideth for ever.

LYING, lying spirit from God, 1 Kin. 22:21-23; 2 Chr. 18:20-22.

MAGICIAN. A person who claims to understand and explain mysteries by magic, Dan. 1:20. Failed to interpret Pharaoh's dreams, Gen. 41:8,24; Nebuchadnezzar's, Dan. 2:2-13; 4:7. Wrought apparent miracles, Ex. 7:11,12,22; 8:7,18.

MAGISTRATE. An officer of civil law, Judg. 18:7; Ezra 7:25; Luke 12:11,58; Acts 16:20,22,35,38. Obedience to, enjoined, Tit. 3:1.

MALICE. Psa. 56:5. Every day they wrest my words: all their thoughts *are* against me for evil. 6. They gather themselves together, they hide themselves, they mark my steps, when they wait for my soul.

Psa. 64:2. Hide me from the secret counsel of the wicked; from the insurrection of the workers of iniquity:

Psa. 69:4. They that hate me without a cause are more than the hairs of mine head: they that would destroy me, *being* mine enemies wrongfully, are mighty:

Psa. 74:20. The dark places of the earth are full of the habitations of cruelty.

Prov. 12:10. The tender mercies of the wicked *are* cruel.

Prov. 15:17. Better *is* a dinner of herbs where love is, than a stalled ox and hatred therewith.

Prov. 17:5. Whoso mocketh the poor reproacheth his Maker: *and* he that is glad at calamities shall not be unpunished.

Mic. 2:1. Woe to them that devise iniquity, and work evil upon their beds! when the morning is light, they practise it, because it is in the power of their hand.

Matt. 5:38. Ye have heard that it hath been said, An eye for an eye, and a tooth for a tooth: 39. But I say unto you, That ye resist not evil: but whosoever shall smite thee on thy right cheek, turn to him the other also. 40. And if any man will sue thee at the law, and take away thy coat, let him have *thy* cloke also. 41. And whosoever shall compel thee to go a mile, go with him twain. Luke 6:29.

Matt. 6:15. If ye forgive not men their trespasses, neither will your Father forgive your trespasses.

Rom. 12:19. Avenge not yourselves, but *rather* give place unto wrath; for it is written, Vengeance *is* mine; I will repay, saith the Lord.

MAN. Created: Gen. 1:26. And God said, Let us make man in our image, after our likeness: and let them have dominion over the fish of the sea, and over the fowl of the air, and over the cattle, and over all the earth, and over every creeping thing that creepeth upon the earth. 27. So God created man in his *own* image, in the image of God created he him; male and female created he them.

Gen. 2:7. And the LORD God formed man *of* the dust of the ground, and breathed into his nostrils the breath of life; and man became a living soul.

Job 33:4. The Spirit of God hath made me, and the breath of the Almighty hath given me life.

Psa. 100:3. Know ye that the LORD he *is* God: *it is* he *that* hath made us, and not we ourselves; *we are* his people, and the sheep of his pasture.

Psa. 139:14. I will praise thee;

for I am fearfully *and* wonderfully made: marvellous *are* thy works; and *that* my soul knoweth right well.

Created in the Image of God: Gen. 1:27. So God created man in his *own* image, in the image of God created he him; male and female created he them.

1 Cor. 11:7. For a man indeed ought not to cover *his* head, forasmuch as he is the image and glory of God: but the woman is the glory of the man.

Design of the Creation of: Psa. 8:6. Thou madest him to have dominion over the works of thy hands; thou hast put all *things* under his feet:

Dominion of: Gen. 9:2. And the fear of you and the dread of you shall be upon every beast of the earth, and upon every fowl of the air, upon all that moveth *upon* the earth, and upon all the fishes of the sea; into your hand are they delivered. 3. Every moving thing that liveth shall be meat for you; even as the green herb have I given you all things.

Equality of: Psa. 33:15. He fashioneth their hearts alike; he considereth all their works.

Prov. 22:2. The rich and poor meet together: the LORD *is* the maker of them all.

Act 17:26. And hath made of one blood all nations of men for to dwell on all the face of the earth, and hath determined the times before appointed, and the bounds of their habitation:

Insignificance of: Psa. 8:3. When I consider thy heavens, the work of thy fingers, the moon and the stars, which thou hast ordained; 4. What is man, that thou art mindful of him? and the son of man, that thou visitest him?

Little Lower than the Angels: Psa. 8:5. For thou hast made him a little lower than [the angels,] and hast crowned him with glory and honour. [R. V. God]

Spirit: Eccl. 1:8. The eye is not satisfied with seeing, nor the ear filled with hearing.

Eccl. 12:7. Then shall the dust return to the earth as it was: and the spirit shall return unto God who gave it.

1 Cor. 2:11. For what man knoweth the things of a man, save the spirit of man which is in him? even so the things of God knoweth no man, but the Spirit of God.

MARRIAGE. Unclassified Scriptures Relating to: Gen. 2:23. And Adam said, This *is* now bone of my bones, and flesh of my flesh: she shall be called Woman, because she was taken out of Man. 24. Therefore shall a man leave his father and his mother, and shall cleave unto his wife: and they shall be one flesh. 1 Cor. 6:16.

Prov. 18:22. *Whoso* findeth a wife findeth a good *thing*, and obtaineth favour of the LORD.

Prov. 21:9. *It is* better to dwell in a corner of the housetop, than with a brawling woman in a wide house. 19. *It is* better to dwell in the wilderness, than with a contentious and an angry woman.

Mal. 2:14. Yet ye say, Wherefore? Because the LORD hath been witness between thee and the wife of thy youth, against whom thou hast dealt treacherously: yet *is* she thy companion, and the wife of thy covenant. 15. And did not he make one? Yet had he the residue of the spirit. And wherefore one? That he might seek a godly seed. Therefore take heed to your spirit, and let none deal treacherously against the wife of his youth. 16. For the LORD, the God of Israel, saith that he hateth putting away: for *one* covereth violence with his garment, saith the LORD of hosts: therefore take heed to your spirit, that ye deal not treacherously.

Matt. 5:31. It hath been said, Whosoever shall put away his wife, let him give her a writing of divorcement: 32. But I say unto you, That whosoever shall put away his wife, saving for the cause of fornication, causeth her to commit adultery: and whosoever shall marry her that is divorced committeth adultery.

Mark 10:9. What therefore God hath joined together, let not man put asunder. 10. And in the house his disciples asked him again of the same *matter*. 11. And he saith unto them, Whosoever shall put away his wife, and marry another, committeth adultery against her. 12. And if a woman shall put away her husband, and be married to another, she committeth adultery. Matt. 19: 2-9.

Luke 16:18. Whosoever putteth away his wife, and marrieth another, committeth adultery: and whosoever marrieth her that is put away from *her* husband committeth adultery.

1 Cor. 7:1. Now concerning the things whereof ye wrote unto me: *It is* good for a man not to touch a woman. 2. Nevertheless, *to avoid* fornication, let every man have his own wife, and let every woman have her own husband. 3. Let the husband render unto the wife due benevolence: and likewise also the wife unto the husband. 4. The wife hath not power of her own body, but the husband: and likewise also the husband hath not power of his own body, but the wife. 5. Defraud ye not one the other, except *it be* with consent for a time, that ye may give yourselves to fasting and prayer; and come together again, that Satan tempt you not for your incontinency. 6. But I speak this by permission, *and* not of commandment. 7. For I would that all men were even as I myself. But every man hath his proper gift of God, one after this manner, and another after that. 8. I say therefore to the unmarried and widows, It is good for them if they abide even as I. 9. But if they cannot contain, let them marry: for it is better to marry than to burn. 10. And unto the married I command, *yet* not I, but the LORD, Let not the wife depart from *her* husband: 11. But and if she depart, let her remain unmarried, or be reconciled to *her* husband: and let not the husband put away *his* wife. 12. But to the rest speak I, not the Lord: If any brother hath a wife that believeth not, and she be pleased to dwell with him, let him not put her away. 13. And the woman which hath an hus-

band that believeth not, and if he be pleased to dwell with her, let her not leave him. 14. For the unbelieving husband is sanctified by the wife, and the unbelieving wife is sanctified by the husband: else were your children unclean; but now are they holy. 15. But if the unbelieving depart, let him depart. A brother or a sister is not under bondage in such *cases:* but God hath called us to peace. 16. For what knowest thou, O wife, whether thou shalt save *thy* husband? or how knowest thou, O man, whether thou shalt save *thy* wife? 32. But I would have you without carefulness. He that is unmarried careth for the things that belong to the Lord, how he may please the Lord: 33. But he that is married careth for the things that are of the world, how he may please *his* wife. 34. There is difference *also* between a wife and a virgin. The unmarried woman careth for the things of the Lord, that she may be holy both in body and in spirit: but she that is married careth for the things of the world, how she may please *her* husband. 35. And this I speak for your own profit; not that I may cast a snare upon you, but for that which is comely, and that ye may attend upon the Lord without distraction. 36. But if any man think that he behaveth himself uncomely toward his virgin, if she pass the flower of *her* age, and need so require, let him do what he will, he sinneth not: let them marry.

1 Tim. 5:14. I will therefore that the younger women marry, bear children, guide the house, give none occasion to the adversary to speak reproachfully.

Heb. 13:4. Marriage *is* honourable in all, and the bed undefiled: but whoremongers and adulterers God will judge.

MARTYRDOM. Matt. 24:9.
Then shall they deliver you up to be afflicted, and shall kill you: and ye shall be hated of all nations for my name's sake.

1 Cor. 13:3. And though I bestow all my goods to feed *the poor,* and though I give my body to be

burned, and have not charity, it profiteth me nothing.

Rev. 6:9. And when he had opened the fifth seal, I saw under the altar the souls of them that were slain for the word of God, and for the testimony which they held: 10. And they cried with a loud voice, saying, How long, O Lord, holy and true, dost thou not judge and avenge our blood on them that dwell on the earth? 11. And white robes were given unto every one of them: and it was said unto them, that they should rest yet for a little season, until their fellow-servants also and their brethren, that should be killed as they *were*, should be fulfilled.

MEASURE. The following modern equivalents of ancient measurements are based upon the latest researches, and are probably as nearly correct as is possible at this time:

Dry: 1. Bushel, about a peck, Matt. 5:15; Mark 4:21; Luke 11:33.

2. Cab, or kab, about two quarts, 2 Kin. 6:25.

3. Cor, equal to one homer or ten ephahs, equal to about eleven and one-ninth bushels, 1 Kin. 4:22; 5: 11; 2 Chr. 2:10; 27:5; Ezra 7:22.

4. Ephah, equal to three seah, and in liquid, to a bath, containing about a bushel and a half, Ex. 16: 36; Lev. 5:11; 6:20; 19:36; Num. 5:15; 28:5; Judg. 6:19; Ruth 2:17; 1 Sam. 1:24; 17:17; Isa. 5:10; Ezek. 45:10,11,13,24; 46:5,7,11,14; Amos 8:5; Zech. 5:6-10.

5. Half-homer, about five and a half bushels, Hos. 3:2.

6. Homer, about eleven bushels, equal to a cor or ten ephahs, Lev. 27:16; Num. 11:32; Isa. 5:10; Ezek. 45:11-14; Hos. 3:2.

7. Omer, about one bushel, Ex. 16:16,18,22,32,33,36.

8. Seah, about a peck and a half, Gen. 18:6; 1 Sam. 25:18; 1 Kin. 18:32; 2 Kin. 7:1,16,18.

9. Tenth deal, about a gallon, equal to one-tenth of an ephah, Ex. 29:40; Lev. 14:10,21; 23:13,17; 24: 5; Num. 15:4,6,9; 28:9,12,13,20,21, 28,29; 29:3,4,9,10,14,15.

Liquid: 1. Bath, about eight gal-

lons and a half, 1 Kin. 7:26,38; 2 Chr. 2:10; 4:5; Ezra 7:22; Isa. 5: 10; Ezek. 45:10,11,14; Luke 16:6.

2. Firkin, nearly nine gallons, John 2:6.

3. Hin, about a gallon and a half, Ex. 29:40; 30:24; Lev. 19:36; 23: 13; Num. 15:4-10; 28:5,7,14; Ezek. 4:11; 45:24; 46:5,7,11,14.

4. Log, about a pint, one-twelfth of a hin, Lev. 14:10,12,15,21,24.

Linear: 1. Finger, Jer. 52:21.

2. Handbreadth, Ex. 25:25; 37:12; 1 Kin. 7:26; 2 Chr. 4:5; Psa. 39:5; Ezek. 40:5,43; 43:13.

3. Span, Ex. 28:16; 1 Sam. 17:4; Isa. 40:12; 48:13; Lam. 2:20; Ezek. 43:13.

4. Cubit, the length of the fore-arm.

5. Reed, probably six cubits, Ezek. 40:5.

6. Fathom, Acts 27:28.

7. Pace, 2 Sam. 6:13.

8. Furlong, Luke 24:13.

9. Mile, probably nine-tenths of an English mile, Matt. 5:41.

10. Sabbath day's journey, two thousand paces, Acts 1:12.

Must Be Just: Deut. 25:13. Thou shalt not have in thy bag divers weights, a great and a small. 14. Thou shalt not have in thine house divers measures, a great and a small. 15. *But* thou shalt have a perfect and just weight, a perfect and just measure shalt thou have: that thy days may be lengthened in the land which the Lord thy God giveth thee. 16. For all that do such things, *and* all that do unrighteously, *are* an abomination unto the Lord thy God.

MEDICINE. Prov. 17:22. A merry heart doeth good *like* a medicine: but a broken spirit drieth the bones.

Isa. 38:21. For Isaiah had said, Let them take a lump of figs, and lay *it* for a plaster upon the boil, and he shall recover.

Jer. 8:22. *Is there* no balm in Gilead; *is there* no physician there? why then is not the health of the daughter of my people recovered?

Rev. 22:2. In the midst of the street of it, and on either side of the river, *was there* the tree of life, which bare twelve *manner of* fruits, *and* yielded her fruit every month: and the leaves of the tree *were* for the healing of the nations.

MEDITATION. Josh. 1:8. This book of the law shall not depart out of thy mouth; but thou shalt meditate therein day and night, that thou mayest observe to do according to all that is written therein: for then thou shalt make thy way prosperous, and then thou shalt have good success.

Psa. 1:2. But his delight *is* in the law of the LORD, and in his law doth he meditate day and night.

Psa. 104:34. My meditation of him shall be sweet: I will be glad in the LORD.

Psa. 139:17. How precious also are thy thoughts unto me, O God! how great is the sum of them! 18. *If* I should count them, they are more in number than the sand: when I awake, I am still with thee.

Psa. 143:5. I remember the days of old; I meditate on all thy works; I muse on the work of thy hands.

MEEKNESS. Psa. 25:9. The meek will he guide in judgment: and the meek will he teach his way.

Psa. 37:11. But the meek shall inherit the earth; and shall delight themselves in the abundance of peace.

Prov. 15:1. A soft answer turneth away wrath: 18. *He that is* slow to anger appeaseth strife.

Matt. 5:5. Blessed *are* the meek: for they shall inherit the earth.

Matt. 11:29. Take my yoke upon you, and learn of me; for I am meek and lowly in heart: and ye shall find rest unto your souls.

2 Tim. 2:24. The servant of the Lord must not strive; but be gentle unto all *men,* apt to teach, patient, 25. In meekness instructing those that oppose themselves;

Heb. 12:14. Follow peace with all *men,*

MEPHIBOSHETH. 1. Son of Saul by Rizpah, whom David surrendered to the Gibeonites to be slain, 2 Sam. 21:8,9.

2. Son of Jonathan, 2 Sam. 4:4. Called MERIB-BAAL, 1 Chr. 8:34; 9: 40. Was lame, 2 Sam. 4:4. David

entertains him at his table, 2 Sam. 9:1-7; 21:7. Property restored to, 2 Sam. 9:9,10. His ingratitude to David at the time of Absalom's usurpation, 2 Sam. 16:1-4; 19:24-30. Property of, confiscated, 2 Sam. 16: 4; 19:29,30.

MERCY. Prov. 3:3. Let not mercy and truth forsake thee: bind them about thy neck; write them upon the table of thine heart: 4. So shalt thou find favour and good understanding in the sight of God and man.

Prov. 11:17. The merciful man doeth good to his own soul: but *he that is* cruel troubleth his own flesh.

Prov. 12:10. A righteous *man* regardeth the life of his beast: but the tender mercies of the wicked *are* cruel.

Matt. 5:7. Blessed *are* the merciful: for they shall obtain mercy.

Luke 6:36. Be ye therefore merciful, as your Father also is merciful.

METEOROLOGY AND CELESTIAL PHENOMENA. Gen. 2:5. The LORD God had not caused it to rain upon the earth, and *there was* not a man to till the ground. 6. But there went up a mist from the earth, and watered the whole face of the ground.

Job. 26:7. He stretcheth out the north over the empty place, *and* hangeth the earth upon nothing. 8. He bindeth up the waters in his thick clouds; and the cloud is not rent under them. 11. The pillars of heaven tremble and are astonished at his reproof.

Job 38:31. Canst thou bind the sweet influences of Pleiades, or loose the bands of Orion? 32. Canst thou bring forth Mazzaroth in his season? or canst thou guide Arcturus with his sons? 33. Knowest thou the ordinances of heaven? canst thou set the dominion thereof in the earth? 34. Canst thou lift up thy voice to the clouds, that abundance of waters may cover thee? 35. Canst thou send lightnings, that they may go, and say unto thee, Here we *are?* 37. Who can number the clouds in wisdom? or who can stay the bottles of heaven?

Isa. 13:13. Therefore I will shake the heavens, and the earth shall remove out of her place, in the wrath of the LORD of hosts, and in the day of his fierce anger.

Joel 2:30. And I will shew wonders in the heavens and in the earth, blood, and fire, and pillars of smoke. 31. The sun shall be turned into darkness, and the moon into blood, before the great and the terrible day of the LORD come.

Matt. 24:27. For as the lightning cometh out of the east, and shineth even unto the west; so shall also the coming of the Son of man be. 29. Immediately after the tribulation of those days shall the sun be darkened, and the moon shall not give her light, and the stars shall fall from heaven, and the powers of the heavens shall be shaken:

Matt. 27:45. Now from the sixth hour there was darkness over all the land and unto the ninth hour. Luke 23:44,45.

Acts 2:19. And I will shew wonders in heaven above, and signs in the earth beneath; blood, and fire, and vapour of smoke: 20. The sun shall be turned into darkness, and the moon into blood, before that great and notable day of the Lord come:

Jas. 5:17. Elias was a man subject to like passions as we are, and he prayed earnestly that it might not rain: and it rained not on the earth by the space of three years and six months. 18. And he prayed again, and the heaven gave rain, and the earth brought forth her fruit.

Rev. 6:12. And I beheld when he had opened the sixth seal, and, lo, there was a great earthquake; and the son became black as sackcloth of hair, and the moon became as blood;

Rev. 7:1. And after these things I saw four angels standing on the four corners of the earth, holding the four winds of the earth, that the wind should not blow on the earth, nor on the sea, nor on any tree.

Rev. 16:21. And there fell upon men a great hail out of heaven, every stone about the weight of a talent: and men blasphemed God because of the plague of the hail; for the plague thereof was exceeding great.

MILLENNIUM. Isa. 65:17. For, behold, I create new heavens and a new earth: and the former shall not be remembered, nor come into mind. 18. But be ye glad and rejoice for ever in that which I create: for, behold, I create Jerusalem a rejoicing, and her people a joy. 19. And I will rejoice in Jerusalem, and joy in my people: and the voice of weeping shall be no more heard in her, nor the voice of crying. 20. There shall be no more thence an infant of days, nor an old man that hath not filled his days: for the child shall die an hundred years old: but the sinner being an hundred years old shall be accursed.

Zech. 9:9. Rejoice greatly, O daughter of Zion; shout, O daughter of Jerusalem: behold, thy King cometh unto thee: he is just, and having salvation; lowly, and riding upon an ass, and upon a colt the foal of an ass. 10. And I will cut off the chariot from Ephraim, and the horse from Jerusalem, and the battle bow shall be cut off: and he shall speak peace unto the heathen: and his dominion shall be from sea even to sea, and from the river even to the ends of the earth.

Zech. 14:16. And it shall come to pass, that every one that is left of all the nations which came against Jerusalem shall even go up from year to year to worship the King, the LORD of hosts, and to keep the feast of tabernacles. 17. And it shall be, that whoso will not come up of all the families of the earth unto Jerusalem to worship the King, the LORD of hosts, even upon them shall be no rain.

Rev. 20:4. And I saw thrones, and they sat upon them, and judgment was given unto them: and I saw the souls of them that were beheaded for the witness of Jesus, and for the word of God, and which had not worshipped the beast, neither his image, neither had received *his* mark upon their foreheads, or in their hands; and they lived and reigned with Christ a thousand years. 5. But the rest of the dead lived not again until the thousand years were finished. This *is* the first resurrection. 6. Blessed and holy *is* he that hath part in the first resurrection: on such the second death hath no power, but they shall be priests of God and of Christ, and shall reign with him a thousand years. *vss.* 7-15.

MINISTER, a sacred teacher.

Call of: Ex. 28:1. And take thou unto thee Aaron thy brother, and his sons with him, from among the children of Israel, that he may minister unto me in the priest's office, *even* Aaron, Nadab and Abihu, Eleazar and Ithamar, Aaron's sons.

1 Sam. 3:4. The LORD called Samuel: and he answered, Here *am* I.

1 Chr. 23:13. Aaron was separated, that he should sanctify the most holy things, he and his sons for ever, to burn incense before the LORD, to minister unto him, and to bless in his name for ever.

Matt. 9:9. And as Jesus passed forth from thence, he saw a man, named Matthew, sitting at the receipt of custom: and he saith unto him, Follow me. And he arose, and followed him. Mark 2:14.

Acts 13:2. As they ministered to the Lord, and fasted, the Holy Ghost said, Separate me Barnabas and Saul for the work whereunto I have called them. 3. And when they had fasted and prayed, and laid *their* hands on them, they sent *them* away.

Acts 26:14. And when we were all fallen to the earth, I heard a voice speaking unto me, and saying in the Hebrew tongue, Saul, Saul, why persecutest thou me? *it is* hard for thee to kick against the pricks. 15. And I said, Who art thou, Lord? And he said, I am Jesus whom thou persecutest. 16. But rise, and stand upon thy feet: for I have appeared unto thee for this purpose, to make thee a minister and a witness both of these

things which thou hast seen, and of those things in the which I will appear unto thee;

Rom. 1:1. Paul, a servant of Jesus Christ, called *to be* an apostle, separated unto the gospel of God,

Col. 4:17. And say to Archippus, Take heed to the ministry which thou hast received in the Lord, that thou fulfil it.

Heb. 5:4. And no man taketh this honour unto himself, but he that is called of God, as *was* Aaron.

Character and Qualifications of: Psa. 68:11. The Lord gave the word: great *was* the company of those that published *it*.

Isa. 32:20. Blessed *are* ye that sow beside all waters, that send forth *thither* the feet of the ox and the ass.

Isa. 52:11. Be ye clean, that bear the vessels of the LORD.

Jer. 3:15. I will give you pastors according to mine heart, which shall feed you with knowledge and understanding.

Matt. 23:11. But he that is greatest among you shall be your servant.

1 Cor. 9:16. For though I preach the gospel, I have nothing to glory of: for necessity is laid upon me; yea, woe is unto me, if I preach not the gospel!

2 Cor. 5:11. Knowing therefore the terror of the Lord, we persuade men; but we are made manifest unto God; and I trust also are made manifest in your consciences.

2 Cor. 6:3. Giving no offence in any thing, that the ministry be not blamed:

1 Tim. 5:17. Let the elders that rule well be counted worthy of double honour, especially they who labour in the word and doctrine. 21. I charge *thee* before God, and the Lord Jesus Christ, and the elect angels, that thou observe these things without preferring one before another, doing nothing by partiality.

1 Tim. 6:11. O man of God, flee these things; and follow after righteousness, godliness, faith, love, patience, meekness.

2 Tim. 1:6. Wherefore I put thee in remembrance that thou stir up

the gift of God, which is in thee by the putting on of my hands.

2 Tim. 2:1. Thou therefore, my son, be strong in the grace that is in Christ Jesus. 2. And the things that thou hast heard of me among many witnesses, the same commit thou to faithful men, who shall be able to teach others also. 14. Of these things put *them* in remembrance, charging *them* before the Lord that they strive not about words to no profit, *but* to the subverting of the hearers. 15. Study to shew thyself approved unto God, a workman that needeth not to be ashamed, rightly dividing the word of truth. 16. But shun profane *and* vain babblings: for they will increase unto more ungodliness.

Tit. 1:5. For this cause left I thee in Crete, that thou shouldest set in order the things that are wanting, and ordain elders in every city, as I had appointed thee: 6. If any be blameless, the husband of one wife, having faithful children not accused of riot or unruly. 7. For a bishop must be blameless, as the steward of God; not selfwilled, not soon angry, [not given to wine,] no striker, not given to filthy lucre; 8. But a lover of hospitality, a lover of good men, sober, just, holy, temperate; 9. Holding fast the faithful word as he hath been taught, that he may be able by sound doctine both to exhort and to convince the gainsayers. [R. V. no brawler]

1 Tim. 3:1. This *is* a true saying, If a man desire the office of a bishop, he desireth a good work. 2. A bishop then must be blameless, the husband of one wife, vigilant, sober, of good behaviour, given to hospitality, apt to teach; 3. Not given to wine, no striker, not greedy of filthy lucre; but patient, not a brawler, not covetous; 4. One that ruleth well his own house, having his children in subjection with all gravity; 5. (For if a man know not how to rule his own house, how shall he take care of the church of God?) 6. Not a novice, lest being lifted up with pride he fall into the condemnation of the devil. 7. Moreover he must have a good report of them which are without: lest he fall into reproach and the snare of the devil.

Duties of: Lev. 10:11. That ye may teach the children of Israel all the statutes which the LORD hath spoken unto them by the hand of Moses. *vss.* 8-11.

Isa. 40:1. Comfort ye, comfort ye my people, saith your God. 2. Speak ye comfortably to Jerusalem, and cry unto her, that her warfare is accomplished, that her iniquity is pardoned:

Isa. 58:1. Cry aloud, spare not, lift up thy voice like a trumpet, and shew my people their transgression, and the house of Jacob their sins.

Jer. 6:27. I have set thee *for* a tower *and* a fortress among my people, that thou mayest know and try their way.

Jer. 23:4. And I will set up shepherds over them which shall feed them: and they shall fear no more, nor be dismayed, neither shall they be lacking, saith the LORD.

Ezek. 6:11. Thus saith the Lord GOD; Smite with thine hand, and stamp with thy foot, and say, Alas for all the evil abominations of the house of Israel!

Ezek. 34:2. Son of man, prophesy against the shepherds of Israel, prophesy, and say unto them, Thus saith the Lord GOD unto the shepherds; Woe *be* to the shepherds of Israel that do feed themselves! should not the shepherds feed the flocks?

Ezek. 44:23. And they shall teach my people *the difference* between the holy and profane, and cause them to discern between the unclean and the clean.

Acts 5:20. Go, stand and speak in the temple to the people all the words of this life.

Acts 20:28. Take heed therefore unto yourselves, and to all the flock, over the which the Holy Ghost hath made you overseers, to feed the church of God, which he hath purchased with his own blood.

1 Cor. 1:16. And I baptized also the household of Stephanas: besides, I know not whether I baptized any other.

1 Cor. 4:1. Let a man so account of us, as of the ministers of Christ, and stewards of the mysteries of God. 2. Moreover it is required in stewards, that a man be found faithful.

1 Cor. 9:16. For though I preach the gospel, I have nothing to glory of: for necessity is laid upon me; yea, woe is unto me, if I preach not the gospel!

2 Cor. 4:5. For we preach not ourselves, but Christ Jesus the Lord; and ourselves your servants for Jesus' sake.

2 Cor. 12:15. And I will very gladly spend and be spent for you; though the more abundantly I love you, the less I be loved.

Eph. 4:11. He gave some, apostles; and some, prophets; and some, evangelists; and some, pastors and teachers; 12. For the perfecting of the saints, for the work of the ministry, for the edifying of the body of Christ:

I Tim. 4:6. If thou put the brethren in remembrance of these things, thou shalt be a good minister of Jesus Christ, nourished up in the words of faith and of good doctrine, whereunto thou hast attained.

2 Tim. 2:2. And the things that thou hast heard of me among many witnesses, the same commit thou to faithful men, who shall be able to teach others also.

2 Tim. 4:1. I charge *thee* therefore before God, and the Lord Jesus Christ, who shall judge the quick and the dead at his appearing and his kingdom; 2. Preach the word; be instant in season, out of season; reprove, rebuke, exhort with all longsuffering and doctrine. 5. But watch thou in all things, endure afflictions, do the work of an evangelist, make full proof of thy ministry.

Duties of the Church to:
Deut. 12:19. Take heed to thyself that thou forsake not the Levite as long as thou livest upon the earth.

I Thess. 5:12. And we beseech you, brethren, to know them which labour among you, and are over you in the Lord, and admonish you; 13. And to esteem them very highly in love for their work's sake.

Heb. 13:17. Obey them that have the rule over you, and submit yourselves: for they watch for your souls, as they that must give account, that they may do it with joy, and not with grief: for that *is* unprofitable for you.

Gal. 6:6. Let him that is taught in the word communicate unto him that teacheth in all good things.

Prayer for, Enjoined: Matt. 9:37. Then saith he unto his disciples, The harvest truly *is* plenteous, but the labourers *are* few; 38. Pray ye therefore the Lord of the harvest, that he will send forth labourers into his harvest. Luke 10:2.

2 Cor. 1:11. Ye also helping together by prayer for us, that for the gift *bestowed* upon us by the means of many persons thanks may be given by many on our behalf.

1 Thess. 5:25. Brethren, pray for us.

Promises to, and Joys of:
Psa. 126:5. They that sow in tears shall reap in joy. 6. He that goeth forth and weepeth, bearing precious seed, shall doubtless come again with rejoicing, bringing his sheaves *with him*.

Dan. 12:3. And they that be wise shall shine as the brightness of the firmament; and they that turn many to righteousness as the stars for ever and ever.

Matt. 28:20. Lo, I am with you alway, *even* unto the end of the world. Amen.

John 4:36. And he that reapeth receiveth wages, and gathereth fruit unto life eternal: that both he that soweth and he that reapeth may rejoice together.

2 Cor. 2:14. Now thanks *be* unto' God, which always causeth us to triumph in Christ, and maketh manifest the savour of his knowledge by us in every place.

Phil. 2:16. Holding forth the word of life; that I may rejoice in the day of Christ.

MIRACLES. Of Jesus, in Chronological Order:
Water made wine, John 2:1-11.
Heals the nobleman's son, John 4:46-54.

Draught of fishes, Luke 5:1-11.

Heals the demoniac, Mark 1:23-26; Luke 4:33-36.

Heals Peter's mother-in-law, Matt. 8:14-17; Mark 1:29-31; Luke 4:38, 39.

Cleanses the leper, Matt. 8:1-4; Mark 1:40-45; Luke 5:12-16.

Heals the paralytic, Matt. 9:1-8; Mark 2:1-12; Luke 5:17-26.

Healing of the impotent man, John 5:1-16.

Restoring the withered hand, Matt. 12:9-13; Mark 3:1-5; Luke 6:6-11.

Restores the centurion's servant, Matt. 8:5-13; Luke 7:1-10.

Raises the widow's son to life, Luke 7:11-16.

Heals a demoniac, Matt. 12:22-37; Mark 3:11; Luke 11:14,15.

Stills the tempest, Matt. 8:23-27; 14:32; Mark 4:35-41; Luke 8:22-25.

Casts devils out of two men of Gadara, Matt. 8:28-34; Mark 5:1-20; Luke 8:26-39.

Raises from the dead the daughter of Jairus, Matt. 9:18,19,23-26; Mark 5:22-24; 35-43; Luke 8:41,42, 49-56.

Cures the woman with the issue of blood. Matt. 9:20-22; Mark 5:25-34; Luke 8:43-48.

Restores two blind men to sight, Matt. 9:27-31.

Heals a demoniac, Matt. 9:32,33.

Feeds five thousand people, Matt. 14:15-21; Mark 6:35-44; Luke 9:12-17; John 6:5-14.

Walks on the sea, Matt. 14:22-23; Mark 6:45-52; John 6:16-21.

Heals the daughter of the Syrophenician woman, Matt. 15:21-28; Mark 7:24-30.

Feeds four thousand people, Matt. 15:32-39; Mark 8:1-9.

Restores one deaf and dumb, Mark 7:31-37.

Restores a blind man, Mark 8:22-26.

Restores lunatic child, Matt. 17:14-21; Mark 9:14-29; Luke 9:37-43.

Tribute money obtained from a fish's mouth, Matt. 17:24-27.

Restores ten lepers, Luke 17:11-19.

Opens the eyes of a man born blind, John 9.

Raises Lazarus from the dead, John 11:1-46.

Heals the woman with the spirit of infirmity, Luke 13:10-17.

Cures a man with dropsy, Luke 14:1-6.

Restores two blind men near Jericho, Matt. 20:29-34; Mark 10:46-52; Luke 18:35-43.

Curses a fig tree, Matt. 21:17-22; Mark 11:12-14,20-24.

Heals the ear of Malchus, Luke 22:49-51.

Second draught of fishes, John 21:6.

Convincing Effect of: John 2:11. This beginning of miracles did Jesus in Cana of Galilee, and manifested forth his glory; and his disciples believed on him.

John 7:31. And many of the people believed on him, and said, When Christ cometh, will he do more miracles than these which this *man* hath done?

John 12:10. But the chief priests consulted that they might put Lazarus also to death; 11. Because that by reason of him many of the Jews went away, and believed on Jesus.

John 20:30. And many other signs truly did Jesus in the presence of his disciples which are not written in this book: 31. But these are written, that ye might believe that Jesus is the Christ, the Son of God; and that believing ye might have life through his name.

Acts 8:6. And the people with one accord gave heed unto those things which Philip spake, hearing and seeing the miracles which he did.

MISCEGENATION. Forbidden by Abraham, Gen. 24:3; Jacob, Gen. 28:1; Moses, Ex. 34:12-16; Deut 7:3,4; Joshua, Josh. 23:12. Reasons for prohibition, Ex. 34:16; Deut. 7:4; Josh. 23:12,13.

Results of, Judg. 3:6,7.

Instances of: Moses, Num. 12:1; Esau, Gen. 26:34,35; Israel, Num. 25:1,6-8; Judg. 3:5-8.

MISER, Eccl. 4:7,8.

MISSIONS. 1 Chr. 16:23. Sing unto the LORD, all the earth; shew forth from day to day his salvation. 24. Declare his glory among the heathen; his marvellous works among all nations.

Isa. 43:6. I will say to the north, Give up; and to the south, Keep not back: bring my sons from far, and my daughters from the ends of the earth;

Matt. 24:14. And this gospel of the kingdom shall be preached in all the world for a witness unto all nations; and then shall the end come.

Matt. 28:19. Go ye therefore, and teach all nations, baptizing them in the name of the Father, and of the Son, and of the Holy Ghost:

Missionary Hymn, Psa. 96.

MODESTY, of women, 1 Tim. 2:9.

Instances of: Saul, 1 Sam. 9: 21. Vashti, Esth. 1:11,12. Elihu, Job 32:4-7.

MONOPOLY. Of lands, Isa. 5:8; Mic. 2:2; by Pharaoh, Gen. 47:19-26; of food, Prov. 11:26.

MORTGAGE, on land, Neh. 5:3.

MOSES. A Levite and son of Amram, Ex. 2:1-4; 6:20; Acts 7:20; Heb. 11:23. Hidden in an ark, Ex. 2:3. Discovered and adopted by the daughter of Pharaoh, Ex. 2:5-10. Learned in all the wisdom of Egypt, Acts 7:22. His loyalty to his race, Heb. 11:24-26. Takes the life of an Egyptian; flees from Egypt; finds refuge among the Midianites, Ex. 2: 11-22; Acts 7:24-29. Joins himself to Jethro, priest of Midian; marries his daughter Zipporah; has two sons, Ex. 2:15-22; 18:3,4. Is herdman for Jethro in the desert of Horeb, Ex. 3:1. Has the vision of the burning bush, Ex. 3:2-6. God reveals to him his purpose to deliver the Israelites and bring them into the land of Canaan, Ex. 3:7-10. Commissioned as leader of the Israelites, Ex. 3:10-22; 6:13. His rod miraculously turned into a serpent, and his hand made leprous, and each restored, Ex. 4:1-9,28. With his wife and sons leaves Jethro to perform his mission, Ex. 4:18-20. His controversy with his wife on account of circumcision, Ex. 4:20-26.

Meets Aaron in the wilderness, Ex. 4:27,28.

With Aaron assembles the leaders of Israel, Ex. 4:29-31. With Aaron goes before Pharaoh, in the name of Jehovah demands the liberties of his people, Ex. 5:1. Rejected by Pharaoh; hardships of the Israelites increased, Ex. 5. People murmur against Moses and Aaron, Ex. 5: 20,21; 15:24; 16:2,3; 17:2,3; Num. 14:2-4; 16:41; 20:2-5; 21:4-6; Deut. 1:12,26-28. Receives comfort and assurance from the Lord, Ex. 6:1-8. Unbelief of the people, Ex. 6:9. Renews his appeal to Pharaoh, Ex. 6:11. Under divine direction brings plagues upon the land of Egypt, Ex. chapters 7-12. Secures the deliverance of the people and leads them out of Egypt, Ex. 13. Crosses the Red Sea; Pharaoh and his army are destroyed, Ex. 14. Composes a song for the children of Israel on their deliverance from Pharaoh, Ex. 15. Joined by his family in the wilderness, Ex. 18:1-12.

Institutes a system of government, Ex. 18:13-26; Num. 11:16-30; Deut. 1:9-18. Receives the law and ordains divers statutes. Face of, transfigured, Ex. 34:29-35; 2 Cor. 3:13. Sets up the tabernacle. Reproves Aaron for making the golden calf, Ex. 32:22,23; for irregularity in the offerings, Lev. 10:16-20. Jealousy of Aaron and Miriam toward, Num. 12. Rebellion of Korah, Dathan, and Abiram against, Num. 16. Appoints Joshua as his successor, Num. 27:22,23; Deut. 31:7,8,14,23; 34:9.

Not permitted to enter Canaan, but views the land from Mount Pisgah, Num. 27:12-14; Deut. 1:37; 3:23-29; 32:48-52; 34:1-8. Death and burial of, Num. 31:2; Deut. 32: 50; 34:1-6. Body of, disputed over, Jude 9. One hundred and twenty years old at death, Deut. 31:2. Mourning for, thirty days in the plains of Moab, Deut. 34:8. His virility, Deut. 31:2; 34:7.

Present with Jesus on the mount of transfiguration, Matt. 17:3,4; Mark 9:4; Luke 9:30.

Type of Christ, Deut. 18:15-18; Acts 3:22; 7:37.

Benedictions of: Upon the people, Lev. 9:23; Num. 10:35,36; Deut. 1:11. Last benediction upon the twelve tribes, Deut. 33.

Character of: Murmurings of, Ex. 5:22,23; Num. 11:10-15. Impatience of, Ex. 5:22,23; 6:12; 32:19; Num. 11:10-15; 16:15; 20: 10; 31:14. Respected and feared, Ex. 33:8. Faith of, Num. 10:29; Deut. 9:1-3; Heb. 11:23-28. Called the man of God, Deut. 33:1. God spake to, as a man to his friend, Ex. 33:11. Magnified of God, Ex. 19:9; Num. 14:12-20; Deut. 9:13-29, with Ex. 32:30. Magnanimity of, toward Eldad and Medad, Num. 11:29. Meekness of, Ex. 14:13,14; 15:24,25; 16:2,3,7,8; Num. 12:3; 16: 4-11. Obedience of, Ex. 7:6; 40:16, 19,21. Unaspiring, Num. 14:12-20; Deut. 9:13-29, with Ex. 32:30.

MOTHER. Ex. 20:12. Honour thy father and thy mother: that thy days may be long upon the land which the LORD thy God giveth thee.

Prov. 1:8. My son, hear the instruction of thy father, and forsake not the law of thy mother:

Prov. 10:1. A foolish son *is* the heaviness of his mother.

Prov. 15:20. A foolish man despiseth his mother.

Prov. 23:22. Despise not thy mother when she is old.

Prov. 29:15. The rod and reproof give wisdom: but a child left *to himself* bringeth his mother to shame.

MOTHER-IN-LAW. Matt. 10: 35. Beloved by Ruth, Ruth 1:14-17. Peter's, healed by Jesus, Mark 1: 30,31.

MOUSE. Forbidden as food, Lev. 11:29; used as food, Isa. 66: 17. Images of, 1 Sam. 6:4,5,11,18.

MOWING. Psa. 72:6; 90:6; 129:7; Amos 7:1.

MULBERRY TREE, 2 Sam. 5:23,24; Psa. 84:6 [marg.].

MULE. Uses of: For royal riders, 2 Sam. 13:29; 18:9; 1 Kin. 1: 33,38; ridden by posts, Esth. 8:10, 14; by saints in Isaiah's prophetic vision of the kingdom of Christ,

Isa. 66:20; as pack animals, 2 Kin. 5:17; 1 Chr. 12:40. Tribute paid in, 1 Kin. 10:25. Used in barter, Ezek. 27:14; by the captivity in returning from Babylon, Ezra 2: 66; Neh. 7: 68; in war, Zech. 14:15.

MURMURING, Against God: Ex. 5:22. And Moses returned unto the LORD, and said, Lord, wherefore hast thou *so* evil entreated this people? why *is* it *that* thou hast sent me? 23. For since I came to Pharaoh to speak in thy name, he hath done evil to this people; neither hast thou delivered thy people at all.

Ex. 16:8. And Moses said, *This shall be,* when the LORD shall give you in the evening flesh to eat, and in the morning bread to the full; for that the LORD heareth your murmurings which ye murmur against him: and what *are* we? your murmurings *are* not against us, but against the LORD.

Job 34:37. He addeth rebellion unto his sin, he clappeth *his hands* among us, and multiplieth his words against God.

Psa. 78:17. And they sinned yet more against him by provoking the most High in the wilderness. 18. And they tempted God in their heart by asking meat for their lust. 19. Yea, they spake against God; they said, Can God furnish a table in the wilderness? 20. Behold, he smote the rock, that the waters gushed out, and the streams overflowed; can he give bread also? can he provide flesh for his people? 21. Therefore the LORD heard *this,* and was wroth: so a fire was kindled against Jacob, and anger also came up against Israel;

Phil. 2:14. Do all things without murmurings and disputings:

MUSIC. Gen. 31:27. Wherefore didst thou flee away secretly, and steal away from me; and didst not tell me, that I might have sent thee away with mirth, and with songs, with tabret, and with harp?

2 Sam. 19:35. I *am* this day fourscore years old: . . . can I hear any more the voice of singing men and singing women?

1 Kin. 1:40. And all the people came up after him, and the people piped with pipes, and rejoiced with great joy, so that the earth rent with the sound of them.

1 Chr. 6:31. And these *are they* whom David set over the service of song in the house of the LORD, after that the ark had rest. 32. And they ministered before the dwelling place of the tabernacle of the congregation with singing, until Solomon had built the house of the LORD in Jerusalem: and *then* they waited on their office according to their order.

1 Chr. 15:16. And David spake to the chief of the Levites to appoint their brethren *to be* the singers with instruments of musick, psalteries and harps and cymbals, sounding, by lifting up the voice with joy.

1 Chr. 16:4. And he appointed *certain* of the Levites to minister before the ark of the LORD, and to record, and to thank and praise the LORD God of Israel:

2 Chr. 5:12. Also the Levites *which were* the singers, all of them of Asaph, of Heman, of Jeduthun, with their sons and their brethren, *being* arrayed in white linen, having cymbals and psalteries and harps, stood at the east end of the altar, and with them an hundred and twenty priests sounding with trumpets: 13. It came even to pass, as the trumpeters and singers *were* as one, to make one sound to be heard in praising and thanking the LORD; and when they lifted up *their* voice with the trumpets and cymbals and instruments of musick, and praised the LORD, *saying,* For *he is* good; for his mercy *endureth* for ever: that *then* the house was filled with a cloud, *even* the house of the LORD;

2 Chr. 23:13. And she looked, and, behold, the king stood at his pillar at the entering in, and the princes and the trumpets by the king: and all the people of the land rejoiced, and sounded with trumpets, also the singers with instruments of musick, and such as taught to sing praise.

Psa. 33:1. Rejoice in the LORD, O ye righteous: *for* praise is comely for the upright. 2. Praise the LORD with harp: sing unto him with the psaltery *and* an instrument of ten strings. 3. Sing unto him a new song; play skilfully with a loud noise. 4. For the word of the LORD is right; and all his works *are done* in truth.

Psa. 92:1. *It is a* good *thing* to give thanks unto the LORD, and to sing praises unto thy name, O most High: 2. To shew forth thy lovingkindness in the morning, and thy faithfulness every night, 3. Upon an instrument of ten strings, and upon the psaltery; upon the harp with a solemn sound.

Psa. 95:1. O come, let us sing unto the LORD: let us make a joyful noise to the rock of our salvation. 2. Let us come before his presence with thanksgiving, and make a joyful noise unto him with psalms.

Ezek. 33:32. And, lo, thou *art* unto them as a very lovely song of one that hath a pleasant voice, and can play well on an instrument: for they hear thy words, but they do them not.

Mark 14:26. And when they had sung an hymn, they went out into the mount of Olives.

Eph. 5:19. Speaking to yourselves in psalms and hymns and spiritual songs, singing and making melody in your heart to the Lord;

MYSTERIES. Of Redemption: Psa. 25:14. The secret of the LORD *is* with them that fear him; and he will shew them his covenant.

Mark 4:11. And he said unto them, Unto you it is given to know the mystery of the kingdom of God: but unto them that are without, all *these* things are done in parables:

Eph. 1:9. Having made known unto us the mystery of his will, according to his good pleasure which he hath purposed in himself:

NAIL. Isa. 41:7; Jer. 10:4. Made of iron, 1 Chr. 22:3; of gold, 2 Chr. 3:9. Jael kills Sisera with, Judg. 4:21.

NAME. Value of a good, Prov.

22:1; Eccl. 7:1. A new name given to persons who have spiritual adoption, Isa. 62:2. To Abraham, Gen. 17:5; Sarah, Gen. 17:15; Jacob, Gen. 32:28; Paul, Acts 13:9.

NATURALIZATION, Acts 22:28; Eph. 2:12,19.

NAVY. Solomon's, 1 Kin. 9:26; Hiram's, 1 Kin. 10:11; of Chittim, Dan. 11:30,40.

NAZARITE. Law concerning, Num. 6:1-21; Judg. 13:5. Character of, Lam. 4:7; Amos 2:11,12.

Instances of: Samson, Judg. 13:5,7; 16:17. Samuel, 1 Sam. 1:11. Rechabites, Jer. 35. John the Baptist, Matt. 11:18; Luke 1:15; 7:33.

NEIGHBOR. Ex. 20:16. Thou shalt not bear false witness against thy neighbour.

Ex. 23:4. If thou meet thine enemy's ox or his ass going astray, thou shalt surely bring it back to him again. 5. If thou see the ass of him that hateth thee lying under his burden, and wouldest forbear to help him, thou shalt surely help with him.

Lev. 19:13. Thou shalt not defraud thy neighbour, neither rob *him:* the wages of him that is hired shall not abide with thee all night until the morning. 16. Thou shalt not go up and down *as* a talebearer among thy people; neither shalt thou stand against the blood of thy neighbour: I *am* the LORD. 17. Thou shalt not hate thy brother in thine heart: thou shalt in any wise rebuke thy neighbour, and not suffer sin upon him.

Prov. 3:28. Say not unto thy neighbour, Go, and come again, and to morrow I will give; when thou hast it by thee. 29. Devise not evil against thy neighbour, seeing he dwelleth securely by thee.

Matt. 7:12. Therefore all things whatsoever ye would that men should do to you, do ye even so to them: for this is the law and the prophets.

Rom. 13:10. Love worketh no ill to his neighbour: therefore love *is* the fulfilling of the law.

Rom. 15:2. Let every one of us please *his* neighbour for *his* good to edification.

Gal. 6:10. As we have therefore opportunity, let us do good unto all *men,* especially unto them who are of the household of faith.

NOAH. Son of Lamech, Gen. 5:28,29. Builds an ark and saves his family from the flood, Gen. 6:14-22; 7;8; Matt. 24:38; Luke 17:27; Heb. 11:7; 1 Pet. 3:20. Builds an altar and offers sacrifices, Gen. 8:20,21. Receives the covenant from God that no flood should again visit the earth; the rainbow instituted as a token of the covenant, Gen. 8:20, 22; 9:9-17. Intoxication of, and his curse upon Canaan, Gen. 9:20-27. His blessing upon Shem and Japheth, Gen. 9:26,27. Dies at the age of nine hundred and fifty years, Gen. 9:28, 29.

OATH, Unclassified Scriptures Relating to: Ex. 20:7. Thou shalt not take the name of the LORD thy God in vain; for the LORD will not hold him guiltless that taketh his name in vain. Deut. 5:11.

Lev. 6:5. Or all that about which he hath sworn falsely; he shall even restore it in the principal, and shall add the fifth part more thereto, *and* give it unto him to whom it appertaineth, in the day of his trespass offering.

Lev. 19:12. And ye shall not swear by my name falsely, neither shalt thou profane the name of thy God: I *am* the LORD.

Deut. 6:13. Thou shalt fear the LORD thy God, and serve him, and shalt swear by his name. chapter 10:20.

OBDURACY. Prov. 1:24. Because I have called, and ye refused; I have stretched out my hand, and no man regarded; 25. But ye have set at nought all my counsel, and would none of my reproof:

Prov. 29:1. He, that being often reproved hardeneth *his* neck, shall suddenly be destroyed, and that without remedy.

Instances of: The antediluvians, Gen. 6:3,5,7. Sodomites, Gen. 19:9, 14. Pharaoh, Ex. 7:14,22,23; 8:15, 19,32; 9:7,12,35; 10:20,28. Israelites, Num. 14:22. Sons of Eli, 1 Sam. 2:22-25.

OBEDIENCE. Ex. 19:5. If ye will obey my voice indeed and keep my covenant, then ye shall be a peculiar treasure unto me above all people:

Psa. 1:2. But his delight *is* in the law of the LORD; and in his law doth he meditate day and night.

Psa. 25:10. All the paths of the LORD *are* mercy and truth unto such as keep his covenant and his testimonies.

Psa. 103:17. The mercy of the LORD *is* from everlasting to everlasting upon them that fear him, and his righteousness unto children's children; 18. To such as keep his covenant, and to those that remember his commandments to do them.

Psa. 111:10. The fear of the LORD *is* the beginning of wisdom: a good understanding have all they that do *his commandments:*

Psa. 119:2. Blessed *are* they that keep his testimonies, *and that* seek him with the whole heart.

Luke 6:46. Why call ye me, Lord, Lord, and do not the things which I say?

John 10:27. My sheep hear my voice, and I know them, and they follow me:

John 14:15. If ye love me, keep my commandments. 23. If a man love me, he will keep my words: and my Father will love him, and we will come unto him, and make our abode with him.

Acts 5:29. Then Peter and the *other* apostles answered and said, We ought to obey God rather than men.

1 John 5:3. This is the love of God, that we keep his commandments: and his commandments are not grievous.

Deut. 5:1. And Moses called all Israel, and said unto them, Hear, O Israel, the statutes and judgments, which I speak in your ears this day, that ye may learn them, and keep and do them. 32. Ye shall observe to do therefore as the LORD your God hath commanded you: ye shall not turn aside to the right hand or to the left. 33. Ye shall walk in all the ways which the LORD your God hath commanded you, that ye may live, and *that it may be* well with you, and *that* ye may prolong *your* days in the land which ye shall possess. *vss.* 1-33.

Josh. 23:6. Be ye therefore very courageous to keep and to do all that is written in the book of the law of Moses, that ye turn not aside therefrom *to* the right hand or *to* the left;

1 Sam. 12:24. Only fear the LORD, and serve him in truth with all your heart: for consider how great *things* he hath done for you.

1 Sam. 15:22. Samuel said, Hath the LORD *as great* delight in burnt offerings and sacrifices, as in obeying the voice of the LORD? Behold, to obey *is* better than sacrifice, *and* to hearken than the fat of rams.

Eccl. 12:13. Let us hear the conclusion of the whole matter: Fear God, and keep his commandments: for this *is* the whole *duty* of man.

Num. 14:24. But my servant Caleb, because he hath another spirit with him, and hath followed me fully, him will I bring into the land whereinto he went; and his seed shall possess it. Josh. 14:6-14.

2 Chr. 24:16. And they buried him in the city of David among the kings, because he had done good in Israel, both toward God, and toward his house.

OFFERINGS. Insufficiency of: Heb. 8:7. For if that first *covenant* had been faultless, then should no place have been sought for the second.

Heb. 10:1. For the law having a shadow of good things to come, *and* not the very image of the things, can never with those sacrifices which they offered year by year continually make the comers thereunto perfect. 4. For *it is* not possible that the blood of bulls and of goats should take away sins.

Unavailing When Not Accompanied by Piety: 1 Sam. 15: 22. And Samuel said, Hath the LORD *as great* delight in burnt offerings and sacrifices, as in obeying the voice of the LORD? Behold, to obey *is* better than sacrifice, *and* to hearken than the fat of rams.

Psa. 51:16. For thou desirest not sacrifice; else would I give it: thou delightest not in burnt offering. 17. The sacrifices of God are a broken spirit: a broken and a contrite heart, O God, thou wilt not despise.

Prov. 21:3. To do justice and judgment is more acceptable to the LORD than sacrifice. 27. The sacrifice of the wicked is abomination: how much more when he bringeth it with a wicked mind?

Hos. 6:6. For I desired mercy, and not sacrifice; and the knowledge of God more than burnt offerings.

Mark 12:33. And to love him with all the heart, and with all the understanding, and with all the soul, and with all the strength, and to love his neighbour as himself, is more than all whole burnt offerings and sacrifices.

OLD AGE. Gen. 47:9. And Jacob said unto Pharaoh, The days of the years of my pilgrimage are an hundred and thirty years: few and evil have the days of the years of my life been, and have not attained unto the days of the years of the life of my fathers in the days of their pilgrimage.

Deut. 34:7. And Moses was an hundred and twenty years old when he died: his eye was not dim, nor his natural force abated.

2 Sam. 19:34. And Barzillai said unto the king, How long have I to live, that I should go up with the king unto Jerusalem? 35. I am this day fourscore years old: and can I discern between good and evil? can thy servant taste what I eat or what I drink? can I hear any more the voice of singing men and singing women? wherefore then should thy servant be yet a burden unto my lord the king? 36. Thy servant will go a little way over Jordan with the king: and why should the king recompense it me with such a reward? 37. Let thy servant, I pray thee, turn back again, that I may die in mine own city, and be buried by the grave of my father and of my mother.

Job 11:17. Thine age shall be clearer than the noonday; thou shalt shine forth, thou shalt be as the morning. Job 42:17.

Job 12:12. With the ancient is wisdom; and in length of days understanding.

Job 32:4. Now Elihu had waited till Job had spoken, because they were elder than he.

Psa. 71:9. Cast me not off in the time of old age; forsake me not when my strength faileth. 18. Now also when I am old and greyheaded, O God, forsake me not; until I have shewed thy strength unto this generation, and thy power to every one that is to come.

Psa. 90:10. The days of our years are threescore years and ten; and if by reason of strength they be fourscore years, yet is their strength labour and sorrow; for it is soon cut off and we fly away.

Psa. 92:14. They shall still bring forth fruit in old age; they shall be fat and flourishing;

Prov. 16:31. The hoary head is a crown of glory, if it be found in the way of righteousness.

Eccl. 12:1. Remember now thy Creator in the days of thy youth, while the evil days come not, nor the years draw nigh, when thou shalt say, I have no pleasure in them;

Isa. 46:4. Even to your old age I am he; and even to hoar hairs will I carry you: I have made, and I will bear; even I will carry, and will deliver you.

Luke 2:37. And she was a widow of about fourscore and four years, which departed not from the temple, but served God with fastings and prayers night and day.

Tit. 2:2. That the aged men be sober, grave, temperate, sound in faith, in charity, in patience. 3. The aged women likewise, that they be in behaviour as becometh holiness, not false accusers, not given to much wine, teachers of good things;

Philem. 9. Yet for love's sake I rather beseech thee, being such an one as Paul the aged, and now also a prisoner of Jesus Christ.

OPPRESSION. Deut 23:15. Thou shalt not deliver unto his

master the servant which is escaped from his master unto thee: 16. He shall dwell with thee, *even* among you, in that place which he shall choose in one of thy gates, where it liketh him best: thou shalt not oppress him.

Deut. 24:14. Thou shalt not oppress an hired servant *that is* poor and needy, *whether he be* of thy brethren, or of thy strangers that *are* in thy land within thy gates: 15. At his day thou shalt give *him* his hire, neither shall the sun go down upon it: lest he cry against thee unto the LORD, and it be sin unto thee.

Psa. 9:9. The LORD also will be a refuge for the oppressed, a refuge in times of trouble.

Psa. 62:10. Trust not in oppression, and become not vain in robbery: if riches increase, set not your heart *upon them.*

Prov. 30:14. *There is* a generation, whose teeth *are as* swords, and their jaw teeth *as* knives, to devour the poor from off the earth, and the needy from *among* men.

Eccl. 7:7. Surely oppression maketh a wise man mad;

Zech. 7:10. And oppress not the widow, nor the fatherless, the stranger, nor the poor; and let none of you imagine evil against his brother in your heart.

ORDINANCE. Gal. 5:6. For in Jesus Christ neither circumcision availeth any thing, nor uncircumcision; but faith which worketh by love.

Eph. 2:15. Having abolished in his flesh the enmity, *even* the law of commandments *contained* in ordinances;

Col. 2:14. Blotting out the handwriting of ordinances that was against us, which was contrary to us, and took it out of the way, nailing it to his cross.

ORPHAN. Ex. 22:22. Ye shall not afflict any widow, or fatherless child. 23. If thou afflict them in any wise, and they cry at all unto me, I will surely hear their cry; 24. And my wrath shall wax hot, and I will kill you with the sword; and your wives shall be widows, and

your children fatherless.

Deut. 16:14. And thou shalt rejoice in thy feast, thou, and thy son, and thy daughter, and thy manservant, and thy maidservant, and the Levite, the stranger, and the fatherless and the widow, that *are* within thy gates.

Deut. 24:17. Thou shalt not pervert the judgment of the stranger, *nor* of the fatherless; nor take a widow's raiment to pledge:

Job 22:9. Thou hast sent widows away empty, and the arms of the fatherless have been broken.

Psa. 82:3. Defend the poor and fatherless: do justice to the afflicted and needy.

Psa. 146:9. The LORD preserveth the strangers; he relieveth the fatherless and widow:

Jer. 49:11. Leave thy fatherless children, I will preserve *them* alive;

Jas. 1:27. Pure religion and undefiled before God and the Father is this, To visit the fatherless and widows in their affliction, *and* to keep himself unspotted from the world.

PAIN. Rev. 21:4. And God shall wipe away all tears from their eyes; and there shall be no more death, neither sorrow, nor crying, neither shall there be any more pain: for the former things are passed away.

PALE HORSE, symbol of death, Rev. 6:8.

PARADOX. Prov. 13:7. There is that maketh himself rich, yet *hath* nothing: *there is* that maketh himself poor, yet *hath* great riches.

Matt. 10:39. He that findeth his life shall lose it: and he that loseth his life for my sake shall find it. chapter 16:25; Mark 8:35; Luke 17:33.

John 12:25. He that loveth his life shall lose it; and he that hateth his life in this world shall keep it unto life eternal.

1 Cor. 3:18. If any man among you seemeth to be wise in this world, let him become a fool, that he may be wise.

2 Cor. 6:4. But in all *things* approving ourselves as the ministers of God, 8. By honour and dis-

honour, by evil report and good report; as deceivers, and *yet* true; 9. As unknown, and *yet* well known; as dying, and, behold, we live; as chastened, and not killed; 10. As sorrowful, yet alway rejoicing; as poor, yet making many rich; as having nothing, and *yet* possessing all things.

Phil. 3:7. But what things were gain to me those I counted loss for Christ.

PARENTS. Unclassified Scriptures Relating to: Gen. 18:19. For I know him, that he will command his children and his household after him, and they shall keep the way of the LORD, to do justice and judgment; that the LORD may bring upon Abraham that which he hath spoken of him.

Deut. 6:7. And thou shalt teach them diligently unto thy children, and shalt talk of them when thou sittest in thine house, and when thou walkest by the way, and when thou liest down, and when thou risest up.

Deut. 32:46. Set your hearts unto all the words which I testify among you this day, which ye shall command your children to observe to do, all the words of this law.

Psa. 103.13. Like as a father pitieth *his* children, *so* the LORD pitieth them that fear him.

Prov. 3:12. Whom the LORD loveth he correcteth; even as a father the son *in whom* he delighteth.

Prov. 13:22. A good *man* leaveth an inheritance to his children's children: 24. He that spareth his rod hateth his son: but he that loveth him chasteneth him betimes.

Prov. 19:18. Chasten thy son while there is hope, and let not thy soul spare for his crying.

Prov. 22:6. Train up a child in the way he should go: and when he is old, he will not depart from it. 15. Foolishness *is* bound in the heart of a child; *but* the rod of correction shall drive it far from him.

Prov. 23:13. Withhold not correction from the child: for *if* thou beatest him with the rod, he shall not die. 14. Thou shalt beat him with the rod, and shalt deliver his soul from hell.

Prov. 29:15. The rod and reproof give wisdom: but a child left *to himself* bringeth his mother to shame. 17. Correct thy son, and he shall give thee rest; yea, he shall give delight unto thy soul.

Joel 1:3. Tell ye your children of it, and *let* your children *tell* their children, and their children another generation.

Mal. 4:6. He shall turn the heart of the fathers to the children, and the heart of the children to their fathers, lest I come and smite the earth with a curse.

Eph. 6:4. Fathers, provoke not your children to wrath: but bring them up in the nurture and admonition of the Lord.

Col. 3:21. Fathers, provoke not your children *to anger,* lest they be discouraged.

1 Tim. 3:4. One that ruleth well his own house, having his children in subjection with all gravity; 5. (For if a man know not how to rule his own house, how shall he take care of the church of God?) 12. Let the deacons be the husbands of one wife, ruling their children and their own houses well.

1 Tim. 5:8. If any provide not for his own, and specially for those of his own house, he hath denied the faith, and is worse than an [infidel.] [R. V. unbeliever]

Tit. 2:4. That they may teach the young women to be sober, to love their husbands, to love their children.

PASSOVER. Institution of, Ex. 12:3-49; 23:15-18; 34:18; Lev. 23:4-8; Num. 9:2-5,13,14; 28:16-25; Deut. 16:1-8,16; Psa. 81:3,5. Design of, Ex. 12:21-28.

Special passover, for those who were unclean, or on journey, to be held in second month, Num. 9:6-12; 2 Chr. 30:2-4. Lamb killed by Levites, for those who were ceremonially unclean, 2 Chr. 30:17; 35:3-11; Ezra 6:20. Strangers authorized to celebrate, Ex. 12:48,49; Num. 9:14.

Observed at place designated by God, Deut. 16:5-7; with unleavened

bread, Ex. 12:8,15-20; 13:3,6; 23:
15; Lev. 23:6; Num. 9:11; 28:17;
Deut. 16:3,4; Mark 14:12; Luke
22:7; Acts 12:3; 1 Cor. 5:8. Penalty for neglecting to observe, Num.
9:13.

Reinstituted by Ezekiel, 45:21-24.

Observation of, renewed by the
Israelites on entering Canaan, Josh.
5:10,11; by Hezekiah, 2 Chr. 30:1;
by Josiah, 2 Kin. 23:22,23; 2 Chr.
35:1,18; after return from captivity, Ezra 6:19,20. Observed by
Jesus, Matt. 26:17-20; Luke 22:15;
John 2:13,23; 13. Jesus in the temple
at time of, Luke 2:41-50. Jesus
crucified at time of, Matt. 26:2;
Mark 14:1,2; John 18:28. The
lamb of, a type of Christ, 1 Cor.
5:7. Lord's supper ordained at,
Matt. 26:26-28; Mark 14:12-25;
Luke 22:7-20.

Prisoner released at, by the Romans, Matt. 27:15; Mark 15:6;
Luke 23:16,17; John 18:39. Peter
imprisoned at time of, Acts 12:3.

Christ called our passover, 1 Cor.
5:7.

PATIENCE. Lam. 3:26. *It is*
good that *a man* should both hope
and quietly wait for the salvation
of the LORD. 27. *It is* good for a
man that he bear the yoke in his
youth.

Rom. 5:3. And not only *so,* but
we glory in tribulations also; knowing that tribulation worketh patience; 4. And patience, experience;
and experience, hope:

Rom. 12:12. Rejoicing in hope;
patient in tribulation;

Gal. 6:9. And let us not be weary
in well doing: for in due season we
shall reap, if we faint not.

2 Tim. 2:24. The servant of the
Lord must not strive; but be gentle
unto all *men,* apt to teach, patient,
25. In meekness instructing those
that oppose themselves;

Heb. 6:12. That ye be not slothful, but followers of them who
through faith and patience inherit
the promises. 15. And so, after he
had patiently endured, he obtained
the promise.

Heb. 10:36. Ye have need of patience, that, after ye have done the
will of God, ye might receive the
promise.

Jas. 1:3. Knowing *this,* that the
trying of your faith worketh patience. 4. But let patience have *her*
perfect work, that ye may be perfect and entire, wanting nothing.
19. Wherefore, my beloved brethren, let every man be swift to hear,
slow to speak, slow to wrath:

PATRIOTISM. Psa. 122:6. Pray
for the peace of Jerusalem: they
shall prosper that love thee. 7.
Peace be within thy walls, *and* prosperity within thy palaces.

Psa. 137:1. By the rivers of
Babylon, there we sat down, yea,
we wept, when we remembered
Zion. 2. We hanged our harps
upon the willows in the midst
thereof. 3. For there they that
carried us away captive required of
us a song; and they that wasted us
required of us mirth, *saying,* Sing
us *one* of the songs of Zion. 4.
How shall we sing the LORD's song
in a strange land? 5. If I forget
thee, O Jerusalem, let my right hand
forget *her* cunning. 6. If I do not
remember thee, let my tongue cleave
to the roof of my mouth; if I prefer not Jerusalem above my chief
joy.

PAUL. Called also SAUL, Acts
8:1; 9:1; 13:9. Of the tribe of Ben-
jamin, Rom. 11:1; Phil. 3:5. Personal appearance of, 2 Cor. 10:
1,10; 11:6. Born in Tarsus, Acts 9:
11; 21:39; 22:3. Educated at Jerusalem in the school of Gamaliel,
Acts 22:3; 26:4. A zealous Pharisee, Acts 22:3; 23:6; 26:5; 2 Cor.
11:22; Gal. 1:14; Phil. 3:5. A
Roman, Acts 16:37; 22:25-28. Per-
secutes the Christians; present at,
and gives consent to, the stoning of
Stephen, Acts 7:58; 8:1,3; 9:1; 22:4.
Sent to Damascus with letters for
the arrest and return to Jerusalem
of Christians, Acts 9:1,2. His vision
and conversion, Acts 9:3-22; 22:4-
19; 26:9-15; 1 Cor. 15:8; Gal.
1:13; 1 Tim. 1:12,13. Is baptized,
Acts 9:18; 22:16. Called to be an
apostle, Acts 22:14-21; 26:16-18;
Rom. 1:1; 1 Cor. 1:1; 9:1,2; 15:9;
Gal. 1:1,15,16; Eph. 1:1; Col. 1:1;
1 Tim. 1:1; 2:7; 2 Tim. 1:1,11;

PAUL

Tit. 1:1,3. Preaches in Damascus, Acts 9:20,22. Is persecuted by the Jews, Acts 9:23,24. Escapes by being let down from the wall in a basket; goes to Arabia, Gal. 1:17; Jerusalem, Acts 9:25,26; Gal. 1: 18,19. Received by the disciples in Jerusalem, Acts 9:26-29. Goes to Cæsarea, Acts 9:30; 18:22. Sent unto the Gentiles, Acts 13:2,3,47,48; 22:17-21; Rom. 11:13; 15:16; Gal. 1:15-24. Has Barnabas as his companion, Acts 11:25,26. Teaches at Antioch one year, Acts 11:26. Conveys the contributions of the Christians in Antioch to the Christians in Jerusalem, Acts 11:27-30. Returns with John to Antioch, Acts 12:25. Visits Seleucia, Acts 13:4; Cyprus, Acts 13:4. Preaches at Salamis, Acts 13:5; at Paphos, Acts 13:6. Sergius Paulus, deputy of the country, is a convert of, Acts 13:7-12. Contends with Elymas the sorcerer, Acts 13:6-12. Visits Perga in Pamphylia, Acts 13:13. John, a companion of, departs for Jerusalem, Acts 13:50,51. Visits Iconium, ia, and preaches in the synagogue, Acts 13:14-41. His message received gladly by the Gentiles, Acts 13:42,49. Persecuted and expelled, Acts 13:50,51. Visits Iconium, and preaches to the Jews and Greeks; is persecuted; escapes to Lystra; goes to Derbe, Acts 14:1-6. Heals an impotent man, Acts 14: 8-10. The people attempt to worship him, Acts 14:11-18. Is persecuted by certain Jews from Antioch and Iconium, and is stoned, Acts 14:19; 2 Cor. 11:25; 2 Tim. 3:11. Escapes to Derbe, where he preaches the gospel, and returns to Lystra, and to Iconium, and to Antioch, confirms the souls of the disciples, exhorts them to continue in the faith, and ordains elders, Acts 14: 19-23. Revisits Pisidia, Pamphylia, Perga, Attalia, and Antioch, in Syria, where he abode, Acts 14: 24-28. Contends with the Judaizing Christians against circumcision, Acts 15:1,2. Refers the question as to circumcision to the apostles and elders at Jerusalem, Acts 15:2,4. He declares to the apostles at Jeru-

salem the miracles and wonders God had wrought among the Gentiles by them, Acts 15:12. Returns to Antioch, accompanied by Barnabas, Judas, and Silas, with letters to the Gentiles, Acts 15:22,25.

Makes his second tour of the churches, Acts 15:36. Chooses Silas as his companion, and passes through Syria and Cilicia, confirming the churches, Acts 15:36-41. Visits Lystra; circumcises Timothy, Acts 16:1-5. Goes through Phrygia and Galatia; is forbidden by the Holy Ghost to preach in Asia; visits Mysia; essays to go to Bithynia, but is restrained by the Spirit; goes to Troas, where he has a vision of a man saying, "Come over into Macedonia, and help us"; immediately proceeds to Macedonia, Acts 16:6-10. Visits Samothracia and Neopolis; comes to Philippi, the chief city of Macedonia; visits a place of prayer at the river side; preaches the word; the merchant, Lydia, of Thyatira, is converted and baptized, Acts 16:11-15. Reproves the soothsayer; causes the evil spirit to come out of the damsel who practices divination, Acts 16:16-18. Persecuted, beaten, and cast into prison with Silas; sings songs of praise in the prison; an earthquake shakes the prison; he preaches to the alarmed jailer, who believes, and is baptized with his household, Acts 16:19-34. Is released by the civil authorities on the ground of his being a Roman citizen, Acts 16:35-39; 2 Cor. 6:5; 11:25; 1 Thess. 2:2. Is received at the house of Lydia, Acts 16:40. Visits Amphipolis, and Apollonia, and Thessalonica, preaches in the synagogue, Acts 17:1-4. Is persecuted, Acts 17:5-9; 2 Thess. 1:1-4. Escapes to Berea by night; preaches in the synagogue; many honorable women, and men, not a few, believe, Acts 17:10-12. Persecuted by the Jews who come from Thessalonica; is conducted by the brethren to Athens, Acts 17:13-15. Disputes on Mars' Hill with Grecians, Acts 17: 16-34. Visits Corinth; dwells with Aquila and his wife, Priscilla, who were tentmakers; joins in their handicraft; reasons in the synagogue

199

PAUL

every Sabbath; is rejected of the Jews; turns to the Gentiles; makes his abode with Justus; continues there one year and six months, teaching the word of God, Acts 18: 1-11. Persecuted by Jews, drawn before the deputy, charged with wicked lewdness; accusation dismissed; takes his leave after many days, and sails unto Syria, accompanied by Aquila and Priscilla, Acts 18:12-18. Visits Ephesus, where he leaves Aquila and Priscilla; enters into a synagogue, where he reasons with the Jews; starts on his return journey to Jerusalem; visits Cæsarea; goes over the country of Galatia and Phrygia, in order, strengthening the disciples, Acts 18: 18-23. Returns to Ephesus; baptizes in the name of the Lord Jesus, and lays his hands upon the disciples, who are baptized with the Holy Ghost; preaches in the synagogue; remains in Ephesus for the space of two years; heals the sick, Acts 19: 1-12. Reproves the exorcists; casts an evil spirit out of a man, and many believe, bringing their books of sorcery to be burned, Acts 19: 13-20; 1 Cor. 16:8,9. Sends Timothy and Erastus into Macedonia, but remains himself in Asia for a season, Acts 19:21,22. The spread of the gospel through his preaching interferes with the makers of idols; he is persecuted, and a great uproar of the city is created; the town clerk appeases the people; dismisses the accusation against Paul, and disperses the people, Acts 19:23-41; 2 Cor. 1:8; 2 Tim. 4:14. Proceeds to Macedonia after confirming the churches in those parts; comes into Greece and abides three months; returns through Macedonia, accompanied by Sopater, Aristarchus, Secundus, Gaius, Timothy, Tychicus, and Trophimus, Acts 20:1-6. Visits Troas; preaches until break of day; restores to life the young man who fell from the window, Acts 20:6-12. Visits Assos, Mitylene, Chios, Samos, Trogyllium, and Miletus, hastening to Jerusalem, to be there at Pentecost, Acts 20:13-16. Sends for the elders of the church of Ephesus; rehearses to them how he had preached in Asia, and his temptations and afflictions testifying repentance toward God; declares he was going bound in spirit to Jerusalem; exhorts them to take heed to themselves and the flock over whom the Holy Ghost had made them overseers; kneels down and prays and takes his departure, Acts 20: 17-38. Visits Coos, Rhodes, Patara; takes ship for Tyre; tarries at Tyre seven days; is brought on his way by the disciples to the outskirts of the city; kneels down and prays; takes ship; comes to Ptolemais; salutes the brethren, and abides one day, Acts 21:1-7. Departs for Cæsarea; enters the house of Philip, the Evangelist; is admonished by Agabus not to go to Jerusalem; proceeds nevertheless to Jerusalem, Acts 21:8-15. Is received by the brethren gladly; talks of the things that had been wrought among the Gentiles by his ministry; enters the temple: the people are stirred against him by Jews from Asia; an uproar is created; he is thrust out of the temple; the chief captain of the garrison interposes and arrests him, Acts 21:17-33. His defense, Acts 21:33-40; 22:1-21. Is confined in the castle, Acts 22:24-30. Is brought before the council; his defense, Acts 22:30; 23:1-5. Is returned to the castle, Acts 23:10. Is cheered by a vision, promising him that he shall bear witness in Rome, Acts 23:11. Jews conspire against his life, Acts 23:12-15; thwarted by his nephew, Acts 23:16-22. Is escorted to Cæsarea by a military guard, Acts 23:23-33. Is confined in Herod's Judgment Hall in Cæsarea, Acts 23:35. His trial before Felix, Acts 24. Remains in custody for two years, Acts 24:27. His trial before Festus, Acts 25:1-12. Appeals to Cæsar, Acts 25:10-12. His examination before Agrippa, Acts 25:13-27; 26. Is taken to Rome in custody of Julius, a centurion, and guard of soldiers; takes shipping, accompanied by other prisoners, and sails by way of the coasts of Asia; stops at Sidon, and at Myra, Acts 27:1-5. Transferred to a ship of Alexandria; sails by way of Cnidus, Crete, Salamis, and the Fair Havens, Acts 27:6-8. Predicts misfortune to the ship; his counsel not heeded, and the voyage resumed, Acts 27:9-13. The ship encounters a tempest; Paul encourages and comforts the officers and crew; the soldiers advise putting the prisoners to death; the centurion interferes, and all on board, consisting of two hundred and seventy-six souls, are saved, Acts 27:14-44. The ship is wrecked, and all on board take refuge on the island of Melita, Acts 27:14-44. Kind treatment by the inhabitants of the island, Acts 28:1,2. Is bitten by a viper and miraculously preserved, Acts 28:3-6. Heals the ruler's father and others, Acts 28:7-10. Is delayed in Melita three months; proceeds on the voyage; delays at Syracuse; sails by Rhegium and Puteoli; meets brethren who accompany him to Rome from Appii forum; arrives at Rome; is delivered to the captain of the guard; is permitted to dwell by himself in custody of a soldier, Acts 28:11-16. Calls the chief Jews together; states his situation; is kindly received; expounds the gospel; testifies to the kingdom of heaven, Acts 28:17-29. Dwells two years in his own hired house, preaching and teaching, Acts 28:30,31.

Supports himself, Acts 18:3; 20:33-35. Sickness of, in Asia, 2 Cor. 1:8-11. His resolute determination to go to Jerusalem against the repeated admonition of the Holy Ghost, Acts 20:22,23; 21:4,10-14. Caught up to the third heavens, 2 Cor. 12:1-4. Has "a thorn in the flesh," 2 Cor. 12:7-9; Gal. 4:13,14. His independence of character, 1 Thess. 2:9; 2 Thess, 3:8. Persecutions of, 1 Thess. 2:2; Heb. 10:34.

PEACE. Psa. 34:14. Seek peace, and pursue it. 1 Pet. 3:11.

Psa. 133:1. Behold, how good and how pleasant *it is* for brethren to dwell together in unity!

Prov. 15:17. Better *is* a dinner of herbs where love is, than a stalled ox and hatred therewith.

Prov. 20:3. *It is* an honour for a man to cease from strife: but every fool will be meddling.

Matt. 5:9. Blessed *are* the peacemakers: for they shall be called the children of God.

Mark 9:50. Have peace one with another.

Rom. 12:18. If it be possible, as much as lieth in you, live peaceably with all men.

Rom. 14:19. Let us therefore follow after the things which make for peace, and things wherewith one may edify another.

1 Cor. 14:33. For God is not *the author* of confusion, but of peace, as in all churches of the saints.

Eph. 4:3. Endeavouring to keep the unity of the Spirit in the bond of peace.

1 Thess. 5:13. Be at peace among yourselves.

1 Tim. 2:2. That we may lead a quiet and peaceable life in all godliness and honesty.

Heb. 12:14. Follow peace with all *men,* and holiness, without which no man shall see the Lord:

Isa. 9:6. His name shall be called Wonderful, Counsellor, The mighty God, The everlasting Father, The Prince of Peace.

Isa. 26:3. Thou wilt keep *him* in perfect peace, *whose* mind *is* stayed *on thee:* because he trusteth in thee.

Phil. 4:7. And the peace of God, which passeth all understanding, shall keep your hearts and minds through Christ Jesus.

Col. 1:20. And having made peace through the blood of his cross, by him to reconcile all things unto himself; by him, *I say,* whether *they be* things in earth, or things in heaven.

Col. 3:15. And let the peace of [God] rule in your hearts, to the which also ye are called in one body; and be ye thankful. [R. V. Christ]

PENITENT. Promises to: Deut. 4:29. But if from thence thou shalt seek the LORD thy God, thou shalt find *him,* if thou seek him with all thy heart and with all thy soul. 30. When thou art in tribulation, and all these things are come upon thee, *even* in the latter days, if thou turn to the LORD thy

God, and shalt be obedient unto his voice; 31. (For the LORD thy God *is* a merciful God;) he will not forsake thee, neither destroy thee, nor forget the covenant of thy fathers which he sware unto them.

2 Kin. 22:19. Because thine heart was tender, and thou hast humbled thyself before the LORD, when thou heardest what I spake against this place, and against the inhabitants thereof, that they should become a desolation and a curse, and hast rent thy clothes, and wept before me; I also have heard *thee*, saith the LORD.

Psa. 6:8. Depart from me, all ye workers of iniquity; for the LORD hath heard the voice of my weeping. 9. The LORD hath heard my supplication; the LORD will receive my prayer.

Psa. 34:18. The LORD *is* nigh unto them that are of a broken heart; and saveth such as be of a contrite spirit.

Psa. 51:17. The sacrifices of God *are* a broken spirit: a broken and a contrite heart, O God, thou wilt not despise.

Psa. 145:18. The LORD *is* nigh unto all them that call upon him, to all that call upon him in truth. 19. He will fulfil the desire of them that fear him: he also will hear their cry, and will save them.

Psa. 147:3. He healeth the broken in heart, and bindeth up their wounds.

Isa. 27:5. Let him take hold of my strength, *that* he may make peace with me.

John 6:37. Him that cometh to me, I will in no wise cast out.

1 John 1:9. If we confess our sins, he is faithful and just to forgive us *our* sins, and to cleanse us from all unrighteousness.

PERFECTION. I Kin. 8:61. Let your heart therefore be perfect with the LORD our God, to walk in his statutes, and to keep his commandments, as at this day.

1 Chr. 29:19. Give unto Solomon my son a perfect heart, to keep thy commandments, thy testimonies, and thy statutes.

2 Chr. 6:36. If they sin against thee, (for *there is* no man which sinneth not,) and thou be angry . . .

Job 9:20. If I justify myself, mine own mouth shall condemn me: *if I say*, I *am* perfect, it shall also prove me perverse. 21. *Though* I *were* perfect, *yet* would I not know my soul; I would despise my life.

Psa. 18:32. *It is* God that girdeth me with strength, and maketh my way perfect.

Eccl. 7:20. For *there is* not a just man upon earth, that doeth good, and sinneth not.

Matt. 5:6. Blessed *are* they which do hunger and thirst after righteousness: for they shall be filled.

48. Be ye therefore perfect, even as your Father which is in heaven is perfect.

Phil. 2:15. That ye may be blameless and harmless, the sons of God, without rebuke, in the midst of a crooked and perverse nation, among whom ye shine as lights in the world;

Col. 2:9. For in him dwelleth all the fulness of the Godhead bodily. 10. And ye are complete in him, which is the head of all principality and power:

Col. 3:14. And above all these things *put on* charity, which is the bond of perfectness.

PERJURY. Lev. 19:12. And ye shall not swear by my name falsely, neither shalt thou profane the name of thy God: I *am* the LORD.

Hos. 10:4. They have spoken words, swearing falsely in making a covenant: thus judgment springeth up as hemlock in the furrows of the field.

Zech. 8:17. And let none of you imagine evil in your hearts against his neighbour; and love no false oath: for all these *are things* that I hate, saith the LORD.

PERSECUTION. Of the Righteous: Job 1:9. Then Satan answered the LORD, and said, Doth Job fear God for nought?

Psa. 11:2. For, lo, the wicked bend *their* bow, they make ready their arrow upon the string, that they may privily shoot at the upright in heart.

Psa. 94:5. They break in pieces thy people, O LORD, and afflict thine heritage.

Isa. 26:20. Come, my people, enter thou into thy chambers, and shut thy doors about thee: hide thyself as it were for a little moment, until the indignation be overpast.

Isa. 51:12. I, *even* I, *am* he that comforteth you: who *art* thou, that thou shouldest be afraid of a man *that* shall die, and of the son of man *which* shall be made *as* grass; 13. And forgettest the LORD thy maker, that hath stretched forth the heavens, and laid the foundations of the earth; and hast feared continually every day because of the fury of the oppressor, as if he were ready to destroy? and where *is* the fury of the oppressor?

Hab. 1:13. *Thou art* of purer eyes than to behold evil, and canst not look on iniquity: wherefore lookest thou upon them that deal treacherously, *and* holdest thy tongue when the wicked devoureth *the man that is* more righteous than he?

Matt. 5:10. Blessed *are* they which are persecuted for righteousness' sake: for their's is the kingdom of heaven. 11. Blessed are ye, when *men* shall revile you, and persecute *you,* and shall say all manner of evil against you falsely, for my sake. 12. Rejoice, and be exceeding glad: for great *is* your reward in heaven: for so persecuted they the prophets which were before you. 44. But I say unto you, Love your enemies, bless them that curse you, do good to them that hate you, and pray for them which despitefully use you, and persecute you; Luke 6:26,27.

Mark 13:9. But take heed to yourselves: for they shall deliver you up to councils; and in the synagogues ye shall be beaten: and ye shall be brought before rulers and kings for my sake, for a testimony against them.

John 15:18. If the world hate you, ye know that it hated me before *it hated* you. 19. If ye were of the world, the world would love

his own: but because ye are not of the world, but I have chosen you out of the world, therefore the world hateth you.

2 Cor. 4:8. *We are* troubled on every side, yet not distressed: *we are* perplexed, but not in despair; 9. Persecuted, but not forsaken; cast down, but not destroyed;

Heb. 12:3. Consider him that endured such contradiction of sinners against himself, lest ye be wearied and faint in your minds. 4. Ye have not yet resisted unto blood, striving against sin.

Heb. 13:13. Let us go forth therefore unto him without the camp, bearing his reproach.

1 John 3:1. The world knoweth us not, because it knew him not. 13. Marvel not, my brethren, if the world hate you.

PERSEVERANCE. 1 Chr. 16:11. Seek the LORD and his strength, seek his face continually,

Psa. 138:8. The LORD will perfect *that which* concerneth me:

Hos. 12:6. Therefore turn thou to thy God: keep mercy and judgment, and wait on thy God continually.

John 8:31. Then said Jesus to those Jews which believed on him, If ye continue in my word, *then* are ye my disciples indeed:

Rom. 2:6. Who will render to every man according to his deeds: 7. To them who by patient continuance in well doing seek for glory and honour and immortality, eternal life:

Gal. 6:9. And let us not be weary in well doing: for in due season we shall reap, if we faint not.

Phil. 4:1. Stand fast in the Lord,

Col. 2:7. Rooted and built up in him, and stablished in the faith,

2 Thess. 3:13. But ye, brethren, be not weary in well doing.

2 Tim. 2:1. Thou therefore, my son, be strong in the grace that is in Christ Jesus. 3. Endure hardness, as a good soldier of Jesus Christ.

Jas. 1:4. Let patience have *her* perfect work, that ye may be perfect and entire, wanting nothing.

PHILOSOPHY. The nature of

things, Eccl. chapters 1-7. A philosophical disquisition on wisdom, Job 28. Philosophical inductions and deductions relating to God and his providence, Job 5:8-20; 9; 10:2-21; 12:6-24; 33:12-30; 37. Reveals the mysteries of providence, Prov. 25:2; Rom. 1:19,20. Is not sufficient for an adequate knowledge of God, 1 Cor. 1:21,22; or of salvation through the atonement of Jesus Christ, 1 Cor. 2:6-10. Employment of, was not Paul's method of preaching the gospel, 1 Cor. 1:17,19,21; 2: 1-5,13. Greek schools of, Acts. 17: 18. Rabbinical, Col. 2:8,16-19; 1 Tim. 6:20.

PHYSICIAN, 2 Chr. 16:12; Matt. 9:12; Mark 5:26; Luke 8:43. Proverbs about, Mark 2:17; Luke 4:23. Luke a physician, Col. 4:14.

Figurative: Job 13:4; Jer. 8:22; Luke 5:31.

PHYSIOLOGY, Job 10:11; Psa. 139:14-16; Prov. 14:30.

PLEASURE. Worldly: Prov. 9:17. Stolen waters are sweet, and bread *eaten* in secret is pleasant.

Prov. 21:17. He that loveth pleasure *shall be* a poor man: he that loveth wine and oil shall not be rich.

Eccl. 2:1. I said in mine heart, Go to now, I will prove thee with mirth, therefore enjoy pleasure: and, behold, this also *is* vanity.

Isa. 5:11. Woe unto them that rise up early in the morning, *that* they may follow strong drink; that continue until night, *till* wine inflame them!

Amos 6:1. Woe to them *that are* at ease in Zion.

Heb. 11:25. Choosing rather to suffer affliction with the people of God, than to enjoy the pleasures of sin for a season;

POLITICS. Corruption in: Psa. 12:8; in the court of Ahasuerus, Esth. 3; of Darius, Dan. 6:4-15.

INSTANCES OF: Absalom, electioneering for the throne, 2 Sam. 15:2-6. Pilate, condemning Jesus to gratify popular clamor, Matt. 27: 23-27; Mark 15:15; Luke 23:13-25; John 18:38,39; 19:4-13.

Ministers in: Zadok the priest,

a partisan of David, 2 Sam. 15:24-29. Nathan, the prophet, influences the selection of David's successor, 1 Kin. 1:11-40.

Women in: The wise woman of Abel, who saved the city through diplomacy, 2 Sam. 20:16-22. Bathsheba, in securing the crown for Solomon, 1 Kin. 1:15-21. Herodias, in influencing the administration of Herod, Matt. 14:3-11; Mark 6:17-28. Mother of Zebedee's children, in seeking favor for her sons, Matt. 20:20-23.

POOR. Job 30:25. Did not I weep for him that was in trouble? was *not* my soul grieved for the poor?

Psa. 37:16. A little that a righteous man hath *is* better than the riches of many wicked.

Psa. 82:3. Defend the poor and fatherless: do justice to the afflicted and needy. 4. Deliver the poor and needy: rid *them* out of the hand of the wicked.

Prov. 13:7. There is that maketh himself rich, yet *hath* nothing: *there is* that maketh himself poor, yet *hath* great riches.

Prov. 19:17. He that hath pity upon the poor lendeth unto the LORD; and that which he hath given will he pay him again.

Prov. 20:13. Love not sleep, lest thou come to poverty; open thine eyes, *and* thou shalt be satisfied with bread.

Jas. 1:9. Let the brother of low degree rejoice in that he is exalted: 10. But the rich, in that he is made low: because as the flower of the grass he shall pass away.

Psa. 41:1. Blessed *is* he that considereth the poor: the LORD will deliver him in time of trouble.

Prov. 28:27. He that giveth unto the poor shall not lack: but he that hideth his eyes shall have many a curse.

Matt. 5:42. Give to him that asketh thee, and from him that would borrow of thee turn not thou away. Luke 6:30.

Matt. 19:21. Jesus said unto him, If thou wilt be perfect, go *and* sell that thou hast, and give to the poor, and thou shalt have treasure in heaven: and come *and* follow me.

Jas. 1:27. Pure religion and undefiled before God and the Father is this, To visit the fatherless and widows in their affliction,

God's Care of: Job 36:6. He preserveth not the life of the wicked: but giveth right to the poor. 15. He delivereth the poor in his affliction, and openeth their ears in oppression.

Psa. 9:18. The needy shall not alway be forgotten: the expectation of the poor shall *not* perish for ever.

Psa. 34:6. This poor man cried, and the LORD heard *him,* and saved him out of all his troubles.

Psa. 74:21. O let not the oppressed return ashamed: let the poor and needy praise thy name.

Psa. 102:17. He will regard the prayer of the destitute, and not despise their prayer.

Psa. 107:9. For he satisfieth the longing soul, and filleth the hungry soul with goodness. 36. There he maketh the hungry to dwell, that they may prepare a city for habitation; 41. Yet setteth he the poor on high from affliction, and maketh *him* families like a flock.

Zeph. 3:12. I will also leave in the midst of thee an afflicted and poor people, and they shall trust in the name of the LORD.

Zech. 11:7. I will feed the flock of slaughter, *even* you, O poor of the flock.

POPULARITY. Instances of: David, 2 Sam. 3:36. Absalom, 2 Sam. 15:2-6,13. Job, Job 29.

POVERTY. Prov. 15:16. Better *is* little with the fear of the LORD, than great treasure and trouble therewith.

Prov. 16:8. Better *is* a little righteousness than great revenues without right. Eccl. 4:6.

Prov. 20:13. Love not sleep, lest thou come to poverty; open thine eyes, *and* thou shalt be satisfied with bread.

Prov. 24:33. *Yet* a little sleep, a little slumber, a little folding of the hands to sleep: 34. So shall thy poverty come *as* one that travelleth; and thy want as an armed man.

POWER. Spiritual: Isa. 40:29. He giveth power to the faint; and to *them that have* no might he increaseth strength. 30. Even the youths shall faint and be weary, and the young men shall utterly fall: 31. But they that wait upon the LORD shall renew *their* strength; they shall mount up with wings as eagles; they shall run, and not be weary; *and* they shall walk, and not faint.

Acts 1:8. But ye shall receive power, after that the Holy Ghost is come upon you: and ye shall be witnesses unto me both in Jerusalem, and in all Judæa, and in Samaria, and unto the uttermost part of the earth.

Acts 6:8. And Stephen, full of faith and power, did great wonders and miracles among the people.

Eph. 1:19. And what *is* the exceeding greatness of his power to us-ward who believe, according to the working of his mighty power, 20. Which he wrought in Christ,

2 Tim. 1:7. For God hath not given us the spirit of fear; but of power, and of love, and of a sound mind.

PRAISE. 2 Sam. 22:4. I will call on the LORD, *who is* worthy to be praised: Psa. 18:3.

1 Chr. 23:30. And to stand every morning to thank and praise the LORD, and likewise at even;

Job 36:24. Remember that thou magnify his work, which men behold.

Psa. 9:11. Sing praises to the LORD, which dwelleth in Zion: declare among the people his doings.

Psa. 28:7. The LORD *is* my strength and my shield; my heart trusted in him, and I am helped: therefore my heart greatly rejoiceth; and with my song will I praise him.

Psa. 34:1. I will bless the LORD at all times: his praise *shall* continually *be* in my mouth. 2. My soul shall make her boast in the LORD: the humble shall hear *thereof,* and be glad. 3. O magnify the LORD with me, and let us exalt his name together.

Psa. 43:3. O send out thy light and thy truth: let them lead me; let them bring me unto thy holy hill, and to thy tabernacles. 4. Then will I go unto the altar of God, unto God my exceeding joy: yea, upon the harp will I praise thee, O God my God.

Psa. 50:23. Whoso offereth praise glorifieth me:

Psa. 92:1. *It is a* good *thing* to give thanks unto the LORD, and to sing praises unto thy name, O most High: 2. To shew forth thy loving-kindness in the morning, and thy faithfulness every night,

Psa. 95:1. O come, let us sing unto the LORD: let us make a joyful noise to the rock of our salvation. 2. Let us come before his presence with thanksgiving, and make a joyful noise unto him with psalms. 6. O come, let us worship and bow down: let us kneel before the LORD our maker. 7. For he *is* our God; and we *are* the people of his pasture, and the sheep of his hand.

Psa. 107:8. Oh that *men* would praise the LORD *for* his goodness, and *for* his wonderful works to the children of men!

Isa. 43:21. This people have I formed for myself; they shall shew forth my praise.

In Heaven: Job 38:7. When the morning stars sang together, and all the sons of God shouted for joy?

Psa. 148:2. Praise ye him, all his angels: praise ye him, all his hosts. 4. Praise him, ye heavens of heavens, and ye waters that *be* above the heavens.

Luke 2:13. Suddenly there was with the angel a multitude of the heavenly host praising God, and saying, 14. Glory to God in the highest, and on earth peace, good will toward men.

Rev. 4:8. They rest not day and night, saying, Holy, holy, holy, Lord God Almighty, which was, and is, and is to come.

PRAYER. 1 Chr. 16:11. Seek the LORD and his strength, seek his face continually. 35. And say ye, Save us, O God of our salvation, and gather us together, and deliver us from the heathen, that we may give thanks to thy holy name, *and* glory in thy praise.

2 Chr. 7:14. If my people, which are called by my name, shall humble themselves, and pray, and seek my face, and turn from their wicked ways; then will I hear from heaven, and will forgive their sin, and will heal their land.

Neh. 4:9. Nevertheless we made our prayer unto our God, and set a watch against them day and night, because of them.

Psa. 145:18. The LORD *is* nigh unto all them that call upon him, to all that call upon him in truth.

Isa. 55:6. Seek ye the LORD while he may be found, call ye upon him while he is near:

Matt. 6:6. But thou, when thou prayest, enter into thy closet, and when thou hast shut thy door, pray to thy Father which is in secret; and thy Father which seeth in secret shall reward thee openly.

Matt. 7:7. Ask, and it shall be given you; seek, and ye shall find; knock, and it shall be opened unto you: 8. For every one that asketh receiveth; and he that seeketh findeth; and to him that knocketh it shall be opened. Matt. 21:22; Mark 11:24.

Col. 4:2. Continue in prayer, and watch in the same with thanksgiving;

1 Thess. 5:17. Pray without ceasing. 18. In every thing give thanks: for this is the will of God in Christ Jesus concerning you.

1 Tim. 2:8. I will therefore that men pray every where, lifting up holy hands, without wrath and doubting.

Heb. 4:16. Let us therefore come boldly unto the throne of grace, that we may obtain mercy, and find grace to help in time of need.

Jas. 5:16. The effectual fervent prayer of a righteous man availeth much.

Answer to, Promised: Deut. 4:7. What nation *is there so* great, who *hath* God *so* nigh unto them, as the LORD our God *is* in all *things that* we call upon him *for?*

Psa. 32:6. For this shall every one that is godly pray unto thee in a time when thou mayest be found: surely in the floods of great waters they shall not come nigh unto him.

Psa. 34:15. The eyes of the LORD *are* upon the righteous, and his ears *are open* unto their cry. 17. *The righteous* cry, and the LORD heareth, and delivereth them out of all their troubles.

Psa. 37:4. Delight thyself also in the LORD; and he shall give thee the desires of thine heart. 5. Commit thy way unto the LORD; trust also in him; and he shall bring *it* to pass.

Psa. 56:9. When I cry *unto thee,* then shall mine enemies turn back: this I know; for God *is* for me.

Psa. 81:10. Open thy mouth wide, and I will fill it.

Psa. 91:15. He shall call upon me, and I will answer him: I *will be* with him in trouble; I will deliver him, and honour him.

Prov. 3:6. In all thy ways acknowledge him, and he shall direct thy paths.

Isa. 65:24. It shall come to pass, that before they call, I will answer; and while they are yet speaking, I will hear.

Jer. 33:3. Call unto me, and I will answer thee, and shew thee great and mighty things, which thou knowest not.

Matt. 18:19. Again I say unto you, That if two of you shall agree on earth as touching any thing that they shall ask, it shall be done for them of my Father which is in heaven. 20. For where two or three are gathered together in my name, there am I in the midst of them.

Matt. 21:22. All things, whatsoever ye shall ask in prayer, believing, ye shall receive.

John 14:13. Whatsoever ye shall ask in my name, that will I do, that the Father may be glorified in the Son. 14. If ye shall ask any thing in my name, I will do *it.*

John 15:7. If ye abide in me, and my words abide in you, ye shall ask what ye will, and it shall be done unto you.

Rom. 8:26. The Spirit also helpeth our infirmities: for we know not what we should pray for as we ought: but the Spirit itself maketh intercession for us with groanings which cannot be uttered.

Eph. 3:20. Now unto him that is able to do exceeding abundantly above all that we ask or think, according to the power that worketh in us,

Heb. 4:16. Let us therefore come boldly unto the throne of grace, that we may obtain mercy, and find grace to help in time of need.

Heb. 11:6. Without faith *it is* impossible to please *him:* for he that cometh to God must believe that he is, and *that* he is a rewarder of them that diligently seek him.

Answered: Psa. 22:4. Our fathers trusted in thee: they trusted, and thou didst deliver them.

Psa. 28:6. Blessed *be* the LORD, because he hath heard the voice of my supplications.

Psa. 34:4. I sought the LORD, and he heard me, and delivered me from all my fears. 5. They looked unto him, and were lightened: and their faces were not ashamed. 6. This poor man cried, and the LORD heard *him,* and saved him out of all his troubles.

Psa. 40:1. I waited patiently for the LORD: and he inclined unto me, and heard my cry.

2 Cor. 12:8. For this thing I besought the Lord thrice, that it might depart from me. 9. And he said unto me, My grace is sufficient for thee: for my strength is made perfect in weakness.

Jas. 5:17. Elias was a man subject to like passions as we are, and he prayed earnestly that it might not rain: and it rained not on the earth by the space of three years and six months. 18. And he prayed again, and the heaven gave rain, and the earth brought forth her fruit.

Confession in: Lev. 5:5. And it shall be, when he shall be guilty in one of these *things,* that he shall confess that he hath sinned in that *thing:*

Psa. 119:176. I have gone astray like a lost sheep; seek thy servant; for I do not forget thy commandments.

I John 1:9. If we confess our sins, he is faithful and just to forgive us *our* sins, and to cleanse us from all unrighteousness.

Importunity in: Ex. 32:32. Yet now, if thou wilt forgive their sin—; and if not, blot me, I pray thee, out of thy book which thou hast written.

Deut. 9:25. Thus I fell down before the LORD forty days and forty nights, as I fell down *at the first;* because the LORD had said he would destroy you.

1 Sam. 12:23. As for me, God forbid that I should sin against the LORD in ceasing to pray for you:

1 Kin. 8:22. And Solomon stood before the altar of the LORD in the presence of all the congregation of Israel, and spread forth his hands toward heaven:

Ezra 9:5. At the evening sacrifice I arose up from my heaviness; and having rent my garment and my mantle, I fell upon my knees, and spread out my hands unto the LORD my God, 6. And said, O my God, I am ashamed and blush to lift up my face to thee, my God: for our iniquities are increased over *our* head, and our trespass is grown up unto the heavens.

Isa. 62:7. And give him no rest, till he establish, and till he make Jerusalem a praise in the earth.

Luke 22:44. And being in an agony he prayed more earnestly: and his sweat was as it were great drops of blood falling down to the ground.

Rom. 8:26. Likewise the Spirit also helpeth our infirmities: for we know not what we should pray for as we ought: but the Spirit itself maketh intercession for us with groanings which cannot be uttered.

Thanksgiving and, Before Taking Food: Matt. 14:19. And he commanded the multitude to sit down on the grass, and took the five loaves, and the two fishes, and looking up to heaven, he blessed, and brake, and gave the loaves to *his* disciples, and the disciples to the multitude. Mark 6:41; Luke 9:16; John 6:11,23.

PRAYERFULNESS. Dan. 6:10. Now when Daniel knew that the writing was signed, he went into his house; and his windows being open in his chamber toward Jerusalem, he kneeled upon his knees three times a day, and prayed, and gave thanks before his God, as he did aforetime.

Luke 2:37. She *was* a widow of about fourscore and four years, which departed not from the temple, but served *God* with fastings and prayers night and day.

Acts 6:4. But we will give ourselves continually to prayer, and to the ministry of the word.

Eph. 1:15. Wherefore I also, ... 16. Cease not to give thanks for you, making mention of you in my prayers;

1 Thess. 5:17. Pray without ceasing.

PREACHING, the act of exhorting, prophesying, reproving, teaching.

1 Cor. 1:17. For Christ sent me not to baptize, but to preach the gospel: not with wisdom of words, lest the cross of Christ should be made of none effect. 18. For the preaching of the cross is to them that perish foolishness; but unto us which are saved it is the power of God. 21. For after that in the wisdom of God the world by wisdom knew not God, it pleased God by the foolishness of preaching to save them that believe.

1 Cor. 2:1. And I, brethren, when I came to you, came not with excellency of speech or of wisdom, declaring unto you the testimony of God. 2. For I determined not to know any thing among you, save Jesus Christ, and him crucified. 3. And I was with you in weakness, and in fear, and in much trembling. 4. And my speech and my preaching *was* not with enticing words of man's wisdom, but in demonstration of the Spirit and of power:

1 Thess. 1:5. For our gospel

came not unto you in word only, but also in power, and in the Holy Ghost.

PREDESTINATION. Josh. 11:20. For it was of the LORD to harden their hearts, that they should come against Israel in battle, that he might destroy them utterly, *and* that they might have no favour, but that he might destroy them, as the LORD commanded Moses.

1 Kin. 12:15. Wherefore the king hearkened not unto the people; for the cause was from the LORD, that he might perform his saying, which the LORD spake by Ahijah the Shilonite unto Jeroboam the son of Nebat.

2 Chr. 6:6. But I have chosen Jerusalem, that my name might be there; and have chosen David to be over my people Israel.

Jer. 1:4. Then the word of the LORD came unto me, saying, 5. Before I formed thee in the belly I knew thee; and before thou camest forth out of the womb I sanctified thee, *and* I ordained thee a prophet unto the nations.

Luke 22:22. And truly the Son of man goeth, as it was determined: but woe unto that man by whom he is betrayed. Matt. 26:24; Mark 14: 21.

John 15:16. Ye have not chosen me, but I have chosen you, and ordained you, that ye should go and bring forth fruit, and *that* your fruit should remain: that whatsoever ye shall ask of the Father in my name, he may give it you.

Rom. 8:28. And we know that all things work together for good to them that love God, to them who are the called according to *his* purpose. 29. For whom he did foreknow, he also did predestinate *to be* conformed to the image of his Son, that he might be the firstborn among many brethren. 30. Moreover whom he did predestinate, them he also called: and whom he called, them he also justified: and whom he justified, them he also glorified. 33. Who shall lay any thing to the charge of God's elect?

Rom. 9:11 (For *the children* being not yet born, neither having

done any good or evil, that the purpose of God according to election might stand, not of works, but of him that calleth;) 12. It was said unto her, The elder shall serve the younger. 13. As it is written, Jacob have I loved, but Esau have I hated. 14. What shall we say then? *Is there* unrighteousness with God? God forbid. 15. For he saith to Moses, I will have mercy on whom I will have mercy, and I will have compassion on whom I will have compassion. 16. So then *it is* not of him that willeth, nor of him that runneth, but of God that sheweth mercy.

Eph. 1:4. According as he hath chosen us in him before the foundation of the world, that we should be holy and without blame before him in love: 5. Having predestinated us unto the adoption of children by Jesus Christ to himself, according to the good pleasure of his will,

Eph. 2:10. For we are his workmanship, created in Christ Jesus unto good works, which God hath before ordained that we should walk in them.

Eph. 3:11. According to the eternal purpose which he purposed in Christ Jesus our Lord:

PRIDE. I Kin. 20:11. And the king of Israel answered and said, Tell *him*, Let not him that girdeth on *his harness* boast himself as he that putteth it off.

Job 32:9. Great men are not *always* wise: neither do the aged understand judgment.

Psa. 49:11. Their inward thought *is, that* their houses *shall continue* for ever, *and* their dwelling places to all generations; they call *their* lands after their own names.

Prov. 6:16. These six *things* doth the LORD hate: yea, seven *are* an abomination unto him: 17. A proud look, . . .

Prov. 8:13. Pride, and arrogancy, . . . do I hate.

Prov. 13:10. Only by pride cometh contention:

Prov. 20:6. Most men will proclaim every one his own goodness: but a faithful man who can find?

Prov. 25:14. Whoso boasteth himself of a false gift *is like* clouds and wind without rain. 27. *For men* to search their own glory *is not* glory.

Prov. 27:2. Let another man praise thee, and not thine own mouth; a stranger, and not thine own lips.

Dan. 4:37. Now I Nebuchadnezzar praise and extol and honour the King of heaven, all whose works *are* truth, and his ways judgment: and those that walk in pride he is able to abase.

1 Cor. 8:1. Knowledge puffeth up, but charity edifieth. 2. If any man think that he knoweth anything, he knoweth nothing yet as he ought to know.

1 Cor. 10:12. Wherefore let him that thinketh he standeth take heed lest he fall.

1 Cor. 13:4. Charity vaunteth not itself, is not puffed up.

1 Tim. 3:6. Not a novice, lest being lifted up with pride he fall into the condemnation of the devil.

PRIEST. Antemosaic: Melchizedek, Gen. 14:18; Heb. 5:6,10, 11; 6:20; 7:1-21. Jethro, Ex. 2:16. Priests in Israel before the giving of the law, Ex. 19:22,24. Called angel, Eccl. 5:6.

Mosaic: Ex. 28:1-4; 29:9,44; Num. 3:10; 18:7; 1 Chr. 23:13. Hereditary descent of office, Ex. 27: 21; 28:43; 29:9. Consecration of, Ex. 29:1-9, 19-35; 40:12-16; Lev. 6: 20-23; 8:6-35; Heb. 7:21. Is holy, Lev. 21:6,7; 22:9; 16. Ablutions of, Ex. 40:30-32; Lev. 16:24; see CONSECRATION OF, above. Must be without blemish, Lev. 21:17-23. Vestments of, Ex. 28:2-43; 39:1-29; Lev. 6:10,11; 8:13; Ezek. 44:17-19. Don vestments in temple, Ezek. 42:14; 44:19. Atonement for, Lev. 16:6, 24; Ezek. 44:27. Defilement and purification of, Ezek. 44:25,26. Marriage of, Lev. 21:7-15; Ezek. 44:22. Chambers for, in temple, Ezek. 40:45,46. Exempt from tax, Ezra 7:24. Armed and organized for war at the time of the disaffection toward Saul, 1 Chr. 12:27, 28. Beard and hair of, Ezek. 44:20. Twenty-four courses of, 1 Chr.

24:1-19; 28:13,21; 2 Chr. 8:14; 31: 2; 35:4,5; Ezra 2:36-39; Neh. 13:30. Chosen by lot, Luke 1:8,9,23.

Usurpations of office of, Num. 3: 10; 16; 18:7; 2 Chr. 26:18. Priests were appointed by Jeroboam who were not of the sons of Levi, 1 Kin. 12:31; 13:33.

Duties of: To offer sacrifices, Lev. 1:4-17; 2:2,16; 3:5,11,13,16; 4:5-12,17,25,26,30-35; 1 Chr. 16:40; 2 Chr. 13:11; 29:34; 35:11-14; Ezra 6:20; Heb. 10:11; see OFFERINGS. To offer the first fruits, Lev. 23:10, 11; Deut. 26:3,4. Pronounce benedictions, Num. 6:22-27; Deut. 21:5; 2 Chr. 30:27. Teach the law, Lev. 10:11; Deut. 24:8; 27:14; 31:9-13; 33:10; Jer. 2:8; Mal. 2:7. Light the lamps in the tabernacle, Ex. 27:20, 21; 2 Chr. 13:11; Lev. 24:3,4. Keep the sacred fire always burning, Lev. 6:12,13. To furnish a quota of wood for the sanctuary, Neh. 10:34. Responsible for the sanctuary, Num. 4:5-15; 18:1,5,7. To act as scribes, Ezra 7:1-6; Neh. 8:9. Be present at and supervise the tithing, Neh. 10:38. Sound the trumpet in calling assemblies and in battle, Num. 10: 2-10; 31:6; Josh. 6; 2 Chr. 13:12. Examine lepers. Purify the unclean, Lev. 15:31. Value things devoted, Lev. 27:8,12. Officiate in the holy place, Heb. 9:6. Chiefs of Levites, Num. 3:9,32; 4:19,28,33; 1 Chr. 9:20. To act as magistrates, Num. 5:14-31; Deut. 17:8-13; 19: 17; 21:5; 2 Chr. 19:8; Ezek. 44:23, 24. To encourage the army on the eve of battle, Deut. 20:2-4. Bear the ark through the Jordan, Josh. 3; 4:15-18; in battle, 1 Sam. 4:3-5.

Emoluments of: No part of the land of Canaan allowed to, Num. 18:20; Deut. 10:9; 14:27; 18: 1,2; Josh. 13:14,33; 14:3; 18:7; Ezek. 44:28. Provided with cities and suburbs, Lev. 25:32-34; Num. 35:2-8; Josh. 21:1-4,13-19,41,42; 1 Chr. 6:57-60; Neh. 11:3,20; Ezek. 45:1-6; 48:8-20. Own lands sanctified to the Lord, Lev. 27:21. Tithes of the tithes, Num. 18:8-18, 26-32; Neh. 10:38. Part of the spoils of war, including captives, Num. 31:25-29. Firstfruits, Lev. 23: 20; 24:9; Num. 18:12,13,17,18;

Deut. 18:3-5; Neh. 10:36. Redemption money, Lev. 27:23; of firstborn, Num. 3:46-51; 18:15,16. Things devoted, Lev. 27:21; Num. 5:9,10; 18:14. Fines, Lev. 5:16; 22:14; Num. 5:8. Trespass money and other trespass offerings, Lev. 5:15, 18; Num. 5:5-10; 18:9; 2 Kin. 12: 16. The shewbread, Ex. 25:30; Lev. 24:5-9; 2 Chr. 2:4; 13:11; Neh. 10: 33; Matt. 12:4; Heb. 9:2. Portions of sacrifices and offerings, Ex. 29: 27-34; Lev. 2:2,3,9,10; 5:12,13,16; 6:15-18,26; 7:6-10,31-34; 10:12-14; 14:12,13; Num. 6:19,20; 18:8-19; Deut. 18:3-5; 1 Sam. 2:13,14; Ezek. 44:28-31; 45:1-4; 1 Cor. 9:13; 10: 18.

Regulations by Hezekiah concerning emoluments, 2 Chr. 31:4-19. Portion of land allotted to, in redistribution in Ezekiel's vision, Ezek. 48:8-14. For sustenance of their families, Lev. 22:11-13; Num. 18: 11,19.

Figurative: Ex. 19:6; Isa. 61:6; 1 Pet. 2:9; Rev. 1:6; 5:10; 20:6.

High Priest: Moses did not denominate Aaron chief or high priest. The function he served was superior to that of other priests. The title appears after the institution of the office, Lev. 21:10-15; Num. 3:32.

Vestments of, Ex. 28:2-43; 39:1-31; Lev. 8:7-9. Respect due to, Acts 23:5.

DUTIES OF: Had charge of the sanctuary and altar, Num. 18:2,5,7. To offer sacrifices, Heb. 5:1; 8:3. To designate subordinate priests for duty, Num. 4:19; 1 Sam. 2:36. To officiate in consecrations of Levites, Num. 8:11-21. To have charge of the treasury, 2 Kin. 12:10; 22:4; 2 Chr. 24:6-14; 34:9. To light the lamps of tabernacle, Ex. 27:20,21; 30:8; Lev. 24:3,4; Num. 8:3. To burn incense, Ex. 30:7,8; 1 Sam. 2:28; 1 Chr. 23:13. To place shewbread on the table every Sabbath, Lev. 24:8. To offer for his own sins of ignorance, Lev. 4:3-12.

On the Day of Atonement, Ex. 30:10; Lev. 16; Heb. 5:3; 9:7,22,23.

Judicial, Num. 5:15; Deut. 17:8-13; 1 Sam. 4:18; Hos. 4:4; Matt. 26:3,50,57,62; Acts 5:21-28; 23:1-5.

To number the people, Num. 1:3. Officiate at choice of ruler, Num. 27:18,19,21. Distribute spoils of war, Num. 31:26-29.

A second priest, under the high priest, Num. 3:32; 4:16; 31:6; 1 Chr. 9:20; 2 Sam. 15:24; 2 Kin. 25: 18; Luke 3:2.

Miscellaneous Facts Concerning: Loyal to Rehoboam at the time of the revolt of the ten tribes, 2 Chr. 11:13. Zeal of, in purging the temple, 2 Chr. 29:4-17. Wickedness of, 2 Chr. 36:14. Taken with the captivity to Babylon, Jer. 29:1. Return from the captivity, Ezra 1:5; 2:36-39,61,70; 3:8; 7:7; 8:24-30; Neh. 7:39-42, 63-73; 10:1-8; 12:1-7. Polluted by marrying idolatrous wives, Ezra 9:1,2; 10:5, 18,19; Neh. 10:28. Restore the altar, and offer sacrifices, Ezra 3:1-7. Supervise the building of the temple, Ezra 3:8-13. Inquire of John the Baptist whether he were the Christ, John 1:19. Conspire to destroy Jesus, Matt. 26:3-5,14,15,47, 51; Mark 14:10,11,43-47, 53-66; 15: 1; Luke 22:1-6,50,54,66-71; 23:1,2; John 11:47; 19:15,16,18. Try and condemn Jesus, Matt. 26:57-68; 27: 1,2; Mark 14:53-65; Luke 22:54-71; 23:13-24; John 18:15-32. Incite the people to ask that Barabbas be released and Jesus destroyed, Matt. 27:20; Mark 15:11; Luke 23:18. Persecute the disciples, Acts 22:5. Reprove and threaten Peter and John, Acts 4:6-21; 5:17-41. Try, condemn, and stone Stephen, Acts 6:12-15; 7. Paul brought before, Acts 22:30, 23:1-5. Many converts among, Acts 6:7.

Corrupt, Jer. 23:11,12; Ezek. 22: 26; Luke 10:31. INSTANCES OF: Eli's sons, 1 Sam. 2:12-17,22; of the captivity, Ezra 9:1,2; 10:18-22; Neh. 13:4-9,13,28,29.

PROCRASTINATION. Ex. 22:29. Thou shalt not delay *to offer* the first of thy ripe fruits, and of thy liquors; the firstborn of thy sons shalt thou give unto me.

Prov. 27:1. Boast not thyself of to morrow; for thou knowest not what a day may bring forth.

Acts 24:25. And as he reasoned

211

of righteousness, temperance, and judgment to come, Felix trembled, and answered, Go thy way for this time; when I have a convenient season, I will call for thee.

Heb. 3:7. Wherefore (as the Holy Ghost saith, To day if ye will hear his voice, 8. Harden not your hearts, as in the provocation, in the day of temptation in the wilderness:

Instances of: Pharaoh, Ex. 8: 10. Elisha, 1 Kin. 19:20,21. Esther, Esth. 5:8.

PRODIGAL SON, Luke 15:11-32.

PROGNOSTICATION, by astrologers, Isa. 47:13.

PROHIBITION, of the use of intoxicating liquors. To priests on duty, Lev. 10:9. To Nazarites, Num. 6:3,4.

PROPERTY. In Real Estate: Gen. 23:17,18; 26:20. Rights in, violated, Gen. 21:25-30; 26:18-22. Dedicated, Lev. 27:16-25.

Dwellings. Alienated for debt, Lev. 25:29,30; by absence, 2 Kin. 8:1-6; in villages, inalienable, Lev. 25:31-33. Dedicated, Lev. 27:14, 15.

Confiscation of (Naboth's vineyard), 1 Kin. 21:15,16. Priests exempt from taxes, Gen. 47:22. Entail of, Num. 27:1-11; 36:1-9. Inherited, Eccl. 2:21. Landmarks of, not to be removed, Deut. 19:14; 27: 17.

Personal: Rights in, sacred, Ex. 20:17; Deut. 5:21. Laws concerning trespass of, and violence to, Ex. 21:28-36; 22:9; Deut. 23:25. Strayed, to be returned to owner, Lev. 6:3,4; Deut. 22:1-3. Hired, Ex. 22:14,15; or loaned, Ex. 22: 10-15. Sold for debt, Prov. 22:26-27; rights of redemption of, Jer. 32: 7. Dedicated to God, redemption of, Lev. 27:9-13, 26-33. In slaves, Ex. 21:4.

PROPHECY. Proof of God's foreknowledge, Isa. 43:9. Sure fulfillment of, Ezek. 12:22-25,28; Hab. 2:3; Matt. 5:18; 24:35; Acts 13:27, 29. Cessation of, Lam. 2:9.

Miscellaneous, Fulfilled: The

birth and zeal of Josiah, 1 Kin. 13: 2; 2 Kin. 23:1-20. Death of the prophet of Judah, 1 Kin. 13:21,22, 24-30. Extinction of Jeroboam's house, 1 Kin. 14:5-17; of Baasha's house, 1 Kin. 16:2,3,9-13. Concerning the rebuilding of Jericho, Josh. 6:26; 1 Kin. 16:34. The drought, foretold by Elijah, 1 Kin. 17:14. Destruction of Ben-hadad's army, 1 Kin. 20:13-30. Of a man who refused to smite a prophet, 1 Kin. 20:35,36. The death of Ahab, 1 Kin. 20:42; 21:18-24; 22:31-38. The death of Ahaziah, 2 Kin. 1:3-17. Elijah's translation, 2 Kin. 2:3-11. Cannibalism among the children of Israel, Lev. 26:29; Deut. 28:53; 2 Kin. 6:28,29; Jer. 19:9; Lam. 4:10. The death of the Samaritan lord, 2 Kin. 7:2,19,20. The end of the famine in Samaria, 2 Kin. 7:1-18. Jezebel's tragic death, 1 Kin. 21:23; 2 Kin. 9:10,33-37. The smiting of Syria by Joash, 2 Kin. 13:16-25. Conquests of Jeroboam, 2 Kin. 14:25-28. Four generations of Jehu to sit upon the throne of Israel, 2 Kin. 10:30, with 2 Kin. 15:12. Destruction of Sennacherib's army, and his death, 2 Kin. 19:6,7,20-37. The captivity of Judah, 2 Kin. 20:17,18; 24:10-16; 25:11-21. Concerning Christ, see JESUS, PROPHECIES CONCERNING. Also see above. Concerning John, Matt. 3:3. Rachel weeping for her children, Jer. 31:15; Matt. 2:17,18. Deliverance of Jeremiah, Jer. 39:15-18. Invasion of Judah by the Chaldeans, Hab. 1:6-11; fulfilled, 2 Kin. 25; 2 Chr. 36:17-21. Betrayal of Jesus by Judas, prophecy, Psa. 41:9; fulfillment, John 13:18; 18:1-9. Judas' self-destruction, Psa. 69:25; Acts 1:16,20; fulfilled, Matt. 27:5; Acts 1:16-20. Outpouring of the Holy Spirit, Joel 2:28,29; fulfilled, Acts 2:16-21. Spiritual blindness of the Jews, Isa. 6:9; 29:13; fulfilled, Mark 7:6,7; Acts 28:25-27. Mission of Jesus, Psa. 68:18; fulfilled, Eph. 4:8,10; see JESUS, MISSION OF. Captivity of the Jews, Jer. 25:11,12; 29:10,14; 32:3-5; Dan. 9:2, with 2 Kin. 25:1-8; Ezra 1. Of the destruction of the ship in which Paul sailed, Acts 27:10,18-44.

PROPHETS. Inspiration of:
Gen. 40:8. And they said unto him, We have dreamed a dream, and *there is* no interpreter of it. And Joseph said unto them, *Do* not interpretations *belong* to God? tell me *them,* I pray you.

Ex. 4:12. Now therefore go, and I will be with thy mouth, and teach thee what thou shalt say. 15. And thou shalt speak unto him, and put words in his mouth: and I will be with thy mouth, and with his mouth, and will teach you what ye shall do.

Ex. 25:22. And there I will meet with thee, and I will commune with thee from above the mercy seat, from between the two cherubims which *are* upon the ark of the testimony, of all *things* which I will give thee in commandment unto the children of Israel.

Ex. 33:9. *The* LORD talked with Moses. 11. And the LORD spake unto Moses face to face, as a man speaketh unto his friend.

Ex. 35:31. And he hath filled him with the spirit of God, in wisdom, in understanding, and in knowledge, and in all manner of workmanship; *v.* 35.

Num. 23:5. And the LORD put a word in Balaam's mouth, and said, Return unto Balak, and thus thou shalt speak. 12. And he answered and said, Must I not take heed to speak that which the LORD hath put in my mouth? 20. Behold, I have received *commandment* to bless: and he hath blessed; and I cannot reverse it. 26. Told not I thee, saying, All that the LORD speaketh, that I must do?

1 Sam. 16:13. And the Spirit of the LORD came upon David from that day forward.

2 Sam. 7:4. And it came to pass that night, that the word of the LORD came unto Nathan, saying, *vss.* 3-7; 2 Sam. 12:1.

2 Sam. 23:2. The Spirit of the LORD spake by me, a his word *was* in my tongue.

Ezek. 8:1. And it came to pass in the sixth year, in the sixth *month,* in the fifth *day* of the month, *as* I sat in mine house, and the elders of Judah sat before me, that the hand of the Lord GOD fell there upon me.

Amos. 3:7. Surely the Lord GOD will do nothing, but he revealeth his secret unto his servants the prophets. 8. The lion hath roared, who will not fear? the Lord GOD hath spoken, who can but prophesy?

Acts 3:18. Those things, which God before had shewed by the mouth of all his prophets, that Christ should suffer, he hath so fulfilled.

Acts 11:28. And there stood up one of them named Agabus, and signified by the spirit that there should be great dearth throughout all the world:

1 Cor. 14:32. The spirits of the prophets are subject to the prophets.

Heb. 1:1. God, who at sundry times and in divers manners spake in time past unto the fathers by the prophets,

2 Pet. 1:21. The prophecy came not in old time by the will of man: but holy men of God spake *as they were* moved by the Holy Ghost.

Jude 14. Enoch also, the seventh from Adam, prophesied of these, saying, Behold, the Lord cometh with ten thousands of his saints,

PROUD. See PRIDE.

PROVERBS. Miscellany of:
1 Kin. 20:11. And the king of Israel answered and said, Tell *him,* Let not him that girdeth on *his harness* boast himself as he that putteth it off.

Prov. 1:17. Surely in vain the net is spread in the sight of any bird.

Ezek. 16:44. Behold, every one that useth proverbs shall use *this* proverb against thee, saying, As *is* the mother, *so is* her daughter.

Hos. 4:9. And there shall be, like people, like priest:

Matt. 12:33. The tree is known by *his* fruit. Luke 6:44.

Luke 4:23. And he said unto them, Ye will surely say unto me this [proverb,] Physician, heal thyself: [R. V. parable]

213

Gal. 6:7. Whatsoever a man soweth, that shall he also reap.

PRUDENCE. Psa. 39:1. I said, I will take heed to my ways, that I sin not with my tongue: I will keep my mouth with a bridle, while the wicked is before me.

Psa. 112:5. He will guide his affairs with discretion.

Prov. 6:1. My son, if thou be surety for thy friend, *if* thou hast stricken thy hand with a stranger, 2. Thou art snared with the words of thy mouth, thou art taken with the words of thy mouth.

Prov. 15:5. He that regardeth reproof is prudent.

Prov. 22:3. A prudent *man* forseeth the evil, and hideth himself: but the simple pass on, and are punished.

Prov. 24:6. By wise counsel thou shalt make thy war: and in multitude of counsellors *there is safety.* 27. Prepare thy work without, and make it fit for thyself in the field; and afterwards build thine house.

Luke 14:28. Which of you, intending to build a tower, sitteth not down first, and counteth the cost, whether he have *sufficient* to finish *it?*

PSALMS. Afflictions: Psalm 3, 4, 5, 7, 11, 13, 16, 17, 22, 26, 27, 28, 31, 35, 41, 42, 43, 44, 54, 55, 56, 57, 59, 60, 61, 62, 63, 64, 69, 70, 71, 74, 77, 79, 80, 83, 84, 86, 88, 89, 94, 102, 109, 120, 123, 129, 137, 140, 141, 142, 143.

Didactic: Psalm 1, 5, 7, 9, 10, 11, 12, 14, 15, 17, 24, 25, 32, 34, 36, 37, 39, 49, 50, 52, 53, 58, 73, 75, 82, 84, 90, 91, 92, 94, 101, 112, 119, 121, 125, 127, 128, 131, 133.

Historical: Psalm 78, 105, 106.

Intercessional: Psalm 20, 67, 122, 132, 144.

Penitential: Psalm 6, 25, 32, 38, 51, 102, 130, 143.

Praise: For God's Attributes: Psalm 8, 19, 24, 29, 33, 47, 50, 65, 66, 76, 77, 93, 95, 96, 97, 99, 104, 111, 113, 114, 115, 134, 139, 147, 148, 150.

Prophetic: Psalm 2, 16, 22, 40, 45, 68, 69, 72, 87, 97, 110, 118.

Thanksgiving: For God's Goodness to Israel. Psalm 21, 46, 48, 65, 66, 68, 76, 81, 85, 98, 105, 124, 126, 129, 135, 136, 149.

For God's Goodness to Good Men: Psalm 23, 34, 36, 91, 100, 103, 107, 117, 121, 145, 146.

For God's Mercies to Individuals: Psalm 9, 18, 30, 34, 40, 75, 103, 108, 116, 118, 138, 144.

PUBLICANS, Roman tax collectors. Disreputable, Matt. 5:46, 47; 9:11; 11:19; 18:17; 21:31; Luke 18:11. Repent under the preaching of John the Baptist, Matt. 21:32; Luke 3:12; 7:29. Matthew, the collector of Capernaum, becomes an apostle, Matt. 9:9; 10:3; Mark 2: 14; Luke 5:27. Parable concerning, Luke 18:9-14. Zacchæus, chief among, receives Jesus into his house, Luke 19:2-10.

PUNISHMENT. Death Penalty: Shall not be remitted, Num. 35:31. In the Mosaic law the death penalty was inflicted for murder, Gen. 9:5,6; Num. 35:16-21, 30-33; Deut. 17:6; adultery, Lev. 20:10; Deut. 22:24; incest, Lev. 20: 11,12,14; bestiality, Lev. 22:19; Lev. 20:15,16; sodomy, Lev. 18:22; 20: 13; incontinence, Deut. 22:21-24; rape of a betrothed virgin, Deut. 22:25; perjury, Zech. 5:4; kidnapping, Ex. 21:16; Deut. 24:7; upon a priest's daughter, who committed fornication, Lev. 21:9; for witchcraft, Ex. 22:18; offering human sacrifice, Lev. 20:2-5; for striking or cursing father or mother, Ex. 21: 15,17; Lev. 20:9; disobedience to parents, Deut. 21:18-21; theft, Zech. 5:3,4; blasphemy, Lev. 24:11-14,16, 23; for Sabbath desecration, Ex. 35: 2; Num. 15:32-36; for prophesying falsely, or propagating false doctrines, Deut. 13:1-10; sacrificing to false gods, Ex. 22:20; refusing to abide by the decision of court, Deut. 17:12; for treason, 1 Kin. 2:25; Esth. 2:23; sedition, Acts 5:36,37.

Modes of Execution of Death Penalty: Burning, Gen. 38:24; Lev. 20:14; 21:9; Jer. 29:22; Ezek. 23: 25; Dan. 3:19-23; stoning, Lev. 20: 2,27; 24:14; Num. 14:10; 15:33-36; Deut. 13:10; 17:5; 22:21,24: Josh. 7:25; 1 Kin. 21:10; Ezek. 16:40;

hanging, Gen. 40:22; Deut. 21:22, 23; Josh. 8:29; beheading, Matt. 14: 10; Mark 6:16,27,28; crucifixion, Matt. 27:35,38; Mark 15:24,27; Luke 23:33; the sword, Ex. 32:27, 28; 1 Kin. 2:25,34,46; Acts 12:2.

Executed by the witnesses, Deut. 13:9; 17:7; Acts 7:58; by the congregation, Num. 15:35,36; Deut. 13:9.

Not inflicted on testimony of less than two witnesses, Num. 35:30; Deut. 17:6; 19:15.

Minor Offenses: Punishable by scourging, Lev. 19:20; Deut. 22: 18; 25:2,3; Prov. 17:10; 19:29; 20:30; Matt. 27:26; Mark 15:15; Luke 23:16; John 19:1; Acts 22: 24,29; imprisonment, Gen. 39:20; 40. Confinement within limits, 1 Kin. 2:26,36-38.

Eternal: Dan. 12:2. And many of them that sleep in the dust of the earth shall awake, some to everlasting life, and some to shame and everlasting contempt.

John 5:29. And shall come forth; they that have done good, unto the resurrection of life; and they that have done evil, unto the resurrection of damnation.

Rev. 20:10. The devil that deceived them was cast into the lake of fire and brimstone, where the beast and the false prophet are, and shall be tormented day and night for ever and ever.

See WICKED, PUNISHMENT OF.

PURITY. Of Heart: Psa. 19: 8. The statutes of the LORD are right, rejoicing the heart: the commandment of the LORD is pure, enlightening the eyes. Psa. 12:6.

Psa. 24:3. Who shall ascend into the hill of the LORD? or who shall stand in his holy place? 4. He that hath clean hands, and a pure heart; who hath not lifted up his soul unto vanity, nor sworn deceitfully. 5. He shall receive the blessing from the LORD, and righteousness from the God of his salvation.

Psa. 65:3. Our transgressions, thou shalt purge them away.

Isa. 1:18. Though your sins be as scarlet, they shall be as white as snow; though they be red like crimson, they shall be as wool.

Matt. 5:8. Blessed are the pure in heart: for they shall see God.

2 Tim. 2:21. If a man therefore purge himself from these, he shall be a vessel unto honour, sanctified, and meet for the master's use, and prepared unto every good work. 22. Flee also youthful lusts: but follow righteousness, faith, charity, peace, with them that call on the Lord out of a pure heart.

RASHNESS. Prov. 14:29. He that is slow to wrath is of great understanding: but he that is hasty of spirit exalteth folly.

Prov. 21:5. The thoughts of the diligent tend only to plenteousness; but of every one that is hasty only to want.

Eccl. 5:2. Be not rash with thy mouth, and let not thine heart be hasty to utter any thing before God: for God is in heaven, and thou upon earth: therefore let thy words be few.

Instances of: Moses, in slaying the Egyptian, Ex. 2:11,12; Acts 7:24,25. When he smote the rock, Num. 20:10-12. Jephtha's vow, Judg. 11:31-39. Israel's vow to destroy the Benjamites, Judg. 21: 1-23. Uzzah, in steadying the ark, 2 Sam. 6:6,7. David, in his generosity to Ziba, 2 Sam. 16:4; with chap. 19:26-29. Rehoboam, in forsaking the counsel of the old men, 1 Kin. 12:8-15. Josiah, in fighting against Necho, 2 Chr. 35:20-24. Naaman, in refusing to wash in Jordan, 2 Kin. 5:11,12. James and John, in desiring to call down fire on the Samaritans, Luke 9:54. Paul, in persisting in going to Jerusalem, against the repeated admonitions of the Holy Ghost, Acts 21:4,10-15. The centurion, in rejecting Paul's counsel, Acts 27:11.

REAPING, Psa. 129:7. The ark of the Lord returned by the Philistines at the time of, 1 Sam. 6:13.

Figurative: Psa. 126:6; Hos. 10:12,13.

REASONING. With God, Job 13:3, 17-28. God reasons with men, Ex. 4:11; 20:5,11; Isa. 1:18; 5:3,4; 43:26; Hos. 4:1; Mic. 6:2.

Natural understanding, Dan. 4:

36. To be applied to religion, 1 Cor. 10:15; 1 Pet. 3:15. Not a sufficient guide in human affairs, Deut. 12:8; Prov. 3:5; 14:12. Of the Pharisees, Luke 5:21,22; 20:5. Of Paul from the Scriptures, Acts 17:2; 18:4,19; 24:25. The gospel cannot be explained by, 1 Cor. 1:18-28; 2:1-14.

REBELLION, treasonable, Prov. 17:11.

Instances of: Absalom, 2 Sam. chapters 15-18. Sheba, 2 Sam. 20. Revolt of the ten tribes, 1 Kin. 12:16-20; 2 Chr. 10; 13:5-12. See SIN.

RECONCILIATION. Between man and man, Matt. 5:23-26. Of Esau and Jacob, Gen. 33:4,11. Between Pilate and Herod, Luke 23:12.

Between God and Man: Lev. 8:15. And he slew *it;* and Moses took the blood, and put *it* upon the horns of the altar round about with his finger, and purified the altar, and poured the blood at the bottom of the altar, and sanctified it, to make reconciliation [*R. V.,* atonement] upon it.

Dan. 9:24. Seventy weeks are determined upon thy people and upon thy holy city, to finish the transgression, and to make an end of sins, and to make reconciliation for iniquity, and to bring in everlasting righteousness, and to seal up the vision and prophecy, and to anoint the Most Holy.

Rom. 5:1. Therefore being justified by faith, [we] have peace with God through our Lord Jesus Christ: 10. For if, when we were enemies, we were reconciled to God by the death of his Son; much more, being reconciled, we shall be saved by his life. [R. V. let us]

Eph. 2:15. Having abolished in his flesh the enmity, *even* the law of commandments *contained* in ordinances; for to make in himself of twain one new man, *so* making peace; 16. And that he might reconcile both unto God in one body by the cross, having slain the enmity thereby; 17. And came and preached peace to you which were afar off, and to them that were nigh. 18. For through him we both

have access by one Spirit unto the Father.

RECREATION, Jesus takes, from the fatigues of his ministry, Mark 6:31,32; 7:24.

REDEMPTION. Of Our Souls: Psa. 130:7. Let Israel hope in the LORD: for with the LORD *there is* mercy, and with him *is* plenteous redemption.

Matt. 20:28. Even as the Son of man came not to be ministered unto, but to minister, and to give his life a ransom for many. Mark 10:45.

Luke 2:38. And she coming in that instant gave thanks likewise unto the Lord, and spake of him to all them that looked for redemption in Jerusalem.

Eph. 1:7. In whom we have redemption through his blood, the forgiveness of sins, according to the riches of his grace;

REGENERATION. 1 Kin. 8:58. That he may incline our hearts unto him, to walk in all ways, and to keep his commandments, and his statutes, and his judgments, which he commanded our fathers.

Psa. 51:2. Wash me throughly from mine iniquity, and cleanse me from my sin. 7. Purge me with hyssop, and I shall be clean: wash me, and I shall be whiter than snow. 10. Create in me a clean heart, O God; and renew a right spirit within me.

Psa. 65:3. *As for* our transgressions, thou shalt purge them away.

Isa. 49:9. That thou mayest say to the prisoners, Go forth; to them that *are* in darkness, Shew yourselves.

Matt. 18:3. Except ye be converted, and become as little children, ye shall not enter into the kingdom of heaven. Mark 10:15; Luke 18:17.

John 1:4. In him was life; and the life was the light of men. 13. Which were born, not of blood, nor of the will of the flesh, nor of the will of man, but of God. 16. And of his fulness have all we received, and grace for grace.

John 5:24. He that heareth my word, and believeth on him that sent me, hath everlasting life, and shall not come into condemnation; but is passed from death unto life.

1 Cor. 6:11. But ye are washed, but ye are sanctified, but ye are justified in the name of the Lord Jesus, and by the Spirit of our God.

Tit. 3:5. Not by works of righteousness which we have done, but according to his mercy he saved us, by the washing of regeneration, and renewing of the Holy Ghost; 6. Which he shed on us abundantly through Jesus Christ our Saviour;

RELIGION. False: Deut. 32:31-33.

Natural: Job 12:7. But ask now the beasts, and they shall teach thee; and the fowls of the air, and they shall tell thee: 8. Or speak to the earth, and it shall teach thee; and the fishes of the sea shall declare unto thee. 9. Who knoweth not in all these that the hand of the Lord hath wrought this?

Psa. 19:1. The heavens declare the glory of God; and the firmament sheweth his handywork. 2. Day unto day uttereth speech, and night unto night sheweth knowledge. 3. There is no speech nor language, where their voice is not heard.

Acts 14:17. Nevertheless he left not himself without witness, in that he did good, and gave us rain from heaven, and fruitful seasons, filling our hearts with food and gladness.

Rom. 1:19. Because that which may be known of God is manifest in them; for God hath shewed it unto them. 20. For the invisible things of him from the creation of the world are clearly seen, being understood by the things that are made, even his eternal power and Godhead; so that they are without excuse:

True: Acts 10:34. Then Peter opened his mouth, and said, Of a truth I perceive that God is no respecter of persons: 35. But in every nation he that feareth him, and worketh righteousness, is accepted with him.

Rom. 8:1. There is therefore now no condemnation to them which are in Christ Jesus, who walk not after the flesh, but after the Spirit.

Rom. 12:1. I beseech you therefore, brethren, by the mercies of God, that ye present your bodies a living sacrifice, holy, acceptable unto God, which is your reasonable service. 2. And be not conformed to this world: but be ye transformed by the renewing of your mind, that ye may prove what is that good, and acceptable, and perfect, will of God.

Jas. 1:27. Pure religion and undefiled before God and the Father is this, To visit the fatherless and widows in their affliction, and to keep himself unspotted from the world.

REMORSE. Psa. 31:10. My life is spent with grief, and my years with sighing: my strength faileth because of mine iniquity, and my bones are consumed.

Psa. 38:2. Thine arrows stick fast in me, and thy hand presseth me sore. 3. There is no soundness in my flesh because of thine anger; neither is there any rest in my bones because of my sin. 4. For mine iniquities are gone over mine head: as an heavy burden they are too heavy for me. 5. My wounds stink and are corrupt because of my foolishness. 6. I am troubled; I am bowed down greatly; I go mourning all the day long.

Psa. 51:17. The sacrifices of God are a broken spirit: a broken and a contrite heart, O God, thou wilt not despise.

Prov. 28:1. The wicked flee when no man pursueth:

Isa. 6:5. Then said I, Woe is me! for I am undone; because I am a man of unclean lips, and I dwell in the midst of a people of unclean lips: for mine eyes have seen the King, the Lord of hosts.

Isa. 57:20. The wicked are like the troubled sea, when it cannot rest, whose waters cast up mire and dirt. 21. There is no peace, saith my God, to the wicked. Isa. 48:22.

Luke 13:28. There shall be weeping and gnashing of teeth, when ye shall see Abraham, and Isaac, and Jacob, and all the prophets, in the kingdom of God, and you yourselves thrust out.

Acts 2:37. Now when they heard

this, they were pricked in their heart, and said unto Peter and to the rest of the apostles, Men *and* brethren, what shall we do?

Instances of: David, Psa. 51. Peter, Matt. 26:75. Judas, Matt. 27:3-5.

REPENTANCE. 2 Chr. 7:14. If my people, which are called by my name, shall humble themselves, and pray, and seek my face, and turn from their wicked ways; then will I hear from heaven, and will forgive their sin, and will heal their land. 2 Chr. 6:36-39.

Neh. 1:9. *If* ye turn unto me, and keep my commandments, and do them; though there were of you cast out unto the uttermost part of the heaven, *yet* will I gather them from thence, and will bring them unto the place that I have chosen to set my name there.

Job 33:26. He shall pray unto God, and he will be favourable unto him: and he shall see his face with joy: for he will render unto man his righteousness. 27. He looketh upon men, and *if any* say, I have sinned, and perverted *that which was* right, and it profited me not; 28. He will deliver his soul from going into the pit, and his life shall see the light.

Job 34:31. Surely it is meet to be said unto God, I have borne *chastisement,* I will not offend *any more:* 32. *That which* I see not teach thou me: if I have done iniquity, I will do no more.

Job 36:10. He openeth also their ear to discipline, and commandeth that they return from iniquity.

Psa. 22:27. All the ends of the world shall remember, and turn unto the LORD:

Psa. 34:14. Depart from evil, and do good; seek peace, and pursue it. 18. The LORD *is* nigh unto them that are of a broken heart; and saveth such as be of a contrite spirit.

Psa. 51:17. The sacrifices of God *are* a broken spirit: a broken and a contrite heart, O God, thou wilt not despise.

Prov. 1:22. How long, ye simple ones, will ye love simplicity? and the scorners delight in their scorning, and fools hate knowledge? 23. Turn you at my reproof: behold, I will pour out my spirit unto you, I will make known my words unto you.

Prov. 28:13. He that covereth his sins shall not prosper: but whoso confesseth and forsaketh *them* shall have mercy.

Isa. 55:6. Seek ye the LORD while he may be found, call ye upon him while he is near: 7. Let the wicked forsake his way, and the unrighteous man his thoughts: and let him return unto the LORD, and he will have mercy upon him; and to our God, for he will abundantly pardon.

Luke 5:32. I came not to call the righteous, but sinners to repentance.

Luke 15:7. I say unto you, that likewise joy shall be in heaven over one sinner that repenteth, more than over ninety and nine just persons, which need no repentance, *vss.* 1-10.

Luke 24:47. And that repentance and remission of sins should be preached in his name among all nations, beginning at Jerusalem.

Acts 3:19. Repent ye therefore, and be converted, that your sins may be blotted out when the times of refreshing shall come from the presence of the LORD;

1 John 1:9. If we confess our sins, he is faithful and just to forgive us *our* sins, and to cleanse us from all unrighteousness.

REPROBACY. Gen. 19:13. For we will destroy this place, because the cry of them is waxen great before the face of the LORD; and the LORD hath sent us to destroy it.

Deut. 28:20. The LORD shall send upon thee cursing, vexation, and rebuke, in all that thou settest thine hand unto for to do, until thou be destroyed, and until thou perish quickly; because of the wickedness of thy doings, whereby thou hast forsaken me.

Psa. 81:11. But my people would not hearken to my voice; and Israel would none of me. 12. So I gave them up unto their own hearts' lust: *and* they walked in their own counsels.

Jer. 6:30. Reprobate silver shall *men* call them, because the LORD hath rejected them.

Jer. 7:16. Therefore pray not thou for this people, neither lift up cry nor prayer for them, neither make intercession to me: for I will not hear thee.

Jer. 15:1. Then said the LORD unto me, Though Moses and Samuel stood before me, *yet* my mind *could* not *be* toward this people: cast *them* out of my sight, and let them go forth.

Hos. 5:6. They shall go with their flocks and with their herds to seek the LORD; but they shall not find *him;* he hath withdrawn himself from them.

Luke 14:24. For I say unto you, That none of those men which were bidden shall taste of my supper.

John 10:26. But ye believe not, because ye are not of my sheep, as I said unto you.

1 John 5:16. If any man see his brother sin a sin *which is* not unto death, he shall ask, and he shall give him life for them that sin not unto death. There is a sin unto death: I do not say that he shall pray for it.

REPROOF. Psa. 141:5. Let the righteous smite me; *it shall be* a kindness: and let him reprove me; *it shall be* a excellent oil, *which* shall not break my head:

Prov. 12:1. Whoso loveth instruction loveth knowledge: but he that hateth reproof *is* brutish.

Prov. 17:10. A reproof entereth more into a wise man than an hundred stripes into a fool.

Prov. 25:12. *As* an earring of gold, and an ornament of fine gold, *so is* a wise reprover upon an obedient ear.

Prov. 27:5. Open rebuke *is* better than secret love. 6. Faithful *are* the wounds of a friend;

Prov. 28:23. He that rebuketh a man afterwards shall find more favour than he that flattereth with the tongue.

REPUTATION, Good: Prov. 22:1; Eccl. 7:1.

RESIGNATION. Job 5:17. Behold, happy *is* the man whom God correcteth: therefore despise not thou the chastening of the Almighty:

Job 34:31. Surely it is meet to be said unto God, I have borne *chastisement,* I will not offend *any more:*

Prov. 3:11. My son, despise not the chastening of the LORD; neither be weary of his correction:

Exemplified: 1 Sam. 3:18. And Samuel told him every whit, and hid nothing from him. And he said, It *is* the LORD: let him do what seemeth him good.

Psa. 39:9. I was dumb, I opened not my mouth; because thou didst *it.*

Acts 21:14. When he would not be persuaded, we ceased, saying, The will of the Lord be done.

2 Cor. 7:4. I am filled with comfort, I am exceeding joyful in all our tribulation.

RESPONSIBILITY. According to Privilege: Matt. 11:20. Then began he to upbraid the cities wherein most of his mighty works were done, because they repented not: 21. Woe unto thee, Chorazin! woe unto thee, Bethsaida! for if the mighty works, which were done in you, had been done in Tyre and Sidon, they would have repented long ago in sackcloth and ashes.

Matt. 12:41. The men of Nineveh shall rise in judgment with this generation, and shall condemn it: because they repented at the preaching of Jonas; and, behold, a greater than Jonas *is* here. 42. The queen of the south shall rise up in the judgment with this generation, and shall condemn it: for she came from the uttermost parts of the earth to hear the wisdom of Solomon; and, behold, a greater than Solomon *is* here. Luke 11:31,32.

Luke 21:1. And he looked up, and saw the rich men casting their gifts into the treasury. 2. And he saw also a certain poor widow casting in thither two mites. 3. And he said, Of a truth I say unto you, that this poor widow hath cast in more than they all: 4. For all these have of their abundance cast in unto the offerings of God: but she of her penury hath cast in all the living that she had.

John 15:22. If I had not come and spoken unto them, they had not had sin: but now they have no cloke for their sin. 24. If I had not done among them the works which none other man did, they had not had sin: but now have they both seen and hated both me and my Father.

RESURRECTION. Psa. 16:9. Therefore my heart is glad, and my glory rejoiceth: my flesh also shall rest in hope. 10. For thou wilt not leave my soul in hell; neither wilt thou suffer thine Holy One to see corruption.

Psa. 17:15. As for me, I will behold thy face in righteousness: I shall be satisfied, when I awake, with thy likeness.

Psa. 49:15. God will redeem my soul from the power of the grave: for he shall receive me.

Isa. 25:8. He will swallow up death [in victory;] and the Lord God will wipe away tears from off all faces; [R. V. for ever]

Dan. 12:2. Many of them that sleep in the dust of the earth shall awake, some to everlasting life, and some to shame *and* everlasting contempt. 3. And they that be wise shall shine as the brightness of the firmament; and they that turn many to righteousness as the stars for ever and ever.

Matt. 24:31. And he shall send his angels with a great sound of a trumpet, and they shall gather together his elect from the four winds, from one end of heaven to the other.

Luke 14:14. And thou shalt be blessed; for they cannot recompense thee: for thou shalt be recompensed at the resurrection of the just.

Acts 17:18. He preached unto them Jesus, and the resurrection. 32. When they heard of the resurrection of the dead, some mocked: and others said, We will hear thee again of this *matter.*

1 Cor. 6:14. God hath both raised up the Lord, and will also raise up us by his own power.

Typified: Isaac, Gen. 22:13, with Heb. 11:19. Jonah, Jonah 2: 10, with Matt. 12:40.

RETALIATION. Lev. 19:18. Thou shalt not avenge, nor bear any grudge against the children of thy people, but thou shalt love thy neighbour as thyself: I *am* the Lord.

Lev. 24:17. And he that killeth any man shall surely be put to death.

Prov. 20:22. Say not thou, I will recompense evil; *but* wait on the Lord, and he shall save thee.

Prov. 26:27. Whoso diggeth a pit shall fall therein: and he that rolleth a stone, it will return upon him.

Rom. 12:17. Recompense to no man evil for evil. 19. Dearly beloved, avenge not yourselves, but *rather* give place unto wrath: for it is written, Vengeance *is* mine; I will repay, saith the Lord.

REVENUE, Solomon's, 2 Chr. 9:13,14.

REVERENCE. For God, Gen. 17:3; Ex. 3:5; 19:16-24; 34:29-35; Isa. 45:9. See Fear of God. For God's house, Lev. 19:30; 26:2. For ministers, 1 Sam. 16:4; Acts 28:10; 1 Cor. 16:18; Phil. 2:29; 1 Thess. 5:12,13; 1 Tim. 5:17; Heb. 13:7,17. See Minister. For kings, 1 Sam. 24:6; 26:9,11; 2 Sam. 1:14; 16:21; Eccl. 10:20; 1 Pet. 2:17. See Rulers. For magistrates, Ex. 22:28; 2 Pet. 2:10; Jude 8. See Rulers. For parents, Ex. 20:12; Lev. 19:3; Isa. 45:10. See Parents. For the aged, Lev. 19:32; Job 32:4-7.

REVIVALS. Religious: Zech. 8:20-23. Prayer for, Hab. 3:2. Prophecies concerning, Isa. 32:15; Joel 2:28; Mic. 4:1-8; Hab. 3:2.

Instances of: Under Joshua, Josh. 5:2-9; Samuel, 1 Sam. 7:1-6; Elijah, 1 Kin. 18:17-40; Jehoash and Jehoiada, 2 Kin. chapters 11; 12; 2 Chr. chapters 23; 24; Hezekiah, 2 Kin. 18:1-7; 2 Chr. chapters 29-31; Josiah, 2 Kin. chapters 22; 23; 2 Chr. chapters 34; 35; Asa, 2 Chr.

14:2-5; 15:1-14; Manasseh, 2 Chr. 33:12-19. In Nineveh, Jonah 3:4-10. At Pentecost, and post-pentecostal times, Acts 2:1-42,46,47; 4:4; 5:14; 6:7; 9:35; 11:20,21; 12:24; 14:1; 19:17-20.

REWARD. A Motive to Faithfulness: Ex. 20:12. Honour thy father and thy mother: that thy days may be long upon the land which the LORD thy God giveth thee. Eph. 6:1-3.

Lev. 25:18. Wherefore ye shall do my statutes, and keep my judgments, and do them; and ye shall dwell in the land in safety. 19. And the land shall yield her fruit, and ye shall eat your fill, and dwell therein in safety.

Deut. 4:40. Thou shalt keep therefore his statutes, and his commandments, which I command thee this day, that it may go well with thee, and with thy children after thee, and that thou mayest prolong *thy* days upon the earth, which the LORD thy God giveth thee, for ever.

Isa. 3:10. Say ye to the righteous, that *it shall be* well *with him:* for they shall eat the fruit of their doings.

Isa. 40:10. Behold, the Lord GOD will come with strong *hand,* and his arm shall rule for him: behold, his reward *is* with him, and his work before him.

Matt. 10:32. Whosoever therefore shall confess me before men, him will I confess also before my Father which is in heaven. Luke 12:8.

Rom. 2:10. But glory, honour, and peace, to every man that worketh good,

Rev. 2:10. Fear none of those things which thou shalt suffer: . . . and ye shall have tribulation ten days: be thou faithful unto death, and I will give thee a crown of life.

Rev. 22:12. And, behold, I come quickly; and my reward *is* with me, to give every man according as his work shall be.

RICH, The: Psa. 49:16. Be not thou afraid when one is made rich, when the glory of his house is increased; 17. For when he dieth he shall carry nothing away: his

glory shall not descend after him. 18. Though while he lived he blessed his soul:

Eccl. 5:13. There is a sore evil *which* I have seen under the sun, *namely,* riches kept for the owners thereof to their hurt. 14. But those riches perish by evil travail: and he begetteth a son, and *there is* nothing in his hand.

Jer. 9:23. Thus saith the LORD, . . . let not the rich *man* glory in his riches:

Jer. 22:13. Woe unto him that buildeth his house by unrighteousness, and his chambers by wrong; *that* useth his neighbour's service without wages, and giveth him not for his work;

Ezek. 28:5. By thy great wisdom *and* by thy traffick hast thou increased thy riches, and thine heart is lifted up because of thy riches:

Zeph. 1:18. Neither their silver nor their gold shall be able to deliver them in the day of the LORD's wrath;

Matt. 19:24. It is easier for a camel to go through the eye of a needle, than for a rich man to enter into the kingdom of God. *v.* 23; Luke 18:24,25.

1 Tim. 6:17. Charge them that are rich in this world, that they be not highminded, nor trust in uncertain riches, but in the living God, who giveth us richly all things to enjoy; 18. That they do good, that they be rich in good works, ready to distribute, willing to communicate; 19. Laying up in store for themselves a good foundation against the time to come that they may lay hold on [eternal life.] [R. V. the life which is life indeed]

Jas. 1:9. Let the brother of low degree rejoice in that he is exalted: 10. But the rich, in that he is made low: because as the flower of the grass he shall pass away.

Jas. 5:1. Go to now, *ye* rich men, weep and howl for your miseries that shall come upon *you.*

Prov. 16:8. Better *is* a little with righteousness than great revenues without right.

RIGHTEOUS. Described: Ex. 33:16. For wherein shall it be known here that I and thy people have found grace in thy sight? *is it* not in that thou goest with us? So shall we be separated, I and thy people, from all the people that *are* upon the face of the earth.

Psa. 1:1. Blessed *is* the man that walketh not in the counsel of the ungodly, nor standeth in the way of sinners, nor sitteth in the seat of the scornful. 2. But his delight *is* in the law of the Lord; and in his law doth he meditate day and night. 3. And he shall be like a tree planted by the rivers of water, that bringeth forth his fruit in his season; his leaf also shall not wither; and whatsoever he doeth shall prosper.

Psa. 4:3. But know that the Lord hath set apart him that is godly for himself:

Psa. 24:3. Who shall ascend into the hill of the Lord? or who shall stand in his holy place? 4. He that hath clean hands, and a pure heart; who hath not lifted up his soul unto vanity, nor sworn deceitfully. 5. He shall receive the blessing from the Lord, and righteousness from the God of his salvation.

Psa. 112:5. A good man sheweth favour, and lendeth: he will guide his affairs with discretion.

Prov. 4:18. But the path of the just *is* as the shining light, that shineth more and more unto the perfect day.

Prov. 13:5. A righteous *man* hateth lying:

Isa. 54:13. And all thy children *shall be* taught of the Lord; and great *shall be* the peace of thy children.

Matt. 7:16. Ye shall know them by their fruits. Do men gather grapes of thorns, or figs of thistles? 17. Even so every good tree bringeth forth good fruit; but a corrupt tree bringeth forth evil fruit.

Matt. 12:50. For whosoever shall do the will of my Father which is in heaven, the same is my brother, and sister, and mother.

John 13:35. By this shall all *men* know that ye are my disciples, if ye have love one to another.

John 15:14. Ye are my friends, if ye do whatsoever I command you.

1 Cor. 2:12. Now we have received, not the spirit of the world, but the spirit which is of God; that we might know the things that are freely given to us of God.

2 Cor. 5:17. Therefore if any man *be* in Christ, *he is* a new creature: old things are passed away; behold, all things are become new.

Gal. 5:22. But the fruit of the Spirit is love, joy, peace, longsuffering, gentleness, goodness, faith, 23. Meekness, temperance: against such there is no law.

Eph. 3:17. That Christ may dwell in your hearts by faith; that ye, being rooted and grounded in love, 18. May be able to comprehend with all saints what *is* the breadth and length, and depth, and height; 19. And to know the love of Christ, which passeth knowledge, that ye might be filled with all the fulness of God.

Phil. 4:8. Whatsoever things are true, whatsoever things *are* honest, whatsoever things *are* just, whatsoever things *are* pure, whatsoever things *are* lovely, whatsoever things *are* of good report; if *there be* any virtue, and if *there be* any praise, think on these things.

Col. 2:7. Rooted and built up in him, and stablished in the faith, as ye have been taught, abounding therein with thanksgiving.

Col. 3:3. For ye are dead, and your life is hid with Christ in God.

2 Tim. 2:19. Let every one that nameth the name of Christ depart from iniquity.

Rev. 17:14. He is Lord of lords, and King of kings: and they that are with him *are* called, and chosen, and faithful.

Promises to, Gen. 22:17. In blessing I will bless thee, and in multiplying I will multiply thy seed as the stars of the heaven, and as the sand which *is* upon the sea shore; and thy seed shall possess the gate of his enemies;

Deut. 33:27. The eternal God *is* thy refuge, and underneath *are* the everlasting arms: and he shall thrust out the enemy from before thee; and shall say, Destroy *them.*

1 Sam. 2:9. He will keep the feet of his saints;

2 Chr. 16:9. For the eyes of the LORD run to and fro throughout the whole earth, to shew himself strong in the behalf of *them* whose heart *is* perfect toward him.

Ezra 8:22. The hand of our God *is* upon all them for good that seek him; but his power and his wrath *is* against all them that forsake him.

Psa. 4:3. But know that the LORD hath set apart him that is godly for himself: the LORD will hear when I call unto him.

Psa. 23:6. Surely goodness and mercy shall follow me all the days of my life: and I will dwell in the house of the LORD for ever.

Psa. 28:8. The LORD *is* their strength, and he *is* the saving strength of his anointed.

Psa. 34:9. O fear the LORD, ye his saints: for *there is* no want to them that fear him. 10. The young lions do lack, and suffer hunger: but they that seek the LORD shall not want any good *thing.* 15. The eyes of the LORD *are* upon the righteous, and his ears *are open* unto their cry. 17. *The righteous* cry, and the LORD heareth, and delivereth them out of all their troubles.

Psa. 37:3. Trust in the LORD, and do good; *so* shalt thou dwell in the land, and verily thou shalt be fed.

23. The steps of a *good* man are ordered by the LORD: and he delighteth in his way.

Psa. 41:1. Blessed *is* he that considereth the poor: the LORD will deliver him in time of trouble.

Psa. 50:15. Call upon me in the day of trouble: I will deliver thee, and thou shalt glorify me.

Psa. 55:22. Cast thy burden upon the LORD, and he shall sustain thee: he shall never suffer the righteous to be moved.

Psa. 73:24. Thou shalt guide me with thy counsel, and afterward receive me *to* glory.

Psa. 84:11. For the LORD God *is* a sun and shield: the LORD will give grace and glory: no good *thing* will

he withhold from them that walk uprightly.

Prov. 3:5. Trust in the LORD with all thine heart; and lean not unto thine own understanding. 6. In all thy ways acknowledge him, and he shall direct thy paths.

Isa. 26:3. Thou wilt keep *him* in perfect peace, *whose* mind *is* stayed *on thee:* because he trusteth in thee.

Isa. 41:10. Fear thou not; for I *am* with thee: be not dismayed; for I *am* thy God: I will strengthen thee; yea, I will help thee; yea, I will uphold thee with the right hand of my righteousness.

Isa. 43:2. When thou passest through the waters, I *will be* with thee; and through the rivers, they shall not overflow thee: when thou walkest through the fire, thou shalt not be burned; neither shall the flame kindle upon thee.

Isa. 58:8. Then shall thy light break forth as the morning, and thine health shall spring forth speedily: and thy righteousness shall go before thee; the glory of the LORD shall be thy rearward.

Jer. 17:7. Blessed *is* the man that trusteth in the LORD, and whose hope the LORD is. 8. For he shall be as a tree planted by the waters, and *that* spreadeth out her roots by the river, and shall not see when heat cometh, but her leaf shall be green; and shall not be careful in the year of drought, neither shall cease from yielding fruit.

Nah. 1:7. The LORD *is* good, a strong hold in the day of trouble; and he knoweth them that trust in him.

Mal. 3:16. Then they that feared the LORD spake often one to another: and the LORD hearkened, and heard *it,* and a book of remembrance was written before him for them that feared the LORD, and that thought upon his name. 17. And they shall be mine, saith the LORD of hosts, in that day when I make up my jewels; and I will spare them, as a man spareth his own son that serveth him.

John 3:16. For God so loved the world, that he gave his only begotten Son, that whosoever believeth in him should not perish, but have everlasting life. 17. For God sent not his Son into the world to condemn the world; but that the world through him might be saved.

36. He that believeth on the Son hath everlasting life:

2 Tim. 4:8. Henceforth there is laid up for me a crown of righteousness, which the Lord, the righteous judge, shall give me at that day: and not to me only, but unto all them also that love his appearing.

Heb. 6:10. For God *is* not unrighteous to forget your work and labour of love, which ye have shewed toward his name, in that ye have ministered to the saints, and do minister.

Jas. 1:5. If any of you lack wisdom, let him ask of God that giveth to all *men* liberally, and upbraideth not; and it shall be given him.

1 Pet. 5:4. And when the chief Shepherd shall appear, ye shall receive a crown of glory that fadeth not away.

Rev. 22:12. And, behold, I come quickly; and my reward *is* with me, to give every man according as his work shall be.

Unity of, with Christ: John 6:56. He that eateth my flesh, and drinketh my blood, dwelleth in me, and I in him. *vss.* 51-57.

John 14:20. At that day ye shall know that I *am* in my Father, and ye in me, and I in you.

John 15:4. Abide in me, and I in you. As the branch cannot bear fruit of itself, except it abide in the vine; no more can ye, except ye abide in me.

John 17:21. That they all may be one; as thou, Father, *art* in me, and I in thee, that they also may be one in us: that the world may believe that thou hast sent me.

Rom. 12:5. So we, *being* many, are one body in Christ, and every one members one of another.

RIGHTEOUSNESS. By faith, Gen. 15:6; Rom. 4:3,5,9,11,13,20, 22,24. Garment of, Job 29:14; Matt. 22:11-14. Imputed on account of obedience, Deut. 6:25; Job 33:26.

Fruits of:

Psa. 1:3. And he shall be like a tree planted by the rivers of water, that bringeth forth his fruit in his season; his leaf also shall not wither; and whatsoever he doeth shall prosper.

Matt. 12:35. A good man out of the good treasure of the heart bringeth forth good things: and an evil man out of the evil treasure bringeth forth evil things.

John 13:35. By this shall all *men* know that ye are my disciples, if ye have love one to another.

Acts 11:29. Then the disciples, every man according to his ability, determined to send relief unto the brethren which dwelt in Judaea:

Rom. 15:1. We then that are strong ought to bear the infirmities of the weak, and not to please ourselves.

2 Cor. 5:17. Therefore if any man *be* in Christ, *he is* a new creature: old things are passed away; behold, all things are become new.

Phil. 2:13. For it is God which worketh in you both to will and to do of *his* good pleasure.

Col. 1:12. Giving thanks unto the Father, which hath made us meet to be partakers of the inheritance of the saints in light: 13. Who hath delivered us from the power of darkness, and hath translated *us* into the kingdom of his dear Son:

2 Tim. 2:22. Flee also youthful lusts: but follow righteousness, faith, charity, peace, with them that call on the Lord out of a pure heart.

Jas. 1:27. Pure religion and undefiled before God and the Father is this, To visit the fatherless and widows in their affliction, *and* to keep himself unspotted from the world.

RISING. Early: Prov. 31:15. For devotions, Psa. 5:3; 59:16; 63:1; 88:13; Song 7:12; Isa. 26:9. Practised by the wicked, Prov. 27:14; Mic. 2:1; Zeph. 3:7; by drunkards, Isa. 5:11. Illustrates spiritual diligence. Rom. 13:11,12.

INSTANCES OF: Lot, Gen. 19:23. Abraham, Gen. 19:27; 21:14; 22:3. Isaac, Gen. 26:31. Abimelech, Gen.

20:8. Jacob, Gen. 28:18; 32:31. Laban, Gen. 31:55. Moses, Ex. 8:20; 9:13. Joshua, Josh. 3:1; 6:12, 15; 7:16. Gideon, Judg. 6:38 Elkanah, 1 Sam. 1:19. Samuel, 1 Sam. 15:12. David, 1 Sam. 17:20. Mary, Mark 16:2; Luke 24:1. Apostles, Acts 5:21.

Late: Consequences of, Prov. 6:9-11; 24:33,34.

ROADS. Public highways, Deut. 2:27. From Gibeon to Beth-horon, Josh. 10:10. From Beth-el to Shechem, Judg. 21:19. From Judæa to Galilee, by way of Samaria, John 4:3-5,43. To the house of God, Judg. 20:31. To cities of refuge, Deut. 19:3. Built by rulers, Num. 20:17; 21:22.

ROBBERS. Prov. 1:11-16. Dens of, Jer. 7:11. Bands of, Hos. 6:9; 7:1.

ROBBERY. Forbidden, Lev. 19:13; Isa. 61:8. Punished with death, Ezek. 18:10,13. Forgiven, Ezek. 33:15.

Instances of: Judg. 9:25; Luke 10:30.

ROBE. Of righteousness, 2 Chr. 6:41; Isa. 61:10; Rev. 6:11; 7:9,13. Parable of the man who was not dressed in a wedding garment, Matt. 22:11.

ROCK. Smitten by Moses for water, Deut. 8:15; Psa. 78:15,16,20. Houses in, Jer. 49:16; Obad. 3; Matt. 7:24,25. Oil from, Job 29:6; Deut. 32:13. Name of deity, Deut. 32:4.

ROMAN EMPIRE. Ruled by Augustus Cæsar, Luke 2:1; Tiberius Cæsar, Luke 3:1; Claudius Cæsar, Acts 18:2; Nero, Phil. 4:22. Citizenship in, by nativity, Acts 22:28; by purchase, Acts 22:28. Rights of citizens, Acts 16:37; 22:25-29; of trial, Acts 25:16; of appeal, Acts 25:10,21.

ROME, the capital of the Roman empire. Jews excluded from, by Claudius, Acts 18:2. Paul's visit to, see PAUL. Visited by Onesiphorus, 2 Tim. 1:16,17. Paul desires to preach in, Rom. 1:15. Abominations in, Rom. 1:18-32. Christians in, Rom. 16:5-17; Phil. 1:12-18; 4:22; 2 Tim. 4:21.

RULERS, Appointed and removed by God. See GOVERNMENT, GOD IN. Chastised, Dan. 4.

Character and Qualifications of: Ex. 18:21. Moreover thou shalt provide out of all the people able men, such as fear God, men of truth, hating covetousness; and place *such* over them, *to be* rulers of thousands, *and* rulers of hundreds, rulers of fifties, and rulers of tens. 22. And let them judge the people at all seasons: and it shall be, *that* every great matter they shall bring unto thee, but every small matter they shall judge: so shall it be easier for thyself, and they shall bear *the burden* with thee.

Ex. 23:8. And thou shalt take no gift: for the gift blindeth the wise, and perverteth the words of the righteous.

Deut. 27:19. Cursed *be* he that perverteth the judgment of the stranger, fatherless, and widow. And all the people shall say, Amen.

2 Sam. 23:3. The God of Israel said, the Rock of Israel spake to me, He that ruleth over men *must be* just, ruling in the fear of God. 4. And *he shall be* as the light of the morning, *when* the sun riseth, *even* a morning without clouds; *as* the tender grass *springing* out of the earth by clear shining after rain.

Rom. 12:8. Or he that exhorteth, on exhortation: he that giveth, *let him do it* with simplicity; he that ruleth, with diligence; he that sheweth mercy, with cheerfulness.

Rom. 13:1. Let every soul be subject unto the higher powers. For there is no power but of God: the powers that be are ordained of God. 2. Whosoever therefore resisteth the power, resisteth the ordinance of God: and they that resist shall receive to themselves damnation.

1 Tim. 2:1. I exhort therefore, that, first of all, supplications, prayers, intercessions, *and* giving of thanks, be made for all men; 2. For kings, and *for* all that are in authority;

Duties of:

Lev. 24:22. Ye shall have one

manner of law, as well for the stranger, as for one of your own country: for I *am* the LORD your God.

Deut. 1:16. And I charged your judges at that time, saying, Hear *the causes* between your brethren, and judge righteously between *every* man and his brother, and the stranger *that is* with him. 17. Ye shall not respect persons in judgment; *but* ye shall hear the small as well as the great; ye shall not be afraid of the face of man; for the judgment *is* God's:

Deut. 19:18. And the judges shall make diligent inquisition: and, behold, *if* the witness *be* a false witness, *and* hath testified falsely against his brother; 19. Then shall ye do unto him, as he had thought to have done unto his brother: so shalt thou put the evil away from among you.

Deut. 24:16. The fathers shall not be put to death for the children, neither shall the children be put to death for the fathers: every man shall be put to death for his own sin.

SABBATH. Unclassified Scriptures Relating to: Gen. 2:2. On the seventh day God ended his work which he had made; and he rested on the seventh day from all his work which he had made. 3. And God blessed the seventh day, and sanctified it; because that in it he had rested from all his work which God created and made.

Ex. 16:5. And it shall come to pass, that on the sixth day they shall prepare *that* which they bring in; and it shall be twice as much as they gather daily. 23. This *is that* which the LORD hath said, To morrow *is* the rest of the holy sabbath unto the LORD: bake *that* which ye will bake *to day,* and seethe that ye will seethe; and that which remaineth over lay up for you to be kept until the morning.

Ex. 20:8. Remember the sabbath day, to keep it holy. 9. Six days shalt thou labour, and do all thy work: 10. But the seventh day *is* the sabbath of the LORD thy God:

in it thou shalt not do any work, thou, nor thy son, nor thy daughter, thy manservant, nor thy maidservant, nor thy cattle, nor thy stranger that *is* within thy gates: 11. For *in* six days the LORD made heaven and earth, the sea, and all that in them *is,* and rested the seventh day: wherefore the LORD blessed the sabbath day, and hallowed it.

Lev. 24:8. Every sabbath he shall set it in order before the LORD continually, *being taken* from the children of Israel by an everlasting covenant. 1 Chr. 9:32.

Psa. 118:24. This *is* the day *which* the LORD hath made; we will rejoice and be glad in it.

Isa. 58:13. If thou turn away thy foot from the sabbath, *from* doing thy pleasure on my holy day; and call the sabbath a delight, the holy of the LORD, honourable; and shalt honour him, not doing thine own ways, nor finding thine own pleasure, nor speaking *thine own* words: 14. Then shalt thou delight thyself in the LORD; and I will cause thee to ride upon the high places of the earth, and feed thee with the heritage of Jacob thy father:

Ezek. 20:12. Moreover also I gave them my sabbaths, to be a sign between me and them, that they might know that I *am* the LORD that sanctify them.

Matt. 12:10. And, behold, there was a man which had *his* hand withered. And they asked him, saying, Is it lawful to heal on the sabbath days? that they might accuse him. 11. And he said unto them, What man shall there be among you, that shall have one sheep, and if it fall into a pit on the sabbath day, will he not lay hold on it, and lift *it* out? 12. How much then is a man better than a sheep? Wherefore it is lawful to do well on the sabbath days. 13. Then saith he to the man, Stretch forth thine hand. And he stretched *it* forth; and it was restored whole, like as the other. Luke 6:1-10.

Mark 2:27. The sabbath was made for man, and not man for the sabbath: *v.* 28.

Col. 2:16. Let no man therefore judge you in meat, or in drink, or in respect of an holyday, or of the new moon, or of the sabbath *days:*

Observance of: By Moses, Num. 15:32-34. By Nehemiah, Neh. 13:15,21. By the women preparing to embalm the body of Jesus, Luke 23:56. By Paul, Acts 13:14. By Disciples, Acts 16:13. By John, Rev. 1:10.

Christian Sabbath: First day of the week, Sunday. Mark 16:9. Now when *Jesus* was risen early the first *day* of the week, he appeared first to Mary Magdalene, Matt. 28: 1,5,6,9.

Acts 20:7. And upon the first *day* of the week when the disciples came together to break bread, Paul preached unto them, ready to depart on the morrow; and continued his speech until midnight.

1 Cor. 16:2. Upon the first *day* of the week, let every one of you lay by him in store, as [God hath prospered him,] that there be no gatherings when I come. [R. V. he may prosper]

Rev. 1:10. I was in the Spirit on the Lord's day, and heard behind me a great voice, as of a trumpet,

SAINTS. See RIGHTEOUS.

SALVATION. See ATONEMENT.

Ex. 15:2. The LORD *is* my strength and song, and he is become my salvation: he *is* my God, and I will prepare him an habitation; my father's God, and I will exalt him.

Psa. 46:4. *There is* a river, the streams whereof shall make glad the city of God, the holy *place* of the tabernacles of the most High.

Isa. 1:18. Come now, and let us reason together, saith the LORD: Though your sins be as scarlet, they shall be as white as snow; though they be red like crimson, they shall be as wool.

Luke 19:10. For the Son of man is come to seek and to save that which was lost.

John 3:14. And as Moses lifted up the serpent in the wilderness even so must the Son of man be lifted up: 15. That whosoever believeth in him should not perish, but have eternal life. 16. For God so loved the world, that he gave his only begotten Son, that whosoever believeth in him should not perish, but have everlasting life. 17. For God sent not his Son into the world to condemn the world; but that the world through him might be saved.

Acts 4:12. Neither is there salvation in any other: for there is none other name under heaven given among men, whereby we must be saved.

Rom. 5:1. Therefore being justified by faith, [we] have peace with God through our Lord Jesus Christ: 2. By whom also we have access by faith into this grace wherein we stand, and rejoice in hope of the glory of God. *vss.* 15-21. [R. V. let us]

Rom. 11:6. And if by grace, then *is it* no more of works: otherwise grace is no more grace. But if *it be* of works, then is it no more grace: otherwise work is no more work.

Eph. 2:1. And you *hath he quickened,* who were dead in trespasses and sins; 3. And were by nature the children of wrath, even as others. 4. But God who is rich in mercy, for his great love wherewith he loved us, 5. Even when we were dead in sins, hath quickened us together with Christ, (by grace ye are saved;) 8. By grace are ye saved through faith; and that not of yourselves; *it is* the gift of God: 9. Not of works, lest any man should boast.

Conditions of: Matt. 3:2. Repent ye: for the kingdom of heaven is at hand.

Matt. 18:3. And said, Verily I say unto you, Except ye be converted, and become as little children, ye shall not enter into the kingdom of heaven.

John 5:24. Verily, verily, I say unto you, He that heareth my word, and believeth on him that sent me, hath everlasting life, and shall not come into condemnation; but is passed from death unto life.

John 6:47. Verily, verily, I say

unto you, He that believeth on me hath everlasting life.

Plan of: John 6:44. No man can come to me, except the Father which hath sent me draw him: and I will raise him up at the last day. *vss.* 37,65.

1 Cor. 1:21. For after that in the wisdom of God the world by wisdom knew not God, it pleased God by the foolishness of preaching to save them that believe.

Col. 1:19. For it pleased *the Father* that in him should all fulness dwell; 20. And, having made peace through the blood of his cross, by him to reconcile all things unto himself; by him, *I say,* whether *they be* things in earth, or things in heaven.

SANCTIFICATION. John 17:17. Sanctify them through thy truth: thy word is truth. 19. And for their sakes I sanctify myself, that they also might be sanctified through the truth.

1 Cor. 6:11. And such were some of you: but ye are washed, but ye are sanctified, but ye are justified in the name of the Lord Jesus, and by the Spirit of our God.

1 Thess. 4:3. For this is the will of God, *even* your sanctification, that ye should abstain from fornication:

1 Thess. 5:23. And the very God of peace sanctify you wholly; and *I pray God* your whole spirit and soul and body be preserved blameless unto the coming of our Lord Jesus Christ.

Heb. 2:11. For both he that sanctifieth and they who are sanctified *are* all of one: for which cause he is not ashamed to call them brethren.

Heb. 9:14. How much more shall the blood of Christ, who through the eternal Spirit offered himself without spot to God, purge your conscience from dead works to serve the living God?

1 John 1:9. If we confess our sins, he is faithful and just to forgive us *our* sins, and to cleanse us from all unrighteousness.

SARCASM. Instances of: Cain's self-justifying argument when

God asked him where Abel was, Gen. 4:9. Israelites reproaching Moses, Ex. 14:11. God reproaching Israel, Num. 11:20; Judg. 10:14. Balak reproaching Balaam, Num. 24:11. Joshua to descendants of Joseph, Josh. 17:15. By Jotham, Judg. 9:7-19; Samson, Judg. 14:18. The men of Jabesh to Nahash, 1 Sam. 11:10. Eliab to David, 1 Sam. 17:28. Elijah to the priests of Baal, 1 Kin. 18:27. David's reply to Michal's irony, 2 Sam. 6:21. Ahab's reply to Ben-hadad, 1 Kin. 20:11. Jehoash to Amaziah, 2 Kin. 14:9,10; 2 Chr. 25:18,19. Rabshakeh to Hezekiah, 2 Kin. 18:23,24. Sanballat's address to the army of Samaria, Neh. 4:2,3. Zophar to Job, Job 11:12. Job to Zophar, Job 12:2,3. Of Solomon, Prov. 26:16. The persecutors of Jesus, Matt. 27:28, 29; Luke 23:11; John 19:2,3,5,15. Paul, 1 Tim. 4:7. Agrippa to Paul, Acts 26:28.

SATAN. Unclassified Scriptures Relating to: Gen. 3:1. Now the serpent was more subtil than any beast of the field which the LORD God had made. And he said unto the woman, Yea, hath God said, Ye shall not eat of every tree of the garden? 4. And the serpent said unto the woman, Ye shall not surely die: 5. For God doth know that in the day ye eat thereof, then your eyes shall be opened, and ye shall be as gods, knowing good and evil.

1 Chr. 21:1. And Satan stood up against Israel, and provoked David to number Israel.

Job 1:6. Now there was a day when the sons of God came to present themselves before the LORD, and Satan came also among them. 7. And the LORD said unto Satan, Whence comest thou? Then Satan answered the LORD, and said, From going to and fro in the earth, and from walking up and down in it.

Zech. 3:1. And he shewed me Joshua the high priest standing before the angel of the LORD, and Satan standing at his right hand to resist him. 2. And the LORD said unto Satan, The LORD rebuke thee, O Satan; even the LORD that hath chosen Jerusalem rebuke thee: *is* not this a brand plucked out of the fire?

Matt. 4:1. Then was Jesus led up of the spirit into the wilderness to be tempted of the devil.

Luke 10:18. And he said unto them, I beheld Satan as lightning fall from heaven.

Luke 13:16. And ought not this woman, being a daughter of Abraham, whom Satan hath bound, lo, these eighteen years, be loosed from this bond on the sabbath day?

Luke 22:31. And the Lord said, Simon, Simon, behold, Satan hath desired *to have* you, that he may sift *you* as wheat:

John 8:44. Ye are of *your* father the devil, and the lusts of your father ye will do. He was a murderer from the beginning, and abode not in the truth, because there is no truth in him. When he speaketh a lie, he speaketh of his own: for he is a liar, and the father of it.

John 13:2. And supper being ended, the devil having now put into the heart of Judas Iscariot, Simon's *son,* to betray him; 27. After the sop Satan entered into him.

Acts 5:3. But Peter said, Ananias, why hath Satan filled thine heart to lie to the Holy Ghost, and to keep back *part* of the price of the land?

Rom. 16:20. And the God of peace shall bruise Satan under your feet shortly.

Eph. 2:2. Wherein in time past ye walked according to the course of this world, according to the prince of the power of the air, the spirit that now worketh in the children of disobedience:

Eph. 4:27. Neither give place to the devil.

Eph. 6:11. Put on the whole armour of God, that ye may be able to stand against the wiles of the devil. 12. For we wrestle not against flesh and blood, but against principalities, against powers, against the rulers of the darkness of this world, against spiritual wickedness in high *places.*

Col. 1:13. Who hath delivered us from the power of darkness, and hath translated *us* into the kingdom of his dear Son:

Col. 2:15. Having spoiled principalities and powers, he made a shew of them openly, triumphing over them in it.

Jude 6. And the angels which kept not their first estate, but left their own habitation, he hath reserved in everlasting chains under darkness unto the judgment of the great day.

Rev. 9:11. They had a king over them, *which is* the angel of the bottomless pit, whose name in the Hebrew tongue *is* Abaddon, but in the Greek tongue hath *his* name Apollyon.

SATIRE. Hannah's song of exultation over Peninnah, 1 Sam. 2:1-10, with chapter 1:5-10. Of Jesus against hypocrites, Matt. 23:2-33; Mark 12:13-40; Luke 11:39-54.

SAVIOUR. See Jesus, Saviour.

SCHOOL. Of the prophets, at Naioth, 1 Sam. 19:20; Beth-el, 2 Kin. 2:3; Jericho, 2 Kin. 2:5,15; Gilgal, 2 Kin. 4:38; Jerusalem, probably, 2 Kin. 22:14; 2 Chr. 34:22. Crowded attendance at, 2 Kin. 6:1.

In the home, Deut. 4:9,10; 6:7, 9; 11:19,20; Psa. 78:5-8. Bible school, Deut. 31:10-13.

State, 2 Chr. 17:7-9; Dan. 1:3-21. Of Gamaliel, Acts 5:34; 22:3. Of Tyrannus, Acts 19:9. Schoolmaster [tutor, *R. V.*], Gal. 3:24, 25.

SCIENCE. Observations of, and deductions from, facts, Job 26:7-14; 28; Eccl. 1:13-17. So-called, false, 1 Tim. 6:20.

SCOFFING: 2 Chr. 36:16. But they mocked the messengers of God, and despised his words, and misused his prophets, until the wrath of the Lord arose against his people, till *there was* no remedy.

Psa. 1:1. Blessed *is* the man that walketh not in the counsel of the ungodly, nor standeth in the way of sinners, nor sitteth in the seat of the scornful.

Prov. 1:22. How long, ye simple ones, will ye love simplicity? and the scorners delight in their scorning, and fools hate knowledge? 25. But ye have set at nought all my counsel, and would none of my reproof:

Prov. 22:10. Cast out the scorner, and contention shall go out; yea, strife and reproach shall cease.

SCRIPTURES. See WORD OF GOD.

SEAL. Figurative: Of secrecy, Dan. 12:9; Rev. 5:1. Of certainty of divine approval, John 6:27; Rom. 15:28; 2 Cor. 1:22; Eph. 1:13; 4:30; Rev. 7:3,4.

An amphibious animal. Skins of, according to the Revised Version, were used as a covering of the tabernacle, Ex. 25:5; 26:14; 35:7, 23; 36:19; 39:34; Num. 4:25.

SECRET. 1 Sam. 16:7. But the LORD said unto Samuel, Look not on his countenance, or on the height of his stature; because I have refused him: for the LORD seeth not as man seeth; for man looketh on the outward appearance, but the LORD looketh on the heart.

Eccl. 12:14. For God shall bring every work into judgment, with every secret thing, whether it be good, or whether it be evil.

Dan. 2:28. But there is a God in heaven that revealeth secrets,

Mark 4:22. For there is nothing hid, which shall not be manifested; neither was any thing kept secret, but that it should come abroad.

1 Cor. 4:5. Therefore judge nothing before the time, until the Lord come, who both will bring to light the hidden things of darkness, and will make manifest the counsels of the heart: and then shall every man have praise of God.

SECRETARY, 2 Sam. 8:17; 20:24; 1 Kin. 4:3; 2 Kin. 12:10-12; 18:18,37; 22:1-14; 1 Chr. 27:32; Esth. 3:12; ˙8:9. Military, 2 Kin. 25:19; 2 Chr. 26:11.

SEEKERS. Job 5:8. I would seek unto God, and unto God would I commit my cause:

Psa. 9:10. And they that know thy name will put their trust in thee: for thou, LORD, hast not forsaken them that seek thee.

Psa. 14:2. The LORD looked down from heaven upon the chil-

dren of men, to see if there were any that did understand, and seek God.

Psa. 22:26. They shall praise the LORD that seek him:

Psa. 34:4. I sought the LORD, and he heard me, and delivered me from all my fears.

Psa. 145:18. The LORD is nigh unto all them that call upon him, to all that call upon him in truth.

Hos. 10:12. It is time to seek the LORD, till he come and rain righteousness upon you.

Heb. 11:6. But without faith it is impossible to please him: for he that cometh to God must believe that he is, and that he is a rewarder of them that diligently seek him.

Jas. 4:8. Draw nigh to God, and he will draw nigh to you.

SELF-CONDEMNATION. Job 9:20. If I justify myself, mine own mouth shall condemn me: if I say, I am perfect, it shall also prove me perverse.

John 8:9. And they which heard it, being convicted by their own conscience, went out one by one, beginning at the eldest, even unto the last: and Jesus was left alone, and the woman standing in the midst.

Instances of: Achan, Josh. 7: 19-25. David, 2 Sam. 12:57. Ahab, 1 Kin. 20:39-42.

SELF-DELUSION. A characteristic of the wicked, Psa. 49:18. Prosperity frequently leads to, Psa. 30:6; Hos. 12:8; Luke 12:17-19. Obstinate sinners often given up to, Psa. 81:11,12; Hos. 4:17; 2 Thess. 2:10,11.

Exemplified: Ahab, 1 Kin. 20: 27,34. Israelites, Hos. 12:8. Jews, John 8:33,41. Church of Laodicea, Rev. 3:17.

SELF-DENIAL. Prov. 16:32. He that is slow to anger is better than the mighty; and he that ruleth his spirit than he that taketh a city.

Prov. 23:2. Put a knife to thy throat, if thou be a man given to appetite.

Matt. 16:24. Then said Jesus unto his disciples, If any man will come after me, let him deny himself, and take up his cross, and follow me. 25. For whosoever will save his life shall lose it: and whosoever will lose his life for my sake shall find it. Mark 8:34,35; Luke 9:23,24.

Luke 5:11. And when they had brought their ships to land, they forsook all, and followed him.

Luke 21:2. And he saw also a certain poor widow casting in thither two mites. 3. And he said, Of a truth I say unto you, that this poor widow hath cast in more than they all: 4. For all these have of their abundance cast in unto the offerings of God: but she of her penury hath cast in all the living that she had. Mark 12:43,44.

John 12:25. He that loveth his life shall lose it; and he that hateth his life in this world shall keep it unto life eternal. Matt. 16:25; Mark 8:35.

1 Cor. 6:12. All things are lawful unto me, but all things are not expedient: all things are lawful for me, but I will not be brought under the power of any.

Phil. 2:4. Look not every man on his own things, but every man also on the things of others. *vss.* 5-8.

Phil. 3:7. But what things were gain to me, those I counted loss for Christ. 8. Yea doubtless, and I count all things *but* loss for the excellency of the knowledge of Christ Jesus my Lord: for whom I have suffered the loss of all things, and do count them *but* dung, that I may win Christ,

SELF-EXALTATION. Gal. 6:3. If a man think himself to be something, when he is nothing, he deceiveth himself.

Instances of: Pharaoh, Ex. 9: 17. Korah, Dathan, and Abiram, Num. 16:1-3. Sennacherib, 2 Chr. 32:9-19. Prince of Tyre, making himself God, Ezek. 28:2,9. Nebuchadnezzar, Dan. 4:30; 5:20. Belshazzar, Dan. 5:23. Simon the sorcerer, Acts 8:9. Herod, when defied by the people, Acts 12:20-23.

SELF-EXAMINATION. Job 13:23. How many *are* mine iniquities and sins? make me to know my transgression and my sin.

Psa. 19:12. Who can understand *his* errors? cleanse thou me from secret *faults.*

Jer. 17:9. The heart *is* deceitful above all *things,* and desperately [wicked:] who can know it? [R. V. sick]

2 Cor. 13:5. Examine yourselves, whether ye be in the faith; prove your own selves. Know ye not your own selves, how that Jesus Christ is in you, except ye be reprobates?

SELFISHNESS. Prov. 24:11. If thou forbear to deliver *them that are* drawn unto death, and *those that are* ready to be slain; 12. If thou sayest, Behold, we knew it not; doth not he that pondereth the heart consider *it?* and he that keepeth thy soul, doth *not* he know *it?* and shall *not* he render to *every* man according to his works?

Prov. 28:27. He that giveth unto the poor shall not lack: but he that hideth his eyes shall have many a curse.

Zech. 7:6. When ye did eat, and when ye did drink, did not ye eat *for yourselves,* and drink *for yourselves?*

Mal. 1:10. Who *is there* even among you that would shut the doors *for nought?* neither do ye kindle *fire* on mine altar for nought.

1 Cor. 10:24. Let no man seek his own, but every man another's *wealth.*

Gal. 6:2. Bear ye one another's burdens, and so fulfil the law of Christ.

Phil. 2:4. Look not every man on his own things, but every man also on the things of others. 20. I have no man likeminded, who will naturally care for your state. 21. For all seek their own, not the things which are Jesus Christ's.

1 John 3:17. Whoso hath this world's good, and seeth his brother have need, and shutteth up his bowels *of compassion* from him, how dwelleth the love of God in him?

SELF-RIGHTEOUSNESS. Job 12:2. No doubt but ye *are* the people, and wisdom shall die with you.

Prov. 12:15. The way of a fool

is right in his own eyes: but he that hearkeneth unto counsel *is* wise.

Prov. 20:6. Most men will proclaim every one his own goodness: but a faithful man who can find?

Prov. 25:14. Whoso boasteth himself of a false gift *is like* clouds and wind without rain. 27. *It is* not good to eat much honey: so *for men* to search their own glory *is not* glory.

Prov. 26:12. Seest thou a man wise in his own conceit? *there is* more hope of a fool than of him.

Prov. 27:2. Let another man praise thee, and not thine own mouth; a stranger, and not thine own lips.

Prov. 28:13. He that covereth his sins shall not prosper: but whoso confesseth and forsaketh *them* shall have mercy. 26. He that trusteth in his own heart is a fool: but whoso walketh wisely, he shall be delivered.

Prov. 30:12. *There is* a generation *that are* pure in their own eyes, and *yet is* not washed from their filthiness. 13. *There is* a generation, O how lofty are their eyes! and their eyelids are lifted up.

Isa. 5:21. Woe unto *them that are* wise in their own eyes, and prudent in their own sight!

Isa. 64:6. But we are all as an unclean *thing*, and all our righteousnesses *are* as filthy rags;

2 Cor. 10:17. But he that glorieth, let him glory in the Lord. 18. For not he that commendeth himself is approved, but whom the Lord commendeth.

Gal. 6:3. For if a man think himself to be something, when he is nothing, he deceiveth himself.

SELF-WILL, stubbornness. Forbidden, 2 Chr. 30:8; Psa. 75:5. Proceeds from unbelief, 2 Kin. 17:14; pride, Neh. 9:16,29; an evil heart, Jer. 7:24. God knows, Isa. 48:4. Exhibited in refusing to hearken to God, Prov. 1:24.

Exemplified: Simeon and Levi, Gen. 49:6. Israelites, Ex. 32:9; Deut. 9:6,13. Saul, 1 Sam. 15:19-23. David, 2 Sam. 24:4. Josiah, 2 Chr. 35:22. Zedekiah, 2 Chr. 36:13.

SENSUALITY: Jas. 5:5. Ye

have lived in pleasure on the earth, and been wanton; ye have nourished your hearts, as in a day of slaughter.

Jude 18. They told you there should be mockers in the last time, who should walk after their own ungodly lusts. 19. These be they who separate themselves, sensual, having not the Spirit.

SHAME. Jesus ashamed of those who deny him, Mark 8:38; Luke 9:26. Of Adam and Eve, Gen. 3:10. Destitute of, the Israelites when they worshiped the golden calf, Ex. 32:25; the unjust, Zeph. 3:5. Of the cross, Heb. 12:2.

SHEEP. Figurative: 1 Chr. 21:17; Psa. 74:1; Jer. 13:20. Of backsliders, Jer. 50:6. Of lost sinners, Matt. 9:36; 10:6. Of the righteous, Jer. 50:17; Ezek. 34; Matt. 26:31; Mark 14:27; John 10:1-16. Of the defenselessness of ministers, Matt. 10:16.

Parable of the lost, Matt. 18:11-13; Luke 15:4-7.

SHEKINAH, the visible sign of God's presence on the ark of testimony in the Holy of holies, Ex. 25:22; Lev. 16:2; 2 Sam. 6:2; 2 Kin. 19:14,15; Psa. 80:1; Isa. 37:16; Ezek. 9:3; 10:18; Heb. 9:5.

SHEOL. See HELL.

SHEPHERD. One who cares for flocks, Gen. 31:38-40; Psa. 78:52,53; Jer. 31:10; Amos 3:12; Luke 2:8. David the, defends his flock against a lion and a bear, 1 Sam. 17:34,35. Causes the flock to rest, Psa. 23:2; Song 1:7; Jer. 33:12. Numbers the flock, Lev. 27:32; Jer. 33:13. Knows his flock by name, John 10:3-5. Keeps the sheep and goats apart, Matt. 25:32. Waters the flocks, Gen. 29:2-10. Keeps the flocks in folds, Num. 32:16; 1 Sam. 24:3; 2 Sam. 7:8; John 10:1. Watch towers of, 2 Chr. 26:10; Mic. 4:8. Dogs of, Job 30:1. Was an abomination to the Egyptians, Gen. 46:34. Angels appeared to, Luke 2:8-20.

Instances of: Abel, Gen. 4:2. Rachel, Gen. 29:9. Daughters of Jethro, Ex. 2:16. Moses, Ex. 3:1. David, 1 Sam. 16:11; 2 Sam. 7:8; Psa. 78:70.

Figurative: Gen. 49:24. Of

God's care, Psa. 23; 78:52; 80:1. Of prophets, priests, Levites, and civil authorities, Ezek. 34. Of Christ, Zech. 13:7; Matt. 26:31; John 10:1-16; Heb. 13:20; 1 Pet. 2:25. Name given to Jesus, Isa. 40:11; Mark 14:27; John 10:11; 1 Pet. 2:25; 5:4.

SHERIFF, Dan. 3:2,3.

SHIELD, Figurative: Of God's protection, Gen. 15:1; Deut. 33:29; 2 Sam. 22:3,36; Psa. 5:12; 18:2,35; 33:20; 59:11; 84:9,11; 89:18; Prov. 30:5. Of God's truth, Psa. 91:4. Of an entire army, Jer. 46:3. Of faith, Eph. 6:16.

SHOE. Taken off on holy ground, Ex. 3:5; Josh. 5:15; Acts 7:33. Put off in mourning, Ezek. 24:17. Of the children of Israel did not wax old, Deut. 29:5. Loosed in token of refusal to observe the levirate marriage, Deut. 25:9; Ruth 4:7,8. Poor sold for a pair of, Amos 2:6; 8:6. Made of iron, Deut. 33:25; of badgers' skins, Ezek. 16:10; latchet of, Gen. 14:23; Isa. 5:27; Mark 1:7; loosing of, a humble service, Luke 3:16.

SHOUTING. In Joy and Praise: 1 Chr. 15:28. Thus all Israel brought up the ark of the covenant of the LORD with shouting, and with sound of the cornet, and with trumpets, and with cymbals, making a noise with psalteries and harps.

2 Chr. 15:12. And they entered into a covenant to seek the LORD God of their fathers with all their heart and with all their soul; 13. That whosoever would not seek the LORD God of Israel should be put to death, whether small or great, whether man or woman. 14. And they sware unto the LORD with a loud voice, and with shouting, and with trumpets, and with cornets.

Psa. 47:1. O clap your hands, all ye people; shout unto God with the voice of triumph.

Acts 3:8. And he leaping up stood, and walked, and entered with them into the temple, walking, and leaping, and praising God. 9. And all the people saw him walking and praising God:

SICK, The. Visiting, Psa. 41:6.

Visiting, a duty, Matt. 25:36,43; Jas. 1:27.

SIN. Job 14:4. Who can bring a clean *thing* out of an unclean? not one.

Isa. 1:6. From the sole of the foot even unto the head *there is* no soundness in it; *but* wounds, and bruises, and putrifying sores; they have not been closed, neither bound up, neither mollified with ointment. 18. Come now, and let us reason together, saith the LORD: though your sins be as scarlet, they shall be as white as snow; though they be red like crimson, they shall be as wool.

Jer. 17:9. The heart *is* deceitful above all *things,* and desperately [wicked:] who can know it? [R. V. sick]

Eph. 2:1. You *hath he quickened,* who were dead in trespasses and sins; 2. Wherein in time past ye walked according to the course of this world, according to the prince of the power of the air, the spirit that now worketh in the children of disobedience:

Confession of: 2 Chr. 29:6. For our fathers have trespassed, and done *that which was* evil in the eyes of the LORD our God, and have forsaken him, and have turned away their faces from the habitation of the LORD, and turned *their* backs.

Job 9:20. If I justify myself, mine own mouth shall condemn me: *if I say,* I *am* perfect, it shall also prove me perverse.

Job 13:23. How many *are* mine iniquities and sins? make me to know my transgression and my sin.

Job 40:4. Behold, I am vile; what shall I answer thee? I will lay mine hand upon my mouth.

Job 42:5. I have heard of thee by the hearing of the ear: but now mine eye seeth thee. 6. Wherefore I abhor *myself,* and repent in dust and ashes.

Psa. 38:3. *There is* no soundness in my flesh because of thine anger; neither *is there any* rest in my bones because of my sin. 4. For mine iniquities are gone over mine head: as an heavy burden they are too heavy for me. 18. For I will declare mine iniquity; I will be sorry for my sin.

Psa. 40:11. Withhold not thou thy tender mercies from me, O LORD: let thy lovingkindness and thy truth continually preserve me. 12. For innumerable evils have compassed me about; mine iniquities have taken hold upon me, so that I am not able to look up; they are more than the hairs of mine head: therefore my heart faileth me.

Psa. 51:2. Wash me throughly from mine iniquity, and cleanse me from my sin. 3. For I acknowledge my transgressions: and my sin *is* ever before me. 4. Against thee, thee only, have I sinned, and done *this* evil in thy sight: that thou mightest be justified when thou speakest, *and* be clear when thou judgest. 5. Behold, I was shapen in iniquity; and in sin did my mother conceive me.

Isa. 6:5. Then said I, Woe *is* me! for I am undone; because I *am* a man of unclean lips, and I dwell in the midst of a people of unclean lips:

Jas. 5:16. Confess *your* faults one to another, and pray one for another, that ye may be healed.

Rom. 5:12. Wherefore, as by one man sin entered into the world, and death by sin; and so death passed upon all men, for that all have sinned:

Forgiveness of: Ex. 34:6. And the LORD passed by before him, and proclaimed, The LORD, The LORD God, merciful and gracious, long-suffering, and abundant in goodness and truth, 7. Keeping mercy for thousands, forgiving iniquity and transgression and sin, Num. 14:18.

2 Sam. 12:13. And David said unto Nathan, I have sinned against the LORD. And Nathan said unto David, The LORD also hath put away thy sin; thou shalt not die.

Psa. 19:12. Who can understand *his* errors? cleanse thou me from secret *faults*.

Psa. 32:1. Blessed *is* he *whose* transgression *is* forgiven, *whose* sin *is* covered. 2. Blessed *is* the man unto whom the LORD imputeth not

iniquity, and in whose spirit *there is* no guile.

Psa. 103:12. As far as the east is from the west, *so* far hath he removed our transgressions from us.

Isa. 1:18. Come now, and let us reason together, saith the LORD: though your sins be as scarlet, they shall be as white as snow; though they be red like crimson, they shall be as wool.

Matt. 1:21. And she shall bring forth a son, and thou shalt call his name JESUS: for he shall save his people from their sins.

Matt. 26:28. This is my blood of the new testament, which is shed for many for the remission of sins.

Eph. 4:32. And be ye kind one to another, tenderhearted, forgiving one another, even as God for Christ's sake hath forgiven you.

Heb. 9:22. Almost all things are by the law purged with blood; and without shedding of blood is no remission.

1 John 2:1. If any man sin, we have an advocate with the Father, Jesus Christ the righteous: 2. And he is the propitiation for our sins: and not for ours only, but also for *the sins of* the whole world. 12. I write unto you, little children, because your sins are forgiven you for his name's sake.

Fruits of: Job 4:8. Even as I have seen, they that plow iniquity, and sow wickedness, reap the same.

Job 20:11. His bones are full [of the sin] of his youth, which shall lie down with him in the dust. [Omitted in R. V.]

Prov. 8:36. He that sinneth against me wrongeth his own soul: all they that hate me love death.

Isa. 57:20. But the wicked *are* like the troubled sea, when it cannot rest, whose waters cast up mire and dirt. 21. *There is* no peace, saith my God, to the wicked.

Hos. 8:7. For they have sown the wind, and they shall reap the whirlwind: it hath no stalk: the bud shall yield no meal: if so be it yield, the strangers shall swallow it up.

Gal. 6:7. Be not deceived; God is not mocked: for whatsoever a man soweth, that shall he also reap. 8. For he that soweth to his flesh shall of the flesh reap corruption; but he that soweth to the Spirit shall of the Spirit reap life everlasting.

Known to God: Gen. 4:10. And he said, What hast thou done? the voice of thy brother's blood crieth unto me from the ground.

Deut. 1:34. And the LORD heard the voice of your words, and was wroth,

Job 10:14. If I sin, then thou markest me, and thou wilt not acquit me from mine iniquity. Josh. 7:10-15.

Psa. 69:5. O God, thou knowest my foolishness; and my sins are not hid from thee.

Jer. 2:22. Though thou wash thee with nitre [lye, *R. V.*], and take thee much soap, *yet* thine iniquity is marked before me, saith the Lord GOD.

Love of: Job 20:12. Though wickedness be sweet in his mouth, *though* he hide it under his tongue; 13. *Though* he spare it, and forsake it not; but keep it still within his mouth:

Prov. 26:11. As a dog returneth to his vomit, *so* a fool returneth to his folly.

John 12:43. For they loved the praise of men more than the praise of God.

National, Punishment of: Isa. 19:4. And the Egyptians will I give over into the hand of a cruel lord; and a fierce king shall rule over them, saith the Lord, the LORD of hosts.

Jer. 12:17. But if they will not obey, I will utterly pluck up and destroy that nation, saith the LORD.

Jonah 1:2. Arise, go to Nineveh, that great city, and cry against it; for their wickedness is come up before me.

Punishment of: Ex. 32:33. And the LORD said unto Moses, Whosoever hath sinned against me, him will I blot out of my book.

Repugnant to God: Deut. 25: 16. For all that do such things, *and* all that do unrighteously, *are*

an abomination unto the LORD thy God.

2 Sam. 11:27. And when the mourning was past, David sent and fetched her to his house, and she became his wife, and bare him a son. But the thing that David had done displeased the LORD.

Psa. 11:5. The LORD trieth the righteous: but the wicked and him that loveth violence his soul hateth.

Repugnant to the Righteous: Psa. 26:5. I have hated the congregation of evil doers; and will not sit with the wicked. 9. Gather not my soul with sinners, nor my life with bloody men:

Psa. 84:10. I had rather be a doorkeeper ·in the house of my God, than to dwell in the tents of wickedness.

Separates from God: Job 13:24. Wherefore hidest thou thy face, and holdest me for thine enemy?

Job 23:3. Oh that I knew where I might find him! *that* I might come *even* to his seat! 8. Behold, I go forward, but he *is* not *there;* and backward, but I cannot perceive him: 9. On the left hand, where he doth work, but I cannot behold *him:* he hideth himself on the right hand, that I cannot see *him:*

Isa. 59:1. Behold, the LORD's hand is not shortened, that it cannot save; neither his ear heavy, that it cannot hear: 2. But your iniquities have separated between you and your God, and your sins have hid *his* face from you, that he will not hear.

SINCERITY. Does not exempt from guilt, Gen. 20.

SLANDER. Comes from the evil heart, Luke 6:45. Often arises from hatred, Psa. 109:3. Idleness leads to, 1 Tim. 5:13. The wicked addicted to, Psa. 50:20. Hypocrites addicted to, Prov. 11:9. A characteristic of the devil, Rev. 12:10. The wicked love, Psa. 52:4. They who indulge in, are fools, Prov. 10:18. Women warned against, Tit. 2:3. Ministers' wives should avoid, 1 Tim. 3:11. Christ was exposed to, Psa. 35:11; Matt. 26:60. Rulers exposed to, Jude 8. Ministers exposed to, Rom. 3:8; 2 Cor. 6:8. The nearest relations exposed to, Psa. 50:20. Saints exposed to, Psa. 38:12; 109:2; 1 Pet. 4:4.

Saints should keep their tongues from, Psa. 34:13, with 1 Pet. 3:10; should lay aside, Eph. 4:31; should be warned against, Tit. 3:1,2; should give no occasion for, 1 Pet. 2:12; 3:16; should return good for, 1 Cor. 4:13; blessed in enduring, Matt. 5:11; characterized as avoiding, Psa. 15:1,3.

Should not be listened to, 1 Sam. 24:9; causes anger, Prov. 25:23 [R. V.].

Effects of: Separating friends, Prov. 16:28; 17:9; deadly wounds, Prov. 18:8; 26:22; strife, Prov. 26: 20; discord among brethren, Prov. 6:19; murder, Psa. 31:13; Ezek. 22:9.

The tongue of, is a scourge, Job 5:21; is venomous, Psa. 140:3; Eccl. 10:11; is destructive, Prov. 11:9. End of, is mischievous madness, Eccl. 10:13. Men shall give account for, Matt. 12:36. Punishment for, Deut. 19:16-21.—*Bible Text-Book.*

Unclassified Scriptures relating to: Ex. 23:1. Thou shalt not raise a false report: put not thine hand with the wicked to be an unrighteous witness.

Psa. 101:5. Whoso privily slandereth his neighbour, him will I cut off:

1 Cor. 4:13. Being defamed, we intreat:

1 Pet. 2:1. Wherefore laying aside all malice, and all guile, and hypocrisies, and envies, and all evil speakings,

SLING. Used for throwing stones, Prov. 26:8. David slays Goliath with, 1 Sam. 17:40-50. Dextrous use of, Judg. 20:16. Used in war, Judg. 20:16; 2 Kin. 3:25; 2 Chr. 26:14.

SLOTHFULNESS. Prov. 6:6. Go to the ant, thou sluggard; consider her ways, and be wise:

Prov. 18:9. He also that is slothful in his work is brother to him that is a great waster.

Prov. 20:4. The sluggard will not plow by reason of the cold;

therefore shall he beg in harvest, and *have* nothing.

Prov. 21:25. The desire of the slothful killeth him; for his hands refuse to labour.

Prov. 23:21. For the drunkard and the glutton shall come to poverty: and drowsiness shall clothe *a man* with rags.

Prov. 24:33. *Yet* a little sleep, a little slumber, a little folding of the hands to sleep: 34. So shall thy poverty come *as* one that travelleth; and thy want as an armed man.

Eccl. 10:18. By much slothfulness the building decayeth; and through idleness of the hands the house droppeth through.

Rom. 12:11. Not slothful in business; fervent in spirit; serving the Lord;

2 Thess. 3:10. For even when we were with you, this we commanded you, that if any would not work, neither should he eat.

Heb. 6:12. That ye be not slothful, but followers of them who through faith and patience inherit the promises.

SOBRIETY. Commanded, 1 Pet. 1:13; 5:8. The gospel designed to teach, Tit. 2:12. With watchfulness, 1 Thess. 5:6. With prayer, 1 Pet. 4:7. Required in ministers, 1 Tim. 3:2,3; Tit. 1:8; wives of ministers, 1 Tim. 3:11; aged men, Tit. 2:2; young men, Tit. 2:6; young women, Tit. 2:4; all saints, 1 Thess. 5:6,8. Women should exhibit in dress, 1 Tim. 2:9. We should estimate our character and talents with, Rom. 12:3. We should live in, Tit. 2:12. Motive for, 1 Pet. 4:7; 5:8. —*Bible Text-Book.*

SON-IN-LAW. Unjust, Jacob, Gen. 30:37-42. Faithful, Peter, Mark 1:29,30; Luke 4:38.

SORCERY, divination by assistance of evil spirits. Forbidden, Lev. 19:26-28,31; 20:6; Deut. 18:9-14. Denounced, Isa. 8:19; Mal. 3:5.

Practised: By the Egyptians, Isa. 19:3,11,12; by the magicians, Ex. 7:11,22; 8:7,18; by Balaam, Num. 22:6; 23:23, with chapters 22; 23; by Jezebel, 2 Kin. 9:22; by the Ninevites, Nah. 3:4,5; by the Babylonians, Isa. 47:9-13; Ezek. 21:21,

22; Dan. 2:2,10,27; by Belshazzar, Dan. 5:7,15; by Simon Magus, Acts 8:9,11; by Elymas, Acts 13:8; by the damsel at Philippi, Acts 16:16; by vagabond Jews, Acts 19:13; by sons of Sceva, Acts 19:14,15; by astrologers, Jer. 10:2; Mic. 3:6,7; by false prophets, Jer. 14:14; 27:9; 29:8,9; Ezek. 13:6-9; 22:28; Matt. 24:24.

SORROW. No sorrow in heaven, Rev. 21:4. Sorrow and sighing shall flee away, Isa. 35:10.

SPEAKING. Evil: Psa. 10:7. His mouth is full of cursing and deceit and fraud: under his tongue *is* mischief and vanity. 8. He sitteth in the lurking places of the villages: in the secret places doth he murder the innocent: his eyes are privily set against the poor.

Psa. 34:13. Keep thy tongue from evil, and thy lips from speaking guile.

Psa. 120:1. In my distress I cried unto the LORD, and he heard me. 2. Deliver my soul, O LORD, from lying lips, *and* from a deceitful tongue. 3. What shall be given unto thee? or what shall be done unto thee, thou false tongue? 4. Sharp arrows of the mighty, with coals of juniper. 5. Woe is me, that I sojourn in Mesech, *that* I dwell in the tents of Kedar! 6. My soul hath long dwelt with him that hateth peace. 7. I *am for* peace: but when I speak, they *are* for war.

Prov. 4:24. Put away from thee a froward mouth, and perverse lips put far from thee.

Prov. 15:1. A soft answer turneth away wrath: but grievous words stir up anger.

Prov. 16:27. An ungodly man diggeth up evil: and in his lips *there is* as a burning fire. 28. A froward man soweth strife: and a whisperer separateth chief friends.

Prov. 26:20. Where no wood is, *there* the fire goeth out: so where *there is* no talebearer, the strife ceaseth. 21. *As* coals *are* to burning coals, and wood to fire; so *is* a contentious man to kindle strife.

Folly in: Job 13:5. O that ye would altogether hold your peace! and it should be your wisdom.

Prov. 18:6. A fool's lips enter into contention, and his mouth calleth for strokes.

Prov. 29:11. A fool uttereth all his mind: but a wise *man* keepeth it in till afterwards. 20. Seest thou a man *that is* hasty in his words? *there is* more hope of a fool than of him.

Matt. 12:36. But I say unto you, That every idle word that men shall speak, they shall give account thereof in the day of judgment. 37. For by thy words thou shalt be justified, and by thy words thou shalt be condemned.

Eph. 5:4. Neither filthiness, nor foolish talking, nor jesting, which are not convenient: but rather giving of thanks.

Wisdom in: Psa. 50:23. Whoso offereth praise glorifieth me: and to him that ordereth *his* conversation *aright* will I shew the salvation of God.

Psa. 141:3. Set a watch, O LORD, before my mouth: keep the door of my lips.

Psa. 145:5. I will speak of the glorious honour of thy majesty, and of thy wondrous works. 6. And *men* shall speak of the might of thy terrible acts: and I will declare thy greatness. 7. They shall abundantly utter the memory of thy great goodness, and shall sing of thy righteousness. 11. They shall speak of the glory of thy kingdom, and talk of thy power; 12. To make known to the sons of men his mighty acts, and the glorious majesty of his kingdom.

Prov. 15:1. A soft answer turneth away wrath: but grievous words stir up anger. 2. The tongue of the wise useth knowledge aright: but the mouth of fools poureth out foolishness. 4. A wholesome tongue *is* a tree of life: but perverseness therein *is* a breach in the spirit. 7. The lips of the wise disperse knowledge: but the heart of the foolish *doeth* not so. 23. A man hath joy by the answer of his mouth: and a word *spoken* in due season, how good *is it!* 26. The thoughts of the wicked *are* an abomination to the

LORD; but *the words* of the pure *are* pleasant words. 28. The heart of the righteous studieth to answer: but the mouth of the wicked poureth out evil things.

Prov. 25:11. A word fitly spoken *is like* apples of gold in pictures of silver.

Matt. 12:37. By thy words thou shalt be justified, and by thy words thou shalt be condemned.

Luke 6:45. A good man out of the good treasure of his heart bringeth forth that which is good; and an evil man out of the evil treasure of his heart bringeth forth that which is evil: for of the abundance of the heart his mouth speaketh. Matt. 12:35.

Jas. 3:2. If any man offend not in word, the same *is* a perfect man, *and* able also to bridle the whole body.

1 Pet. 3:15. But sanctify the Lord God in your hearts: and *be* ready always to *give* an answer to every man that asketh you a reason of the hope that is in you with meekness and fear:

SPIES. Gen. 42:9. Sent to investigate Canaan, Num. 13; Jaazer, Num. 21:32; Jericho, Josh. 2:1. Used by David, 1 Sam. 26:4; at the court of Absalom, 2 Sam. 15:10; 17:1-17. Pharisees acted as, Luke 20:20. In the church of Galatia, Gal. 2:4.

SPIRIT, called inner man, Rom. 7:22; Eph. 3:16.

SPIRITUAL BLESSINGS. See BLESSINGS, SPIRITUAL; HOLY SPIRIT; SANCTIFICATION.

STABILITY, of Character: Psa. 57:7. My heart is fixed, O God, my heart is fixed: I will sing and give praise. Psa. 108:1; 112:7.

1 Cor. 15:58. Therefore, my beloved brethren, be ye stedfast, unmoveable, always abounding in the work of the Lord, forasmuch as ye know that your labour is not in vain in the Lord.

STARS. Created by God, Gen. 1:16; Job. 26:13; Psa. 8:3; 33:6; 136:7,9; Amos 5:8. Differ in splendor, 1 Cor. 15:41. Worship of, forbidden, Deut. 4:19. Worshiped, 2 Kin. 17:16; 21:3; 23:5; Jer. 19:13;

Amos 5:26; Zeph. 1:5; Acts 7:42,43. Constellations of, Isa. 13:10; Orion, Job 9:9; Amos 5:8; serpent, Job 26:13. Planets, 2 Kin. 23:5; the morning star, Job 38:7; Rev. 2:28; 22:16. Darkening of, Job 9:7; Eccl. 12:2; Isa. 13:10; 34:4; Joel 2:10; 3:15; Rev. 8:11,12. Comets, Jude 13. Falling of, Dan. 8:10; Matt. 24:29; Mark 13:25; Rev. 6:13; 8:10; 9:1; 12:4. Guides the wise men, Matt. 2:2,7,9,10.

STRANGERS. Kindness to, required, Lev. 19:33,34. Love of, enjoined, Deut. 10:18,19. Abhorrence of, forbidden, Deut. 23:7. Marriage with, forbidden, Deut. 25:5.

STRAW. Used for provender, Gen. 24:32; Isa. 65:25; for brick, Ex. 5:7.

STRAY. Animals straying to be returned, Ex. 23:4; Deut. 22:1-3. Instance of animals straying, Kish's, 1 Sam. 9.

STRIFE. Gen. 13:8. And Abram said unto Lot, Let there be no strife, I pray thee, between me and thee, and between my herdmen and thy herdmen; for we *be* brethren.

Psa. 80:6. Thou makest us a strife unto our neighbours: and our enemies laugh among themselves.

Prov. 10:12. Hatred stirreth up strifes: but love covereth all sins.

Prov. 16:28. A froward man soweth strife: and a whisperer separateth chief friends.

Prov. 18:19. A brother offended *is harder to be won* than a strong city: and *their* contentions *are* like the bars of a castle.

Prov. 20:3. *It is* an honour for a. man to cease from strife: but every fool will be meddling.

Prov. 21:19. *It is* better to dwell in the wilderness than with a contentious and an angry woman.

Prov. 22:10. Cast out the scorner, and contention shall go out; yea, strife and reproach shall cease.

Prov. 23:29. Who hath woe? who hath sorrow? who hath contentions? who hath babbling? who hath wounds without cause? who hath redness of eyes? 30. They that tarry

SUFFERING

long at the wine; they that go to seek mixed wine.

Prov. 26:17. He that passeth by, *and* meddleth with strife *belonging* not to him, *is like* one that taketh a dog by the ears.

Prov. 27:15. A continual dropping in a very rainy day and a contentious woman are alike.

Prov. 28:25. He that is of a proud heart stirreth up strife:

Matt. 18:15. Moreover if thy brother shall trespass against thee, go and tell him his fault between thee and him alone: if he shall hear thee, thou hast gained thy brother. 16. But if he will not hear *thee, then* take with thee one or two more, that in the mouth of two or three witnesses every word may be established. 17. And if he shall neglect to hear them, tell *it* unto the church: but if he neglect to hear the church, let him be unto thee as an heathen man and a publican.

Rom. 12:18. If it be possible, as much as lieth in you, live peaceably with all men.

Rom. 13:13. Let us walk honestly, as in the day; . . . not in strife and envying.

Rom. 16:17. Now I beseech you, brethren, mark them which cause divisions and offences contrary to the doctrine which ye have learned; and avoid them.

1 Cor. 1:10. I beseech you, brethren, by the name of our Lord Jesus Christ, that ye all speak the same thing, and *that* there be no divisions among you; but *that* ye be perfectly joined together in the same mind and in the same judgment.

Phil. 2:3. *Let* nothing *be done* through strife or vainglory; but in lowliness of mind let each esteem other better than themselves.

Jas. 4:1. From whence *come* wars and fightings among you? *come they* not hence, *even* of your lusts that war in your members?

Instances of: Between Abraham and Lot's herdmen, Gen. 13:6, 7; Abimelech's, Gen. 21:25; Isaac's and those of Gerar, Gen. 26:20-22. Laban and Jacob, Gen. 31:36. Israelites, Deut. 1:12. Jephthah and

his brethren, Judg. 11:2; and Ephraimites, Judg. 12:1-6. Israel and Judah, about David, 2 Sam. 19:41-43. Disciples, over who might be greatest, Mark 9:34; Luke 22:24. Jews, concerning Jesus, John 10:19. Christians at Antioch, about circumcision, Acts 15:2. Paul and Barnabas, about Mark, Acts 15:38, 39. Pharisees and Sadducees, concerning the resurrection, Acts 23:7-10. Corinthians, 1 Cor. 1:11,12; 6:6.

STUDENTS. Poverty of, 2 Kin. 4:1. In state school, Dan. 1. In schools of the prophets, 1 Sam. 19:20; 1 Kin. 20:35; 2 Kin. 2:2,3,5, 7,15; 4:1.

SUBMISSION. To authority: Jesus an example of, Matt. 26:39, 42; Mark 14:36; Luke 22:42; Heb. 5:8.

Of Paul, 1 Cor. 16:7.

SUBSTITUTION, Ex. 28:38. The offering for the offerer, Lev. 1:4; 16:21,22. The Levites for the firstborn of the Israelites, Num. 3:12,41,45; 8:18. The life of Ahab for that of Ben-hadad, I Kin. 20:42.

SUBURBS. Num. 35:3-5; Josh. 14:4.

SUFFERING. For Christ: Acts 9:16. For I will show him how great things he must suffer for my name's sake.

2 Cor. 1:7. And our hope of you *is* stedfast, knowing, that as ye are partakers of the sufferings, so *shall ye be* also of the consolation.

Phil. 1:29. For unto you it is given in the behalf of Christ, not only to believe on him, but also to suffer for his sake;

Phil. 3:10. That I may know him, and the power of his resurrection, and the fellowship of his sufferings, being made conformable unto his death.

Vicarious: John 15:13. Greater love hath no man than this, that a man lay down his life for his friends.

Rom. 9:3. For I could wish that myself were accursed from Christ for my brethren, my kinsmen according to the flesh:

1 John 3:16. We ought to lay down *our* lives for the brethren.

SUICIDE. Amos 9:2; Rev. 9:6. Temptation to, of Jesus, Matt. 4:5,6; Luke 4:9,10,11. Of the Philippian jailer, Acts 16:27.

SUNSTROKE, 2 Kin. 4:19.

SUPEREROGATION, the doctrine of excessive and meritorious righteousness, Ezek. 33:12,13; Luke 17:10.

SYMPATHY. Phil. 2:1. If *there be* therefore any consolation in Christ, if any comfort of love, if any fellowship of the Spirit, if any bowels and mercies, 2. Fulfil ye my joy, that ye be likeminded, having the same love, *being* of one accord, of one mind.

Jas. 1:27. Pure religion and undefiled before God and the Father is this, To visit the fatherless and widows in their affliction, *and* to keep himself unspotted from the world.

1 Pet. 3:8. *Be* pitiful,

TALEBEARER. Lev. 19:16. Thou shalt not go up and down *as* a talebearer among thy people; neither shalt thou stand against the blood of thy neighbour; I *am* the LORD.

Prov. 11:13. A talebearer revealeth secrets: but he that is of a faithful spirit concealeth the matter.

Prov. 16:28. A froward man soweth strife: and a whisperer separateth chief friends.

Prov. 17:9. He that repeateth a matter separateth *very* friends.

Prov. 26:20. Where no wood is, *there* the fire goeth out. So where *there is* no talebearer, the strife ceaseth.

TEACHING. See INSTRUCTION.

TEARS, Psa. 6:6; 39:12; 42:3. Observed by God, Psa. 56:8; Isa. 38:3-5. Wiped away, Rev. 7:17. None in heaven, Rev. 21:4.

Figurative: Psa. 80:5.

TEMPERANCE. Esth. 1:8. And the drinking *was* according to the law; none did compel: for so the king had appointed to all the officers of his house, that they should do according to every man's pleasure.

Prov. 25:16. Hast thou found honey? eat so much as is sufficient for thee, lest thou be filled therewith, and vomit it.

Dan. 1:8. But Daniel purposed in his heart that he would not defile himself with the portion of the king's meat, nor with the wine which he drank.

Rom. 13:14. But put ye on the Lord Jesus Christ, and make not provision for the flesh, to *fulfil* the lusts *thereof.*

1 Tim. 3:3. Not given to wine. [Tit. 1:7,8.]

TEMPTATION. Gen. 3:1. Now the serpent was more subtil than any beast of the field which the LORD God had made. And he said unto the woman, Yea, hath God said, Ye shall not eat of every tree of the garden?

Prov. 1:10. My son, if sinners entice thee, consent thou not.

Prov. 4:14. Enter not into the path of the wicked, and go not in the way of evil *men.*

Prov. 6:27. Can a man take fire in his bosom, and his clothes not be burned? 28. Can one go upon hot coals, and his feet not be burned?

Prov. 14:27. The fear of the LORD *is* a fountain of life, to depart from the snares of death. Prov. 13:14.

Rom. 12:21. Be not overcome of evil, but overcome evil with good.

1 Cor. 10:13. There hath no temptation taken you but such as [is common to man:] but God *is* faithful, who will not suffer you to be tempted above that ye are able; but will with the temptation also make a way to escape, that ye may be able to bear it. [R. V. man can bear]

Eph. 4:27. Neither give place to the devil.

Jas. 4:7. Resist the devil, and he will flee from you.

I Pet. 5:8. Be sober, be vigilant; because your adversary the devil, as a roaring lion, walketh about, seeking whom he may devour: 9. Whom resist stedfast in the faith, knowing that the same afflictions are accomplished in your brethren that are in the world.

2 Pet. 2:9. The Lord knoweth how to deliver the godly out of

temptations, and to reserve the unjust unto the day of judgment to be punished:

Neh. 4:9. Nevertheless we made our prayer unto our God, and set a watch against them day and night, because of them.

Job 31:1. I made a covenant with mine eyes; why then should I think upon a maid?

TESTIMONY. Religious: 1 Chr. 16:8. Give thanks unto the LORD, call upon his name, make known his deeds among the people. 9. Sing unto him, sing psalms unto him, talk ye of all his wondrous works.

Psa. 18:49. Therefore will I give thanks unto thee, O LORD, among the heathen, and sing praises unto thy name.

Luke 24:48. And ye are witnesses of these things.

John 15:27. And ye also shall bear witness, because ye have been with me from the beginning.

Acts 1:8. But ye shall receive power, after that the Holy Ghost is come upon you: and ye shall be witnesses unto me both in Jerusalem, and in all Judæa, and in Samaria, and unto the uttermost part of the earth.

Psa. 145:4. One generation shall praise thy works to another, and shall declare thy mighty acts.

Dan. 4:37. Now I Nebuchadnezzar praise and extol and honour the King of heaven, all whose works *are* truth, and his ways judgment: and those that walk in pride he is able to abase. *vss.* 1-37.

THANKFULNESS. Enjoined: Psa. 50:14. Offer unto God thanksgiving; and pay thy vows unto the most High: 15. And call upon me in the day of trouble: I will deliver thee, and thou shalt glorify me.

Psa. 106:1. Praise ye the LORD. O give thanks unto the LORD: for *he is* good: for his mercy *endureth* for ever.

Phil. 4:6. Be careful for nothing; but in every thing by prayer and supplication with thanksgiving let your requests be made known unto God.

Col. 3:15. And let the peace of God rule in your hearts, to the which also ye are called in one body; and be ye thankful.

1 Thess. 5:18. In every thing give thanks: for this is the will of God in Christ Jesus concerning you.

1 Tim. 2:1. I exhort therefore, that, first of all, supplications, prayers, intercessions, *and* giving of thanks, be made for all men;

THANKSGIVING. See PRAISE; THANKFULNESS.

THEFT AND THIEVES. Ex. 20:15. Thou shalt not steal. Deut. 5:19; Matt. 19:18; Luke 18:20; Rom. 13:9.

Ex. 21:16. And he that stealeth a man, and selleth him, or if he be found in his hand, he shall surely be put to death.

Lev. 19:11. Ye shall not steal, neither deal falsely, 13. Thou shalt not defraud thy neighbour, neither rob *him*:

Eph. 4:28. Let him that stole steal no more: but rather let him labour, working with *his* hands the thing which is good, that he may have to give to him that needeth.

Tit. 2:10. Not purloining, but shewing all good fidelity; that they may adorn the doctrine of God our Saviour in all things.

TITHES. Paid by Abraham to Melchizedek, Gen. 14:20; Heb. 7:2-6. Jacob vows a tenth of all his property to God, Gen. 28:22.

Mosaic laws instituting, Lev. 27:30-33; Num. 18:21-24; Deut. 12:6,7, 17-19; 14:22-29; 26:12-15. Customs relating to, Neh. 10:37,38; Amos 4:4; Heb. 7:5-9. Tithe of tithes for priests, Num. 18:26; Neh. 10:38. Stored in the temple, Neh. 10:38, 39; 12:44; 13:5,12; 2 Chr. 31:11,12; Mal. 3:10.

Payment of, resumed in Hezekiah's reign, 2 Chr. 31:5-10. Under Nehemiah, Neh. 13:12. Withheld, Neh. 13:10; Mal. 3:8.

Customary in later times, Matt. 23:23; Luke 11:42; 18:12. Observed by idolaters, Amos 4:4,5.

TONGUES, miraculous gift, 1 Cor. 12:10,28,30; 13:8; 14:2-19,21-28,39.

TRINITY. The Holy: Matt.

28:19. Go ye therefore, and teach all nations, baptizing them in the name of the Father, and of the Son, and of the Holy Ghost:

Luke 1:35. The angel answered and said unto her, The Holy Ghost shall come upon thee, and the power of the Highest shall overshadow thee: therefore also that holy thing which shall be born of thee shall be called the Son of God.

Luke 3:22. The Holy Ghost descended in a bodily shape like a dove upon him, and a voice came from heaven, which said, Thou art my beloved Son; in thee I am well pleased. Matt. 3:16.

1 Cor. 8:6. But to us *there is but* one God, the Father, of whom *are* all things, and we in him: and one Lord Jesus Christ, by whom *are* all things, and we by him.

2 Cor. 3:17. The Lord is that Spirit: and where the Spirit of the Lord *is*, there *is* liberty.

Tit. 3:4. But after that the kindness and love of God our Saviour toward man appeared, 5. Not by works of righteousness which we have done, but according to his mercy he saved us, by the washing of regeneration, and renewing of the Holy Ghost: 6. Which he shed on us abundantly through Jesus Christ our Saviour:

Heb. 9:14. How much more shall the blood of Christ, who through the eternal Spirit offered himself without spot to God, purge your conscience from dead works to serve the living God?

1 Pet. 1:2. Elect according to the foreknowledge of God the Father, through sanctification of the Spirit, unto obedience and sprinkling of the blood of Jesus Christ:

TRUST. See FAITH.

TRUTH. Psa. 51:6. Behold, thou desirest truth in the inward parts:

Psa. 89:14. Justice and judgment *are* the habitation of thy throne: mercy and truth shall go before thy face.

Psa. 100:5. For the LORD *is* good; his mercy *is* everlasting; and his truth *endureth* to all generations.

Prov. 12:19. The lip of truth shall be established for ever: but a lying tonge *is* but for a moment.

John 14:6. Jesus saith unto him, I am the way, the truth, and the life:

John 16:13. Howbeit when he, the Spirit of truth, is come, he will guide you into all truth:

John 17:17. Sanctify them through thy truth: thy word is truth.

TYPES. Miscellaneous: Bride, a type of the Church, Rev. 21:2,9; 22:17. The sanctuary a type of the heavenly sanctuary, Ex. 40:2,24; Heb. 8:2,5; 9:1-12. The saving of Noah and his family, of the salvation through the gospel, 1 Pet. 3:20, 21.

Of the Saviour: Col. 2:17; Heb. 9:7-15,18-28; 10:1-10. High Priest, typical of the mediatorship, Ex. 28:1,12,29,30,38; Lev. 16:15; Zech. 6:12,13, with Heb. 5; 8:2; 10:21. The institutions ordained by Moses, Matt. 26:54; Luke 24:25-27,44-47; Col. 2:14-17; Heb. 10:1-14. The sacrifices, Lev. 4:2,3,12; Heb. 9:7-15,18-25; 10:1-22,29; 13: 11-13; 1 Pet. 1:19; Rev. 5:6. The morning and evening sacrifice, John 1:29,36. The red heifer, Num. 19:2-6, with Heb. 9:13,14. The paschal lamb, 1 Cor. 5:7. The brazen altar, Ex. 27:1,2, with Heb. 13:10. The laver of brass, Ex. 30:18-20, with Zech. 13:1; Eph. 5:26,27. Mercy seat, Ex. 25:17-22, with Heb. 4:16. The veil, Ex. 40:21; 2 Chr. 3:14, with Heb. 10:20. Manna, John 6: 32-35; 1 Cor. 10:3. Cities of refuge, Num. 35:6, with Heb. 6:18. Brazen serpent, Num. 21:9; John 3:14,15. Tree of life, Gen. 2:9, with John 1:4; Rev. 22:2.

Adam, Rom. 5:14; 1 Cor. 15:45. Abel, Gen. 4:8,10, with Heb. 12:24. Noah, Gen. 5:29, with 2 Cor. 1:5. Melchizedek, Heb. 7:1-17. Moses, Deut. 8:15,18; Acts 3:20,22; 7:37; Heb. 3:2-6. David, 2 Sam. 8:15; Psa. 89:19,20; Ezek. 37:24; Phil. 2:9. Eliakim, Isa. 22:20-22; Rev. 3:7. Jonah, Jonah 1:17, with Matt. 12:40.

UNBELIEF. Num. 11:23. And the LORD said unto Moses, Is the LORD's hand waxed short? thou shalt see now whether my word shall come to pass unto thee or not.

Psa. 78:19. Yea, they spake against God; they said, Can God furnish a table in the wilderness? 32. For all this they sinned still, and believed not for his wondrous works.

Matt. 13:58. And he did not many mighty works there because of their unbelief.

Mark 6:4. But Jesus said unto them, A prophet is not without honour, but in his own country, and among his own kin, and in his own house. 5. And he could there do no mighty work, save that he laid his hands upon a few sick folk, and healed *them*. 6. And he marvelled because of their unbelief.

Luke 16:31. And he said unto him, If they hear not Moses and the prophets, neither will they be persuaded, though one rose from the dead.

John 1:10. He was in the world, and the world was made by him, and the world knew him not. 11. He came unto his own, and his own received him not.

Rom. 4:20. He staggered not at the promise of God through unbelief; but was strong in faith, giving glory to God;

2 Cor. 6:14. Be ye not unequally yoked together with unbelievers: for what fellowship hath righteousness with unrighteousness? and what communion hath light with darkness?

UNCHARITABLE-NESS. Matt. 7:1. Judge not, that ye be not judged.

1 Cor. 13:1. Though I speak with the tongues of men and of angels, and have not charity, I am become *as* sounding brass, or a tinkling cymbal.

UNFRUITFULNESS. Matt. 7:19. Every tree that bringeth not forth good fruit is hewn down, and cast into the fire.

Matt. 13:4. And when he sowed, some *seeds* fell by the way side, and the fowls came and devoured them up: 5. Some fell upon stony places, where they had not much earth: and forthwith they sprung up,

because they had no deepness of earth: 6. And when the sun was up, they were scorched; and because they had no root, they withered away. 7. And some fell among thorns; and the thorns sprung up, and choked them:

John 15:2. Every branch in me that beareth not fruit he taketh away: and every *branch* that beareth fruit, he purgeth it, that it may bring forth more fruit. 4. Abide in me, and I in you. As the branch cannot bear fruit of itself, except it abide in the vine; no more can ye, except ye abide in me. 6. If a man abide not in me, he is cast forth as a branch, and is withered: and men gather them, and cast *them* into the fire, and they are burned.

UNITY. Of the Righteous: Psa. 133:1. Behold, how good and how pleasant *it is* for brethren to dwell together in unity!

Rom. 12:16. *Be* of the same mind one toward another.

Rom. 14:19. Let us therefore follow after the things which make for peace, and things wherewith one may edify another.

Rom. 15:5. Now the God of patience and consolation grant you to be likeminded one toward another, according to Christ Jesus: 6. That ye may with one mind *and* one mouth glorify God, even the Father of our Lord Jesus Christ.

Eph. 4:3. Endeavouring to keep the unity of the Spirit in the bond of peace.

Phil. 2:2. Fulfil ye my joy, that ye be likeminded, having the same love, *being* of one accord, of one mind.

UNPARDONABLE SIN, 2 Kin. 24:4; Matt. 12:31,32; Luke 12:10; Heb. 6:4-6; 1 John 5:16.

Instances of: Israel, Num. 14: 26-45. Eli's house, 1 Sam. 3:14.

UNSELFISHNESS. Rom. 12:10. *Be* kindly affectioned one to another with brotherly love; in honour preferring one another;

Rom. 15:1. We then that are strong ought to bear the infirmities of the weak, and not to please ourselves. 2. Let every one of us please *his* neighbour for *his* good

UPRIGHTNESS

to edification. 3. For even Christ pleased not himself; but, as it is written, The reproaches of them that reproached thee fell on me.

1 Cor. 10:24. Let no man seek his own, but every man another's *wealth.* 33. Even as I please all *men* in all *things,* not seeking mine own profit, but the *profit* of many, that they may be saved.

Phil. 2:3. *Let* nothing *be done* through strife or vainglory: but in lowliness of mind let each esteem other better than themselves.

UPRIGHTNESS. See RIGHT-EOUSNESS.

URIM AND THUMMIM, signifying light and perfection. In the breastplate, Ex. 28:30; Lev. 8:8. Eleazar to ask counsel for Joshua, after the judgment of, Num. 27:21. Priests only might interpret, Deut. 33:8; Ezra 2:63; Neh. 7:65. Israelites consult, Judg. 1:1; 20:18,23. Withheld answer from King Saul, 1 Sam. 28:6.

VAIL. Of the temple, 2 Chr. 3:14. Rent at the time of the crucifixion of Jesus, Matt. 27:51; Mark 15:38; Luke 23:45.

VEGETARIANS, persons who eat no flesh, Rom. 14:2.

VENGEANCE, belongs to God, Psa. 94:1; Rom. 12:19.

VENTRILOQUISM, Isa. 29:4. Divination by, Acts 16:16.

VIPER. A serpent, Job 20:16; Isa. 30:6; 59:5. Fastens on Paul's hand, Acts 28:3.

VOWS. Num. 30:2. If a man vow a vow unto the LORD, or swear an oath to bind his soul with a bond; he shall not break his word, he shall do according to all that proceedeth out of his mouth. 3. If a woman also vow a vow unto the LORD, and bind *herself* by a bond, *being* in her father's house in her youth; 4. And her father hear her vow, and her bond wherewith she hath bound her soul, and her father shall hold his peace at her: then all her vows shall stand, and every bond wherewith she hath bound her soul shall stand. 5. But if her father disallow her in the day that he heareth; not any of her vows, or of her bonds wherewith she hath

bound her soul, shall stand: and the LORD shall forgive her, because her father disallowed her. 6. And if she had at all an husband, when she vowed, or uttered ought out of her lips, wherewith she bound her soul; 7. And her husband heard *it,* and held his peace at her in the day that he heard *it:* then her vows shall stand, and her bonds wherewith she bound her soul shall stand. 8. But if her husband disallowed her on the day that he heard *it;* then he shall make her vow which she vowed, and that which she uttered with her lips, wherewith she bound her soul, of none effect: and the LORD shall forgive her. 9. But every vow of a widow, and of her that is divorced, wherewith they have bound their souls, shall stand against her.

Eccl. 5:4. When thou vowest a vow unto God, defer not to pay it; for *he hath* no pleasure in fools: pay that which thou hast vowed. 5. Better *is it* that thou shouldest not vow, than that thou shouldest vow and not pay. 6. Suffer not thy mouth to cause thy flesh to sin; neither say thou before the angel, that it *was* an error: wherefore should God be angry at thy voice, and destroy the work of thine hands?

WAGES, Unclassified Scriptures Relating to: Lev. 19:13. Thou shalt not defraud thy neighbour, neither rob *him:* the wages of him that is hired shall not abide with thee all night until the morning.

Deut. 25:4. Thou shalt not muzzle the ox when he treadeth out *the corn.*

Jer. 22:13. Woe unto him that buildeth his house by unrighteousness, and his chambers by wrong; *that* useth his neighbour's service without wages, and giveth him not for his work;

Luke 10:7. For the labourer is worthy of his hire. Matt. 10:10.

Rom. 6:23. For the wages of sin *is* death; but the gift of God *is* eternal life through Jesus Christ our Lord.

Col. 4:1. Masters, give unto *your*

servants that which is just and equal; knowing that ye also have a Master in heaven.

WAR. Figurative: Warfare of saints: Is not after the flesh, 2 Cor. 10:3. Is a good warfare, 1 Tim. 1:18,19. Called the good fight of faith, 1 Tim. 6:12.

Is against the devil, Gen. 3:15; 2 Cor. 2:11; Eph. 6:12; Jas. 4:7; 1 Pet. 5:8; Rev. 12:17; the flesh, Rom. 7:23; 1 Cor. 9:25-27; 2 Cor. 12:7; Gal. 5:17; 1 Pet. 2:11; enemies, Psa. 38:19; 56:2; 59:3; the world, John 16:33; 1 John 5:4,5; death, 1 Cor. 15:26, with Heb. 2:14,15.

Armor for: a girdle of truth, Eph. 6:14; the breastplate of righteousness, Eph. 6:14;

Victory in, is from God, 1 Cor. 15:57; 2 Cor. 2:14; through Christ, Rom. 7:25;

WATCHFULNESS. Deut. 4:9. Only take heed to thyself, and keep thy soul diligently, lest thou forget the things which thine eyes have seen, and lest they depart from thy heart all the days of thy life: but teach them thy sons, and thy sons' sons:

Psa. 39:1. I said, I will take heed to my ways, that I sin not with my tongue: I will keep my mouth with a bridle, while the wicked is before me.

Psa. 119:9. Wherewithal shall a young man cleanse his way? by taking heed *thereto* according to thy word.

Psa. 141:3. Set a watch, O LORD, before my mouth; keep the door of my lips.

Prov. 4:23. Keep thy heart with all diligence; for out of it *are* the issues of life. 25. Let thine eyes look right on, and let thine eyelids look straight before thee. 26. Ponder the path of thy feet, and let all thy ways be established.

Mark 13:35. Watch ye therefore: for ye know not when the master of the house cometh, at even, or at midnight, or at the cockcrowing, or in the morning: 36. Lest coming suddenly he find you sleeping. 37. And what I say unto you I say unto all, Watch. Matt. 24:42-51; Luke 21:8-36.

1 Cor. 10:12. Wherefore let him that thinketh he standeth take heed lest he fall.

1 Cor. 11:28. But let a man examine himself, and so let him eat of *that* bread, and drink of *that* cup.

Col. 4:2. Continue in prayer, and watch in the same with thanksgiving;

WATCHMAN, a sentinel. On the walls of cities, Song 3:3; 5:7; of Jerusalem, 2 Sam. 13:34; 18:24,25; Neh. 4:9; 7:3; Isa. 52:8; 62:6; of Babylon, Jer. 51:12. On towers, 2 Kin. 9:17; 2 Chr. 20:24; Isa. 21:5-12; Jer. 31:6. At the gates of the temple, 2 Kin. 11:6,7. Alarm of, given by trumpets, Ezek. 33:3-6. Unfaithfulness in the discharge of duty of, punished by death, Ezek. 33:6; Matt. 28:14; Acts 12:19.

WATER. Figurative: Water of life, John 4:14; 7:37-39; Rev. 21:6; 22:17. Of affliction, 2 Sam. 22:17; Psa. 69:1; Isa. 30:20; 43:2. Of salvation, Isa. 12:3; 49:10; 55:1; Ezek. 36:25; John 4:10; 7:38. Domestic love, Prov. 5:15.

SYMBOLICAL: Isa. 8:7; Rev. 8:11; 12:15; 16:4; 17:1,15.

WEATHER. Signs of, Matt. 16:2,3. Sayings concerning, Job. 37:9,17,22.

WEDDING. See MARRIAGE.

WEEPING, Rom. 12:15; 1 Cor. 7:30. In perdition, Matt. 8:12; 22:13; 24:51; 25:30. None in heaven, Rev. 7:17. Penitential, Jer. 50:4; Joel 2:12. Instances of penitential: The Israelites, Judg. 2:4,5. Peter, Matt. 26:75; Mark 14:72; Luke 22:62. While doing good, Psa. 126:5,6. For others, Jer. 9:1. On account of tribulation, Jer. 22:10; Amos 5:16,17.

Instances of: Of Abraham for Sarah, Gen. 23:2. Of Esau, Gen. 27:38. Of Jacob and Esau, Gen. 33:4. Of Jacob, Gen. 37:35. Of Joseph, Gen. 42:24; 43:30; 45:2,14; 46:29; 50:1,17. Of Hannah, 1 Sam. 1:7. Of Jonathan and David, 1 Sam. 20:41. Of David, 2 Sam. 1:17; 3:32; 13:36; 15:23,30; 18:33. Of Hezekiah, 2 Kin. 20:3; Isa. 38:3. Of Jesus, over Jerusalem, Luke 19:41; at the grave of Lazarus, John 11:35. Of Mary, when she washed the

feet of Jesus, Luke 7:38; John 11:
2,33. Of Mary Magdalene, John
20:11. Of Paul, Acts 20:19; Phil.
3:18.

WELLS. The occasion of feuds:
Between Abraham and Abimelech,
Gen. 21:25-30; between Isaac and
Abimelech, Gen. 26:15-22,32,33. Of
Jacob, John 4:6. Of Solomon, Eccl.
2:6. Of Uzziah, 2 Chr. 26:10. Of
Hezekiah, see GIHON. At Haran,
Gen. 24:16.

Figurative: Of salvation, Isa.
12:3; John 4:14. Without water,
Jer. 15:18; 2 Pet. 2:17.

WHEAT, Rev. 6:6. Grown in
Palestine, 1 Kin. 5:11; Psa. 81:16;
147:14. Offerings of, Num. 18:12.
Prophecy of the sale of a measure
of, for a penny, Rev. 6:6.

Parables of, Matt. 13:25; Luke
16:7. Winnowing of, Matt. 3:12;
Luke 3:17. Ground in a mortar,
Prov. 27:22. Chaff of, Jer. 23:28;
Matt. 3:12; Luke 3:17. Growth of,
figurative of vicarious death, John
12:24.

Figurative: Of God's mercy,
Psa. 81:16; 147:14. Of self-righteousness, Jer. 12:13.

WHIRLWIND. Figurative:
Of the judgment of God, Jer. 23:
19; 30:23. Of the fruits of unrighteousness, Hos. 8:7. Of divine
judgments, Ezek. 1:4.

WHISPERER, a slanderer,
Rom. 1:29; 2 Cor. 12:20.

WHORE, revenues of, not to
be brought to the sanctuary, Deut.
23:18.

WHOREDOM, licentious rites
of, in idolatrous worship, Lev. 19:
29; Deut. 31:16; Judg. 2:17; 2 Kin.
9:22.

Figurative: Ezek. 16; 23; Rev.
17:1-6.

WHOREMONGER, Rev. 21:
8; 22:15.

**WICKED. Contrasted With
the Righteous:** Psa. 1:1. Blessed
is the man that walketh not in the
counsel of the ungodly, nor standeth in the way of sinners, nor sitteth
in the seat of the scornful.

Psa. 32:10. Many sorrows *shall
be* to the wicked: but he that trusteth in the LORD, mercy shall compass him about.

Psa. 91:7. A thousand shall fall
at thy side, and ten thousand at thy
right hand; *but* it shall not come
nigh thee. 8. Only with thine eyes
shalt thou behold and see the reward of the wicked.

Prov. 11:3. The integrity of the
upright shall guide them: but the
perverseness of transgressors shall
destroy them.

Described: Lev. 18:25. The
land is defiled: therefore I do visit
the iniquity thereof upon it, and
the land itself vomiteth out her inhabitants.

1 Kin. 21:20. And Ahab said to
Elijah, Hast thou found me, O
mine enemy? And he answered, I
have found *thee:* because thou hast
sold thyself to work evil in the
sight of the LORD.

Job 14:4. Who can bring a
clean *thing* out of an unclean? not
one.

Job 20:12. Though wickedness be
sweet in his mouth, *though* he hide
it under his tongue; 13. *Though*
he spare it, and forsake it not; but
keep it still within his mouth:

Psa. 49:20. Man *that is* in honour, and understandeth not, is like
the beasts *that* perish.

Psa. 53:1. The fool hath said in
his heart, There *is* no God. Corrupt are they, and have done
abominable iniquity: *there is* none
that doeth good.

Prov. 14:9. Fools make a mock
at sin:

Isa. 57:20. The wicked *are* like
the troubled sea, when it cannot
rest, whose waters cast up mire and
dirt. 21. *There is* no peace, saith
my God, to the wicked.

Jer. 30:12. For thus saith the
LORD, Thy bruise *is* incurable, *and*
thy wound *is* grievous. 13. *There is*
none to plead thy cause, that thou
mayest be bound up: thou hast no
healing medicines.

Luke 1:79. Them that sit in
darkness and *in* the shadow of
death,

John 3:18. He that believeth not
is condemned already, because he
hath not believed in the name of
the only begotten Son of God.

John 5:42. But I know you, that

ye have not the love of God in you.

Rom. 1:20. So that they are without excuse: 21. Because that, when they knew God, they glorified *him* not as God, neither were thankful; but became vain in their imaginations, and their foolish heart was darkened. 22. Professing themselves to be wise, they became fools.

Prayer of: Job 27:9. Will God hear his cry when trouble cometh upon him?

Psa. 18:41. They cried, but *there was* none to save *them; even* unto the LORD, but he answered them not.

Psa. 66:18. If I regard iniquity in my heart, the Lord will not hear me:

Prov. 21:13. Whoso stoppeth his ears at the cry of the poor, he also shall cry himself, but shall not be heard.

Isa. 1:15. And when ye spread forth your hands, I will hide mine eyes from you: yea, when ye make many prayers, I will not hear: your hands are full of blood.

Isa. 59:2. But your iniquities have separated between you and your God, and your sins have hid *his* face from you, that he will not hear.

Jas. 4:3. Ye ask, and receive not, because ye ask amiss, that ye may consume *it* upon your lusts.

Punishment of: Num. 15:31. Because he hath despised the word of the LORD, and hath broken his commandment, that soul shall utterly be cut off; his iniquity *shall be* upon him.

Job 34:22. *There is* no darkness, nor shadow of death, where the workers of iniquity may hide themselves.

Psa. 2:4. He that sitteth in the heavens shall laugh: the Lord shall have them in derision. 5. Then shall he speak unto them in his wrath, and vex them in his sore displeasure. 9. Thou shalt break them with a rod of iron; thou shalt dash them in pieces like a potter's vessel.

Psa. 7:11. God judgeth the righteous, and God is angry *with the wicked* every day.

Psa. 32:10. Many sorrows *shall be* to the wicked:

Isa. 48:22. *There is* no peace, saith the LORD, unto the wicked.

Isa. 57:20. But the wicked *are* like the troubled sea, when it cannot rest, whose waters cast up mire and dirt. 21. *There is* no peace, saith my God, to the wicked.

Ezek. 7:4. Mine eyes shall not spare thee, neither will I have pity: but I will recompense thy ways upon thee, and thine abominations shall be in the midst of thee: and ye shall know that I *am* the LORD.

Dan. 12:2. And many of them that sleep in the dust of the earth shall awake, some to everlasting life, and some to shame *and* everlasting contempt.

Hos. 10:8. They shall say to the mountains, Cover us; and to the hills, Fall on us. Luke 23:30; Rev. 6:16; 9:6.

Matt. 8:12. But the children of the kingdom shall be cast out into outer darkness: there shall be weeping and gnashing of teeth.

Matt. 10:28. And fear not them which kill the body, but are not able to kill the soul: but rather fear him which is able to destroy both soul and body in hell. [Luke 12:4, 5.]

Matt. 23:33. *Ye* serpents, *ye* generation of vipers, how can ye escape the [damnation] of hell? Matt. 12:34. [R. V. judgment]

Heb. 10:27. But a certain fearful looking for of judgment and fiery indignation, which shall devour the adversaries.

2 Pet. 2:4. For if God spared not the angels that sinned, but cast *them* down to hell, and delivered *them* into chains of darkness, to be reserved unto judgment:

WIDOW. Deut. 10:18. He doth execute the judgment of the fatherless and widow, and loveth the stranger, in giving him food and raiment.

Jer. 49:11. Let thy widows trust in me.

Jas. 1:27. Pure religion and undefiled before God and the Father is this, To visit the fatherless and widows in their affliction, *and* to keep himself unspotted from the world.

WIFE.

Unclassified Scriptures Relating to: Gen. 2:18. And the LORD God said, *It is* not good that the man should be alone; I will make him an help meet for him. 24. Therefore shall a man leave his father and his mother, and shall cleave unto his wife: and they shall be one flesh.

Gen. 3:16. Unto the woman he said, I will greatly multiply thy sorrow and thy conception; in sorrow thou shalt bring forth children; and thy desire *shall be* to thy husband, and he shall rule over thee.

Psa. 128:3. Thy wife *shall be* as a fruitful vine by the side of thine house: thy children like olive plants round about thy table. 4. Behold, that thus shall the man be blessed that feareth the LORD.

Prov. 18:22. *Whoso* findeth a wife findeth a good *thing*, and obtaineth favour of the LORD.

Prov. 19:13. The contentions of a wife *are* a continual dropping. 14. And a prudent wife *is* from the LORD.

Prov. 25:24. *It is* better to dwell in the corner of the housetop, than with a brawling woman and in a wide house. Prov. 21:9,19.

1 Cor. 7:2. Nevertheless, *to avoid* fornication, let every man have his own wife, and let every woman have her own husband. 3. Let the husband render unto the wife due benevolence: and likewise also the wife unto the husband. 4. The wife hath not power of her own body, but the husband: and likewise also the husband hath not power of his own body, but the wife. 5. Defraud ye not one the other, except *it be* with consent for a time, that ye may give yourselves to fasting and prayer; and come together again, that Satan tempt you not for your incontinency.

Eph. 5:22. Wives, submit yourselves unto your own husbands, as unto the Lord. 23. For the husband is the head of the wife, even as Christ is the head of the church: and he is the saviour of the body.

24. Therefore as the church is subject unto Christ, so *let* the wives *be* to their own husbands in every thing. 25. Husbands, love your wives, even as Christ also loved the church, and gave himself for it;

Col. 3:18. Wives, submit yourselves unto your own husbands, as it is fit in the Lord. 19. Husbands, love *your* wives, and be not bitter against them.

WINE. Psa. 104:14. He causeth the grass to grow for the cattle, and herb for the service of man: that he may bring forth food out of the earth; 15. And wine *that* maketh glad the heart of man, *and* oil to make *his* face to shine, and bread *which* strengtheneth man's heart.

Joel 1:5. Awake, ye drunkards, and weep; and howl, all ye drinkers of wine, because of the new wine; for it is cut off from your mouth.

Hab. 2:5. Yea [also, because he transgresseth by wine, *he is* a proud] man, neither keepeth at home, who enlargeth his desire as hell, and *is* as death, and cannot be satisfied, but gathereth unto him all nations, and heapeth unto him all people:

1 Tim. 5:23. Drink no longer water, but use a little wine for thy stomach's sake and thine often infirmities.

Admonitions Against the Use of: Lev. 10:9. Do not drink wine nor strong drink, thou, nor thy sons with thee, when ye go into the tabernacle of the congregation, lest ye die: *it shall be* a statute for ever throughout your generations.

Prov. 20:1. Wine *is* a mocker, strong drink *is* raging: and whosoever is deceived thereby is not wise.

Prov. 21:17. He that loveth pleasure *shall be* a poor man: he that loveth wine and oil shall not be rich.

Prov. 23:29. Who hath woe? who hath sorrow? who hath contentions? who hath babbling? who hath wounds without cause? who hath redness of eyes? 30. They that tarry long at the wine; they that go to seek mixed wine. 31. Look not thou upon the wine when it is red, when it giveth his colour in the cup, *when* it moveth itself aright. 32. At the last it biteth like a serpent, and stingeth like an adder.

Isa. 5:11. Woe unto them that rise up early in the morning, *that* they may follow strong drink: that continue until night, *till* wine inflame them! 22. Woe unto *them that are* mighty to drink wine, and men of strength to mingle strong drink:

Hos. 4:11. Whoredom and wine and new wine take away the heart.

Rom. 14:21. *It is* good neither to eat flesh, nor to drink wine, nor *any thing* whereby thy brother stumbleth.

Eph. 5:18. And be not drunk with wine, wherein is excess; but be filled with the Spirit.

WISDOM. Job 12:2. No doubt but ye *are* the people, and wisdom shall die with you.

Psa. 111:10. The fear of the LORD *is* the beginning of wisdom: a good understanding have all they that do *his* commandments:

Prov. 1:5. A wise *man* will hear, and will increase learning; and a man of understanding shall attain unto wise counsel:

Dan. 12:3. And they that be wise shall shine as the brightness of the firmament; and they that turn many to righteousness as the stars for ever and ever.

John 7:17. If any man will do his will, he shall know of the doctrine, whether it be of God, or *whether* I speak of myself.

John 8:32. Ye shall know the truth, and the truth shall make you free.

John 17:3. This is life eternal, that they might know thee the only true God, and Jesus Christ, whom thou has sent.

1 Cor. 3:18. Let no man deceive himself. If any man among you seemeth to be wise in this world, let him become a fool, that he may be wise.

1 Cor. 13:11. When I was a child, I spake as a child, I understood as a child, I thought as a child: but when I became a man, I put away childish things.

1 Cor. 14:20. Brethren, be not children in understanding: howbeit in malice be ye children, but in understanding be men.

Eph. 5:15. See then that ye walk circumspectly, not as fools, but as wise, 16. Redeeming the time, because the days are evil. 17. Wherefore be ye not unwise, but understanding what the will of the Lord *is*.

2 Tim. 3:15. And that from a child thou hast known the holy scriptures, which are able to make thee wise unto salvation through faith which is in Christ Jesus.

Jas. 3:13. Who *is* a wise man and endued with knowledge among you? let him shew out of a good conversation his works with meekness of wisdom.

Spiritual, From God: 1 Chr. 22:12. Only the LORD give thee wisdom and understanding, and give thee charge concerning Israel, that thou mayest keep the law of the LORD thy God.

Psa. 32:8. I will instruct thee and teach thee in the way which thou shalt go: I will guide thee with mine eye.

Psa. 119:130. The entrance of thy words giveth light; it giveth understanding unto the simple.

Prov. 1:23. Turn you at my reproof: behold, I will pour out my spirit unto you, I will make known my words unto you.

Prov. 3:5. Trust in the LORD with all thine heart; and lean not unto thine own understanding. 6. In all thy ways acknowledge him, and he shall direct thy paths.

Eccl. 2:26. For *God* giveth to a man that *is* good in his sight wisdom, and knowledge, and joy:

Isa. 30:21. And thine ears shall hear a word behind thee, saying, This *is* the way, walk ye in it, when ye turn to the right hand, and when ye turn to the left.

Isa. 48:17. Thus saith the LORD, thy Redeemer, the Holy One of Israel; I *am* the LORD thy God which teacheth thee to profit, which leadeth thee by the way *that* thou shouldest go.

Luke 21:15. I will give you a

mouth and wisdom, which all your adversaries shall not be able to gainsay nor resist.

1 Cor. 2:9. But as it is written, Eye hath not seen, nor ear heard, neither have entered into the heart of man, the things which God hath prepared for them that love him. 10. But God hath revealed *them* unto us by his Spirit: for the Spirit searcheth all things, yea, the deep things of God.

1 Cor. 12:8. For to one is given by the Spirit the word of wisdom; to another the word of knowledge by the same Spirit;

2 Tim. 1:7. God hath not given us the spirit of fear; but of power, and of love, and of a sound mind.

Jas. 3:17. But the wisdom that is from above is first pure, then peaceable, gentle, *and* easy to be intreated, full of mercy and good fruits, without partiality, and without hypocrisy.

Worldly: Prov. 3:7. Be not wise in thine own eyes: fear the LORD, and depart from evil.

Prov. 28:11. The rich man *is* wise in his own conceit; but the poor that hath understanding searcheth him out.

Isa. 5:21. Woe unto *them that are* wise in their own eyes, and prudent in their own sight!

Luke 16:8. And the lord commended the unjust steward, because he had done wisely: for the children of this world are in their generation wiser than the children of light.

WITCHCRAFT. Law concerning, Ex. 22:18; Lev. 19:31; 20:6,27. Witch of Endor, 1 Sam. 28:7-25. Witches destroyed, 1 Sam. 28:3,9.

WIZARD. See SORCERY.

WOMEN. Creation of, Gen. 1:27; 2:21,22. Named, Gen. 2:23. Fall of, and curse upon, Gen. 3:1-16; 2 Cor. 11:3; 1 Tim. 2:14. Promise to, Gen. 3:15.

Weaker than men, 1 Pet. 3:7. Are timid, Isa. 19:16; Jer. 50:37; 51:30; Nah. 3:13; affectionate, 2 Sam. 1:26; tender to her offspring, Isa. 49:15; Lam. 4:10; mirthsome, Judg. 11:34; 21:21; Jer. 31:13; Zech. 9:17; courteous to strangers,

Gen. 24:17. Could not marry without consent of parents, Gen. 24:3,4; 34:6; Ex. 22:17. Not to be given in marriage considered a calamity, Judg. 11:37; Psa. 78:63; Isa. 4:1. Taken captive, Num. 31:9,15,17,18, 35; Lam. 1:18; Ezek. 30:17,18. Shrewd, 2 Sam. 20:16-22.

Virtuous, held in high estimation, Ruth 3:11; Prov. 31:10-30.

Fond of self-indulgence, Isa. 32:9-11; of ornaments, Jer. 2:32. Subtle and deceitful, Prov. 6:24-29, 32-35; 7:6-27; Eccl. 7:26. Silly, and easily led into error, 2 Tim. 3:6. Zealous in promoting superstition and idolatry, Jer. 7:18; Ezek. 13:17,23. Active in instigating iniquity, Num. 31:15,16; 1 Kin. 21:25; Neh. 13:26. Guilty of sodomy, 2 Kin. 23:7; Rom. 1:26.

As rulers: Isa. 3:12; Deborah, Judg. 4:4; Athaliah, 2 Kin. 11:1-16; 2 Chr. 22:2,3,10-12; Queen of Sheba, 1 Kin. 10:1-13; Candace, Acts 8:27; Persian queen sat on throne with the king, Neh. 2:6. Patriotic: Miriam, Ex. 15:20; Deborah, Judg. 5; women of Israel, 1 Sam. 18:6; of the Philistines, 2 Sam. 1:20. Aid in defensive operations, Judg. 9:53.

As poets: Miriam, Ex. 15:21; Deborah, Judg. 5; Hannah, 1 Sam. 2:1-10; Elisabeth, Luke 1:42-45; Mary, Luke 1:46-55.

As prophets: Miriam, Ex. 15:20, 21; Mic. 6:4; Deborah, Judg. 4:4,5; Huldah, 2 Kin. 22:14-20; 2 Chr. 34:22-28; Noadiah, Neh. 6:14; Anna, Luke 2:36-38; Philip's daughters, Acts 21:9. False prophets, Ezek. 13:17-23.

In business, Prov. 31:14-18,24. Property rights of: In inheritance, Num. 27:1-11; 36; Josh. 17:3-6; Job 42:15; to sell real estate, Ruth 4:3-9.

First to sin, Gen. 3:6. Last at the cross, Matt. 27:55,56; Mark 15:40,41. First at the sepulcher, Mark 15:46,47; 16:1-6; Luke 23:27,28,49, 55,56; 24:1-10. First to whom the risen Lord appeared, Mark 16:9; John 20:14-18.

Unclassified Scriptures Relating to: Gen. 2:18. And the LORD God said, It is not good that the man should be alone; I will make him an help meet for him.

Gen. 3:16. Unto the woman he said, I will greatly multiply thy sorrow and thy conception; in sorrow thou shalt bring forth children; and thy desire *shall be* to thy husband, and he shall rule over thee.

Prov. 18:22. *Whoso* findeth a wife findeth a good *thing*, and obtaineth favour of the LORD.

1 Tim. 3:11. Even so *must their* wives *be* grave, not slanderous, sober, faithful in all things.

WONDERFUL, a name of the Messiah, Isa. 9:6. See Judg. 13:18. See JESUS, NAMES OF.

WORD, a title of Jesus, John 1:1,14; 1 John 5:7; Rev. 19:13.

WORD OF GOD. Deut. 30:11. For this commandment which I command thee this day, it *is* not hidden from thee, neither *is* it far off. 12. It *is* not in heaven, that thou shouldest say, Who shall go up for us to heaven, and bring it unto us, that we may hear it, and do it? 13. Neither *is* it beyond the sea, that thou shouldest say, Who shall go over the sea for us, and bring it unto us, that we may hear it, and do it? 14. But the word *is* very nigh unto thee, in thy mouth, and in thy heart, that thou mayest do it.

Deut. 31:26. Take this book of the law, and put it in the side of the ark of the covenant of the LORD your God, that it may be there for a witness against thee.

Josh. 1:8. This book of the law shall not depart out of thy mouth; but thou shalt meditate therein day and night, that thou mayest observe to do according to all that is written therein: for then thou shalt make thy way prosperous, and then thou shalt have good success.

1 Chr. 16:15. Be ye mindful always of his covenant; the word *which* he commanded to a thousand generations;

Psa. 19:7. The law of the LORD *is* perfect, converting the soul: the testimony of the LORD *is* sure, making wise the simple.

Psa. 33:4. For the word of the LORD *is* right; 6. By the word of the LORD were the heavens made;

and all the host of them by the breath of his mouth.

Psa. 107:20. He sent his word, and healed them, and delivered *them* from their destructions.

Jer. 22:29. O earth, earth, earth, hear the word of the LORD.

Matt. 22:29. Ye do err, not knowing the scriptures, nor the power of God.

Mark 13:31. Heaven and earth shall pass away, but my words shall not pass away.

Luke 1:37. For no word from God shall be void of power. [*R. V.*]

Luke 11:28. But he said, Yea rather, blessed *are* they that hear the word of God, and keep it.

John 6:63. It is the spirit that quickeneth; the flesh profiteth nothing: the words that I speak unto you, *they* are spirit, and *they* are life.

John 15:3. Now ye are clean through the word which I have spoken unto you.

John 17:8. For I have given unto them the words which thou gavest me; and they have received *them,* and have known surely that I came out from thee, and they have believed that thou didst send me. [*v.* 14.]

John 20:31. But these are written, that ye might believe that Jesus is the Christ, the Son of God; and that believing ye might have life through his name.

Col. 3:16. Let the word of Christ dwell in you richly in all wisdom; teaching and admonishing one another in psalms and hymns and spiritual songs, singing with grace in your hearts to the Lord.

1 Thess. 5:20. Despise not prophesyings.

2 Tim. 1:13. Hold fast the form of sound words, which thou hast heard of me, in faith and love which is in Christ Jesus.

2 Tim. 3:15. And that from a child thou hast known the holy scriptures, which are able to make thee wise unto salvation through faith which is in Christ Jesus. 16. All scripture *is* given by inspiration of God, and *is* profitable for doctrine, for reproof, for correction, for instruction in righteousness:

Heb. 10:7. Then said I, Lo, I come (in the volume of the book it is written of me,) to do thy will, O God.

1 Pet. 2:2. As newborn babes, desire the sincere milk of the word, that ye may grow thereby: 3. If so be ye have tasted that the Lord is gracious.

Inspiration: Ex. 20:1. And God spake all these words.

Dan. 10:21. But I will shew thee that which is noted in the scripture of truth:

Rev. 2:7. He that hath an ear, let him hear what the Spirit saith unto the churches;

Unbelief In: Prov. 13:13. Who-so despiseth the word shall be destroyed: but he that feareth the commandment shall be rewarded.

Luke 16:31. And he said unto him, If they hear not Moses and the prophets, neither will they be persuaded, though one rose from the dead.

Luke 24:25. Then he said unto them, O fools, and slow of heart to believe all that the prophets have spoken:

1 Cor. 1:18. For the preaching of the cross is to them that perish foolishness; but unto us which are saved it is the power of God.

2 Tim. 4:3. For the time will come when they will not endure sound doctrine; but after their own lusts shall they heap to themselves teachers, having itching ears: 4. And they shall turn away their ears from the truth, and shall be turned unto fables.

Rev. 22:19. And if any man shall take away from the words of the book of this prophecy, God shall take away his part out of the book of life, and out of the holy city, and from the things which are written in this book.

WORKS. Good: Psa. 37:3. Trust in the LORD, and do good; so shalt thou dwell in the land, and verily thou shalt be fed.

Matt. 3:8. Bring forth therefore fruits meet for repentance:

Matt. 10:42. And whosoever shall give to drink unto one of these little ones a cup of cold water only in the name of a disciple, verily I say unto you, he shall in no wise lose his reward.

Matt. 18:5. And whoso shall receive one such little child in my name receiveth me.

John 15:14. Ye are my friends, if ye do whatsoever I command you.

2 Cor. 9:8. And God is able to make all grace abound toward you; that ye, always having all sufficiency in all things, may abound to every good work:

Eph. 2:10. For we are his workmanship, created in Christ Jesus unto good works, which God hath before ordained that we should walk in them.

Phil. 1:11. Being filled with the fruits of righteousness, which are by Jesus Christ, unto the glory and praise of God.

2 Thess. 2:17. Comfort your hearts, and stablish you in every good word and work.

1 Tim. 2:10. But (which becometh women professing godliness) with good works.

Heb. 6:10. For God is not unrighteous to forget your work and labour of love, which ye have shewed toward his name, in that ye have ministered to the saints, and do minister.

Heb. 10:24. And let us consider one another to provoke unto love and to good works:

Heb. 21. Make you perfect in every ood work to do his will, working n you that which is well-pleasing in his sight, through Jesus Christ; to whom be glory for ever and ever.

Insufficiency of, for Salvation: Psa. 49:7. None of them can by any means redeem his brother, nor give to God a ransom for him: 8. (For the redemption of their soul is precious, and it ceaseth for ever:)

Isa. 64:6. But we are all as an unclean thing, and all our righteousnesses are as filthy rags; and we all do fade as a leaf; and our iniquities, like the wind, have taken us away.

Acts 13:39. And by him all that believe are justified from all things, from which ye could not be justified by the law of Moses.

Rom. 8:3. For what the law could not do, in that it was weak through the flesh, God sending his own Son in the likeness of sinful flesh, and for sin, condemned sin in the flesh:

Rom. 11:6. If by grace, then *is it* no more of works: otherwise grace is no more grace. But if *it be* of works, then is it no more grace: otherwise work is no more work.

Gal. 2:16. Knowing that a man is not justified by the works of the law, but by the faith of Jesus Christ, even we have believed in Jesus Christ, that we might be justified by the faith of Christ, and not by the works of the law: for by the works of the law shall no flesh be justified.

Eph. 2:8. For by grace are ye saved through faith; and that not of yourselves: *it is* the gift of God: 9. Not of works, lest any man should boast.

2 Tim. 1:9. Who hath saved us, and called *us* with an holy calling, not according to our works, but according to his own purpose and grace, which was given us in Christ Jesus.

WORLDLINESS. 1 Sam. 8: 19. Nevertheless the people refused to obey the voice of Samuel; and they said, Nay; but we will have a king over us; 20. That we also may be like all the nations;

Job 21:11. They send forth their little ones like a flock, and their children dance. 12. They take the timbrel and harp, and rejoice at the sound of the organ. 13. They spend their days in wealth, and in a moment go down to the grave. 14. Therefore they say unto God, Depart from us, for we desire not the knowledge of thy ways. 15. What *is* the Almighty, that we should serve him? and what profit should we have, if we pray unto him?

Prov. 14:12. There is a way which seemeth right unto a man, but the end thereof *are* the ways

of death. 13. Even in laughter the heart is sorrowful; and the end of that mirth *is* heaviness.

Isa. 28:4. And the glorious beauty, which *is* on the head of the fat valley, shall be a fading flower, *and* as the hasty fruit before the summer; which *when* he that looketh upon it seeth, while it is yet in his hand he eateth it up.

Isa. 47:7. And thou saidst, I shall be a lady for ever: *so* that thou didst not lay these *things* to thy heart, neither didst remember the latter end of it.

Mic. 2:10. Arise ye, and depart; for this *is* not *your* rest: because it is polluted, it shall destroy *you,* even with a sore destruction.

Matt. 10:39. He that findeth his life shall lose it: and he that loseth his life for my sake shall find it. Matt. 16:25; Mark 8:35; Luke 17: 33; John 12:25.

Matt. 16:26. For what is a man profited, if he shall gain the whole world, and lose his own soul? or what shall a man give in exchange for his soul? Mark 8:36,37.

Luke 12:19. And I will say to my soul, Soul, thou hast much goods laid up for many years; take thine ease, eat, drink, *and* be merry.

John 5:44. How can ye believe, which receive honour one of another, and seek not the honour that *cometh* from God only?

John 12:43. For they loved the praise of men more than the praise of God.

John 15:19. If ye were of the world, the world would love his own: but because ye are not of the world, but I have chosen you out of the world, therefore the world hateth you.

Rom. 12:2. And be not conformed to this world: but be ye transformed by the renewing of your mind, that ye may prove what *is* that good, and acceptable, and perfect, will of God.

Col. 3:2. Set your affection on things above, not on things on the earth.

1 Tim. 5:6. But she that liveth in pleasure is dead while she liveth.

Jas. 4:4. Ye adulterers and

adulteresses, know ye not that the friendship of the world is enmity with God? whosoever therefore will be a friend of the world is the enemy of God.

1 Pet. 2:11. Dearly beloved, I beseech *you* as strangers and pilgrims, abstain from fleshly lusts, which war against the soul;

1 John 2:15. Love not the world, neither the things *that are* in the world. If any man love the world, the love of the Father is not in him. 16. For all that *is* in the world, the lust of the flesh, and the lust of the eyes, and the pride of life, is not of the Father, but is of the world. 17. And the world passeth away, and the lust thereof: but he that doeth the will of God abideth for ever.

WORSHIP, Psa. 29:2. Give unto the LORD the glory due unto his name; worship the LORD in the beauty of holiness.

Psa. 35:18. I will give thee thanks in the great congregation: I will praise thee among much people.

Psa. 55:14. We took sweet counsel together, *and* walked unto the house of God in company.

Psa. 84:1. How amiable *are* thy tabernacles, O LORD of hosts! 2. My soul longeth, yea, even fainteth for the courts of the LORD: my heart and my flesh crieth out for the living God. 3. Yea, the sparrow hath found an house, and the swallow a nest for herself, where she may lay her young, *even* thine altars, O LORD of hosts, my King, and my God. 4. Blessed *are* they that dwell in thy house: they will be still praising thee. 10. For a day in thy courts *is* better than a thousand. I had rather be a doorkeeper in the house of my God, than to dwell in the tents of wickedness.

Psa. 95:6. O come, let us worship and bow down: let us kneel before the LORD our maker.

Isa. 40:31. But they that wait upon the LORD shall renew *their* strength; they shall mount up with wings as eagles; they shall run, and not be weary; *and* they shall walk, and not faint.

Rev. 15:4. Who shall not fear thee, O Lord, and glorify thy name? for *thou* only *art* holy: for all nations shall come and worship before thee; for thy judgments are made manifest.

Heb. 10:25. Not forsaking the assembling of ourselves together, as the manner of some *is;* but exhorting *one another:* and so much the more, as ye see the day approaching.

YOUNG MEN. Psa. 119:9. Wherewithal shall a young man cleanse his way? by taking heed *thereto* according to thy word.

Psa. 148:12. Both young men, and maidens; old men, and children: 13. Let them praise the name of the LORD: for his name alone is excellent; his glory *is* above the earth and heaven.

Prov. 3:1. My son, forget not my law; but let thine heart keep my commandments: 2. For length of days, and long life, and peace, shall they add to thee.

Prov. 4:1. Hear, ye children, the instruction of a father, and attend to know understanding. 2. For I give you good doctrine, forsake ye not my law. 3. For I was my father's son, tender and only *beloved* in the sight of my mother. 4. He taught me also, and said unto me, Let thine heart retain my words: keep my commandments, and live.

Prov. 15:5. A fool despiseth his father's instruction: but he that regardeth reproof is prudent. 20. A wise son maketh a glad father: but a foolish man despiseth his mother.

Prov. 19:13. A foolish son *is* the calamity of his father:

Prov. 20:29. The glory of young men *is* their strength: and the beauty of old men *is* the gray head.

Prov. 23:15. My son, if thine heart be wise, my heart shall rejoice, even mine.

Prov. 24:1. Be not thou envious against evil men, neither desire to be with them.

Prov. 28:7. Whoso keepeth the law *is* a wise son: but he that is a companion of riotous *men* shameth his father.

1 Tim. 4:12. Let no man despise

thy youth; but be thou an example of the believers, in word, in conversation, in charity, in spirit, in faith, in purity.

2 Tim. 2:22. Flee also youthful lusts: but follow righteousness, faith, charity, peace, with them that call on the Lord out of a pure heart. 23. But foolish and unlearned questions avoid, knowing that they do gender strifes.

Tit. 2:6. Young men likewise exhort to be sober minded.

1 John 2:13. I write unto you, young men, because ye have overcome the wicked one. I write unto you, little children, because ye have known the Father.

ZEAL, Religious. Eccl. 9:10. Whatsoever thy hand findeth to do, do *it* with thy might; for *there is* no work, nor device, nor knowledge, nor wisdom, in the grave, whither thou goest.

1 Cor. 13:3. And though I bestow all my goods to feed *the poor,* and though I give my body to be burned, and have not charity, it profiteth me nothing.

1 Cor. 14:12. Even so ye, forasmuch as ye are zealous of spiritual *gifts,* seek that ye may excel to the edifying of the church.

1 Cor. 15:58. Therefore, my beloved brethren, be ye stedfast, unmoveable, always abounding in the work of the Lord, forasmuch as ye know that your labour is not in vain in the Lord.

2 Cor. 9:2. For I know the forwardness of your mind, for which I boast of you to them of Macedonia, that Achaia was ready a year ago; and your zeal hath provoked very many.

Gal. 4:18. But *it is* good to be zealously affected always in a good *thing.*

Gal. 6:9. Let us not be weary in well doing: for in due season we shall reap, if we faint not. 2 Thess. 3:13.

Rev. 3:19. As many as I love, I rebuke and chasten: be zealous therefore, and repent.

Exemplified: Ex. 32:31. Oh, this people have sinned a great sin, and have made them gods of gold. 32. Yet now, if thou wilt forgive their sin—; and if not, blot me, I pray thee, out of thy book which thou hast written.

Deut. 9:18. I fell down before the LORD, as at the first, forty days and forty nights: I did neither eat bread, nor drink water, because of all your sins which ye sinned, in doing wickedly in the sight of the LORD, to provoke him to anger. *v.* 19.

Jer. 13:17. If ye will not hear it, my soul shall weep in secret places for *your* pride; and mine eye shall weep sore, and run down with tears, because the LORD'S flock is carried away captive.

Luke 19:41. When he was come near, he beheld the city, and wept over it, *v.* 42; Matt. 23:37.

Rom. 9:1. I say the truth in Christ, I lie not, my conscience also bearing me witness in the Holy Ghost, 2. That I have great heaviness and continual sorrow in my heart. 3. For I could wish that myself were accursed from Christ for my brethren, my kinsmen according to the flesh:

2 Cor. 6:11. O *ye* Corinthians, our mouth is open unto you, our heart is enlarged.

Without Knowledge: John 16:2. They shall put you out of the synagogues: yea, the time cometh, that whosoever killeth you will think that he doeth God service.

Rom. 10:2. For I bear them record that they have a zeal of God, but not according to knowledge. 3. For they being ignorant of God's righteousness, and going about to establish their own righteousness, have not submitted themselves unto the righteousness of God.